The
WILEY
advantage

Dear Valued Customer,

We realize you're a busy professional with deadlines to hit. Whether your goal is to learn a new technology or solve a critical problem, we want to be there to lend you a hand. Our primary objective is to provide you with the insight and knowledge you need to stay atop the highly competitive and ever-changing technology industry.

Wiley Publishing, Inc., offers books on a wide variety of technical categories, including security, data warehousing, software development tools, and networking — everything you need to reach your peak. Regardless of your level of expertise, the Wiley family of books has you covered.

- For Dummies® – The *fun* and *easy* way® to learn
- The Weekend Crash Course® –The *fastest* way to learn a new tool or technology
- Visual™ – For those who prefer to learn a new topic *visually*
- The Bible – The *100% comprehensive* tutorial and reference
- The Wiley Professional list – *Practical* and *reliable* resources for IT professionals

The book you now hold, *Common Warehouse Metamodel Developer's Guide,* is your complete and authoritative guide to developing datawarehousing and business intelligence applications via the Common Warehouse Metamodel (CWM) framework. Written by several of the core developers of the CWM standard, the book will show you all the steps you'll need for planning and implementing a CWM-enabled datawarehousing environment. The authors provide you with detailed guidelines and in-depth code examples that will allow you to put the Common Warehouse Metamodel to work in your business.

Our commitment to you does not end at the last page of this book. We'd want to open a dialog with you to see what other solutions we can provide. Please be sure to visit us at www.wiley.com/compbooks to review our complete title list and explore the other resources we offer. If you have a comment, suggestion, or any other inquiry, please locate the "contact us" link at www.wiley.com.

Finally, we encourage you to review the following page for a list of Wiley titles on related topics. Thank you for your support and we look forward to hearing from you and serving your needs again in the future.

Sincerely,

Richard K Swadley

Richard K. Swadley
Vice President & Executive Group Publisher
Wiley Technology Publishing

Bible

DUMMIES

Independent Thinkers

more information on related titles

Also from OMG Press
▬▬ Available from Wiley Publishing ▬▬▬▬▬▬▬▬▬▬▬

ADVANCED

INTERMEDIATE

Common Warehouse Metamodel Developer's Guide

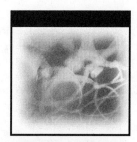

Common Warehouse Metamodel Developer's Guide

John Poole, Dan Chang,
Douglas Tolbert, and David Mellor

Wiley Publishing, Inc.

Publisher: Joe Wikert
Executive Editor: Robert M. Elliott
Assistant Developmental Editor: Emilie Herman
Managing Editor: Pamela Hanley
New Media Editor: Brian Snapp
Text Design & Composition: Wiley Composition Services

Published by Wiley Publishing, Inc., Indianapolis, Indiana

Published simultaneously in Canada

For general information on our other products and services please contact our Customer Care Department within the United States at (800) 762-2974, outside the United States at (317) 572-3993 or fax (317) 572-4002.

Wiley also publishes its books in a variety of electronic formats. Some content that appears in print may not be available in electronic books.

ISBN 0-471-20243-6

Printed in the United States of America

10 9 8 7 6 5 4 3 2 1

Advance Praise for
Common Warehouse Metamodel Developer's Guide

"*CWM Developer's Guide* breaks new ground by providing an in-depth overview of Model Driven Integration for the data warehouse and Business Intelligence tool chain using innovative meta data design patterns. The use of UML and MOF to define platform-independent models while simultaneously targeting both XML and Java-based meta data management using XMI and JMI is supported with numerous examples. Software architects, CTOs, systems integrators, and vendors grappling with the complexity of tool, data, and application integration can learn firsthand the power of OMG Model Driven Architecture from this pioneering book."

Sridhar Iyengar
IBM Distinguished Engineer, OMG Architecture Board

"The first CWM book, *Common Warehouse Metamodel: An Introduction,* has become a great complement to the CWM specifications. This follow-on book delves even deeper into the implementation world, which is critical to the success of any standard. This developer's guide establishes a key transition from 'paper standards' to actual adopted standards for tool integration.

Common Warehouse Metamodel Developer's Guide is not only well written, but also well focused on applications related to the standards. I highly recommend this second book to anyone who wants to transform standards into reality in their product strategy."

Christian H. Bremeau
President and CEO, Meta Integration Technology, Inc. (MITI)

"*Common Warehouse Metamodel Developer's Guide* is a highly practical guide to a powerful new way of integrating systems in the data warehousing and business analysis domains. By leveraging this new standard for modeling and exchanging application, tool, and instance meta data, the authors show how representing common business and domain concepts as higher-level abstractions can solve complex, real-world integration problems.

Model-based development has the potential to vastly simplify the increasingly complex issues faced by developers in building integrated solutions in today's distributed, heterogeneous environments, and CWM is the leading example of the success of this approach."

Chuck Mosher
Staff Engineer, Market Development Engineering, Sun Microsystems

"This book illustrates how CWM is used not only to describe complex data warehousing systems, but also to facilitate interoperability and integration. It is an excellent guide for anyone interested in developing platform-independent domain models and leveraging domain models for integration and information exchange."

Ravi Dirckze
JMI 1.0 Specification Lead and Senior Software Engineer, Unisys Corporation

OMG Advisory Board

David Frankel
Chief Consulting Architect
IONA

Sridhar Iyengar
Distinguished Engineer
IBM Corporation

Cris Kobryn
Chief Technologist
Telelogic

Nilo Mitra, Ph.D.
Principal System Engineer
Ericsson

Jishnu Mukerji
Senior Systems Architect
Hewlett-Packard Company

Jon Siegel, Ph.D.
Vice President, Technology Transfer
Object Management Group, Inc.

Richard Mark Soley, Ph.D.
Chairman and Chief Executive
    Officer
Object Management Group, Inc.

About the OMG

The Object Management Group (OMG) is an open membership, not-for-profit consortium that produces and maintains computer industry specifications for interoperable applications. To achieve this goal, the OMG specifies open standards for every aspect of distributed computing from analysis and design, through infrastructure, to application objects and components defined on virtually every enterprise middleware platform. OMG's membership roster includes virtually every large company in the computer industry, and hundreds of smaller ones. Most of the companies that shape enterprise and Internet computing today are represented on OMG's Board of Directors.

OMG's flagship specification, and the basis for future OMG specifications, is the multi-platform Model Driven Architecture (MDA). Unifying the modeling and middleware spaces, the MDA supports applications over their entire lifecycle from Analysis and Design, through implementation and deployment, to maintenance and evolution. Based on normative, platform-independent Unified Modeling Language (UML) models, MDA-based applications and standards may be expressed and implemented, equivalently, on multiple middleware platforms; implementations are produced automatically, for the most part, by MDA-enabled tools, which also generate cross-platform invocations making for a truly interoperable environment. Because the UML models remain stable as the technological landscape changes around them over time, MDA-based development maximizes software ROI as it integrates applications across the enterprise, and one enterprise with another. Adopted by members as the basis for OMG specifications in September 2001, the MDA is truly a unique advance in distributed computing. To learn more about the MDA, see www.omg.org/mda.

OMG's modeling specifications form the foundation for the MDA. These include the UML, the MetaObject Facility (MOF), XML Metadata Interchange

(XMI), and the Common Warehouse Metamodel (CWM). The industry's standard for representation of analysis and design, the UML defines Use Case and Activity diagrams for requirements gathering, Class and Object diagrams for design, Package and Subsystem diagrams for deployment, and six other diagram types. The MOF defines a standard metamodel for applications, allowing UML models to be interchanged among tools and repositories; and XMI standardizes the format for these interchanges. Finally, CWM establishes metamodels in the field of data warehousing, completing OMG's standardization in the modeling space.

The Common Object Request Broker Architecture (CORBA) is OMG's vendor-neutral, system-independent middleware standard. Based on the OMG/ISO Interface Definition language (OMG IDL) and the Internet Inter-ORB Protocol (IIOP), CORBA is a mature technology represented on the market by more than 70 ORBs (Object Request Brokers) plus hundreds of other products. Scalable to Internet and Enterprise levels, CORBA more than meets business computing requirements through its robust services providing directory, distributed event handling, transactionality, fault tolerance, and security. Specialized versions of CORBA form the basis for distributed Realtime computing, and distributed embedded systems.

Building on this foundation, OMG Domain Facilities standardize common objects throughout the supply and service chains in industries such as Telecommunications, Healthcare, Manufacturing, Transportation, Finance/Insurance, Biotechnology, Utilities, Space, and Military and Civil Defense Logistics. OMG members are now extending these Domain Facilities, originally written in OMG IDL and restricted to CORBA, into the MDA by constructing UML models corresponding to their underlying architecture; standard MDA procedures will then produce standards and implementations on such platforms as Web Services, XML/SOAP, Enterprise JavaBeans, and others. OMG's first MDA-based specification, the Gene Expression Facility, was adopted less than six months after the organization embraced the MDA; based on a detailed UML model, this specification is implemented entirely in the popular language XML.

In summary, the OMG provides the computing industry with an open, vendor-neutral, proven process for establishing and promoting standards. OMG makes all of its specifications available without charge from its Web site, www.omg.org. Delegates from the hundreds of OMG member companies convene at week-long meetings held five times each year at varying sites around the world, to advance OMG technologies. The OMG welcomes guests to their meetings; for an invitation, send your email request to info@omg.org or see www.omg.org/news/meetings/tc/guest.htm.

Membership in OMG is open to any company, educational institution, or government agency. For more information on the OMG, contact OMG headquarters by telephone at +1-781-444-0404, by fax at +1-781-444-0320, by email to info@omg.org, or on the Web at www.omg.org.

Contents

Acknowledgments

The authors wish to acknowledge Sridhar Iyengar for his vision, foresight, and ongoing championing of the CWM effort, ever since the time of its earliest inception. The authors also wish to acknowledge the significant contributions made by both Jean-Jacques Daudenarde and David Last in the development of the CWM model.

Of course, no effort of the magnitude of CWM would ever have been possible without the hard work and contributions of many individuals, and the authors also wish to acknowledge and thank their many colleagues, both within and outside of the Object Management Group, who participated in, contributed materially to, reviewed, and strongly supported, the CWM effort.

And finally, the authors wish to express their gratitude to the fine editorial staff at Wiley Publishing Inc., who recognized the importance of this book from early on, and made its publication possible.

Introduction

Meta data is widely recognized as the single most important factor in achieving seamless integration and interoperability between dissimilar software products and applications. For software components to interoperate effectively, they must be capable of easily sharing data. And sharing data requires a common definition of how the data is structured (its organization and data types), as well as its meaning (or semantics). Since data is generally defined by meta data, having a common definition of meta data is a necessary prerequisite for achieving integration at the data level. What is required is a common language for describing or expressing meta data and an agreed-upon format or interface for exchanging meta data between components. If both a descriptive language and interchange mechanism for meta data can be standardized and agreed upon by software vendors, then the first and most fundamental roadblock to having truly interoperable systems will have been removed.

The Common Warehouse Metamodel (CWM) is an interoperability standard of the Object Management Group (OMG) that defines a common language and interchange mechanism for meta data in the data warehousing and business analysis domains. CWM provides the long-sought-after common metamodel for describing data warehousing and business analysis meta data, along with an XML-based interchange facility. It has long been acknowledged by leaders and analysts in this particular industry segment that the long-term Return on Investment (ROI) of any complex data warehousing or supply chain effort would be greatly enhanced by the standardization of just such a common metamodel and eXtensible Markup Language (XML) interchange format. CWM enables vendors to build truly interoperable databases, tools, and applications. Customers benefit by being able to select from best-of-breed product offerings and avoiding single-vendor lock-in, while remaining confident that their investments will not be diluted by the inability of diverse tools to interoperate. CWM has established itself as the meta data interchange standard of choice in the data warehousing and business analysis communities, and has been incorporated into many vendors' product suites.

From a technical standpoint, CWM extends the OMG's established metamodeling architecture to include data warehousing and business analysis domain concepts. CWM supports a model-driven approach to meta data interchange, in which formal models representing shared meta data are constructed according to the specifications of the CWM metamodel (essentially an object technology approach to achieving data warehouse integration). These models are stored and interchanged in the form of XML documents. Meta data can be defined independently of any product-specific considerations or formats. It can be stored externally to products as an information commodity within its own right, and is readily used by products as generic definitions of information structures.

Data warehousing and business analysis tools that agree on the fundamental domain concepts and relationships defined by CWM can understand a wide range of models representing particular meta data instances. Tools, products, and applications can integrate at the meta data level, because they have a common language with which to externalize their meta data and do not require knowledge of each other's proprietary information structures and interfaces. And, although CWM is focused primarily on data warehousing and business analysis, its basic components and methodologies are easily extended to include subject areas of other domains, as well.

Mission of This Book

The mission of this book is to provide a comprehensive and highly practical guide for software practitioners who need to implement CWM solutions within their software product offerings, or use CWM-enabled tools in the construction or evolution of their own corporate data warehouses, information factories, and supply chains.

As a developer's guide to developing CWM-enabled technologies and meta data integration solutions, this book is a particularly novel approach to this subject. In the spirit of Ralph Kimball's seminal work, *The Data Warehouse Toolkit* (Kimball, 1996), this book approaches the general problem of how to implement CWM by providing four highly representative vertical models of data warehousing that all greatly benefit from a standards-based approach to meta data integration:

- Data warehouse realization and loading
- Dimensional modeling
- Web-enabled data warehouse
- Meta Data Repository

The reader is led through the development and implementation of complete CWM meta data integration solutions for each of the four vertical models. The Meta Data Repository vertical is then used to tie the other three together in the form of fully integrated meta data solution architecture.

Another important aspect of this book is that it provides a complete treatment of the pattern-based approach to CWM meta data integration. This area represents the next phase in providing truly interoperable meta data architectures, and greatly enhances the power, expressiveness, and flexibility of CWM by providing a means of specifying domain-specific semantic contexts for the interchange of CWM models. Both the theory and practice of meta data interchange patterns are fully developed within this book and applied in the creation of CWM solutions for each of the vertical models.

This book is a companion to *Common Warehouse Metamodel: An Introduction to the Standard for Data Warehouse Integration* (2002), also published by John Wiley & Sons. *Common Warehouse Metamodel: An Introduction* is a concise and very readable primer on CWM that provides a complete picture of the CWM standard. It introduces the value proposition and economic rationale for CWM and CWM's foundational technologies and architecture, using CWM to model basic data warehousing and business analysis meta data, implementing and extending CWM, and the role CWM plays in defining wide-scale meta data integration solutions. This book significantly augments the content and goals of the introductory book by providing technical specifics on developing complete CWM solutions, from initial analysis of requirements, to detailed design, to implementation in code.

While a competent software developer can succeed in implementing a CWM solution based on this book alone, readers are generally more likely to acquire a fuller appreciation of CWM rationale and technology after having read the introductory volume. Many of the foundational concepts of CWM summarized in this book are presented in greater detail in the first volume. Hence, *Common Warehouse Metamodel: An Introduction* is highly recommended as a starting point for those wishing a comprehensive overview of the CWM domain prior to embarking on an implementation effort based on *Common Warehouse Metamodel Developer's Guide.*

How This Book Is Organized

This book provides a logical and straightforward approach to developing CWM solutions. The following is a roadmap to the chapters of this book. Readers who are generally familiar with CWM concepts might consider skipping the first two chapters and begin with Chapter 3, "Modeling Meta Data Using CWM." Those who are already comfortable with the approach taken by CWM in modeling meta data solutions might also consider skipping Chapter 3 and begin with Chapter 4, "Meta Data Interchange Patterns." Chapter 3 introduces substantial new material that forms the basis for much of what follows in the rest of the book.

Part One, "Introduction," provides all necessary introductory material required for the book as a whole:

- Chapter 1, "Introducing CWM: Model-Based Integration of the Supply Chain," summarizes the economic justification for developing CWM-based meta data integration solutions by describing how standards-based meta data integration maximizes the long-term Return on Investment (ROI) of the information supply chain.

- Chapter 2, "An Architectural Survey of CWM," provides an architectural overview of CWM and its foundational technologies. Collectively, Chapters 1 and 2 largely summarize much of the detailed information provided by Chapters 1 through 4 of Common Warehouse Metamodel: An Introduction.

- Chapter 3, "Modeling Meta Data Using CWM," provides a detailed treatment of using CWM as a modeling language for describing meta data in a vendor- and product-neutral manner, and largely formalizes the techniques used in developing the modeling examples of Chapter 5 of the introductory book.

- Chapter 4, "Meta Data Interchange Patterns," introduces the new area of employing pattern-based structuring techniques when formulating meta data models. The pattern-based approach enhances interoperability and greatly simplifies the construction of CWM-enabled tools. This topic was alluded to in Chapter 8 of the introductory book, but not given full treatment there.

Part Two, "Introducing the Vertical Models," develops the comprehensive data warehousing and business analysis vertical models, using CWM to model and implement all aspects of these models, from logical to physical design, to the modeling of underlying implementation resources.

- Chapter 5, "Data Warehouse Management Model," presents the design and implementation of a general data warehousing vertical model using CWM. Specifies the overall dimensional organization of the data warehouse model. Develops meta data describing source-to-target mappings and transformations, as part of the overall data warehouse load process. Further develops the models to include descriptions of processes that schedule, control, and track the data warehouse load process. Finally, develops examples of extending the core data warehouse model to provide additional, specialized meta data structures to handle tool-specific meta data. Emphasis is placed on using the built-in CWM extension mechanisms, as well as extending the CWM metamodel itself.

- Chapter 6, "Dimensional Model," presents the design and implementation of a large, dimensional vertical model, using CWM. Illustrates the use of CWM in modeling all of the basic multidimensional structures used throughout this model: Dimensions, Levels, Hierarchies, Cubes, and Measures. Develops a physical relational database design, as a model of an underlying implementation structure of the dimensional model in terms of a relational star-schema: Tables, columns, keys, foreign keys, and join relationships. Illustrates the modeling of deployment mapping by developing a CWM mapping model linking the logical dimensional model to the underlying relational resource model. Emphasis is placed on the specification and resolution of logical concepts to their underlying, physical realization. Then covers the development of an alternative logical-to-physical mapping, in which the same logical dimensional model is deployed on top of another underlying resource model. Emphasis is placed on how the physical model is modified to provide various optimizations while the logical model is preserved. Finally, the dimensional model is extended via extension of the core dimensional model to provide additional, specialized meta data structures to handle tool-specific meta data. Emphasis is placed on using the built-in CWM extension mechanisms, as well as extending the CWM metamodel itself.

- Chapter 7, "Web-Enabled Data Warehouse Model," develops additional dimensional and operational concepts that allow the data warehouse to participate in a distributed, highly collaborative, Web-based computing environment. It is demonstrated how CWM can be used to model situations in which a data warehouse is used to back-end a Web server, providing new dimensional structures and other meta data constructs supporting clickstream analysis. As with Chapters 5 and 6, examples of extending the core CWM metamodel to more adequately cover the additional domain semantics required by the Web environment are also demonstrated.

- Chapter 8, "CWM Metastore," builds upon and unifies the previous three, domain-oriented scenarios by demonstrating how CWM can be used to define the overall modeling and meta data management environment. In this particular case, the advanced facilities provided by CWM's inheritance from the OMG's standard metamodeling architecture and foundational technologies are given full demonstration. This chapter, in particular, provides much of the basis for the subsequent implementation-oriented chapters of the book, as well as the CWM implementation software provided on the companion Web site.

Part Three, "Implementation and Deployment," describes, in depth, the implementation of the meta data store developed as part of the vertical modeling chapters. This provides a concrete example of a complete CWM implementation.

- Chapter 9, "Integration Architecture," builds upon material originally introduced in Chapter 6 of the introductory book by defining a concrete meta data management strategy for the combined scenarios of the detailed design. The strategy is then refined into technical and integration architectural models that guide the subsequent development of the CWM implementation.

- Chapter 10, "Interface Rendering," describes the process of translating the CWM metaclasses to programmatic interfaces in some target implementation language, according to some formal mapping standard. In this case, the mapping standard is the Java Meta Data Interface, a mapping of OMG's MOF to the Java programming language. The reader is guided through the steps required to generate the Java interfaces representing the CWM meta objects, using the software tools provided with the book.

- Chapter 11, "Implementation Development," gives an overview of the development of an overall meta data integration architecture, centered on the meta data store modeled largely in Chapter 8, "Meta Data Interchange Patterns"; the various integration architectural patterns introduced in Chapter 9, "Integration Architecture"; and the CWM interfaces defined in Chapter 10, "Interface Rendering." The intent of this chapter is to give the reader an idea of what is required in order to implement a working CWM implementation, and covers various topics, including adapter construction, the extension of CWM to Web services, and the development of largely automated meta data integration services.

- Finally, Chapter 12, "Conclusions," recaps all major results covered by the book, provides speculation on the future evolution of the CWM standard and related technologies, and proposes areas for future research and investigation.

Who Should Read This Book

While *Common Warehouse Metamodel: An Introduction* provides a conceptual overview of CWM intended for moderately technical audiences, this book is targeted toward a highly technical audience, consisting primarily of developers who are responsible for developing or integrating and deploying CWM-enabled software products and tools. The term developer, in this context, means any person with a strong background in both software design and implementation, including system, database, and data warehouse architects, software engineers, analysts, modelers, and system integrators. This book will also be of tremendous value to highly technical managers and planners who need sufficiently detailed technical information to effectively plan and budget their CWM-enabled solutions.

Those readers desiring a less technical and more conceptual understanding of CWM are, of course, referred to the first CWM book, *Common Warehouse Metamodel: An Introduction to the Standard for Data Warehouse Integration* (2002). The first book is of great benefit to anyone who needs to rapidly acquire a coherent CWM knowledge base, without delving into the nuts and bolts of constructing a CWM solution. On the other hand, given that *Common Warehouse Metamodel Developer's Guide* builds on many of the key concepts presented in *Common Warehouse Metamodel: An Introduction*, it is highly recommended that serious students of CWM read the introductory book first, or at least have it available as a reference.

What's on the Web Site

This book is accompanied by the Web site www.wiley.com/compbooks/ poole. This site provides all of the models, source code, meta data interchange pattern catalog, standard pattern template, and other artifacts developed throughout the chapters of this book, with instructions on downloading, installing, and using these work products. The site also specifies any other third-party software needed to compile and run the CWM solution source code, along with summaries of system requirements, licensing terms, and pointers to the various vendors' Web sites.

Also provided on the Web site are errata listings for both the book and supplied code, along with any upgraded software versions. Summaries of bug fixes are also provided, as part of the release notes for each posted software upgrade.

Onward and Upward

Most people (even highly experienced modelers and designers) find OMG modeling technologies such as MOF, UML, XMI, and CWM decidedly difficult to understand. But one should keep in mind that these technologies are aimed at solving notoriously difficult problems. As tools for solving highly complex system integration problems, these technologies strive to be as simple as possible while still providing robust, effective, and broadly applicable solutions. Anyone in the situation of having to effectively apply a technology like CWM should rest assured that the extra time and effort invested in thoroughly learning the intricacies of such standards will result in superior implementations and longer-term benefit to the ultimate end users of seamlessly integrated systems.

Also, while CWM and related technologies may sometimes appear difficult to use at this point in time, such standards will generally become easier to apply as more experience is gained in their implementation. The development of certain formal techniques for simplifying the development of CWM-based solutions (for example, the ongoing codification of meta data interchange patterns) will ultimately make CWM far more acceptable in the near term. And, of course, the forthcoming availability of a large assortment of automated tools for designing, implementing, deploying, and managing model-driven architectures will greatly aid in alleviating the current implementation burden. Getting to that point will require a lot of hard work and persistence, but the rewards are expected to be considerable. This book will prove to be of valuable assistance in your own efforts to build truly interoperable and intelligent systems. You now have everything you need to get started.

Happy modeling!

About the Authors

JOHN POOLE is a Distinguished Software Engineer at Hyperion Solutions and a coauthor of the CWM specification.

DAN CHANG is a member of the Database Technology Institute at IBM, a visiting professor at San Jose State University, and a coauthor of the CWM specification.

DOUGLAS TOLBERT is a Consulting Engineer at Unisys Corporation, a coauthor of the CWM specification, and a current co-chair of the CWM Revision Task Force within the Object Management Group.

DAVID MELLOR is a Consulting Engineer at Oracle Corporation, a coauthor of the CWM specification, and a current co-chair of the CWM Revision Task Force within the Object Management Group.

The UML class diagrams in this book represent class inheritance using an open arrow head rather than the closed, "hollow triangle" normally prescribed by UML notation. While this is not standard UML notation, it helped to simplify much of the composition process of the book's artwork. On the other hand, the fact that this non-standard symbol is being used to denote class inheritance is very clear in each diagram in which it occurs, and no where does it conflict with the other known usages of open arrow heads in UML models (for example, to represent non-navigable association ends, dependencies, or instantiation, none of which are used in the CWM metamodel).

PART

One

Introduction

Introducing CWM: Model-Based Integration of the Supply Chain

The Common Warehouse Metamodel (CWM) is an open industry standard defining a common metamodel and eXtensible Markup Language (XML)-based interchange format for meta data in the data warehousing and business analysis domains. CWM is a generic domain model of the data warehousing and business analysis domains, with a standards-based mapping to the XML. CWM provides the long-sought-after common language for describing meta data, along with an XML-based meta data interchange facility. CWM has established itself within the data warehousing and business analysis communities and is being incorporated into many next-generation data warehousing and business analysis products and tools.

This chapter describes the economic benefits ultimately realized by CWM-enabled data warehousing and analysis products and tools. In this chapter, we analyze the economic impact facing the data warehousing community when meta data integration is not readily available, why the CWM approach is the best bet to achieving integration, and how CWM is used to integrate diverse, multivendor software products and applications. Because all useful technologies also have their limitations, this chapter delineates the boundaries of CWM and describes aspects of data warehouse integration that CWM is not intended to solve.

Integrating the Information Supply Chain

The typical data warehousing and business analysis environment is often described in terms of an Information Supply Chain (ISC) (Kimball, 1996) or *information economy* (Thomsen, 1997). These metaphors reflect the fact that information in this environment flows from its sources (that is, providers of *raw data*) through a sequence of refinements that ultimately yields *information products* that are of great strategic value to corporate decision-makers. Figure 1.1 provides an illustration of a typical ISC.

Components of the Information Supply Chain

The typical ISC closely resembles the manufacturing and distribution of durable goods. In a durable goods supply chain, raw materials (wood, iron or steel ore, petroleum, and so on) are refined through a number of distinct manufacturing steps and are finally assembled into useful consumer products. These products are stored in a warehouse until customer orders for the products are secured, at which point products are shipped out of the warehouse, either directly to the customer or perhaps to some intermediate distribution center. In the ISC analog to the manufacturing-distribution process, raw data is first acquired at the start of the chain and then is subjected to a number of refining transformations before being passed to the end consumer (the corporate decision-maker, in this context).

The first refinement step in the ISC usually consists of reconciling diverse transactional data into something with a more uniform representation. This step comes under various names, including *data extraction, transformation, and loading* (ETL); *data normalization*; *data warehouse building*; *data cleansing and reconciliation*; and so on. Regardless of the terminology used, this step consists of scheduled acquisitions of data from the various transaction systems, the translation of that data into some common format, and the subsequent storage of that transformed data in a special-purpose database. This special-purpose database greatly enhances the transformed data's capability to serve as strategic information to decision-makers, as opposed to detailed records of individual business events. Interestingly enough, this specialized database of strategic information (refined and assembled information products) is often called a *data warehouse*, in a manner consistent with our manufacturing-distribution analogy.

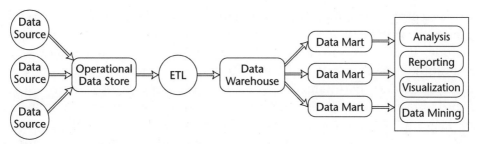

Figure 1.1 The information supply chain.

Perhaps the most significant feature about the data warehouse is that it organizes refined data in a manner that greatly facilitates advanced analyses, which are critical to the ongoing success of a business. Data warehouses are usually *dimensional* in nature; that is, they organize data in a uniform manner according to the various *dimensions* of the business: accounts, products, geographic regions, sales units, stores, and so on. These business dimensions serve as search keys that identify the data. Data warehouses are invariably organized by time, as well. For example, a business analyst might use a data warehouse to compare sales of a particular product line for different geographic regions over different fiscal periods. The data residing in a data warehouse may have been acquired from highly diverse transaction systems, but the variations in the transaction data are abstracted away by the dimensional organization of the data warehouse. Data warehouses ultimately facilitate business analysis by transforming raw business data into *strategic business information*.

Advanced analysis and reporting tools may work directly off the data warehouse or may attach to departmental data marts. These tools add considerable value to the information available from the data warehouse. Although the data warehouse establishes the dimensional view of information, analysis and reporting tools provide unique capabilities, such as manipulation of dimensionally organized data and specialized operations or visualization. For example, an advanced financial analysis and modeling package might perform complex statistical analyses of the basic dimensional information. The analysis package also might leverage the capabilities of an Online Analytical Processing (OLAP) server or data-mining tool.

Advanced reporting and visualization tools add value by enabling the end user to view the analysis results in highly useful and diverse ways. This includes the use of various types of charts, graphs, color codes, alerts, or multidimensional visual constructs and images that the end user can manipulate directly (rotate, pivot, reshape, resize, and so on).

Data marts, advanced analysis tools (including software-based analysis packages, OLAP servers, and data mining packages), and reporting and visualization tools collectively represent the final refinement step in the ISC, in which strategic, dimensional business information is effectively transformed into *business knowledge, insight,* or *vision*.

The Economics of Integrating the ISC

One of the most profound characteristics of any ISC is that it consists of a well-defined (and highly purposeful) flow of data, from its initial sources, through a series of transformations, and then on to some ultimate destination (usually, the end users of analysis and reporting tools). Each refinement step in the ISC is implemented using one or more software products that are relevant to the specific objectives of that refinement step (see Figure 1.1). To effectively implement an ISC, the suite of tools must be fully capable of participating in this data interchange. Each tool must have an understanding of the nature of the data it is to consume: where it came from, what its various fields mean, what transformations it needs to perform on the data, where the results need to be stored, what target processes require these results, and so on.

Meta data is key to understanding what data means and how it is to be used. All the various software tools and products implementing the stages of any ISC rely on meta data to describe the data that they consume and transform. For a given product to properly operate on its data, that product must have a complete understanding of both the structure and semantic meaning of its data. This understanding is invariably provided by meta data. Meta data is a key input to the internal processing logic of the products and tools comprising an ISC. This product-internal logic uses meta data as the basis for making decisions on how to process the data. For a given collection of software products to effectively participate in an ISC and interoperate at the level of data, it must have a common understanding of the meta data describing that data. Put another way, each of the software products and tools comprising an ISC must be integrated at the meta data level before it can be effectively integrated at the data level.

Meta data-level integration, however, is difficult because most commercial products store meta data in widely varying formats. A given product's meta data is usually accessible to the rest of the world through some interface provided by the product, but just because meta data is *readily accessible* does not necessarily mean that it is *universally understandable*. The form and semantics of the meta data, as well as the interfaces providing access to it, are rarely uniform between products and are generally geared more toward the effective operation of each product, rather than toward integration with other products.

This diversity is largely the result of product development histories. Often, software products and tools are designed and built in relative isolation from one another. For example, an OLAP server produced by one vendor might be designed with an internal definition of meta data that is ideal for the server itself, but not necessarily adequate for the various reporting tools that need to work with the server. In other cases, vendors may have been reluctant to standardize on their meta data for fear of losing market share to competitors. When companies merge or acquire other companies, they find themselves having to support multiple product lines that, regardless of their similarities, support vastly different meta data structures.

In practice, tools with dissimilar meta data are integrated through the building of complex *meta data bridges*. A meta data bridge is a piece of software capable of translating meta data of one product into a format required by another product. Such a bridge needs to have detailed knowledge of the meta data structures and interfaces of each product that it attempts to integrate. Figure 1.2 illustrates several ISC components interconnected via meta data bridges. The hollow arrows illustrate the overall data flow, but each shaded arrow represents a distinct meta data bridge and its associated meta data flow. Note that a separate bridge is required for each unique pair of tools being integrated. Furthermore, the bridge usually needs to be bidirectional (that is, capable of understanding meta data mappings in either direction). For example, moving data from a transaction system to a data warehouse requires a bridge that maps transactional meta data to dimensional meta data (for example, mapping a transaction table definition to a relational star-schema). Providing data warehouse users with the ability to drill back to transactions requires a bridge that maps the dimensional meta data back to the transactional meta data. Each mapping is not necessarily an inverse of the other. Often, a certain amount of information loss occurs when translating from one form of meta data to another, and the bridge somehow needs to account for this.

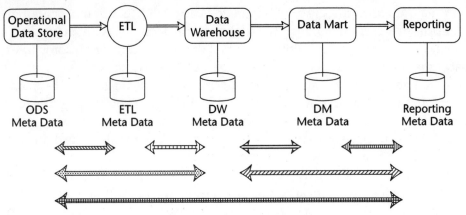

Figure 1.2 Meta data integration via point-to-point bridges.

Bridge building, whether performed by product vendors, third-party consultants, or the implementers of ISCs and data warehouses, is a very difficult and costly process. Bridges must have detailed knowledge of proprietary meta data models and interfaces, and knowledge of how the different models map to one another must be infused into the bridge. Furthermore, the processing logic comprising a particular bridge is not necessarily reusable in the construction of other bridges. Integrating software products in this manner diminishes the level of Return on Investment (ROI) of the data warehouse by adding considerably to its development and maintenance costs.

The need for globally available and universally understood meta data is partially addressed through the use of a *meta data repository*. A meta data repository is a special-purpose database that stores, controls, and makes available to the rest of the environment all relevant meta data components. Figure 1.3 shows a meta data repository deployed in the ISC of Figure 1.1. The various software products comprising the ISC retrieve global meta data from the central repository. The repository contains a single definition of the total meta data defining the ISC, based on a single metamodel specific to the repository product itself. Each product must implement its own repository access layer (yet another form of bridge), which understands the repository-specific meta data structures and knows how to map these repository-specific structures to product-specific meta data structures.

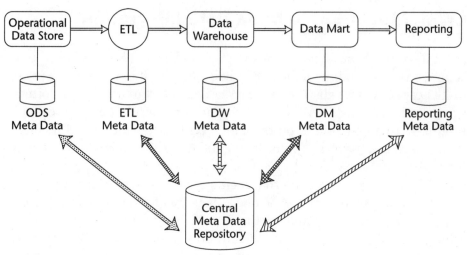

Figure 1.3   Meta data integration via a centralized repository.

Although this approach mitigates the need to build many point-to-point bridges (as shown in Figure 1.2), the bridging problem has not been completely eliminated. A different access layer needs to be developed for each software product participating in the ISC (either by the product vendor, repository vendor, or third-party integrator), and each access layer is still specific to a particular repository product. Although this solution has reduced overall cost, it has not reduced cost to its lowest possible level, nor has it eliminated the vendor lock-in issue. The repository is yet one more tool that needs to be integrated with other products and tools deployed throughout the environment.

Because the repository is built around its own proprietary metamodel, interfaces, and delivery services, a need exists to build meta data bridges (that is, the product-specific, repository access layers), although less so than in a point-to-point integration architecture. The cost of a meta data repository, whether purchased or custom built, and its integration with the rest of the environment additionally impact the ROI of the overall ISC effort. Thus, an implementer of an ISC solution must weigh the cost incurred by one meta data integration strategy versus the other (for example, point-to-point versus a central meta data repository). Although point-to-point solutions are expensive because of the proliferation of product-wise bridges, meta data repository solutions are costly as well.

CWM: Model-Based Meta Data Integration

Several software products can be integrated effectively only if they have a common understanding of the data flowing among them. Meta data is used in this capacity, as well. The same meta data used internally by software products is also used as the basis for data integration among different products. This situation is problematic because considerable difficulty is involved in using product-internal meta data as the basis for the external integration of those products. As described previously, most products have differing or incompatible internal metamodels and proprietary interfaces exposing their meta data. CWM overcomes this fundamental problem by providing a common metamodel that is sufficient for representing the most domain-oriented concepts with which tools need to deal. This representation is in the form of an abstract model that is completely platform-independent. To understand how this might be the case, let's first consider what it means to provide a model-based perspective on meta data.

The Model-Based Approach to Meta Data

For a given element of meta data to be an effective representation of the data it describes, it must describe its data precisely. Otherwise, no guarantee can be given that data operations based on that meta data will be performed correctly. Meta data does not usually describe all aspects of its data, only certain essential characteristics. For example, the meta data describing a numeric field in a record might define the field's position within the record and its type (for example, integer or real), but the meta data need not define the rules for adding two numeric values together. Presumably, an addition operation implemented within some software product already knows how to do this. All that's required by the addition operation is a limited amount of descriptive information about the data fields that are to be added together (for example, their location within the record and their numeric types). Meta data can generally afford to be abstract and concise. It need not describe all possible characteristics of the data, just the minimum information required by any operations to be performed on the data. What meta data does describe, however, it must describe precisely and unambiguously.

Often, the term *model* is used to describe such a precise, yet abstract, representation of something in the real world. For example, an architect might create a model of a house in the form of a blueprint. The blueprint precisely describes the house to be built but doesn't describe how to build the house (nor does it need to; the building contractor already knows how to do this).

Nor does the blueprint describe all aspects of the house, only the minimal information that the contractor requires. Furthermore, separate blueprints may be used to provide different viewpoints on the same house. Each is used by a different type of contractor in the construction of the house (plumbing, electrical, and so on). Although the blueprint is an abstract description of the house, it must still be a precise description. Otherwise, the contractor may not be totally sure about how to build certain features of the house. Furthermore, to ensure that any contractor can understand it, the architect must draw the blueprint in accordance with well-established rules on the formation of blueprints (a limited collection of well-defined notational symbols, specific rules for combining or connecting these symbols, and so on). A model is an abstract and precise description of something, and in the interest of correctness, models must be constructed according to certain formal rules. Otherwise, we could build models that are nonsensical.

Given all of these considerations, it is now easy to see why meta data is essentially a *formal model* of its data. Meta data is an abstract description of data that describes data precisely. Meta data must also be formulated according to certain rules ensuring that it is correctly formed. This guarantees that any software product aware of the meta data description rules will always be able to correctly interpret meta data when performing operations on the corresponding data.

Consider the simple relational table model shown in Figure 1.4. This simple model is expressed in the Unified Modeling Language (UML), which abstractly describes any relational table in terms of a named collection of columns. A relational table has a name. A column has a name and a data type. The data type is specified as a string whose value denotes the data type (for example, "integer"). A table may contain any number of columns, as indicated by the association line joining the table to the column. The "*" on the column end of the line denotes zero or more occurrences of a column, and the black diamond and the "1" at the table end denote a column as being owned by precisely one table.

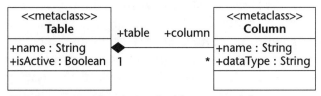

Figure 1.4 Simple relational table metamodel.

Note that this relational table model does not describe any particular relational table, but rather describes in general how a relational table might be defined. To specify an actual table, we need to create an *instance* of the table model. Figure 1.5 shows a UML *instance diagram* describing a simple relational table that stores data about products. The Product table consists of three columns: ID, which uniquely identifies each product; Name, which defines each product's name; and Color, which identifies the color of a particular product. The instance diagram represents an instance of the generic relational table model. Note that the generic model prescribes that a table may have multiple columns, and the instance has three such columns. Each of the three columns has a name and a data type, as prescribed by the generic model. The Product table also has a name, as prescribed by the generic model.

The instance diagram in Figure 1.5 describes the structure of some particular relational table (the "Product" table) that could be implemented in a relational database management system. Table 1.1 shows an outline of that table and some possible data values as rows within the table. Following is a statement in the Structured Query Language Data Definition Language (SQL DDL) that, when submitted to a relational database management system, results in the actual construction of the Product table:

```
CREATE TABLE Product (
     ID              INTEGER NOT NULL,
     Name              CHARACTER NOT NULL,
     Color           CHARACTER NOT NULL
);
```

It should be clear from this example that the instance diagram of Figure 1.5 is a *model* of the Product table. Furthermore, the abstract relational table model in Figure 1.4 is a *model of the model* (that is, a *metamodel*) of the Product table. Also, note that the SQL DDL for building the Product table could easily be derived from the Product table model (for example, via a software process that reads the UML instance diagram and translates it into equivalent table creation statements in SQL DDL). When a relational database engine processes the SQL DDL statement, it generates internal meta data describing the Product table and stores this meta data in the relational database *catalog*, which is essentially a local repository of meta data describing all databases currently maintained by the relational database engine. The relational engine also allocates all of the necessary physical resources for actually implementing the table in the database and storing its data rows, indexes, and so on, as part of the table-building process.

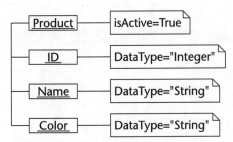

Figure 1.5   Product table meta data.

Users of various *data modeling tools* should be familiar with the scenario just described. Data modeling tools provide database architects or designers with the ability to visually define database schemas at various levels of abstraction, in the form of *entity-relationship diagrams*. In an entity-relationship diagram, an *entity* represents a type of object from the business domain being modeled (for example, Product entity, Customer entity, Account entity, and so on). Entities are connected via relationships that are very similar to the associations connecting Table and Column in the relational table metamodel of Figure 1.4. Entity-relationship diagrams generally start off as logical models, capturing the basic entities and relationships from the business domain. At some point, when the logical model is reasonably complete, the logical entity-relationship diagram is transformed by the data modeler into a physical entity-relationship diagram, through the further specification of primary and foreign keys, data types, referential integrity constraints, and so on. The physical entity-relationship diagram is then directly translated into a collection of SQL DDL statements capable of building the corresponding physical database schema. This capability of a data modeling tool might be viewed largely as a matter of convenience; it makes it unnecessary for the database modeler to hand code the SQL DDL from the visual entity-relationship diagram. A much more profound implication is that the entity-relationship diagram, like the Product table instance diagram in the previous example, effectively defines the meta data of the target information structures. The data modeling tool should be viewed not merely as a means of drawing entity-relationship models, but rather as a source of meta data, or perhaps even more profoundly, as a *meta data authoring tool*.

Table 1.1   Product Table and Its Data Values

PRODUCT ID	NAME	COLOR
1001	Widget	Red
2002	Gizmo	Blue
2022	Sproget	Teal
4034	Thingamagiger	Gray
5035	Gadget	Yellow

We have demonstrated that a model expressed in a formal language, such as UML, can be used to define the meta data describing some information structure or schema. We have also demonstrated that this formal model can be translated (by some software process created specifically for this purpose) into an equivalent meta data definition that can be used to create an actual instance of the information structure itself. What is perhaps not immediately obvious is the fact that these various formal models, such as the instance diagram of Figure 1.5, are generally *platform-independent*. They do not exhibit physical features of the computing platform used to deploy the actual information structure, because formal modeling languages (such as UML or the various data modeling notations) are generally platform-independent specification languages. A collection of SQL DDL statements can be viewed as a *platform-specific model* because it specifies the target information structure in the language of a particular computing platform (for example, a SQL-compliant relational database engine). The hypothetical translation process that converts a formal model, such as the UML instance diagram of Figure 1.5, into SQL DDL is said to *map* the platform-independent model to a platform-specific model, based on some set of formal *mapping rules* that the translation process implements.

Three very important conclusions can readily be drawn from the preceding observations:

- Any formal model of an information structure effectively *is* the meta data defining that information structure.

- Meta data, as a formal and platform-independent model, can exist *outside*, and *independently of*, any particular platform.

- Meta data, as a formal and platform-independent model, can be translated to any of a number of different platform-specific models, each representing a different target platform.

These conclusions are important because they give us our first step toward solving the meta data integration problem for diverse software products and tools. We see that one compelling approach is to develop an *external representation of meta data*, which is not dependent upon any particular product or tool. Such a representation is based on formal and platform-independent models of information structures, described using an appropriate formal language, such as UML. A product uses such a formal model as the basis for its own meta data by invoking an appropriate *import mapping* process to translate the formal model into an instance of its own product-specific meta data. Similarly, a product may expose its proprietary meta data to other products through an *export mapping* process that translates its internal meta data into a platform-independent, formal model.

How is this proposed solution any better than the meta data bridge solution described earlier? Recall that the main problem with meta data bridges is that each bridge must map between two proprietary, product-specific models. The bridge essentially needs to convert meta data from the format prescribed by one product's metamodel (the product's proprietary model of its own meta data) to that prescribed by the other product-specific metamodel. Now, if the metamodel itself is externalized and made independent of any particular implementation platform, and the products interchanging meta data agree on this common, external metamodel, then the problem of translating between proprietary implementation models is solved.

This approach to meta data-level integration and interoperability can be described as a *model-based approach to meta data integration*. It consists of exchanging shared meta data between software products in the form of externalized meta data definitions expressed as formal and product-independent models. Software products and tools participating in this environment agree on the common metamodel defining the overall domain, enabling them to readily understand any instances of that metamodel (for example, any shared meta data that might be interchanged). Each product maps this shared meta data to its own internal meta data representations. This requires that the metamodel be a reasonably complete representation of its domain and that the metamodel further provide some means of extension, whereby any semantic gaps in the metamodel can be compensated for in a standard, agreed-upon manner by participating products.

The model-based approach to meta data integration eliminates or significantly reduces the cost and complexities associated with the traditional point-to-point meta data integration architectures based on meta data bridges. This approach provides the same benefit to central repository-based, hub-and-spoke-style meta data architectures, as well. In point-to-point architectures, the model-based approach eliminates the need to build multiple meta data bridges, which interconnect each pair of product types that need to be integrated. Instead, each software product implements a *meta data adapter* (a layer of software) that understands the common metamodel and the internal, implementation metamodel of the product. The adapter is, of course, another form of a meta data bridge, but one that needs to be written only once for a given product, because all products agree on the common metamodel. This is in sharp contrast to the traditional meta data bridging approach, in which pair-wise bridges are built for every pair of product types that are to be integrated. The model-based solution clearly reduces the costs and complexities of repeatedly building and maintaining product-wise meta data bridges. This enhances the long-term ROI of the ISC or data warehouse effort.

Figure 1.6 illustrates a fully integrated ISC based on a model-based meta data integration architecture (in which the common metamodel, of course, is CWM).

An Overview of CWM

CWM is a complete metamodel of the data warehousing and business analysis problem domain. As a metamodel, CWM provides both the syntax and semantics required to construct meta data describing all components of a complete ISC.

CWM actually is comprised of a number of different but closely related metamodels. Each metamodel represents some sub-domain of the ISC environment. A block diagram describing the overall organization of CWM is shown in Figure 1.7. Each block represents a constituent metamodel, or *package*, of CWM and corresponds to an important functional area of a typical ISC. A given model derived from one of the CWM packages (for example, an instance of one of the constituent metamodels) defines a piece of meta data that, in turn, describes some data within the corresponding functional area. For example, a model derived from the relational metamodel is meta data describing some instance of relational data (that is, a collection of rows from our Product table). Note that whether or not this data actually exists out there in the real world doesn't really matter. The key point here is that regardless of whether or not the data exists right now or at some future point in time, we can still *describe it*, because models derived from CWM exist independently of any particular software product, technology, or platform.

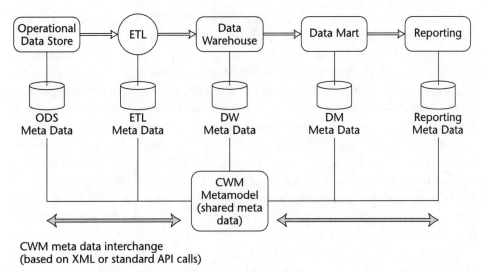

CWM meta data interchange
(based on XML or standard API calls)

Figure 1.6   An ISC integrated via a common metamodel.

We stated previously that a model-based meta data integration architecture requires a formal language capable of representing meta data in terms of shared platform-independent models. In CWM, this language is UML (actually, a very specific subset of UML). UML is an Object Management Group (OMG) standard language for specifying abstract models of discrete systems (Booch et al., 1999; Rumbaugh et al., 1999). UML is the notational basis for CWM, and CWM likewise *extends* a subset of the UML language to include data warehousing and business analysis domain concepts. CWM relies on the expressiveness and power of UML as a means of defining complex meta data structures and relationships.

Management	Warehouse Process			Warehouse Operation		
Analysis	Transformation	OLAP		Data Mining	Information Visualization	Business Nomenclature
Resource	Object	Relational		Record	Multi-dimensional	XML
Foundation	Business Information	Data Types	Expressions	Keys and Indexes	Software Deployment	Type Mapping
Object Model	Core		Behavioral		Relationships	Instance

Figure 1.7   CWM metamodel layering.

Note the lowest layer in the CWM block diagram of Figure 1.7, referred to as the *Object* layer. This UML subset layer is used by CWM as its base metamodel. The Object layer consists of four metamodels: *Core*, *Behavioral*, *Relationships*, and *Instance*. The Core metamodel defines the most basic, static modeling elements residing within the core of the UML language. The Behavioral metamodel extends those static structures to define behavioral things, such as operations and procedures. The Relationships metamodel defines the basic relationships between model elements, such as the association between Table and Column. Finally, the Instance metamodel defines modeling elements used to represent the actual instances of certain other modeling elements (for example, the association between a *class* and a specific *object*, as an instance of that class, can be modeled using constructs from the Instance metamodel).

CWM uses the object-oriented concept of *inheritance* to extend the modeling elements of this UML subset to define new modeling elements representing data warehousing and business analysis concepts. These new elements provide one with the capability to completely specify an instance of an ISC. To gain a better understanding of what these extended modeling elements consist of, let's continue with our examination of the various CWM sub-metamodels.

The next layer, called the *Foundation* layer, consists of metamodels that extend the Object layer modeling elements to produce representations of common services required by all components of an ISC. For example, the *Data Types* metamodel extends certain modeling elements in the Object layer to define new elements representing basic data types that we must be able to express in our meta data. *Type Mapping* defines new modeling elements that enable us to create models of mappings between dissimilar type systems (obviously necessary for ensuring interoperability between dissimilar software tools and platforms). The *Keys Indexes* metamodel similarly builds upon the basic modeling elements defined by the Object layer to define the abstract concepts of unique and foreign keys, as well as ordering constraints imposed on data sets. These concepts are fundamentally important to building models of relational database structures, but the notion of a unique key is not limited to a relational database. It is also important to record-oriented and multidimensional databases (for example, an OLAP dimension can define a unique key).

The *Business Information* metamodel defines elements that support the modeling of basic business information pertaining to the environment (for example, contact names and descriptions of modeling element instances). *Software Deployment* facilitates the modeling of component-oriented applications and their deployment across nodes in a distributed computing platform, and *Expressions* defines elements used to construct explicit expression structures (as expression trees) in a standard and interchangeable way. The key point to this layer is that, by defining these concepts at a very abstract level of the CWM architecture, we ensure that these concepts are defined only once and that they can be reused in more specific contexts.

The next layer of CWM, *Resource*, defines metamodels of the various types of data resources comprising an information supply chain. The *Relational, Record, Multidimensional*, and *XML* metamodels extend both the Object and Foundation layers to define new modeling elements used to construct meta data defining relational databases, record-oriented databases, multidimensional servers, and XML document-based data resources. Note that object-oriented databases are not explicitly represented, because the Object layer, as a subset of UML, is replete with object-oriented modeling concepts. We can use CWM to define any conceivable meta data representing the various types of data resources that need to be managed by a data warehouse or ISC.

Business analysis concepts, the real heart and purpose of the data warehouse and ISC, are represented by metamodels comprising the fourth layer of CWM, the *Analysis* layer. Perhaps one of the most important metamodels in the Analysis layer is the *Transformation* metamodel. This metamodel defines modeling elements that can be used to specify source and target mappings and transformations between data resource models (instances of the Resource layer metamodels), as well as source and target mappings and transformations between data resource models and any of the various *analysis models*. These mappings often cross one or more levels of abstraction. For example, a purely logical OLAP model satisfying some business analysis requirement might be formulated using the OLAP metamodel. Similarly, a physical model of a relational *star-schema* might be specified using the Relational metamodel. The two models, logical and physical, then are linked together using instances of transformation mappings. The dimensional tables of the star-schema relational database are *semantically identified* as the *physical implementations* of *logical dimension* by virtue of this semantic mapping.

The Analysis layer provides additional metamodels that support the modeling of analysis-oriented meta data: *data mining, business nomenclature*, and *information visualization*. Data mining defines modeling elements used to specify meta data associated with various data mining tools that are often applied against the various data resources to extract important patterns and trends from the data. Business nomenclature allows for the construction of meta data defining and relating taxonomies of business terms and concepts. Elements defined by the Visualization metamodel enable the construction of meta data that is relevant to advanced reporting and visualization tools. Collectively, these metamodels provide the necessary semantic constructs required to build meta data supporting the analysis phases of the ISC.

Finally, the *Management* layer defines two metamodels that are critical to defining meta data describing the ISC processing as a whole. The *Warehouse Process* metamodel enables us to model specific warehouse processes, such as ETL processes. *Warehouse Operation* defines modeling elements that are used to construct meta data defining the specific, periodic, and routine operations, such as scheduled events and their interdependencies. Also provided are elements that model the mechanisms used to track these activities. This meta data is of interest to ETL tools, time-dependent schedulers, and other warehouse management tools.

We've shown that CWM provides the semantically replete, common metamodel describing the problem domain that a model-based, meta data integration architecture for data warehousing and business analysis would require. If the various software products, tools, applications, and databases used in the construction of an ISC agree on the CWM metamodel, all are fundamentally capable of understanding the same instances of the CWM metamodel (models or meta data). Meta data can readily be interchanged (shared or reused) between the software components comprising the ISC. In fact, the collection of metamodels provided by CWM is comprehensive enough to model an entire data warehouse and ISC environment. A complete model of an entire ISC, from front-end data resources, to transformation and cleansing, to end-user analysis, to data warehouse management, can be constructed using the CWM metamodel. Such a model is essentially a top-to-bottom *slice* through the layers of the CWM metamodel.

This ISC model can be made available to the entire environment (for example, via either a meta data repository or through point-wise interchange) and consumed by CWM-aware tools comprising the ISC. Each tool consumes those portions of the shared, global model that are relevant to its operations. A relational server would read that portion of the ISC model defining the relational schema of the data warehouse and use this sub-model to build its internal catalog. Similarly, an OLAP server would extract an OLAP schema, along with transformation mappings back to the relational database schema, and use this particular sub-model as the basis for constructing its internal multidimensional structures and data resource links. Therefore, from a single model-based definition, an entire ISC could be generated from CWM-aware warehouse construction tools.

We also stated earlier that the common metamodel, serving as the heart of the model-based meta data integration approach, must be formulated according to certain formal rules (an abstract language) to ensure that all software tools will interpret the common metamodel in the same intended manner. In the case of CWM, the OMG's Meta Object Facility (MOF) provides this required set of formal rules. MOF is an OMG standard defining a common abstract language for the specification of metamodels. MOF is essentially a meta-metamodel, or model of the metamodel. It defines the essential elements, syntax, and structure of metamodels that are used to construct models of discrete systems. MOF serves as the common model of both CWM and UML. MOF semantics generally define certain meta data repository services that support model construction, discovery, traversal, and update. In particular, MOF defines meta data management semantics that define effective meta data authoring and publishing functions, especially if combined with support for visual modeling.

The model-based approach to meta data integration also requires a common interchange format for exchanging instances of shared meta data, as well as a common programming interface for meta data access. We had previously discussed the advantages of using the XML for this purpose, and this viewpoint is supported by much of the industry and advocated by leading meta data experts. The XML interchange encoding used by CWM is XML Metadata Interchange (XMI), an OMG standard that defines a formal mapping of MOF-compliant metamodels, such as CWM, to XML. XMI defines precisely how XML tags are to be used to store CWM metamodel instances in XML documents. The CWM metamodel is used to define a collection of XML tags expressed in the form of an XML Document Type Definition (DTD). CWM meta data (for example, instances of the CWM metamodel) then is serialized in XML documents. Each instance of meta data is stored as XML element content, delimited by appropriate metamodel tags. Communication of meta data content is both self-describing and inherently asynchronous, which is why XMI- and XML-based interchange is so important in distributed and heterogeneous environments.

Programmatic access to CWM-enabled meta data resources is defined via standard mappings from MOF-compliant metamodels to various programming languages. The MOF specification, in particular, defines a mapping from any MOF-compliant metamodel, such as CWM, to the OMG's Interface Definition Language (IDL), a language-neutral notation for specifying programmatic interfaces. The CWM specification includes the complete IDL definition for CWM. Defining a programmatic interface in some programming language of choice (for example, Java or C++) requires compiling the CWM IDL into interface definitions expressed in the syntax of the target language, using an appropriate IDL compiler for the target language.

Finally, we stated that a model-based, meta data integration solution must also provide some standard means of extending models, which is necessary to define highly product-specific meta data not accounted for by CWM. It is also necessary to be able to extend the metamodel by including new metamodels representing additional sub-domains that we might later want to include in our overall ISC solution. Because CWM is based on UML, we can rely on standard UML extension mechanisms to extend our models. These standard UML extension mechanisms consist of the modeling elements *Tagged Value*, *Stereotype*, and *Constraint*. These modeling elements are defined within the Core metamodel of the CWM Object layer. Extending the CWM metamodel, on the other hand, involves defining a new metamodel representing some new sub-domain. Both types of extension mechanism are treated in depth in the vertical model case studies in Part Two.

We have demonstrated throughout this chapter that CWM satisfies all of the model-specific characteristics of the model-based meta data integration approach. Much of the material described here is discussed in greater detail in subsequent chapters.

Summary

In this chapter, we thoroughly examined the need for comprehensive meta data integration in the data warehousing and business analysis environments. We used the metaphor of the Information Supply Chain (ISC) to describe the movement of data through this environment, and described why effective meta data integration between software products and tools supporting this environment is critical to ensuring that the supply chain flows smoothly.

We determined that a lack of meta data standards (that is, in terms of a commonly agreed-upon metamodel and an associated interchange format and programmatic interfaces) greatly inhibits meta data integration across the ISC. We concluded that this inability to integrate ISC tools and to share meta data in a standard way has a major impact on the economic ROI of data warehousing and business analysis efforts. In fact, we might even conclude that meta data integration (or the lack thereof) is perhaps the single greatest economic issue in the deployment of data warehousing and business analysis solutions.

The Object Management Group's (OMG's) Common Warehouse Metamodel (CWM) standard was described in detail, and we discussed how CWM is used in realizing completely integrated information supply chains comprised of multivendor software products and tools. CWM enhances the overall value-proposition for the ISC implementation effort, reducing integration costs and allowing for an optimal mixture of low-cost and best-of-breed tools. It does this by providing a model-based approach to meta data integration. We also delved considerably into the underlying OMG technologies for metamodeling and meta data interchange and interoperability that CWM leverages.

In Chapter 2, "An Architectural Survey of CWM," we investigate each of the major constituent metamodels of CWM, and describe how each metamodel represents its corresponding sub-domain of the data warehousing and business analysis environment.

An Architectural Survey of CWM

Chapter 1 provided a comprehensive overview of the Common Warehouse Metamodel (CWM) in terms of a model-based approach to solving meta data integration problems within the Information Supply Chain (ISC). The underlying Object Management Group (OMG) technical architecture for metamodeling and meta data interchange was also described, and an overview of CWM in terms of the layering of its constituent metamodels was also discussed in some detail.

This chapter further investigates the layered model architecture of CWM. In particular, each of the component metamodels of CWM is closely examined. Each metamodel (or *package*) solves a particular modeling problem within the data warehousing and business analysis domains. Complete CWM solutions are crafted by piecing together instances of modeling elements from one or more CWM packages. So one of the objectives of this survey is to demonstrate how each package effectively models the main sub-domain concepts it is intended to represent.

We also describe the reasonably fine-grained, modular organization of the CWM metamodel. When using CWM to construct models of data warehouses and ISC environments, and particularly when extending CWM to introduce new sub-domains, this high degree of modularity greatly facilitates the reuse of CWM. It also tends to lighten the overall implementation *footprint*, in that implementations of CWM solutions generally deploy only what they need from the core metamodel and no more.

The CWM Metamodel Packages

In Chapter 1 we gave a brief overview of the layered architecture of the CWM metamodel. Figure 2.1 illustrates the package structure of CWM that was first presented in Figure 1.7. It was pointed out that CWM consists of a total of 21 packages distributed over five functional layers of varying degrees of abstraction. We will investigate each of these layers and their constituent packages in turn, starting first with the core packages of the Object Model layer.

In the subsequent descriptions of each of the CWM packages, super-classes are shown in the diagrams for packages in the Object Model, Foundation, and Resource layers. However, at the higher, more abstract Analysis and Management layers, superclasses are not shown. This has been done to simplify the diagrams at the higher layers because packages in higher layers tend to have more classes than those at lower layers. The absence of superclasses in the diagrams at these layers makes them simpler to understand because the number of classes is reduced. The complete set of superclasses for the Analysis and Management layers can be found in the CWM specification.

Also, after discussing the first three layers, we will take a break from package descriptions for a while to explore how the CWM accomplishes three important tasks. We will then examine how:

- CWM uses inheritance to achieve reuse
- Meta data definitions are tied to the physical data resources
- Resource packages support creation of instance data objects

By the time we get to Part Two, "Introducing the Vertical Models," we will have acquired enough fundamental training in the basics of CWM organization to appreciate how CWM is used to construct such complex domain models.

Management	Warehouse Process			Warehouse Operation		
Analysis	Transformation	OLAP	Data Mining	Information Visualization	Business Nomenclature	
Resource	Object	Relational	Record	Multi-dimensional	XML	
Foundation	Business Information	Data Types	Expressions	Keys and Indexes	Software Deployment	Type Mapping
Object Model	Core	Behavioral		Relationships	Instance	

Figure 2.1   CWM 21 metamodel packages spanning five functional layers.

The Object Model Layer

The Object Model layer contains packages that define fundamental meta-model concepts, relationships, and constraints required by the rest of the CWM packages. These concepts create an environment in which the remainder of the CWM packages can be defined in a crisp and clear fashion, enabling them to concentrate on their individual purposes and minimizing the extent to which they must deal with infrastructure and other house-keeping details. The Object Model packages constitute the complete set of fundamental metamodel services needed by the other CWM packages; no other services are necessary for the definition of the CWM.

The Object Model is essentially a subset of the Unified Modeling Language (UML). Most of its classes and associations directly correspond to UML classes and associations. This correspondence is intentional. UML provides a strong, widely used modeling foundation, and CWM attempts to leverage the substantial strengths of its UML heritage. It includes portions of UML that CWM heavily depends on without requiring support for the unused parts. Furthermore, the Object Model package structure minimizes the number of object-oriented capabilities inherited by widely used, non-object-oriented concepts.

The Core Package

The Core package contains basic classes and associations used by all other CWM packages. As such, it depends on no other packages. Core includes the basic UML infrastructure required to define non-object-oriented data stores, such as relational databases and record files, without introducing exclusively object-oriented concepts. Core also contains support classes and data types widely used by other packages. The principal classes of the Core package are shown in Figure 2.2.

In CWM, every class in every package is a sub-class of the Element class. Element has no attributes and provides no services beyond being a single point from which all objects in a CWM description can be found. If you think of CWM as a tree-structured arrangement of classes, then Element is the root of the tree.

With the exception of a few support classes, such as TaggedValue, all CWM classes are also sub-classes of the ModelElement class. ModelElement provides a number of basic attributes (for example, *name*) for all of its sub-classes. Although perhaps subtle in appearance, this technique of relating general-purpose classes to ModelElement is used throughout CWM to provide metamodel services to every model element. The notion of model elements is pervasive in CWM, and is used frequently to refer to any named CWM object (that is, any instance of the ModelElement class).

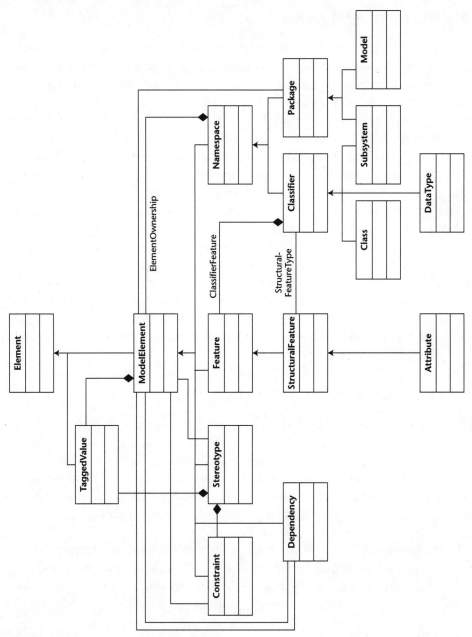

Figure 2.2 Classes of the Core package.

At its heart, the Core package provides for the description of things that have structure. Structured things include familiar computer system objects like relational database tables, records in a file, and members of Online Analytical Processing (OLAP) cube dimensions. In UML terms, the individual items of a thing's structure are called *features* and are represented by the StructuralFeature class. For example, the features of a relational table are the columns in the table; for a record, they are an ordered list of the record's fields. CWM allows for nonstructural features as well; they are described by the Behavioral package. The Attribute class represents structural features that can have an initial value.

Features are owned by Classifiers through a composite association called *ClassifierFeature*. A classifier is a thing that has structure; for example, both records and relational tables are types of classifiers. The notion of *classifier* is very similar to the idea of *type* used in modern programming languages. *Integer* and *character* are simple, frequently encountered programming language types; they are classifiers in CWM, but they have no features. *Address*, in contrast, is a compound type (classifier) whose features might consist of *street*, *city*, *state*, and *zip code*. In the same way, a relational table is a classifier whose features are its columns, and a record is a classifier whose features are its fields. Note that StructuralFeatures are owned by one classifier and are related to another classifier. The former is the StructuralFeature's owner, and the latter, reached via the association called *StructuralFeatureType*, is its type. A StructuralFeature cannot have the same classifier as both its owner and its type.

The class named *Class* represents classifiers that can have multiple instances. So, Tables are really instances of Class because they can contain multiple data rows. In contrast, the DataType class represents classifiers that have only one instance; *integer* and *character* are instances of DataType.

Although Namespaces have no attributes, they are critically important because they ensure that individual objects can be uniquely identified by their names. Consequently, *nearly every model element in a CWM description will be owned by some Namespace*. Normally, the only model elements that are not owned by Namespaces are those representing top-level Namespaces (that is, Namespaces not owned by other Namespaces). The composite association between Namespace and ModelElement, called *ElementOwnership*, allows Namespaces to own ModelElements, and hence, other Namespaces. This association is one of the primary structuring mechanisms within the CWM. This association enables model elements to be organized in hierarchical, or treelike, arrangements in which the parent Namespace is said to contain, or own, its child ModelElements regardless of their ultimate type. ElementOwnership is reused extensively throughout the CWM to indicate ownership relationships between classes at every level.

Because of the package structure of the CWM, model elements must be able to reference objects in other packages. This is achieved by the Package sub-class of Namespace. Packages, because they are Namespaces, allow model elements of arbitrary types to be collected into hierarchies. However, because a ModelElement can be owned by, at most, one Namespace, we cannot use this mechanism to pull in ModelElements owned by different Namespaces. Instead, the Package class provides the notion of *importing* ModelElements from other packages. This technique, based on rules established by the underlying Meta Object Facility (MOF) specification, is used to associate objects across package boundaries and is the foundation for linking descriptions of database schemas and file layouts to their physical deployments within an enterprise. We will see extensive examples of this in Part Two. Also, refer to the *Software Deployment Package* section later in this chapter for more information on this technique.

Behavioral Package

The Behavioral package collects classes that provide CWM classes in other packages with behavioral characteristics frequently found in object-oriented systems. Software systems that include the Behavioral package can create classifiers capable of having the object-oriented concepts of *operation*, *method*, *interface*, and *event* specified as part of their definition in a CWM model. The organization of the Behavioral package is shown in Figure 2.3.

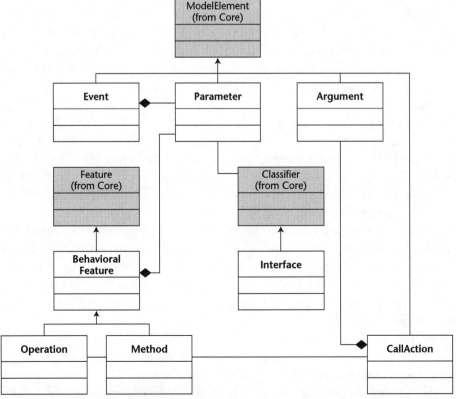

Figure 2.3 Classes of the Behavioral package.

The package's object-oriented features are centered on the Behavioral-Feature class. BehavioralFeature is similar to the StructuralFeature class described in the Core package in that both are classes of Feature and can be owned by classifiers. In everyday terms, BehavioralFeature can be thought of as representing executable units of program logic that an object can perform. As such, they have a name, a set of parameter definitions describing their input and output values, and, optionally, a returned value. The parameters of a behavioral feature are described by the Parameter class.

A BehavioralFeature is either an operation or a method. An operation is a specification of a callable unit of programmatic logic shared by all of the methods that implement the operation. In contrast, a method represents the implementation of a particular programmatic unit in some programming language. The methods implementing a particular operation all perform the same task but may do so in different ways or may be written in different programming languages. Actual invocations of methods can be recorded using the CallAction class. The ownership association between the CallAction class and the Argument class enables the recording of the actual values of parameters used in the call.

An interface is a collection of operations that defines some service that classifiers can provide to their clients. Individual classifiers may provide multiple interfaces.

The Event class represents an observable occurrence and may have parameters. CWM, however, does not record the action taken when a particular event occurs. This decision is left to individual application programs.

Relationships Package

Classes in the Relationships package describe how CWM objects are related to one another. Two types of relationships are defined by CWM: Generalization and Association, as shown in Figure 2.4. Because CWM classes are defined at the M2 level in the OMG metamodel architecture, the Generalization, Association, and AssociationEnd classes allow specific instances of other CWM classes to be related and arranged in hierarchies at the M1 level. MOF classes defined at the M3 level also provide the framework that allows the M2 CWM classes shown in this chapter to be related and arranged in hierarchies.

Generalization is a relationship between more general objects and more specific objects that enables them to be organized into an abstraction *hierarchy*. In abstraction hierarchies, the more general objects occupy the *parental*, or superclass, position, and more specific objects occupy the *child*, or sub-class, position. Although generalization hierarchies are very similar in appearance to organizational structure diagrams, the semantic relationships between the parent and child objects more closely match that of taxonomic relationships in biology in which the child is considered to be a type of the parent. The Generalization class identifies two classifiers, one representing a parent and the other representing its child. Because a child can have children of its own, arbitrarily deep hierarchies can be created. The CWM allows children to have more than one parent classifier. Although multiple parent situations are not encountered frequently in CWM, they do exist. For example, the Subsystem class defined in the Core package has the classes Classifier and Package as parents. This means that Subsystems have the characteristics of both Classifiers (the ability to have features) and Packages (the ability to own and import model elements).

Associations define specific relationships between two (or more!) classifiers. Associations that relate two classifiers are *binary*, and those that relate more than two classifiers are *n-ary*. N-ary relationships are quite rare, and most applications of CWM will have no need to create them. The end points of an association are represented by the AssociationEnd class. Associations own their ends using the ClassifierFeature association defined in the Core package. AssociationEnds identify the classifiers to which they are connected via the Core package's type association between StructuralFeature and Classifier.

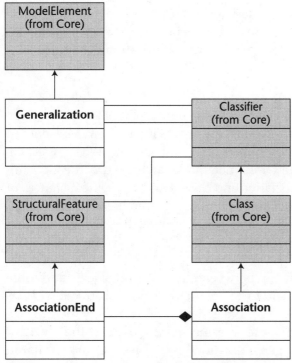

Figure 2.4   Classes of the Relationships package.

Instance Package

In addition to interchanging meta data with CWM, it is often useful to include small quantities of data as well. This capability can be especially useful for data that represents the allowed values for some attribute, such as a column in a relational table. Such columns are sometimes categorical, because they define the allowed types of rows that can be stored in the table. For example, a library database might have a table containing books with a column describing the type of each book; the type column would contain values like "fiction," "nonfiction," "reference," and so on. CWM's Instance package provides the infrastructure required to include data values along with meta data in a CWM interchange. The Instance package is shown in Figure 2.5.

All data instances are either DataValues or Objects. An object is an instance of some classifier that defines the structure of the object. Objects own a collection of slots. Each slot represents the value of one of the StructuralFeatures (usually Attributes) of the classifier that describes the structure of the object. If a slot represents a StructuralFeature that is itself a classifier, the slot contains another object that owns still other slots. Otherwise, the slot contains a DataValue that specifies the data value.

Extent class is a sub-class of the Package class from the Core package. This class is used to collect multiple objects of the same kind using the ElementOwnership association. Extents might be used, for example, to own all of the objects comprising the instance values of some classifier.

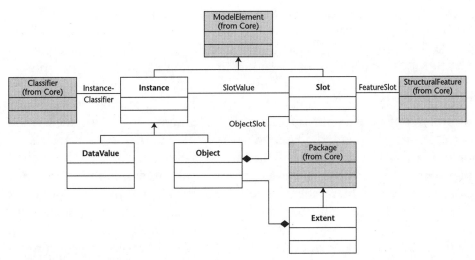

Figure 2.5   Classes of the Instance package.

Foundation Layer

CWM's Foundation Layer contains packages that provide common services to other packages residing at higher layers. In this respect, Foundation packages differ from Object Model packages, whose services are of a general-purpose nature and not specifically designed for CWM.

Business Information Package

The Business Information package provides general-purpose services to other CWM packages for recording facts about the business environment in which a data warehouse interchange takes place. The package is not meant to be a complete representation of business environments but rather to provide just those services that the CWM design team felt were necessary to accomplish the interchange of data warehouse meta data. Although it is not complete, the Business Information package provides a framework in which specific CWM applications can create extensions to meet their particular business meta data needs. This package is shown in Figure 2.6.

Three classes provide access to business information services: Description, Document, and ResponsibleParty. Description allows general-purpose textual information to be stored within the CWM model element. Typically, Descriptions contain comment, help, or tutorial text about some Model-Element. However, descriptive text can service any required purpose. Descriptions can be tied to a single model element or shared by many. Descriptions can even contain text describing other Descriptions, because the model elements that the text is linked to are themselves Description objects.

Document is very similar to Description, except that they are assumed to be stored at some location outside of the CWM meta data. For example, you would find the text of a Description embedded in a CWM XMI interchange file, but a Document might be found in a filing cabinet in the corporate records department. In the XMI interchange file, you would find that the Document class has the notation "look in the filing cabinet in corporate records," but you would not find the Document's text. This distinction between descriptions and documents was created so that CWM interchange files would not be unnecessarily burdened with large or structurally complex text blocks. Because Documents are a sub-class of Namespace, they can be arranged in hierarchies as well, permitting the complete structure of a complicated document (that is, all of its chapters, sections, subheadings, and so on) to be represented, if necessary. In this way, any ModelElement could be linked to its formal definition in a particular section of a complicated design document.

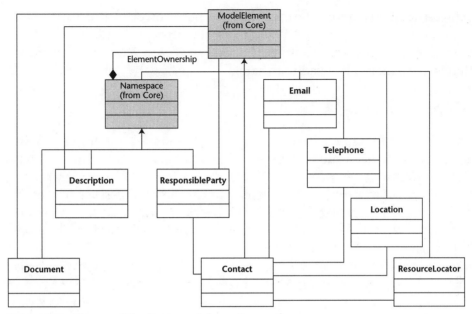

Figure 2.6 Classes of the Business Information package.

ResponsibleParty enables people or organizational units, such as the Information Technology (IT) department, to be identified as responsible for, or at least, as interested in hearing about, every ModelElement. As with Descriptions and Documents, ResponsibleParties can be arranged in numerous ways including hierarchical ownership trees. Because of the close structural correspondence between trees and organizational structures, ResponsibleParty objects can be used to represent complete organization charts, allowing responsibility for particular model elements in an information system to be closely tied to the organizational units directly responsible for them.

ResponsibleParties also can be associated with multiple sets of contact information. Each set of contact information can have multiple telephone numbers, email addresses, locations, or resource locators (typically, these would be in the form of Internet Uniform Resource Locators, or URLs, but this is not a requirement). The associations between Contact objects and Telephone, Email, Location, and ResourceLocators are ordered so that contact priorities can be retained as well. For example, you might want to call the IT director's office first, mobile phone second, and home third.

Because Descriptions, Documents, and ResponsibleParties can be arranged in tree structures with the ElementOwnership association and linked to ad hoc ModelElements with their individual associations to ModelElement, complex relationships can be constructed. These powerful structuring techniques were included in the CWM so that potentially complicated business scenarios could be accurately expressed. However, as with all complex things, they should be used with care.

DataTypes Package

The notion of *type* (a name that describes what kind of a thing something *is*) is central to most modern programming languages and data management systems. Types provide the foundation from which programming systems begin to capture the meaning and behavior, or *semantics*, of the real-world activities that they mimic by restricting the kinds of values and operations that are relevant for particular computer memory locations. Types have evolved from the loosely defined and easily circumvented memory overlays of assemblers and COBOL through primitive data types, such as *integer* and *boolean*, and structured types, such as C's *struct* and Pascal's *record*, to become perhaps *the* central idea in modern type-safe programming languages, such as Java and C++. In object-oriented programming languages and modeling languages like UML and CWM, the *class* construct is fully equivalent to the type concept. A class is merely a user-definable type. The concept of type most closely corresponds to the semantics of the CWM's Classifier class.

The collection of primitive types and type structuring capabilities of a programming language or database system is its *type system*. Most modern type systems share many important types in common. The notions of integer number, Boolean, float-point number, and fixed-precision number are widely supported. Within the boundaries imposed by various value representation techniques on their underlying hardware platforms, data characterized by such types can be exchanged between systems. However, seldom do multiple type systems share collections of types that completely overlap. The success of an exchange can even be influenced by low-level hardware details of the particular systems involved. The result is that the exchange of data values between systems is fraught with difficulties and challenges. No guarantee exists that exchanging data between matching releases of the same software system running under identical operating systems on architecturally equivalent hardware platforms will always be trouble-free.

In the realm of meta data interchange, a CWM-based tool must be able to recognize type system incompatibilities and respond accordingly. To do this, the CWM designer must be able to describe the type system of data resources that participate in CWM-mediated interchanges. After a data resource's type system is described in CWM, it can be exchanged with other CWM-compliant tools. The DataTypes package, shown in Figure 2.7, provides the infrastructure required to support the definition of both primitive and structured data types. Defining type systems and mapping data types between them is dealt with by the TypeMapping package, which is described later in this chapter.

Primitive numeric data types like *byte*, *short*, *integer*, *long*, *float*, *real*, and (single) *character* are defined by creating an instance of the Core's DataType class to represent them. The DataType instance appropriate for a particular attribute is referenced via the StructuralFeatureType association defined in the Core package. Primitive numeric data types that require additional information to complete their definitions, such as *decimal* and *fixed*, whose definitions require precision and scale, are also created as instances of DataType. The values required to complete their definitions are, however, stored in the Attribute instance rather than with the DataType itself. Modeling parameterized data types in this way keeps the number of DataType instances to a manageable level. To enforce this style, a constraint defined on the DataType class prevents it from having attributes that could be used to store parameter attributes, such as precision and scale.

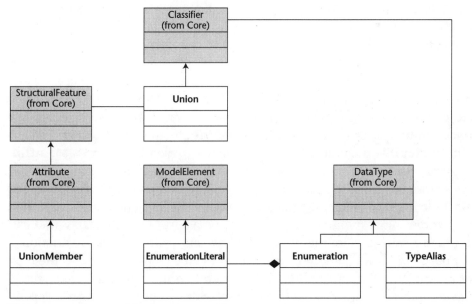

Figure 2.7 Classes of the DataTypes package.

The representation of string data types can be done in several ways; the appropriate choice usually is dictated by the semantics of the programming language whose types are being described. In languages whose strings do not have defined lengths, an instance of DataType can be used. If the language, even optionally, defines string lengths, creating a parameterized data type like that described for *decimal* and *fixed* might be appropriate, with the string length being recorded in the corresponding Attribute instance. If strings have the semantics of an array of characters (as is the case in the C language), strings might be better treated as a sub-class of the language's array constructs. When exchanging strings that use different representations, the TypeMapping or Transformation packages can be used to identify correct handling protocols.

CWM does not define the concept of an *array*. Array definitions are left to extension packages supporting specific programming languages, which require them because of the semantic differences that exist between the implementation of arrays by various languages and operating systems; however, direct interchange can be problematic. An example of how to define arrays for CORBA IDL language is provided in the CWM specification.

The DataTypes package does provide general-purpose support for structured types like C's *struct* and Pascal's *record* data types, union data types, and enumerations. Simple structured types are handled directly by creating instances of the Core package's Classifier class. The values or fields owned by simple structured types are StructuralFeatures of their Classifier and can be found via the ClassifierFeature association.

Unions are more complex structured data types. They can best be thought of as a set of simple, alternative structured types. The choice of which union member is present is fully dynamic and can be changed by the user at any time. For example, the *Variant* data type defined by Microsoft's Visual Basic language is implemented using a union data structure. In some programming languages, unions can contain an attribute, the union's *discriminator*, which identifies the union member currently present. Discriminator attributes can reside either outside or inside the union members. (When placing discriminators inside union members, be sure to include the discriminator attribute in every union member!) Although some implementations of union data types allow the union members to be a sort of type overlay that can access the same area of memory, CWM does not support this distinction.

Enumerations are named sets of constant values that can serve as the type of an attribute. The individual values in an enumeration are *enumeration literals* and are referenced by their names. For example, an attribute specifying a day of the week might have a data type called Weekday whose enumerated values are Sunday, Monday, Tuesday, Wednesday, Thursday, Friday, and Saturday. CWM allows optional numeric values to be associated with enumeration literals.

The TypeAlias class allows aliases, or other names, to be defined for data types but does not change the definition of a data type alias in any other way. Although type aliases can be useful in any language, they were added to CWM specifically to support the needs of the CORBA IDL languages.

We will see a number of examples of application of CWM DataTypes in Part Two.

Expressions Package

In programming systems, an expression is an ordered combination of values and operations that can be evaluated to produce a value, set of values, or effect. As such, expressions can be used to describe logical relationships between their component values and to describe algorithmic sequences of steps. Indeed, some programming languages are considered to be elaborate expressions. Because one of CWM's chief goals is to promote meta data interchange in environments, the capability to exchange expressions is paramount. Unfortunately, this capability often does not exist in data warehousing systems. Rather, senders and receivers generally share little or no common language syntax or semantics.

Normally, expressions are encoded in the syntax of a specific language. However, in this form, their interchange can be achieved only if both the sender and receiver share the same language syntax and semantics. Such expressions are called *black box* expressions because their content cannot be discerned by an entity that does not share knowledge of the common expression format. For example, a C language expression is meaningless to a Fortran compiler. CWM provides direct support for the exchange of black box expressions with the Expression class and its sub-classes in the Core package. (Expression classes were not explicitly discussed in the previous discussion of the Core package.) The Expression class allows an expression's text, as well as the name of the language in which the text was written, to be recorded. Understanding of the content of a black box expression is left, however, to the sender and receiver. CWM has no knowledge of the meaning of the content of the expression text.

CWM also provides for *white box* expressions so that expressions can be exchanged between senders and receivers that do not share a common language. In a white box expression, the individual components within an expression (that is, its values and operations) are exposed to CWM, permitting reference to operations and attributes already defined in CWM. In addition, white box expressions permit the tracking of the participation of individual attributes in expressions to facilitate analysis of the moment of data within a data warehouse process. White box expressions are defined using the metamodel shown in Figure 2.8.

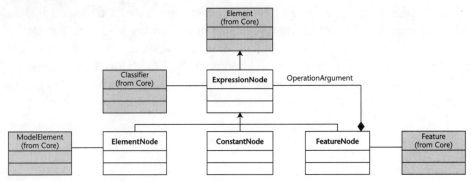

Figure 2.8   Classes of the Expression package.

To record an expression in the Expression package, it first must be con-verted to a form that is compatible with the structure of the classes in the package and at the same time be language-neutral. In principle, virtually any expression, irrespective of the language in which it is written, can be converted to a (possibly nested) sequence of function calls. Converting expressions to a function representation matches the object-oriented nature of the CWM and is a technique that can be executed by the vast majority of experienced programmers. For example, the famous equation $E = mc^2$ can be represented in a functional notation as follows:

```
Assign(E, Multiply(m, Power(c, 2)))
```

Reading from the inside out, an equivalent English form of this functional expression might be, "Raise c to the second power, multiply the square by m, and assign the result to E."

To place a functional expression in the CWM, first define each of the functions as an operation of some classifier (perhaps even one that was defined specifically for this purpose). In our example, operations named *Assign*, *Multiply*, and *Power* would be required. Second, create attributes to define the variables E, m, and c, and create DataValue instances to hold each of their values. Finally, create instances of FeatureNode for each of the functions and values and a ConstantNode instance to hold the value 2. (A more complete description of this example is available in the CWM specification.)

Functional expressions can be stored directly in a hierarchical data struc-ture. The tree-structure of the CWM Expression package is provided by the nested relationships between functions in which the result of one function (for example, *Power*) acts as an actual parameter to its containing function (*Multiply*). These tree relationships are recorded by the OperationArgument composite association between FeatureNode and ExpressionNode. Feature-Nodes representing functions are linked to operations that define them via the association between FeatureNode and Feature (a superclass of Operation). Similarly, FeatureNodes representing variables are linked Attributes (a sub-class of Feature) that define them via the same association. ConstantNodes directly hold the values of constants in a locally declared attribute and do not need to be linked to some Feature. The ElementNode class permits CWM expression elements access to any object in the CWM store that is not a Feature.

Every node in a CWM expression is an ExpressionNode. The association between ExpressionNode and Classifier allows the type of any node in an expression tree to be specified. However, specifying ExpressionNode types is optional and needs to be done only for the root ExpressionNode (the *Assign* FeatureNode in our example) when a return value is required. Type classifiers can be recorded for intermediate nodes whenever there is reason to do so. Each ExpressionNode also contains an attribute of type Expression; this attribute can be used at any node to record useful information about the node. For example, in an ExpressionNode tree describing a SQL query, the Expression attribute of the root ExpressionNode instance might be used to record the text of the complete query.

When creating expression attributes in CWM, it may not always be clear whether a black box or white box expression will be needed. In such situations, declare the type of the attribute as an ExpressionNode (a white box) rather than as an Expression (a black box). In this way, you can store either type of expression in the attribute. If a black box expression is needed, place the language name and expression text in the expression attribute of the ExpressionNode and create no expression nodes for it.

Keys and Indexes Package

Much like the one at the back of this book, an *index* is a list of elements arranged in an order other than the physical sequence of the elements themselves. In a database management system, an index is used as a performance optimization technique to specify alternative orderings of data objects. When an index exists that matches the structure of a query, database management software can use it to return data objects more quickly than it could if the index were not present.

A *key* is a set of one or more values that identifies, often uniquely, some record within a database. Also, keys may be used in indexes to identify the record at this index location and, in relational databases, as the basis upon which relationships between data rows are constructed.

Because keys and indexes are used by several CWM packages and by some extension packages (see Volume 2 of the CWM specification for examples), classes supporting them have been included at the CWM Foundation layer. The Keys and Indexes package is shown in Figure 2.9.

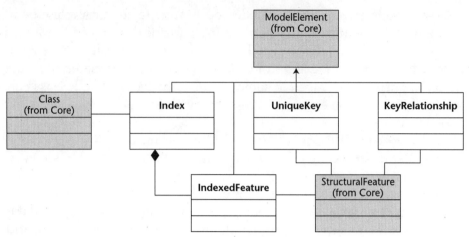

Figure 2.9 Classes of the Keys and Indexes package.

The Index class represents index data structures and is said to *span* a class. The association between these classes records this relationship and is required because an index that doesn't span a class is meaningless. Instances of the IndexedFeature provide links to the attributes of the spanned class; these links describe the index's key and are owned and ordered via the composite association to Index. Mapping index key features in this way allows them to remain attributes of their owning class and still participate in the definition of spanning indexes.

The UniqueKey class defines the notion of a key that uniquely identifies a member of a class. Although not shown in the figure, classes own their UniqueKey instances using the ElementOwnership association. Much like index keys, UniqueKeys are linked to, and ordered by, the association to StructuralFeature (usually, its Attribute sub-class). UniqueKey is a super-class of the relational database notion of a *primary key*.

KeyRelationship instances represent relationships that are based on shared key values, similar to the *foreign key* of relational databases. Like UniqueKeys, KeyRelationships are owned by the class that contains them. In relational database terms, the KeyRelationship is owned by the class that contains the foreign key, not the class containing the primary key. KeyRelationships are key fields linked by an ordering association to StructuralFeature.

To better understand how CWM models keys, note that they are *not* modeled as classifiers. Rather, they are ModelElements that represent the roles played by collections of fields. This distinction is important because the definition of the Core package does not permit Features to be owned by more than one classifier. Consequently, if keys were modeled as classifiers, fields could not be owned by both their class and the possibly multiple keys in which they might participate.

Software Deployment Package

The Software Deployment package records how software and hardware in a data warehouse are used. CWM-enabled warehouse management tools can use the information found here to locate hardware and software components of the warehouse. The package attempts to capture only as much of the operational configurations as is needed to service other CWM packages; it does not try to be a complete or general-purpose model of any data-processing configuration. Figure 2.10 shows the package classes and associations.

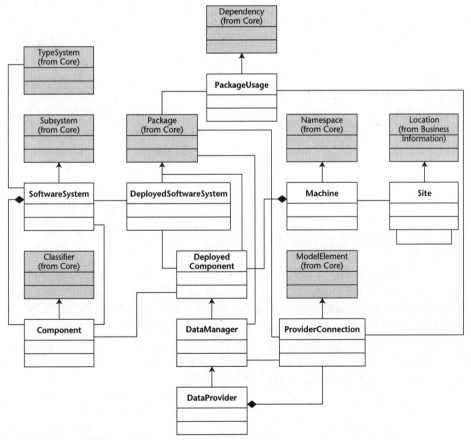

Figure 2.10   Classes of the Software Deployment package.

Software packages are modeled as SoftwareSystem instances. A SoftwareSystem can be thought of as representing an installable unit of software that you might purchase from a software vendor. Each SoftwareSystem can record identifying information such as *name, type, subtype, vendor,* and *version*. A TypeSystem instance can be associated with a SoftwareSystem providing a link to the data types that it defines. Individual parts of an installable software system are modeled by the Component class. Components are owned by SoftwareSystems. So that they can be shared without violating the single ownership nature of the ElementOwnership association, components can be imported by other SoftwareSystems.

The actual installation of a software package on a computer is modeled by the DeployedSoftwareSystem class, and an installed component is represented by the DeployedComponent class. DeployedComponents are linked to the Machines on which they are deployed, and Machines are owned by Sites, which may be arranged hierarchically to reflect organizational structure or similar relationships.

DataManagers represent software components that provide access to data, such as database management systems and file systems. As discussed in the following section, each of the Resource layer packages has a subclass of the Core's Package class, which inherits the relationship between Package and DataManager that is used to link the meta data resource's meta data to its physical deployment.

A DataProvider is a kind of DataManager that provides access to data stored in other DataManagers. This class is used to model data interfaces like Open Data Base Connectivity (ODBC) and Java Data Base Connectivity (JDBC) that do not actually own the data to which they provide access. The PackageUsage class allows DataProviders to provide access to other DataManager's data under names not used by the DataManager itself.

TypeMapping Package

As discussed in the DataTypes package, a key component of successful data warehouse interchange is the capability to correctly transfer data defined by the type systems of different software products. The DataTypes package provides the capability to define data types. In contrast, the TypeMapping package defines the notion of type systems as a collection of data types and supports the mapping of data types between type systems. The package metamodel is shown in Figure 2.11.

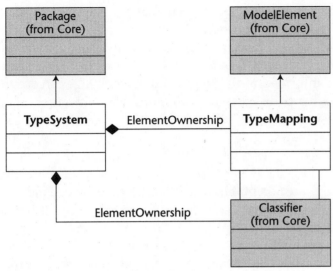

Figure 2.11 The TypeMapping metamodel.

The TypeSystem class represents a collection of data types defined by some software package or programming language. Type systems can be recognized by the names or the content of the version information attributes they contain. Best practice guidelines suggest that a convention about how type system names are constructed within an organization will simplify the process of finding a specific TypeSystem instance.

TypeSystem instances own two separate sets of objects. One set describes the data types that the TypeSystem defines; the other set identifies the TypeMapping instances, which describe how the TypeSystem's data types are mapped into the type systems of other products. Because both sets of objects are owned via the ElementOwnership association, you will need to examine the type of each object to determine what it might be. Any object that is a TypeMapping instance represents how type mapping occurs; any other object type is a data type.

TypeMapping instances are unidirectional; they define movement of data from a source type in the current TypeSystem to a target type in another TypeSystem. Consequently, a reciprocal pair of TypeMapping instances is required to model a two-way transfer, one in each of the type systems involved. It is, however, perfectly acceptable for a type mapping to be defined in only one direction.

If a TypeMapping instance exists, the mapping that it describes is considered *permissible*. If no TypeMapping instance exists for a pair of data types, any desired mappings between them must be handled by the Transformation package in the Analysis layer. TypeMapping instances have two flags that provide additional information about how data interchange can occur. Because a type may be mapped successfully to more than one target type, the *isBestMatch* flag usually will be true for whichever of the available mappings is the *preferred* mapping.

If more than one TypeMapping instance between a source and a target is marked as a best match, it is up to the application to decide which one to use. Some type mappings are acceptable within some value ranges and not acceptable elsewhere; the *isLossy* attribute should be set to true in the latter case and false in the former. For example, a long data type can be mapped to another compatible long data type regardless of the value being interchanged. However, a long data type can be interchanged successfully to an integer data type only when the value of the data being transferred is less than the maximum value that can be stored in an integer data type. *isLossy* can be set to true in the latter case to indicate that the mapping may be subject to value truncation errors, depending upon the value interchanged.

Resource Layer

CWM packages in the Resource layer describe the structure of data resources that act as either sources or targets of a CWM-mediated interchange. The layer contains metamodel packages that permit descriptions of object-oriented databases and applications, relational database management systems, traditional record-oriented data sources such as files and record model database management systems, multidimensional databases created by OLAP tools, and eXtensible Markup Language (XML) streams.

Object Package

The CWM already contains a perfectly good object model, in the form of the Object Model layer. Consequently, CWM does not attempt to create another one. Instead, the Object Model layer Core, Behavioral, Relationship, and Instance packages can be used directly to create descriptions of object-oriented data resources. These packages can be used to describe the structure of object-oriented databases and of object-oriented application components that act as data sources (for example, Component Object Model (COM) and Enterprise Java Bean (EJB) objects).

If you encounter an object-oriented data source with features or capabilities that cannot be handled by the Object Model packages, an extension package can be defined to add support for the additional capabilities. If you need to create an extension package, it will need to define only those classes and associations required to support the additional features. The modeling capabilities of the existing Object Model packages can continue to be used as they are; you should not need to duplicate any metamodel features already provided.

Relational Package

Relational database schemata can be described by the Relational package. The metamodel for the Relational package, a portion of which is shown in Figure 2.12, supports the description of SQL99-compliant relational databases, including its object-oriented extensions. This standard was selected because of its widespread acceptance in the data processing community and because it is vendor-neutral. Although the CWM design team knew of no vendor's relational database that had fully implemented the SQL99 standard, virtually all commercially important relational database managements implement significant portions of this standard. The result is that the CWM design team believes the Relational metamodel is sufficient to support general-purpose, CWM-mediated interchange between relational databases from the majority of relational vendor database management systems. This conclusion has been tested and verified by the various verification and production efforts of CWM-submitting companies who build relational Database Management System (DBMS) products.

Although the Relational metamodel package is sufficient for the interchange of relational data, it is unlikely that it can hold a complete description of any commercial relational database schema. This is because the metamodel supports the logical aspects (for example, tables, columns, views, triggers, procedures, and so forth) but not the physical aspects (such as file locations and attributes, index blocking factors, and similar characteristics) of relational databases. The physical schemata of relational databases are highly vendor-specific and are not generally the kind of information that needs to be interchanged, especially between products from different vendors. However, experimental work by the CWM design team indicates that creating extension packages supporting the physical schemata of specific database products is likely to be a straightforward exercise.

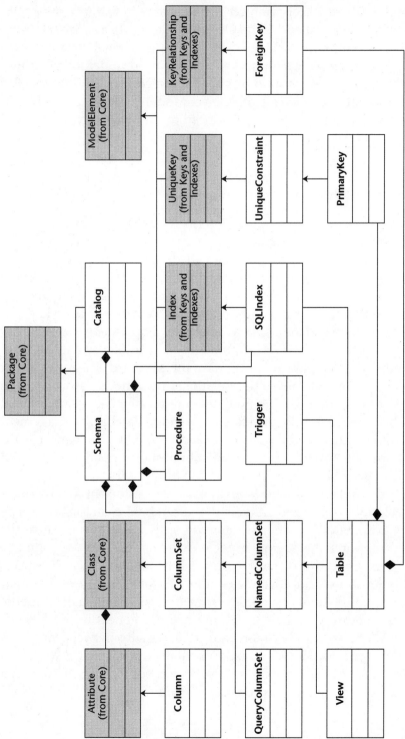

Figure 2.12   Classes of the Relational package.

The logical components of relational databases (their tables, columns, and key relationships, among others) are already widely understood. However, note that the Schema class is the common point that brings together all of the parts of a single database schema, and that the package illustrates how higher-level packages inherit from the Object Model and Foundation layers.

Record Package

The record concept, a linear arrangement of simple and structured fields, predates computers and is one of the most widely used data organization methods today. Records are highly flexible data structures ranging from character stream files (in which each character is a record) to complex structures of interlinked records. Because of their flexibility and longevity, record-based files are pervasive in today's computing environments. Because they were compatible with disk and memory structures, records could be transferred directly between the two storage media without translation. Records became the foundation upon which first-generation database management systems were built, and they still underlie the physical storage of many of today's more advanced databases. The CWM Record package, shown in Figure 2.13, provides the infrastructure needed to describe a wide variety of record-oriented data structures.

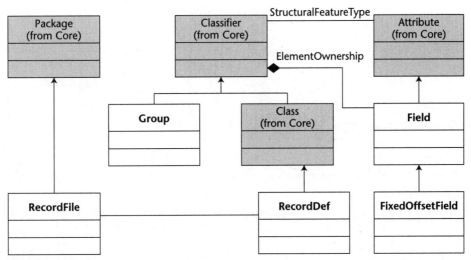

Figure 2.13 Classes of the Record package.

The RecordDef class describes the field layout of a record. Each Record-Def owns an ordered list of Field instances via the ClassifierFeature association. Each Field instance defines a semantically meaningful area of the RecordDef. Because they are attributes, Fields inherit a data type via the StructuralFeatureType association. This classifier may be a DataType instance for simple field types like integer, or it may be a structured classifier, a Group, which describes the internal structure of the field itself. Note that Groups are not actually embedded directly into RecordDefs, but instead serve as the types of Field instances. Although Groups can be thought of as an inline data type that has meaning only where they are directly declared, CWM permits Group definitions to be shared as needed by fields in multiple RecordDefs.

The FixedOffsetField class allows fields to be mapped to particular byte offsets with a RecordDef and can be used to record memory boundary alignments when required.

A RecordFile is an ordered collection of RecordDefs that can be instantiated physically as a file in some file system. The ordering on the association between RecordFiles and RecordDefs can be used to record required sequences of records in a file.

Multidimensional Package

Multidimensional databases are physical support structures created and used by OLAP tools. The objects in a multidimensional database directly represent OLAP concepts, such as dimensions and hierarchies, in a form that tends to maximize performance and flexibility in ways that will benefit the OLAP tools. The magnitude of improvements achieved can be sufficient to justify unloading warehouse data from more traditional data stores, such as relational databases and spreadsheets, and placing it in specialized multidimensional constructs. The CWM metamodel for multidimensional databases is shown in Figure 2.14.

The CWM Multidimensional metamodel does not attempt to provide a complete representation of all aspects of commercially available, multidimensional databases. Unlike relational database management systems, multidimensional databases tend to be proprietary in structure, and no published, widely agreed upon, standard representations of the logical schema of a multidimensional database exist. Instead, the CWM Multidimensional Database metamodel is oriented toward complete specification generality and is meant to serve as a foundation on which tool-specific extensions to the metamodel can be built. In situations like this, providing a stub metamodel like the Multidimensional package is valuable, because it allows tool-specific extensions that inherit directly from the stub to receive the breadth of other services that CWM packages can offer. For example, tying a tool-specific extension to the Multidimensional package allows the extension package to participate in transformations. In this way, the original sources of data in a warehouse and the transformations that move it into an OLAP cube can be recorded and shared with other tools. Fortunately, tool-specific extension packages are relatively easy to formulate, and examples of several popular OLAP tools are provided in Volume 2 of the CWM specification.

XML Package

The XML developed by W3C (www.w3c.org) is a vendor-neutral data interchange language that has rapidly become an integral part of many data processing environments, especially those with significant Internet activity. Because XML documents can be stored as standalone files and because they can be adapted easily to the structure of any particular data structures to be exchanged, they are becoming a popular storage format for data. The CWM XML package shown in Figure 2.15 defines metamodel classes needed to support the description of XML documents as data resources in a data warehouse and is compatible with the XML 1.0 specification.

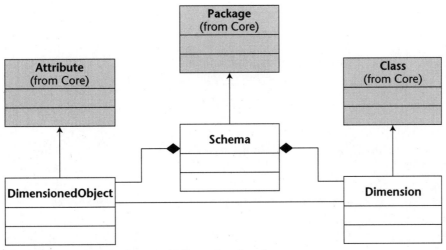

Figure 2.14   Classes of the Multidimensional package.

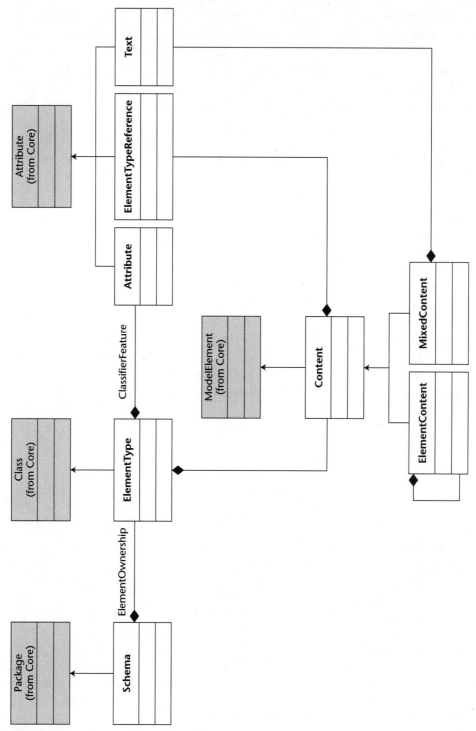

Figure 2.15   Classes of the XML package.

The CWM XML metamodel does not contain an XML document with data to be interchanged. Rather, it contains the XML Document Type Definition that describes the structure of XML documents that can be interchanged. If you think of an XML stream as a database containing information to be exchanged, the Document Type Definition (DTD) is the schema of that database and is represented by the Schema class. An XML Schema owns a set of ElementTypes. Each ElementType owns a set of attributes that describe the element type and, optionally, one Content instance that specifies the kind of data that the ElementType can contain. The Content can be either an ElementContent, which limits the content to XML tags, or MixedContent, which permits both XML tags and character data. Content instances can also own other ElementTypes. In this case, the ownership is of the weak kind, as is the ownership relationship between ElementType and Content and the recursive ownership on ElementContent.

XML DTDs have been criticized because they are not strongly typed. To respond to this and other problems with DTDs, W3C continues to evolve the way in which XML documents can be described. The next step in this process will occur with the acceptance of the XML Schema specification, which will provide improved type support and other features and will replace DTDs as the preferred method for describing the structure of XML documents. Unfortunately, when the CWM was adopted by OMG, the XML Schema specification was not yet ready. Although the present XML package correctly describes DTDs and is fully usable for that purpose, you should expect that the XML package will be extended to include XML schemas soon after the specifications are adopted by W3C.

Analysis Layer

Packages in the Analysis layer support warehouse activities not directly related to the description of data sources and targets. Rather, Analysis layer packages describe services that operate on the data sources and targets described by Resource layer packages. The layer includes a Transformation package supporting extraction, transformation, and loading (ETL). It also includes data lineage services, an OLAP model for viewing warehouse data as cubes and dimensions, a data mining support metamodel, a foundation for storing visually displayed objects, and a terminology package supporting the definition of logical business concepts that cannot be directly defined by Resource layer packages.

Transformation Package

Two technical concerns are chiefly responsible for the separation of data warehousing and operational databases in today's enterprises. First, fundamental resource tradeoffs and consistency requirements in database management systems make it exceptionally difficult (most would say impossible) to tune a single data storage engine so that it simultaneously serves both update-intensive transactional application and retrieval-intensive warehousing applications with optimal efficiency. A database that tries to do both simultaneously does neither well. Second, high throughput retrieval can best be provided when data is organized in a fashion distinctly different from that used by operational databases. Many data warehouse retrievals are optimized through the use of data summarization techniques. Invoking those aggregation operations could easily destroy the performance of any operational data store.

The cost of having separate operational and warehouse databases is that data must be moved, and transformed, from operational databases to warehouse databases on a regular basis without losing integrity in either the source or the target systems. Conversely, business analysts must be able to examine the source operational data supporting conclusions drawn from summarized data in the warehouse, regardless of the complexities induced by any transformations that may have occurred. These requirements are addressed by the Transformation package. This is shown in Figure 2.16.

The Transformation class records the data sources and targets in a single transformation. Source and target data items are members of the transformation's DataObjectSet and can reference any ModelElement. Related transformations can be grouped into larger sets, TransformationTasks, which, in turn, can be collected into TransformationSteps that can be sequenced using the StepPrecedence and PrecedenceConstraint classes. TransformationTasks own Transformations weakly so that Transformations can participate in multiple TransformationTasks. A TransformationActivity owns an unordered set of TransformationSteps and is the top-level class in the Transformation package. Execution of TransformationActivities and TransformationSteps can be scheduled using the Warehouse Process package described in the *Warehouse Process Package* section later in this chapter.

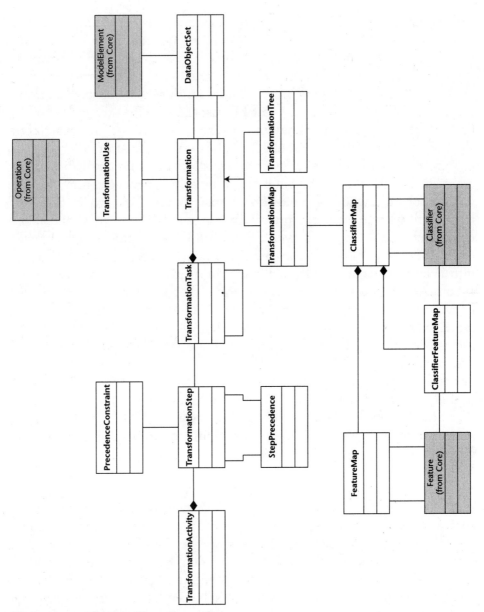

Figure 2.16   The Transformation package.

In conjunction with the Warehouse Process package, transformations can be scheduled for execution. The Warehouse Operation package records the execution activities of transformations and is the basis for determining the data lineage of information in the warehouse. Transformations may operate sequentially, passing intermediate result sets of subsequent transformations, or in parallel and can be associated with any operation or method recorded by the Behavioral package to indicate the exact code module that is responsible for effecting the desired transformation.

Transformations may be *white box* or *black box*. Black box transformations record information movement at large granularities, between entire systems or components, whereas white box transformations record information movement at a fine level of granularity, between individual classes and attributes. Transformations may even record information movement between objects of different granularities, such as moving an entire XML document into a column of a table, if the semantics of the situation so require.

Some detailed white box transformations that are commonly reused can be recorded as TransformationMaps or as TransformationTrees. TransformationMaps can be used to preserve a detailed record of multiple movements of data between specific classifiers and attributes using the ClassifierMap, FeatureMap, and ClassifierFeatureMap classes, which might be performed by external agents (such as a method described in the CWM). In this way, detailed records can be kept to track the lineage of individual data items as they move from operation data sources to the warehouse. The TransformationTree class allows a transformation to be represented as an expression tree using the Expressions package metamodel.

As an example of how the Transformation package can be used, you can coordinate the evolution of systems that have multiple levels of abstraction. For example, as shown in Figure 2.17, conceptual business objects, such as customers, might be modeled as concepts in the Business Nomenclature package. The customer concept can be mapped to a less abstract description in a logical data model, such as the Entity class in the CWM's Entity-Relationship (ER) extension package. At an even lower abstraction level, a table in a relational database might be used to implement customer Entities. Transformations can be used to evolve each of the abstraction levels forward, and TransformationMaps can be used to record how transitions between abstraction levels are accomplished. In this way, full data lineage can be recorded and traversed for multiple versions of multilayered systems. (For more examples of interesting things that can be done with TransformationMaps, refer to the OLAP chapter of the CWM specification.)

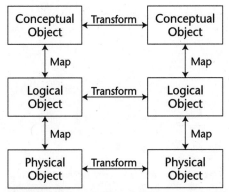

Figure 2.17 Transformations are used within abstraction layers, and mappings are used between layers.

OLAP Package

Online Analytical Processing (OLAP) is an analysis technique in which business data originating from multiple, diverse operational sources is consolidated and exposed in a multidimensional format that allows business analysts to explore it in a retrieval-friendly environment. The ultimate goal of OLAP tools is to transform operational business data into strategic business insights.

OLAP tools can be used in many ways. However, many commercially important tools directly support the storage of multidimensional data in relational databases (ROLAP), multidimensional databases (MOLAP), or a hybrid of the two, making data resources described by the CWM's Relational and Multidimensional packages ideal candidates for OLAP analysis techniques. Mapping these data resources into OLAP systems and tracing the lineage of OLAP data back to its sources can be accomplished with CWM's Transformation package. The OLAP package metamodel is shown in Figure 2.18.

Chapter 6, "Dimensional Model," provides an extensive example of using CWM Transformation Mappings to map a logical OLAP model to a physical, Relational resource model.

The Schema class owns all elements of an OLAP model and contains Dimensions and Cubes.

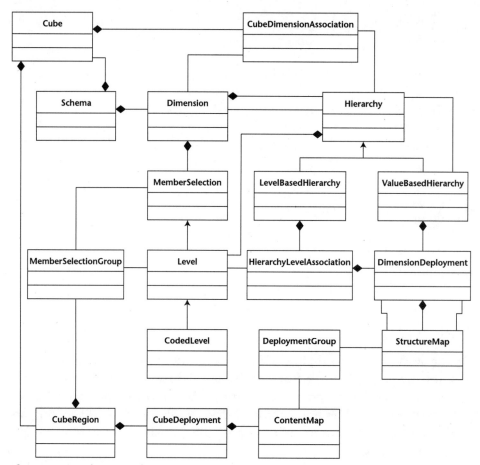

Figure 2.18   Classes of the OLAP package.

Each Dimension is a collection of Members representing ordinal positions along the Dimension. Dimensions (because they inherit from Classifier) describe attributes of their Members, which can be used to identify individual Members. The MemberSelection and MemberSelectionGroup classes support limiting the portions of a Dimension that are currently viewed. Dimensions can also contain multiple hierarchical arrangements of Members, including two specialized hierarchies that support ordering Members by hierarchy levels and value.

The OLAP metamodel also supports two special-purpose dimensions: Time and Measure. The Time dimension supports time-series data in a form that supports consolidation at various levels. The Measure dimension describes the values available within each cell of a Cube.

A Cube is a collection of values described by the same set of Dimensions. Conceptually, each Dimension represents one edge of the Cube. A set of Dimension members, one for each dimension, uniquely identifies one, and only one, cell within the Cube. This cell contains one value for each member of the Measure dimension. The value of a Measure in a cell is often an aggregate value that represents a consolidation (often a simple sum, but other aggregate functions are allowed) of the values subsumed by the cell.

Cubes are constructed from a set of CubeRegions, each of which defines some subset of a larger Cube. CubeRegions are also used by some implementations as a device for controlling the physical location of data corresponding to CubeRegions. The CubeDeployment and Dimension-Deployment classes are used to map portions of a cube to particular implementation strategies.

Data Mining Package

Data mining applies mathematical and statistical techniques to large data sets to detect patterns or trends that are not immediately obvious through visual inspection. For example, data mining tools can detect patterns that are present in the data but that would likely be missed by human business analysts because the patterns become apparent only after statistical analysis. Often, this happens because patterns are based on interactions of several measured values. Statistical and learning techniques such as factor analysis, principle component analysis, clustering, and neural networks can detect these types of patterns, but with visual inspection of the sort offered by OLAP tools, detection is much less certain. Data mining techniques are also attractive because, being discovery-oriented, they do not require analysts to form and test hypotheses about possible relationships.

The Data Mining package contains descriptions of the results of data mining activities by representing the models they discover and the attribute values that were used in the exploration. The Data Mining metamodel is shown in Figure 2.19.

Data Mining metamodel classes are grouped into three main areas: the core model, settings, and attributes. The core model represents the result of a data mining operation (that is, a mathematical model of some aspect of the information described in the CWM) and includes the MiningModel, SupervisedMiningModel, MiningModelResult, MiningSetting, Application-InputSpecification, and ApplicationAttribute classes.

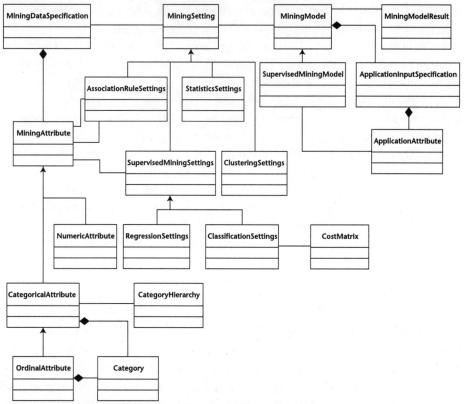

Figure 2.19 Classes of the Data Mining package.

The settings area describes input parameters and values for model attributes that were (or will be) used to construct a mining model. MiningSettings are a collection of mining model attributes, and five specific types of settings are defined: Statistics, Clustering, AssociationRule, Classification, and Regression, along with a CostMatrix indicating the cost of a misclassification for classification settings. The AttributeUsageRelation class provides additional information about how settings use mining attributes.

The attributes area elaborates on the MiningAttribute class, allowing for numerical and categorical attributes. Categorical attributes are arranged into taxonomic hierarchies and may have a collection of properties describing the Category. The OrdinalAttribute class is used to describe categories in which the ordering of category levels is significant.

Information Visualization Package

Because of the volume and complexity of data that can reside in a data warehouse, graphical presentation and summarization capabilities are essential for the effective analysis and understanding of business information gleaned from warehouses. Information recorded in the warehouse must be able to be presented in any of an ever-growing number of presentation styles (*renderings*) and on a dynamically evolving collection of traditional display media, such as paper and screens. Information must be able to be presented in more modern media like Web browsers, XML/eXtensible Stylesheet Language (XSL) rendering, and audio players. Because of the breadth and rapid pace of this problem domain, CWM provides a very generic visualization package whose primary purpose is to permit the rendering of information of any type to be interchanged for any object in CWM. The metamodel classes defined here provide a framework in which more elaborate and capable models can be defined to interchange complex M1 level models of relevant to specific rendering environments and tool sets. The Information Visualization metamodel is presented in Figure 2.20.

The RenderedObject class acts as a stand-in for any ModelElement in CWM and contains specific information about the rendering of the object, such as its relationship to neighboring objects or its location on a display grid. RenderedObjects can reference a number of Renderings that indicate how the objects are actually presented. Renderings can be thought of as transformations that turn a RenderedObject into a displayable object in some rendering style (for example, table, chart, graph, and so on) or rendering tool. RenderedObjects describe the logical rendering aspects of ModelElements, whereas Renderings alter how they are represented without changing their logical rendering information.

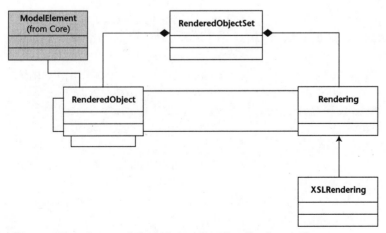

Figure 2.20   Classes of the Information Visualization package.

RenderedObjects can be composed of an arbitrary number of other RenderedObjects and can reference neighboring RenderedObjects. In this way, complex RenderedObjects can be constructed from simpler ones. Indeed, RenderedObjects may themselves be the targets of complex transformations described using the Transformation package. XSLRendering is a useful sub-class of Renderings that uses XSL to create HyperText Markup Language (HTML) documents for display by Web browsers.

Business Nomenclature Package

Most of the CWM packages are focused on information that is already organized and structured in ways that can be easily represented in computer systems. However, computer systems, at their core, model real-world systems and processes that are not necessarily so tidily defined. In fact, many of the business concepts and ideas that computer systems represent are structured, artificially limited expressions of ideas and concepts that are best defined in natural languages. For example, the business notion of a customer is a clearly understood concept in most situations (even though we might disagree about how to describe it). Taking an understandable intellectual shortcut, computer professionals can come to equate the business notion of a customer with a specific set of tables in some database that contains customer information. Although nothing is particularly wrong with this transition, the businessperson understands that the customer tables in the database are merely one of possibly many representations of a useful idea. The idea of customers and their importance to a business remains very real no matter how many times or in what formats they are presented in computer systems. In fact, customers are just as real as ever to businesses, even if they have never been computerized.

Representing generic ideas, like customer, in a form that is purely conceptual and not tied to any particular implementation technique is useful because it conveys an independent existence to ideas. It is the foundation for permitting the lineage of ideas to be traced across the multiple implementations that are likely in a data warehouse environment. The CWM Business Nomenclature package captures generic business concepts in the form of a structured vocabulary (an *ontology*) that is independent of any computer implementation format or data model and is shown in Figure 2.21. An important side-effect of having a generic description of business concepts close at hand is that they can foster communication between business- and technically oriented employees and can help clarify a business's understanding of its own processes.

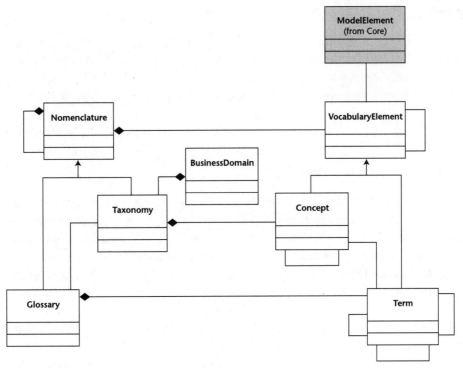

Figure 2.21   Classes of the Business Nomenclature package.

The Business Nomenclature package expresses concepts as collections of terms that can be organized into hierarchies of taxonomies and glossaries. Concepts capture semantic relationships, can be related to similar concepts, and identify terms that describe them. Taxonomy is a collection of concepts, and a BusinessDomain is a definable business area that owns a set of taxonomies that are relevant to its activities.

Terms are collected into glossaries and may be related to each other. Terms may be *preferred* (that is, the best term representing a concept) or may be *synonyms* that reference preferred terms and allow for shades of meaning. Hierarchical arrangements of terms into more general and more specific elements allow the substitution of narrower terms for more specific terms where appropriate.

A VocabularyElement, the superclass of Concept and Term, is a stand-in for any ModelElement in the CWM, captures conceptual descriptive information about the ModelElement that documents its business meaning, and allows it to be related to other VocabularyElements. VocabularyElements are the words and phrases of the Business Nomenclature package.

Management Layer

Packages in the Management layer provide service functions that can support the day-to-day operation and management of a data warehouse. These packages can make the CWM an active, well-integrated part of your data warehouse environment. Besides acting in the roles described here, these packages can serve as a foundation upon which more elaborate warehouse management activities can be built using CWM extension packages.

Warehouse Process Package

The Warehouse Process package, shown in Figure 2.22, describes the flow of information in a data warehouse. Information flows are expressed as transformations described by the Transformation package and may be documented at the level of a complete TransformationActivity or one of its TransformationSteps. Warehouse events are the triggers that begin the flow of information between data warehouse components; they can be scheduled or provoked by either internal or external events.

A Warehouse Process is either a WarehouseActivity or a WarehouseStep, depending on whether it represents a TransformationActivity or a TransformationStep, respectively. Related Warehouse Processes can be collected into Process packages as needed. WarehouseEvents trigger the initiation of Warehouse processes. A scheduled WarehouseEvent occurs at a predetermined point in time, or it can recur after a specific period of time has elapsed. An external WarehouseEvent is a response to some happening or stimulus that has occurred outside the data warehouse. Finally, CascadeEvents and RetryEvents can fire internal WarehouseEvents at the completion of a preceding WarehouseEvent. These events can be used for many activities, including starting the next WarehouseProcess, scheduling a retry or the next occurrence of the current WarehouseProcess, and posting activity records to the ActivityExecution and StepExecution classes in the Warehouse Operations package.

Warehouse Operation Package

The Warehouse Operation package, shown in Figure 2.23, records events of interest in a data warehouse. Three types of events are recorded: transformation executions, measurements, and change requests.

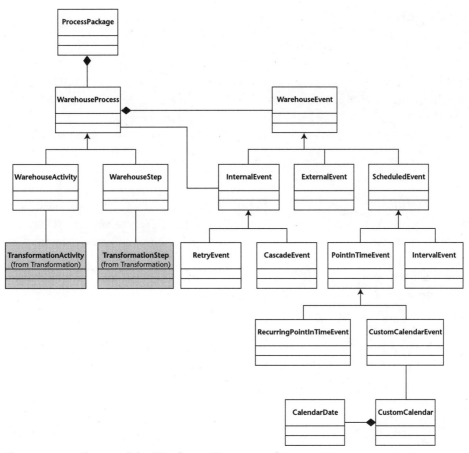

Figure 2.22   Classes of the Warehouse Process package.

After transformations have been completed, the results of their activity can be recorded by the ActivityExecution and StepExecution sub-classes of TransformationExecution. This recording can be done in response to the occurrence of an InternalEvent in the Warehouse Process package or by any other equivalent means. Start time, end time, and various progress and result indications can be recorded for each TransformationExecution. For StepExecutions, the actual arguments used in executing the transformations can be recorded using the CallAction class from the Object Model's Behavioral package.

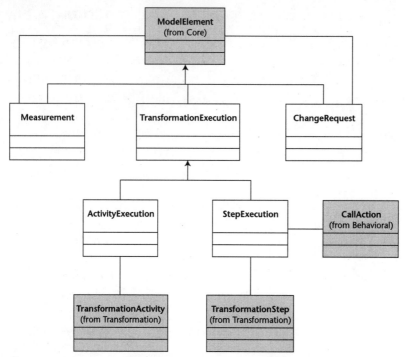

Figure 2.23   Classes of the Warehouse Operation package.

Measurement allows metrics to be recorded for any ModelElement. Measurements can hold actual, planned, or estimated values for any item of interest in a particular tooling, analytic, or administrative function. ChangeRequests permit the recording of proposed alterations affecting any ModelElement. A number of attributes describing the change are provided, and historical as well as planned changes can be kept as needed.

Key Architectural Concepts: Extending CWM

The previous section presented all of the major metamodel packages comprising CWM in depth. In this section, we examine several key architectural properties of CWM that are important to understand. These architectural features ultimately affect how modelers will use CWM in modeling meta data. They also affect how users of CWM can extend CWM in various ways to accommodate new conceptual domains, as well as provide support for highly tool-specific meta data. These key architectural properties will come into play in Chapter 5, "Data Warehouse Management Model," as well as throughout much of Part Two, "Introducing the Vertical Models."

Meta Data Reuse and Extension Based on Inheritance

We emphasized a number of times in Chapter 1, and extensively throughout Chapter 2 of *Common Warehouse MetaModel: An Introduction* (Poole, 2002), that meta data reuse across participants in a data warehousing or ISC environment is a key factor for enhancing the overall Return on Investment (ROI) of the supply chain.

From a modeling perspective, ROI is also greatly enhanced when established model resources can be readily reused in the creation of new models. CWM employs the object-oriented concept of *inheritance* (or sub-classing) to provide this. This is expressed in the structure of CWM, and is also available to users who might need to extend the existing CWM metamodel into new conceptual sub-domains.

For example, Figure 2.24 contains a fragment of CWM's XML package. Notice that the composite associations between Schema and ElementType and between ElementType and Attribute are labeled with the names of associations defined in the Object Model's Core package. By redrawing these Core associations as if they were part of the XML package, we have shown which associations are reused to achieve the desired owner relationships without having to reproduce all of the superclass structure of the Core package to do so.

How can classes be kept from owning other classes that they are not allowed to own? For example, what prevents an XML Schema from owning a Relational Trigger? There is nothing in the Core package that prevents the creation of such nonsensical relationships. The CWM specification contains rules, *integrity constraints*, which are encoded in a special-purpose language, Object Constraint Language (OCL) (Warmer, 1999), which is a part of UML. OCL ensures that XML schemas can own only XML Element-Types.

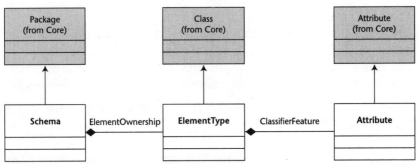

Figure 2.24   A fragment of the XML metamodel showing reused Core associations.

To understand exactly what is really going on, let's expand this fragment of the XML package to see how the relationships and inheritance really work. The complete inheritance tree for the XML classes Schema, ElementType, and Attribute is shown in Figure 2.25 from the perspective of the XML package.

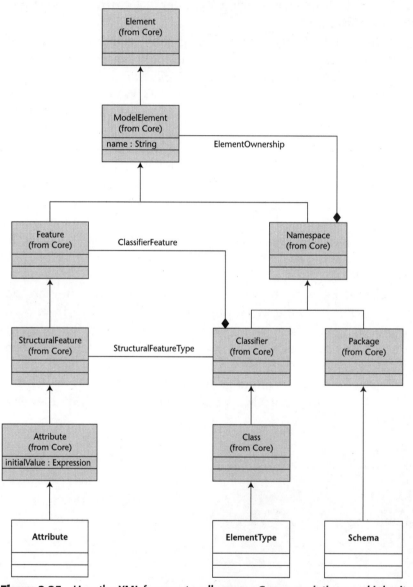

Figure 2.25   How the XML fragment really reuses Core associations and inherits attributes.

The expanded figure makes the semantics of the Core associations and classes easier to see. Because inheritance provides classes with the attributes and associations of all of their superclasses and prevents the inheritance of attributes and associations of classes that are not superclasses, the XML classes acquire from the Core only those capabilities that are relevant to their location in the inheritance tree. For example, the Schema and ElementType classes can own other elements because they are sub-classses of Namespace, even though remotely. Similarly, the XML Attribute class cannot own other elements because it is not a sub-class of Namespace. Attributes can, however, be owned by Namespaces (via ElementOwnership) and by Classifiers (via ClassifierFeature), whereas ElementType and Schema can be owned by Namespaces but not by Classifiers. This distinction is important because the semantics of the ownership associations involved convey different capabilities.

To further illustrate the power of inheritance to control shared capabilities, two attributes have been added to Figure 2.25 (ModelElement::name and Attribute::*initialValue*). Every class in the figure, except Element, has a *name* attribute, because it is a sub-class of ModelElement. Referring to the *name* of an ElementType is perfectly valid, even though no attribute called *name* is declared directly for ElementType. In contrast, the *initialValue* attribute is defined only for the Core's Attribute class and for XML's Attribute class. The concept of an initial value is not meaningful for the other classes in the figure, and they do not inherit it because they are not attributes.

So we see that CWM has largely been built using inheritance. The same technique is generally used to extend the metamodel packages of the CWM metamodel proper to create new metamodels. The Entity-Relationship package from Volume 2 of the CWM Specification provides just such an example. This is illustrated in Figure 2.26.

Except for RelationshipEnd and Domain, the ER extension classes are all sub-classes of corresponding CWM classes. Because these extension classes do not add attributes, the only function they serve is to rename the CWM class so that they match the names expected by users familiar with the ER model. That so many of the ER classes rename existing CWM classes speaks to the model power of CWM. Nearly all of the concepts required by ER were already present in CWM, except that their names were spelled wrong!

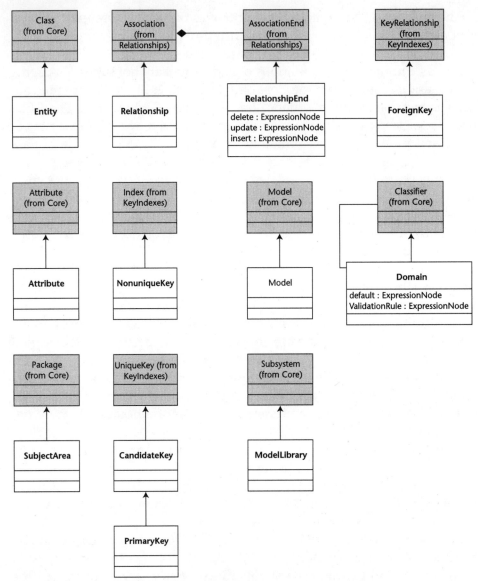

Figure 2.26   Classes of the Entity-Relationship extension package.

Relationship and Domain are true extension classes because they add attributes that are unique to the ER model. In addition, the ER package adds two associations that are unique to this model (between RelationshipEnd and ForeignKey and from Domain to Classifier). Notice that the Attribute and Model classes were added, even though they have the same name as their sub-classes from the Core package. Sub-classing these two classes was not strictly necessary; the corresponding Core classes could have been reused as they are. They were sub-classed so that it was clear that they were included in the ER model.

In the various vertical domain models developed throughout Part Two of this book, we shall see numerous examples of the use of inheritance to create new metamodel extensions to CWM.

Lightweight Extension Mechanisms: Stereotypes and TaggedValues

A sometimes-heard complaint about inheritance as an extension technique is that it is too heavyweight for most simple situations, especially when the only extension that may be needed is to add an attribute or two. Although such concerns are generally based on worry that inheritance techniques will have detrimental performance impacts, in some legitimate situations, inheritance techniques may be pretty heavy-handed. The CWM Core Stereotype and TaggedValue classes were created to address these situations. As an example of the use of these simpler extension techniques, the ER extension package has been recrafted in Figure 2.27 using Stereotypes and TaggedValues instead of inheritance.

In the figure, the labels on classes enclosed in double brackets indicate stereotypes; for example, <<Entity>> is a stereotype of the Class class from the Core package. Stereotypes are special-purpose labels that convey extra semantic information about the intended use of the class they adorn. The meaning of a stereotype is usually significant only to humans; it does not directly carry significance for software systems. Note that the Attribute and Model classes from the Core package are reused and do not require stereotypes because their current names completely convey their semantic intent.

TaggedValues are arbitrary name-value pairs that can be added to any ModelElement. In Figure 2.27, they are used to hold the values of needed attributes unique to the ER model and are shown as instances of the TaggedValue class owned by the relevant classes. The tag attribute of the TaggedValue instances holds the name of the extended attribute. However, the modeling of extended attributes does not work completely in this case, because the data type of the new attribute *must* be *string*. This means that nonstring values, such as *integers* or *ExpressionNodes*, must be converted to strings prior to saving them in TaggedValues and must be reconverted to their native data types when they are retrieved.

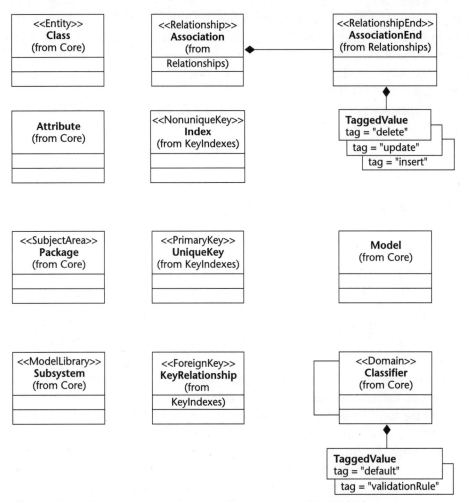

Figure 2.27   ER package modeled using Stereotypes and TaggedValues.

Stereotype and TaggedValue extensions are created as instances of their respective classes in the Core package. These classes provide the necessary links that allow the extensions to be owned by ModelElements and allow Stereotypes to own a set of TaggedValues. This latter mechanism allows a set of TaggedValues to be associated with any class that has been assigned the Stereotype that owns the set.

These extension techniques are simpler to use than sub-classing, but they fall short of sub-classing in another way because they provide no mechanism for adding associations to the ER model. Consequently, the association between the RelationshipEnd and ForeignKey classes in Figure 2.26 could not be modeled in Figure 2.27.

As with inheritance, opinions differ as to the value of Stereotypes and TaggedValues as extension mechanisms. Their chief advantages are their simplicity and ease of use; they require no additional metamodel changes and are lightweight. Complaints about Stereotypes and TaggedValues as extension mechanisms often revolve around their incomplete modeling of the desired extensions. In our example, the string problem and the inability to add associations are indicative of these complaints. Most of the problems that these simple extension mechanisms experience stem from the fact that they are seen as degenerate inheritance mechanisms: They do only part of the job.

You can see that any user-definable character string, which both Stereotypes and TaggedValues are, whose base purpose is to add some extra information about the role or function of particular instances of some classes is little more than a shorthand for a sub-class hierarchy. The unfortunate aspect of taking such shortcuts is that the sending and receiving applications must be aware of the meaning of specific strings, which limits the interchange to tools aware of the extensions. Ultimately, the question of which to use comes down to whether the simpler Stereotypes and Tagged-Values will provide you with the modeling power that you need in your application. If they do, use them, but if you are unsure, inheritance is safer, more robust, and semantically cleaner.

The various vertical models developed throughout Part Two of this book include numerous examples of model extensions based on Stereotypes and TaggedValues. Many of the patterns developed throughout this book also explicitly specify Stereotype and TaggedValue as key components of their various *projections* of the CWM metamodel.

Summary

In this chapter, we surveyed the architecture of CWM in considerable detail. We showed how CWM is structured as a collection of interrelated packages, where each package addresses the modeling requirements of some particular sub-domain of data warehousing and business analysis. This is a key characteristic of CWM that facilitates the management of complexity in the modeling of large data warehouses and information supply chain architectures by breaking up the descriptions of both the problem domain and its solutions into easily managed and reusable chunks.

We provided a comprehensive survey of the architectural layers of CWM and each of the metamodel packages residing at each layer. In particular:

- ObjectModel, which effectively represents a subset of the UML and is used as the base metamodel for all other CWM packages.

- Foundation layer, which defines a number of packages that facilitate the modeling of common services and constructs found in most data warehouses and ISCs, such as the modeling of data types and key and index structures.

- Resource layer, which supports the modeling of the various, physical information resources found in a typical ISC, such as relational and multidimensional databases.

- Analysis layer, in which typical business analysis meta data is defined on top of the various resource models. This includes the modeling of data transformations, logical OLAP schemas, data mining and information visualization, and business nomenclature.

- Management layer, which allows for the modeling of common data warehouse management tasks and processes, and supports the tracking of these activities and other significant events within the data warehouse.

We also discussed several key aspects of CWM that fundamentally relate the architecture to its use in modeling, including how the object-oriented concept of inheritance is leveraged, both in the construction of the core CWM metamodel as well as a standard mechanism for extending CWM. This further demonstrates the support that CWM provides for meta data reuse, and enables users of CWM to develop their own metamodels. What is perhaps most relevant about this is the fact that the very same architectural nuances that characterize the structure of CWM itself (for example, the use of inheritance and package structuring) automatically provide the means by which CWM may be extended and customized.

Chapter 3, "Modeling Meta Data Using CWM," follows naturally from this chapter by demonstrating how many of these concepts are leveraged in the modeling of meta data structures using CWM.

Modeling Meta Data Using CWM

Common Warehouse Metamodel (CWM) is a meta data standard for data warehousing and business analysis, consisting of the following components:

- A common metamodel defining shared meta data for data warehousing and business analysis

- A common interchange format for interchanging shared meta data for data warehousing and business analysis

- A common programming interface for accessing shared meta data for data warehousing and business analysis

As such, CWM provides the core components of a model-based, meta data integration solution for data warehousing and business analysis (Poole, 2002).

Additional components, nevertheless, are required to form a complete solution. The most important component is software adapters that facilitate product-specific meta data interchange and access in CWM.

Without such adapters, CWM is just a paper standard of only theoretical interest and with little practical value. With such adapters available for all required data warehousing and business analysis tools in an Information Supply Chain (ISC), CWM can truly provide the ideal architecture for meta data integration as shown in Figure 3.1.

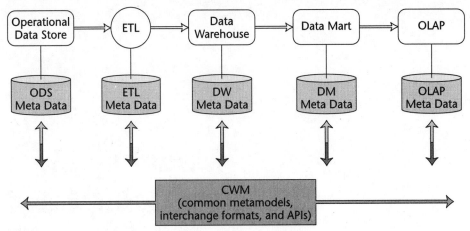

Figure 3.1   A CWM-based meta data integration architecture.

The software adapters shown in the architecture each consist of two parts: one that is common to all adapters and handles CWM objects, and the other that is product-specific and handles meta data unique to that product. (By CWM objects we mean "objects" that represent shared meta data conforming to the CWM metamodel.) Therefore, the key to developing a software adapter is to map product-specific meta data to CWM objects or, to put it another way, to model product-specific meta data using the CWM metamodel.

In this chapter we will discuss how to model data warehousing and business analysis meta data using the CWM metamodel. First, we will discuss the modeling language that is used to specify the CWM metamodel, namely Unified Modeling Language (UML). A good understanding of UML is needed to understand the modeling constructs used by the CWM metamodel, the power they offer, and the constraints they impose. We will then give an overview of the salient design features of the CWM metamodel: how it is modularly structured, what the common thread is among all sub-metamodels, and how the sub-metamodels can be used independently of and with other sub-metamodels. This overview complements what was discussed in Chapter 2. We finish by discussing the use of the CWM metamodel (or actually various CWM sub-metamodels) to model relational, record-based, transformation, and Online Analytical Processing (OLAP) meta data. The discussion is comprehensive, but not exhaustive, either in scope or in depth. By discussing these examples of using the CWM metamodel to model some of the most important data warehousing and business analysis meta data, we hope to provide a good understanding of the power and flexibility of the CWM metamodel. You will then be in a position to follow the detailed discussions, in subsequent chapters, of four major scenarios of using CWM to provide meta data integration solutions for data warehousing and business analysis.

UML

UML is a language for specifying, visualizing, constructing, and documenting the artifacts of systems, particularly software systems. Before UML, more than 50 object-oriented modeling languages existed. Among these, the most prominent ones included Grady Booch's Booch Method, Ivar Jacobson's Object-Oriented Software Engineering (OOSE), and Jim Rumbaugh's Object Modeling Technique (OMT). In 1996, these three modeling languages were unified and published as UML 0.9. A revised version, UML 1.1, was adopted by the Object Management Group (OMG) as a standard in November 1997 (Rumbaugh et al., 1999).

CWM is based on UML 1.3, which was adopted by the OMG in June 1999. The UML 1.3 specification consists of the following major parts that CWM depends on:

UML Semantics.   Defines the semantics of the UML metamodel. The UML metamodel is layered architecturally and organized by packages. Within each package, the model elements are defined in terms of abstract syntax (using class diagrams), well-formedness rules (in OCL, see below), and semantics (in English).

UML Notation Guide.   Specifies the graphic syntax (for example, class diagram) for expressing the semantics of the UML metamodel.

Object Constraint Language Specification.   Defines the Object Constraint Language (OCL) syntax, semantics, and grammar. OCL is a formal language for expressing constraints (Warmer and Kleppe, 1999).

Building Blocks and Well-Formedness Rules

UML provides an object-oriented modeling language that consists of building blocks and well-formedness rules. The basic building blocks of UML are as follows:

Model elements. Common object-oriented concepts such as classes, objects, interfaces, components, use cases, and so on.

Relationships. Connections among model elements such as associations, generalization, dependencies, and so on.

Diagrams. Groups of graphic symbols that can be used to represent model elements and their relationships, such as class diagrams, object diagrams, use case diagrams, and so on.

Simple building blocks can be used together to construct large, complex models as illustrated in Figure 3.2, which shows a class diagram representing a model of carbon-hydrogen compounds. In the model, a chemical element is represented as a UML class. Because both carbon and hydrogen are chemical elements, they are represented as UML classes as well, specifically as a specialization of the class that represents the chemical element. The bonding between carbon and hydrogen is represented as a UML association, with a special label <<covalent>>. The two ends of the covalent bond are represented as UML *Association Ends* and are marked with role names "C" and "H" (for carbon and hydrogen, respectively). The bonding between carbon and carbon is represented in a similar fashion.

Figure 3.3 shows an object diagram representing a specific instance of the model of a carbon-hydrogen compound, which represents the C_2H_6 molecule. In the diagram are two instances of the Carbon class with both instances linked together. The link is an instance of the <<covalent>> association between Carbon classes. Six instances of the Hydrogen class, with three instances each, are linked to an instance of the Carbon class. The link is an instance of the <<covalent>> association between the Carbon class and the Hydrogen class.

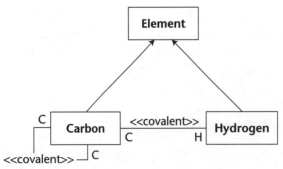

Figure 3.2 Class diagram: carbon-hydrogen compounds.

Well-formedness rules can be used to ensure that a model or model fragment adheres to all syntactic and semantic rules that apply to it. As an example of syntactic rules, a class is drawn as a solid-outline rectangle with three compartments separated by horizontal lines. The top compartment contains the class name, and the other compartments contain attributes and operations, respectively. Only the top compartment is required; either or both of the attribute and operation compartments may be suppressed. We have already seen this in Figure 3.2, where only the required top compartment is shown. Also shown is an example of syntactic guidelines: Class names begin with an uppercase letter.

Some semantic rules can be expressed using graphic notations. These include scope, visibility, and multiplicity. We will see examples of these when we discuss attributes, operations, and associations. Most semantic rules can be expressed using only OCL. An example is the following semantic constraint on a concrete class: If a class is concrete, all the operations of the class must have a realizing method in the full descriptor. In OCL, this constraint is expressed as follows:

```
not self.isAbstract implies self.allOperations->
    forAll(op | self.allMethods->exists(m | m.specification->includes(op)))
```

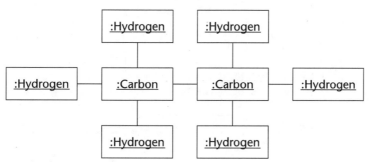

Figure 3.3 Object diagram: C_2H_6.

Static Structure Modeling

UML can be used to model different aspects of a system including the following:

Structural modeling.   Emphasizes the structure of objects of the system including their classes, relationships, attributes, and operations. Structural modeling consists of static structure modeling using class diagrams and object diagrams, and implementation modeling using component diagrams and deployment diagrams.

Use case modeling.   Emphasizes the functionality of the system as it appears to outside users. A use case model partitions system functionality into transactions (use cases) that are meaningful to users (actors). Use case modeling is done utilizing use case diagrams.

Behavioral modeling.   Emphasizes the behavior of objects of the system including their interactions, events, and control and data flow. Behavioral modeling consists of interaction modeling using sequence diagrams and collaboration diagrams, event modeling using state chart diagrams, and control and data flow modeling using activity diagrams.

CWM only uses static structural modeling for modeling shared meta data for data warehousing and business analysis. As such, in the following discussion, we will only elaborate on static structured modeling.

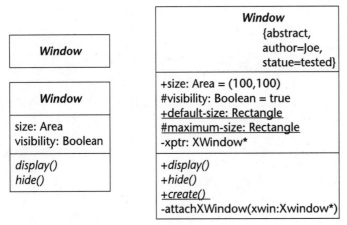

Figure 3.4   Class diagrams: Window.

The core elements of static structures are classes, objects, attributes, and operations. A *class* is a description of a set of objects that share the same attributes, operations, and semantics. All *objects* are instances of a class. A class has attributes that describe the characteristics of the objects. A class also may have operations that manipulate the attributes and perform other actions. An *attribute* has a name and type, which can be a primitive type or class. An attribute can have different scope—class-scope or instance-scope, and different visibility—public (+), protected (#), or private (-). An *operation* has a name, type, and zero or more parameters. Similar to attributes, an operation can have different scope—class-scope or instance-scope, and different visibility—public (+), protected (#), or private (-). These core elements are illustrated in Figure 3.4, which shows a Window class represented in varying levels of detail. The first class diagram shows only the class name, the second class diagram also shows the public and protected attributes and operations, and the third class diagram shows all attributes and operations as well as the class name with annotations.

The core relationships of static structures include the following: association, aggregation, generalization, dependency, and refinement. *Association* is a relationship between two or more classes, which involves connections among their objects. An association normally is bidirectional, but may be unidirectional. It has multiplicity at both ends, which expresses how many objects can be linked: zero-to-one (0..1), one-to-one (1..1), zero-to-many (0..* or *), or one-to-many (1..*). *Aggregation* is a special form of association that specifies a whole-part relationship between the aggregate (whole) and the component (part). An aggregation may be *shared*, in which case the parts may be parts in any wholes, or the aggregation may be a *Composition*, in which case the whole owns the parts, and the multiplicity on the whole must be zero-to-one. *Generalization* is a taxonomic relationship between a more general and a more specific element. An instance of the more specific element may be used wherever the more general element is allowed. *Dependency* is a relationship between two elements in which a change to one element (the independent element) will affect the other element (the dependent element). *Realization* is a relationship between a specification and its implementation. Examples of associations are shown in Figure 3.5. An association named Job exists between the Person class and Company class, with role names employee and employer, respectively. The Job association has an associated class by the same name, which is used to describe its characteristics. The Job class is related to itself by an association named Manages, with role names boss and worker. Examples of Compositions are shown in Figure 3.6. The Window class owns the Slider, Header, and Panel classes.

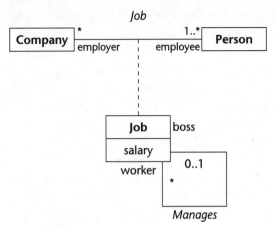

Figure 3.5   Associations.

Model Management

UML uses *package* as the mechanism for organizing model elements into semantically related groups. A package owns its model elements, and a model element cannot be owned by more than one package. A package can import model elements from other packages, which means that the public contents of the target package are added to the namespace of the source package. A package can have different visibility: public (+), protected (#), or private (-). Figure 3.7 shows a Warehouse package owning three classes and an association.

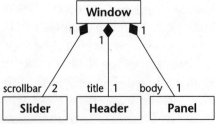

Figure 3.6   Compositions.

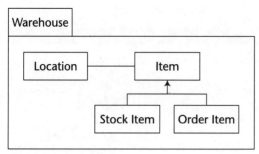

Figure 3.7   Package.

Meta Object Facility

UML, a general-purpose modeling language, can be used to model any system, natural or artificial, as we have illustrated in the examples used above. When UML is used to model meta data, it should be used within the context of MOF.

Meta Object Facility (MOF) is a model-driven, distributed object framework for specifying, constructing, managing, interchanging, and integrating meta data in software systems. The aim of the framework is to support any kind of meta data and to allow new kinds of meta data to be added as required. In order to achieve this, MOF uses a four-layer meta data architecture, the so-called OMG Meta Data Architecture, as shown in Table 3.1. This architecture treats meta data (M1) as data (M0) and formally models each distinct type of meta data. These formal models, the so-called metamodels (M2), are expressed using the meta-modeling constructs provided by a single meta-metamodel (M3), which is called the MOF Model. Figure 3.8 shows an example of the OMG Meta Data Architecture, which further illustrates the relationships between the MOF Model (the meta-metamodel), the UML metamodel (an example of a metamodel), a user model (an example of model or meta data), and user objects (examples of object or data).

Table 3.1 OMG Meta Data Architecture

META-LEVEL	MOF TERMS	EXAMPLES
M3	Meta-metamodel	MOF Model
M2	Metamodel Meta-meta data	UML Metamodel CWM Metamodel
M1	Model Meta data	UML models Warehouse meta data
M0	Object Data	Modeled systems Warehouse data

CWM is based on MOF 1.3, which was adopted by the OMG in September 1999. The MOF 1.3 specification consists of the following parts:

The MOF Model. Defines the modeling elements, including the rules for their use, which can be used to construct metamodels.

MOF reflective interfaces. Allow a program to create, update, access, navigate, and invoke operations on meta data without using metamodel-specific interfaces.

MOF to IDL mapping. Defines the standard mapping from a metamodel defined using the MOF Model onto CORBA IDL, thus allowing the automatic generation of metamodel-specific interfaces for accessing and manipulating meta data.

For the purpose of modeling meta data, only the MOF Model is relevant, which is discussed below, especially how it relates to UML.

The MOF Model

The MOF Model is based on the concepts and constructs of UML, particularly its static structure model and model management. As such, the MOF Model does not define its own graphical notation or constraint language, but uses the UML notation and OCL for such purposes, respectively. Like UML, the MOF Model is layered architecturally and organized by packages. Within each package, the model elements are defined in terms of abstract syntax (using class diagrams), well-formedness rules (in OCL), and semantics (in English).

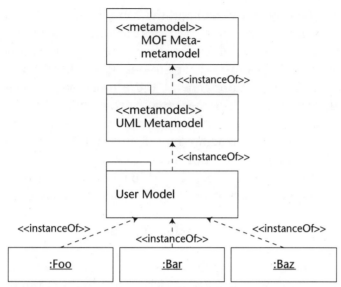

Figure 3.8 OMG Meta Data Architecture: An example.

The core elements of the MOF Model are classes, objects, attributes, and operations. A *class* is a description of a set of objects that share the same attributes, operations, and semantics. All *objects* are instances of a class. A class has attributes that describe the characteristics of the objects. A class also may have operations that manipulate the attributes and perform other actions. An *attribute* has a name and type, which can be a primitive type or class. It can have different scope—class-scope or instance-scope, and different visibility—public (+), protected (#), or private (-). An *operation* has a name, type, and zero or more parameters. Similar to attributes, an operation can have different scope—class-scope or instance-scope, and different visibility—public (+), protected (#), or private (-). These concepts and constructs are identical to those in the UML static structure model, but at a higher meta level. That is, MOF classes, objects, attributes, and operations are at the M3 level and are used to define metamodels (M2); whereas UML classes, objects, attributes, and operations are at the M2 level and are used to define models (M1).

The core relationships of the MOF Model include the following: association, aggregation, and generalization. *Association* is a relationship between two or more classes that involves connections among their objects. An association usually is bidirectional but may be unidirectional. It has multiplicity at both ends, which expresses how many objects can be linked: zero-to-one (0..1), one-to-one (1..1), zero-to-many (0..* or *), or one-to-many (1..*). *Aggregation* is a special form of association that specifies a whole-part relationship between the aggregate (whole) and the component (part). An aggregation may be *shared*, in which case the parts may be parts in any wholes, or it may be a *Composition*, in which case the whole owns the parts and the multiplicity on the whole must be zero-to-one. *Generalization* is a taxonomic relationship between a more general and a more specific element. An instance of the more specific element may be used wherever the more general element is allowed. These concepts and constructs again are identical to those in the UML static structure model, but at a higher meta level. That is, MOF associations, aggregations, and generalizations are at the M3 level and are used to define metamodels (M2); whereas UML associations, aggregations, and generalizations are at the M2 level and are used to define models (M1).

MOF uses *package* as the mechanism for organizing model elements into semantically related groups. A package owns its model elements, and a model element cannot be owned by more than one package. A package can import model elements from other packages, which means that the public contents of the target package are added to the namespace of the source package. A package can have different visibility: public (+), protected (#), or private (-). This mechanism is identical to that used in UML model management.

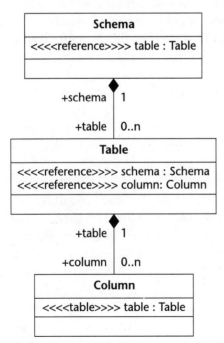

Figure 3.9   MOF-based metamodel: Relational database.

Although the MOF Model is identical to the UML static structure model and model management in most concepts and constructs, major differences do exist. First, an MOF association is restricted to be binary: It is defined between two classes, and it has two association ends. Each association end has a name, type, and multiplicity. Second, an MOF association cannot have an attached class (the *association class* in UML, see Figure 3.5). Third, an MOF class can have references. A reference defines the class's knowledge of, and access to, links that are instances of an association. A reference has a name and the referenced AssociationEnd. Figure 3.9 shows a simple MOF-based metamodel of a relational database that consists of Schema, Table, and Column, with binary associations and references.

The CWM Metamodel

In Chapters 1 and 2 we showed that CWM is a complete metamodel representing the data warehousing and business analysis domain. In particular, CWM provides both the syntax and semantics required to construct meta data describing all of the components of a complete ISC.

We have also shown that CWM actually is comprised of a number of different but closely related metamodels. Each metamodel represents some sub-domain of the ISC environment. A block diagram describing the overall organization of the CWM metamodel is shown in Figure 3.10. Each block in the top three layers represents a constituent metamodel of CWM that corresponds to an important functional area of a typical ISC.

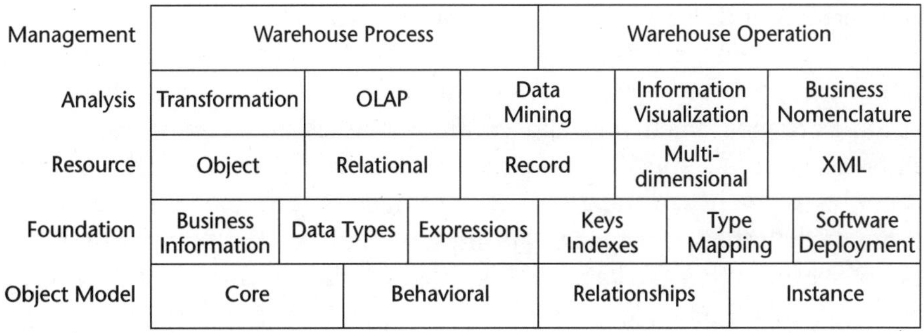

Management	Warehouse Process			Warehouse Operation	
Analysis	Transformation	OLAP	Data Mining	Information Visualization	Business Nomenclature
Resource	Object	Relational	Record	Multi-dimensional	XML
Foundation	Business Information	Data Types	Expressions	Keys Indexes	Type Mapping	Software Deployment
Object Model	Core	Behavioral	Relationships	Instance

Figure 3.10 The CWM metamodel.

The lowest layer in the CWM block diagram is referred to as the *Object Model* layer. This layer is a subset of the UML metamodel and is used by CWM as its base metamodel. The Object Model layer consists of four meta-models: *Core, Behavioral, Relationships,* and *Instance.* CWM uses the object-oriented concept of *inheritance* to extend the modeling elements of this UML subset to define new modeling elements representing data warehousing and business analysis concepts. Previously, we mentioned that CWM is specified in UML. While UML is the modeling language for defining CWM, it is important to note that CWM also uses a subset of the UML metamodel, namely, the Object Model layer, as the base metamodel and *extends* it to represent data warehousing and business analysis domain concepts. Therefore, CWM relies on the expressiveness and power of UML as a means of defining complex meta data structures and relationships.

The next layer, called the *Foundation* layer, consists of metamodels that extend the Object Model layer modeling elements to produce representations of common services required by all components of an ISC. The Foundation layer consists of six metamodels: *Business Information, Data Types, Expressions, Keys Indexes, Type Mapping,* and *Software Deployment.* The third layer of CWM, *Resource,* defines metamodels of the various types of data resources comprising an information supply chain. This layer consists of five metamodels: *Object, Relational, Record, Multidimensional,* and *eXtensible Markup Language (XML).* Note that the Object metamodel here is the same as the Object Model layer. Business analysis concepts, the real heart and purpose of the data warehouse and ISC, are represented by metamodels comprising the fourth layer of CWM, the *Analysis* layer. The Analysis layer consists of five metamodels: *Transformation, OLAP, Data Mining, Information Visualization,* and *Business Nomenclature.* Finally, the *Management* layer defines two metamodels that are critical to defining meta data describing the ISC processing as a whole: *Warehouse Process* and *Warehouse Operation.*

CWM is designed for deployment in production-quality software. It consists of small, modular packages that can be easily understood and implemented. Small packages also make learning the CWM a much less daunting task that can be done in incremental chunks. In total, CWM consists of 21 separate packages. Each package contains classes, associations, and constraints relevant to a specific area of interest in data warehousing and business analysis. Twenty of the 21 CWM packages require the presence of one or more of the other packages in an implementation. The one package that does not require other packages is the most fundamental part of the CWM, upon which all other packages ultimately depend. This is the *Core* package. To understand and use a particular CWM package, one must understand only that package and the packages it depends on; other packages can be ignored.

To help you understand the structure of the CWM metamodel and how to use its modular package design to best advantage in modeling meta data, we will take a look at how CWM accomplishes three important tasks:

- CWM uses inheritance to achieve reuse.
- Meta data definitions are tied to the physical data resources.
- Resource packages support creation of instance data objects.

How CWM Uses Inheritance to Achieve Reuse

The notion of *inheritance* in which *sub-classes* acquire the attributes, operations, and associations of all of their *superclasses* is one of the most useful features of object-oriented technology. Inheritance is a powerful organizing principle that allows complexity to be managed in an orderly fashion. However, inheritance is well known only to those familiar with object-oriented technology; no direct counterparts exist in the relational model, and none can be found in the Record model. Because classes receive inherited features through their immediate superclasses only, inheritance hides much of the complexities of more ancestral superclasses (that is, those above the immediate superclass).

In the following, we will see how inheritance achieves reuse and acquires a feeling for the true structural nature of the CWM metamodel. For illustration, we will use Figure 3.11, which contains a fragment of the XML package. Notice that composite associations between Schema and ElementType and between ElementType and Attribute are labeled with the names of associations defined in the Object Model's Core package. By redrawing these Core associations as if they were explicit parts of the XML package, we have shown which associations are reused to achieve the desired owner relationships without having to reproduce all of the superclass structure of the Core package to do so. This technique has been used repeatedly in the CWM specification and dramatically simplifies the metamodel diagrams. Diagrams redrawn in this way are completely correct representations of the desired relationships.

How can classes be kept from owning other classes that they are not allowed to own? For example, what prevents an XML Schema from owning a Relational Trigger? Apparently there is nothing in the Core package that would prevent the creation of such nonsensical relationships. The CWM specification contains rules—*integrity constraints*—which are encoded in OCL, which is a part of UML as described previously. These constraints ensure that XML schemas can own only XML ElementTypes.

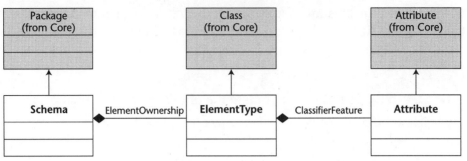

Figure 3.11   A fragment of the XML metamodel showing reused Core associations.

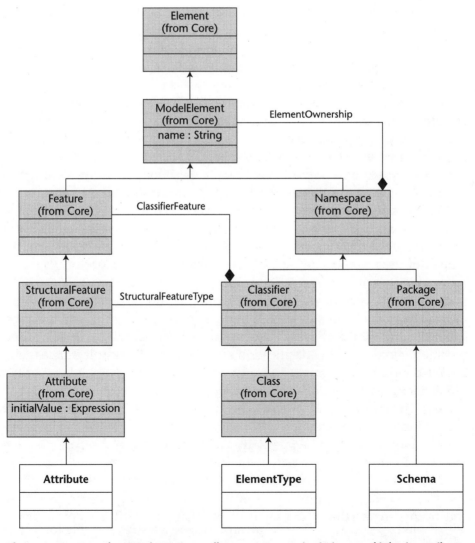

Figure 3.12   How the XML fragment really reuses Core associations and inherits attributes.

To understand exactly what is really going on, let's expand this fragment of the XML package to see how the relationships and inheritance really work. The CWM specification frequently resorts to expanded diagrams of this sort to clearly illustrate relationships across inherited classes of the CWM metamodel. The complete inheritance tree for the XML classes Schema, ElementType, and Attribute is shown in Figure 3.12 from the perspective of the XML package.

The expanded figure makes the semantics of the Core associations and classes easier to see. Because inheritance provides classes with the attributes and associations of all of their superclasses and prevents the inheritance of attributes and associations of classes that are not superclasses, the XML classes acquire from the Core only those capabilities that are relevant to their location in the inheritance tree. For example, the Schema and ElementType classes can own other elements because they are sub-classes of Namespace. Similarly, the XML Attribute class cannot own other elements because it is not a sub-class of Namespace. However, Attributes can be owned by Namespaces (via ElementOwnership) and by Classifiers (via ClassifierFeature), whereas ElementType and Schema can be owned by Namespaces but not by Classifiers. This distinction is important because the semantics of the ownership associations involved convey different capabilities.

To further illustrate the power of inheritance to control shared capabilities, two attributes have been added to Figure 3.12: the *name* attribute of ModelElements and the *initialValue* attribute of Attribute. Every class in the figure, except Element, has a *name* attribute, because it is a sub-class of ModelElement; referring to the *name* of an ElementType is perfectly valid even though no attribute called *name* is declared directly for ElementType. In contrast, the *initialValue* attribute is defined only for the Core's Attribute class and for XML's Attribute class. The concept of an initial value is not meaningful for the other classes in Figure 3.12, and they do not inherit it because they are not Attributes.

Finally, note that the reuse of class names is not prohibited. There is no confusion between the Core's Attribute class and XML's Attribute class in a CWM implementation because rules defined by the MOF at level M3 in the OMG meta data architecture require that all names be qualified by the name of the package in which they occur.

How Meta Data Links to Physical Data Resources

In a data warehousing and business analysis environment, meta data does not exist independently. It is always associated with physical data resources. The primary purpose of the SoftwareDeployment package is to allow you to record the location of, and the software responsible for, physical data resources in the warehouse. Figure 3.13 shows how you can link the physical data resources with the meta data that describes its structure and characteristics.

Each Resource layer package contains a class that is a sub-class of the Core's Package class. These sub-classes of Package collect the meta data information in their respective packages. Recall that for object-oriented data resources, the Core's Package class fills this role directly, and no sub-class is needed. The link to the corresponding physical data resources (that is, the corresponding relational databases, record files, multidimensional databases, or XML documents) is created by the DataManagerDataPackage association between SoftwareDeployment's DataManager class and the Core's Package class. In yet another example of the value of inheritance, a single association is reused for all data resources defined today, as well as any extension packages and data resource packages that may be added in the future. All that is necessary is to make the top-level meta data container in a new data resource package a sub-class of the Core's Package class.

Normally, this link technique might not be worthy of this much attention. However, because the DataManagerDataPackage association crosses the package boundary between SoftwareDeployment and Core, the MOF makes the situation more interesting. The MOF requires cross-package associations to be implemented in a way that provides maximum flexibility but that may reduce their performance in some implementations. The reason for this is not really important here. Cross-package associations in MOF are guaranteed to be semantically correct; the only effect is on the performance of accesses across such associations in some implementations. By using a single cross-package association to capture the deployment relationship between data resources and their descriptive meta data, implementation of the DataManagerDataPackage association can be done once and leveraged for all data resources, present or future.

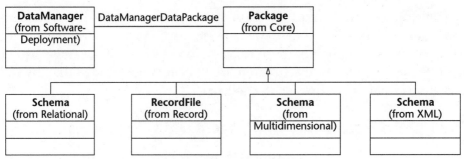

Figure 3.13   How meta data links to physical data resources.

How Resource Packages Support Instance Objects

Each data resource package in the Resource layer provides classes that directly sub-class the Object Model's Instance package classes. These classes allow data instances, such as the DataType instances defined by a programming language's type system or the predefined values of categorical data fields, to be included in a CWM-mediated meta data interchange. The instance classes for each data resource package are shown in Figure 3.14. Data resource classes in each column are sub-classes of the Object Model's Instance package class at the top of the column. For example, a relational RowSet is a sub-class of the Extent class in the Instance package, and Row is a sub-class of Object. The XML package has no sub-class of DataValue, because it simply reuses the Instance package's DataValue class directly.

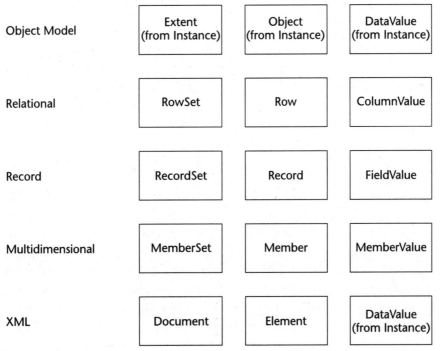

Object Model	Extent (from Instance)	Object (from Instance)	DataValue (from Instance)
Relational	RowSet	Row	ColumnValue
Record	RecordSet	Record	FieldValue
Multidimensional	MemberSet	Member	MemberValue
XML	Document	Element	DataValue (from Instance)

Figure 3.14 Data resource package Instance classes.

Using CWM to Model Meta Data

In this section we would like to provide you with a good understanding of how CWM is used in practice to construct models of typical data warehousing and business analysis use cases, and how these models are subsequently used as meta data for integrating the information supply chain. A *use case* is a description of how a typical function within a system is performed, most often from the perspective of an end user of the system. In the case of CWM, we are primarily concerned with use cases describing the construction or specification of system models in the data warehouse, which translate directly to meta data. We will first present a simple use case that is used as the basis for constructing relational meta data using the CWM Relational package as well as record-based meta data using the CWM Record package. Then, the relational model is expanded into a dimensional model using the CWM OLAP and Transformation packages. This model refinement process should illustrate both the logical and physical modeling of the same use case, using CWM as the modeling language.

CWM covers a broad spectrum of meta data information about the data warehouse. Our discussion of CWM use is based on a single, and comprehensive, use-case scenario. To cover as much of the model as possible, this use case takes you through a complete data warehouse scenario, from concepts to design, implementation, and end-user analysis. Although this use case is rather large, it represents only a fraction of the total CWM metamodel. This particular use case was chosen because it covers many of the basic concepts and constructs used throughout the CWM metamodel and describes the complete data warehouse life cycle, from concept to end-user analysis. The CWM metamodel supports the wide variety of definitions required to go from one end of the life cycle to the other. To set the stage, let's consider Figure 3.15.

In Figure 3.15, we see that the process of traversing from one level to the next level is called *mapping*, and traversing between levels is called *transforming*. CWM uses this paradigm extensively in the construction of models, and it is one of the most important aspects of the overall CWM design. With this basic understanding of how the CWM modeling process moves between conceptual levels, we can begin the discussion of the use case.

First, we need to define what a use case is, in terms of CWM: A *use case* is some standard way of using meta data, from the viewpoint of an end user of that meta data. Use cases can be very simple, describing a specific low-level meta data definition, such as how a Relational table is defined and used. Use cases also can be very complex, describing the entire interaction of meta data from concept to analysis. In this chapter, we use a series of use cases to describe how to use the CWM metamodel. At the end of this chapter, the series of individual use cases is put together to form a single use case that will describe the complete interaction of meta data, from its use in a conceptual design tool to its use in an end-user analysis tool. Note that the descriptions in this chapter attempt to give you a feel for how to use CWM to solve real-world problems.

Secondly, you should not feel intimidated by the notation used to describe how CWM satisfies the use cases. We will use instance diagrams to depict the CWM objects necessary to satisfy the use cases. These diagrams are a convenient and compact way to describe CWM meta data. You don't need a highly technical background or any knowledge of object-oriented programming to understand the instance diagrams.

To illustrate how an instance diagram works, let's consider the simple metamodel found in Figure 3.16, as well as an instance of that metamodel.

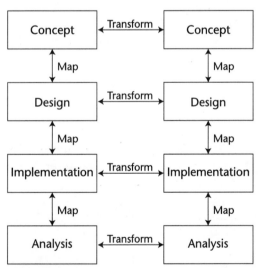

Figure 3.15 Data warehouse life-cycle conceptual levels and activities.

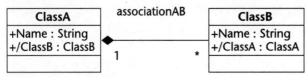

Figure 3.16 Simple metamodel.

Figure 3.16 shows a simple UML metamodel containing two class definitions: ClassA and ClassB. An association between the two classes indicates that ClassA *owns* all instances of ClassB. Each class has a pair of attributes, one naming each instance of the class, and the other defining a link between the two classes.

Figure 3.17 shows four object instances of the classes defined by the metamodel in Figure 3.16. The metamodel governs how the objects are constructed and associated. The metamodel indicates that a ClassA object can *own* a collection of ClassB objects. The instance diagram in Figure 3.17 depicts a particular instance of the metamodel (a *model* or *meta data*). The object named SampleClassA is an instance of ClassA. This object owns three instances of ClassB: SampleClassB1, SampleClassB2, and Sample-ClassB3.

Now that we have a basic understanding of instance diagrams, let's begin the use-case studies by describing a few simple CWM objects. We start in the Design layer of Figure 3.15, with the definition of two physical structures: a Relational table and a record file.

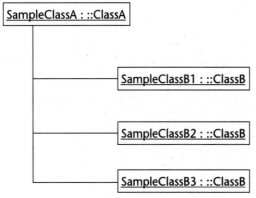

Figure 3.17 An instance of the simple metamodel.

Modeling Relational Meta Data

The first use case demonstrates how to physically represent a set of data. The data we want to model is shown in Table 3.2. The data is presented in tabular form, but we will use this data in the two different physical representations.

To model the data in Table 3.2 as a physical Relational table, we will use CWM's Relational metamodel. The use case will define a Relational table called *Product* with five columns, with one column for each of the data columns in Table 3.2. The use case also will define a key on the Relational table that will be used to uniquely identify the different rows of data. To produce the use-case instances, we first must determine which CWM packages we actually need.

Figure 3.18 shows the layered CWM metamodel structure originally presented in Figure 3.10. One of the basic design principles of CWM is that metamodels residing at one particular layer are dependent only on metamodels residing at a lower layer. This structure allows individual implementations to use only those portions of the CWM metamodel that are germane to their problem space. A result of this dependency structure is that little or no *package coupling* exists between metamodels on the same level, or from a lower level to a higher level. This means that a given CWM metamodel is dependent only on packages below itself in the block diagram (but not necessarily all packages below). In addition, no dependencies exist along any horizontal plane of the packages. An implementation of a given metamodel package requires the accompanying implementation of all other metamodel packages that it depends on, but no others.

Table 3.2 Sample Data for the Use-Case Study

UPC	NAME	SIZE	BRAND	CATEGORY
111222	Dave's Candy Bar	4 oz.	CompanyA	Candy
111223	Michele's Cookie	24 oz.	CompanyA	Food
112222	Good Cola	8 oz.	CompanyA	Beverage
112223	Better Cola	8 oz.	CompanyB	Beverage

Management	Warehouse Process			Warehouse Operation	
Analysis	Transformation	OLAP	Data Mining	Business Nomenclature	Information Visualization
Resource	Relational	Record		Multidimensional	XML
Foundation	Business Information	Data Types	Software Deployment	Keys Indexes	Expressions	Type Mapping
Object	Core	Behavioral		Relationships	Instance

Figure 3.18   Layered CWM metamodel.

The relational use case, therefore, requires the selection of only a subset of the entire metamodel. The packages required are illustrated in Figure 3.19. Notice that not all the packages from any one horizontal level were selected. In this example, the Relational package was selected because the Relational table and relational column modeling elements reside in that package. In addition, we need to define a unique key on the table, so, we also need a relational constraint. These objects are dependent on the Keys and Indexes metamodel from the Foundation layer and are dependent on the Core metamodel from the Object layer.

The actual use-case instance described previously is shown in Figure 3.20. In this figure is an instance of a Relational table called Product. The Product table has five columns: UPC, Name, Size, Brand, and Category.

Management	Warehouse Process			Warehouse Operation	
Analysis	Transformation	OLAP	Data Mining	Business Nomenclature	Information Visualization
Resource	Relational	Record		Multidimensional	XML
Foundation	Business Information	Data Types	Software Deployment	Keys Indexes	Expressions	Type Mapping
Object	Core	Behavioral		Relationships	Instance

Figure 3.19   CWM packages required for the relational use case.

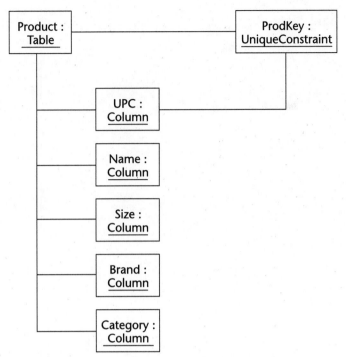

Figure 3.20   Instance diagram of the Relational table.

The Product table also has a unique constraint, ProdKey. This example shows how the CWM metamodel can represent the Relational table as a design element. In the next use case, we take the same data and use the Record package to represent the design of a Record File.

A tool that can be used to validate or illustrate the CWM metamodel is a sequence diagram; sequence diagrams show the message interaction between objects in the system. We introduce these diagrams to give you a flavor of how an Application Programming Interface (API) of the CWM metamodel might work. Another reason to introduce sequence diagrams is to give you more insight into how to use the *classifier equality* feature of the CWM metamodel. We will completely define this feature a little later in this section and show you how it solves certain problems.

The easiest way to describe a sequence diagram is to look at the diagram and walk through the syntax. The sequence diagram shown in Figure 3.21 is for the instances of the Relational table shown in Figure 3.20.

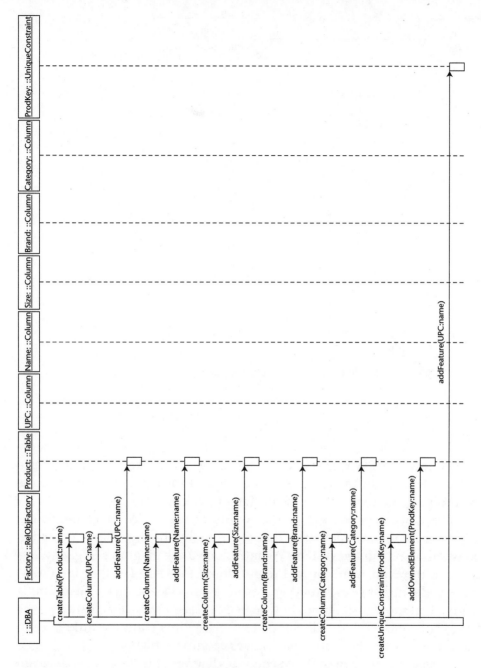

Figure 3.21 Sequence diagram for creating the Relational table.

The sequence diagram in Figure 3.21 shows a sample set of API calls to create and associate the Relational objects. The CWM specification does not contain this API. Rather, this API is a projection based on best practices of API design used by the authors. A slight embellishment exists in Figure 3.20:

No RelationalObjectFactory object exists in the CWM metamodel. This object is used to show that the objects must be created in some fashion, and the sequence diagram provides a convenient vehicle with which such an object can be used. In the preceding sequence diagram, messages are sent to the factory object. These method calls are used to create the Relational objects. These messages are also directed to the Product table object. Notice that the method is addFeature. The addFeature method is used because in the CWM metamodel, a Relational table is a type of classifier and, as such, inherits an association to a Feature from Classifier. In the Relational meta-model, a column is a type of feature and, as a result, no special association is necessary to link Relational tables to Columns. This same type of association reuse is found in the UniqueConstraint class in the Relational package. The UniqueConstraint is a type of UniqueKey found in the Keys and Indexes package. The UniqueKey object provides a relationship to some Structural Feature. Therefore, a UniqueConstraint in the Relational package can be related to a Relational Column via this inherited relationship. This feature of the CWM metamodel turns out to be very powerful to users of CWM. We will show how this feature works later in this section in the context of a dimensional modeling scenario, because we need an example of another resource to fully understand the significance of the UniqueConstraint.

Modeling Record-Based Meta Data

In the next use-case scenario, we will take the same data definition shown in Table 3.2 and use the Record package of CWM to produce the design of a Record File. The structure of the file will be the same as the structure of the Relational table, but we will replace the Relational table with a Record File. The Relational Columns will be replaced with fields, and the Unique-Constraint will be replaced with a UniqueKey. To start this use-case scenario, we again use the block diagram depicting the CWM packages and identify the packages necessary to solve this use case.

Figure 3.22 shows the packages required for this use-case scenario. The diagram differs from the Relational scenario only at the Resource level. The instances of the Record Package are shown in Figure 3.23. This figure shows an instance of RecordFile called Product, which correlates to the Relational table. The CWM definition of RecordFile is that it can support multiple record definitions per file, so we must add a RecordDef object. The next set of instances are Field objects. These objects correspond directly to the Column definitions from before. The last object is that of a UniqueKey. This object represents the intention of the designer to identify one of the fields of the record that can be used for record identity. This idea is a parallel concept to the Relational UniqueConstraint.

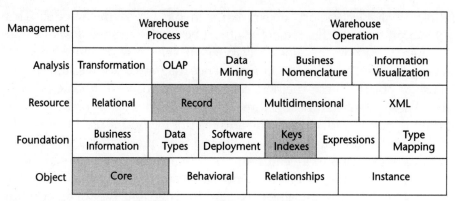

Figure 3.22   Packages required for producing a record file.

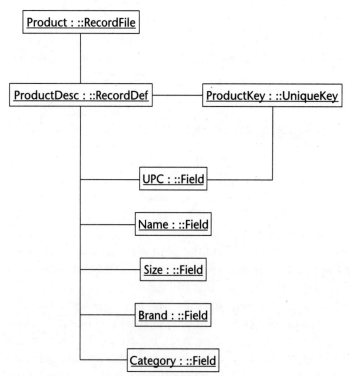

Figure 3.23   Instance of a record file.

Figure 3.24 shows the sequence diagram that describes the API calls, which might be made to create the Object instances shown in Figure 3.23. This set of API calls is again only a projection based on the definition of the Record Package in CWM. The sequence diagram uses an Object factory for the creation of the objects.

The most important aspect of illustrating these two use-case scenarios is the resulting instance and sequence diagram. An important result is that if you take a close look at both examples, you will realize that the only differences are in the object creation and the base types of objects. The structures of both the Relational table and the Record File are identical. In fact, even the projected API calls are the same. This is no accident. Further investigation will result in the discovery of what we previously called classifier equality.

These two use-case scenarios show the need for a user of CWM to first learn the nomenclature and definitions used in the CWM metamodel. In both use-case scenarios, the method used to add both Columns to Tables and Fields to Files was addFeature. Using the same method, addFeature, may seem strange at first, but this is a good example of why the user of CWM must become familiar with the overall methodology used to design the CWM metamodel. In this case, if the user was looking for an addColumn method on Tables and didn't find it, she may have come to the conclusion that the CWM metamodel didn't have the correct semantics for her use. This could not be farther from the truth. The CWM metamodel has the complete definitions necessary to model Relational Database objects. The important thing to remember is that CWM has abstracted many common features that belong to warehouse definitions and placed them in one place. These features are inherited from the metamodel and used by a great number of object definitions. This design technique is used throughout the construction of the CWM metamodel.

The benefits are twofold: First, this technique allows users of CWM to slice and dice the implementation of the model down to exactly the portions of the metamodel needed for their specific tool. The design eliminates package coupling by placing the commonly used associations between class definitions in the lowest-level packages. As more specific packages and specific class definitions were added to those packages, most of the common structural associations were already there in the lower levels of the metamodel.

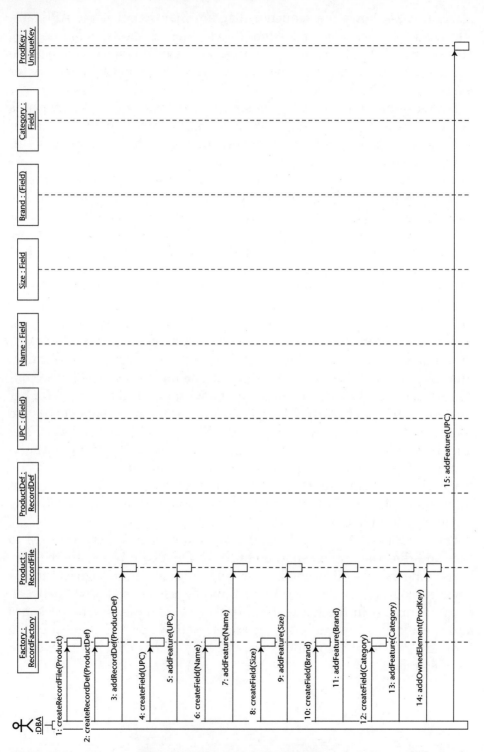

Figure 3.24   Sequence diagram for the product file instance.

Second, this design creates the classifier equality that we have been talking about. *Classifier equality* means all classifiers are created equal, and all features are also created equal. In data warehouse meta data, this turns out to be very important. The CWM metamodel can model constructs from concepts to analysis, with design and implementation in between. The underlying construct behind this methodology is that at their core, all these types of objects inherit from the same common root—the classifier. This classifier equality made trivial the construction of a common way to navigate from any type of resource to any other type of resource. In fact, this construct is the basis for the design of a very, very small transformation package that effectively can describe the movement of data from any resource to any other resource. This package also can describe the logical mapping from any level of classifier to any other level of classifier. Figure 3.25 shows the classifier equality in the model. The diagram depicts that Schemas, Packages, and Record files are equal. The diagram also depicts that Classifier, Table, RecordDef, Dimension, and ElementType are equal. Finally, the diagram shows that Feature, Column, Field, DimensionedObject, and Attribute are equal. This equality also provides CWM users with the benefit of learning how one package works; they get a greater understanding as to how other similar packages will work. This can reduce the ramp-up time in adding new packages to a given implementation.

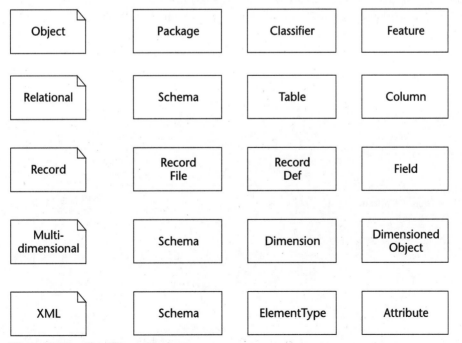

Figure 3.25   Classifier equivalence.

Modeling Physical Data Resources

To cover more of the CWM metamodel, the use-case scenario can be extended to include a physical implementation of the preceding example. The Relational use case will be extended to place the Relational table into a Schema. The Schema, in turn, will be placed into a Relational catalog. By adding these two objects, the object graph now can be associated with a particular installed database instance. This use-case scenario will use the fictitious database company TablesAreUs. This company makes a relational database that will house the Table definition from the preceding use-case scenario. CompanyA has purchased the TablesAreUs relational database and will install it on one of their servers, Ethel. This new use-case scenario now describes the meta data necessary to locate a particular database table in a particular instance of a relational database running on a machine. Again, we use the block diagram in Figure 3.19 to identify the packages necessary to complete this use case. Figure 3.26 shows the packages necessary for this use case. Notice that it was only necessary to augment the packages by one. The SoftwareDeployment package contains both the definition of the software package and the machine object. The meta data associated with the additional objects is shown in Figure 3.27. The physical link, from the table definition to where it is located, is through a Deployed Software System. In terms of the CWM metamodel, implementing the physical location was as simple as adding one package implementation and providing the associated objects and object associations.

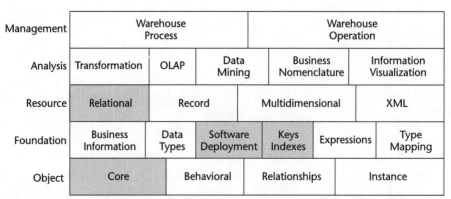

Figure 3.26 Packages needed to physically locate the Relational table.

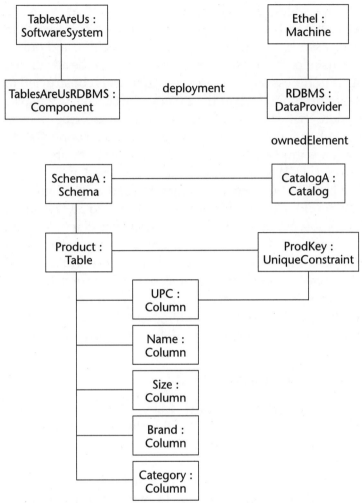

Figure 3.27   Physical deployment of the Product table.

This use-case scenario demonstrates another important aspect of the design of the CWM metamodel: its use of Namespaces. A *Namespace* as defined by CWM is:

A part of a model that contains a set of ModelElements, each of whose names designates a unique element within the Namespace.

In the metamodel, a Namespace is a ModelElement that can own other ModelElements, such as Classifiers. The name of each owned ModelElement must be unique within the Namespace. Moreover, each contained ModelElement is owned by at most one Namespace. The concrete sub-classes of Namespace may have additional constraints on which kind of elements may be contained. (CWM, 2001)

This definition allows users of CWM to use Namespace as a logical demarcation between local and enterprisewide definitions. In the preceding use-case scenario, let's assume that there was only one machine and only a single instance of the installed database. In that case, carrying the additional enterprise meta data is unnecessary. The CWM metamodel is constructed to allow the meta data definition to stop at the catalog object. This use makes an implicit assumption that the meta data is used to describe a local instance. In addition, when a user of such a system makes a connection to the meta data, a location is implied, and all meta data definitions are part of the connection. This type of CWM use is completely supported by the metamodel, but care must be used when determining where an implementation can set up meta data boundaries. A good rule of thumb is to always use a Namespace (or some subtype) as the implementation boundary. Another rule is that if the Namespace selected is generally an owned element of another Namespace, walk the owner relationships until you find a Namespace that stands on its own. The topmost Namespace is where the logical demarcation should be applied. In the preceding example, the demarcation would be the Relational Catalog object. A user logging into a particular Catalog will find the owned Schemas and, in turn, Tables, Columns, and so on.

Modeling Transformation Meta Data

The use case up to this point has shown the design of both a Relational table and a Record file. The use case then added the physical location to the Relational table definition, thereby making it an implementation. We can use the same use-case scenario to show another aspect of the CWM metamodel by introducing the mapping section of CWM. In CWM there are two types of mappings. The first is generally used to map from the different levels shown in Figure 3.15. That CWM mechanism is Transformation-Maps, which is a general mechanism to describe how objects are built from or defined by other objects. We will use this mechanism later in the overall use-case scenario to map from the Analytic level to the Implementation level. Dependency is a second lightweight mapping mechanism. We will use that here to show how to map from design to implementation. (Note: The TransformationMaps also could have been used; however, they will be used where dependency could not. We decided to show this part of the use-case scenario with Dependency.)

This time, instead of adding the association from the physical database to the catalog, we will make a *deep copy* of the Catalog object. A deep copy means that we will copy the Catalog object and all objects owned by the Catalog. In this specific case, it means a copy of the Catalog, the Schema, the Product Table, the Columns, and the Unique Constraint. We will use the Dependency mechanism to link the first Catalog object to the copied Catalog object. The second Catalog then will be associated to the physical database. We will repeat the process a second time with a second instance of the database on a different machine. This new set of instances will show that the CWM metamodel can be used to design a Relational table and implement that table on two different database instances.

The instances shown in Figure 3.28 could represent the meta data test and production instances of the TablesAreUs database. The set of instances representing the design of the table are shared via a dependency between the two database instances. This mechanism can be used to provide both dependency tracking and design to implementation specification. In Figure 3.28 we have shown the dependency object used to link the design specification of the table to the implementation of the table. In fact, additional Dependency objects probably would be between the columns to complete the use case. These objects were omitted for brevity and because they look identical to the Dependency objects between the Table objects.

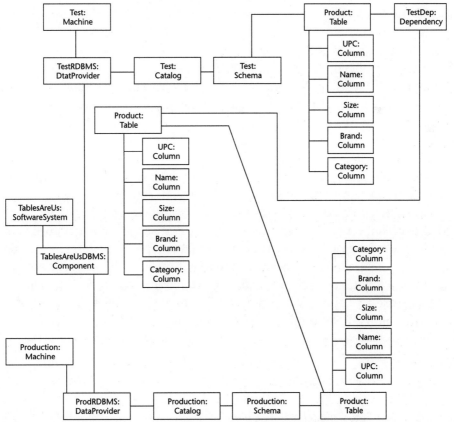

Figure 3.28 Test and production implementation of the Product table.

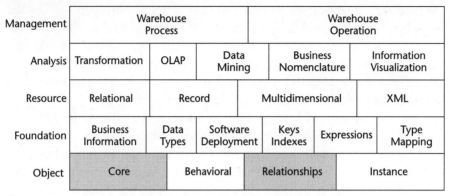

Management	Warehouse Process			Warehouse Operation	
Analysis	Transformation	OLAP	Data Mining	Business Nomenclature	Information Visualization
Resource	Relational	Record		Multidimensional	XML
Foundation	Business Information	Data Types	Software Deployment	Keys Indexes	Expressions	Type Mapping
Object	Core	Behavioral		Relationships	Instance

Figure 3.29   Core package is the only package needed for conceptual modeling.

The use-case scenario has now covered the middle two portions of Figure 3.15. Two levels remain in the diagram: Concept and Analysis. The decision as to which to cover first is arbitrary, but to make a cleaner flow of the overall concepts, we will discuss the conceptual level first.

To add the conceptual level, no further packages of the CWM metamodel have to be implemented. No other packages are needed because in the CWM metamodel, the design and implementation structures are dependent on the conceptual level. This fact is highlighted in Figure 3.29, which shows the packages necessary to implement the conceptual area of the metamodel.

If we apply the concepts of the Object Model layer to the Relational use-case scenario, we can add a conceptual design to the overall use case. To make the use-case scenario concrete, assume that we have some visual modeling tool to construct our conceptual model. This particular tool has the capability to model data entities as classes and data attributes as features of those classes. In addition, we will model the connection between the two associations that connect the classes via an association end object. This long-winded explanation is another way of saying that some data structure will have some set of data attributes. The nature of this type of modeling requires us to use very abstract words, but the meaning is simple. These words enable us to equate a Relational table and a file with a fixed record type at this level. In this use-case scenario, we can now define an abstract data structure and design it for both a Relational table and a Record file.

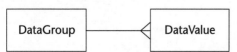

Figure 3.30   Conceptual model of a data group.

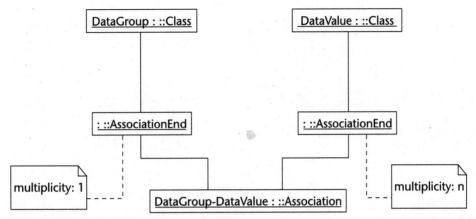

Figure 3.31 Object instances from the Object package representing a conceptual model.

The Conceptual model shown in Figure 3.30 defines a DataGroup that can have many DataValues. The set of CWM instances from the Object package is shown in Figure 3.31.

To complete the use-case scenario, we need to map the conceptual model to the design model (see Figure 3.32). As we did earlier in this section, we will use the Dependency object to map the DataGroup to a Relational table and a DataValue to a Column.

The modeling tool used in this portion of the use-case scenario used classes and other objects from the Core package. The example could have been done just as easily with an Entity-Relationship (ER) modeling tool. The objects in the Core package were used as the basis for one of the CWM extension packages—the ER extension. We mention this here because many of the conceptual or design tools used provide ER diagramming tools. The ER extension package is not part of the normative part of the CWM specification. However, it is supplied in the specification to show how to extend the CWM metamodel. Supplying the ER package also solved another issue for CWM. The use of ER diagramming tools is very pervasive in the data warehouse community, and we wanted to show how such a tool could use CWM. The ER extension is mostly a renaming of specific Core package object definitions. Some very slight differences exist, and these were added as domain-specific attributes and associations in the ER package. CWM is a good choice to capture meta data from ER design tools, even though the ER package is supplied as an extension to the specification.

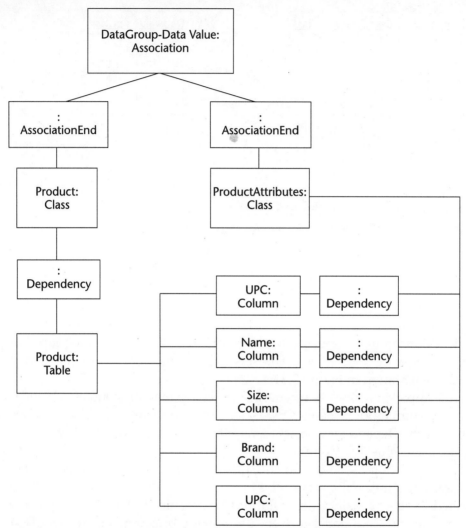

Figure 3.32   Instance diagram mapping the conceptual and design levels.

Modeling OLAP Meta Data

We will conclude this use-case scenario by adding the last portion of the diagram shown in Figure 3.15. This time the augmented use-case scenario will describe a Dimensional metamodel that is implemented in a relational database. The first step is to start with the block CWM package diagram shown in Figure 3.33 to identify the packages needed by this use-case scenario.

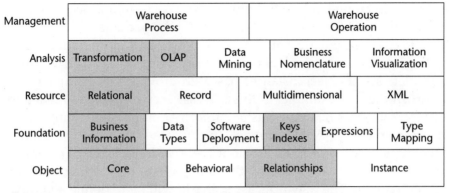

Management	Warehouse Process			Warehouse Operation	
Analysis	Transformation	OLAP	Data Mining	Business Nomenclature	Information Visualization
Resource	Relational	Record		Multidimensional	XML
Foundation	Business Information	Data Types	Software Deployment	Keys Indexes	Expressions	Type Mapping
Object	Core	Behavioral		Relationships	Instance

Figure 3.33   Packages required for dimensional use-case scenario.

In this use-case scenario, we will introduce two new portions of the CWM metamodel: Transformation and Online Analytical Processing (OLAP). To complete this use-case scenario, we must now map from the OLAP meta-model to the Relational metamodel. It is necessary to use a map because of the way the OLAP metamodel is defined. The OLAP metamodel must be implemented by some physical resource. As we stated earlier in this section, we have two mapping options available. In this case, we will use the more robust mapping objects supplied by the Transformation package. To imple-ment the OLAP metamodel as a Relational table, we will use a set of objects from the Transformation package. These new objects are the TransformMap, ClassifierMap, and the FeatureMap. These three objects are all that is neces-sary to map from the OLAP metamodel to the Relational metamodel. The Transformation package is very compact, and the mapping portion is even smaller. The compact representation of the Transformation package is made possible by the same overall architecture that CWM uses in a number of areas in the metamodel. The particular feature exploited here is that all phys-ical warehouse structures are a subtype of Classifier. This feature means that a metamodel that can link classifiers can link any two objects that are of type Classifier. This design methodology was also extended to the OLAP pack-age. By creating the CWM metamodel in this way, a CWM user can map any OLAP metamodel to any type of Classifier. In turn, Attributes of the OLAP metamodel can be mapped to any type of Feature. The mapping metamodel does support one additional type of mapping from Feature to Classifier. This additional object was defined because certain types of features, more specif-ically collections of features, will result in a Classifier. A good example of this is a set of Relational columns that is often equated with a single Dimension of a Multidimensional database. This Dimension object is the physical

Dimension object found in the Multidimensional package, and should not be confused with the Dimension object from the OLAP package.

The following use-case scenario may seem long and intimidating; however, a large portion is a rehash of the use cases we have already examined. The complete set of object instances has been provided for completeness and as an end-to-end example. In this use-case scenario, we also will add some object instances from the BusinessInformation package to introduce that portion of the CWM metamodel. In this use-case scenario, we will omit the deployment information about the Relational tables. This information could be inferred by adding the deployment information from the preceding use case. The new use-case scenario will be to define an OLAP metamodel that consists of a single Dimension and a Cube dimensioned by that Dimension with one measure. Cubes will have more Dimensions in the real world in general, but adding more dimensions would only lengthen the description and instance diagrams and add little additional information. The OLAP metamodel in this example is implemented as a standard star-schema in a relational database (Kimball, 1996). The specifics of the use-case scenario are shown in Figure 3.34.

The following set of figures describes the object instances to fulfill this use-case scenario. We start with the instances of the Relational metamodel that represent the star-schema shown in Figure 3.34.

Figure 3.35 contains the object instances for both the Product table as well as the Fact table. In this example, we have introduced a new Relational object type: ForeignKey. This object is the standard Relational foreign key definition and is used to connect tables with many-to-one relationships.

- Dimension: Product
    - Attributes: ID, Name
    - Levels: UPC, BRAND, and CATEGORY
    - Hierarchy: Standard
        - Levels in Hierachy
            - CATEGORY
            - BRAND
            - UPC
        - Cube: SalesCube
            - Cube Dimensions: Product
            - Cube Measures: Sales
            - Tables: Product, and SalesFact

Figure 3.34 Physical layout of the star-schema.

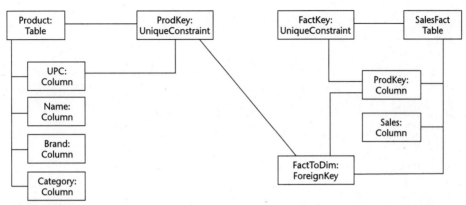

Figure 3.35 Star-schema instances.

Now, we start to define the Dimensional OLAP metamodel. The initial set of diagrams presents the Dimension and the Dimension's related structures. We then map the Dimension to the Product table of the star-schema.

Figure 3.36 shows a set of instances that describe the Product dimension. Notice that the Dimension has a UniqueKey object attached to it. The use of *keys* is another concept that has been abstracted for use in almost all parts of the metamodel. The intended use is to describe some set of Dimension attributes that will return a unique list of Dimension values. Figure 3.36 also depicts the standard hierarchy of the Product dimension. The diagram has numbered the associations from the hierarchy to the HierarchyLevelAssociation objects. The numbers have been placed in the diagram to show the ordered association. The diagram should be read from the bottom up; Category is at the top of the hierarchy followed by Brand and finally UPC.

In the CWM metamodel, Dimensions, Levels, Hierarchies, and HierarchyLevelAssociations are all types of classifiers. All these objects are types of classifiers because in a Dimensional metamodel, each one of these types of objects can expose a set of attributes. In addition to exposing attributes, the Dimensional metamodel could be mapped at any and all of these objects. In general, the physical mapping is done on Levels and Level attributes and HierarchyLevelAssociations and their attributes. In this example, we will map only the HierarchyLevelAssociation attributes to the star-schema. The other object mappings have been omitted for brevity of the example, and showing the additional mappings would add no new information. However, we will supply the mapping from the Dimension to its associated Levels. This mapping could have been done between the Dimension and the HierarchyLevelAssociations, but again we are trying to describe the various features of the metamodel, and the two types of mappings are identical.

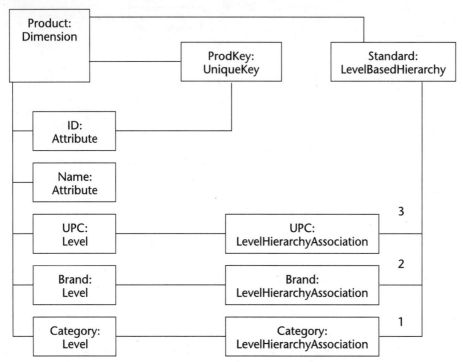

Figure 3.36   Instance of the Product dimension.

Figure 3.37 looks very complicated, but it really isn't. The key feature that this diagram depicts is that the Product dimension is made up of a logical union of its components. The logical union is shown by the ClassifierMap with a single target (the Product dimension) and three sources (the three Levels). This diagram shows the next important CWM concept: It illustrates a particular Attribute of a Dimension, which is also composed as a logical union of its components. In Figure 3.37 notice that the names of the Level attributes are different from the Dimension attributes. This was done to show that the mapping between these items is based on the FeatureMaps and not some naming convention. It is also worth pointing out that the various Levels expose a differing number of attributes. This was one of the requirements of the OLAP metamodel. The last thing to notice about Figure 3.37 is that in the Category level, one of the attributes is used as a source for both the ID and Name attribute of the Dimension. An important feature of the OLAP metamodel not shown is that the Attributes of the Levels are independent of the Attributes of the Dimension. This means that Attributes defined for the Levels may or may not be exposed by the Dimension. The reason for this is that many Level attributes make

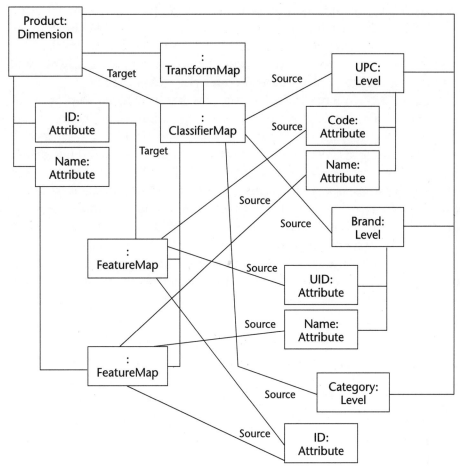

Figure 3.37   Mapping from a dimension to its levels.

sense only for a particular Level. Forcing the Dimension to expose these Attributes is arbitrary and may not match a user's view of the system. This design provides a CWM user with the most flexibility to solve the demands of their users. In general, the Attributes exposed by the Dimension will be a subset of the union of all Attributes exposed by the Levels. This is a general use of the metamodel but is not mandated.

Next, we turn our attention to mapping the OLAP metamodel onto an implementation. Before we can do that, we need to add some structure to the LevelBasedHierarchy and its owned objects. HierarchyLevelAssociations are a type of classifier. We also indicated that the maps support mapping only between classifiers and attributes. To link the OLAP metamodel to the Relational metamodel, we must now define a set of attributes on the HierarchychyLevelAssociations. In this example, we will define a special attribute for each named ID. This will be used when retrieving the set of values for the Hierarchy. In addition, we will add another special attribute, PARENT, to the HierarchyLevelAssociations representing the Brand and UPC levels. This attribute will serve as the immediate parent in the hierarchy. Finally, we will add a Name attribute to each of the HierarchyLevelAssociations.

In Figure 3.38, we have introduced a new set of objects: Deployment-Group and DimensionDeployment. These object definitions enable users of CWM to provide multiple deployments of a specific OLAP metamodel. A few key features of CWM are highlighted by the instances in Figure 3.38. First, the LOV StructureMap is connected to the DimensionDeployment via the listOfValues association. This set of objects should be navigated to provide the list of values for the Category level in the Standard hierarchy. This activity is critical to the construction of a hierarchy and was, therefore, given a special association to navigate in the OLAP metamodel. Second, users can reuse physical structures in mapping to the OLAP model. This is shown by the Category column, which represents both the list of values and the name of the Category elements in the hierarchy.

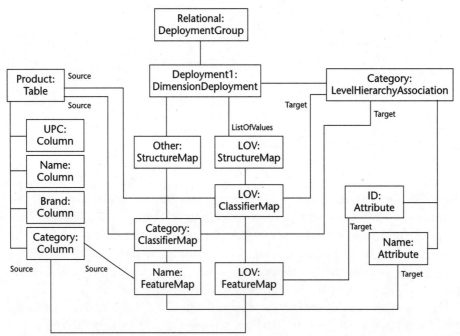

Figure 3.38   Mapping of Category level in the standard hierarchy to a Relational table.

Figure 3.39, which depicts how to create an instance for a lower level in the hierarchy, is almost identical to the top-most level shown in Figure 3.38. The main difference is the introduction of the second special association, immediateParent. The capability to navigate an association to the immediate parent in the hierarchy also was considered critical to the construction of the Hierarchy metamodel. Thus, a special association was added. The proper interpretation of the instances from Figures 3.38 and 3.39, with regard to retrieving both the values of the Hierarchy and the immediate parent in the Hierarchy, is that of the logical union of the various pairs of listOfValues and immediateParent associations for the set of levels of the hierarchy.

(In Figure 3.39, the mapping of the Attribute name was omitted to keep the diagram simple. The mapping is identical to that shown in Figure 3.38 except that the FeatureMap source would be the Brand column.)

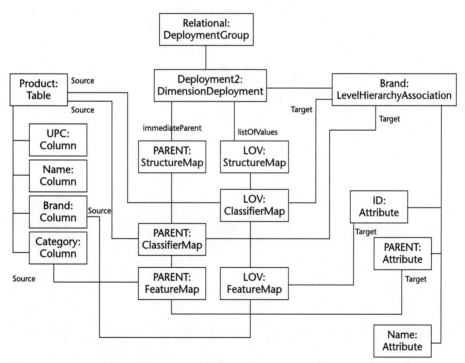

Figure 3.39   Mapping of category level in standard hierarchy to a Relational table.

To complete the mapping of the Standard hierarchy to the star-schema, we would produce a third set of mapping structures similar to those shown in Figure 3.39. This set of objects would be for the UPC level in the Standard hierarchy. These mappings are not shown, but would essentially map the listOfValues to the UPC column, the immediateParent to the Brand column, and the Name attribute to the Name column. With the Dimension now mapped, we turn our attention to the other side of the OLAP metamodel: Cubes.

In this use-case scenario, we have a single Cube with one Dimension and one Measure. The process for Cubes is similar to that of Dimensions. First, we define the logical Cube model, and then we map that model onto a physical implementation. In this case, we will map the Cube onto the SalesFact fact table. Figure 3.40 shows the instance of the logical Sales cube. In the OLAP metamodel, the Cube is dimensioned by using a set of CubeDimensionAssociation objects to identify the Dimensions of the Cube. This structure is used to enable a CWM user to identify sparsity patterns in Cubes. A Dimension may be dense in one Cube and sparse in another. This functionality is made available by the intermediate CubeDimensionAssociation object. Figure 3.40 also shows that the Cube has a Measure called Sales. This association is not shown directly in the CWM specification, which, rather, shows another instance of the reuse of associations. The Cube is a subtype of Classifier, and the Measure is a subtype of Feature. The Cube reuses the Classifier-Feature association to imply that a Cube can contain a set of Measures.

Like Dimensions, Cubes must be implemented to represent actual values of the data warehouse. The process of implementing a Cube is slightly different than that of implementing a Dimension. The OLAP metamodel uses the CubeRegion construct to provide this functionality. A CubeRegion is necessary because of the varied ways in which data is stored in Data warehouses. The main difference between mapping a Cube and a Dimension is that the data represented by the Cube could be many orders of magnitude larger than the data represented by the Dimension. To illustrate how the volume of data represented by the Cube could explode, consider Table 3.3.

Table 3.3   Data Volume Explosion

STRUCTURE	NUMBER OF DATA VALUES
Product dimension	100,000
Geography dimension	1,000
Time dimension	1,000

Table 3.3 *(Continued)*

STRUCTURE	NUMBER OF DATA VALUES
Channel dimension	100
Sales: Product × Geography	100,000,000
Sales: Product × Geography × Time	100,000,000,000
Sales: Product × Geography × Time × Channel	10,000,000,000,000

By definition, the Cube represents a set of data equal to the cross product of the number of values of its Dimensions. As Table 3.3 shows, a single structure representing the entire Cube might need to be enormous. A Cube structure this large could be either too large to be efficiently handled or may not be implementable in a given database technology. In general, Cubes are split into sections that represent some manageable slice of Cube data because of the possibility of data explosion. The data slice usually represents some predefined section of each Dimension of the Cube. The various types of physical implementations lead CWM to construct the OLAP metamodel to parallel the storage flexibility needed by the implementers of Cubes. The definition of a CubeRegion is that the Dimensionality of the region is exactly the same as that of the Cube and represents some proper subset of the Measures of the Cube. In this use-case scenario, there is only one Measure. Thus, the CubeRegion defined in Figure 3.41 represents all the Measures of the Cube, but this is not mandated by the OLAP metamodel.

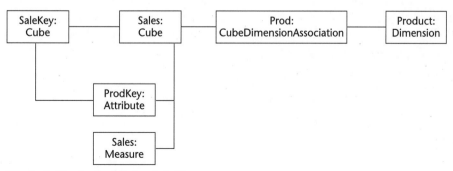

Figure 3.40 Logical Cube definition.

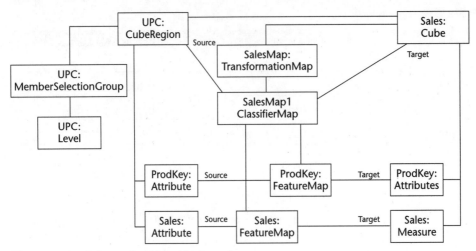

Figure 3.41   Cube region object instances.

Figure 3.41 depicts the object instances to create a CubeRegion for the Sales Cube. This CubeRegion represents a slice of data at the UPC level. This is defined in Figure 3.42 by the MemberSelectionGroup linked to the UPC level. The OLAP metamodel MemberSelectionGroup should contain one association for every Dimension of the Cube. This structure completely describes the slice of data represented by the CubeRegion. In the OLAP metamodel, the CubeRegion can contain any number of MemberSelection-Groups. This is because a particular physical slice of data may represent many logical slices of data. This metamodel can represent any portion of the Cube, with the smallest MemberSelectionGroup identifying a single value of the Cube. The next portion of this use-case scenario is to map the CubeRegion to a physical implementation: the SalesFact Table. By combining the object instances in Figures 3.41 and 3.42, a complete definition of the UPC CubeRegion is provided. The object instances show the specific mapping of the Cube to a physical implementation. In this case, the Sales Cube has a single physical implementation at the lowest level through the UPC Cube region.

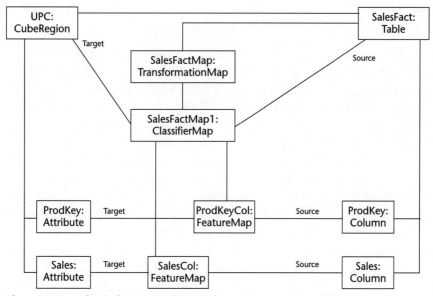

Figure 3.42   Physical mapping from Cube region to a fact table.

The last portion of this use-case scenario is to link the Cube and Dimension objects. In CWM, a type of Namespace is typically used, which is provided by the CWM OLAP metamodel as an object called a schema. The Schema object is a Namespace and the entry point to the OLAP metamodel. The Schema object also serves to provide an overall namespace for Cubes and Dimensions. Figure 3.43 depicts the OLAP Schema object instance along with the SalesCube and Product Dimension.

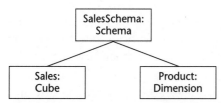

Figure 3.43   The OLAP Schema and owned Cubes and Dimensions.

Summary

In this chapter we have shown how to model data warehousing and business analysis meta data using the CWM metamodel. First, we reviewed the modeling language that is used to specify the CWM metamodel, namely UML. We provided an example of using UML to create a static model of a small, discrete system (a simple molecular compound), and we discussed the fundamental components of UML class diagrams, such as Classes, Associations, Features (that is, Operations and Attributes), and Packages. Secondly, we gave an overview of the salient design features of the CWM metamodel: how it is modularly structured, what the common thread is among all sub-metamodels, and how the sub-metamodels can be used independently of and with other sub-metamodels.

We then demonstrated the use of the CWM metamodel (that is, various CWM sub-metamodels) to model relational, record-based, transformation, and OLAP meta data. We saw how a CWM model is constructed from a simple use case. In the process, we illustrated several standard usage patterns for the CWM metamodel. We also demonstrated that a particular usage of the CWM metamodel (that is, to solve a specific modeling problem of interest to a particular CWM user) could be restricted to only those packages germane to the task at hand. The CWM metamodel covers a great number of features and functions available in data warehousing. The ability to implement and use portions of the overall model is a very important feature of the CWM metamodel and should lower the entrance barrier to tools looking to use CWM as an interchange vehicle. Another central theme in this chapter, and an important aspect of CWM, is the reuse of associations. Our use-case modeling showed that the model doesn't always appear to have the structure we would have expected. This fact was clearly illustrated in the Relational table and Column example. In general, if an association looks like it's missing from an object definition, look to a superclass in the model; chances are that the missing association has been abstracted for use by like objects.

The discussion provided in this chapter is comprehensive, but not exhaustive. By focusing on a few important examples of using the CWM metamodel to model data warehousing and business analysis meta data, we hope we have enabled you to obtain a good understanding of the power and flexibility of the CWM metamodel. We hope you are now in a position to follow the detailed discussions in subsequent chapters of four major scenarios of using CWM to provide meta data integration solutions for data warehousing and business analysis.

Meta Data Interchange Patterns

This chapter establishes a complete theory and methodology of Common Warehouse Metamodel (CWM) Meta Data Interchange Patterns. In particular, the need to develop meta data interchange patterns is first investigated through a number of illustrative examples. It is demonstrated that truly interoperable meta data integration is not necessarily guaranteed by CWM syntax alone, but that some means of both specifying a semantic context for model interpretation, as well as a means of managing the sizes of CWM instances, are required.

We propose and fully define the notion of a pattern-based approach to solving these interoperability issues. We then demonstrate the effectiveness of this approach, both through detailed examples, as well as references to other areas of computer science and software engineering that have already successfully leveraged solutions analogous to the use of patterns. We also fully develop a practical methodology for developing meta data interchange patterns based on CWM. This methodology is demonstrated in the actual construction of a fundamental meta data interchange pattern that will serve as the basis for much of the rest of this book.

To achieve their objective of nearly seamless and highly interoperable meta data interchange, patterns need to be developed by the people who intend to use them: the various domain experts, meta data modelers, and integrators of data warehousing and business analysis solutions. To that end, this chapter also defines a standard way of specifying meta data interchange patterns, and then publishing them in the form of public *pattern catalogs*. (The companion Web site provides just such a public catalog of the patterns developed throughout this book.) This manner of specifying and publishing meta data interchange patterns is specifically engineered toward a distributed, Web-based environment.

Introducing Meta Data Interchange Patterns

CWM is a generic metamodel of data warehousing and business analysis meta data that has been engineered to cover a broad spectrum of meta data interchange requirements. Since the designers of CWM could never anticipate in advance all of the possible ways in which CWM users might go about solving integration problems, CWM was designed to be flexible, expressive, and completely independent of platform and environmental considerations. However, this high degree of expressiveness and flexibility also makes interchanging CWM models in a truly seamless manner rather difficult. Specifically:

- CWM defines a formal syntax for defining meta data, but there is also a need to somehow be able to express the particular *context* in which a given CWM model is to be interpreted or understood. The problem of describing the context of an interchange is outside the scope of CWM itself.

- Any CWM model potentially consists of an unlimited number of valid arrangements of modeling elements. Without some formal criteria for limiting the physical extent of a particular CWM model, processes consuming that model must either be prepared to accept models of unbounded size and complexity, or judge what portions of the model to process and what portions to ignore.

The next two subsections investigate these problems in detail, using several concrete examples. The fundamental concepts of the pattern-based approach to meta data interchange are established in the process of illustrating the problems with establishing common context and placing boundaries on solution extents. In the next two subsections, these intuitive concepts are fully developed into both a complete theory of meta data interchange patterns, as well as a practical methodology for developing and publishing them.

The Need to Establish a Common Context for Meta Data Interchange

Consider the following two diagrams from the CWM Relational metamodel. The first diagram, shown in Figure 4.1, illustrates the subset of the CWM Relational metamodel defining packages that might be used as containers of NamedColumnSet.

Figure 4.2 shows the subset to the CWM Relational metamodel in which Table is defined as a subtype of NamedColumnSet and Column is defined as a subtype of Attribute. This diagram also illustrates that an instance of Table may own instances of Column via the inherited *owner-feature* composition relating Classifier to StructuralFeature.

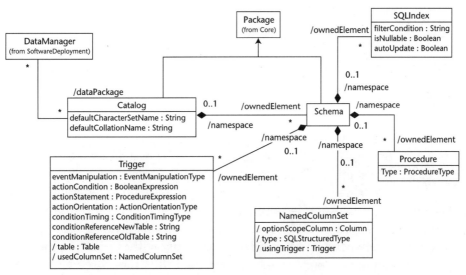

Figure 4.1   CWM Relational metamodel: Catalog and Schema.

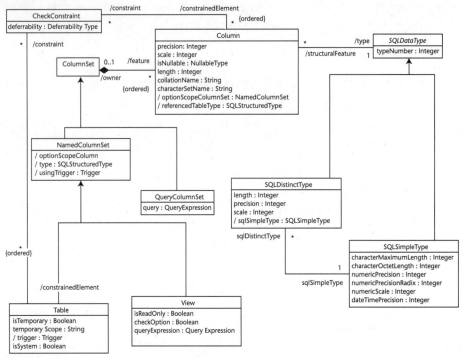

Figure 4.2   CWM Relational metamodel: Table and Column.

Note in Figure 4.1 that a Catalog may contain Tables via the inherited *namespace-ownedElement* composition, since Table, as a subtype of Named-ColumnSet, is therefore a descendent of ModelElement, and since Catalog, as a subtype of Package, is therefore a descendent of Namespace. On the other hand, a Table may also be owned by a Schema (a named collection of Tables), and Schema, in turn, may (or may not) be owned by a Catalog. In either case, an instance of Table can only have a single owner (it cannot be shared). Its owner may be a Catalog, a Schema, or even a generic instance of Package, since Package is not abstract. On the other hand, there is no strict requirement that a Table have an owner. An instance of Table can be interchanged between CWM-enabled tools as is, without being placed in any kind of container. Figures 4.3 through 4.5 illustrate three alternative ways of modeling and interchanging meta data.

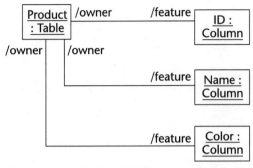

Figure 4.3   Relational Table: Instance diagram.

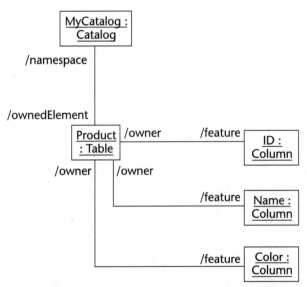

Figure 4.4   Relational Catalog: Instance diagram.

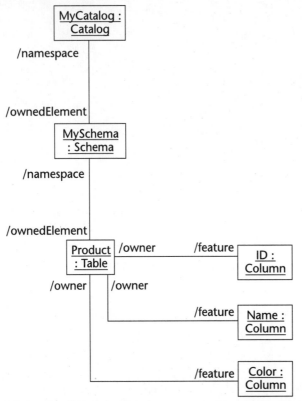

Figure 4.5 Relational Catalog and Schema: Instance diagram.

Now, the question that naturally comes to mind: When using CWM to interchange a relational table model, which of these three alternative configurations is correct? Well, there is no wrong or right answer. Each configuration is correct relative to some assumed *context*. For example, let's assume that a database modeling tool and a relational engine both agree that relational tables should always be registered by a catalog. In that case, we say, informally, that the common interchange context of the tools stipulates a certain expectation (or convention) that Tables are always owned by Catalogs. In this case, the scenario represented by Figure 4.4 will be intelligible to those tools, but the other two scenarios will not. Not that there is anything inherently wrong or incorrect with either of the other two scenarios, but they simply are just not meaningful within the established context.

The modeling tool always emits XML Metadata Interchange (XMI) files in which Tables are contained by Catalogs, and the relational engine, when consuming an XMI file, always tests for the presence of a Catalog first, and then searches any Catalogs for their contained Tables. If the relational engine were to import an XMI file containing Table definitions alone, it would most likely not be able to process the imported meta data, because it is expecting the highest level meta data content in the XMI file to consist of instances of Catalog.

As another example of what is meant by context, consider the interchange of an Online Analytical Processing (OLAP) model together with meta data representing multidimensional visualization concepts. Figure 4.6 shows the subset of the CWM OLAP metamodel defining Cube, Dimension, Schema, and their interrelationships. (Note that the Schema class shown here is an OLAP Schema, and should not be confused with the Relational Schema described earlier.) Figure 4.7 shows the complete CWM Information Visualization metamodel.

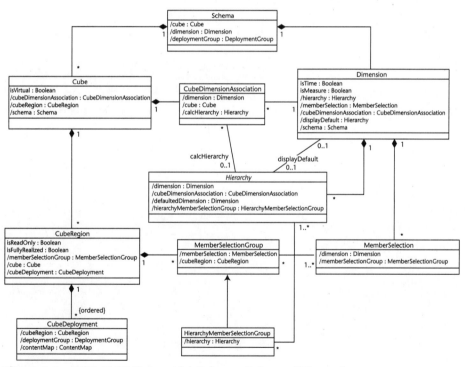

Figure 4.6 CWM OLAP Metamodel: Schema, Cube, and Dimension.

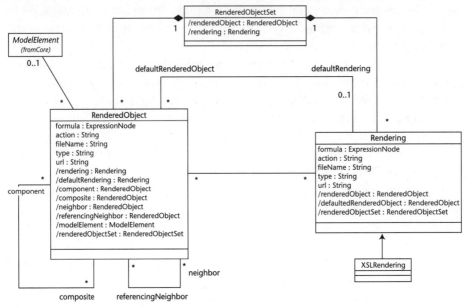

Figure 4.7   CWM Information Visualization Metamodel.

As shown in Figure 4.6, the CWM OLAP metamodel requires Cubes to be owned by Schemas. This is by virtue of the "1" cardinality on the Schema end of the composition relating Schema to Cube. So it is not unreasonable for any tool importing a CWM OLAP model to search the XMI file for instances of OLAP Schema first, and then query each Schema for its Cubes. Figure 4.8 shows an example of an OLAP model consisting of a single Schema with multiple Cubes.

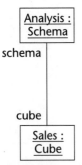

Figure 4.8   OLAP Schema and Cube: Instance diagram.

Now, let's assume we want to augment the OLAP model with some additional meta data that would be useful to advanced visualization software in representing the data content of the Cube. How can we combine this with the OLAP model of Figure 4.8? Figure 4.9 illustrates an enhanced version of the OLAP model in which an instance of RenderedObjectSet has been added to the Schema. RenderedObjectSet contains an instance of RenderedObject for each Cube in the Schema. RenderedObject serves as a logical proxy for a model element that is to be rendered in some manner (for example, projected onto a two-dimensional surface, or possibly translated to some nonvisual format, such as an audio stream). The Rendering class models the actual rendering transformation. RenderedObjectSet groups both Renderings and their related RenderedObjects together within a single package.

In the model of Figure 4.9, Schema owns the RenderedObjectSet that provides visualization transformations for its Cubes. Schema is a Package, and RenderedObjectSet is also a Package, but Package is a type of ModelElement, so there is nothing syntactically wrong in adding the RenderedObjectSet to the Schema as an owned element.

What if we had chosen to make the RenderedObjectSet an owned element of one of the Cubes instead? That would also be valid, from a purely syntactical standpoint, since a Cube is a Namespace. However, since the visualization transformations apply across the various Cubes of the Schema, it seems a bit odd to have one of the Cubes in particular own the RenderedObjectSet.

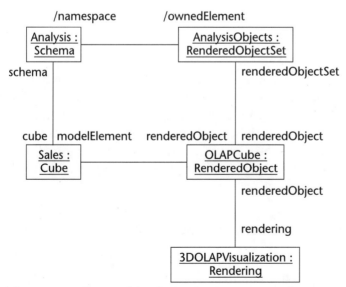

Figure 4.9   OLAP Model with visualization: Instance diagram.

On the other hand, we could also let the RenderedObjectSet reside outside the Schema in the XMI file, and not have it owned by any element of the model. All these possibilities are syntactically valid, as far as the CWM metamodel is concerned. But given the fact that we are using CWM classes to represent rendering transformations that are, presumably, specialized for use with OLAP Cubes, it seems reasonable that these transformations and their associations to Cubes should be owned by the Schema.

Once again, there is no wrong or right answer here, so we need to strive to do what seems most reasonable. If all tools in the environment agree that visualization meta data should be owned by the Schemas containing the OLAP elements being visualized, then we say (again, informally) that the common interchange context expects or stipulates this particular way of structuring visualization meta data for OLAP models. This has the following consequences for tools that process OLAP models:

- Software tools not concerned with visual renderings can simply ignore any visualization models when processing the content of an imported XMI file. This does not necessarily mean that these tools have not acknowledged the contextual convention for visualization, but that they simply have no interest in visualizing anything, and avoid searching for visualization models.

- Software tools interested in extracting visualization meta data from the OLAP model (for example, graphically oriented, multidimensional reporting tools) know precisely where to find the visualization model relative to the rest of the OLAP model. They do not have to exhaustively search the contents of an XMI file beyond locating instances of the OLAP Schema. So the construction of internal search logic is simplified in this case.

- Software tools that disregard the established context for interchange run the risk of exporting meta data that is not completely interchangeable. For example, if a visualization model is placed in an XMI file at the same level as the OLAP Schema, the visualization model will most likely not be discovered by tools subscribing to the convention that all OLAP visualization models are stored within their relevant Schemas.

The Need to Place Boundaries on Solution Extents

Along with establishing a common semantic context, effective meta data interchange also requires constraining the numbers of certain types of model elements within a model. In this case, we are setting limits or boundaries on the size of a model's physical extent. The physical extents of most CWM models are usually unlimited, by virtue of certain CWM and Meta Object Facility (MOF) metamodeling contentions. As with the common context problem, examples will help to illustrate why this is important.

Consider once again the subset of the CWM Relational metamodel illustrated in Figure 4.2, which shows how Columns (as descendents of Feature) are related to Tables (as descendents of Classifier) via the inherited *owner-feature* composition. The Feature end of the association specifies that the number of Column instances that may be owned by a Table is *unbounded*, meaning that CWM specifies no particular limit on this number (or perhaps, more precisely, *avoids* specifying any limit). This is because CWM has no way of anticipating in advance what reasonable maximum values for such cardinalities might be. In fact, there is no reasonable maximum value. It is strictly up to the end user's implementation of a given model to make such decisions.

As an example, let's assume that we have a relational database engine that limits the total number of columns on any relational table to 64K. This limit, of course, exceeds the number of useful columns normally defined on most relational tables in practice, but it does represent a practical limitation in the design of a software tool. In this case, we might want to ensure that relational models in our environment never define tables with more than 64K columns. This means that our relational modeling tool will have to ensure that any relational model selected for export via an XMI file does not contain table definitions with greater than 64K columns. Similarly, the relational engine needs to ensure that it correctly handles any relational table model it might import with more than 64K columns. But what exactly does that mean? Should it accept all columns up to the 64Kth and simply ignore the rest? Or should it reject the table definition outright? Probably the latter rather than the former is the preferred behavior. But in either case, some sort of exception should be made, signaling the detection of an unacceptable (although not necessarily syntactically invalid) relational model.

A properly constrained relational model for this particular environment is illustrated in the instance diagram of Figure 4.10. This model contains a single relational Table with an attached Constraint that limits the total number of Columns that may be added to the Table. If more Tables were added to this model, the Constraint could be reused, in the sense that an instance of a CWM Constraint can be made to reference any number of CWM ModelElements.

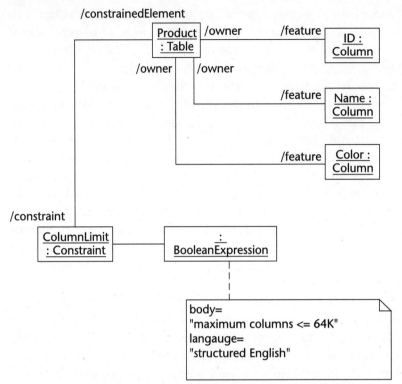

Figure 4.10 Relational Table with a constrained number of columns.

As another example, consider the fact that CWM, like Unified Modeling Language (UML), provides Stereotypes and TaggedValues as instance-level extension mechanisms for CWM models. Returning to the subset of the CWM OLAP metamodel illustrated in Figure 4.9, note that the Cube class has but a single Boolean attribute, *isVirtual*, which indicates whether or not a particular instance of Cube models a *virtual cube*. Let's assume, however, that we'd like to be able to model Cubes containing converted currencies. In particular, we would like to be able to define at most a single *currency cube* per OLAP Schema. What we need, of course, is an *isCurrency* attribute on the Cube class, but this isn't defined by CWM. One way around this is to introduce a new subtype of Cube (for example, CurrencyCube), but this requires physically extending the CWM metamodel itself, which has the effect of limiting our ability to readily interchange models. An alternative approach is to create a Stereotype instance named *currency* that we can attach to a Cube to mark it as a currency cube. The new Stereotype is readily interchanged in any CWM XMI file, of course, but is only meaningful to those tools that have agreed in advance on the precise meaning of the currency Stereotype. (Note that such an agreement is yet another aspect of establishing a common context.) Figure 4.11 illustrates this extended OLAP model.

Now, one of the problems with our new currency Stereotype is that the CWM metamodel permits a Stereotype instance to extend any number of ModelElements. This is a result of the unbounded association end, *extendedElement*, that relates Stereotype to ModelElement in the CWM Core metamodel. This is generally reasonable, since we would usually want to be able to reuse Stereotypes in extending any number of different model elements. However, in this particular case, we need to limit the number of currency Cubes in our model to at most one occurrence per OLAP Schema. So we need to limit the number of Cubes extended by the currency Stereotype to one. But we do not want that limit to apply to any other Stereotype instances defined by our OLAP model. Figure 4.12 illustrates an enhanced version of the OLAP model of Figure 4.11 in which the type and number of model elements the Stereotype can be used to extend is constrained to the Cube class and an upper bound of one, respectively. In this case, we've once again accomplished this by defining a Constraint whose text references the model's meta level, as a means of placing a finite upper bound on the association end.

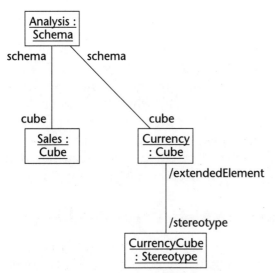

Figure 4.11 Extending an OLAP model to include a currency cube.

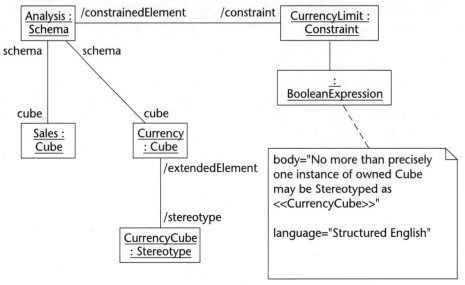

Figure 4.12   Constrained currency Cube model.

As a final example, consider again the OLAP model enhanced with visualization meta data. In this particular example, only a single instance of RenderedObjectSet has been added to the Schema. But there is nothing restricting us from adding multiple occurrences of RenderedObjectSet to the Schema, if we want to. In fact, we can add as many as we want (as long as they are uniquely named). There are many conceivable situations in which this might make sense, and others in which it does not. For example, if a visualization tool discovers that a Schema contains not one, but several, RenderedObjectSets, which one should the tool use as the basis for its subsequent activities? Perhaps it can select the correct one by name. But if that's the case, then we will need to establish some naming convention for these different visualization models. On the other hand, it might be easier simply to restrict the cardinality of the ownedElement end of the *namespaceownedElement* association to a value of one, with respect to our contextual requirement that Schemas contain any RenderedObjectSets that they use. The result is that any Schema may carry at most one visualization model.

The Pattern-Based Approach to Meta Data Interchange

The previous two subsections demonstrated, by way of example, that there are many situations in which a particular instance of CWM meta data, though syntactically valid, is not necessarily guaranteed to be useful to all intended consumers. Here is a synopsis of the key points:

- CWM, as a formal modeling language for expressing data warehousing and business analysis meta data, cannot possibly anticipate in advance all of the ways in which it might be put to use. No more so than MOF or UML can anticipate all possible ways in which they might be used to model object-oriented software systems. Thus, all such formal modeling languages must allow for a high degree of flexibility and expressiveness. But this also means that users are free to build models that do not necessarily make sense (even though these models are correct in terms of language syntax).

- What "makes sense" in terms of the overall content and structure of any CWM model directly depends on the reasonable expectations of both the producers and consumers of CWM meta data. This collection of expections is informally defined as the *context* of the meta data interchange. A common context for meta data interchange must be agreed upon by all participants in the interchange. It is beyond the scope of CWM to decide what valid interchange contexts are. As a metamodel, CWM deliberately limits itself to defining the semantic meanings of its individual classes, and describing how models are to be physically structured.

- Relative to a particular interchange context, it is also necessary to constrain the number of instances of certain classes that may occur in a particular model. In general, any CWM class may be instantiated any number of times in the construction of a CWM model, and most association ends specify unbounded cardinalities. This means that importing tools are faced with the possibility of having to deal with a potentially unlimited number of model elements. And as we previously demonstrated, there are also situations in which having multiple elements of a particular type might make the meaning of certain parts of a model ambiguous. In this case, a tool must formulate its own interpretation of what the model means. This has the effect of unduly complicating the tool's internal logic, as well as ultimately reducing the reliability of the meta data interchange process. (Note that it is not necessary that a particular model ever introduce such multiple occurrences of elements. The fact that it *can happen* has to be accounted for by the tool, or, alternatively, *not accounted for*, which might possibly be even worse.) The ability to place certain limits on model extents, then, has the desirable effect of minimizing the amount of meta data that an importing tool needs to sift through, as well as simplifying the decisions that that tool needs to make regarding how to process the imported meta data.

REGULAR EXPRESSIONS

Readers familiar with the use of grammars in defining formal languages over finite alphabets (for example, programming languages like Java and C++) will readily recognize many of the issues cited previously. For example, consider the simple grammar expressed by the following *regular expression*:

    01(001)*01 + (010)*1

Any string of 0's and 1's that conforms to this regular expression is said to be a valid instance of the regular expression, or, alternatively, a valid sentence of the language defined by the regular expression over the finite alphabet {0, 1}. For example, the following strings are all valid instances of the regular expression:

    0101
    0100101
    0100100101
    1
    0101

On the other hand, the following strings are not valid instances of the regular expression:

    0110
    0
    001100

However, validity here means that the strings are *syntactically valid* relative to the formal definition of the expression. We have not yet established what it means for any of the syntactically valid strings to be *semantically valid*. We might take an initial step in this direction by ascribing some particular semantic meaning to each of the alphabetic symbols 0 and 1: for example, if we agree that 0 represents the concept of logical falsity, while 1 represents logical truth. In this case, we could possibly interpret the valid strings as instances of certain logical propositions. On the other hand, we could equate the symbols 0 and 1 with specific voltage levels in an electronic device. In this case, we might interpret the above strings as traces of sequences of activities performed by this device (such as the lighting of an LCD). Or, we might agree that each string represents some sequence of instructions telling the device to perform certain actions (much like small machine-language programs stored in some digital computer). In this case, do certain valid sequences make more sense than other valid sequences? Is it possible to have sequences that are perfectly valid (syntactically), but are otherwise unusable by some implementation or language processor?

The main point of this example is that none of the possible interpretations of the strings produced by the regular expression (that is, those strings that are syntactically valid, relative to the regular expression) are absolutely correct or absolutely incorrect. It all depends upon the context in which a given string is being interpreted, and that context is determined by some agent external to the regular expression itself (for example, a human observer or some machine that takes meaningful actions based on the content of each valid string). In fact, even if each individual symbol is ascribed some particular semantic meaning, it is still not always clear what a complex of such symbols means. There is a need for a broader semantic context to meaningfully interpret such strings. And, finally, note that the presence of the "*" operator in the regular expression specifies an unbounded number of occurrences of a particular sub-string of the expression. This is good for logical simplicity and flexibility, as far as the formulation of the regular expression is concerned. However, in a real implementation of our regular expression *processor* (whatever that happens to mean!), we would undoubtedly be faced with many practical limits on how large these strings could actually be. So we find that we require both a context and some means of constraining the number or sizes of instances we have to deal with.

We can view CWM (or any other similar, MOF-compliant model or metamodel, for that matter) in a similar manner: CWM is essentially a grammar for generating expressions representing meta data. We usually refer to these meta data expressions as models. In the interests of flexibility and widest possible application, the CWM grammar imposes very few restrictions on the meta data expressions that one may generate using CWM. Thus, just as with other grammars defining formal languages, the effective use of CWM requires participants to further establish a common semantic context in which to understand meta data expressions. And in addition, they must also set some practical limitations on the number of instances of those expressions (or their sub-expressions) that one may reasonably expect to have to deal with in the process of interchanging meta data.

It should be noted that the issues discussed above are not specific to meta data model or interchange. They have emerged many times before, in other areas of endeavor (computer science, discrete mathematics, and linguistics, to name but a few). In most cases, these issues are invariably dealt with using some sort of machinery already available to the domain in which they arise. The sidebar Regular Expressions provides yet another viewpoint on this problem.

It should be fairly obvious from much of the preceding discussion that what we are heading toward, as a general approach to resolving the interchange issues previously described, is the establishment of some sort of regular and well-known patterns for meta data usage. We are not suggesting modifications to the CWM metamodel itself. Rather, we are proposing taking steps toward establishing standard ways of forming and interpreting instances of the CWM metamodel that enable us to overcome the problems of correctly interpreting the meaning of constructs expressed in a highly flexible formal modeling language. We assert that a patterns-based approach is currently the simplest and most effective way of resolving these issues.

We informally define a *meta data interchange pattern* as a structural pattern imposed on meta data content that has been agreed upon in advance by both the producers and consumers of the interchanged meta data. To manage all of the issues previously cited, each given meta data interchange pattern must identify the common context that makes the intended meaning of interchanged meta data clear to all tools participating in the interchange. Patterns must also (wherever necessary) constrain the cardinalities of certain model elements in order to reduce the overall number of elements that might potentially exist within a model, as well as eliminate problems of ambiguous interpretation that sometimes result from having a multiplicity of certain types of model elements.

The use of such patterns for structuring interchanged meta data greatly simplifies the construction and logic of CWM-aware software. Importing tools or adapters know in advance what to look for; their search space is constrained to specific structural patterns, with the top-level anchor points of patterned content known well in advance. Tools do not have to contain extensive checking logic to detect and handle the potentially ambiguous situations that might occur when meta data structures are relatively unconstrained in multiplicity (relative to some particular context). Tools can go about the task of identifying or interpreting an otherwise unknown model in a *highly deterministic* and *intentional* manner. The construction of export logic is also greatly simplified, since the pattern provides an established guideline to follow in structuring meta data for export. And, of course, the overall reliability of the entire meta data interchange process is greatly enhanced.

The next section formally defines the fundamental concepts of a pattern-based approach to meta data interchange, and describes how these concepts relate to CWM. As part of our comprehensive approach to pattern-based meta data interchange, we will also leverage a number of established concepts from the much more widely known discipline of *Software Design Patterns* (Gamma et al., 1995; Grand, 1998; and Grand, 1999). We will see that a meta data interchange pattern is not quite the same thing as a software design pattern, but that many of the more traditional design pattern concepts have applicability in the formulation, specification, and publication of useful meta data interchange patterns. The sidebar *Software Design Patterns* provides a general overview of the discipline of software design patterns, describing both its history and its significant contributions to modern software engineering practices.

SOFTWARE DESIGN PATTERNS

A *software design pattern* is a description of communicating objects and classes that are customized to solve a general problem within a particular context (Gamma, 1995).

Over the past two decades, the computer software industry was fundamentally transformed by the evolution and widespread adoption of object-oriented software and programming. One of the reasons for the tremendous success of the object-oriented approach is that it enabled programmers to finally build software systems more in terms of the real-world objects that they were attempting to model in software. Another was that object technology better supported the hiding (*encapsulation*) of how a particular object might be implemented, versus the functionality that the object chose to expose through its public interfaces. This has led to the ability of software designers and engineers to produce software in terms of discrete components that were more reliable, and much more readily reusable, than what was possible under the more traditional *structured* development techniques.

Along with object-oriented programming, a number of corresponding analysis and software design methodologies and corresponding notations based on object-oriented techniques also became prevalent. One of the better known of these was the object-oriented design notation and methodology defined by Grady Booch's seminal book, *Object Oriented Design with Applications* (Booch, 1991). The Unified Modeling Language, which CWM is heavily aligned with, is a more recent notation that was formed largely as an effort to combine the Booch notation along with the Object Modeling Technique (OMT) and Object Oriented Software Engineering (OOSE) formalisms.

Once object-oriented programming, analysis, and design firmly took hold, software developers found they had a superior collection of tools and techniques for designing and building software systems that were far more reliable and capable of much greater, and yet more manageable, complexity. However, another interesting trend began to reveal itself sometime around the early 1990s. It was becoming apparent that many object-oriented developers had, independently of one another, devised a number of ways of effectively structuring certain types of objects in order to solve a number of frequently recurring problems. Developers found that the mechanisms of object-oriented software were, by themselves, necessary but not sufficient to solve certain standard problems. They found that they could readily leverage object-oriented techniques as powerful building blocks in the (now relatively straightforward) construction of more complete solutions.

(continues)

SOFTWARE DESIGN PATTERNS *(Continued)*

These solutions invariably involved organizing objects into very specific *patterns* that could be readily recognized and described. In time, these patterns became known as *software design patterns*, and owed much of their prominence to a single book known as *Design Patterns: Elements of Reusable Object-Oriented Software*, authored by Erich Gamma, Richard Helm, Ralph Johnson, and John Vlissedes (Gamma, 1995). This book not only represented the first attempt to codify and publish known, useful patterns for developing object-oriented software solutions; it also provided something of a methodology for organizing, classifying, describing, and specifying these software patterns. This ultimately led to the creation of an entire school of thinking on software engineering based on the use of formal patterns. In time, the patterns, methodology, and mindset manifested themselves in many key areas of commercial software development (for example, Java and Enterprise Java Bean (EJB) development (Grand, 1998; Grand, 1999; Marinescu, 2002).

The pervasiveness of software pattern discipline is an acknowledgment that object-oriented techniques are very powerful, but still not quite sufficient by themselves for crafting solutions to many complex problems. The discovery of the pattern approach helped to largely resolve this. Of course, the pattern-based approach to software design would not have been possible without the power of Object Oriented (OO) techniques in the first place.

In a similar manner, CWM, for all of its immense power, expressiveness, and flexibility, requires a similar, parallel discipline for overcoming the problems of semantic context and boundaries on search space size. Meta data interchange is arguably one of the most fertile areas to benefit from the application of patterns-based techniques.

Conversely, a patterns-based approach to meta data can also make significant contributions back to the software patterns community in general, since the meta data interchange problem requires new and unique ways of viewing pattern application. For example, a meta data interchange pattern is very similar to, but not quite the same thing as, a software design pattern, given the definition for software design pattern stated above. In particular, meta data patterns are fundamentally bound to their defining metamodel. This is not generally the case with the more general software patterns, and any patterns-based approach to meta data interchange must take this fact into account. Similarly, as we will see subsequently, the overall approach to meta data interchange pattern specification and publishing (to the meta data community) can benefit greatly by co-opting much of the formal methodology developed for publishing software patterns and constructing pattern catalogs. However, as will be shown subsequently, the current methodology used for pattern specification and publishing also needs to be extended with new ideas and concepts to accommodate meta data interchange patterns.

Formal Definitions of Meta Data Interchange Pattern Concepts

The previous sections helped build a strong intuitive understanding of the concept of a meta data interchange pattern. In this section, we formalize these concepts by introducing a series of precise definitions, starting from relatively basic principles and ending with a complete definition of a meta data interchange pattern. Each definition is accompanied by commentary describing how it applies specifically to CWM. In the following section, *Developing Meta Data Interchange Patterns for CWM,* we present a practical methodology for developing and publishing meta data interchange patterns that builds directly on the formal definitions presented here.

> **Definition 4.1.** Any given instance of a metamodel is a *solution* to some meta data modeling problem within the overall domain prescribed by that metamodel. A solution is sometimes referred to as having been *generated* from the metamodel.

> **Commentary on Definition 4.1.** The overall domain prescribed by the CWM metamodel is, of course, the data warehousing and business analysis domain (or, perhaps more precisely, the particular viewpoint of that domain captured by the CWM metamodel). Whether or not any particular solution is actually meaningful can only be decided relative to some particular semantic context; that is, some limited portion of the overall domain that is currently of interest to the parties interchanging the solution. For example, if a solution can be interpreted in a sensible way by a human modeler, relative to some very specific portion of the data warehousing and business analysis domain, then it is deemed to be meaningful. Or, if the solution causes an automated agent or process (such as a data warehousing tool) to produce some useful result, again, relative to some limited aspect of the overall domain, then it can likewise be deemed meaningful. All of the instance diagrams shown in Figures 4.3 through 4.17 are examples of CWM solutions.

> **Definition 4.2.** The *solution space* of a metamodel is the collection of all possible solutions (that is, all possible instances) generated from that metamodel.

> **Commentary on Definition 4.2.** The solution space of CWM is generally unbounded in extent; that is, the total number of all possible CWM solutions has no specified limit. This is by virtue of the fact that CWM, as a MOF metamodel expressed in UML notation, contains many unbounded association ends, as well as unbounded

cardinalities on instances of metamodel classes. The instance diagrams of Figures 4.3 through 4.17 are but a very small subset of the CWM solution space.

Definition 4.3. A *subset* of a metamodel is some portion of the metamodel that has been (in a strictly conceptual sense) partitioned or separated from the rest of the metamodel in a manner allowable by the metamodel definition.

Commentary on Definition 4.3. The CWM metamodel can be legally partitioned into subsets wherever association ends with lower bounds of zero are present. The two portions of the CWM Relational metamodel shown in Figures 4.1 and 4.2 are both examples of (partitioned) subsets of the CWM metamodel.

Definition 4.4. The *subset space* of a metamodel is the collection of all possible subsets of the metamodel.

Commentary on Definition 4.4. The subset space of CWM is the collection of all possible, legally partitioned arrangements of the various metaclasses and associations comprising the CWM metamodel. Another way of viewing this space is as the collection of all *tracings* or *trajectories* through the UML diagram that defines CWM. If you think of the UML diagram as a generalized *graph* (in computer science terminology), then the subset space of CWM is the set of all legally partitioned sub-graphs of the single graph defining the complete CWM metamodel. The CWM Relational metamodel subsets illustrated in Figures 4.1 and 4.2 are both members of the CWM subset space.

The subset space of CWM is bounded (finite) in size, but vastly large. The vastness of this space is an example of *combinatorial explosion*, a phenomenon that often arises in computer science problems dealing with permutations of finite sets. Much of the important work in this area deals with finding ways of efficiently extracting useful results from vast, combinatorial spaces (for example, *nondeterministic algorithms* and *heuristic search*).

Effectively handling the vast CWM subset space is important, because it is precisely from this combinatorial space that we obtain the *semantic context* required for the meaningful and unambiguous interpretation of interchanged meta data when using the patterns-based approach. In fact, the process of developing meta data patterns is equivalent to performing just such a heuristic search through the CWM subset space. The sidebar The *Library of Babel* provides an unusual perspective on the challenges of dealing with combinatorial search spaces, recasting the patterns-based approach in terms of these broader issues.

Definition 4.5. A *projection* on a metamodel is a specified collection of subsets of the metamodel. The subsets included in a projection need not be physically connected; that is, a projection may be formed from completely partitioned (separated or disconnected) subsets of the metamodel.

Commentary on Definition 4.5. A projection on the CWM metamodel (that is, a collection of subsets of the CWM metamodel) is *precisely* what specifies the domain-specific, semantic context for interchange. We stated earlier that the CWM metamodel is essentially a definition of the "overall domain" of data warehousing and business analysis (or, more precisely, that the CWM metamodel is a particular *interpretation* of that domain). For a particular interchange of meta data to be effective, we must establish a very specific context for that interchange. But we are not permitted to stray *outside* of the language defined by the CWM metamodel. For example, a human user of CWM may have a good, intuitive notion of what some particular semantic context *should be*, but whatever that is, it eventually must be expressed only in terms of the CWM metamodel if it is actually to be used as the basis for interchange. Providing such a precise and *semantically grounded* interchange context, therefore, equates to selecting one or more subsets of the CWM metamodel, and then simply declaring that they collectively define that precise, semantic context needed to make sense of some particular CWM solution.

In Object Management Group (OMG) modeling terminology, a projection of the CWM metamodel is inherently an M2-level partitioning, or selection, of elements of the CWM metamodel.

Note that any projection on the CWM metamodel is necessarily of finite size, and only needs to be as large as is necessary to provide the complete semantic context required by some CWM solution. However, the total set of solutions generated by a particular CWM projection may or may not be bounded in size. In particular, if the projection contains at least one unbounded association end, or a class of unbounded cardinality (which is very likely indeed), then the complete set of related solutions is fundamentally unbounded in size. Of course, there are, most likely, only a very small number of solutions that we are actually interested in interchanging. But this is still an issue for an importing tool. Once a projection has been established, meta data interchange can now be grounded in terms of a very precise semantic context. However, importers of meta data still need to properly handle the unbounded nature of the projection's solution space. This does not mean that we actually expect to have to sift through an intractable number of solutions. (There is, after all, only a single solution being interchanged.) Rather, the fundamentally unbounded nature of the solution space makes it impossible to construct a deterministic algorithm for *identification* or *interpretation* of any one of its elements. This means that some heuristic is needed in advance before we can even consider how to go about interpreting any imported (and hence, *unknown*) solution. This leads us to our next definition.

Definition 4.6. A *restriction* on a projection is a specified subset of the solutions that can be generated from the projection.

Commentary on Definition 4.6. Within an established projection (context), a restriction further tightens the boundaries on the possible solution space of the projection, ensuring that any interchanged solution is of some predictable configuration, relative to the projection's (potential) combinatorial properties. For example, a restriction might be formulated in such a manner that there is precisely one instance of a certain type of model element specified by the projection. Or, perhaps, a restriction might be formulated by enforcing that multiple occurrences of some particular type of projected model element are at least unique. In either case, the restriction facilitates obtaining a handle or anchor point on the instance as a whole. The currency Cube example of Figure 4.17 illustrates just this sort of restriction. In that example, we deliberately constrained both the type and number of model elements that the Stereotype may extend to the Cube class and an upper bound of one, respectively, thus ensuring that any instance of an OLAP Schema will have at most a single currency Cube. This relieves the importing tool of having to check for, and somehow resolve, a potentially ambiguous situation, that is, the (potential) presence in the meta data of multiple currency Cubes for a target OLAP system that supports the deployment of at most a single currency Cube.

In OMG modeling terminology, a restriction on a projection of the CWM metamodel is inherently an M2-level constraint on the M1-level instances of that projection on the CWM metamodel.

Definition 4.7. A *parameter* is the specification of some value that must be used in forming the restricted solution set of the projection.

Commentary on Definition 4.7. Parameter values are used either to provide initial values to the instance variables of the CWM objects comprising a model, or to identify any subtypes that are to be substituted for occurrences of their super-types in the definition of the projection. In the construction of a CWM model, the tool-building model is responsible for supplying any required parameter values.

Definition 4.8. A *meta data interchange pattern*, relative to some meta-model, is a specified projection on that metamodel, optionally with one or more restrictions on that projection, and possibly with a set of parameters for binding the pattern to some set of realizing solutions.

Commentary on Definition 4.8. A meta data interchange pattern for CWM, therefore, consists of the specification of some projection on the CWM metamodel, optionally with restrictions on the solutions generated from that projection, and possibly a specified set of binding parameters.

Definition 4.9. A *realization* of a meta data interchange pattern is an actual instance of meta data conforming to, or generated from, the interchange pattern. A meta data interchange pattern is said to be *bound* to any of its realizations, and any given realization is said to *realize* its defining pattern.

Commentary on Definition 4.9. Any instance of CWM meta data conforming to some established CWM meta data interchange pattern is a realization of that pattern.

Figure 4.13 illustrates how all of these concepts relate to one another.

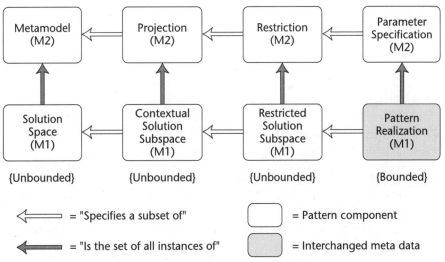

Figure 4.13   Components of a CWM meta data interchange pattern.

THE LIBRARY OF BABEL

In *Labyrinths*, Jorge Luis Borges (1962) describes "The Library of Babel," a hypothetical library of seemingly infinite expanse. The library is comprised of a vast number of galleries, each gallery containing 700 books, with 410 pages per book, 40 lines per page, and 80 characters per line, for a total of 1,312,000 characters per book. Each character consists either of a space, a period, a comma, or one of the 22 lowercase letters of the Spanish alphabet. The books are not arranged in any particular order. No two books in the library are identical, and there is precisely one book for each combination of 1,312,000 characters selected from the 25 orthographic symbols. Thus, the library is finite in size, but immensely vast, containing a total of $25^{1312000}$ (or, equivalently, $\sim 10^{1834097}$) books.

It's interesting to note that, despite the library's incomprehensible size, its content can be described completely in just a few sentences. And although the Library itself could never exist in any physical sense (the number of books it contains far exceeds the number of atoms in the known universe), it nonetheless is still very real, and readily accessible. For example, one could easily write a simple computer program that repeatedly generates 1,312,000-character strings, with each character randomly selected from the 25 orthographic symbols. With each string that is generated, the program has effectively retrieved (at random) a single book from the library. This program could be allowed to run for a very long time, and subsequently obtain a very large collection of these books. And every such book obtained is almost absolutely guaranteed to contain nothing but indecipherable, random text. In Borges's narrative, the occupants of the library encountered the same results. Although many generations spent many centuries searching the various galleries of the library, no one ever discovered any meaningful books.

And yet, despite the pervasive randomness of its content, the library contains *all possible knowledge* expressible in straight text. The library contains the greatest works of literature, reference, engineering, and science, by authors past, present, and future, and also by authors who never had, nor ever will, exist. The library also contains countless facsimiles of each of these works (of all conceivable degrees of fidelity to the originals), as well as all possible commentaries. And, for any conceivable subject, the library also contains numerous true and false accounts of that subject, of all possible degrees of truth and falsity. All of this is guaranteed by virtue of nothing more than the simple definition at the beginning of this sidebar.

There is, however, a fundamental point of difficulty regarding the library: All of the truly useful books are largely and forever inaccessible. There simply is no tractable way of discovering them, or even determining their locations. Even if the Library were conceived as an ideal information retrieval system, with a complete directory, an optimized search engine, and no physical limitations (for example, no delays due to signal propagation), such that directory searches and retrievals of content could be performed instantaneously, the library would still be unusable. And the reason why is because formulating effective search criteria in this situation is itself an intractable problem. How could one possibly even begin to formulate any sort of reasonable criteria for a match? How much information would have to be supplied (short of having to replicate the very same book one is attempting to discover) to ensure reasonable matches? And how do we even begin to discriminate between the various true and false accounts of some particular subject? It's not at all clear if a meaningful predicate can even be formulated for such a search, never mind evaluated. But, then again, the library itself contains numerous books describing solutions to this very same problem.

The Library of Babel is a powerful thought experiment for investigating issues related to the nature of finite combinatorial spaces, and the difficulties encountered when attempting to extract useful information from them. Such problems recur frequently in computer science, mainly in the areas of classical artificial intelligence, theory of computation, and the study of discrete structures. Often, we can prove the existence of certain elements within these spaces, but cannot compute their locations deterministically in any reasonable amount of time. Solutions to such problems invariably involve the formulation of *heuristics* (nondeterministic methods, or "good tricks") that enable us to obtain approximate results in reasonable time that are satisfactory for most purposes. The use of heuristic search is equivalent to being able to obtain one or more reasonable facsimiles of some ideal book in the library. Perhaps not quite the book that we want, but the trade-off is that we obtain these facsimiles in hours, weeks, or years, rather than running the risk of possibly never finding the ideal target.

In fact, heuristics have already been successfully applied many times in searching the library of Babel. Consider all of the numerous, useful books surrounding us right now. All of these have effectively been extracted from the library. All are approximations to "ideal" books, but they nonetheless still largely satisfy our needs. And exactly what *are* the heuristics that have been employed in finding those useful facsimiles in the library? Well, they are essentially all of the typical human activities we engage in that are directed toward acquiring and codifying knowledge. The act of *writing* a new book is equivalent to *finding* that book in the library, using some (experiential) heuristic that enables the author to search the vast combinatorial space of the library in a reasonable amount of time.

The model-based approach to meta data integration also falls within this class of problems dealing with combinatorial search spaces. In particular, the problem of finding an appropriate common context as part of the solution to one or more meta data interchange problems effectively requires finding a suitable member of the CWM subset space we alluded to earlier. Like the Library of Babel, the subset space of the CWM metamodel is also finite in size, but immensely vast. And most of its content is useless. A CWM projection randomly selected from the CWM subset space most likely does not define a meaningful context for any practical, real-world meta data interchange. Thus, part of the challenge of providing nearly seamless and highly interoperable meta data interchange based on CWM involves being able to isolate the truly useful CWM projections. And this can only be accomplished, of course, by employing some adequate heuristic. We propose that the process of formulating meta data interchange patterns, based on domain-specific knowledge and experience, is just such an application of heuristic search through a vast, combinatorial space. It is fundamentally no different than our attempts to extract useful books from the Library of Babel.

Developing Meta Data Interchange Patterns for CWM

The preceding sections provided the conceptual underpinnings supporting the notion of a meta data interchange pattern. This section first describes the sequence of steps involved in developing a meta data interchange pattern. Then, an actual pattern, *Unit of Interchange*, is developed in a step-by-step fashion that provides an overall framework for organizing all other pattern-based meta data. Taking this approach not only illustrates the pattern development process in concrete terms but it also establishes a very fundamental pattern that we will use subsequently throughout the rest of the book.

Steps for Developing Interchange Patterns

The following is a step-by-step description of a general process for identifying and specifying meta data interchange patterns. This is the process followed in the development of the CWM meta data interchange patterns defined on the companion Web site to this book.

Step 1: Identify the interchange problem to be solved

The first step, of course, is determining the particular meta data interchange problem that needs to be solved. The best way to do this is by attempting to describe the problem in a few short, concise sentences. Attempt to identify the major or most obvious elements of the problem. Also try to establish clear boundaries for the problem (that is, what the scope or limits of the problem statement are, and what is not a part of this problem).

Step 2: Propose a pattern that solves the problem

Again, in a few short sentences, formulate a proposed pattern that solves the interchange problem. Remember that this is just an overview or draft proposal. Avoid the temptation to develop a complete solution at this point. The overall effectiveness of the proposed solution should be relatively obvious from the draft description. Otherwise, the proposed solution, or even the problem statement itself, might be in need of further refinement.

Step 3: Identify several scenarios in which the proposed pattern would be used

If you can identify several real-world scenarios in which the problem statement manifests itself, and for which the proposed pattern-based solution clearly resolves the problem, then this will greatly help to validate the overall solution approach. Think of this as an initial "proof-of-concept" exercise for your proposed solution.

Step 4: Determine how the proposed pattern reuses, or otherwise relates to, known patterns

Once the interchange problem and corresponding pattern-based solution are both clearly understood, survey any available descriptions of meta data interchange patterns (by scanning known *pattern catalogs*—see the subsection *Developing and Publishing a Pattern Specification*) to determine if a usable solution might already exist. It is quite possible that some established pattern largely solves the interchange problem, in which case, you would not need to design a complete solution from scratch, but rather reuse an existing pattern, possibly with some modification. On the other hand, developing a new pattern might involve reusing a number of known, existing patterns. In general, a new pattern is often constructed partly by combining or layering a number of known patterns. The resulting complex of patterns is generally referred to as a *composite pattern*. Any instance (realization) of a composite pattern naturally contains instances of its constituent patterns.

Step 5: Identify the structural classification of the proposed pattern

A large composite pattern, when viewed as a whole, tends to exhibit various levels of *structural resolution* as a result of the process of composition. Each component pattern resides at some particular structural level relative to other component patterns. We can classify a pattern by the relative level of structural resolution at which it is to be used. Structural classifications consist of the following:

Macro pattern.   A coarse-grain pattern that represents an overall organizational framework for meta data.

Domain pattern.   A medium-grain pattern that represents some
domain-specific context. In general, the notion of providing *context* in
meta data interchange is largely realized by specifying and combining various domain patterns.

Micro pattern.   A fine-grain pattern that represents some frequently
occurring way of organizing basic meta data structures. Higher-level
patterns, such as domain patterns, are generally comprised of many
different micro patterns.

Classifying a pattern in this manner assists others in reusing the pattern.
For example, a pattern user designing a new domain-level pattern might
wish to survey a number of pattern catalogs for various micro patterns that
provide standard ways of organizing lower-level meta data constructs.
This ensures that the new domain pattern will still make use of standard,
known ways of organizing lower-level, constituent meta data structures.
The Unit of Interchange pattern, developed in the subsection *Developing a
Fundamental Pattern: Unit of Interchange,* is an example of a macro pattern.

Step 6: Identify the usage category of the proposed pattern

Interchange patterns are used in very specific ways. As with structural
classifications, being able to categorize a new pattern according to its
intended use will assist others in reusing the pattern. Note that some patterns may fall into more than one category of usage. The following list
defines standard usage categories for meta data interchange patterns:

Interchange.   Any pattern that facilitates meta data interchange and
model organization

Mapping.   Any pattern that facilitates mapping or relating models to
other models: for example, linking models across abstraction layers
or conceptual-to-logical and logical-to-physical model resolutions

Typing.   Any pattern that facilitates the typing or domain-specific
classification of models or model elements

Extension.   Any pattern that facilitates the extension or augmentation
of existing models or model elements

Interpretation.   Any pattern that facilitates or disambiguates the interpretation of some model

Generation.   Any pattern that facilitates the automated generation of an implementation from a model

Structural or constructive.   Any pattern that provides a cleaner or more manageable organization of models or model elements

Step 7: Identify the metamodel projection

As was established in the earlier subsection, *Formal Definitions of Meta Data Interchange Pattern Concepts*, the common context for meta data interchange must be expressed in terms of some clearly delineated subset of the CWM metamodel. Anyone responsible for designing a meta data integration architectural solution probably has a very strong intuitive concept of the various contexts required within their environment. For example, this is something that might be based largely on the known meta data requirements of the various data warehousing and integration tools comprising the integration architecture. These various interchange contexts must be formalized in terms of the CWM metamodel. In general, each distinct, identifiable context is mapped to some subset of the CWM metamodel (more precisely, one or more of the constituent metamodels comprising CWM).

Each distinct context has its own projection, and each projection may be specified in terms of a sub-graph of the global UML model graph that defines CWM. A projection may be specified by listing each of the CWM classes and associations (including derived or inherited associations) comprising the projection. In the interests of simplicity, individual patterns are generally developed around a single common context and/or projection, although this is not strictly required. When documenting the projection, a diagram of the CWM sub-graph helps to easily visualize the structure of the projection. Note that in OMG modeling terms, the elements comprising any projection of the CWM metamodel are inherently at the M2-level.

When formulating a projection on the CWM metamodel, the pattern designer should generally strive to include the highest possible base classes that fulfill a particular role in establishing a context for interchange (for example, specify Package rather than Schema). This enables greater flexibility in the application of the projection. A broader range of realizations can ultimately be bound to the pattern description by simply substituting required sub-class instances at run time. This is described more fully in the discussion of *binding parameters* below.

Step 8: Determine any restrictions on instances of the projection

Once the context and its corresponding CWM metamodel projection has been established, the next step is to determine if the solutions generated from the projection need to be constrained. Although the set of all solutions generated from a projection is a proper subset of the complete CWM solution space, it may still be unbounded in size. The projection helps to establish this subspace of the solution space by binding it to a very specific context. But the solution subspace often still needs to be constrained in some manner in order to be effectively searched. For example, some specific model element in the projection might be constrained to a single instance in the solution subspace, or at least a sequence of unique values. This makes it possible for an importing process to get a *handle* (or *anchor point*) on an imported instance. Restrictions may be specified as constraints expressed in some natural language (for example, English), or more preferably in some formal language, such as OCL (Warmer, 1999). Note that in OMG modeling terms, the elements comprising any restrictions on a CWM metamodel projection are, like the projection itself, inherently at the M2 level.

Step 9: Determine the parameters for binding pattern realizations

Now that both the projection and restrictions of the pattern have been established, we can determine what particular values we need to assign to specific elements of the restricted solution subspace to tailor the generic pattern description to some pattern realization. Recall that the pattern realization is some actual instance of CWM meta data that conforms to a pattern and provides some particular meta data interchange solution. For our purposes, there are essentially two types of binding parameters:

Value-oriented. These parameter descriptions specify how values of CWM class variables are to be computed, or are to specify explicit, fixed values that are to be assigned to those variables directly.

Subtype-oriented. These parameter descriptions specify particular subtypes of CWM classes of the projection that are to be substituted (at the instance level) for their corresponding base classes in any solution realizing the projection.

At the point when these values are actually supplied (for example, as values of class variables in actual CWM objects that are to be rendered in an XMI file), we say that the formal pattern description (that is, projection plus restriction) has been *bound to a realization*. This binding takes place at the last possible moment (for example, when the CWM object model is created or when its serialized representation in the form of an XMI file is written). For the most part, the values of binding parameters are provided by the exporting process, and subsequently recognized and handled by some (pattern-aware) importing process. Note that in OMG modeling terms, the identification of any binding parameter concerns modeling elements at the M2 level, but the values themselves are M1-level instances of those M2-level elements.

The specification of the parameters may state that certain parameter values are fixed, in which case, the exporting process simply provides the value required by the pattern specification. On the other hand, other parameters may not necessarily have fixed values determined by the pattern specification. Rather, the pattern specification provides a description of the variable that the exporting process needs to abide by. The exporting process is responsible for obtaining or calculating suitable values for these variables, and the pattern specification merely provides an overall description.

Parameters enable formal pattern definitions to be tailored to particular interchange situations. One can thus view the pattern definition with non-fixed binding parameter values as a template for the delayed generation of a concrete realization of the pattern.

Step 10: Validate the pattern

Once the designer is satisfied that the formal pattern description provides the desired meta data interchange solution, the pattern should be validated. This generally involves creating a small prototypical model of one or more instances of meta data that are made to conform to the pattern. The approach taken in validating the pattern depends largely, of course, on the tools available to assist in the process. But, at a minimum, the designer should attempt to generate an XMI file rendering of the prototypical model. The resulting XMI file should be validated against the CWM Document Type Definition (DTD) (whichever version is supported by the target interchange architecture). This would be followed by attempting to import the XMI file into one or more meta data consumers. Then, the designer would inspect the imported meta data model via any front-end or reporting facilities provided by the consumer, and judge whether or not the pattern appears to work. The designer may conclude that the pattern simply needs some fine-tuning, in which case, the formal pattern description is revised somewhat and then revalidated. On the other hand, it may be determined that the pattern has some fundamental conceptual flaw, and the pattern description (or even the problem statement itself) might need to be completely reconsidered.

How much work actually is required to successfully perform the import largely depends on the current architecture of the importing tool. For example, if the tool is already CWM pattern-aware, then a minimal amount of work should be required to perform this validation. Otherwise, getting the import to work might require hand-coding a new import adapter for the tool. But if the prototype model is kept reasonably small, and the tool already supports the ability to readily integrate CWM import adapters, this should not be too much of an effort.

Developing and Publishing a Pattern Specification

To ensure that a pattern accomplishes its intended goal (that is, the relatively seamless interchange of shared meta data between multiple vendors' tools), a pattern must be published. And to ensure that published patterns are readily understandable by their prospective users, published pattern specifications should conform to the same standards of language and format. This was one of the most important steps taken in the book *Design Patterns: Elements of Reusable Object-Oriented Software* (Gamma, 1995) in its approach to specifying and publishing software design patterns. The *Design Patterns* book presents a standard template for describing software design patterns and subsequently organizing them into a catalog. In fact, much of the book consists of just that: a comprehensive catalog of useful software design patterns formulated according to the guidelines put forth in the beginning of the book. Other authors in the software design patterns community have followed a similar approach to organizing and publishing their patterns [for example, see Grand (1998) and Grand (1999)].

We adopt many of the fundamentals of this approach, but also make some modifications. In particular, we developed our own standard template for pattern specification that is specific to meta data. Our template is closely based on the standard template defined in *Design Patterns*. However, it replaces many specification elements that are particular to object-oriented software (for example, *Collaborations*) with analogous specification elements based on the meta data pattern definitions formulated in this chapter (for example, the concepts of *Projection*, *Restriction*, and *Parameters*). Furthermore, we advocate a highly democratic, Web-oriented approach to the publishing of meta data interchange patterns. In our approach, we attempt to establish an overall framework for developing and publishing meta data interchange patterns for CWM, but also assume that the CWM user community at large will play a very big role in developing most of the truly useful patterns. This makes sense to us, because the meta data users, integrators, and various other domain experts are ultimately the final authorities on what makes sense as far as establishing common patterns for interoperable meta data. We foresee users developing their own pattern catalogs and publishing them, largely in a distributed fashion, over the World Wide Web. While we provide our own pattern catalog on the companion Web site , we view this as our own contribution to this effort. It is certainly a good starting point, but by no means the definitive expression of useful meta data interchange patterns for CWM.

With that in mind, the following describes each of the elements of our standard template for specifying meta data interchange patterns. The specification elements consist of:

Pattern Name.   The pattern specification should have a simple and descriptive name that more or less indicates what purpose the pattern serves.

Pattern Version.   The pattern specification should be versioned to support subsequent evolution of the pattern. We recommend a simple version and dot-release format, for example, "1.2".

URL.   The Uniform Resource Locator that uniquely identifies and provides the location for a particular meta data interchange pattern specification. This greatly facilitates publishing the pattern in catalogs distributed over the Web. The URL does not necessarily have to be a complete path. It could, for example, consist of an address to a home page that, among other things, contains an easily found link to the pattern catalog. This is generally sufficient, because pattern specifications by themselves are intended for human consumption. We will see in a subsequent treatment of the explicit modeling of patterns that pattern models require greater resolution in terms of their exact identity and location. This is because the consumers of explicit pattern models are more likely to be automated processes, rather than human users.

Contributor(s).   The name of the person or organization who defined and published this pattern to the catalog or pattern community. May include email or Web page addresses.

Structural Classification.   The structural classification of the pattern, as described previously. This is an important component of the specification, because it assists individuals who are searching pattern catalogs to find patterns that conform to a specific level of structural resolution. Structural classification is determined during the fifth step of pattern development. Identify the structural classification of the proposed pattern.

Usage Category.   The usage category of the pattern, as described previously. Like structural classification, this is also an important component of the specification, because it assists individuals who are searching pattern catalogs to find patterns that conform to specific types of usage. Usage category is determined during the sixth step of pattern development. Identify the usage category of the proposed pattern.

Intent.   A one-sentence description of the overall intent of the pattern. Like structural classification and usage category, this is also an important component of the pattern specification, because it facilitates finding patterns that solve a very specific interchange problem. Intent can be derived from the activities of the second step in pattern development. Propose a pattern that solves the problem.

Also Known As.   A listing of any other well-known synonyms for this pattern. This information might be obtained during the third step in pattern development. Determine how the proposed pattern reuses, or otherwise relates to, known patterns.

Motivation.   A detailed description of the meta data interchange problem that the pattern solves. This description is formulated during the first step in pattern development. Identify the interchange problem to be solved.

Applicability.   A description of real-world situations in which the pattern would typically be applied. This description is formulated during the third step in pattern development. Identify several scenarios in which the proposed pattern would be used.

Projection.   A description of the M2-level projection used to establish a common context for meta data interchange. The projection is formulated during the seventh step in pattern development. Identify the Metamodel Projection. The projection can be specified as a list of the CWM classes and associations (including inherited or derived associations) forming the projection. If possible, an M2-level UML diagram should also be provided, as this greatly enhances the reader's ability to understand that pattern. The M2-level diagram is essentially a UML diagram depicting the subset of the CWM metamodel forming the projection.

Restriction.   A description of the M2-level constraints used to restrict or limit the extent of instances of the projection. This may be expressed in some natural language (for example, English), but it is preferable to provide some formal language representation of these constraints (for example, OCL). The restriction is determined during the eighth step in pattern development. Determine any restrictions on instances of the projection.

Usage.   Describes the general usage conventions for instances (realizations) of this pattern, including values assigned to object attributes and sub-class substitutions. This is intended to provide an overview of how the formal pattern description is realized via parameter binding. This description generally follows from the activities of the ninth step in pattern development. Determine the parameters for binding pattern realizations.

Parameters.   Describes the set of formal parameters that are used to realize an instance of the pattern. As with the Usage description, these follow from the ninth step in pattern development. Determine the parameters for binding pattern realizations. Parameters are M2-level identifications of the class attributes of CWM classes included in the projection, along with their corresponding M1-level values that result in the binding of the formal pattern to a particular realization. Parameters may also consist of M2-level identifications of base classes in the projection, along with the specification of corresponding M1-level instances of subtypes of those base classes that are to be substituted in place of those base classes in the actual pattern realization. Parameters are best specified in terms of a table listing each M2-level parameter, its corresponding M1-level value, and any relevant comments.

Commentary.   Any informal, additional commentary that might be helpful in describing how this pattern should generally be used.

Consequences.   A description of the ramifications and trade-offs, both positive and negative, in the application of this pattern.

Known Uses.   A citation of any known examples of actual software systems employing this pattern.

Related Patterns.   A list of any other meta data interchange patterns that this pattern is closely related to, collaborates with, or is composed from. This description should include any URLs pointing to the associated pattern descriptions, if possible. Much of this information is established as part of the third step of pattern development. Determine how the proposed pattern reuses, or otherwise relates to, known patterns.

Sample Solution.   A detailed example of how to use this pattern to solve its related meta data interchange pattern. If possible, this example should consist of both UML instance diagrams and equivalent XMI fragments to illustrate the solution. Much of this material may be created as part of the tenth and final step in pattern development. Validate the pattern.

An equivalent HyperText Markup Language (HTML) rendering of the standard template for the construction of meta data interchange pattern specifications is available on the companion Web site. The companion Web site provides a number of actual meta data interchange pattern specifications that are specific to the various vertical meta data models developed throughout this book. These are based on a standard pattern template, also located on the companion Web site.

Developing a Fundamental Pattern: Unit of Interchange

Now that we've established all of the practical steps involved in the development of a CWM meta data interchange pattern, as well as its subsequent publication, let's illustrate how these steps actually work by developing a very fundamental pattern that we need for all subsequent meta data interchange.

Unit of Interchange is a macro pattern that provides an overall organizing framework for CWM meta data that is to be interchanged using the pattern-based approach. Unit of Interchange provides a standard way of defining the expected structure of the outermost container of pattern-based meta data. A particular realization of Unit of Interchange contains some realization of a more domain-oriented (contextual) pattern. Unit of Interchange provides a means of both organizing and identifying this domain-specific pattern realization.

We will develop Unit of Interchange in a step-by-step fashion, using the steps defined in the previous subsection titled *Steps for Developing Interchange Patterns*. A specification of Unit of Interchange, conforming to the guidelines for formulating pattern specification was presented in the previous subsection. The details of each pattern development step are presented in each of the following subsections.

Identify the interchange problem to be solved

CWM meta data interchange via XMI is greatly simplified (particularly in the case of meta data import) when the XMI file contains a single outermost, or top-level, package organizing the rest of the meta data content. The package should have a predefined set of attributes that further identifies the package's content and internal structuring.

Propose a pattern that solves the problem

Unit of Interchange provides a consistently structured, identifiable unit of meta data interchange required by the problem description. It does so by specifying how instances of existing model elements of the CWM metamodel are to be organized to provide a standard unit of meta data interchange.

Identify several scenarios in which the proposed pattern would be used

The Unit of Interchange pattern is used in all interchange situations as a means of organizing the highest level of content of CWM meta data within a single XMI file. A software process importing an XMI file tests that the high-level elements in <XMI.content> conform to the Unit of Interchange pattern. If so, then the importing process tests further for an instance of some Domain pattern that the process is particularly interested in. Otherwise, the importing process may ignore the XMI file, or take some other action (such as signaling an exception). Similarly, an exporting process uses the Unit of Interchange pattern as the basis for organizing the high-level content of the XMI file it is writing.

Note that, in normal usage, it is generally expected that any XMI file will contain a single instance (realization) of the Unit of Interchange pattern. However, there is nothing incorrect in having multiple occurrences of Unit of Interchange within a given XMI file. Each represents a discrete unit of meta data interchange.

Determine how the proposed pattern reuses, or otherwise relates to, known patterns

Unit of Interchange does not directly reuse any other patterns, since it is intended to serve as an outermost wrapper or container of other patterns. However, since the content of any instance (realization) of Unit of Interchange is expected to conform to some specified Domain pattern, Unit of Interchange is fundamentally related to all possible Domain patterns.

Unit of Interchange is sometimes referred to by a number of other pattern names, including Unit of Work, Unit of Exchange, and Unit of Transfer.

Identify the structural classification of the proposed pattern

Unit of Interchange is clearly a Macro pattern.

Identify the usage category of the proposed pattern

Unit of Interchange exists for no other reason than to directly facilitate ease of interchange; hence, its usage category is Interchange.

Identify the metamodel projection

The Unit of Interchange pattern is based on a sub-graph of the CWM meta-model consisting of the following meta classes and associations:

- org.omg.cwm.objectmodel.core.Package
- org.omg.cwm.objectmodel.core.Stereotype
- org.omg.cwm.objectmodel.core.TaggedValue
- org.omg.cwm.objectmodel.core.ElementOwnership
- org.omg.cwm.objectmodel.core.StereotypeElement
- org.omg.cwm.objectmodel.core.StereotypeTaggedValues

This sub-graph is illustrated in Figure 4.14.

Determine any restrictions on instances of the projection

The Unit of Interchange pattern requires that instances of its projection be restricted as follows:

- The Package instance must not be owned by any Namespace; that is, it must be the outermost element of the interchange meta data.
- The Package instance is extended by an instance of Stereotype; this Stereotype is owned by the Package instance and extends no other model elements.
- The single Stereotype extending the Package instance has precisely one requiredTag with the class attribute TaggedValue.tag set to "version."

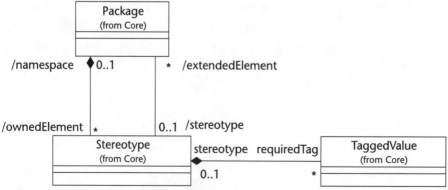

Figure 4.14 Unit of Interchange projection.

The above restrictions are formally expressed by the following OCL constraint:

```
Context Package
Inv: self.namespace->isEmpty
Inv: self.ownedElement->collect( oclType = Stereotype )
->forAll( s | s.extendedElement->includes( self ) Implies
( s.extendedElement->size = 1 and
s.requiredTag->Includes( tag = "version" ) and
s.requiredTag->size = 1 ) )
Inv: self.ownedElement->collect( oclType = Stereotype )
->collect( extendedElement->Includes( self ) )->size = 1
```

Determine the parameters for binding pattern realizations

It is generally expected that the Unit of Interchange pattern is bound to its various realizations in the following manner:

- The name of the single Package instance is user-defined, and its value is not in any way prescribed by the definition of the Unit of Interchange pattern.

- The single Stereotype instance specifies the Domain pattern that the Package content conforms to. The attribute Stereotype.Model-lement::name is set to the Domain pattern's name.

- The single instance of TaggedValue specifies the version of the Domain pattern; that is, TaggedValue.tag is fixed to the value "version," and TaggedValue.value is set to the relevant version number of the Domain pattern.

These binding requirements are expressed in terms of parameters and parameter values in Table 4.1.

Table 4.1 Unit of Interchange Parameters

M2 PARAMETER	M1 VALUE	COMMENTS
Package.Model-Element::name	User-defined	Value is arbitrary; up to the end user
Stereotype.Model-Element::name	User-defined	Value should be the name of a published Domain pattern that the Package content realizes
TaggedValue.tag	"version"	Value is fixed by the pattern definition
TaggedValue.value	User-defined	Value is the version of the Domain pattern, usually expressed in the form m.n (for example, "1.0")

Validate the pattern

We shall validate the Unit of Interchange pattern by determining if it can be used to package a realization of some Domain pattern. We shall assume that the Domain pattern we're interested in is version 1.0 of a published pattern known as "DataWebhouse." Therefore, the single Package instance prescribed by the Unit of Interchange will contain some realization of this Domain pattern, and the Domain pattern name and version will be identified via the single Stereotype instance attached to the Package. The Package name itself is user-specified; we will assume that the user has chosen the name "CwmModel."

The instance diagram in Figure 4.15 shows an instance of the Unit of Interchange projection that represents a realization of Unit of Interchange based on the parameter values previously specified. Figure 4.16 shows the equivalent XMI file. Because the structures in Figures 4.15 and 4.16 are valid instances of the CWM metamodel, and because we can freely substitute those parameter values not fixed by the Unit of Interchange pattern definition without altering the model structures in the two figures, we can conclude that Unit of Interchange, as specified, is a valid solution to the stated meta data interchange problem.

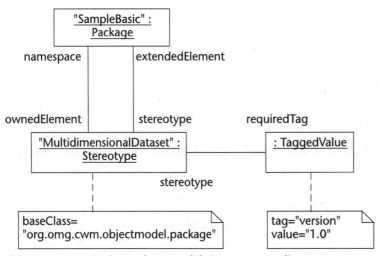

Figure 4.15 Unit of Interchange validation: Instance diagram.

```
<?xml version="1.0" encoding="UTF-8"?>
<XMI xmlns:CWM="org.omg.java.cwm.objectmodel.core"
xmlns:CWMOLAP="org.omg.java.cwm.analysis.olap"
    xmlns:CWMREC="org.omg.java.cwm.resource.record"
    xmlns:CWMTFM="org.omg.java.cwm.analysis.transformation"
    xmlns:CWMMDB="org.omg.java.cwm.resource.multidimensional"
    xmi.version="1.1" timestamp="Wed Jan 23 18:25:50 EST 2002">
  <XMI.header>
    <XMI.documentation>
      <XMI.exporter>Generic CWM Toolkit</XMI.exporter>
      <XMI.exporterVersion>1.0</XMI.exporterVersion>
    </XMI.documentation>
  </XMI.header>
  <XMI.content>
    <CWM:Package xmi.id="_1" name="CwmModel">
      <CWM:Namespace.ownedElement>
        <CWM:Stereotype xmi.id="_1.1" name="DataWebhouse"
baseClass="org.omg.java.cwm.objectmodel.package" namespace="_1"
extendedElement="_1">
          <CWM:Stereotype.requiredTag>
            <CWM:TaggedValue xmi.id="_1.1.1" tag="version" value="1.0"
stereotype="_1.1"/>
          </CWM:Stereotype.requiredTag>
        </CWM:Stereotype>
      </CWM:Package>
    </XMI.content>
</XMI>
```

Figure 4.16   Unit of Interchange validation: XMI rendering

Summary

This chapter established both a theory and development methodology for meta data interchange patterns based on CWM. We first established the need for meta data interchange patterns through a number of examples of meta data interchange problems that are not solved by CWM syntax alone. We then demonstrated the efficacy of applying a pattern-based approach to resolving the issue of both specifying a semantic context for model interpretation, as well as a means of managing the sizes of CWM instances. We then went on to fully develop a practical methodology for developing meta data interchange patterns based on CWM. This methodology was demonstrated in the construction of an actual meta data interchange pattern, Unit of Interchange, that will play a fundamental role in the interchange examples developed throughout much of the rest of this book.

This chapter has also defined a standard way of specifying meta data interchange patterns, and publishing them in the form of public pattern catalogs. This methodology is aligned with similar methods developed in the area of software design patterns. A standard template for developing specifications of meta data interchange patterns was developed. This template is provided on the companion Web site. Throughout subsequent chapters of this book, a number of meta data patterns will be developed using the methodologies for both development and specification presented here. Those patterns form the basis for the complete meta data interchange catalog provided on the companion Web site for this book.

We view the pattern-based approach as being critical to ensuring the widespread use of CWM as a meta data integration and interoperability mechanism. In particular, we see a meta data interchange pattern user community developing in fairly short order, once the pattern-based solution approach and its associated tools for the specification and publishing of meta data interchange patterns become well established. This will undoubtedly lead to the development of a large class of CWM-based data warehousing and business analysis integration tools that are fundamentally pattern-driven and pattern-aware.

PART

Two

Introducing the
Vertical Models

CHAPTER 5

Data Warehouse Management Model

This chapter discusses two major data warehouse management scenarios and demonstrates how Common Warehouse Metamodel (CWM) can be used to facilitate the meta data integration required for the operation of an Information Supply Chain (ISC). The two major data warehouse scenarios that will be discussed are the operational data store and the Extraction, Transformation, and Loading (ETL) process. These two scenarios together cover the first three components (and their meta data) of the information supply chain discussed in previous chapters and shown in Figure 5.1. The fourth ISC component, the data mart, is very much like the dimensional data warehouse, and the process of creating a data mart from a data warehouse is generally a special case of the ETL process. Therefore, the only component of the information supply chain that we will not cover in this chapter is the Online Analytical Processing (OLAP) component, which will be covered by the OLAP model discussed in Chapter 6.

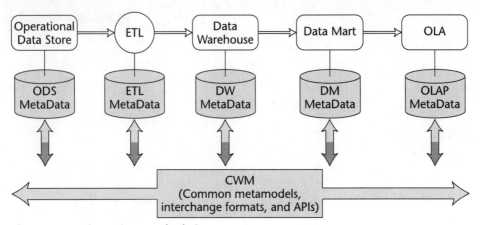

Figure 5.1   Information supply chain.

The operational data store scenario deals with extracting all essential meta data from a relational database, which is the most dominant type of operational data store, and exporting these meta data using CWM. The ETL scenario deals with modeling the ETL process required to transform raw operational data into aggregate business information and exporting the ETL process meta data using CWM. As can be seen from Figure 5.1, these two scenarios, put together end-to-end, form a complete data warehouse scenario producing meta data and data suitable for use by OLAP for decision-making, either directly or indirectly through data marts.

We will discuss in detail the major CWM packages used in the two scenarios, including CWM Relational, CWM Transformation, and CWM Warehouse Process. In addition, for the operational data store scenario we will provide code examples to illustrate how to actually implement meta data interchange using CWM.

The Operational Data Store Scenario

In the old days, there was no distinction between the operational data store and the data warehouse. That is, query and reporting facilities were built directly on top of the operational data store to provide business analysts access to "business information" for decision support. However, since the operational data store contains raw, operational data running daily transactions of the business, there would be several problems if the business analysts were to access the operational data directly:

- The business analysts might not have the expertise to query the operational data store, given that it was not designed with business analysts in mind.

- Operational data generally is not in the best format to be used by business analysts. Operational data normally is cast in the format optimized for daily transactions.

- Performance is critical for the operational data store. Long-running queries by business analysts cannot be allowed, except during off-hours.

The data warehouse, according to W. H. Inmon, is "a *subject-oriented, integrated, time-variant, nonvolatile* collection of data in support of management's decisions." A data warehouse consists of a set of hardware and software components that can be used to better prepare and analyze the massive amounts of data that companies are accumulating to make better business decisions. The data warehouse provides the following major benefits:

- Provides a dedicated database for decision support

- Transforms and integrates raw operational data into business information suitable for use in decision support

- Offloads processing from the operational data store

For comparison, the main differences between the data warehouse and the operational data store are summarized in Table 5.1.

Table 5.1. Differences between the Data Warehouse and Operational Data Store

	DATA WAREHOUSE	OPERATIONAL DATA STORE
Data Volume	Extremely large (can be terabytes)	Orders of magnitude smaller
Data Access	Static (mainly read only)	Dynamic (continually updated)
Time Variance	Mostly historical data	Very recent information
Integration	Integrated	Different formats coexist
Summarization	A lot of summary data	No

(continues)

Table 5.1. Differences between the Data Warehouse and Operational Data Store *(Continued)*

	DATA WAREHOUSE	OPERATIONAL DATA STORE
Planning	Predefined query	
Periodically run query		
Long running query	No	
Design	Subject oriented	Application oriented
Data Model	Multidimensional	Mainly relational

Most operational data stores are relational databases or nonrelational systems (e.g., hierarchical databases) supporting a relational interface (e.g., Java Data Base Connectivity [JDBC] or Open Data Base Connectivity [ODBC]). We will focus our attention on relational databases as operational data stores, specifically on extracting all essential meta data from a relational database and exporting these meta data using CWM.

The Exemplar Operational Data Store

Before we discuss how to export relational meta data using CWM, we will give a brief description of the exemplar operational data store, CwmOds, that we will use for illustration in this scenario. CwmOds is an operational data store maintained by a fictitious national retailer that has stores located across the country, which sell all sorts of products, from clothing to stationery to utensils, and so on. CwmOds contains raw operational data, that is, daily transactional data recorded by all stores within a given region. We are interested in CwmOds, since in the next scenario (the ETL Scenario) we will discuss how the raw operational data stored in it can be extracted, transformed, and loaded into the exemplar data warehouse, CwmStore, as shown in Figure 5.2.

CwmOds is a relational database that consists of three tables: Store, Product, and Sales. The definitions of these tables are shown in Tables 5.2 to 5.4. The Store table contains information on all stores within a given region. The Product table contains information on all products carried by the stores within the region. The Sales table contains daily sales information on all products sold by the stores within the region.

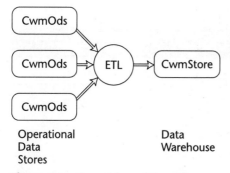

Operational
Data
Stores

Data
Warehouse

Figure 5.2   CwmOds and CwmStore.

Table 5.2.   CwmOds Store Table

COLUMN	DATATYPE	LENGTH	NOT NULL	PRIMARY KEY
Store_id	Integer		Yes	Yes
Name	Varchar	128		
City	Varchar	80		
State	Character	2		

Table 5.3.   CwmOds Product Table

COLUMN	DATATYPE	LENGTH	NOT NULL	PRIMARY KEY
Product_id	Integer		Yes	Yes
Price	Double			
Cost	Double			
Description	Varchar	128		
Prod_size	Varchar	7		
Color	Varchar	32		
Brand	Varchar	64		
Department	Varchar	64		
Category	Varchar	32		

Table 5.4. CwmOds Sales Table

COLUMN	DATATYPE	LENGTH	NOT NULL	PRIMARY KEY	FOREIGN KEY
Store_id	Integer		Yes		Yes
Product_id	Integer		Yes		Yes
Quantity	Integer				
Revenue	Double				
Cost	Double				
Date	Varchar	32			

Tables 5.5 to 5.7 show some sample data contained in each of the three tables. Please note that the Store and Product tables contain relatively stable information about stores and products, whereas the Sales table contains constantly added data about sales. As such, this table needs to be processed and off-loaded periodically to avoid overflow.

Table 5.5. Sample Data in the CwmOds Store Table

STORE_ID	NAME	CITY	STATE
1	Store1	Boston	MA
2	Store2	Boston	MA
5	Store5	Boston	MA
17	Store17	Milford	CT
18	Store18	New Haven	CT
19	Store19	New Haven	CT
21	Store21	New York	NY
22	Store22	New York	NY
23	Store23	New York	NY
24	Store24	New York	NY

Table 5.6.   Sample Data in the CwmOds Product Table

STORE_ID	PRODUCT_ID	QUANTITY	REVENUE	COST	DATE
1	5	3	30	24	1/1/1999
1	17	2	64	54	1/1/1999
1	18	1	19	16	1/1/1999
2	17	3	96	81	1/1/1999
2	21	1	45	37	1/1/1999
2	22	1	38	33	1/1/1999
5	18	2	38	32	1/1/1999
5	18	1	19	16	1/1/1999
5	24	5	25	20	1/1/1999
5	25	2	10	8	1/1/1999

Table 5.7.   Sample Data in the CwmOds Sales Table

STORE_ID	PRODUCT_ID	QUANTITY	REVENUE	COST	DATE
1	5	3	30	24	1/1/1999
1	17	2	64	54	1/1/1999
1	18	1	19	16	1/1/1999
2	17	3	96	81	1/1/1999
2	21	1	45	37	1/1/1999
2	22	1	38	33	1/1/1999
5	18	2	38	32	1/1/1999
5	18	1	19	16	1/1/1999
5	24	5	25	20	1/1/1999
5	25	2	10	8	1/1/1999

The Relational Meta Data

There are a number of mechanisms you can use to access and extract the meta data, or schema information, from a relational database. For example, you can directly query the schema tables of a relational database using Structured Query Language (SQL). The advantage of this approach is that you can access and extract all meta data of the relational database. The disadvantage of this approach is that it is not at all straightforward to write all the SQL statements required. In addition, the SQL statements will be vendor-product-specific. As another example, you can use JDBC to access and extract the meta data of a relational database. The advantage of this approach is that the same code can work with any relational database that supports JDBC. In fact, the same code can work with even nonrelational systems that support JDBC. The disadvantage of this approach is that not all meta data can be accessed and extracted, only those provided through JDBC. For our purpose, the JDBC approach is desirable. Since our goal is to export shared relational meta data using CWM, by intent, the same kind of meta data should be accessible from any vendor product. As such, JDBC is an ideal choice; it is designed to provide a uniform meta data access Application Program Interface (API) for all relational database products.

JDBC provides a single interface for accessing the meta data of a relational database: DatabaseMetaData. In addition, it also provides an interface for accessing the meta data of the result set of a SQL query: ResultSetMetaData. In the following, we will describe first the methods of DatabaseMetaData, and then those of ResultSetMetaData, that we will use to export meta data using CWM. As can be seen in Figures 5.3 and 5.5, these methods are only a subset of all the methods provided by DatabaseMetaData and ResultSetMetaData, respectively. Please also note that in each of the method descriptions that follow, the column descriptions of the result set are copied verbatim from the corresponding JDBC JavaDoc documentation to avoid any potential misrepresentation.

Database Meta Data

The methods that we will use to access the meta data of a relational database are listed in Figure 5.3. The database objects, whose meta data can be accessed, are shown in Figure 5.4.

```
public interface DatabaseMetaData
{
    public ResultSet getCatalogs() throws SQLException
    public ResultSet getSchemas() throws SQLException

// Table meta data

    public ResultSet getTables(String catalog,
                               String schemaPattern,
                               String tableNamePattern,
                               String[] types)
        throws SQLException
    public ResultSet getColumns(String catalog,
                                String schemaPattern,
                                String tableNamePattern,
                                String columnNamePattern)
        throws SQLException
    public ResultSet getPrimaryKeys(String catalog,
                                    String schema,
                                    String table)
        throws SQLException
    public ResultSet getExportedKeys(String catalog,
                                     String schema,
                                     String table)
        throws SQLException
    public ResultSet getIndexInfo(String catalog,
                                  String schema,
                                  String table,
                                  boolean unique,
                                  boolean approximate)
        throws SQLException

// Data type meta data

    public ResultSet getTypeInfo()
                  throws SQLException
    public ResultSet getUDTs(String catalog,
                             String schemaPattern,
                             String typeNamePattern,
                             int[] types)
        throws SQLException
    public ResultSet getAttributes(String catalog,
                                   String schemaPattern,
```

Figure 5.3 DatabaseMetaData: methods used. *(continues)*

```
                                    String typeNamePattern,
                                    String attributeNamePattern)
        throws SQLException

// Stored procedure meta data

    public ResultSet getProcedures(String catalog,
                                   String schemaPattern,
                                   String procedureNamePattern)
        throws SQLException
    public ResultSet getProcedureColumns(String catalog,
                                         String schemaPattern,
                                         String procedureNamePattern,
                                         String columnNamePattern)
        throws SQLException
}
```

Figure 5.3   DatabaseMetaData: methods used. *(continued)*

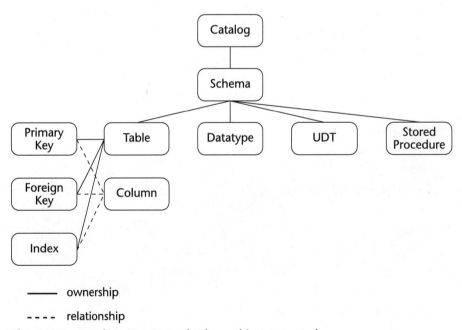

———— ownership

- - - - relationship

Figure 5.4.   DatabaseMetaData: database objects exported.

Catalog and Schema Meta Data

Taking a top-down approach, the first method of DatabaseMetaData that we will use is getCatalogs(). This method retrieves the catalog names available in the database. The results are ordered by catalog name. Each catalog description has only one column:

```
1. TABLE_CAT String => catalog name
```

Please note that not all relational database products support this method. That is, this method may always return null for certain relational database products. When that is the case, the following method on the Connection interface should be used instead, which returns the current catalog name:

```
public String getCatalog() throws SQLException
```

The next method we will use is getSchemas(). This method retrieves the schema names available in the database. The results are ordered by schema name. Each schema description has the following columns:

```
1. TABLE_SCHEM String => schema name
2. TABLE_CATALOG String => catalog name (may be null)
```

Once the catalog and schema names are known, they can be used to retrieve all meta data information owned by the proper catalog and schema names pair, including those related to tables, data types, and stored procedures, as shown below.

Table Meta Data

There are five methods that we will use to export meta data on tables and their related database objects. The getTables() method will retrieve a description of the tables available in the given catalog. Only table descriptions matching the catalog, schema pattern, table name pattern, and type criteria are returned. They are ordered by TABLE_TYPE, TABLE_SCHEM, and TABLE_NAME. Each table description has the following columns (columns 6 to 10 are applicable only to typed tables, that is, tables created on structured types):

```
1. TABLE_CAT String => table catalog (may be null)
2. TABLE_SCHEM String => table schema (may be null)
3. TABLE_NAME String => table name
```

4. TABLE_TYPE String => table type. Typical types are "TABLE", "VIEW", "SYSTEM TABLE","GLOBAL TEMPORARY", "LOCAL TEMPORARY", "ALIAS", "SYNONYM".
5. REMARKS String => explanatory comment on the table
6. TYPE_CAT String => the types catalog (may be null)
7. TYPE_SCHEM String => the types schema (may be null)
8. TYPE_NAME String => type name (may be null)
9. SELF_REFERENCING_COL_NAME String => name of the designated "identifier" column of a typed table (may be null)
10. REF_GENERATION String => specifies how values in SELF_REFERENCING_COL_NAME are created. Values are "SYSTEM", "USER", "DERIVED". (may be null)

The getColumns() method retrieves a description of table columns available in the given catalog. Only column descriptions matching the catalog, schema pattern, table name pattern, and column name criteria are returned. They are ordered by TABLE_SCHEM, TABLE_NAME, and ORDINAL_POSITION. Each column description has the following columns:

1. TABLE_CAT String => table catalog (may be null)
2. TABLE_SCHEM String => table schema (may be null)
3. TABLE_NAME String => table name
4. COLUMN_NAME String => column name
5. DATA_TYPE short => SQL type from java.sql.Types
6. TYPE_NAME String => Data source dependent type name, for a UDT the type name is fully qualified
7. COLUMN_SIZE int => column size. For char or date types this is the maximum number of characters, for numeric or decimal types this is precision.
8. BUFFER_LENGTH is not used.
9. DECIMAL_DIGITS int => the number of fractional digits
10. NUM_PREC_RADIX int => Radix (typically either 10 or 2)
11. NULLABLE int => is NULL allowed.
columnNoNulls - might not allow NULL values
columnNullable - definitely allows NULL values
columnNullableUnknown - nullability unknown
12. REMARKS String => comment describing column (may be null)
13. COLUMN_DEF String => default value (may be null)
14. SQL_DATA_TYPE int => unused
15. SQL_DATETIME_SUB int => unused
16. CHAR_OCTET_LENGTH int => for char types the maximum number of bytes in the column
17. ORDINAL_POSITION int => index of column in table (starting at 1)
18. IS_NULLABLE String => "NO" means column definitely does not allow NULL values; "YES" means the column might allow NULL values. An empty string means nobody knows.
19. SCOPE_CATALOG String => catalog of table that is the scope of a reference attribute (null if DATA_TYPE isn't REF)
20. SCOPE_SCHEMA String => schema of table that is the scope of a

```
                reference attribute (null if the DATA_TYPE isn't REF)
     21. SCOPE_TABLE String => table name that is the scope of a
                reference attribute (null if the DATA_TYPE isn't REF)
     22. SOURCE_DATA_TYPE short => source type of a distinct type or
                user-generated Ref type, SQL type from java.sql.Types (null if
                DATA_TYPE isn't DISTINCT or user-generated REF)
```

The getPrimaryKeys() method retrieves a description of the given table's primary key columns. They are ordered by COLUMN_NAME. Each primary key column description has the following columns:

```
     1. TABLE_CAT String => table catalog (may be null)
     2. TABLE_SCHEM String => table schema (may be null)
     3. TABLE_NAME String => table name
     4. COLUMN_NAME String => column name
     5. KEY_SEQ short => sequence number within primary key
     6. PK_NAME String => primary key name (may be null)
```

The getExportedKeys() method retrieves a description of the foreign key columns that references the given table's primary key columns (the foreign keys exported by a table). They are ordered by FKTABLE_CAT, FKTABLE_SCHEM, FKTABLE_NAME, and KEY_SEQ. Each foreign key column description has the following columns:

```
     1. PKTABLE_CAT String => primary key table catalog (may be null)
     2. PKTABLE_SCHEM String => primary key table schema (may be null)
     3. PKTABLE_NAME String => primary key table name
     4. PKCOLUMN_NAME String => primary key column name
     5. FKTABLE_CAT String => foreign key table catalog (may be null) being
                exported (may be null)
     6. FKTABLE_SCHEM String => foreign key table schema (may be null)
                being exported (may be null)
     7. FKTABLE_NAME String => foreign key table name being exported
     8. FKCOLUMN_NAME String => foreign key column name being exported
     9. KEY_SEQ short => sequence number within foreign key
     10. UPDATE_RULE short => What happens to foreign key when primary is
                updated:
importedNoAction - do not allow update of primary key if it has been
imported
importedKeyCascade - change imported key to agree with primary key update
importedKeySetNull - change imported key to NULL if its primary key has
been updated
importedKeySetDefault - change imported key to default values if its
primary key has been updated
importedKeyRestrict - same as importedKeyNoAction (for ODBC 2.x
compatibility)
     11. DELETE_RULE short => What happens to the foreign key when
primary
```

```
            is deleted:
importedKeyNoAction - do not allow delete of primary key if it has been
imported
importedKeyCascade - delete rows that import a deleted key
importedKeySetNull - change imported key to NULL if its primary key has
been deleted
importedKeyRestrict - same as importedKeyNoAction (for ODBC 2.x
compatibility)
importedKeySetDefault - change imported key to default if its primary
key has been deleted
    12. FK_NAME String => foreign key name (may be null)
    13. PK_NAME String => primary key name (may be null)
    14. DEFERRABILITY short => can the evaluation of foreign key
        constraints be deferred until commit:
importedKeyInitiallyDeferred - see SQL92 for definition
importedKeyInitiallyImmediate - see SQL92 for definition
importedKeyNotDeferrable - see SQL92 for definition
```

The getIndexInfo() method retrieves a description of the indexes and statistics of the given table. They are ordered by NON_UNIQUE, TYPE, INDEX_NAME, and ORDINAL_POSITION. Each index column description has the following columns:

```
    1. TABLE_CAT String => table catalog (may be null)
    2. TABLE_SCHEM String => table schema (may be null)
    3. TABLE_NAME String => table name
    4. NON_UNIQUE boolean => Can index values be non-unique. false when
        TYPE is tableIndexStatistic
    5. INDEX_QUALIFIER String => index catalog (may be null); null when
        TYPE is tableIndexStatistic
    6. INDEX_NAME String => index name; null when TYPE is
        tableIndexStatistic
    7. TYPE short => index type:
tableIndexStatistic - this identifies table statistics that are returned
in conjunction with a table's index descriptions
tableIndexClustered - this is a clustered index
tableIndexHashed - this is a hashed index
tableIndexOther - this is some other style of index
    8. ORDINAL_POSITION short => column sequence number within index; zero
        when TYPE is tableIndexStatistic
    9. COLUMN_NAME String => column name; null when TYPE is
        tableIndexStatistic
    10. ASC_OR_DESC String => column sort sequence, "A" => ascending, "D"
        => descending, may be null if sort sequence is not supported; null
        when TYPE is tableIndexStatistic
    11. CARDINALITY int => When TYPE is tableIndexStatistic, then this is
        the number of rows in the table; otherwise, it is the number of
```

unique values in the index.

12. PAGES int => When TYPE is tableIndexStatisic then this is the number of pages used for the table, otherwise it is the number of pages used for the current index.

13. FILTER_CONDITION String => Filter condition, if any. (may be null)

Data Type Meta Data

There are three methods that we will use to export the meta data on data types, including standard (built-in) data types and user-defined data types (Java objects, distinct types, or structured types). The getTypeInfo() method retrieves a description of all the standard SQL types supported by the database. They are ordered by DATA_TYPE and then by how closely the data type maps to the corresponding JDBC SQL type. Each type description has the following columns:

1. TYPE_NAME String => Type name
2. DATA_TYPE short => SQL data type from java.sql.Types
3. PRECISION int => maximum precision
4. LITERAL_PREFIX String => prefix used to quote a literal (may be null)
5. LITERAL_SUFFIX String => suffix used to quote a literal (may be null)
6. CREATE_PARAMS String => parameters used in creating the type (may be null)
7. NULLABLE short => can you use NULL for this type.
typeNoNulls - does not allow NULL values
typeNullable - allows NULL values
typeNullableUnknown - nullability unknown
8. CASE_SENSITIVE boolean => is it case sensitive.
9. SEARCHABLE short => can you use "WHERE" based on this type:
typePredNone - No support
typePredChar - Only supported with WHERE .. LIKE
typePredBasic - Supported except for WHERE .. LIKE
typeSearchable - Supported for all WHERE ..
10. UNSIGNED_ATTRIBUTE boolean => is it unsigned.
11. FIXED_PREC_SCALE boolean => can it be a money value.
12. AUTO_INCREMENT boolean => can it be used for an auto-increment value.
13. LOCAL_TYPE_NAME String => localized version of type name (may be null)
14. MINIMUM_SCALE short => minimum scale supported
15. MAXIMUM_SCALE short => maximum scale supported
16. SQL_DATA_TYPE int => unused
17. SQL_DATETIME_SUB int => unused
18. NUM_PREC_RADIX int => usually 2 or 10

The getUDTs() method retrieves a description of the user-defined types (UDTs) defined in a given catalog. UDTs may have type JAVA_OBJECT, STRUCT, or DISTINCT. Only types matching the catalog, schema, type name, and type criteria are returned. They are ordered by DATA_TYPE, TYPE_SCHEM, and TYPE_NAME. The type name parameter may be a fully qualified name. In this case, the catalog and schemaPattern parameters are ignored. Each type of description has the following columns:

```
1. TYPE_CAT String => the type's catalog (may be null)
2. TYPE_SCHEM String => type's schema (may be null)
3. TYPE_NAME String => type name
4. CLASS_NAME String => Java class name
5. DATA_TYPE String => type value defined in java.sql.Types. One of
     JAVA_OBJECT, STRUCT, or DISTINCT
6. REMARKS String => explanatory comment on the type
7. BASE_TYPE short => type code of the source type of a DISTINCT type
     or the type that implements the user-generated reference type of
     the SELF_REFERENCING_COLUMN of a structured type as defined in
     java.sql.Types (null if DATA_TYPE is not DISTINCT or not STRUCT
     with REFERENCE_GENERATION = USER_DEFINED)
```

The getAttributes() method retrieves a description of the given attribute of the given type for a UDT that is available in the given catalog. Descriptions are returned only for attributes of UDTs matching the catalog, schema, type, and attribute name criteria. They are ordered by TYPE_SCHEM, TYPE_NAME, and ORDINAL_POSITION. This description does not contain inherited attributes. Each attribute description has the following columns:

```
 1. TYPE_CAT String => type catalog (may be null)
 2. TYPE_SCHEM String => type schema (may be null)
 3. TYPE_NAME String => type name
 4. ATTR_NAME String => attribute name
 5. DATA_TYPE short => attribute type SQL type from java.sql.Types
 6. ATTR_TYPE_NAME String => Data source dependent type name. For a
      UDT, the type name is fully qualified. For a REF, the type name is
      fully qualified and represents the target type of the reference
      type.
 7. ATTR_SIZE int => column size. For char or date types this is the
      maximum number of characters; for numeric or decimal types this is
      precision.
 8. DECIMAL_DIGITS int => the number of fractional digits
 9. NUM_PREC_RADIX int => Radix (typically either 10 or 2)
10. NULLABLE int => whether NULL is allowed
attributeNoNulls - might not allow NULL values
attributeNullable - definitely allows NULL values
attributeNullableUnknown - nullability unknown
```

11. REMARKS String => comment describing column (may be null)

12. ATTR_DEF String => default value (may be null)

13. SQL_DATA_TYPE int => unused

14. SQL_DATETIME_SUB int => unused

15. CHAR_OCTET_LENGTH int => for char types the maximum number of bytes in the column

16. ORDINAL_POSITION int => index of column in table (starting at 1)

17. IS_NULLABLE String => "NO" means column definitely does not allow NULL values; "YES" means the column might allow NULL values. An empty string means unknown.

18. SCOPE_CATALOG String => catalog of table that is the scope of a reference attribute (null if DATA_TYPE isn't REF)

19. SCOPE_SCHEMA String => schema of table that is the scope of a reference attribute (null if DATA_TYPE isn't REF)

20. SCOPE_TABLE String => table name that is the scope of a reference attribute (null if the DATA_TYPE isn't REF)

21. SOURCE_DATA_TYPE short => source type of a distinct type or user-generated Ref type, SQL type from java.sql.Types (null if DATA_TYPE isn't DISTINCT or user-generated REF)

Stored Procedure Meta Data

There are two methods that we will use to export meta data on stored procedures. The getProcedures() method retrieves a description of the stored procedures available in the given catalog. Only procedure descriptions matching the schema and procedure name criteria are returned. They are ordered by PROCEDURE_SCHEM and PROCEDURE_NAME. Each procedure description has the following columns:

1. PROCEDURE_CAT String => procedure catalog (may be null)

2. PROCEDURE_SCHEM String => procedure schema (may be null)

3. PROCEDURE_NAME String => procedure name

4. reserved for future use

5. reserved for future use

6. reserved for future use

7. REMARKS String => explanatory comment on the procedure

8. PROCEDURE_TYPE short => kind of procedure:

procedureResultUnknown - May return a result

procedureNoResult - Does not return a result

procedureReturnsResult - Returns a result

The getProcedureColumns() method retrieves a description of the given catalog's stored procedure parameter and result columns. Only descriptions matching the schema, procedure, and parameter name criteria are returned. They are ordered by PROCEDURE_SCHEM and PROCEDURE_NAME. Within this, the return value, if any, is first. Next are the parameter descriptions in call order. The column descriptions follow in column number order. Each row in the ResultSet is a parameter description or column description with the following fields:

```
1. PROCEDURE_CAT String => procedure catalog (may be null)
2. PROCEDURE_SCHEM String => procedure schema (may be null)
3. PROCEDURE_NAME String => procedure name
4. COLUMN_NAME String => column/parameter name
5. COLUMN_TYPE Short => kind of column/parameter:
procedureColumnUnknown - nobody knows
procedureColumnIn - IN parameter
procedureColumnInOut - INOUT parameter
procedureColumnOut - OUT parameter
procedureColumnReturn - procedure return value
procedureColumnResult - result column in ResultSet
6. DATA_TYPE short => SQL type from java.sql.Types
7. TYPE_NAME String => SQL type name, for a UDT type the type name is
   fully qualified
8. PRECISION int => precision
9. LENGTH int => length in bytes of data
10. SCALE short => scale
11. RADIX short => radix
12. NULLABLE short => can it contain NULL.
procedureNoNulls - does not allow NULL values
procedureNullable - allows NULL values
procedureNullableUnknown - nullability unknown
13.REMARKS String => comment describing parameter/column
```

Function and Trigger Meta Data

JDBC provides four methods for accessing the meta data on functions:

```
public String getNumericFunctions()
    throws SQLException
public String getStringFunctions()
    throws SQLException
public String getSystemFunctions()
    throws SQLException
public String getTimeDateFunctions()
    throws SQLException
```

The CWM Relational package, however, does not contain an explicit model on functions. Instead, it provides a Procedure, which can be used to represent functions (in addition to stored procedures).

The CWM Relational package contains a model on triggers. Unfortunately, JDBC does not provide any method for accessing trigger meta data. Therefore, if needed, the trigger meta data must be obtained using a mechanism other than JDBC.

```
public interface ResultSetMetaData
{
    public int getColumnCount()
        throws SQLException
    public String getColumnName(int column)
        throws SQLException
    public int getColumnType(int column)
        throws SQLException
}
```

Figure 5.5 ResultSetMetaData: methods used.

ResultSet Meta Data

The methods that we will use to access the meta data of the result set returned from a SQL query are listed in Figure 5.5.

The getColumnCount() method returns the number of columns in the result set. The getColumnName() method returns the name of the given column. The getColumnType() method returns the SQL datatype of the given column.

The CWM Relational Package

Now that we know how to access various relational meta data using JDBC, next we will discuss the CWM Relational package. This package defines what relational meta data can be interchanged using CWM and what their structures and semantics are. In doing so, along the way, we will also show the Java Meta Data Interface (JMI) mappings of the CWM Relational package. The JMI mappings provide Java interfaces for constructing and manipulating CWM Relational meta objects (that is, objects that represent meta data). As such, they can conveniently serve as the intermediary when accessing relational meta data using JDBC and exporting relational meta data using CWM, as we will discuss in the next section.

The CWM Relational package and its dependent packages are shown in Figure 5.6. It can be seen that the Relational package depends on the following packages:

Object Model layer: Core, Behavior, Instance

Foundation layer: DataTypes, KeyIndexes

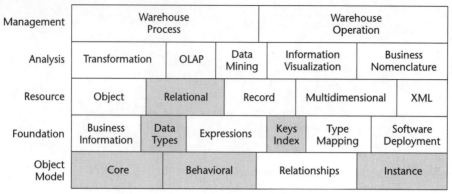

Management	Warehouse Process			Warehouse Operation	
Analysis	Transformation	OLAP	Data Mining	Information Visualization	Business Nomenclature
Resource	Object	Relational	Record	Multidimensional	XML
Foundation	Business Information	Data Types	Expressions	Keys Index	Type Mapping	Software Deployment
Object Model	Core		Behavioral	Relationships	Instance

Figure 5.6 CWM Relational and dependent packages.

This dependency is explicitly illustrated in the class inheritance diagram shown in Figures 5.7 and 5.8. It can be seen that the Relational package depends on the following classes:

Core package: ModelElement, Package, Classifier, Class, DataType, Attribute, Constraint

Behavior package: Method, Parameter

Instance package: Extent, Instance, DataValue, Object, Slot

DataTypes package: TypeAlias

KeyIndexes package: UniqueKey, KeyRelationship, Index, IndexedFeature

CWM Relational Dependent Classes and JMI Mappings

In the following, we will first discuss the CWM Relational dependent classes and their JMI mappings. This is necessary in order to understand the CWM Relational classes and their JMI mappings.

Exporting Relational Meta Data Using CWM

We have gone over a lot of material in order to get ready to discuss how to export relational meta data using CWM. We are now ready, but before we do so, let us summarize what we have done so far:

- We gave a brief description of the exemplar operational data store, CwmOds, which we will use for illustration.

- We discussed how to use JDBC to access and extract relational meta data.

- We discussed the CWM Relational package and its dependent packages, which define what relational meta data can be interchanged using CWM and what their structures and semantics are. In doing so, we also showed their JMI mappings, which provide Java interfaces for constructing and manipulating CWM Relational and dependent meta objects.

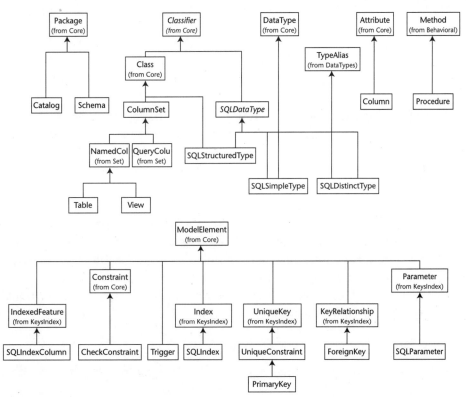

Figure 5.7   CWM Relational package inheritance.

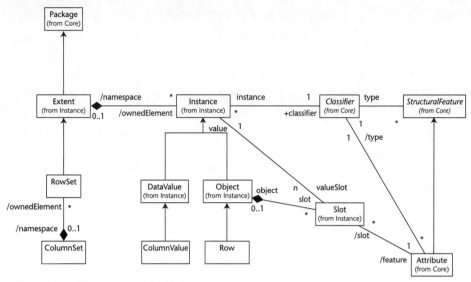

Figure 5.8 CWM Relational instance classes.

In the following discussions, we will assume that a generic tool is available to take a group of JMI meta objects and export them in proper XML Meta Data Interchange (XMI) format. Therefore, the code fragments we will show only deal with constructing JMI meta objects and not with the final XMI export. (We will, nevertheless, at the end show sample CWM XMI files generated from exporting the meta data contained in CwmOds.)

Please note that the code fragments provided below are for illustration purposes only. While attempts have been made to ensure their correctness and consistency, they may not be executable as is or combined as is. Also, for convenience, no exception-handling code is provided.

To access relational meta data using JDBC, we will first make a JDBC connection to the database (e.g., CwmOds):

```
Connection con = DriverManager.getConnection(url)
```

The URL above points to the database (e.g., jdbc:db2:cwmods). In addition, we will assume that we have obtained a reference to a JMI Relational meta object server that implements the RelationalPackage interface:

```
RelationalPackage relPkg = <obtain reference to a JMI Relational
    meta object server>
```

Simple Type

The first thing we will export is the SQL simple type meta data. There are two reasons why we want to do this first:

- We need them when exporting, for example, column meta data.
- They are not owned by any other relational meta data. This is because SQL simple types are independent of any database and/or catalog or schema.

But before we can do so, however, we must first obtain access to the database meta data object:

```
DatabaseMetaData dbmd = con.getMetaData();
```

With this object in hand, we can export the SQL simple type meta data as follows:

```
Vector dtv = new Vector();
ResultSet rs = _dbmd.getTypeInfo();
while (rs.next())
{
    SQLSimpleType type = relPkg.getSQLSimpleType().
createSQLSimpleType();
    type.setName(rs.getString(1));
    type.setTypeNumber(rs.getInt(2));

    dtv.addElement(type);
}
```

In the above, please note:

- Since there is more than one SQL simple type, we have used a vector to collect all exported SQL simple type meta objects.
- We have chosen not to export optional meta data such as character-MaximumLength. If it is important to do so, the code segment must be modified accordingly.

Catalog and Schema

Now we are ready to export all other relational meta data. Starting from the top, we will first export the catalog meta data as follows:

```
String catName = con.getCatalog();
Catalog cat = relPkg.getCatalog().createCatalog();
cat.setName(catName);
```

In the above, please note:

- We have used the getCatalog() method on the Connection interface since it is applicable to all database products, as we have discussed previously. The assumption made here and in the following discussion is that only one catalog exists for a given JDBC connection.

- We have chosen not to export optional meta data such as default-CharacterSetName. If it is important to do so, the code segment must be modified accordingly.

Next we will export the schema meta data, as follows:

```
Vector sv = new Vector();
ResultSet rs = dbmd.getSchemas();
while (rs.next())
{
    String schName = rs.getString(1);
    Schema sch = relPkg.getSchema().createSchema();
    sch.setName(schName);

    // export meta data (e.g., table) owned by the schema here

    sv.addElement(sch);
}
```

In the above, please note:

- Since there may be more than one schema in the catalog, we have used a vector to collect all exported schema meta objects. The assumption made here is that we are interested in exporting all schema meta data in the catalog. If we are interested in exporting only certain schema meta data (e.g., a schema with a given name), the code segment must be modified accordingly.

- We have reserved a place for exporting meta data (e.g., table) owned by the schema. The actual code for doing so will be discussed in the following sections.

Since schema meta data is owned by the catalog (or in CWM terms, the Schema class is owned by the Catalog class), we must associate the schema meta objects with the catalog meta objects as follows:

```
for (int j = 0; j < sv.size(); j++)
{
    Schema sch = (Schema) sv.elementAt(j);
    cat.addOwnedElement(sch);
    sch.addNamespace(cat);
}
```

Table and Column

Among the meta data owned by the schema, we will first export the table
meta data as follows:

```
Vector tiv = new Vector();
Result rs = dbmd.getTables(null, schName, null, "TABLE");
while (rs.next())
{
    String tabName = rs.getString(3);
    Table tab = relPkg.gettable().createTable();
    tab.setName(tabName);

    // export column meta data owned by the table

    Vector cv = new Vector();
    ResultSet rs2 = dbmd.getColumns(null, schName, tabName, null);
    while (rs2.next())
    {
        Column col = relPkg.getColumn().createColumn();
        col.setName(rs2.getString(4));
        col.setLength(rs2.getInt(7));
        int ctn = rs2.getInt(5);

        for (int j = 0; j < dtv.size(); j++)
        {
            SQLSimpleType type = (SQLSimpleType) dtv.elementAt(j);
            if (type.getTypeNumber() == ctn)
            {
                col.addType(type);
                break;
            }
        }

        tab.addFeature(col);
        col.addOwner(tab);

        cv.addElement(col);
    }

    // export other meta data (e.g., primary key) owned by the table
    // which references the table here

    tiv.addElement(tab);
}
```

`or`

In the above, please note:

- Since there may be more than one table in the schema, we have used
  a vector to collect all exported table meta objects. The assumption

made here is that we are interested in exporting all table meta data in the schema. If we are interested in exporting only certain table meta data (e.g., a table with a given name), the code segment must be modified accordingly.

- We have chosen to export meta data only for base tables. If we are interested in exporting other types of tables (e.g., view), the code segment must be modified accordingly.

- Since there may be more than one column in a table, we have used a vector to collect all exported column meta objects. The assumption made here is that we are interested in exporting all column meta data in a given table. If we are interested in exporting only certain column meta data (e.g., a column with a given name), the code segment must be modified accordingly.

- We have chosen to export only certain meta data (e.g., name) for columns. If we are interested in exporting other types of meta data (e.g., system isNullable), the code segment must be modified accordingly.

- We have used the SQL simple types meta objects exported earlier to associate a column meta object with its corresponding SQL simple type meta object.

- Since column meta data is owned by the table, we have associated all column meta objects with their owning table meta object.

- We have reserved a place for exporting meta data (e.g., primary key) which is owned by the table or which references the table. The actual code for doing so will be discussed in the following section.

Since table meta data is owned by the schema, we must associate the table meta objects with the schema meta objects as follows:

```
for (int j = 0; j < tiv.size(); j++)
{
    ModelElement tabInd = (ModelElement)tiv.elementAt(j);
    sch.addOwnedElement(tabInd);
    tabInd.addNamespace(sch);
}
```

Primary and Foreign Keys

We will continue by exporting primary and foreign keys meta data owned by each table as follows:

```
// export primary key meta data owned by the table
```

```
Vector pkv = new Vector();
PrimaryKey pk = null;
ResultSet rs2 = dbmd.getPrimaryKeys(null, schName, tabName);
while (rs2.next())
{
    if (pk == null)
    {
        pk = relPkg.getPrimaryKeys().createPrimaryKey();
    }
    pk.setName(rs2.getString(6));
    String cn = rs2.getString(4);

    for (int j = 0; j < cv.size(); j++)
    {
        Column col = (Column) cv.elementAt(j);
        if (col.getName().equals(cn))
        {
            pk.addFeature(col);
            break;
        }
    }
}


if (pk != null)
{
    tab.addOwnedElement(pk);
    pk.addNamespace(tab);

    pkv.addElement(pk);
}

// export foreign key meta data owned by the table

Vector fkv = new Vector();
Vector pknv = new Vector();
String pkn = null;
ForeignKey fk = null;
ResultSet rs2 = dbmd.getImportedKeys(null, schName, tabName);
while (rs2.next())
{
    String fkn = rs2.getString(12);

    if (fk == null)
    {
        fk = relPkg.getForeignKey().createForeignKey();
    }          }
    else if (!fk.getName().equals(fkn))
    {
        tab.addOwnedElement(fk);
        fk.addNamespace(tab);

        fkv.addElement(fk);
```

```
                pknv.addElement(pkn);

                fk = relPkg.getForeignKey().createForeignKey();
            }

            fk.setName(fkn);
            pkn = rs2.getString(13);
            String cn = rs2.getString(8);

            for (int j = 0; j < cv.size(); j++)
            {
                Column col = (Column) cv.elementAt(j);
                if (col.getName().equals(cn))
                {
                    fk.addFeature(col);
                    break;
                }
            }
        }

        if (fk != null)
        {
            tab.addOwnedElement(fk);
            fk.addNamespace(tab);

            fkv.addElement(fk);
            pknv.addElement(pkn);
        }
```

In the above, please note:

- Since there may be more than one primary key in a table, we have used a vector to collect all exported primary key meta objects.

- We have used the column meta objects exported earlier to associate primary key meta objects with their corresponding column meta objects.

- Since primary key meta data is owned by the table, we have associated all primary key meta objects with their owning table meta objects.

- Since there may be more than one foreign key in a table, we have used a vector to collect all exported foreign key meta objects.

- We have used the column meta objects exported earlier to associate foreign key meta objects with their corresponding column meta objects.

- Since foreign key meta data is owned by the table, we have associated all foreign key meta objects with their owning table meta objects.

We have used a vector to collect all primary key names referenced by the foreign keys. We will need this later to associate each foreign key with its corresponding primary key.

Since the foreign key of a table generally references the primary key of a different table, we must wait until we have completed constructing all table meta objects, and therefore all primary key meta objects, before we can associate each foreign key with its corresponding primary key as follows:

```
for (int i = 0; i < fkv.size(); i++)
{
    ForeignKey fk = (ForeignKey) fkv.elementAt(i);
    String pkn = (String) pknv.elementAt(i);

    for (int j = 0; j < pkv.size(); j++)
    {
        PrimaryKey pk = (PrimaryKey) pkv.elementAt(j);
        if (pkn.equals(pk.getName()))
         {
            fk.addUniqueKey(pk);
            pk.addKeyRelationship(fk);
            break;
        }
    }
}
```

In the above, please note that we used three vectors built earlier to facilitate the matching between foreign keys and primary keys: foreign key vector, primary key name vector, and primary key vector.

Index

In CWM, index meta data is owned by the schema. We can export it as follows:

```
// export index meta data for each table

SQLIndex index = null;
ResultSet rs2 = _dbmd.getIndexInfo(null, schemaName, tabName, false,
true);
while(rs2.next())
{
    String indexName = rs2.getString(6);
    if (indexName == null)continue;

    if (index == null)
    {
        index = relPkg.getSQLIndex().createSQLIndex();
        index.addSpannedClass(tab);
    }
```

```
            else if (!index.getName().equals(indexName))
            {
                tiv.addElement(index);

                index = relPkg.getSQLIndex().createSQLIndex();
                index.addSpannedClass(tab);
            }

            index.setName(indexName);
            String cn = rs2.getString(9);

            for (int j = 0; j < cv.size(); j++)
            {
                Column col = (Column) cv.elementAt(j);
                if (col.getName().equals(cn))
                 {
                     SQLIndexColumn idxCol=
                         relPkg.getSQLIndexColumn().createSQLIndexColumn();
                     index.addIndexedFeature(idxCol);
                     idxCol.addIndex(index);
                     idxCol.addFeature(col);

                     break;
                 }
            }

        }

        if (index != null)
        {
            tiv.addElement(index);
        }
```

In the above, please note:

■ Since index meta data is owned by the schema, we have used the same vector that we used to collect table meta objects to collect index meta objects. (This is why we have named the vector *tiv*.)

Since index meta data is owned by the schema, we must associate the index meta objects with the schema meta objects. However, this is the same code as has been used previously for associating table meta objects with the schema meta objects (this is why we have named the model element *tabInd*):

```
    for (int j = 0; j < tiv.size(); j++)
    {
        ModelElement tabInd = (ModelElement)tiv.elementAt(j);
        sch.addOwnedElement(tabInd);
        tabInd.addNamespace(sch);
    }
```

Types of Meta Data Not Exported

The exemplar operational data store, CwmOds, does not contain the following features:

- Check constraint
- View
- Distinct type
- Structured type
- User-defined function
- Stored procedure and parameter
- Trigger

As a result, we need not be concerned about exporting any of the above types of meta data.

The CWM XMI File

Assuming the existence of a generic tool that can take a group of JMI meta objects and serialize them in proper XMI format, the final CWM XMI file produced when exporting the meta data of CwmOds is shown in Figure 5.9.

```
<?xml version="1.0" encoding="UTF-8"?>
<!DOCTYPE XMI SYSTEM "CWM_1.0.dtd" [
<!ELEMENT ixafs (ixaftv)+ >
<!ATTLIST ixafs
            n CDATA #REQUIRED
>
<!ELEMENT ixaftv EMPTY >
<!ATTLIST ixaftv
            t CDATA #REQUIRED
            v CDATA #REQUIRED
>]>
<XMI xmi.version="1.1" timestamp="Tue May 21 20:20:46 PDT 2002"
xmlns:CWMRDB="org.omg.CWM1.0/Relational" xmlns:CWM="org.omg.CWM1.0">
  <XMI.header>
    <XMI.documentation>
      <XMI.exporter>XMI Application Framework</XMI.exporter>
      <XMI.exporterVersion>1.15</XMI.exporterVersion>
    </XMI.documentation>
  </XMI.header>
  <XMI.content>
```

Figure 5.9 CwmOdsCatalog.xml. *(continues)*

```
    <CWMRDB:Catalog xmi.id="_1" name="CWMODS">
      <CWM:Namespace.ownedElement>
        <CWMRDB:Schema xmi.id="_1.1" name="CWM" namespace="_1">
          <CWM:Namespace.ownedElement>
            <CWMRDB:Table xmi.id="_1.1.1" name="PRODUCT"
namespace="_1.1">
              <CWM:Classifier.feature>
                <CWMRDB:Column xmi.id="_1.1.1.1" name="PRODUCT_ID"
length="10"
                    type="_11" owner="_1.1.1"/>
                <CWMRDB:Column xmi.id="_1.1.1.2" name="PRICE"
length="15"
                    type="_15" owner="_1.1.1"/>
                <CWMRDB:Column xmi.id="_1.1.1.3" name="COST" length="15"
                    type="_15" owner="_1.1.1"/>
                <CWMRDB:Column xmi.id="_1.1.1.4" name="DESCRIPTION"
length="128"
                    type="_19" owner="_1.1.1"/>
                <CWMRDB:Column xmi.id="_1.1.1.5" name="PROD_SIZE"
length="7"
                    type="_19" owner="_1.1.1"/>
                <CWMRDB:Column xmi.id="_1.1.1.6" name="COLOR"
length="32"
                    type="_19" owner="_1.1.1"/>
                <CWMRDB:Column xmi.id="_1.1.1.7" name="BRAND"
length="64"
                    type="_19" owner="_1.1.1"/>
                <CWMRDB:Column xmi.id="_1.1.1.8" name="DEPARTMENT"
length="64"
                    type="_19" owner="_1.1.1"/>
                <CWMRDB:Column xmi.id="_1.1.1.9" name="CATEGORY"
length="32"
                    type="_19" owner="_1.1.1"/>
              </CWM:Classifier.feature>
              <CWM:Namespace.ownedElement>
                <CWMRDB:PrimaryKey xmi.id="_1.1.1.10"
name="SQL020428133231090"
                    feature="_1.1.1.1" namespace="_1.1.1"
                    keyRelationship="_1.1.3.7"/>
              </CWM:Namespace.ownedElement>
            </CWMRDB:Table>
            <CWMRDB:SQLIndex xmi.id="_1.1.2" name="SQL020428133230920"
                spannedClass="_1.1.1" namespace="_1.1">
              <CWM:Index.indexedFeature>
                <CWMRDB:SQLIndexColumn xmi.id="_1.1.2.1" index="_1.1.2"
                    feature="_1.1.1.1"/>
              </CWM:Index.indexedFeature>
            </CWMRDB:SQLIndex>
```

Figure 5.9 CwmOdsCatalog.xml. *(continued)*

```
            <CWMRDB:Table xmi.id="_1.1.3" name="SALES" namespace="_1.1">
              <CWM:Classifier.feature>
                <CWMRDB:Column xmi.id="_1.1.3.1" name="STORE_ID"
length="10"
                    type="_11" owner="_1.1.3"/>
                <CWMRDB:Column xmi.id="_1.1.3.2" name="PRODUCT_ID"
length="10"
                    type="_11" owner="_1.1.3"/>
                <CWMRDB:Column xmi.id="_1.1.3.3" name="QUANTITY"
length="10"
                    type="_11" owner="_1.1.3"/>
                <CWMRDB:Column xmi.id="_1.1.3.4" name="REVENUE"
length="15"
                    type="_15" owner="_1.1.3"/>
                <CWMRDB:Column xmi.id="_1.1.3.5" name="COST" length="15"
                    type="_15" owner="_1.1.3"/>
                <CWMRDB:Column xmi.id="_1.1.3.6" name="DATE" length="32"
                    type="_19" owner="_1.1.3"/>
              </CWM:Classifier.feature>
              <CWM:Namespace.ownedElement>
                <CWMRDB:ForeignKey xmi.id="_1.1.3.7"
name="SQL020428133231171"
                    feature="_1.1.3.2" namespace="_1.1.3"
uniqueKey="_1.1.1.10"/>
                <CWMRDB:ForeignKey xmi.id="_1.1.3.8"
name="SQL020428133231170"
                    feature="_1.1.3.1" namespace="_1.1.3"
uniqueKey="_1.1.4.5"/>
              </CWM:Namespace.ownedElement>
            </CWMRDB:Table>
            <CWMRDB:Table xmi.id="_1.1.4" name="STORE" namespace="_1.1">
              <CWM:Classifier.feature>
                <CWMRDB:Column xmi.id="_1.1.4.1" name="STORE_ID"
length="10"
                    type="_11" owner="_1.1.4"/>
                <CWMRDB:Column xmi.id="_1.1.4.2" name="NAME"
length="128"
                    type="_19" owner="_1.1.4"/>
                <CWMRDB:Column xmi.id="_1.1.4.3" name="CITY" length="80"
                    type="_19" owner="_1.1.4"/>
                <CWMRDB:Column xmi.id="_1.1.4.4" name="STATE" length="2"
                    type="_8" owner="_1.1.4"/>
              </CWM:Classifier.feature>
              <CWM:Namespace.ownedElement>
                <CWMRDB:PrimaryKey xmi.id="_1.1.4.5"
name="SQL020428133230850"
                    feature="_1.1.4.1" namespace="_1.1.4"
                    keyRelationship="_1.1.3.8"/>
```

Figure 5.9   CwmOdsCatalog.xml. *(continues)*

```
                </CWM:Namespace.ownedElement>
            </CWMRDB:Table>
            <CWMRDB:SQLIndex xmi.id="_1.1.5" name="SQL020428133230660"
                spannedClass="_1.1.4" namespace="_1.1">
              <CWM:Index.indexedFeature>
                <CWMRDB:SQLIndexColumn xmi.id="_1.1.5.1" index="_1.1.5"
                    feature="_1.1.4.1"/>
              </CWM:Index.indexedFeature>
            </CWMRDB:SQLIndex>
          </CWM:Namespace.ownedElement>
        </CWMRDB:Schema>
        <CWMRDB:Schema xmi.id="_1.2" name="SYSCAT" namespace="_1"/>
        <CWMRDB:Schema xmi.id="_1.3" name="SYSIBM" namespace="_1"/>
        <CWMRDB:Schema xmi.id="_1.4" name="SYSSTAT" namespace="_1"/>
      </CWM:Namespace.ownedElement>
    </CWMRDB:Catalog>
    <CWMRDB:SQLSimpleType xmi.id="_2" name="BLOB" typeNumber="1111"/>
    <CWMRDB:SQLSimpleType xmi.id="_3" name="CLOB" typeNumber="1111"/>
    <CWMRDB:SQLSimpleType xmi.id="_4" name="LONG VARCHAR FOR BIT DATA"
        typeNumber="-4"/>
    <CWMRDB:SQLSimpleType xmi.id="_5"
        name="VARCHAR () FOR BIT DATA" typeNumber="-3"/>
    <CWMRDB:SQLSimpleType xmi.id="_6" name="CHARacter () FOR BIT DATA"
        typeNumber="-2"/>
    <CWMRDB:SQLSimpleType xmi.id="_7" name="LONG VARCHAR" typeNumber="-
1"/>
    <CWMRDB:SQLSimpleType xmi.id="_8" name="CHARacter" typeNumber="1"/>
    <CWMRDB:SQLSimpleType xmi.id="_9" name="NUMeric" typeNumber="2"/>
    <CWMRDB:SQLSimpleType xmi.id="_10" name="DECimal" typeNumber="3"/>
    <CWMRDB:SQLSimpleType xmi.id="_11" name="INTeger" typeNumber="4"/>
    <CWMRDB:SQLSimpleType xmi.id="_12" name="SMALLINT" typeNumber="5"/>
    <CWMRDB:SQLSimpleType xmi.id="_13" name="FLOAT" typeNumber="6"/>
    <CWMRDB:SQLSimpleType xmi.id="_14" name="REAL" typeNumber="7"/>
    <CWMRDB:SQLSimpleType xmi.id="_15" name="FLOAT" typeNumber="8"/>
    <CWMRDB:SQLSimpleType xmi.id="_16" name="DATE" typeNumber="91"/>
    <CWMRDB:SQLSimpleType xmi.id="_17" name="TIME" typeNumber="92"/>
    <CWMRDB:SQLSimpleType xmi.id="_18" name="TIMESTAMP"
typeNumber="93"/>
    <CWMRDB:SQLSimpleType xmi.id="_19" name="VARCHAR" typeNumber="12"/>
    <CWMRDB:SQLSimpleType xmi.id="_20" name="DATALINK"
typeNumber="1111"/>
    <CWMRDB:SQLSimpleType xmi.id="_21" name="BIGINT" typeNumber="-5"/>
  </XMI.content>
</XMI>
```

Figure 5.9   CwmOdsCatalog.xml. *(continued)*

Exporting Relational Data Using CWM

Even though CWM can be used to export relational data, it is not well suited to do so. You will see that the exported CWM XMI file is quite convoluted and very verbose. This is partly due to the fact that the CWM ObjectModel (and really the UML Metamodel from which the CWM ObjectModel is derived) treats primitive values (e.g., 3) as objects and every instance of a primitive value as a distinct object. Therefore, CWM should only be used to export small amounts of relational data, e.g., sample data. Please note that this caution applies to all types of data (e.g., record-based), not just relational data.

To access relational data using JDBC, we will again first make a JDBC connection to the database (e.g., CwmOds):

```
Connection con = DriverManager.getConnection(url)
```

The url in the above points to the database (e.g., jdbc:db2:cwmods). We will then execute a SQL query against the database and obtain a result set:

```
Statement stmt = con.createStatement();
Result rs = stmt.executeQuery(query);
```

In addition, we will assume that we have obtained references to the following JMI meta object servers that implement various CWM package interfaces:

```
DataTypesPackage dtPkg = <obtain reference to a JMI DataTypes
    meta object server>
InstancePackage instPkg = <obtain reference to a JMI Instance
    meta object server>
RelationalPackage relPkg = <obtain reference to a JMI Relational
    meta object server>
```

QueryColumnSet

When exporting relational data, it is important to also export the associated meta data so that the exported data is self-describing and can be understood and processed as is, without the need to obtain the meta data separately. This is done by exporting the meta data of the result set using QueryColumnSet:

```
        Vector v = new Vector();

        ResultSetMetaData rsmd = rs.getMetaData();

        QueryColumnSet sqlq =
relPkg.getQueryColumnSet().createQueryColumnSet();

        QueryExpression qe =
dtPkg.getQueryExpression().createQueryExpression;
        qe.setLanguage("SQL");
        qe.setBody(query);
        sqlq.setQuery(qe);

        int cc = rsmd.getColumnCount();
        Vector cv = new Vector();
        for (int i = 1; i <= cc; i++)
        {
            Column col = relPkg.getColumn().createColumn();
            col.setName(rsmd.getColumnName(i));
            int ct = rsmd.getColumnType(i);

            for (int j = 0; j < dtv.size(); j++)
            {
                SQLSimpleType type = (SQLSimpleType) dtv.elementAt(j);
                if (type.getTypeNumber() == ct)
                 {
                    col.addType(type);
                    break;
                }
            }

            sqlq.addFeature(col);
            col.addOwner(sqlq);

            cv.addElement(col);
        }

        v.addElement(sqlq);
```

In the above, please note:

- We have used a vector to collect the QueryColumnSet meta object. (We will use the same vector later to collect the RowSet and ColumnValue meta objects.)

- We assume that the SQL simple types meta objects have been exported (as we have done previously when we exported the relational meta data) and, therefore, we have used them to associate a column meta object with its corresponding SQL simple type meta object.

RowSet, Row, and ColumnValue

Next we will export the data of the result set using RowSet, Row, and ColumnValue as follows:

```
Vector cvv = new Vector();

RowSet rowset = relPkg.getRowSet().createRowSet();
while (rs.next())
{
    Row row = relPkg.getRow().createRow();
    row.addClassifier(sqlq);

    for(int i = 1; i <= cc; i++)
    {
        Slot sl = instPkg.getSlot().createSlot();
         sl.addObject(row);
        row.addSlot(sl);

        sl.addFeature((Column) cv.elementAt(i-1));


        // data value
        java.lang.Object obj = rs.getObject(i);
        if (obj != null)
         {
            String val = obj.toString();
            ColumnValue cval =
relPkg.getColumnValue().createColumnValue();
            cval.setValue(val);

            sl.addValue(cval);
            cvv.addElement(cval);
        }
    }

    rowset.addOwnedElement(row);
    row.addNamespace(rowset);
}

v.addElement(rowset);
v.addAll(cvv);
```

In the above, please note:

As promised, we have used the same vector to collect the RowSet and ColumnValue meta objects.

The Row, Column, and ColumnValue meta objects are connected to each other through the Slot meta object. That is, a Row owns Slots and each Slot is associated with a Column and ColumnValue. By the way, Rows are owned by a RowSet.

The CWM XMI File

Assuming the existence of a generic tool that can take a group of JMI meta objects and serialize them in proper XMI format, the final CWM XMI file produced when exporting some sample data (and associated meta data) of CwmOds is shown in Figure 5.10.

```
<?xml version="1.0" encoding="UTF-8"?>
<!DOCTYPE XMI SYSTEM "CWM_1.0.dtd" [
<!ELEMENT ixafs (ixaftv)+ >
<!ATTLIST ixafs
          n CDATA #REQUIRED
>
<!ELEMENT ixaftv EMPTY >
<!ATTLIST ixaftv
          t CDATA #REQUIRED
          v CDATA #REQUIRED
>]>
<XMI xmi.version="1.1" timestamp="Thu Jun 06 10:29:03 PDT 2002"
xmlns:CWMRDB="org.omg.CWM1.0/Relational" xmlns:CWM="org.omg.CWM1.0">
  <XMI.header>
    <XMI.documentation>
      <XMI.exporter>XMI Application Framework</XMI.exporter>
      <XMI.exporterVersion>1.15</XMI.exporterVersion>
    </XMI.documentation>
  </XMI.header>
  <XMI.content>
    <CWMRDB:QueryColumnSet xmi.id="_1">
      <CWMRDB:QueryColumnSet.query>
        <CWM:QueryExpression xmi.id="_1.1" language="SQL" body="SELECT
name, city, state, description, brand,        quantity, revenue,
Sales.cost, date FROM Store, Product, Sales WHERE Store.store_id =
Sales.store_id AND        Product.product_id = Sales.product_id AND
city = 'Boston' AND Sales.date = '1/1/1999'"/>
      </CWMRDB:QueryColumnSet.query>
      <CWM:Classifier.feature>
        <CWMRDB:Column xmi.id="_1.2" name="NAME" type="_110"
owner="_1"/>
        <CWMRDB:Column xmi.id="_1.3" name="CITY" type="_110"
owner="_1"/>
        <CWMRDB:Column xmi.id="_1.4" name="STATE" type="_99"
owner="_1"/>
        <CWMRDB:Column xmi.id="_1.5" name="DESCRIPTION" type="_110"
owner="_1"/>
        <CWMRDB:Column xmi.id="_1.6" name="BRAND" type="_110"
owner="_1"/>
        <CWMRDB:Column xmi.id="_1.7" name="QUANTITY" type="_102"
owner="_1"/>
```

Figure 5.10 CwmOdsResultSet.xml.

```
        <CWMRDB:Column xmi.id="_1.8" name="REVENUE" type="_106"
owner="_1"/>
        <CWMRDB:Column xmi.id="_1.9" name="COST" type="_106"
owner="_1"/>
        <CWMRDB:Column xmi.id="_1.10" name="DATE" type="_110"
owner="_1"/>
      </CWM:Classifier.feature>
    </CWMRDB:QueryColumnSet>
    <CWMRDB:RowSet xmi.id="_2">
      <CWM:Namespace.ownedElement>
        <CWMRDB:Row xmi.id="_2.1" classifier="_1" namespace="_2">
          <CWM:Object.slot>
            <CWM:Slot xmi.id="_2.1.1" object="_2.1" feature="_1.2"
value="_3"/>
            <CWM:Slot xmi.id="_2.1.2" object="_2.1" feature="_1.3"
value="_4"/>
            <CWM:Slot xmi.id="_2.1.3" object="_2.1" feature="_1.4"
value="_5"/>
            <CWM:Slot xmi.id="_2.1.4" object="_2.1" feature="_1.5"
value="_6"/>
            <CWM:Slot xmi.id="_2.1.5" object="_2.1" feature="_1.6"
value="_7"/>
            <CWM:Slot xmi.id="_2.1.6" object="_2.1" feature="_1.7"
value="_8"/>
            <CWM:Slot xmi.id="_2.1.7" object="_2.1" feature="_1.8"
value="_9"/>
            <CWM:Slot xmi.id="_2.1.8" object="_2.1" feature="_1.9"
value="_10"/>
            <CWM:Slot xmi.id="_2.1.9" object="_2.1" feature="_1.10"
value="_11"/>
          </CWM:Object.slot>
        </CWMRDB:Row>
        <CWMRDB:Row xmi.id="_2.2" classifier="_1" namespace="_2">
          <CWM:Object.slot>
            <CWM:Slot xmi.id="_2.2.1" object="_2.2" feature="_1.2"
value="_12"/>
            <CWM:Slot xmi.id="_2.2.2" object="_2.2" feature="_1.3"
value="_13"/>
            <CWM:Slot xmi.id="_2.2.3" object="_2.2" feature="_1.4"
value="_14"/>
            <CWM:Slot xmi.id="_2.2.4" object="_2.2" feature="_1.5"
value="_15"/>
            <CWM:Slot xmi.id="_2.2.5" object="_2.2" feature="_1.6"
value="_16"/>
            <CWM:Slot xmi.id="_2.2.6" object="_2.2" feature="_1.7"
value="_17"/>
            <CWM:Slot xmi.id="_2.2.7" object="_2.2" feature="_1.8"
value="_18"/>
```

Figure 5.10 CwmOdsResultSet.xml. *(continues)*

```
            <CWM:Slot xmi.id="_2.2.8" object="_2.2" feature="_1.9"
value="_19"/>
            <CWM:Slot xmi.id="_2.2.9" object="_2.2" feature="_1.10"
value="_20"/>
          </CWM:Object.slot>
        </CWMRDB:Row>
        <CWMRDB:Row xmi.id="_2.3" classifier="_1" namespace="_2">
          <CWM:Object.slot>
            <CWM:Slot xmi.id="_2.3.1" object="_2.3" feature="_1.2"
value="_21"/>
            <CWM:Slot xmi.id="_2.3.2" object="_2.3" feature="_1.3"
value="_22"/>
            <CWM:Slot xmi.id="_2.3.3" object="_2.3" feature="_1.4"
value="_23"/>
            <CWM:Slot xmi.id="_2.3.4" object="_2.3" feature="_1.5"
value="_24"/>
            <CWM:Slot xmi.id="_2.3.5" object="_2.3" feature="_1.6"
value="_25"/>
            <CWM:Slot xmi.id="_2.3.6" object="_2.3" feature="_1.7"
value="_26"/>
            <CWM:Slot xmi.id="_2.3.7" object="_2.3" feature="_1.8"
value="_27"/>
            <CWM:Slot xmi.id="_2.3.8" object="_2.3" feature="_1.9"
value="_28"/>
            <CWM:Slot xmi.id="_2.3.9" object="_2.3" feature="_1.10"
value="_29"/>
          </CWM:Object.slot>
        </CWMRDB:Row>
        <CWMRDB:Row xmi.id="_2.4" classifier="_1" namespace="_2">
          <CWM:Object.slot>
            <CWM:Slot xmi.id="_2.4.1" object="_2.4" feature="_1.2"
value="_30"/>
            <CWM:Slot xmi.id="_2.4.2" object="_2.4" feature="_1.3"
value="_31"/>
            <CWM:Slot xmi.id="_2.4.3" object="_2.4" feature="_1.4"
value="_32"/>
            <CWM:Slot xmi.id="_2.4.4" object="_2.4" feature="_1.5"
value="_33"/>
            <CWM:Slot xmi.id="_2.4.5" object="_2.4" feature="_1.6"
value="_34"/>
            <CWM:Slot xmi.id="_2.4.6" object="_2.4" feature="_1.7"
value="_35"/>
            <CWM:Slot xmi.id="_2.4.7" object="_2.4" feature="_1.8"
value="_36"/>
            <CWM:Slot xmi.id="_2.4.8" object="_2.4" feature="_1.9"
value="_37"/>
            <CWM:Slot xmi.id="_2.4.9" object="_2.4" feature="_1.10"
value="_38"/>
          </CWM:Object.slot>
```

Figure 5.10 CwmOdsResultSet.xml. *(continued)*

```
          </CWMRDB:Row>
        <CWMRDB:Row xmi.id="_2.5" classifier="_1" namespace="_2">
          <CWM:Object.slot>
            <CWM:Slot xmi.id="_2.5.1" object="_2.5" feature="_1.2"
value="_39"/>
            <CWM:Slot xmi.id="_2.5.2" object="_2.5" feature="_1.3"
value="_40"/>
            <CWM:Slot xmi.id="_2.5.3" object="_2.5" feature="_1.4"
value="_41"/>
            <CWM:Slot xmi.id="_2.5.4" object="_2.5" feature="_1.5"
value="_42"/>
            <CWM:Slot xmi.id="_2.5.5" object="_2.5" feature="_1.6"
value="_43"/>
            <CWM:Slot xmi.id="_2.5.6" object="_2.5" feature="_1.7"
value="_44"/>
            <CWM:Slot xmi.id="_2.5.7" object="_2.5" feature="_1.8"
value="_45"/>
            <CWM:Slot xmi.id="_2.5.8" object="_2.5" feature="_1.9"
value="_46"/>
            <CWM:Slot xmi.id="_2.5.9" object="_2.5" feature="_1.10"
value="_47"/>
          </CWM:Object.slot>
        </CWMRDB:Row>
        <CWMRDB:Row xmi.id="_2.6" classifier="_1" namespace="_2">
          <CWM:Object.slot>
            <CWM:Slot xmi.id="_2.6.1" object="_2.6" feature="_1.2"
value="_48"/>
            <CWM:Slot xmi.id="_2.6.2" object="_2.6" feature="_1.3"
value="_49"/>
            <CWM:Slot xmi.id="_2.6.3" object="_2.6" feature="_1.4"
value="_50"/>
            <CWM:Slot xmi.id="_2.6.4" object="_2.6" feature="_1.5"
value="_51"/>
            <CWM:Slot xmi.id="_2.6.5" object="_2.6" feature="_1.6"
value="_52"/>
            <CWM:Slot xmi.id="_2.6.6" object="_2.6" feature="_1.7"
value="_53"/>
            <CWM:Slot xmi.id="_2.6.7" object="_2.6" feature="_1.8"
value="_54"/>
            <CWM:Slot xmi.id="_2.6.8" object="_2.6" feature="_1.9"
value="_55"/>
            <CWM:Slot xmi.id="_2.6.9" object="_2.6" feature="_1.10"
value="_56"/>
          </CWM:Object.slot>
        </CWMRDB:Row>
        <CWMRDB:Row xmi.id="_2.7" classifier="_1" namespace="_2">
          <CWM:Object.slot>
            <CWM:Slot xmi.id="_2.7.1" object="_2.7" feature="_1.2"
value="_57"/>
```

Figure 5.10 CwmOdsResultSet.xml. *(continues)*

```
            <CWM:Slot xmi.id="_2.7.2" object="_2.7" feature="_1.3"
value="_58"/>
            <CWM:Slot xmi.id="_2.7.3" object="_2.7" feature="_1.4"
value="_59"/>
            <CWM:Slot xmi.id="_2.7.4" object="_2.7" feature="_1.5"
value="_60"/>
            <CWM:Slot xmi.id="_2.7.5" object="_2.7" feature="_1.6"
value="_61"/>
            <CWM:Slot xmi.id="_2.7.6" object="_2.7" feature="_1.7"
value="_62"/>
            <CWM:Slot xmi.id="_2.7.7" object="_2.7" feature="_1.8"
value="_63"/>
            <CWM:Slot xmi.id="_2.7.8" object="_2.7" feature="_1.9"
value="_64"/>
            <CWM:Slot xmi.id="_2.7.9" object="_2.7" feature="_1.10"
value="_65"/>
          </CWM:Object.slot>
        </CWMRDB:Row>
        <CWMRDB:Row xmi.id="_2.8" classifier="_1" namespace="_2">
          <CWM:Object.slot>
            <CWM:Slot xmi.id="_2.8.1" object="_2.8" feature="_1.2"
value="_66"/>
            <CWM:Slot xmi.id="_2.8.2" object="_2.8" feature="_1.3"
value="_67"/>
            <CWM:Slot xmi.id="_2.8.3" object="_2.8" feature="_1.4"
value="_68"/>
            <CWM:Slot xmi.id="_2.8.4" object="_2.8" feature="_1.5"
value="_69"/>
            <CWM:Slot xmi.id="_2.8.5" object="_2.8" feature="_1.6"
value="_70"/>
            <CWM:Slot xmi.id="_2.8.6" object="_2.8" feature="_1.7"
value="_71"/>
            <CWM:Slot xmi.id="_2.8.7" object="_2.8" feature="_1.8"
value="_72"/>
            <CWM:Slot xmi.id="_2.8.8" object="_2.8" feature="_1.9"
value="_73"/>
            <CWM:Slot xmi.id="_2.8.9" object="_2.8" feature="_1.10"
value="_74"/>
          </CWM:Object.slot>
        </CWMRDB:Row>
        <CWMRDB:Row xmi.id="_2.9" classifier="_1" namespace="_2">
          <CWM:Object.slot>
            <CWM:Slot xmi.id="_2.9.1" object="_2.9" feature="_1.2"
value="_75"/>
            <CWM:Slot xmi.id="_2.9.2" object="_2.9" feature="_1.3"
value="_76"/>
            <CWM:Slot xmi.id="_2.9.3" object="_2.9" feature="_1.4"
value="_77"/>
```

Figure 5.10 CwmOdsResultSet.xml. *(continued)*

```
            <CWM:Slot xmi.id="_2.9.4" object="_2.9" feature="_1.5"
value="_78"/>
            <CWM:Slot xmi.id="_2.9.5" object="_2.9" feature="_1.6"
value="_79"/>
            <CWM:Slot xmi.id="_2.9.6" object="_2.9" feature="_1.7"
value="_80"/>
            <CWM:Slot xmi.id="_2.9.7" object="_2.9" feature="_1.8"
value="_81"/>
            <CWM:Slot xmi.id="_2.9.8" object="_2.9" feature="_1.9"
value="_82"/>
            <CWM:Slot xmi.id="_2.9.9" object="_2.9" feature="_1.10"
value="_83"/>
          </CWM:Object.slot>
        </CWMRDB:Row>
        <CWMRDB:Row xmi.id="_2.10" classifier="_1" namespace="_2">
          <CWM:Object.slot>
            <CWM:Slot xmi.id="_2.10.1" object="_2.10" feature="_1.2"
value="_84"/>
            <CWM:Slot xmi.id="_2.10.2" object="_2.10" feature="_1.3"
value="_85"/>
            <CWM:Slot xmi.id="_2.10.3" object="_2.10" feature="_1.4"
value="_86"/>
            <CWM:Slot xmi.id="_2.10.4" object="_2.10" feature="_1.5"
value="_87"/>
            <CWM:Slot xmi.id="_2.10.5" object="_2.10" feature="_1.6"
value="_88"/>
            <CWM:Slot xmi.id="_2.10.6" object="_2.10" feature="_1.7"
value="_89"/>
            <CWM:Slot xmi.id="_2.10.7" object="_2.10" feature="_1.8"
value="_90"/>
            <CWM:Slot xmi.id="_2.10.8" object="_2.10" feature="_1.9"
value="_91"/>
            <CWM:Slot xmi.id="_2.10.9" object="_2.10" feature="_1.10"
value="_92"/>
          </CWM:Object.slot>
        </CWMRDB:Row>
      </CWM:Namespace.ownedElement>
    </CWMRDB:RowSet>
    <CWMRDB:ColumnValue xmi.id="_3" value="Store1"/>
    <CWMRDB:ColumnValue xmi.id="_4" value="Boston"/>
    <CWMRDB:ColumnValue xmi.id="_5" value="MA"/>
    <CWMRDB:ColumnValue xmi.id="_6" value="Tie"/>
    <CWMRDB:ColumnValue xmi.id="_7" value="BrandA"/>
    <CWMRDB:ColumnValue xmi.id="_8" value="3"/>
    <CWMRDB:ColumnValue xmi.id="_9" value="30.0"/>
    <CWMRDB:ColumnValue xmi.id="_10" value="24.0"/>
    <CWMRDB:ColumnValue xmi.id="_11" value="1/1/1999"/>
    <CWMRDB:ColumnValue xmi.id="_12" value="Store1"/>
```

Figure 5.10 CwmOdsResultSet.xml. *(continues)*

```
<CWMRDB:ColumnValue xmi.id="_13" value="Boston"/>
<CWMRDB:ColumnValue xmi.id="_14" value="MA"/>
<CWMRDB:ColumnValue xmi.id="_15" value="Sweatshirt"/>
<CWMRDB:ColumnValue xmi.id="_16" value="BrandA"/>
<CWMRDB:ColumnValue xmi.id="_17" value="2"/>
<CWMRDB:ColumnValue xmi.id="_18" value="64.0"/>
<CWMRDB:ColumnValue xmi.id="_19" value="54.0"/>
<CWMRDB:ColumnValue xmi.id="_20" value="1/1/1999"/>
<CWMRDB:ColumnValue xmi.id="_21" value="Store1"/>
<CWMRDB:ColumnValue xmi.id="_22" value="Boston"/>
<CWMRDB:ColumnValue xmi.id="_23" value="MA"/>
<CWMRDB:ColumnValue xmi.id="_24" value="Hat"/>
<CWMRDB:ColumnValue xmi.id="_25" value="BrandA"/>
<CWMRDB:ColumnValue xmi.id="_26" value="1"/>
<CWMRDB:ColumnValue xmi.id="_27" value="19.0"/>
<CWMRDB:ColumnValue xmi.id="_28" value="16.0"/>
<CWMRDB:ColumnValue xmi.id="_29" value="1/1/1999"/>
<CWMRDB:ColumnValue xmi.id="_30" value="Store2"/>
<CWMRDB:ColumnValue xmi.id="_31" value="Boston"/>
<CWMRDB:ColumnValue xmi.id="_32" value="MA"/>
<CWMRDB:ColumnValue xmi.id="_33" value="Sweatshirt"/>
<CWMRDB:ColumnValue xmi.id="_34" value="BrandA"/>
<CWMRDB:ColumnValue xmi.id="_35" value="3"/>
<CWMRDB:ColumnValue xmi.id="_36" value="96.0"/>
<CWMRDB:ColumnValue xmi.id="_37" value="81.0"/>
<CWMRDB:ColumnValue xmi.id="_38" value="1/1/1999"/>
<CWMRDB:ColumnValue xmi.id="_39" value="Store2"/>
<CWMRDB:ColumnValue xmi.id="_40" value="Boston"/>
<CWMRDB:ColumnValue xmi.id="_41" value="MA"/>
<CWMRDB:ColumnValue xmi.id="_42" value="Jacket"/>
<CWMRDB:ColumnValue xmi.id="_43" value="BrandA"/>
<CWMRDB:ColumnValue xmi.id="_44" value="1"/>
<CWMRDB:ColumnValue xmi.id="_45" value="45.0"/>
<CWMRDB:ColumnValue xmi.id="_46" value="37.0"/>
<CWMRDB:ColumnValue xmi.id="_47" value="1/1/1999"/>
<CWMRDB:ColumnValue xmi.id="_48" value="Store2"/>
<CWMRDB:ColumnValue xmi.id="_49" value="Boston"/>
<CWMRDB:ColumnValue xmi.id="_50" value="MA"/>
<CWMRDB:ColumnValue xmi.id="_51" value="Jacket"/>
<CWMRDB:ColumnValue xmi.id="_52" value="BrandB"/>
<CWMRDB:ColumnValue xmi.id="_53" value="1"/>
<CWMRDB:ColumnValue xmi.id="_54" value="38.0"/>
<CWMRDB:ColumnValue xmi.id="_55" value="33.0"/>
<CWMRDB:ColumnValue xmi.id="_56" value="1/1/1999"/>
<CWMRDB:ColumnValue xmi.id="_57" value="Store5"/>
<CWMRDB:ColumnValue xmi.id="_58" value="Boston"/>
<CWMRDB:ColumnValue xmi.id="_59" value="MA"/>
<CWMRDB:ColumnValue xmi.id="_60" value="Hat"/>
<CWMRDB:ColumnValue xmi.id="_61" value="BrandA"/>
```

Figure 5.10   CwmOdsResultSet.xml. *(continued)*

```
<CWMRDB:ColumnValue xmi.id="_62" value="2"/>
<CWMRDB:ColumnValue xmi.id="_63" value="38.0"/>
<CWMRDB:ColumnValue xmi.id="_64" value="32.0"/>
<CWMRDB:ColumnValue xmi.id="_65" value="1/1/1999"/>
<CWMRDB:ColumnValue xmi.id="_66" value="Store5"/>
<CWMRDB:ColumnValue xmi.id="_67" value="Boston"/>
<CWMRDB:ColumnValue xmi.id="_68" value="MA"/>
<CWMRDB:ColumnValue xmi.id="_69" value="Hat"/>
<CWMRDB:ColumnValue xmi.id="_70" value="BrandA"/>
<CWMRDB:ColumnValue xmi.id="_71" value="1"/>
<CWMRDB:ColumnValue xmi.id="_72" value="19.0"/>
<CWMRDB:ColumnValue xmi.id="_73" value="16.0"/>
<CWMRDB:ColumnValue xmi.id="_74" value="1/1/1999"/>
<CWMRDB:ColumnValue xmi.id="_75" value="Store5"/>
<CWMRDB:ColumnValue xmi.id="_76" value="Boston"/>
<CWMRDB:ColumnValue xmi.id="_77" value="MA"/>
<CWMRDB:ColumnValue xmi.id="_78" value="Pen"/>
<CWMRDB:ColumnValue xmi.id="_79" value="BrandC"/>
<CWMRDB:ColumnValue xmi.id="_80" value="5"/>
<CWMRDB:ColumnValue xmi.id="_81" value="25.0"/>
<CWMRDB:ColumnValue xmi.id="_82" value="20.0"/>
<CWMRDB:ColumnValue xmi.id="_83" value="1/1/1999"/>
<CWMRDB:ColumnValue xmi.id="_84" value="Store5"/>
<CWMRDB:ColumnValue xmi.id="_85" value="Boston"/>
<CWMRDB:ColumnValue xmi.id="_86" value="MA"/>
<CWMRDB:ColumnValue xmi.id="_87" value="Pen"/>
<CWMRDB:ColumnValue xmi.id="_88" value="BrandC"/>
<CWMRDB:ColumnValue xmi.id="_89" value="2"/>
<CWMRDB:ColumnValue xmi.id="_90" value="10.0"/>
<CWMRDB:ColumnValue xmi.id="_91" value="8.0"/>
<CWMRDB:ColumnValue xmi.id="_92" value="1/1/1999"/>
<CWMRDB:SQLSimpleType xmi.id="_93" name="BLOB" typeNumber="1111"/>
<CWMRDB:SQLSimpleType xmi.id="_94" name="CLOB" typeNumber="1111"/>
<CWMRDB:SQLSimpleType xmi.id="_95"
    name="LONG VARCHAR FOR BIT DATA" typeNumber="-4"/>
<CWMRDB:SQLSimpleType xmi.id="_96" name="VARCHAR () FOR BIT DATA"
typeNumber="-3"/>
<CWMRDB:SQLSimpleType xmi.id="_97"
    name="CHARacter () FOR BIT DATA" typeNumber="-2"/>
<CWMRDB:SQLSimpleType xmi.id="_98" name="LONG VARCHAR" typeNumber="-
1"/>
<CWMRDB:SQLSimpleType xmi.id="_99" name="CHARacter" typeNumber="1"/>
<CWMRDB:SQLSimpleType xmi.id="_100" name="NUMeric" typeNumber="2"/>
<CWMRDB:SQLSimpleType xmi.id="_101" name="DECimal" typeNumber="3"/>
<CWMRDB:SQLSimpleType xmi.id="_102" name="INTeger" typeNumber="4"/>
<CWMRDB:SQLSimpleType xmi.id="_103" name="SMALLINT" typeNumber="5"/>
<CWMRDB:SQLSimpleType xmi.id="_104" name="FLOAT" typeNumber="6"/>
<CWMRDB:SQLSimpleType xmi.id="_105" name="REAL" typeNumber="7"/>
<CWMRDB:SQLSimpleType xmi.id="_106" name="FLOAT" typeNumber="8"/>
```

Figure 5.10   CwmOdsResultSet.xml. *(continues)*

```
    <CWMRDB:SQLSimpleType xmi.id="_107" name="DATE" typeNumber="91"/>
    <CWMRDB:SQLSimpleType xmi.id="_108" name="TIME" typeNumber="92"/>
    <CWMRDB:SQLSimpleType xmi.id="_109" name="TIMESTAMP"
typeNumber="93"/>
    <CWMRDB:SQLSimpleType xmi.id="_110" name="VARCHAR" typeNumber="12"/>
    <CWMRDB:SQLSimpleType xmi.id="_111" name="DATALINK"
typeNumber="1111"/>
    <CWMRDB:SQLSimpleType xmi.id="_112" name="BIGINT" typeNumber="-5"/>
  </XMI.content>
</XMI>
```

Figure 5.10   CwmOdsResultSet.xml. *(continued)*

The ETL Scenario

As mentioned previously, the focus of the ETL scenario is on extracting, transforming, and loading the raw operational data stored in the exemplar operational data store, CwmOds, into the exemplar data warehouse, CwmStore, as shown in Figure 5.2. As a reminder on why we are interested in the scenario, the following is the recast of the major benefits that a data warehouse provides:

- Provides a dedicated database for decision support
- Transforms and integrates raw operational data into business information suitable for use in decision support
- Offloads processing from the operational data store

The informational data stored in CwmStore is ready for use in decision-making (e.g., OLAP, data mining) either directly or through data marts, as shown in Figure 5.11.

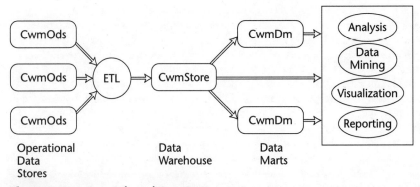

Figure 5.11.   CwmOds and CwmStore.

The Exemplar Data Warehouse

CwmStore is a relational database with a star-schema, designed to store informational data that is historical and aggregated in nature. CwmStore consists of four tables: Store, Product, Period, and Sales. The definitions of these tables are shown in Tables 5.8 to 5.11. The Store table contains information on all stores within the United States, including information about their county, territory, and region, which is useful for analysis. The Product table contains information on all products carried by the stores within the United States. Please note that transient product information, such as price, is not kept. The Period table contains information on time that is useful for analysis. The Sales table contains accumulated sales information on all products sold by the stores within the United States.

Table 5.8. CwmStore Store Table

COLUMN	DATATYPE	LENGTH	NOT NULL	PRIMARY KEY
Store_id	Integer		Yes	Yes
Name	Varchar	128		
City	Varchar	80		
County	Varchar	32		
State	Character	2		
Territory	Varchar	32		
Region	Varchar	16		

Table 5.9. CwmStore Product Table

COLUMN	DATATYPE	LENGTH	NOT NULL	PRIMARY KEY
Product_id	Integer		Yes	Yes
Description	Varchar	128		
Prod_size	Varchar	7		
Color	Varchar	32		
Brand	Varchar	64		
Department	Varchar	64		
Category	Varchar	32		

Table 5.10. CwmStore Period Table

COLUMN	DATATYPE	LENGTH	NOT NULL	PRIMARY KEY
Period_id	Integer		Yes	Yes
End_date	Varchar	32		
Holiday	Character	1		
Week_in_year	Integer			
Week_overall	Varchar	7		
Month_in_year	Integer			
Month_overall	Varchar	8		
Year	Integer			

Tables 5.12 to 5.15 show some sample data contained in each of the four tables. Please note that the Store, Product, and Period tables contain information about the store, product, and time dimensions, respectively, whereas the Sales table contains historical facts on sales. As might be expected, the amount of data stored in the Sales table is massive.

Table 5.11. CwmStore Sales Table

COLUMN	DATATYPE	LENGTH	NOT NULL	PRIMARY KEY	FOREIGN KEY
Store_id	Integer		Yes	Yes	Yes
Product_id	Integer		Yes	Yes	Yes
Period_id	Integer		Yes	Yes	Yes
Quantity	Integer				
Gross_revenue	Double				
Gross_cost	Double				
Gross_profit	Double				

Table 5.12. Sample Data in the CwmStore Store Table

STORE_ID	NAME	CITY	COUNTY	STATE	TERRITORY	REGION
1	Store1	Boston	MA_1	MA	East_1	East
2	Store2	Boston	MA_1	MA	East_1	East
5	Store5	Boston	MA_1	MA	East_1	East
17	Store17	Milford	CT_2	CT	East-2	East
18	Store18	New Haven	CT_1	CT	East-2	East
19	Store19	New Haven	CT_1	CT	East-2	East
21	Store21	New York	NY_3	NY	East_2	East
22	Store22	New York	NY_3	NY	East_2	East
23	Store23	New York	NY-3	NY	East_2	East
24	Store24	New York	NY_3	NY	East_2	East

Table 5.13. Sample Data in the CwmStore Product Table

PRODUCT_ID	DESCRIPTION	PROD_SIZE	COLOR	BRAND	DEPARTMENT	CATEGORY
1	Tshirt	Small	Red	BrandA	Clothing	Personal
2	Tshirt	Small	Brown	BrandB	Clothing	Personal
5	Tie	Small	Brown	BrandA	Clothing	Personal
17	Sweatshirt	Small	Grey	BrandA	Clothing	Personal
18	Hat	Small	Purple	BrandA	Clothing	Personal
19	Hat	Small	White	BrandB	Clothing	Personal
21	Jacket	Small	Purple	BrandA	Clothing	Personal
22	Jacket	Small	Brown	BrandB	Clothing	Personal
24	Pen	Regular	Black	BrandC	Stationery	Personal
25	Pen	Regular	Blue	BrandC	Stationery	Personal

Table 5.14. Sample Data in the CwmStore Period Table

PERIOD_ID	END_DATE	HOLIDAY	WEEK_IN_ YEAR	WEEK_ OVERALL	MONTH_IN_ YEAR	MONTH_ OVERALL	YEAR
1	1/1/1999	Y	1	1999_1	1	JAN_1999	1999
2	1/2/1999	N	1	1999_1	1	JAN_1999	1999
3	1/3/1999	N	1	1999_1	1	JAN_1999	1999
11	1/11/1999	N	2	1999_2	1	JAN_1999	1999
21	1/21/1999	N	3	1999_3	1	JAN_1999	1999
31	1/31/1999	N	5	1999_5	1	JAN_1999	1999
51	2/20/1999	N	8	1999_8	2	FEB_1999	1999
91	4/1/1999	N	13	1999_13	4	APR_1999	1999
171	6/20/1999	N	25	1999_25	6	JUN_1999	1999
251	9/8/1999	N	36	1999_36	9	SEP_1999	1999

Table 5.15.   Sample Data in the CwmStore Sales Table

STORE_ID	PRODUCT_ID	PERIOD_ID	QUANTITY	GROSS_REVENUE	GROSS_COST	GROSS_PROFIT
51	201	610	5	10	8.75	1.25
51	201	613	10	20	17.5	25
52	201	688	16	32	28	4
52	201	694	3	6	5.25	0.75
86	205	721	4	8	7	1
87	205	628	2	4	3.5	0.5
59	234	697	1	2	1.75	0.25
59	234	718	10	20	17.5	2.5
96	262	664	12	24	21	3
96	262	715	4	8	7	1

The ETL Process Meta Data

Currently there is no standard mechanism one can use to access and extract the meta data of ETL processes. As such, we will not discuss it here, since any vendor-product-specific mechanism is proprietary and not suitable for use as an example in this book. Hopefully, in the near future, the situation will change and there will be a standard mechanism defined in the industry to access meta data of ETL processes.

In the following, we will discuss the CWM Transformation and WarehouseProcess packages. These packages together define what ETL process meta data can be interchanged using CWM and what their structures and semantics are. In doing so, we will also show their JMI mappings, as we have done previously with the CWM Relational package. As was the case, the JMI mappings provide Java interfaces for constructing and manipulating CWM meta objects (in this case the CWM Transformation and WarehouseProcess meta objects).

The CWM Transformation Package

The CWM Transformation package and its dependent packages are shown in Figure 5.12. It can be seen that the Transformation package depends on the following packages:

> **Object Model layer:** Core, Behavioral
>
> **Foundation layer:** Expression, SoftwareDeployment

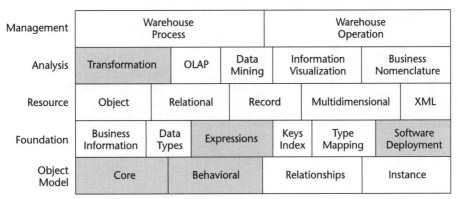

Figure 5.12 CWM Transformation and dependent packages.

The class inheritance diagrams are shown in Figures 5.13 and 5.14. Most of the dependencies are either explicitly or implicitly shown in these diagrams.

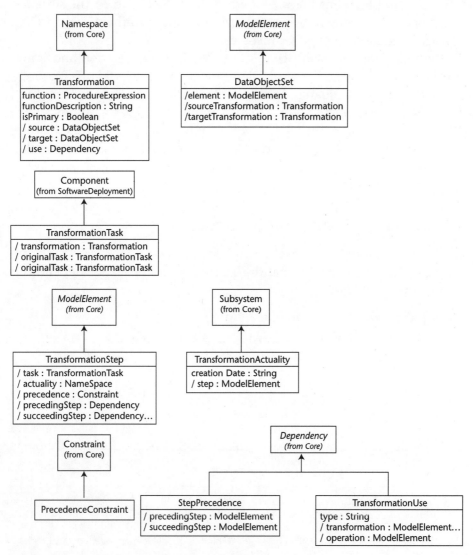

Figure 5.13   CWM Transformation package inheritance—1.

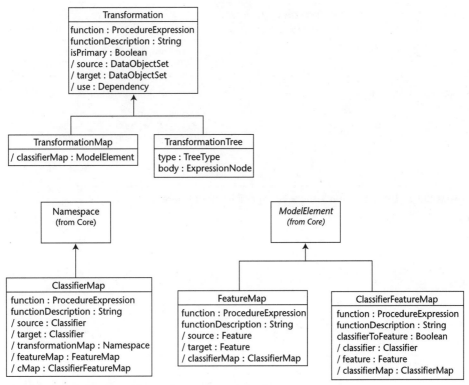

Figure 5.14 CWM Transformation package inheritance—2.

The CWM WarehouseProcess Package

The CWM WarehouseProcess package and its dependent packages are shown in Figure 5.15. It can be seen that the Warehouse package depends on the following packages:

Object Model layer: Core, Behavior

Analysis layer: Transformation

Most of the dependency is explicitly illustrated in the class inheritance diagram shown in Figure 5.16.

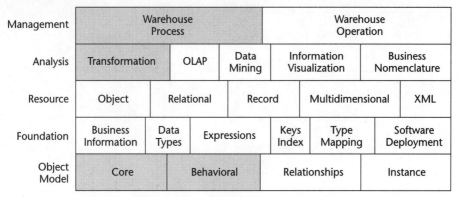

Figure 5.15   CWM WarehouseProcess and dependent packages.

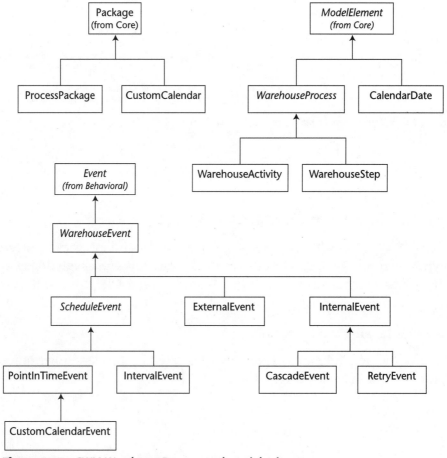

Figure 5.16   CWM WarehouseProcess package inheritance.

Note that we omit discussion of warehouse events (that is, the WarehouseEvent class, its subclasses, and its associated classes) since the ETL scenario does not include any use of warehouse events.

Exporting ETL Meta Data Using CWM

The following is a summary of what we have done for the ETL scenario:

- We gave a brief description of the exemplar data warehouse, CwmStore.

- We mentioned that there is no standard mechanism to access and export ETL meta data.

- We discussed the CWM Transformation and WarehouseProcess, which define what ETL meta data can be interchanged using CWM and what their structures and semantics are. In doing so, we also showed the JMI mappings, which provide Java interfaces for constructing and manipulating CWM Transformation and WarehouseProcess meta objects.

Had it not been for the lack of standard mechanisms to access and export ETL meta data, we would have provided code fragments and discussions that show how one can construct JMI meta objects per the CWM Transformation and WarehouseProcess packages. Using a generic toll that can take the JMI meta objects and export them in proper XMI format, we would then be able to show some sample CWM XMI files generated from exporting the meta data contained in the ETL process that can transform the data in CwmOds into the one in CwmStore.

The CWM XMI File

The CWM XMI file produced when exporting the meta data of CwmStore is shown below. This meta data can be used as input in the OLAP scenario to be discussed in Chapter 6 (see Figure 5.17).

```
<?xml version="1.0" encoding="UTF-8"?>
<!DOCTYPE XMI SYSTEM "CWM_1.0.dtd" [
<!ELEMENT ixafs (ixaftv)+ >
<!ATTLIST ixafs
          n CDATA #REQUIRED
>
<!ELEMENT ixaftv EMPTY >
```

Figure 5.17 CWMStore meta data rendered in XMI. *(continues)*

```
<!ATTLIST ixaftv
           t CDATA #REQUIRED
           v CDATA #REQUIRED
>]>
<XMI xmi.version="1.1" timestamp="Tue May 21 20:10:15 PDT 2002"
xmlns:CWMRDB="org.omg.CWM1.0/Relational" xmlns:CWM="org.omg.CWM1.0">
  <XMI.header>
    <XMI.documentation>
      <XMI.exporter>XMI Application Framework</XMI.exporter>
      <XMI.exporterVersion>1.15</XMI.exporterVersion>
    </XMI.documentation>
  </XMI.header>
  <XMI.content>
    <CWMRDB:Catalog xmi.id="_1" name="CWMSTORE">
    <CWM:Namespace.ownedElement>
      <CWMRDB:Schema xmi.id="_1.1" name="CWM" namespace="_1">
        <CWM:Namespace.ownedElement>
          <CWMRDB:Table xmi.id="_1.1.1" name="PERIOD"
namespace="_1.1">
              <CWM:Classifier.feature>
                <CWMRDB:Column xmi.id="_1.1.1.1" name="PERIOD_ID"
length="10"
                     type="_11" owner="_1.1.1"/>
                <CWMRDB:Column xmi.id="_1.1.1.2" name="END_DATE"
length="32"
                     type="_19" owner="_1.1.1"/>
                <CWMRDB:Column xmi.id="_1.1.1.3" name="HOLIDAY"
length="1" type="_8"
                     owner="_1.1.1"/>
                <CWMRDB:Column xmi.id="_1.1.1.4" name="WEEK_IN_YEAR"
length="10"
                     type="_11" owner="_1.1.1"/>
                <CWMRDB:Column xmi.id="_1.1.1.5" name="WEEK_OVERALL"
length="7"
                     type="_19" owner="_1.1.1"/>
                <CWMRDB:Column xmi.id="_1.1.1.6" name="MONTH_IN_YEAR"
length="10"
                     type="_11" owner="_1.1.1"/>
                <CWMRDB:Column xmi.id="_1.1.1.7" name="MONTH_OVERALL"
length="8"
                     type="_19" owner="_1.1.1"/>
                <CWMRDB:Column xmi.id="_1.1.1.8" name="YEAR" length="10"
type="_11"
                     owner="_1.1.1"/>
              </CWM:Classifier.feature>
              <CWM:Namespace.ownedElement>
                <CWMRDB:PrimaryKey xmi.id="_1.1.1.9"
name="SQL020407112031790"
```

Figure 5.17 CWMStore meta data rendered in XMI. *(continued)*

```
                        feature="_1.1.1.1" namespace="_1.1.1"
                        keyRelationship="_1.1.5.9"/>
                  </CWM:Namespace.ownedElement>
              </CWMRDB:Table>
              <CWMRDB:SQLIndex xmi.id="_1.1.2" name="SQL020407112031640"
                  spannedClass="_1.1.1" namespace="_1.1">
                <CWM:Index.indexedFeature>
                  <CWMRDB:SQLIndexColumn xmi.id="_1.1.2.1" index="_1.1.2"
                      feature="_1.1.1.1"/>
                </CWM:Index.indexedFeature>
              </CWMRDB:SQLIndex>
              <CWMRDB:Table xmi.id="_1.1.3" name="PRODUCT"
namespace="_1.1">
                <CWM:Classifier.feature>
                  <CWMRDB:Column xmi.id="_1.1.3.1" name="PRODUCT_ID"
length="10"
                      type="_11" owner="_1.1.3"/>
                  <CWMRDB:Column xmi.id="_1.1.3.2" name="DESCRIPTION"
length="128"
                      type="_19" owner="_1.1.3"/>
                  <CWMRDB:Column xmi.id="_1.1.3.3" name="PROD_SIZE"
length="7"
                      type="_19" owner="_1.1.3"/>
                  <CWMRDB:Column xmi.id="_1.1.3.4" name="COLOR"
length="32" type="_19"
                      owner="_1.1.3"/>
                  <CWMRDB:Column xmi.id="_1.1.3.5" name="BRAND"
length="64" type="_19"
                      owner="_1.1.3"/>
                  <CWMRDB:Column xmi.id="_1.1.3.6" name="DEPARTMENT"
length="64"
                      type="_19" owner="_1.1.3"/>
                  <CWMRDB:Column xmi.id="_1.1.3.7" name="CATEGORY"
length="32"
                      type="_19" owner="_1.1.3"/>
                </CWM:Classifier.feature>
                <CWM:Namespace.ownedElement>
                  <CWMRDB:PrimaryKey xmi.id="_1.1.3.8"
name="SQL020407112032230"
                      feature="_1.1.3.1" namespace="_1.1.3"
                      keyRelationship="_1.1.5.10"/>
                </CWM:Namespace.ownedElement>
              </CWMRDB:Table>
              <CWMRDB:SQLIndex xmi.id="_1.1.4" name="SQL020407112032090"
                  spannedClass="_1.1.3" namespace="_1.1">
                <CWM:Index.indexedFeature>
                  <CWMRDB:SQLIndexColumn xmi.id="_1.1.4.1" index="_1.1.4"
                      feature="_1.1.3.1"/>
```

Figure 5.17   CWMStore meta data rendered in XMI. *(continues)*

```
                </CWM:Index.indexedFeature>
            </CWMRDB:SQLIndex>
            <CWMRDB:Table xmi.id="_1.1.5" name="SALES" namespace="_1.1">
                <CWM:Classifier.feature>
                    <CWMRDB:Column xmi.id="_1.1.5.1" name="PERIOD_ID"
length="10"
                        type="_11" owner="_1.1.5"/>
                    <CWMRDB:Column xmi.id="_1.1.5.2" name="STORE_ID"
length="10"
                        type="_11" owner="_1.1.5"/>
                    <CWMRDB:Column xmi.id="_1.1.5.3" name="PRODUCT_ID"
length="10"
                        type="_11" owner="_1.1.5"/>
                    <CWMRDB:Column xmi.id="_1.1.5.4" name="QUANTITY"
length="10"
                        type="_11" owner="_1.1.5"/>
                    <CWMRDB:Column xmi.id="_1.1.5.5" name="GROSS_REVENUE"
length="15"
                        type="_15" owner="_1.1.5"/>
                    <CWMRDB:Column xmi.id="_1.1.5.6" name="GROSS_COST"
length="15"
                        type="_15" owner="_1.1.5"/>
                    <CWMRDB:Column xmi.id="_1.1.5.7" name="GROSS_PROFIT"
length="15"
                        type="_15" owner="_1.1.5"/>
                </CWM:Classifier.feature>
                <CWM:Namespace.ownedElement>
                    <CWMRDB:PrimaryKey xmi.id="_1.1.5.8"
name="SQL020407112032500"
                        feature="_1.1.5.1 _1.1.5.2 _1.1.5.3"
namespace="_1.1.5"/>
                    <CWMRDB:ForeignKey xmi.id="_1.1.5.9"
name="SQL020407112032501"
                        feature="_1.1.5.1" namespace="_1.1.5"
uniqueKey="_1.1.1.9"/>
                    <CWMRDB:ForeignKey xmi.id="_1.1.5.10"
name="SQL020407112032503"
                        feature="_1.1.5.3" namespace="_1.1.5"
uniqueKey="_1.1.3.8"/>
                    <CWMRDB:ForeignKey xmi.id="_1.1.5.11"
name="SQL020407112032502"
                        feature="_1.1.5.2" namespace="_1.1.5"
uniqueKey="_1.1.7.8"/>
                </CWM:Namespace.ownedElement>
            </CWMRDB:Table>
            <CWMRDB:SQLIndex xmi.id="_1.1.6" name="SQL020407112032350"
                spannedClass="_1.1.5" namespace="_1.1">
                <CWM:Index.indexedFeature>
```

Figure 5.17 CWMStore meta data rendered in XMI. *(continued)*

```
                    <CWMRDB:SQLIndexColumn xmi.id="_1.1.6.1" index="_1.1.6"
                        feature="_1.1.5.1"/>
                    <CWMRDB:SQLIndexColumn xmi.id="_1.1.6.2" index="_1.1.6"
                        feature="_1.1.5.2"/>
                    <CWMRDB:SQLIndexColumn xmi.id="_1.1.6.3" index="_1.1.6"
                        feature="_1.1.5.3"/>
                </CWM:Index.indexedFeature>
            </CWMRDB:SQLIndex>
            <CWMRDB:Table xmi.id="_1.1.7" name="STORE" namespace="_1.1">
                <CWM:Classifier.feature>
                    <CWMRDB:Column xmi.id="_1.1.7.1" name="STORE_ID"
length="10"
                        type="_11" owner="_1.1.7"/>
                    <CWMRDB:Column xmi.id="_1.1.7.2" name="NAME"
length="128" type="_19"
                        owner="_1.1.7"/>
                    <CWMRDB:Column xmi.id="_1.1.7.3" name="CITY" length="80"
type="_19"
                        owner="_1.1.7"/>
                    <CWMRDB:Column xmi.id="_1.1.7.4" name="COUNTY"
length="32"
                        type="_19" owner="_1.1.7"/>
                    <CWMRDB:Column xmi.id="_1.1.7.5" name="STATE" length="2"
type="_8"
                        owner="_1.1.7"/>
                    <CWMRDB:Column xmi.id="_1.1.7.6" name="TERRITORY"
length="32"
                        type="_19" owner="_1.1.7"/>
                    <CWMRDB:Column xmi.id="_1.1.7.7" name="REGION"
length="16"
                        type="_19" owner="_1.1.7"/>
                </CWM:Classifier.feature>
                <CWM:Namespace.ownedElement>
                    <CWMRDB:PrimaryKey xmi.id="_1.1.7.8"
name="SQL020407112032010"
                        feature="_1.1.7.1" namespace="_1.1.7"
                        keyRelationship="_1.1.5.11"/>
                </CWM:Namespace.ownedElement>
            </CWMRDB:Table>
            <CWMRDB:SQLIndex xmi.id="_1.1.8" name="SQL020407112031860"
                spannedClass="_1.1.7" namespace="_1.1">
                <CWM:Index.indexedFeature>
                    <CWMRDB:SQLIndexColumn xmi.id="_1.1.8.1" index="_1.1.8"
                        feature="_1.1.7.1"/>
                </CWM:Index.indexedFeature>
            </CWMRDB:SQLIndex>
        </CWM:Namespace.ownedElement>
    </CWMRDB:Schema>
```

Figure 5.17   CWMStore meta data rendered in XMI. *(continues)*

```
            <CWMRDB:Schema xmi.id="_1.2" name="SYSCAT" namespace="_1"/>
            <CWMRDB:Schema xmi.id="_1.3" name="SYSIBM" namespace="_1"/>
            <CWMRDB:Schema xmi.id="_1.4" name="SYSSTAT" namespace="_1"/>
        </CWM:Namespace.ownedElement>
    </CWMRDB:Catalog>
    <CWMRDB:SQLSimpleType xmi.id="_2" name="BLOB" typeNumber="1111"/>
    <CWMRDB:SQLSimpleType xmi.id="_3" name="CLOB" typeNumber="1111"/>
    <CWMRDB:SQLSimpleType xmi.id="_4" name="LONG VARCHAR FOR BIT DATA"
        typeNumber="-4"/>
    <CWMRDB:SQLSimpleType xmi.id="_5" name="VARCHAR () FOR BIT DATA"
        typeNumber="-3"/>
    <CWMRDB:SQLSimpleType xmi.id="_6" name="CHARacter () FOR BIT DATA"
        typeNumber="-2"/>
    <CWMRDB:SQLSimpleType xmi.id="_7" name="LONG VARCHAR" typeNumber="-
1"/>
    <CWMRDB:SQLSimpleType xmi.id="_8" name="CHARacter" typeNumber="1"/>
    <CWMRDB:SQLSimpleType xmi.id="_9" name="NUMeric" typeNumber="2"/>
    <CWMRDB:SQLSimpleType xmi.id="_10" name="DECimal" typeNumber="3"/>
    <CWMRDB:SQLSimpleType xmi.id="_11" name="INTeger" typeNumber="4"/>
    <CWMRDB:SQLSimpleType xmi.id="_12" name="SMALLINT" typeNumber="5"/>
    <CWMRDB:SQLSimpleType xmi.id="_13" name="FLOAT" typeNumber="6"/>
    <CWMRDB:SQLSimpleType xmi.id="_14" name="REAL" typeNumber="7"/>
    <CWMRDB:SQLSimpleType xmi.id="_15" name="FLOAT" typeNumber="8"/>
    <CWMRDB:SQLSimpleType xmi.id="_16" name="DATE" typeNumber="91"/>
    <CWMRDB:SQLSimpleType xmi.id="_17" name="TIME" typeNumber="92"/>
    <CWMRDB:SQLSimpleType xmi.id="_18" name="TIMESTAMP"
typeNumber="93"/>
    <CWMRDB:SQLSimpleType xmi.id="_19" name="VARCHAR" typeNumber="12"/>
    <CWMRDB:SQLSimpleType xmi.id="_20" name="DATALINK"
typeNumber="1111"/>
    <CWMRDB:SQLSimpleType xmi.id="_21" name="BIGINT" typeNumber="-5"/>
    </XMI.content>
</XMI>
```

Figure 5.17   CWMStore meta data rendered in XMI. *(continued)*

Summary

In this chapter we have discussed two major data warehouse scenarios and demonstrated how CWM can be used to facilitate the meta data integration required for the operation of an information supply chain. The two major data warehouse scenarios that have been discussed are the operational data store scenario and the ETL (Extraction, Transformation, and Loading) scenario. These two scenarios together cover the first three components (and their meta data) of the information supply chain. The last component, OLAP, will be covered in the OLAP scenario to be discussed in Chapter 6.

For the first—operational data store scenario—we have provided begin-to-end code examples and discussions that clearly and explicitly show how CWM can be used to interchange the meta data stored in an operational data store, such as CwmOds. For the second—ETL scenario—we have provided detailed descriptions of the CWM Transformation and WarehouseProcess packages that define what ETL process meta data can be interchanged using CWM and what their structures and semantics are. Unfortunately, due to the lack of standard mechanisms for accessing ETL process meta data, we were not able to provide begin-to-end code examples.

Please refer to this book's companion Web site for the formal specification of meta data interchange patterns that are relevant to this particular chapter.

CHAPTER 6

Dimensional Model

This chapter explores how the Common Warehouse Metamodel (CWM) Online Analytical Processing (OLAP) package is used in *dimensional modeling*. Creating dimensional models of various business domain problems often provides solutions to the meta data requirements of many OLAP application tools and multidimensional databases. This chapter will concentrate on the set of CWM packages outlined in Figure 6.1.

Management	Warehouse Process			Warehouse Operation	
Analysis	Transformation	OLAP	Data Mining	Business Nomenclature	Information Visualization
Resource	Relational		Record	Multidimensional	XML
Foundation	Business Information	Data Types	Software Deployment	Keys Indexes	Expressions	Type Mapping
Object	Core		Behavioral	Relationships	Instance

Figure 6.1 Featured packages of the CWM model.

The CWM OLAP model separates the concepts of logical and physical models of a multidimensional system. A logical dimensional model generally consists of purely logical OLAP concepts, such as Dimensions, Hierarchies, Cubes, and their various attributes. A physical OLAP model, on the other hand, generally consists of some sort of model of the physical data structures that underly (or *realize*) the logical OLAP model. Such a physical model is often referred to as a *deployment model*. A single, logical OLAP model might be realized by any of several possible deployment models, such as a Relational database model (for example, a relational star or snowflake schema), or a vendor-specific model of a memory-based, multidimensional server.

In CWM, the logical and physical models are mapped together using the CWM transformation metamodel. In this case, the end user creates a logical model consisting of Dimension, Levels, Hierarchies, and Cubes. These definitions represent how end users view their business model. This business model has a corresponding deployment model representing some underlying database management system. The connection between the business model and the database representation requires a mapping between the logical constructs and physical layout of the data, and this is generally accomplished in CWM via CWM Transformation mappings.

This chapter provides a complete example of using the OLAP metamodel in the manner described above. First, a logical OLAP model is developed using the CWM OLAP package (see Figure 6.1). A simple logical model is initially constructed and then further refined by adding Attribute and Key instances from the CWM Core and KeysIndexes packages, respectively. Then, a physical model is constructed representing a deployment based on the use of relational database technology. This is constructed using the CWM Relational metamodel package. Mappings from the logical OLAP model to this physical realization are then created using modeling elements from the CWM Transformation package.

Next, an example of a second OLAP deployment model is constructed. This model is based on the CWM Multidimensional metamodel, which is used to represent the core components of a physical, memory-based, OLAP server. In this particular example, the core Multidimensional metamodel is first extended to represent key features of the Oracle Express multidimensional server. Then, a mapping from the logical OLAP model to a model of an Express instance is constructed, once again using CWM Transformation mappings.

Finally, an example of extending the second deployment model with vendor-specific constructs using CWM Stereotypes and Tagged Values is provided.

The overall approach to constructing this detailed example is to identify specific features of applicable CWM metamodels and show the construction of meta data objects using instance diagrams. This is then followed by fragments of the actual implementation code (expressed in terms of a Java Meta Data Interface (JMI) mapping based on the CWM metamodel) used to produce the instances. Note that, in many cases, several sets of instance diagrams are needed to provide a clear picture of the required instances. In these cases, instances may sometimes be replicated; the actual number of object instances being created can be determined by the code examples.

The Logical Model

A sample logical model has been selected from an imaginary consumer package goods company. This company has several product lines and sells its products around the world. The company requires the ability to do trend analysis along time for a variety of measures. The creation of the logical model is broken down into a series of tasks, with each task delving deeper and deeper into the logical model.

Dimensions, Attributes, Levels, and Hierarchies

The first task in defining the logical model is to identify the dimensions. These will form the basis for the types of analysis the system can support. The CWM model supports a wide variety of dimensional modeling capabilities. The CWM OLAP model contains the following high-level features:

- Dimensions
- Levels
- Hierarchies
- Attributes
- Cubes
- Measures

A CWM dimension can contain any number of attributes, levels, and hierarchies. A CWM level can contain any number of attributes. This was done to allow users of CWM to maintain a separation of constructs between what is exposed at the dimension "level" and what is exposed at the level "level." A CWM hierarchy can also contain its own set of attributes. This is again necessary to keep a clear separation between objects exposed by the dimension and objects exposed by the hierarchy. In addition, a level

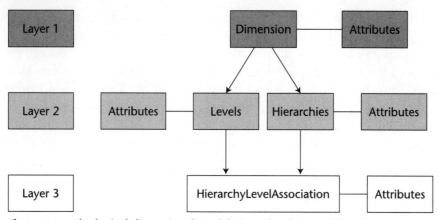

Figure 6.2 The logical dimensional model viewed as layers of detail.

hierarchy is comprised of a set of references to certain levels. In this case, the model again needs to support the distinction between attributes exposed by the intersection of a specific level as used by a level hierarchy. The logical model of CWM can be represented as layers of detail, as shown in Figure 6.2.

This feature in CWM allows users to maintain complete control over the visibility of attributes and was an early design goal for CWM. The example provided in this chapter shows users how to take advantage of this and many others features in CWM.

The CWM Model

This portion of the example will concentrate on the aspects of the CWM model illustrated in Figures 6.3 and 6.4. The next few sections of this chapter will use the metamodels shown in Figures 6.3 and 6.4 to create the logical model. The logical model used as the basis for this example is a relatively simple dimensional model consisting of the following OLAP elements:

- A Product dimension consisting of four Levels and two Hierarchies
- A Geography dimension consisting of three Levels and a single Hierarchy

- A Time dimension consisting of four Levels and a single Hierarchy
- A Sales Cube defined as consisting of three Measures, each dimensioned by Product, Geography, and Time
- A Population Cube consisting of a single Measure dimensioned by Geography and Time

To create the Product dimension, an instance of the OLAP Package dimension object is created. The instance diagram in Figure 6.5 illustrates that the Product dimension will have four attributes. One of those attributes, "Id," will be used later in the example to represent a unique key for the dimension. The remaining three attributes represent description attributes of the dimension. In CWM, the OLAP model represents a logical model. This model must be mapped to either finer-grained logical structures or a physical representation. The mappings will be covered later in the example. The instance diagram in Figure 6.5 represents the Product dimension and its attributes.

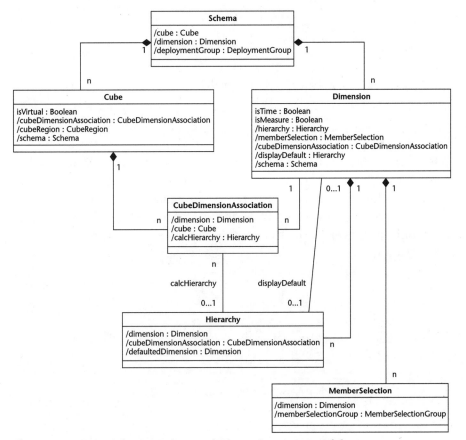

Figure 6.3 CWM Schema, Cubes, and Dimensions metamodel.

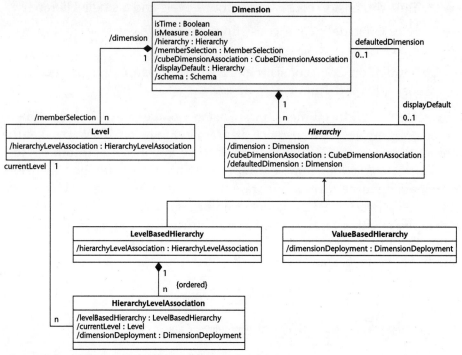

Figure 6.4 CWM Levels and Hierarchies metamodel.

Defining the Dimensions and Attributes

The Application Program Interface (API) used in this book follows the JMI specification. This specification was used to generate a set of APIs, which correspond to the CWM model. The first set of statements in the following code segment represents object factories as specified by JMI and will be used throughout this example to generate the object instances.

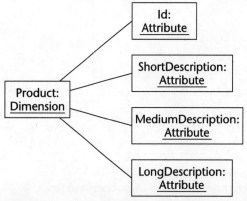

Figure 6.5 The Product dimension and its attributes.

An important feature of the CWM model is the lack of package coupling. In order to achieve this goal, many of the model associations have been generalized as high in the model as possible. This provides for the greatest reuse of object definitions and prevents package coupling. The problem with this approach is that some of the constructs in the model have been generalized. Users of CWM may feel on first inspection that some concepts they expect to find in an individual metamodel are missing. Usually, the missing concept has been generalized in some parent structure. A good example of this is that a dimension can have attributes. The Attribute class, however, is not defined in the OLAP package. Attribute actually belongs to the Core package, and a dimension's ability to have attributes is inherited from Classifier. Note the way an attribute is added to the dimension using the addFeature method. The following code snippet represents the code to create the instances of the Product dimension in Figure 6.5.

```
//bootstrap code
     CWMCompletePackage cwmComplete = new CWMCompletePackageImpl();
     OlapPackage olapPackage = cwmComplete.getOlap();
     RelationalPackage relationalPackage = cwmComplete.getRelational();
     CorePackage corePackage = cwmComplete.getCore();
     KeysIndexesPackage keysIndexes = cwmComplete.getKeysIndexes();

     //create the dimensional objects
     //create the product dimension
     Dimension product = olapPackage.getDimension().createDimension();
     product.setName("Product");
     //create the product attributes
     Attribute prodId = corePackage.getAttribute().createAttribute();
     prodId.setName("ID");

     Attribute prodSDesc =
          corePackage.getAttribute().createAttribute();

     prodSDesc.setName("Short Description");
  Attribute prodMDesc = corePackage.getAttribute().createAttribute();
 prodMDesc.setName("Medium Description");
  Attribute prodLDesc = corePackage.getAttribute().createAttribute();
     prodLDesc.setName("Long Description");

     //add the attributes to the dimension
     product.addFeature(prodId);
     product.addFeature(prodSDesc);
     product.addFeature(prodMDesc);
     product.addFeature(prodLDesc);
```

The Geography dimension will also have four attributes. One attribute will represent a unique id for the dimension (Id). Another attribute will represent a description for every dimension value. Lastly, two attributes will represent the longitude and latitude of a given geography. The CWM instances in Figure 6.6 will be used to describe the Geography dimension.

The code shown below describes the creation of the Geography dimension object instances. This code relies on the factories described above to create the object instances. As in the first example, the dimension's attributes are instances of the Core metamodel Attribute class. They are associated with the dimension using the addFeature method.

```
//create the geography dimension
    Dimension geog = olapPackage.getDimension().createDimension();
    geog.setName("Geography");
    //create the geography attributes
    Attribute geogId = corePackage.getAttribute().createAttribute();
    geogId.setName("ID");
    Attribute geodSDesc =
corePackage.getAttribute().createAttribute();
    geogDesc.setName("Description");
    Attribute geogLongitude =
        corePackage.getAttribute().createAttribute();
    geogLongitude.setName("Longitude");
    Attribute geogLatitude =
        corePackage.getAttribute().createAttribute();
    geogLatitude.setName("Latitude");

    //add the attributes to the dimension
    geog.addFeature(geogId);
    geog.addFeature(geogDesc);
    geog.addFeature(geogLongitude);
    geog.addFeature(geogLatitude);
```

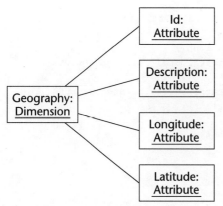

Figure 6.6 The Geography dimension and its attributes.

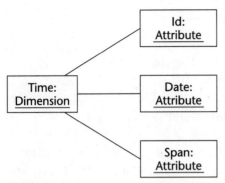

Figure 6.7 The Time dimension and its attributes.

In the example, the Time dimension will have three attributes. The first attribute, "Id," will represent both a unique identifier for the dimension and a description for the dimension values. The remaining two attributes, "date" and "span," will be used to represent the ending date of the period and the span of the period in days, respectively. These two attributes can be used in combination to provide an application with date-based calculations. See Figure 6.7.

The following code snippet represents the code necessary to create the Time dimension and its supporting attributes.

```
//create the Time dimension
Dimension time = olapPackage.getDimension().createDimension();
time.setName("Time");

//create the product attributes
Attribute timeId = corePackage.getAttribute().createAttribute();
timeId.setName("ID");

Attribute timeSpan = corePackage.getAttribute().createAttribute();
timeSpan.setName("Time Span");
Attribute endingDate =
  corePackage.getAttribute().createAttribute();
endingDate.setName("Ending Date");

//add the attributes to the dimension
time.addFeature(timeId);
time.addFeature(timeSpan);
time.addFeature(endingDate);
```

Defining Levels and Level Attributes

In the CWM metamodel, a dimension can be described as a set of levels. In the metamodel, a level is a specialization of the class memberSelection.

Note that there is an association between dimension and level with role names preceded by a "/". This is a convention the CWM specification uses when one would expect to see an association between two classes and that association is actually provided higher in the object hierarchy. In this case, the association between dimension and level is actually between dimension and memberSelection. As such, the role names are /dimension and /memberSelection in the diagram.

The CWM level class is a type of Class and, as such, can expose its own set of attributes. These attributes are intentionally different from the attributes exposed by the dimension. The dimension attributes can be mapped to the level's attributes when there is equivalence between them; but, in general, mapping is required only when the user wishes to provide this functionality. This layering of the logical model provides the CWM user with maximum flexibility in defining where attributes are visible. This feature allows users to define attributes that only make sense at specific levels; they need not be exposed by the dimension to be a part of a level.

The instance diagram in Figure 6.8 defines six independent levels in the Product dimension. Each level exposes a set of attributes that are associated to the level using the addFeature method. Note that level attributes have different names than the Product dimension attributes. CWM provides this functionality in the metamodel because the dimension is connected to its levels and level attributes using the mapping metamodel. This will be covered later in the example, but it is an important feature that level attributes and dimension attributes are independent.

The following code snippet represents the code necessary to create the product levels and level attributes. It is important to note that the specific API calls used by levels are the same API calls used by the dimension. This is because both dimension and level are types of classes. They inherit attributes from the same structure in the hierarchy, so the manipulation of these classes is identical with respect to attributes. Also note that to add a level to the Product dimension, the addMemberSelection method is used. As stated above, the level concept has been generalized as memberSelection.

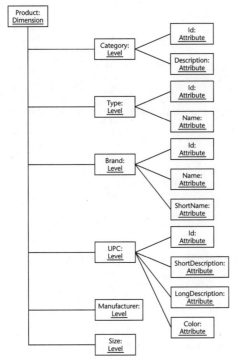

Figure 6.8 The Product levels and level attributes.

```
//create the product dimension levels
Level category = olapPackage.getLevel().createLevel();
category.setName("Category");
product.addMemberSelection(category);

//add the category attributes
Attribute categoryId = corePackage.getAttribute().createAttribute();
categoryId.setName("ID");
categoryId.setOwner(category);
Attribute categoryDesc = corePackage.getAttribute().createAttribute();
categoryDesc.setName("Description");
categoryDesc.setOwner(category);

//create the type level
Level type = olapPackage.getLevel().createLevel();
```

```
type.setName("Type");
product.addMemberSelection(type);

//add the type attributes
Attribute typeId = corePackage.getAttribute().createAttribute();
typeId.setName("ID");
typeId.setOwner(type);
Attribute typeName = corePackage.getAttribute().createAttribute();
typeName.setName("Name");
typeName.setOwner(type);

//create the brand level
Level brand = olapPackage.getLevel().createLevel();
brand.setName("Brand");
product.addMemberSelection(brand);

//add the type attributes
Attribute brandId = corePackage.getAttribute().createAttribute();
brandId.setName("ID");
brandId.setOwner(brand);
Attribute brandName = corePackage.getAttribute().createAttribute();
brandName.setName("Name");
brandName.setOwner(brand);
Attribute brandSName = corePackage.getAttribute().createAttribute();
brandSName.setName("Short Name");
brandSName.setOwner(brand);

//create the UPC level
Level UPC = olapPackage.getLevel().createLevel();
UPC.setName("UPC");
product.addMemberSelection(UPC);

//add the type attributes
Attribute UPCId = corePackage.getAttribute().createAttribute();
UPCId.setName("ID");
UPCId.setOwner(UPC);
Attribute UPCLName = corePackage.getAttribute().createAttribute();
UPCLName.setName("Long Name");
UPCLName.setOwner(UPC);
Attribute UPCSName = corePackage.getAttribute().createAttribute();
UPCSName.setName("Short Name");
UPCSName.setOwner(UPC);

//create the manufacturer and size level
Level manufacturer = olapPackage.getLevel().createLevel();
manufacturer.setName("Manufacturer");
product.addMemberSelection(manufacturer);

Level size = olapPackage.getLevel().createLevel();
size.setName("Size");
product.addMemberSelection(size);
```

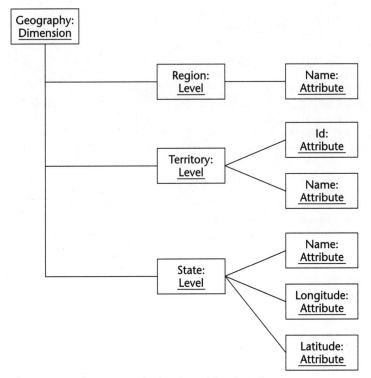

Figure 6.9 The Geography levels and level attributes.

The Geography dimension will contain three levels. The individual levels will expose a set of attributes unique to the owning level. In this case, only one level will expose all the dimension attributes. The longitude and latitude dimension attributes will only have meaning at the state level. As such, only the state level will have attributes that can be mapped to the product attributes. The instance diagram in Figure 6.9 represents the Geography dimension's levels and level attributes.

The following code snippet represents the API calls necessary to create the Geography level instances.

```
//create the geography levels
Level region = olapPackage.getLevel().createLevel();
region.setName("Region");
geog.addMemberSelection(region);

//create the region attribute
Attribute name = corePackage.getAttribute().createAttribute();
name.setName("Name");
name.setOwner(region);
```

```
//create the territory level
Level territory = olapPackage.getLevel().createLevel();
territory.setName("Territory");
geog.addMemberSelection(territory);

//create the region attribute
Attribute territoryId = corePackage.getAttribute().createAttribute();
territoryId.setName("Id");
territoryId.setOwner(territory);
Attribute territoryName = corePackage.getAttribute().createAttribute();
territoryName.setName("Name");
territoryName.setOwner(territory);

//create the state level
Level state = olapPackage.getLevel().createLevel();
state.setName("state");
geog.addMemberSelection(state);

//create the region attribute
Attribute stateName = corePackage.getAttribute().createAttribute();
stateName.setName("Name");
stateName.setOwner(state);
Attribute stateLongitude = corePackage.getAttribute().createAttribute();
stateLongitude.setName("Longitude");
stateLongitude.setOwner(state);
Attribute stateLatitude = corePackage.getAttribute().createAttribute();
stateLatitude.setName("Latitude");
stateLatitude.setOwner(state);
```

The Time dimension will contain four levels, and each level will expose all of the Time dimension attributes. In many systems, this will be the norm and is fully supported by CWM. One of the goals of the CWM team was to cover as much of the data warehouse space as possible. For this reason, it is possible to provide a very complex dimension to level mapping. This is not to say that such a structure is necessary and, in fact, many of the systems that CWM used to unit test the model had uniform structures between levels and dimensions. The instance diagrams in Figure 6.10 represent the Time dimension levels and their supporting structures.

The following code snippet represents the API calls to create the Time dimension's levels and level attributes. Note that the code to create the various dimensions, levels, and attributes is all very similar. This is a side effect of pushing many of the common constructs into the Core package. The CWM team felt this was desirable and limited the number of API calls needed to understand the model.

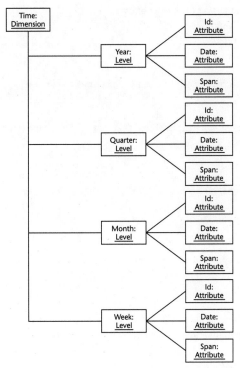

Figure 6.10   The Time levels and level attributes.

```
//create the time levels
Level year = olapPackage.getLevel().createLevel();
year.setName("Year");
time.addMemberSelection(year);

//create the year attribute
Attribute yearId = corePackage.getAttribute().createAttribute();
yearId.setName("Id");
yearId.setOwner(year);
Attribute yearDate = corePackage.getAttribute().createAttribute();
yearDate.setName("Date");
yearDate.setOwner(year);
Attribute yearTimeSpan =
corePackage.getAttribute().createAttribute();
yearTimeSpan.setName("Span");
yearTimeSpan.setOwner(year);

//create the time levels
```

```
Level quarter = olapPackage.getLevel().createLevel();
quarter.setName("Quarter");
time.addMemberSelection(quarter);

//create the year attribute
Attribute quarterId = corePackage.getAttribute().createAttribute();
quarterId.setName("Id");
quarterId.setOwner(year);
Attribute quarterDate = corePackage.getAttribute().createAttribute();
quarterDate.setName("Date");
quarterDate.setOwner(year);
Attribute quarterTimeSpan =
corePackage.getAttribute().createAttribute();
quarterTimeSpan.setName("Span");
quarterTimeSpan.setOwner(year);

//create the time levels
Level month = olapPackage.getLevel().createLevel();
month.setName("Month");
time.addMemberSelection(month);

//create the year attribute
Attribute monthId = corePackage.getAttribute().createAttribute();
monthId.setName("Id");
monthId.setOwner(year);
Attribute monthDate = corePackage.getAttribute().createAttribute();
monthDate.setName("Date");
monthDate.setOwner(year);
Attribute monthTimeSpan = corePackage.getAttribute().createAttribute();
monthTimeSpan.setName("Span");
monthTimeSpan.setOwner(year);

//create the time levels
Level week = olapPackage.getLevel().createLevel();
week.setName("Week");
time.addMemberSelection(week);

//create the year attribute
Attribute weekId = corePackage.getAttribute().createAttribute();
weekId.setName("Id");
weekId.setOwner(year);
Attribute weekDate = corePackage.getAttribute().createAttribute();
weekDate.setName("Date");
weekDate.setOwner(year);
Attribute weekTimeSpan = corePackage.getAttribute().createAttribute();
weekTimeSpan.setName("Span");
weekTimeSpan.setOwner(year);
```

Defining Hierarchies and Hierarchical Attributes

In this subsection, we will use CWM OLAP and Core metamodel elements to define the various Hierarchies and Attributes of our logical dimensions.

We shall start with the Product dimension. The Product dimension has a primary Hierarchy that intersects with four of the Product dimension's defined levels. The instance diagram of Figure 6.11 shows how this Hierarchy and the various level-based attributes are represented as a CWM object model. Product dimension has a single LevelBased Hierarchy called *Standard*, and the attributes particular to this single Hierarchy consist of *Id*, which specifies a unique key for members of the product dimension; *LongDescription*, which specifies any long, textual description associated with the member; and *Parent*, an attribute used to specify any given member's parent member in the Standard Hierarchy.

The *Category* level, which is the highest level of the Product dimension, and is represented via the Level 0 HierarchyLevelAssociation intersection object, consists of the attributes Id and LongDescription. Note that the Id and LongDescription attributes are identical in intent to the Id and LongDescription attributes of the Product dimension as a whole. That is, they are used to specify the unique IDs and long descriptions, respectively, of all Product dimension members residing within the intersection of Level 0 and the Standard Hierarchy. Although these Level 0 attributes are identical in name and semantics to those of the Product dimension as a whole, note that they are still different attributes; they are specific to members occupying the uppermost level (Level 0) of the Product dimension, and do not apply to all members described by the Product dimension as a whole. (Also, note that even if the Product dimension had one, and only one, Hierarchy, specifying this intersection explicitly using a HierarchyLevelAssociation object is still required, as this is a standard, intended usage of the CWM OLAP model.) Note that the Level 0 HierarchyLevelAssociation object also has an explicit link to the Category level of the Product dimension.

The *Type* level, which is the second highest level of the Product dimension, is represented via the Level 1 HierarchyLevelAssociation intersection object, and consists of the attributes Id, LongDescription, and *Parent*. Here, Parent represents an attribute of the members occupying the intersection between the Type level and Standard Hierarchy that specifies values used to uniquely identify the member parent residing at Level 0, of any given member residing at Level 1 (the Type level). Otherwise, the other attributes have the same names and semantic intent as the correspondingly named attributes in Level 0. Note that the Level 1 HierarchyLevelAssociation object also has an explicit link to the Type level object of the Product dimension.

The *Brand* level, which is the third level of the Product dimension, is represented via the Level 2 HierarchyLevelAssociation intersection object, and consists of the attributes Id, LongDescription, and Parent, and also contains an explicit link to the Brand level object.

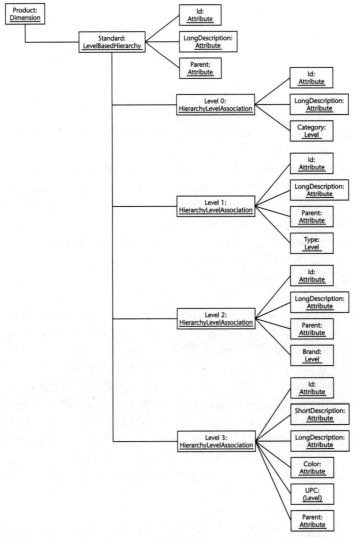

Figure 6.11   Product Standard Level Hierarchy and Hierarchical attributes.

Finally, the *Universal Package Code (UPC)* level, which represents the lowest possible level of the Product dimension, is represented via the Level 3 HierarchyLevelAssociation intersection object, and consists of the attributes Id, ShortDescription, LongDescription, Color, and Parent, and also, of course, contains an explicit link to the UPC level object. Note that Color is a good example of an attribute that can only exist at this particular level; that is, at the level of the individual products or items. An attribute like Color could not logically apply to such higher levels of the hierarchy such as Brand, Type, and Category.

The code fragment below illustrates the JMI code used to construct the Product dimension Standard Hierarchy using the various CWM modeling elements.

```
//create the standard product Hierarchy
LevelBasedHierarchy prodStdH =
olapPackage.getLevelBasedHierarchy(). createLevelBasedHierarchy();
prodStdH.setName("Standard");
product.addHierarchy(prodStdH);

//create the hierarchy attributes
Attribute stdId = corePackage.getAttribute().createAttribute();
stdId.setName("Id");
stdId.setOwner(prodStdH);
Attribute stdLongDescription =
corePackage.getAttribute().createAttribute();
stdLongDescription.setName("Long Description");
stdLongDescription.setOwner(prodStdH);
Attribute stdParent =
corePackage.getAttribute().createAttribute();
stdParent.setName("Parent");
stdParent.setOwner(prodStdH);

//create the hierarchyLevelRelationships
HierarchyLevelAssociation catHLR =

olapPackage.getHierarchyLevelAssociation().createHierarchyLevel
Association();
catHLR.setName("Category");
catHLR.setCurrentLevel(category);
prodStdH.addHierarchyLevelAssociation(catHLR);

Attribute catHLRId = corePackage.getAttribute().createAttribute();
catHLRId.setName("Id");
catHLRId.setOwner(catHLR);
Attribute catHLRLongDescription =
corePackage.getAttribute().createAttribute();
catHLRLongDescription.setName("Long Description");
catHLRLongDescription.setOwner(catHLR);
```

```
        //create the hierarchyLevelRelationships
        HierarchyLevelAssociation typeHLR =

olapPackage.getHierarchyLevelAssociation().createHierarchyLevel
Association();
        typeHLR.setName("Type");
        typeHLR.setCurrentLevel(type);
        prodStdH.addHierarchyLevelAssociation(typeHLR);

        Attribute typeHLRId =
corePackage.getAttribute().createAttribute();
        typeHLRId.setName("Id");
        typeHLRId.setOwner(typeHLR);
        Attribute typeHLRLongDescription =
corePackage.getAttribute().createAttribute();
        typeHLRLongDescription.setName("Long Description");
        typeHLRLongDescription.setOwner(typeHLR);
        Attribute typeHLRparent =
corePackage.getAttribute().createAttribute();
        typeHLRparent.setName("Parent");
        typeHLRparent.setOwner(typeHLR);


        //create the hierarchyLevelRelationships
        HierarchyLevelAssociation brandHLR =
olapPackage.getHierarchyLevelAssociation().createHierarchyLevel
Association();
        brandHLR.setName("Brand");
        brandHLR.setCurrentLevel(brand);
        prodStdH.addHierarchyLevelAssociation(brandHLR);

        Attribute brandHLRId =
corePackage.getAttribute().createAttribute();
        brandHLRId.setName("Id");
        brandHLRId.setOwner(brandHLR);
        Attribute brandHLRLongDescription =
corePackage.getAttribute().createAttribute();
        brandHLRLongDescription.setName("Long Description");
        brandHLRLongDescription.setOwner(brandHLR);
        Attribute brandHLRparent =
corePackage.getAttribute().createAttribute();
        brandHLRparent.setName("Parent");
        brandHLRparent.setOwner(brandHLR);

        //create the hierarchyLevelRelationships
        HierarchyLevelAssociation upcHLR =

olapPackage.getHierarchyLevelAssociation().createHierarchyLevel
Association();
        upcHLR.setName("UPC");
        upcHLR.setCurrentLevel(UPC);
        prodStdH.addHierarchyLevelAssociation(upcHLR);
```

```
    Attribute upcHLRId = corePackage.getAttribute().createAttribute();
    upcHLRId.setName("Id");
    upcHLRId.setOwner(upcHLR);
    Attribute upcHLRLongDescription =
corePackage.getAttribute().createAttribute();
    upcHLRLongDescription.setName("Long Description");
    upcHLRLongDescription.setOwner(upcHLR);
    Attribute upcHLRShortDescription =
corePackage.getAttribute().createAttribute();
    upcHLRLongDescription.setName("Short Description");
    upcHLRLongDescription.setOwner(upcHLR);
    Attribute upcHLRColor =
corePackage.getAttribute().createAttribute();
    upcHLRColor.setName("Color");
    upcHLRColor.setOwner(upcHLR);
    Attribute upcHLRparent =
corePackage.getAttribute().createAttribute();
    upcHLRparent.setName("Parent");
    upcHLRparent.setOwner(upcHLR);
```

The Product dimension has a secondary Hierarchy called *Alternate* that intersects with three of the Product dimension's defined levels. The instance diagram of Figure 6.12 shows how this secondary Hierarchy and its various level-based attributes are represented as a CWM object model. The Alternate Hierarchy is a LevelBased Hierarchy, and the attributes particular to this Hierarchy consist of *Id*, which specifies a unique key for members of the Product dimension; *Description*, which specifies any long, textual description associated with the member; and *Parent*, an attribute used to specify any given member's parent member in the Alternate Hierarchy.

The *Manufacturer* level, which is the highest level of the Product dimension, relative to the Alternate Hierarchy, is represented via the Level 0 HierarchyLevelAssociation intersection object, and consists of the Attributes Id and Description, as well as an explicit link to the Manufacturer level object.

Next, the *Size* level, which is the second highest level of the Product dimension, relative to the Alternate Hierarchy, is represented via the Level 1 HierarchyLevelAssociation intersection object, and consists of the attributes Id, Description, and Parent. The Level 1 HierarchyLevelAssociation object also has an explicit link to the Size level object of the Product dimension, as expected.

Finally, the *UPC* level, which is the lowest level of the Product dimension, relative to the Alternate Hierarchy, is represented via the Level 2 HierarchyLevelAssociation intersection object, and consists of the attributes Id, Description, Parent, and Color, and also contains an explicit link to the UPC level object.

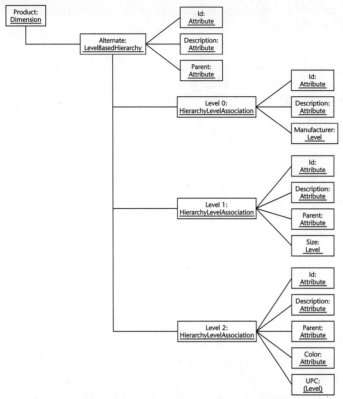

Figure 6.12 Product Alternate Hierarchy level and Hierarchical attributes.

The code fragment below illustrates the JMI code used to construct the Product dimension Alternate Hierarchy using the various CWM modeling elements.

```
        //create the alternate product Hierarchy
     LevelBasedHierarchy prodAltH =

olapPackage.getLevelBasedHierarchy().createLevelBasedHierarchy();
     prodAltH.setName("Alternate");
     product.addHierarchy(prodAltH);

     //create the hierarchy attributes
     Attribute altId = corePackage.getAttribute().createAttribute();
     altId.setName("Id");
     altId.setOwner(prodAltH);
     Attribute atlLongDescription =
corePackage.getAttribute().createAttribute();
     atlLongDescription.setName("Long Description");
     atlLongDescription.setOwner(prodAltH);
```

```
        Attribute altParent = corePackage.getAttribute().createAttribute();
        altParent.setName("Parent");
        altParent.setOwner(prodAltH);

        //create the hierarchyLevelRelationships
        HierarchyLevelAssociation manuHLR =

olapPackage.getHierarchyLevelAssociation().createHierarchyLevel
Association();
        manuHLR.setName("Manufacturer");
        manuHLR.setCurrentLevel(manufacturer);
        prodAltH.addHierarchyLevelAssociation(manuHLR);

        Attribute manuHLRId =
corePackage.getAttribute().createAttribute();
        manuHLRId.setName("Id");
        manuHLRId.setOwner(manuHLR);
        Attribute manuHLRLongDescription =
corePackage.getAttribute().createAttribute();
        manuHLRLongDescription.setName("Long Description");
        manuHLRLongDescription.setOwner(manuHLR);


        //create the hierarchyLevelRelationships
        HierarchyLevelAssociation sizeHLR =

olapPackage.getHierarchyLevelAssociation().createHierarchyLevel
Association();
        sizeHLR.setName("Size");
        sizeHLR.setCurrentLevel(size);
        prodAltH.addHierarchyLevelAssociation(sizeHLR);

        Attribute sizeHLRId = corePackage.getAttribute().createAttribute();
        sizeHLRId.setName("Id");
        sizeHLRId.setOwner(sizeHLR);
        Attribute sizeHLRLongDescription =
corePackage.getAttribute().createAttribute();
        sizeHLRLongDescription.setName("Long Description");
        sizeHLRLongDescription.setOwner(sizeHLR);
        Attribute sizeHLRparent =
corePackage.getAttribute().createAttribute();
        sizeHLRparent.setName("Parent");
        sizeHLRparent.setOwner(sizeHLR);

        //create the hierarchyLevelRelationships
        HierarchyLevelAssociation altupcHLR =
olapPackage.getHierarchyLevelAssociation().createHierarchyLevel
Association();
        altupcHLR.setName("UPC");
        altupcHLR.setCurrentLevel(UPC);
        prodAltH.addHierarchyLevelAssociation(altupcHLR);
```

```
        Attribute altupcHLRId =
corePackage.getAttribute().createAttribute();
        altupcHLRId.setName("Id");
        altupcHLRId.setOwner(altupcHLR);
        Attribute altupcHLRDescription =
corePackage.getAttribute().createAttribute();
        altupcHLRDescription.setName("Description");
        altupcHLRDescription.setOwner(altupcHLR);
        Attribute altupcHLRColor =
corePackage.getAttribute().createAttribute();
        altupcHLRColor.setName("Color");
        altupcHLRColor.setOwner(altupcHLR);
        Attribute altupcHLRparent =
corePackage.getAttribute().createAttribute();
        altupcHLRparent.setName("Parent");
        altupcHLRparent.setOwner(altupcHLR);
```

The Geography dimension has a single, primary Hierarchy, also called *Standard*, that intersects with three of the Geography dimension's defined levels. The instance diagram in Figure 6.13 shows how this Hierarchy and its various level-based attributes are represented as a CWM object model. The Standard Hierarchy is a LevelBased Hierarchy, and the attributes particular to this Hierarchy consist of *Id*, which specifies a unique key for members of the Geography dimension; *Name*, which specifies any textual description associated with the member (identical in intent to the LongDescription, ShortDescription, and Description Attributes presented for the Product dimension); and *Parent*, an attribute used to specify any given member's parent member in the Standard Hierarchy.

The *Region* level, which is the highest level of the Geography dimension, relative to the Standard Hierarchy, is represented via the Region HierarchyLevelAssociation intersection object, and consists of the attributes Id and Name, as well as an explicit link to the Region level object.

Next, the *Territory* level, which is the second highest level of the Geography dimension, relative to the Standard Hierarchy, is represented via the Territory HierarchyLevelAssociation intersection object, and consists of the attributes Id, Name, and Parent. The Region HierarchyLevelAssociation object also has an explicit link to the Size level object of the Geography dimension, as expected.

Finally, the *State* level, which is the lowest level of the Geography dimension, relative to the Standard Hierarchy, is represented via the State HierarchyLevelAssociation intersection object, and consists of the attributes Id, Name, and Parent, and also contains an explicit link to the State level object.

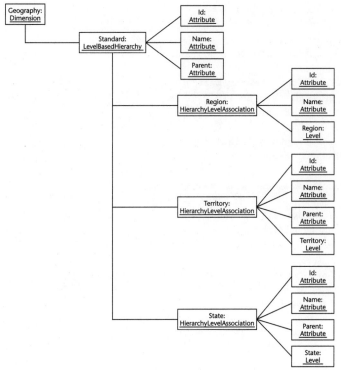

Figure 6.13 Geography Hierarchy and Hierarchical attributes.

The code fragment below illustrates the JMI code used to construct the Geography dimension Standard Hierarchy using the various CWM modeling elements.

```
//create the standard geog Hierarchy
    LevelBasedHierarchy geogStdH =

olapPackage.getLevelBasedHierarchy().createLevelBasedHierarchy();
    geogStdH.setName("Standard");
    geog.addHierarchy(geogStdH);

    //create the hierarchy attributes
    Attribute geogstdId =
corePackage.getAttribute().createAttribute();
    geogstdId.setName("Id");
    geogstdId.setOwner(geogStdH);
```

```
        Attribute geogstdLongDescription =
corePackage.getAttribute().createAttribute();
        geogstdLongDescription.setName("Long Description");
        geogstdLongDescription.setOwner(geogStdH);
        Attribute geogstdParent =
corePackage.getAttribute().createAttribute();
        geogstdParent.setName("Parent");
        geogstdParent.setOwner(geogStdH);

        //create the hierarchyLevelRelationships
        HierarchyLevelAssociation regHLR =

olapPackage.getHierarchyLevelAssociation().createHierarchyLevelAssociati
on();
        regHLR.setName("Region");
        regHLR.setCurrentLevel(region);
        geogStdH.addHierarchyLevelAssociation(regHLR);

        Attribute regHLRId = corePackage.getAttribute().createAttribute();
        regHLRId.setName("Id");
        regHLRId.setOwner(regHLR);
        Attribute regHLRName =
corePackage.getAttribute().createAttribute();
        regHLRName.setName("Name");
        regHLRName.setOwner(regHLR);


        //create the hierarchyLevelRelationships
        HierarchyLevelAssociation terrHLR =

olapPackage.getHierarchyLevelAssociation().createHierarchyLevelAssociati
on();
        terrHLR.setName("Territory");
        terrHLR.setCurrentLevel(territory);
        geogStdH.addHierarchyLevelAssociation(terrHLR);

        Attribute terrHLRId =
corePackage.getAttribute().createAttribute();
        terrHLRId.setName("Id");
        terrHLRId.setOwner(terrHLR);
        Attribute terrHLRName =
corePackage.getAttribute().createAttribute();
        terrHLRName.setName("Name");
        terrHLRName.setOwner(terrHLR);
        Attribute terrHLRparent =
corePackage.getAttribute().createAttribute();
        terrHLRparent.setName("Parent");
        terrHLRparent.setOwner(terrHLR);


            //create the hierarchyLevelRelationships
```

```
      HierarchyLevelAssociation stateHLR =

olapPackage.getHierarchyLevelAssociation().createHierarchyLevelAssociati
on();
      stateHLR.setName("State");
      stateHLR.setCurrentLevel(state);
      geogStdH.addHierarchyLevelAssociation(stateHLR);

      Attribute stateHLRId =
corePackage.getAttribute().createAttribute();
      stateHLRId.setName("Id");
      stateHLRId.setOwner(stateHLR);
      Attribute stateHLRName =
corePackage.getAttribute().createAttribute();
      stateHLRName.setName("Name");
      stateHLRName.setOwner(stateHLR);
      Attribute stateHLRparent =
corePackage.getAttribute().createAttribute();
      stateHLRparent.setName("Parent");
      stateHLRparent.setOwner(stateHLR);
```

The Time dimension has a single, primary Hierarchy, called *Calendar*, that intersects with four of the Time dimension's defined levels. The instance diagram in Figure 6.14 shows how this Hierarchy and its various level-based attributes are represented as a CWM object model. The Calendar Hierarchy is a LevelBasedHierarchy, and the attributes particular to this Hierarchy consist of *Id*, which specifies a unique key for members of the Time dimension; *Date*, which specifies the calendar date of the beginning of any time period represented by a given member; and *Span*, an attribute used to specify the length or duration of that time period.

The *Year* level, which is the highest level of the Time dimension, relative to the Calendar Hierarchy, is represented via the Year HierarchyLevelAssociation intersection object, and consists of the attributes Id, Date, and Span, as well as an explicit link to the Year level object.

The *Quarter* level, which is the second highest level of the Time dimension, relative to the Calendar Hierarchy, is represented via the Quarter HierarchyLevelAssociation intersection object, and consists of the attributes Id, Date, Span, and Parent. The Quarter HierarchyLevelAssociation object also has an explicit link to the Quarter level object of the Time dimension, as expected.

Next, the *Month* level, which is the third level of the Time dimension, relative to the Calendar Hierarchy, is represented via the Month HierarchyLevelAssociation intersection object, and consists of the attributes Id, Date, Span, and Parent. The Month HierarchyLevelAssociation object also has an explicit link to the Month level object of the Time dimension, as expected.

Finally, the *Week* level, which is the lowest level of the Time dimension, relative to the Calendar Hierarchy, is represented via the Week HierarchyLevelAssociation intersection object, and consists of the attributes Id, Date, Span, and Parent, and also contains an explicit link to the Week level object.

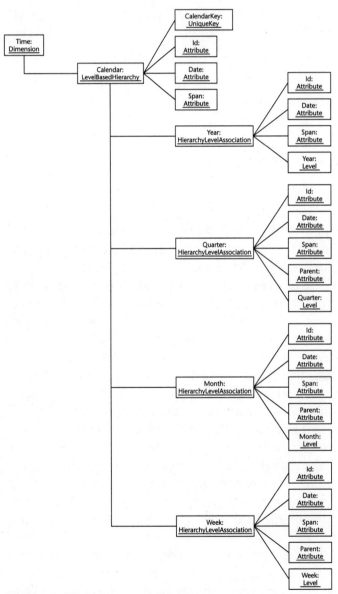

Figure 6.14 Time Hierarchy and Hierarchical attributes.

Add the Dimensions to the Schema

The dimensions and their logical structures have been completed. The OLAP Schema class provides a container to group sets of cooperating dimensions and cubes. The dimensions created above can be added to the logical schema. Later in the example, a set of Cubes will also be added to the logical schema. The set of dimensions and Cubes represents an analysis domain for end users. Figure 6.15 and the code fragment below illustrate the addition of dimensions to an OLAP Schema.

```
//create an overall holding schema
org.omg.java.cwm.analysis.olap.Schema dimensionalSchema =
    olapPackage.getSchema().createSchema();

dimensionalSchema.addDimension(product);
dimensionalSchema.addDimension(geog);
dimensionalSchema.addDimension(time);
```

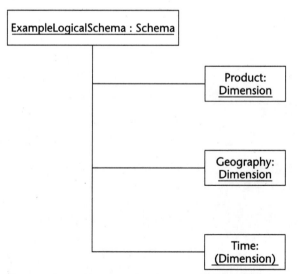

Figure 6.15   The ExampleSchema with its dimensions.

Defining Cubes and Measures

CWM contains the concept of a Cube. This structure is supplied to allow users to combine measures that share the same dimensionality into a single entity. Creating a CubeDimensionAssociation object for each dimension of the Cube identifies the dimensionality. The Cube's association to CubeDimensionAssociation is an ordered association because dimension order is important to the structure of the Cube. The CubeDimensionAssociation class contains a reference to the associated dimension. The Cube can contain a set of attributes and measures. The measures of the Cube represent some user-defined measurement. The attributes represent either the framework of the Cube or properties about the Cube. The use of framework attributes will be discussed later in the section called *Defining Keys*.

This example will define two Cubes. The first Cube will represent sales measures. These measures—sales cost and profit—will be dimensioned by all three dimensions defined earlier. The instances required to define the Sales Cube are shown in Figure 6.16.

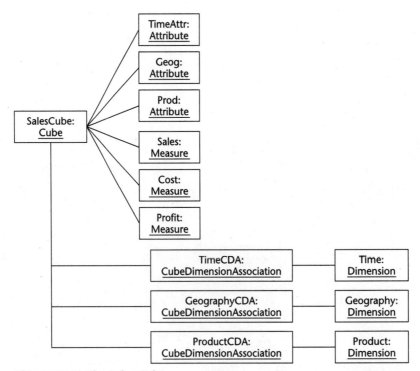

Figure 6.16   The Sales Cube.

In the Sales Cube example, there will be an attribute that represents the dimension member for each dimension of the Cube. The Cube is a type classifier so like dimension, it inherits the ability to contain attributes from its parent in the object hierarchy. The Cube also has a set of measures. The Measure class is a type of attribute. The addition of measures to the Cube is done using the addFeature method. The Cube is associated to the dimensions by an ordered set of CubeDimensionAssociations. Each CubeDimensionAssociation is then associated to a dimension using the setDimension method.

```
//create the cube
Cube salesCube = olapPackage.getCube().createCube();
salesCube.setName("Sales Cube");

//add the attributes and measures to the cube

//add an attribute that will represent each dimension and the key
of the
//cube
Attribute timeAttr = corePackage.getAttribute().createAttribute();
timeAttr.setName("Time");
timeAttr.setOwner(salesCube);

Attribute geogAttr = corePackage.getAttribute().createAttribute();
geogAttr.setName("Geog");
geogAttr.setOwner(salesCube);

Attribute prodAttr = corePackage.getAttribute().createAttribute();
prodAttr.setName("Prod");
prodAttr.setOwner(salesCube);

//add the measures
Measure sales = olapPackage.getMeasure().createMeasure();
sales.setName("Sales");
sales.setOwner(salesCube);

Measure cost = olapPackage.getMeasure().createMeasure();
cost.setName("Cost");
cost.setOwner(salesCube);

Measure Profit = olapPackage.getMeasure().createMeasure();
Profit.setName("Profit");
Profit.setOwner(salesCube);

//create the three cube dimension associations
CubeDimensionAssociation timeAsso =

olapPackage.getCubeDimensionAssociation().createCubeDimensionAssociation
();
```

```
        timeAsso.setDimension(time);
        salesCube.addCubeDimensionAssociation(timeAsso);

        CubeDimensionAssociation geogAsso =

olapPackage.getCubeDimensionAssociation().createCubeDimensionAssociation
();
        geogAsso.setDimension(geog);
        salesCube.addCubeDimensionAssociation(geogAsso);

        CubeDimensionAssociation prodAsso =

olapPackage.getCubeDimensionAssociation().createCubeDimensionAssociation
();
        prodAsso.setDimension(product);
        salesCube.addCubeDimensionAssociation(prodAsso);
```

A second example Cube called the *Population Cube* will contain two measures: *population* and *total revenue*. The Time and Geography dimensions are used to define the dimensionality of these measures. In Figure 6.17 and in the following code, note that there is a separate CubeDimensionAssociation for each dimension in each Cube. The CubeDimensionAssociation objects are not shared across Cubes. This was done to allow a different calculation hierarchy to be defined on a Cube-by-Cube basis. The instances for the population Cube are shown in Figure 6.17.

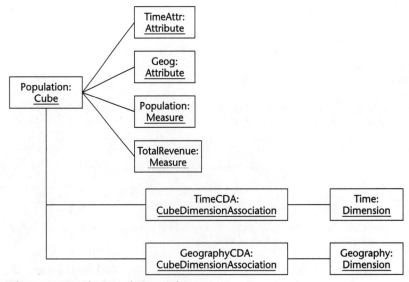

Figure 6.17   The Population Cube.

The code fragment below illustrates the JMI code used to construct the Population Cube using the various CWM modeling elements.

```
//create the cube
    Cube populationCube = olapPackage.getCube().createCube();
    populationCube.setName("Population Cube");

    //add the attributes and measures to the cube

    //add an attribute that will represent each dimension and the key
of the
    //cube
    Attribute poptimeAttr =
corePackage.getAttribute().createAttribute();
    poptimeAttr.setName("Time");
    poptimeAttr.setOwner(populationCube);

    Attribute popgeogAttr =
corePackage.getAttribute().createAttribute();
    popgeogAttr.setName("Geog");
    popgeogAttr.setOwner(populationCube);

    //add the measures
    Measure totalRevenue = olapPackage.getMeasure().createMeasure();
    sales.setName("Total Revenue");
    sales.setOwner(populationCube);

    //create the two cube dimension associations
    CubeDimensionAssociation poptimeAsso =

olapPackage.getCubeDimensionAssociation().createCubeDimensionAssociation
();
    poptimeAsso.setDimension(time);
    populationCube.addCubeDimensionAssociation(poptimeAsso);

    CubeDimensionAssociation popgeogAsso =

olapPackage.getCubeDimensionAssociation().createCubeDimensionAssociation
();
    popgeogAsso.setDimension(geog);
    populationCube.addCubeDimensionAssociation(popgeogAsso);
```

Add the Cubes to the Schema

The logical model is now nearly complete. Before moving on to the mapping portion of the logical model, the Cubes will be added to the OLAP Schema. In the example above, the dimensions were added to logical schema; now the Cubes can be added. The logical schema is shown in Figure 6.18 with both the dimensions and Cubes.

The following code fragment illustrates the code for adding the Cubes to the logical schema:

```
//add the cubes to the schema
dimensionalSchema.addCube(salesCube);
dimensionalSchema.addCube(populationCube);
```

Defining Keys

Users of the CWM OLAP model need the ability to identify which objects represent the unique set of values for certain OLAP structures. To add clarity to this statement, consider a dimension object. A question that will most certainly be posed to the dimension object is: What is your list of values? To answer this question, a "key" will be added to the dimension. This key will be mapped to some set of the dimension's attributes that, when evaluated, represents the unique set of members that make up the dimension. This same technique is used for the other parts of the OLAP model that will be required to answer the list of values question; namely, Levels, Hierarchies, and HierarchyLevelAssociations. The following set of instance diagrams and code fragments will walk through the objects required to create keys for the various levels of the logical model.

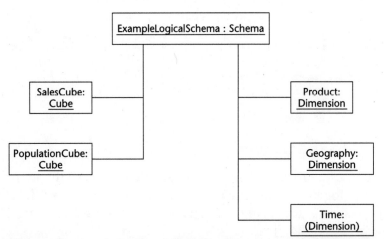

Figure 6.18   The ExampleSchema with its dimensions and Cubes.

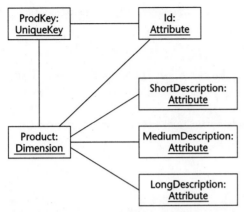

Figure 6.19   Product dimension Key.

Adding Keys to the Dimensions

The Product dimension will be required to respond to the list of values question; to that end, a unique key will be defined. The instance diagram in Figure 6.19 shows that the key on the Product dimension is mapped to the Id attribute. This means that the Id attribute is evaluated to return the list of values of the Product dimension. To add the key to the Product dimension, the addOwnedElement method is used. Figure 6.19 is also another example of using a generalized association CWM.

```
UniqueKey prodKey = keysIndexes.getUniqueKey().createUniqueKey();
prodKey.addFeature(prodId);
product.addOwnedElement(prodKey);
```

The instance diagram in Figure 6.20 and the code snippet that follows illustrate how to create a key for the Geography dimension.

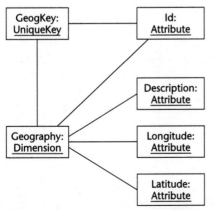

Figure 6.20   Geography dimension Key.

```
UniqueKey geogKey = keysIndexes.getUniqueKey().createUniqueKey();
geogKey.addFeature(geogId);
geog.addOwnedElement(geogKey);
```

Finally, to complete the dimension keys, a key is added to the Time dimension. See Figure 6.21.

```
UniqueKey timeKey = keysIndexes.getUniqueKey().createUniqueKey();
timeKey.addFeature(timeId);
time.addOwnedElement(timeKey);
```

Adding Keys to the Levels

In CWM, the list of values question can be applied to any individual level. The technique used for dimensions will now be applied to the levels. This can be done because both dimensions and levels are both types of classifiers. The designers of CWM reused as many concepts as possible to maintain as much symmetry in the model as possible. The process of adding a key to a level is identical to the process of adding a key to a dimension. This is illustrated in the sequence of instance diagrams in Figures 6.22 to 6.24.

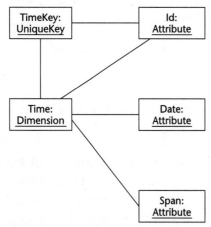

Figure 6.21   Time dimension Key.

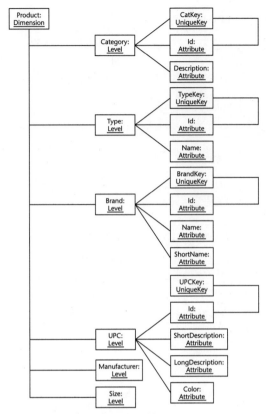

Figure 6.22   Product level keys.

Adding Keys to the Hierarchies

In CWM, the list of values question can be applied to hierarchies in the same way it was applied to individual levels. The key concept was reused across the entire logical OLAP model. The process of adding a key to a level is identical to the process of adding a key to a dimension. This is illustrated in Figures 6.25 to 6.28.

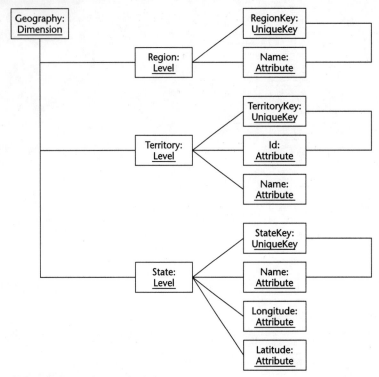

Figure 6.23   Geography keys.

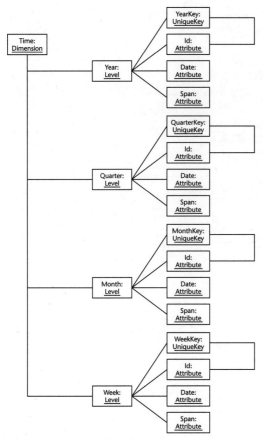

Figure 6.24   Time level keys.

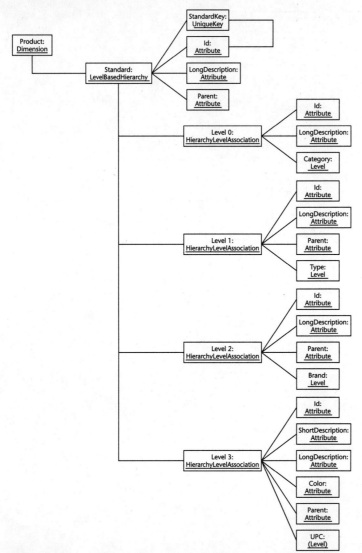

Figure 6.25 Standard Product Hierarchy key.

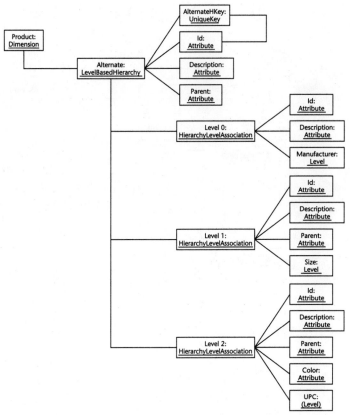

Figure 6.26   Alternate Product Hierarchy key.

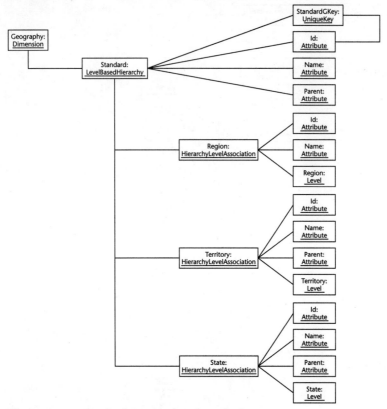

Figure 6.27 Standard Geography Hierarchy key.

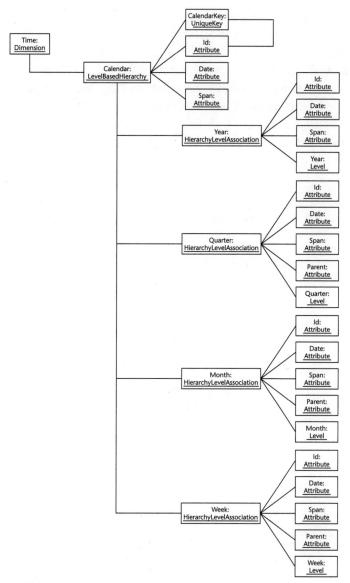

Figure 6.28 Standard Time Hierarchy key.

Adding Keys to the Cubes

Adding a key to the Cube serves a slightly different purpose than adding a key to a dimension. The main function of the Cube key is to identify how certain Cube attributes play a framework role in the Cube. In the Sales

Cube, there are three attributes labeled Time, Geography, and Product. These attributes as a set represent an intersection of dimension member values in the Cube where data is present. When data is returned from the Cube, these attributes will represent dimension members and define the ordinates for the measure values. To identify the set of attributes that plays this role, the CWM designers reused the key concept. The instance diagrams in Figures 6.29 and 6.30 and the following code fragments represent the objects and implementation code necessary to create keys for the Sales and Population Cubes.

```
//create keys on the cubes
UniqueKey salesCubeKey =
keysIndexes.getUniqueKey().createUniqueKey();
salesCubeKey.addFeature(timeAttr);
salesCubeKey.addFeature(geogAttr);
salesCubeKey.addFeature(prodAttr);
salesCube.addOwnedElement(salesCubeKey);
```

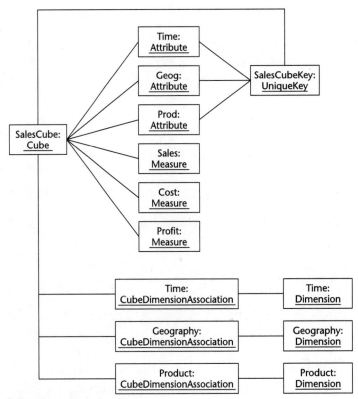

Figure 6.29 Sales Cube key.

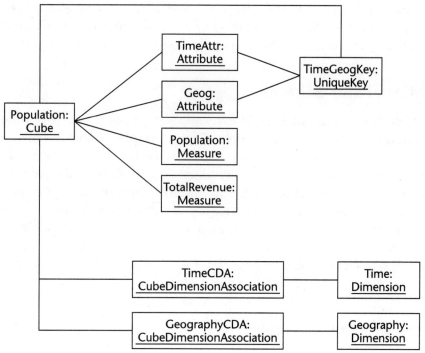

Figure 6.30 Population Cube key.

```
//create keys on the cubes

    UniqueKey popCubeKey =
keysIndexes.getUniqueKey().createUniqueKey();
    popCubeKey.addFeature(poptimeAttr);
    popCubeKey.addFeature(popgeogAttr);
    populationCube.addOwnedElement(popCubeKey);
```

The Physical Model

The CWM metamodel represents several common physical models in the Resource package. This example will show the use of two Resource meta-models: the Relational metamodel and the Multidimensional metamodel. The CWM OLAP metamodel represents a logical view of the data available in an organization. These representations ultimately need some physical counterpart, which stores the actual data. CWM maintains a complete separation between the logical and physical models in the data warehouse. This gives CWM users the greatest level of flexibility in providing logical views driven by end users and the physical needs of database technologies.

A Relational Star-Schema

The first physical representation shown in this example will be from the Relational metamodel. The key features of this example are that the physical representation is completely independent of the logical OLAP view. In this Relational example, a star-schema will be defined to store the data for the logical model defined above. The star-schema will contain a dimension table for each dimension defined above. The dimension tables will contain a column for each level in the hierarchy and a column for each attribute defined at the lowest level in the respective hierarchies. The star-schema will contain two fact tables: one for each OLAP Cube. Each table will have columns representing the Cube's keys and measures.

Defining the Physical Objects

To define the Relational metamodel objects, the diagrams in Figures 6.31 and 6.32 show the portions of the Relational metamodel that will be used. Like the OLAP metamodel, the CWM modeling conventions are used by the Relational metamodel. As such, there are a number of instances of derived associations that will be leveraged in this portion of the example. Note the association between ColumnSet and Column. This association is marked as inherited from their respective parent classes—Classifier/ Feature. The association between Tables and Keys is inherited from NameSpace/ModelElement. Take a moment to note the remaining inherited association in the following metamodels.

Defining the Tables and Columns

The relational example will provide a lookup table for each dimension defined above. In the case of the Product dimension, a relational table called the Product table has six columns. There will be a column called UPC, which will represent the unique UPC values in the system. This column will be used later to define a Primary key for the Product table. There are two attribute columns representing attributes of the UPCs called Description and Color. The remaining columns represent levels in the product hierarchy. The instances of the Relational metamodel and the implementation code fragment are shown in Figures 6.33 to 6.35 and in the coding that follows.

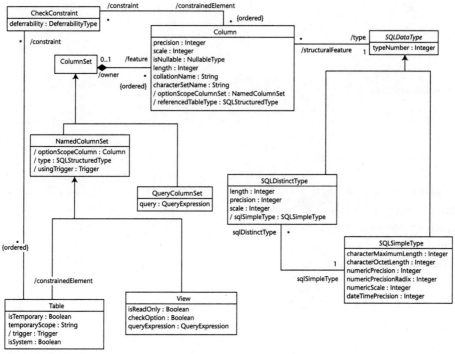

Figure 6.31 The CWM Relational model major components.

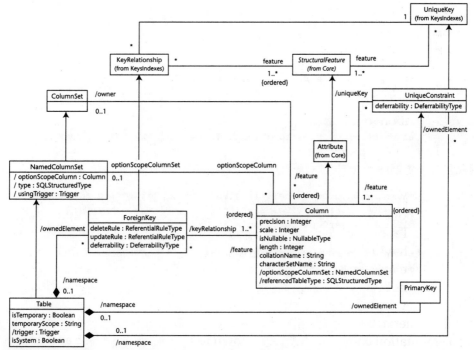

Figure 6.32 The CWM Relational model Keys and Foreign Keys.

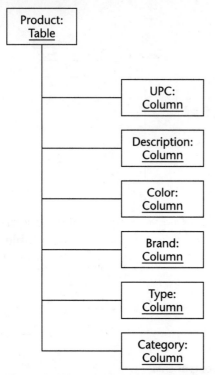

Figure 6.33 The Product Lookup table.

```
//create the relational schema
Table prodTable = relationalPackage.getTable().createTable();
prodTable.setName("Product");

//create the columns
Column relUPC = relationalPackage.getColumn().createColumn();
relUPC.setName("UPC");
relUPC.setOwner(prodTable);

Column relProdDesc = relationalPackage.getColumn().createColumn();
relProdDesc.setName("Description");
relProdDesc.setOwner(prodTable);

Column relBrand = relationalPackage.getColumn().createColumn();
relBrand.setName("Brand");
```

```
relBrand.setOwner(prodTable);

Column relType = relationalPackage.getColumn().createColumn();
relType.setName("Type");
relType.setOwner(prodTable);

Column relCat = relationalPackage.getColumn().createColumn();
relCat.setName("Category");
relCat.setOwner(prodTable);

Column relColor = relationalPackage.getColumn().createColumn();
relColor.setName("Color");
relColor.setOwner(prodTable);
```

A Relational table called the Geography table will support the Geography dimension. This table will have a structure similar to the Product table. The table will contain four columns; a state column represents the lowest level in the hierarchy. The example will define a column to represent the description of the states and columns to represent the rest of the levels in the hierarchy. The state column will be used later as the Primary key for the Geography table. The instances representing the Geography table are shown in Figure 6.34.

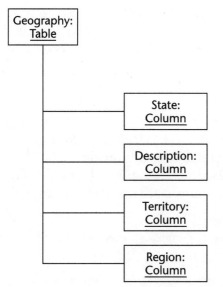

Figure 6.34 The Geography Lookup table.

The code fragment below illustrates the JMI code used to construct the Geography Lookup table using the various CWM modeling elements.

```
//create the geography table

    Table geogTable = relationalPackage.getTable().createTable();
    geogTable.setName("Geography");

    //create the columns
    Column relState = relationalPackage.getColumn().createColumn();
    relState.setName("State");
    relState.setOwner(geogTable);

    Column relGeogDesc = relationalPackage.getColumn().createColumn();
    relGeogDesc.setName("Description");
    relGeogDesc.setOwner(geogTable);

    Column relTerr = relationalPackage.getColumn().createColumn();
    relTerr.setName("Territory");
    relTerr.setOwner(geogTable);

    Column relRegion = relationalPackage.getColumn().createColumn();
    relRegion.setName("Region");
    relRegion.setOwner(geogTable);
```

To complete the dimension lookup tables, a Time table will be created to represent the Time dimension. This table will be constructed with a week column representing the lowest level of the Time dimension and columns that contain the start date and end date of the week period. This may seem odd because many relational systems have date data types that can represent the week column as a date. In this particular example, the proposed dates will be used to represent a nonuniform calendar. Using a start and end date is a common technique to provide date calculations for nonuniform or non-Gregorian calendars. The remaining columns in this table—month, quarter, and year—represent the levels in the time hierarchy. The instance diagrams for the Time table and columns are shown in Figure 6.35.

```
        //create the time table
        Table timeTable = relationalPackage.getTable().createTable();
        timeTable.setName("Time");

        //create the columns
        Column relWeek = relationalPackage.getColumn().createColumn();
        relWeek.setName("Week");
        relWeek.setOwner(timeTable);

        Column relStartDate =
```

```
relationalPackage.getColumn().createColumn();
    relStartDate.setName("Start Date");
    relStartDate.setOwner(timeTable);

    Column relEndDate = relationalPackage.getColumn().createColumn();
    relEndDate.setName("End Date");
    relEndDate.setOwner(timeTable);

    Column relMonth = relationalPackage.getColumn().createColumn();
    relMonth.setName("Month");
    relMonth.setOwner(timeTable);

    Column relQuarter = relationalPackage.getColumn().createColumn();
    relQuarter.setName("Quarter");
    relQuarter.setOwner(timeTable);

    Column relYear = relationalPackage.getColumn().createColumn();
    relYear.setName("Year");
    relYear.setOwner(timeTable);
```

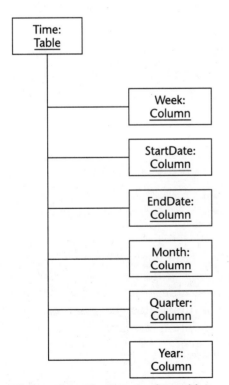

Figure 6.35 The Time Lookup table.

The next step is to define the Fact tables. In a star-schema, the fact tables contain the data for the OLAP Cubes. The Sales table will represent the Sales Cube by defining a table with five columns (see Figure 6.36). The first three columns represent the key of the fact table with the individual columns of the key providing Foreign Key semantics to the dimension tables. The remaining columns—sales and cost—will represent the OLAP measures Sales and Cost. The diagram in Figure 6.36 contains the instances required to create the Sales table.

```
//create the sales fact table

Table salesFactTable = relationalPackage.getTable().createTable();
salesFactTable.setName("Sales Fact Table");

//create the columns
Column relsalesTimeId =
relationalPackage.getColumn().createColumn();
    relsalesTimeId.setName("Time");
    relsalesTimeId.setOwner(salesFactTable);

    Column relSalesGeogId =
relationalPackage.getColumn().createColumn();
    relSalesGeogId.setName("Geography");
    relSalesGeogId.setOwner(salesFactTable);

    Column relSalesProdId =
relationalPackage.getColumn().createColumn();
    relSalesProdId.setName("Product");
    relSalesProdId.setOwner(salesFactTable);

    Column relSales = relationalPackage.getColumn().createColumn();
    relSales.setName("Sales");
    relSales.setOwner(salesFactTable);

    Column relCost = relationalPackage.getColumn().createColumn();
    relCost.setName("Cost");
    relCost.setOwner(salesFactTable);
```

The Population fact table will be the physical representation of the Population Cube. The diagram in Figure 6.37 illustrates the instances and implementation code necessary for the Population fact table.

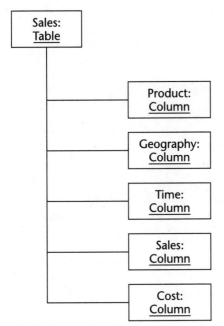

Figure 6.36   The Sales Fact table.

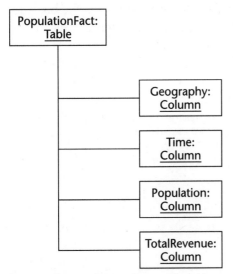

Figure 6.37   The Population Fact table.

```
        //create the population fact table

        Table popFactTable = relationalPackage.getTable().createTable();
        popFactTable.setName("Population Fact Table");

        //create the columns
        Column relpopTimeId =
relationalPackage.getColumn().createColumn();
        relpopTimeId.setName("Time");
        relpopTimeId.setOwner(popFactTable);

        Column relpopGeogId =
relationalPackage.getColumn().createColumn();
        relpopGeogId.setName("Geography");
        relpopGeogId.setOwner(popFactTable);

        Column relTotalRevenue =
relationalPackage.getColumn().createColumn();
        relTotalRevenue.setName("Total Revenue");
        relTotalRevenue.setOwner(popFactTable);
```

Adding Primary Keys and Foreign Keys

The CWM Relational metamodel contains a representation for relational Primary and Foreign keys. The CWM Foundation model supplies the basis for these keys. The Relational metamodel contains specific definitions for the Relational keys, but the keys are added into the model using an inherited association. In the case of Primary and Foreign keys, they are added using the addOwnedElement method on Table. The diagrams in Figures 6.38 through 6.42 and the implementation code that follows illustrate how to add Primary and Foreign keys to the various components of the star-schema.

```
    //add keys to the product table
        PrimaryKey prodPrimaryKey =
relationalPackage.getPrimaryKey().createPrimaryKey();
        prodTable.addOwnedElement(prodPrimaryKey);
        prodPrimaryKey.addFeature(relUPC);
```

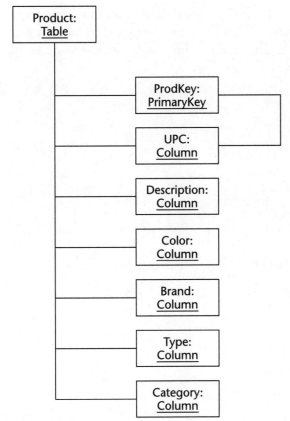

Figure 6.38   The Product Lookup table keys.

A relational star-schema is formed by connecting a fact table to its supporting lookup or dimension tables using Primary key to Foreign key pairs. A Primary key was added to each dimension table above and can now be used by the fact table to provide the star-schema linking. In this example, both the Sales fact table as well as the Population fact table will be connected to their supporting dimension tables using Foreign keys. In addition, each fact table will be defined with a Primary key. In the case of a fact table, the Primary key mimics the structure of the star and contains a set of columns, one for each dimension table. The instance diagrams in Figures 6.41 and 6.42 and the code fragments below illustrate the creation of Primary and Foreign keys for the fact tables.

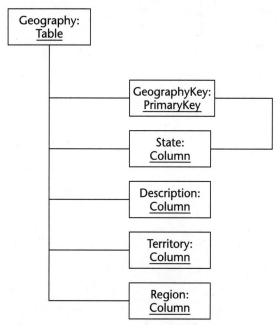

Figure 6.39 The Geography Lookup table keys.

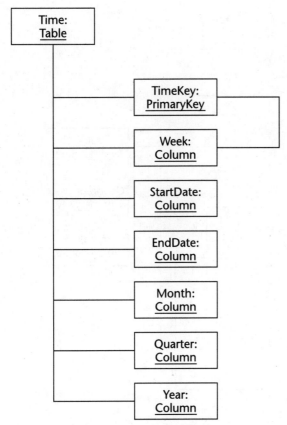

Figure 6.40   The Time Lookup table keys.

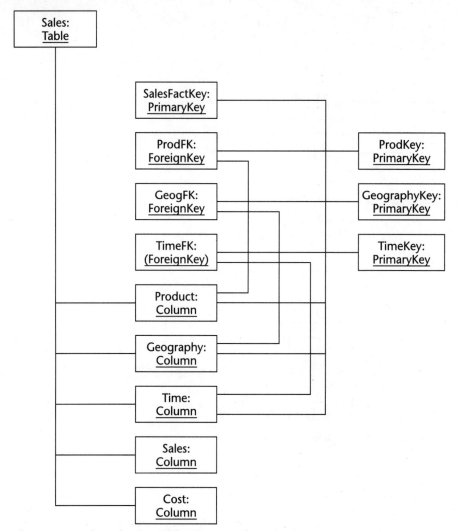

Figure 6.41 The Sales fact table Primary and Foreign keys.

```
//add keys to the sales fact table
    PrimaryKey salesPrimaryKey =
relationalPackage.getPrimaryKey().createPrimaryKey();
    salesFactTable.addOwnedElement(salesPrimaryKey);
    salesPrimaryKey.addFeature(relsalesTimeId);
    salesPrimaryKey.addFeature(relSalesGeogId);
    salesPrimaryKey.addFeature(relSalesProdId);
```

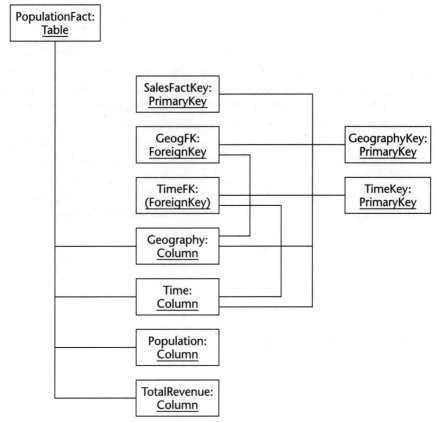

Figure 6.42   The Population fact table Primary and Foreign keys.

```
//add the foreign key(s)
     ForeignKey salesToProd =
relationalPackage.getForeignKey().createForeignKey();
     salesFactTable.addOwnedElement(salesToProd);
     salesToProd.addFeature(relSalesProdId);
     salesToProd.setUniqueKey(prodPrimaryKey);
```

Physical Deployment Models

The CWM metamodel uses deployments to group the various logical and physical mappings together to create a cohesive set of objects. This is necessary to allow tools to register different mappings for different purposes. A typical example of this is production versus test. In many cases, end users will want to try different physical configurations and test them before moving them into production. The deployment metamodel provides the "glue" to allow these groupings. The deployments are grouped by the DeploymentGroup class, which is owned by the OLAP Schema. A user of CWM will most likely select a DeploymentGroup as part of the application startup, and this will govern the available physical deployments for a particular session. This is not the only way to use deployments; this is just one usage foreseen by the CWM designers. The CWM deployment model is shown in Figure 6.43.

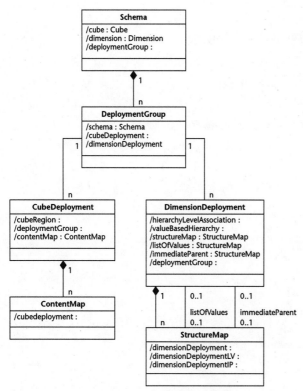

Figure 6.43 The Deployment metamodel.

Creating the DeploymentGroup

To create a deployment, an instance of DeploymentGroup is created and added to the OLAP Schema. The instances and code to do this are shown in Figure 6.44.

In the following code fragment, the DeploymentGroup is added to the ExampleSchema instance using the addOwnedElement method. This is another case of using an inherited association to represent the desired effect instead of adding a specific association.

```
//create the deployment group
DeploymentGroup deploy1 =
olapPackage.getDeploymentGroup().createDeploymentGroup();
dimensionalSchema.addOwnedElement(deploy1);
```

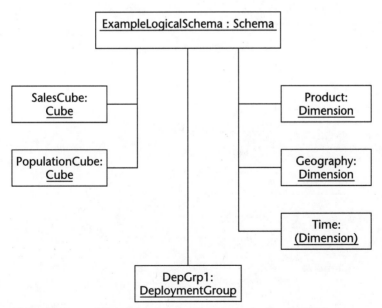

Figure 6.44 Adding a DeploymentGroup to the ExampleSchema.

The CWM Mapping Model

The CWM Transformation metamodel is used for both transformations as well as mappings. The CWM metamodel can represent a wide range of transformations. Transformations are traditionally viewed as rules to move data from one form to another. This activity is generally in the domain of ETL-oriented tools, which include straight transformations as well as data cleansing. In this example, the transformation metamodel will be used as a mapping model. These mappings will describe how to navigate between the various logical levels of the OLAP metamodel and the physical representation of the logical model. The Transformation metamodel is intended to cover a wide range of transformation and mapping activity. Figure 6.45 illustrates the various types of mappings and transformations available in CWM.

In Figure 6.45, to move between levels of similar types a transformation is used. To move between levels, a mapping is used. This concept will be used next to show how the elements of the logical model can be mapped together to form a complete picture of the end-user needs of the logical model.

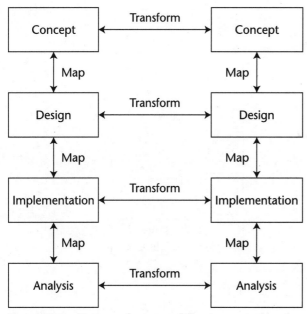

Figure 6.45 Data warehouse modeling conceptual levels, activities, and their transformations and mappings.

Mapping the Logical Model

The CWM mapping metamodel is shown in Figure 6.46. This model is relatively small, but represents a wide variety of possible mappings. This is made possible by the overall design philosophy that the CWM designers used with regard to the object hierarchy. The major components of the CWM metamodel all share common ancestors, which converge at either classifier or feature. For this reason, the mappings are all done between instances of classifiers and instances of features. A special mapping is provided to map between a classifier and a feature. This is necessary to provide functionality that can bridge the gap between certain types of physical models and the logical OLAP models. An example of this classifier to feature mapping is mapping a multidimensional dimension instance to an OLAP attribute.

The first mapping example that will be considered is the mapping of the Product Hierarchy to its component structures. In this case, a portion of the logical is mapped to subordinate logical objects. This style of mapping indicates that the data for the hierarchy is actually retrieved by navigating the

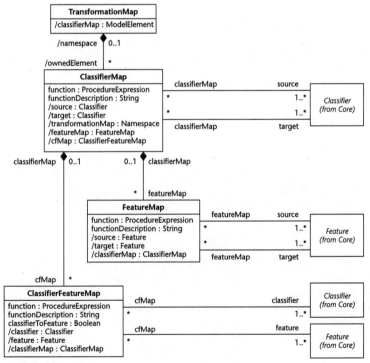

Figure 6.46 The CWM mapping metamodel.

hierarchy structure to a set of finer-grained objects that may be mapped to a physical representation. In this specific example, the mappings are shown as a sequence of diagrams to keep the pictures clean and easy to read. The instance diagrams in Figures 6.47 to 6.49 show that the ID attribute in the Standard hierarchy is really the union of the ID attributes from the various HierarchyLevelAssociation objects owned by the hierarchy. This is shown in the picture by the feature map having four distinct sources. This same technique is applied to the other two attributes of the Standard hierarchy, and both are represented as unions of their components. This mapping will allow a user of CWM to retrieve all values of the Standard hierarchy by requesting the ID attribute. The code evaluating this request will have an explicit roadmap to follow to a lower portion of the model to retrieve the data. This technique will be reused later in the example and is a commonly used feature of CWM. Figures 6.47 to 6.49 show a set of instance diagrams with the objects required to create the mappings. The implementation code is shown below.

```
TransformationMap standardProdHierTM =

transformationPackage.getTransformationMap().createTransformationMap();
    prodStdH.addOwnedElement(standardProdHierTM);

ClassifierMap standardProdHierCM =
    transformationPackage.getClassifierMap().createClassifierMap();
standardProdHierTM.addOwnedElement(standardProdHierCM);

//create the featuremaps and assign target and sources
FeatureMap stdProdHierFMId =
    transformationPackage.getFeatureMap().createFeatureMap();
standardProdHierCM.addFeatureMap(stdProdHierFMId);
stdProdHierFMId.addTarget(stdId);
stdProdHierFMId.addSource(catHLRId);
stdProdHierFMId.addSource(typeHLRId);
stdProdHierFMId.addSource(brandHLRId);
stdProdHierFMId.addSource(upcHLRId);


FeatureMap stdProdHierFMDesc =
    transformationPackage.getFeatureMap().createFeatureMap();
standardProdHierCM.addFeatureMap(stdProdHierFMDesc);
stdProdHierFMDesc.addTarget(stdLongDescription);
stdProdHierFMDesc.addSource(catHLRLongDescription);
stdProdHierFMDesc.addSource(typeHLRLongDescription);
stdProdHierFMDesc.addSource(brandHLRLongDescription);
stdProdHierFMDesc.addSource(upcHLRLongDescription);

FeatureMap stdProdHierFMParent =
    transformationPackage.getFeatureMap().createFeatureMap();
standardProdHierCM.addFeatureMap(stdProdHierFMParent);
```

```
stdProdHierFMParent.addTarget(stdParent);
stdProdHierFMParent.addSource(typeHLRparent);
stdProdHierFMParent.addSource(brandHLRparent);
stdProdHierFMParent.addSource(upcHLRparent);
```

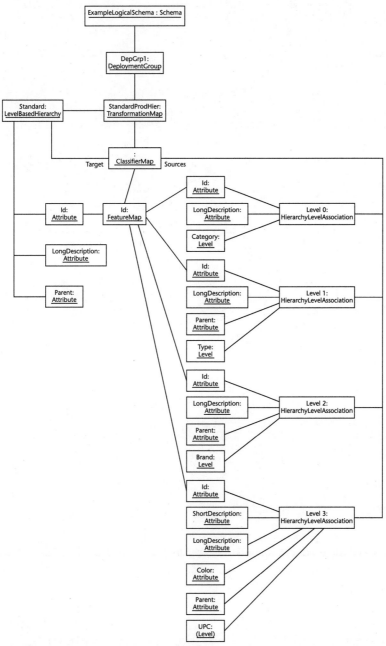

Figure 6.47 Mapping the Product Standard Hierarchy to its Components: ID attribute.

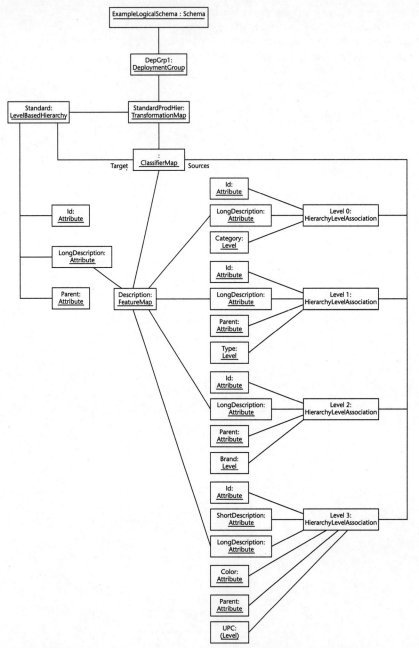

Figure 6.48 Mapping the Product Standard Hierarchy to its components: LongDescription attribute.

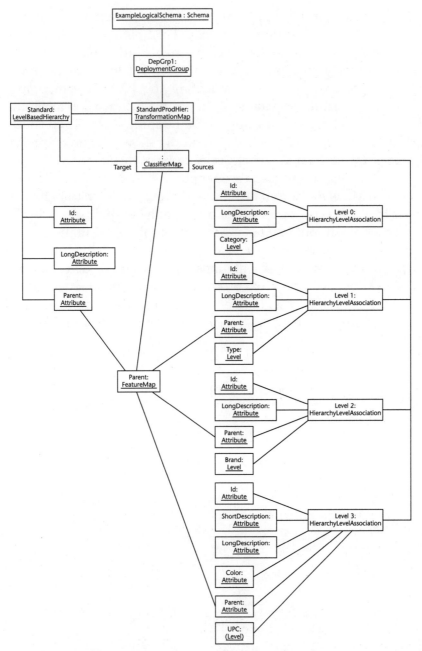

Figure 6.49 Mapping the Product Standard Hierarchy to its components: Parent attribute.

The next set of mapping examples is to provide a mapping from the Product dimension to the Standard hierarchy. This mapping is similar to the mappings from the hierarchy to its components but moves up in the logical model hierarchy. In this case, the Product dimension is mapped directly to the Standard hierarchy. Navigating the ID source mapping processes a user request for all values of the Product dimension attribute ID. The data is now retrieved according to the mapping of the ID attribute in the Standard hierarchy. The preceding example shows the union of the ID attributes with the HierarchyLevelAssociations of the Standard hierarchy. This type of navigation is used throughout the CWM model and will give a user of CWM the maximum flexibility in providing physical links. It also indicates that users can retrieve data from a number of different levels of the logical model without having a direct physical representation. This is a very important feature of the CWM model and keeps the division between logical and physical representations separate and flexible. Figures 6.50 to 6.53 show how the individual product attributes are mapped to the hierarchy attributes. In this case, unlike in the previous example, the feature maps have a target with a single source. The implementation code is also shown.

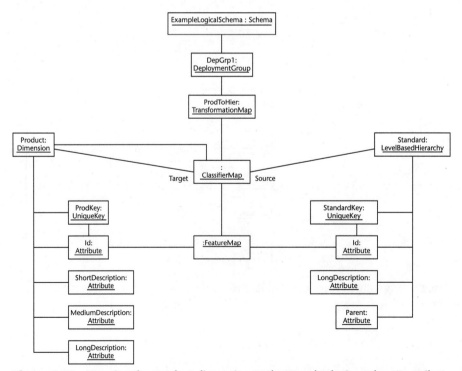

Figure 6.50 Mapping the Product dimension to the Standard Hierarchy: ID attribute.

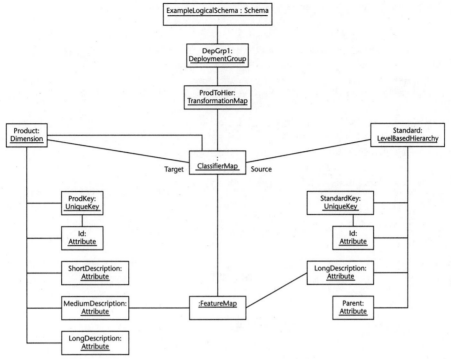

Figure 6.51 Mapping the Product dimension to the Standard Hierarchy: ShortDescription attribute.

```
        TransformationMap ProdtoHierTM =

transformationPackage.getTransformationMap().createTransformationMap();
        product.addOwnedElement(standardProdHierTM);

        ClassifierMap ProdtoHierCM =
            transformationPackage.getClassifierMap().createClassifierMap();
        standardProdHierTM.addOwnedElement(standardProdHierCM);

        //create the featuremaps and assign target and sources
        FeatureMap ProdtoHierFMId =
          transformationPackage.getFeatureMap().createFeatureMap();
        ProdtoHierCM.addFeatureMap(ProdtoHierFMId);
        ProdtoHierFMId.addTarget(stdId);
        ProdtoHierFMId.addSource(stdId);

        FeatureMap ProdtoHierFMSDesc =
            transformationPackage.getFeatureMap().createFeatureMap();
        ProdtoHierCM.addFeatureMap(ProdtoHierFMSDesc);
        ProdtoHierFMSDesc.addTarget(prodSDesc);
```

```
ProdtoHierFMSDesc.addSource(stdLongDescription);

FeatureMap ProdtoHierFMMDesc =
  transformationPackage.getFeatureMap().createFeatureMap();
ProdtoHierCM.addFeatureMap(ProdtoHierFMMDesc);
ProdtoHierFMMDesc.addTarget(prodMDesc);
ProdtoHierFMMDesc.addSource(stdLongDescription);

FeatureMap ProdtoHierFMLDesc =
  transformationPackage.getFeatureMap().createFeatureMap();
ProdtoHierCM.addFeatureMap(ProdtoHierFMLDesc);
ProdtoHierFMLDesc.addTarget(prodLDesc);
ProdtoHierFMLDesc.addSource(stdLongDescription);
```

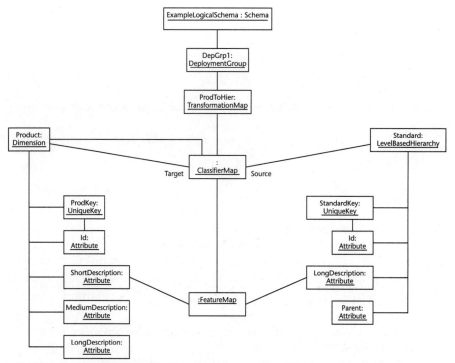

Figure 6.52 Mapping the Product dimension to the Standard Hierarchy: MediumDescription attribute.

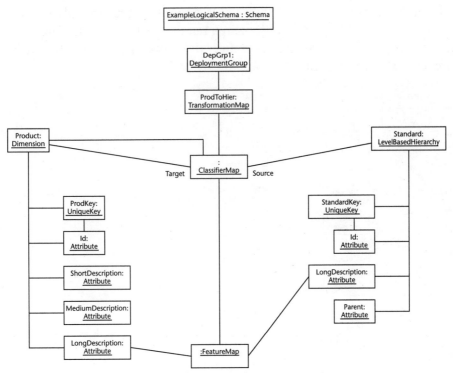

Figure 6.53 Mapping the Product dimension to the Standard Hierarchy: LongDescription attribute.

The CubeRegion is part of the deployment of the Cube. CubeRegions are subcomponents of a Cube that represent some portion of the Cube. An instance of a CubeRegion always has the same dimensionality as the parent Cube but can contain only a subset of the measures. This CWM functionality was driven by the needs of various storage systems that will house the data representing the Cube. A CubeRegion also represents some slice of Cube dimension's values. To represent this, the CWM metamodel uses a MemberSelectionGroup. A MemberSelectionGroup will contain a reference to one MemberSelection for each dimension of the Cube. A CubeRegion can contain more than one MemberSelectionGroup if there is more than a single level of data in the CubeRegion. In the following example, a CubeRegion will be defined with a structure that mimics the Cube itself and represents data from the lowest levels of all the dimensions. This type of CubeRegion is typical of physical implementations in a relational database that are star-schemas. The instances needed to define the CubeRegion are shown in Figure 6.54. The implementation code follows.

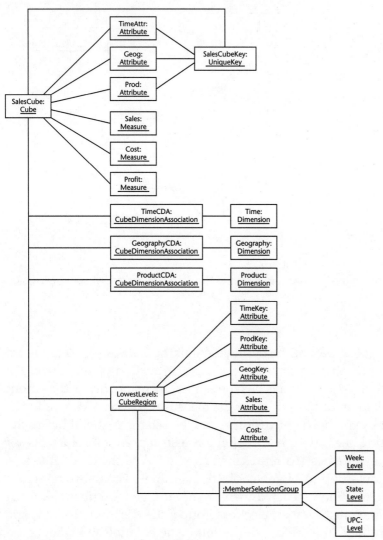

Figure 6.54 Creating the CubeRegions.

In the following code fragment, note that the structure of the CubeRegion is identical to the Cube itself. This will be typical when the physical implementation is a Relational database. A feature of CubeRegion not shown in the examples is that the CubeRegion can represent the entire Cube. In this case, a special flag is FullyRealized, which can be set to true. This feature will be frequently used with the physical implementation in a multidimensional database.

```
//create the cube region
CubeRegion lowestLevels =
olapPackage.getCubeRegion().createCubeRegion();
    lowestLevels.setCube(salesCube);
    Attribute LLTimeKey =
corePackage.getAttribute().createAttribute();
    Attribute LLProdKey =
corePackage.getAttribute().createAttribute();
    Attribute LLGeogKey =
corePackage.getAttribute().createAttribute();
    Attribute LLSales   =
corePackage.getAttribute().createAttribute();
    Attribute LLCost    =
corePackage.getAttribute().createAttribute();

    lowestLevels.addFeature(LLTimeKey);
    lowestLevels.addFeature(LLProdKey);
    lowestLevels.addFeature(LLGeogKey);
    lowestLevels.addFeature(LLSales);
    lowestLevels.addFeature(LLCost);

    MemberSelectionGroup LLMSG =

olapPackage.getMemberSelectionGroup().createMemberSelectionGroup();
    LLMSG.setCubeRegion(lowestLevels);
    LLMSG.addMemberSelection(week);
    LLMSG.addMemberSelection(state);
    LLMSG.addMemberSelection(UPC);
```

To complete the set of CubeRegions required by this example, Figure 6.55 represents the Population CubeRegion required by the Population Cube.

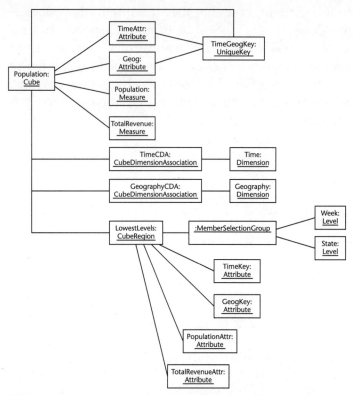

Figure 6.55 CubeRegions required by the Population Cube.

Cubes and CubeRegions are tied together using the Transformation package-mapping model. The mappings are similar to the mappings shown from the Product dimension to its components. In the case of the Sales Cube and SalesCubeRegion, the mappings are one to one from the Cube's various attributes. Figures 6.56 to 6.60 represent the mapping required to link the Cube to its CubeRegion. It may seem that a lot of instances are required, but the diagrams are split into a series of diagrams to keep the pictures clean. The actual number of instances required is one transformationMap, one classifierMap, and six feature maps. These mappings are linked to the dimension mappings by sharing the same deployment group.

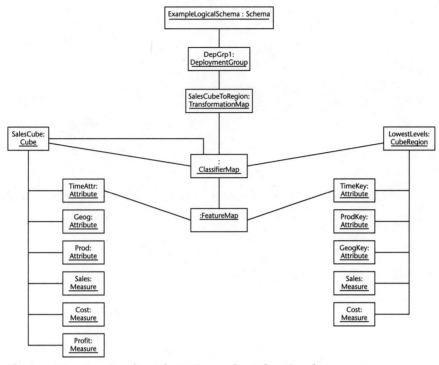

Figure 6.56   Mapping the CubeRegion to the Cube: Time key.

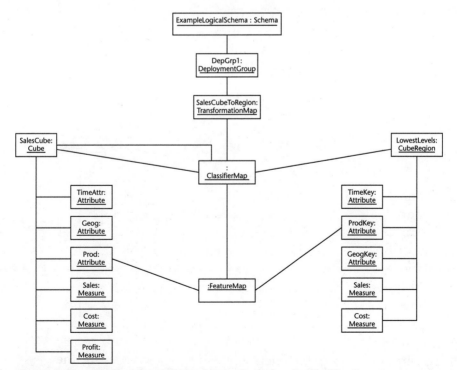

Figure 6.57   Mapping the CubeRegion to the Cube: Product key.

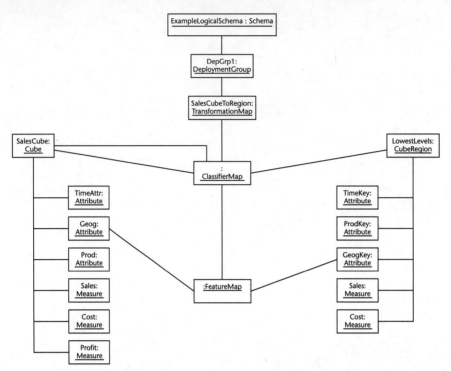

Figure 6.58 Mapping the CubeRegion to the Cube: Geography key.

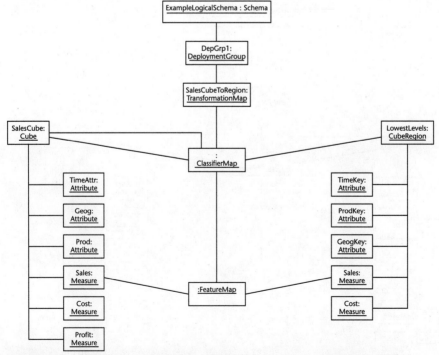

Figure 6.59 Mapping the CubeRegion to the Cube: Sales measure.

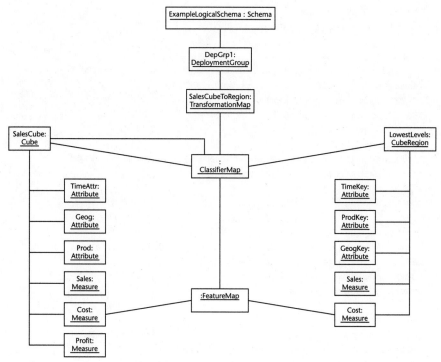

Figure 6.60 Mapping the CubeRegion to the Cube: Cost measure.

Figure 6.61 introduces how CWM can support a derived attribute. In this case, instead of mapping the profit measure to the CubeRegion, it is mapped to two other measures. The feature map has a function, which defines that the profit measure is a calculated measure of sales minus cost. This is a very simple calculated attribute; the mapping function can be as simple or complex as the user needs.

```
    //map the cuberegion to the cube
    TransformationMap salesCubeToRegion =

transformationPackage.getTransformationMap().createTransformationMap();
    salesCube.addOwnedElement(salesCubeToRegion);
    ClassifierMap salesCubeToRegionCM =
      transformationPackage.getClassifierMap().createClassifierMap();
    salesCubeToRegion.addClassifierMap(salesCubeToRegionCM);
    salesCubeToRegionCM.addSource(lowestLevels);
    salesCubeToRegionCM.addTarget(salesCube);

    FeatureMap SCRFM1 =
      transformationPackage.getFeatureMap().createFeatureMap();
    salesCubeToRegionCM.addFeatureMap(SCRFM1);
```

```
SCRFM1.addTarget(timeAttr);
SCRFM1.addSource(LLTimeKey);

FeatureMap SCRFM2 =
    transformationPackage.getFeatureMap().createFeatureMap();
salesCubeToRegionCM.addFeatureMap(SCRFM2);
SCRFM2.addTarget(prodAttr);
SCRFM2.addSource(LLProdKey);

FeatureMap SCRFM3 =
    transformationPackage.getFeatureMap().createFeatureMap();
salesCubeToRegionCM.addFeatureMap(SCRFM3);
SCRFM3.addTarget(geogAttr);
SCRFM3.addSource(LLGeogKey);

FeatureMap SCRFM4 =
    transformationPackage.getFeatureMap().createFeatureMap();
salesCubeToRegionCM.addFeatureMap(SCRFM4);
SCRFM4.addTarget(sales);
SCRFM4.addSource(LLCost);

FeatureMap SCRFM5 =
    transformationPackage.getFeatureMap().createFeatureMap();
salesCubeToRegionCM.addFeatureMap(SCRFM5);
SCRFM5.addTarget(cost);
SCRFM5.addSource(LLSales);
```

Mapping the Physical Model

The next set of mappings is mapping logical structures to physical structures. These mappings follow the same general flow as the logical-to-logical mappings shown previously. Their usage generally signifies an endpoint to provide the data for a logical structure. In this example, there will be three different types of logical-to-physical mappings. The first type of mapping will be illustrated by mapping the levels of the OLAP model to the Relational database. In this case, the intended use is for when a user has navigated to a specific level and within that level wishes to retrieve data. The instance diagrams in Figures 6.62 to 6.65 show how to link the levels of the Product dimension to the Product table. This mapping creates a transformationMap, a classifierMap, and a series of feature Maps. Note the targets of the feature maps. In many instances, the source column is used by any number of logical target features.

Figures 6.62 to 6.65 illustrate the instances required to map all the product levels and their associated attributes to a single physical table. This table will also be used later in the example to provide physical data for the product hierarchy. These mappings will ultimately be added to the deployment group defined above. This provides a cohesive set of mappings, which contains the logical structures and their physical representation. The implementation code required to produce the object instances follows.

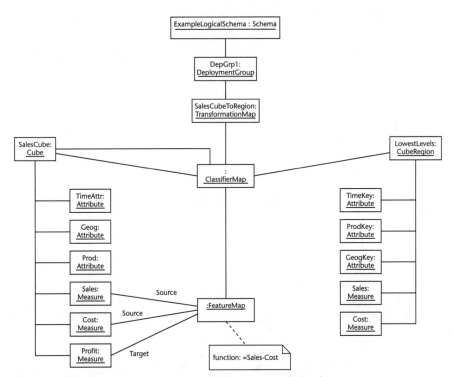

Figure 6.61 Using the mapping model to create a derived measure.

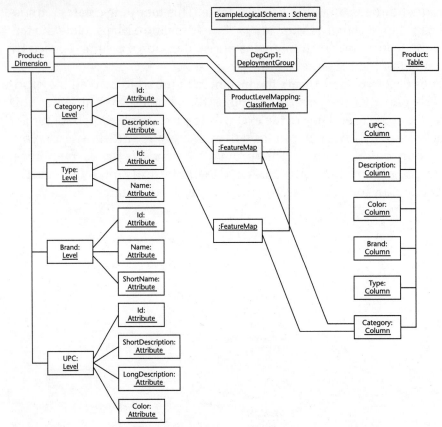

Figure 6.62 Map the levels to the relational database: Category level.

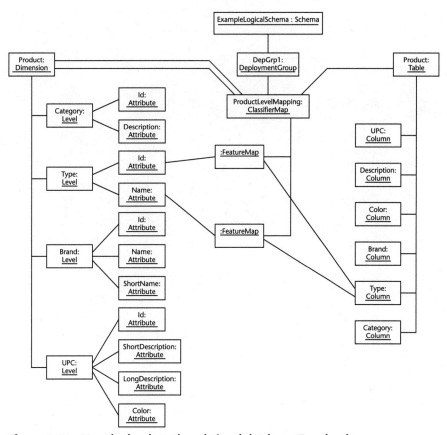

Figure 6.63 Map the levels to the relational database: Type level.

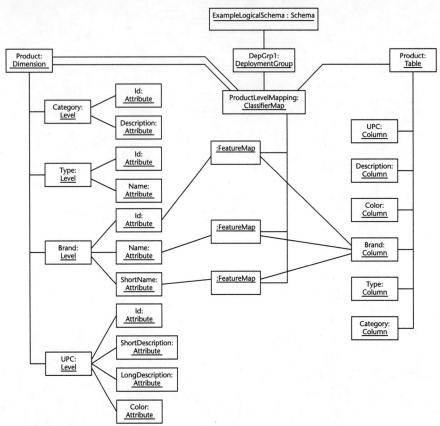

Figure 6.64   Map the levels to the relational database: Brand level.

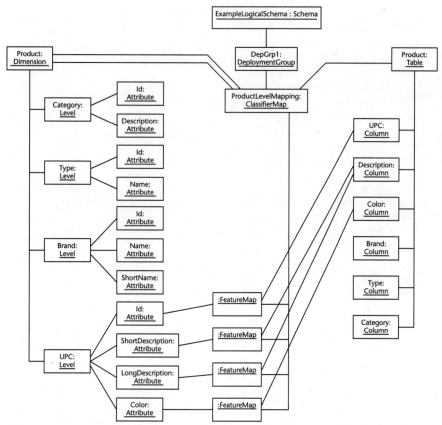

Figure 6.65   Map the levels to the relational database: UPC level.

```
            //now map the levels to the physical database
            TransformationMap catTM =

transformationPackage.getTransformationMap().createTransformationMap();
            category.addOwnedElement(catTM);
            ClassifierMap catCM =
               transformationPackage.getClassifierMap().createClassifierMap();
            category.addOwnedElement(catCM);

            catCM.addSource(prodTable);
            catCM.addTarget(category);

            FeatureMap catId =
               transformationPackage.getFeatureMap().createFeatureMap();
            catCM.addFeatureMap(catId);
            catId.addTarget(categoryId);
            catId.addSource(relCat);

            FeatureMap catDesc =
               transformationPackage.getFeatureMap().createFeatureMap();
            catCM.addFeatureMap(catDesc);
            catDesc.addTarget(categoryDesc);
            catDesc.addSource(relCat);

            TransformationMap typeTM =

transformationPackage.getTransformationMap().createTransformationMap();
            type.addOwnedElement(typeTM);
            ClassifierMap typeCM =
               transformationPackage.getClassifierMap().createClassifierMap();
            type.addOwnedElement(typeCM);

            typeCM.addSource(prodTable);
            typeCM.addTarget(type);

            FeatureMap typeIdFM =
               transformationPackage.getFeatureMap().createFeatureMap();
            typeCM.addFeatureMap(typeIdFM);
            typeIdFM.addTarget(typeId);
            typeIdFM.addSource(relType);

            FeatureMap typeDescFM =
               transformationPackage.getFeatureMap().createFeatureMap();
            typeCM.addFeatureMap(typeDescFM);
            typeDescFM.addTarget(typeName);
            typeDescFM.addSource(relType);

            TransformationMap brandTM =

transformationPackage.getTransformationMap().createTransformationMap();
            brand.addOwnedElement(brandTM);
            ClassifierMap brandCM =
```

```
        transformationPackage.getClassifierMap().createClassifierMap();
    brand.addOwnedElement(brandCM);

    brandCM.addSource(prodTable);
    brandCM.addTarget(category);

    FeatureMap brandIdFM =
        transformationPackage.getFeatureMap().createFeatureMap();
    brandCM.addFeatureMap(brandIdFM);
    brandIdFM.addTarget(brandId);
    brandIdFM.addSource(relBrand);

    FeatureMap brandDescFM =
        transformationPackage.getFeatureMap().createFeatureMap();
    brandCM.addFeatureMap(brandDescFM);
    brandDescFM.addTarget(brandName);
    brandDescFM.addSource(relBrand);

    TransformationMap upcTM =

transformationPackage.getTransformationMap().createTransformationMap();
    category.addOwnedElement(upcTM);
    ClassifierMap upcCM =
        transformationPackage.getClassifierMap().createClassifierMap();
    UPC.addOwnedElement(upcCM);

    upcCM.addSource(prodTable);
    upcCM.addTarget(UPC);

    FeatureMap upcIdFM =
        transformationPackage.getFeatureMap().createFeatureMap();
    upcCM.addFeatureMap(upcIdFM);
    upcIdFM.addTarget(UPCId);
    upcIdFM.addSource(relUPC);

    FeatureMap upcSDescFM =
        transformationPackage.getFeatureMap().createFeatureMap();
    upcCM.addFeatureMap(upcSDescFM);
    upcSDescFM.addTarget(UPCSName);
    upcSDescFM.addSource(relProdDesc);

    FeatureMap upcLDescFM =
        transformationPackage.getFeatureMap().createFeatureMap();
    upcCM.addFeatureMap(upcLDescFM);
    upcLDescFM.addTarget(UPCLName);
    upcLDescFM.addSource(relProdDesc);
```

The next set of mappings that the example will show is dimension deployments. The metamodel containing the DimensionDeployment is shown in Figure 6.66. This metamodel will be used to create the linkage between the HierarchyLevelRelationships and their physical representation. This type of mapping is pervasive enough in the industry that the designers of CWM decided to provide a specialized mapping object. This object has a couple of special associations that provide commonly used model semantics. The first is listOfValues; this association is used to provide a physical mapping that, when evaluated, returns a unique list of values for the associated feature. The second is immediateParent; this association represents the immediate parent in the hierarchy. Figures 6.66 to 6.73 show how to use DimensionDeployments and their associations to StructureMaps to identify a mapping path to provide both a list of values and immediate parent for the Product Standard hierarchy. As with the other mapping diagrams, the diagrams have been broken into a series of pictures to maintain clarity. The actual number of instances is not as large as the number of diagrams might indicate at first glance. The best view of these structures is found in the implementation code shown below.

The DimensionDeployment metamodel is shown in Figure 6.66. Implementers of CWM should note that either a HierarchyLevelAssociation or a ValueBasedHierarchy owns a DimensionDeployment. These objects cannot be shared and this type of model indicates an exclusive "OR" with respect to ownership.

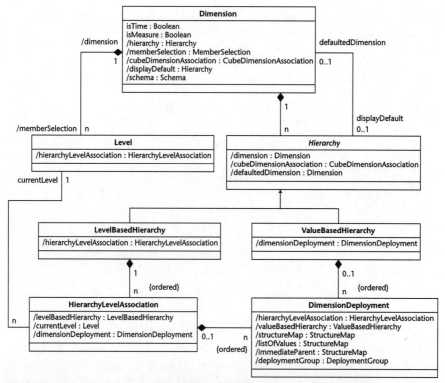

Figure 6.66 CWM Metamodel: Dimensional deployment metamodel.

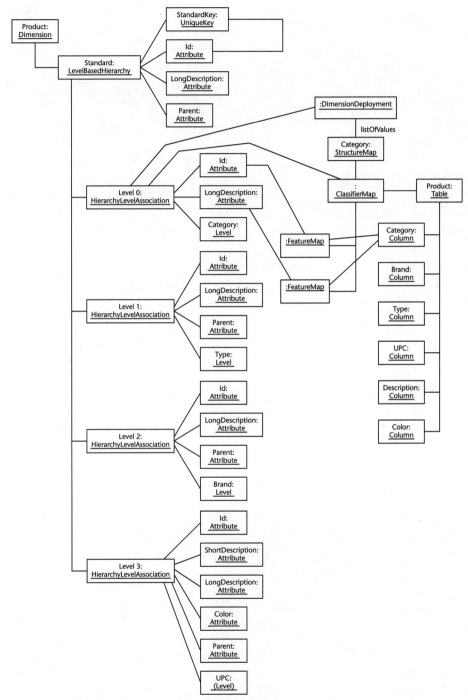

Figure 6.67   Mapping the Category Level's listOfValues.

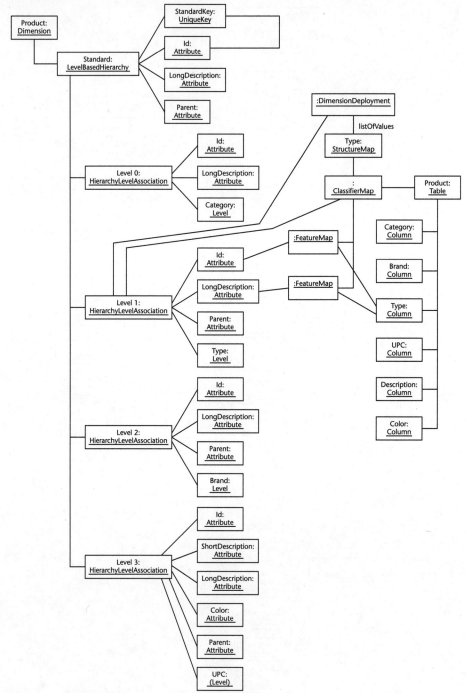

Figure 6.68 Mapping the Type Level's listOfValues.

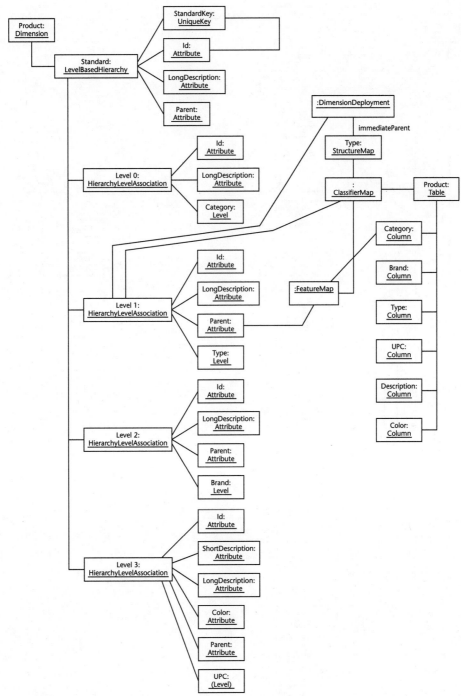

Figure 6.69 Mapping the Type Level's immediateParent.

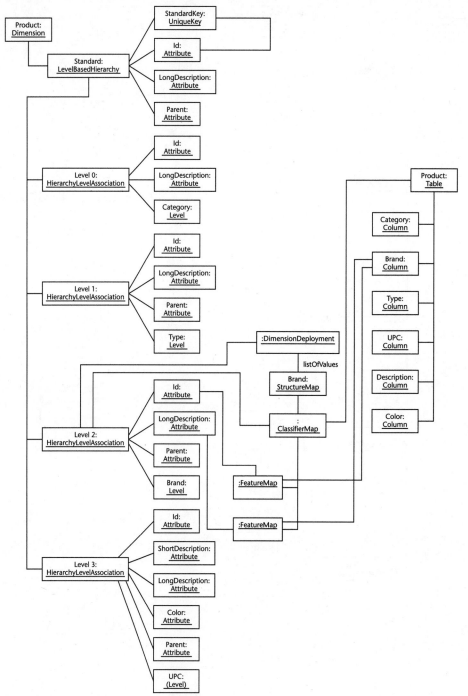

Figure 6.70   Mapping the Brand Level's listOfValues.

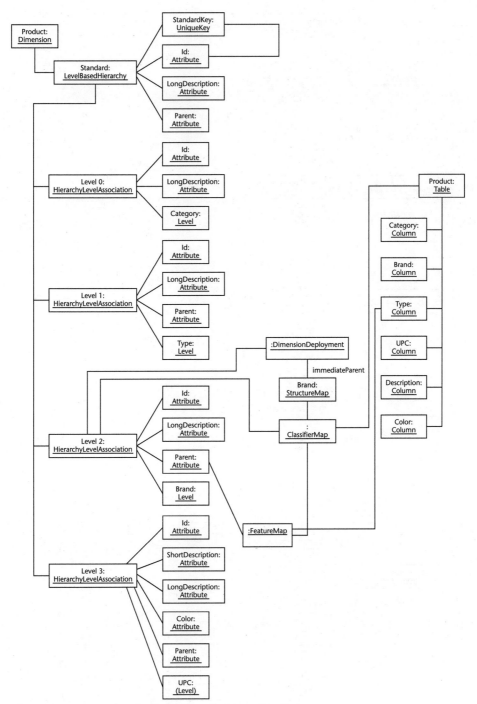

Figure 6.71 Mapping the Brand Level's immediateParent.

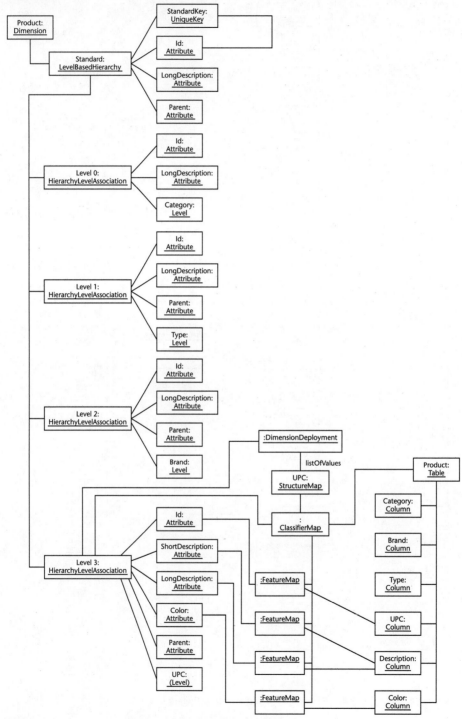

Figure 6.72   Mapping the UPC Level's listOfValues.

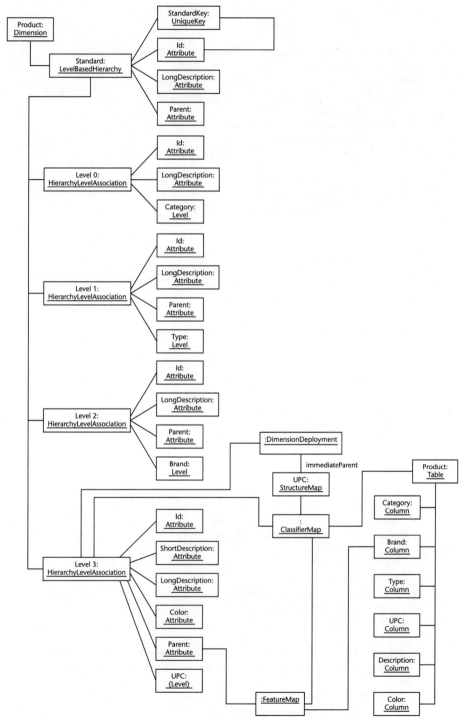

Figure 6.73   Mapping the UPC Level's immediateParent.

```
            //map the hierarchy to the relational database
            DimensionDeployment catDD =

olapPackage.getDimensionDeployment().createDimensionDeployment();
            catHLR.addOwnedElement(catDD);
            StructureMap catLOVSM =
                olapPackage.getStructureMap().createStructureMap();
            catHLR.addOwnedElement(catLOVSM);
            catDD.addStructureMap(catLOVSM);
            ClassifierMap catStdCM =
                transformationPackage.getClassifierMap().createClassifierMap();
            catLOVSM.addClassifierMap(catStdCM);
            catHLR.addOwnedElement(catStdCM);
            catStdCM.addTarget(catHLR);
            catStdCM.addSource(prodTable);

            FeatureMap catStdIdFM =
                transformationPackage.getFeatureMap().createFeatureMap();
            catStdCM.addFeatureMap(catStdIdFM);
            catStdIdFM.addTarget(catHLRId);
            catStdIdFM.addSource(relCat);

            FeatureMap catStdLongDescriptionFM =
                transformationPackage.getFeatureMap().createFeatureMap();
            catStdCM.addFeatureMap(catStdLongDescriptionFM);
            catStdLongDescriptionFM.addTarget(catHLRLongDescription);
            catStdLongDescriptionFM.addSource(relCat);

            //type
            DimensionDeployment typeDD =

olapPackage.getDimensionDeployment().createDimensionDeployment();
            typeHLR.addOwnedElement(typeDD);
            StructureMap typeLOVSM =
                olapPackage.getStructureMap().createStructureMap();
            typeHLR.addOwnedElement(typeLOVSM);
            typeDD.addStructureMap(typeLOVSM);
            ClassifierMap typeStdCM =
                transformationPackage.getClassifierMap().createClassifierMap();
            typeLOVSM.addClassifierMap(typeStdCM);
            typeHLR.addOwnedElement(typeStdCM);
            typeStdCM.addTarget(typeHLR);
            typeStdCM.addSource(prodTable);

            FeatureMap typeStdIdFM =
                transformationPackage.getFeatureMap().createFeatureMap();
            typeStdCM.addFeatureMap(typeStdIdFM);
            typeStdIdFM.addTarget(typeHLRId);
            typeStdIdFM.addSource(relType);

            FeatureMap typeStdLongDescriptionFM =
                transformationPackage.getFeatureMap().createFeatureMap();
```

```
typeStdCM.addFeatureMap(typeStdLongDescriptionFM);
typeStdLongDescriptionFM.addTarget(typeHLRLongDescription);
typeStdLongDescriptionFM.addSource(relType);

StructureMap typeParentSM =
   olapPackage.getStructureMap().createStructureMap();
typeHLR.addOwnedElement(typeParentSM);
typeDD.addStructureMap(typeParentSM);
ClassifierMap typeStdParentCM =
   transformationPackage.getClassifierMap().createClassifierMap();
typeParentSM.addClassifierMap(typeStdParentCM);
typeHLR.addOwnedElement(typeStdParentCM);
typeStdParentCM.addTarget(typeHLR);
typeStdParentCM.addSource(prodTable);

FeatureMap typeStdParentFM =
   transformationPackage.getFeatureMap().createFeatureMap();
typeStdParentCM.addFeatureMap(typeStdParentFM);
typeStdParentFM.addTarget(typeHLRparent);
typeStdParentFM.addSource(relCat);

//brand
DimensionDeployment brandDD =

olapPackage.getDimensionDeployment().createDimensionDeployment();
brandHLR.addOwnedElement(brandDD);
StructureMap brandLOVSM =
   olapPackage.getStructureMap().createStructureMap();
brandHLR.addOwnedElement(brandLOVSM);
brandDD.addStructureMap(brandLOVSM);
ClassifierMap brandStdCM =
   transformationPackage.getClassifierMap().createClassifierMap();
brandLOVSM.addClassifierMap(brandStdCM);
brandHLR.addOwnedElement(brandStdCM);
brandStdCM.addTarget(brandHLR);
brandStdCM.addSource(prodTable);

FeatureMap brandStdIdFM =
   transformationPackage.getFeatureMap().createFeatureMap();
brandStdCM.addFeatureMap(brandStdIdFM);
brandStdIdFM.addTarget(brandHLRId);
brandStdIdFM.addSource(relBrand);

FeatureMap brandStdLongDescriptionFM =
   transformationPackage.getFeatureMap().createFeatureMap();
brandStdCM.addFeatureMap(brandStdLongDescriptionFM);
brandStdLongDescriptionFM.addTarget(catHLRLongDescription);
brandStdLongDescriptionFM.addSource(relBrand);

StructureMap brandParentSM =
   olapPackage.getStructureMap().createStructureMap();
brandHLR.addOwnedElement(brandParentSM);
```

```
brandDD.addStructureMap(brandParentSM);
ClassifierMap brandStdParentCM =
   transformationPackage.getClassifierMap().createClassifierMap();
brandParentSM.addClassifierMap(brandStdParentCM);
brandHLR.addOwnedElement(brandStdParentCM);
brandStdParentCM.addTarget(brandHLR);
brandStdParentCM.addSource(prodTable);

FeatureMap brandStdParentFM =
   transformationPackage.getFeatureMap().createFeatureMap();
brandStdParentCM.addFeatureMap(brandStdParentFM);
brandStdParentFM.addTarget(brandHLRparent);
brandStdParentFM.addSource(relType);

//upc
DimensionDeployment upcDD =

olapPackage.getDimensionDeployment().createDimensionDeployment();
   upcHLR.addOwnedElement(upcDD);
   StructureMap upcLOVSM =
      olapPackage.getStructureMap().createStructureMap();
   upcHLR.addOwnedElement(upcLOVSM);
   upcDD.addStructureMap(upcLOVSM);
   ClassifierMap upcStdCM =
      transformationPackage.getClassifierMap().createClassifierMap();
   upcLOVSM.addClassifierMap(upcStdCM);
   upcHLR.addOwnedElement(upcStdCM);
   upcStdCM.addTarget(upcHLR);
   upcStdCM.addSource(prodTable);

FeatureMap upcStdIdFM =
   transformationPackage.getFeatureMap().createFeatureMap();
upcStdCM.addFeatureMap(upcStdIdFM);
upcStdIdFM.addTarget(upcHLRId);
upcStdIdFM.addSource(relUPC);

FeatureMap upcStdLongDescriptionFM =
   transformationPackage.getFeatureMap().createFeatureMap();
upcStdCM.addFeatureMap(upcStdLongDescriptionFM);
upcStdLongDescriptionFM.addTarget(upcHLRLongDescription);
upcStdLongDescriptionFM.addSource(relProdDesc);

FeatureMap upcStdColorFM =
   transformationPackage.getFeatureMap().createFeatureMap();
upcStdCM.addFeatureMap(upcStdColorFM);
upcStdColorFM.addTarget(upcHLRColor);
upcStdColorFM.addSource(relColor);

StructureMap upcParentSM =
   olapPackage.getStructureMap().createStructureMap();
upcHLR.addOwnedElement(upcParentSM);
upcDD.addStructureMap(upcParentSM);
```

```
ClassifierMap upcStdParentCM =
   transformationPackage.getClassifierMap().createClassifierMap();
upcParentSM.addClassifierMap(brandStdParentCM);
upcHLR.addOwnedElement(upcStdParentCM);
upcStdParentCM.addTarget(upcHLR);
upcStdParentCM.addSource(prodTable);

FeatureMap upcStdParentFM =
   transformationPackage.getFeatureMap().createFeatureMap();
upcStdParentCM.addFeatureMap(upcStdParentFM);
upcStdParentFM.addTarget(upcHLRparent);
upcStdParentFM.addSource(relBrand);
```

The final phase of this example is to map the CubeRegion to the Relational database. In CWM, there is a metamodel that provides a specific type of mapping class definition for CubeRegions called CubeDeployment. Creating a CubeDeployment for the CubeRegion provides the physical mapping. The CWM CubeDeployment metamodel is shown in Figure 6.74.

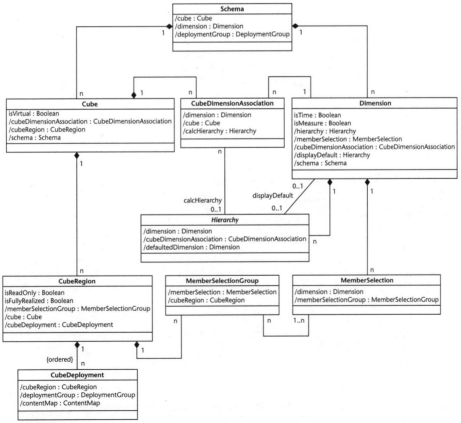

Figure 6.74 CWM Cube deployment metamodel.

The process of mapping the Sales CubeRegion to the Sales fact table is very similar to the mappings already described. It starts with the creation of a CubeDeployment class. This is followed by the creation of a ContentMap and a ClassifierMap. The attributes of the CubeRegion are then mapped to the Relational Columns using FeatureMaps. In this example, the structure of the CubeRegion mimics the structure of the fact table so the mapping is straightforward. These mappings are added to the set of mappings associated to the DeploymentGroup. This completes a deployment of the logical model. The instances necessary to map the CubeRegion to the fact table are shown in Figures 6.75 to 6.79. For clarity, each diagram shows only one FeatureMap. The implementation code to create and populate the mappings is shown below.

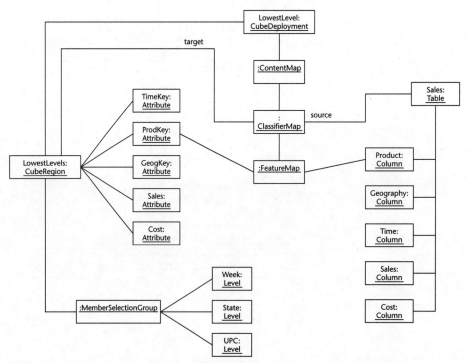

Figure 6.75 Map the Cube Region to the relational database: Product key.

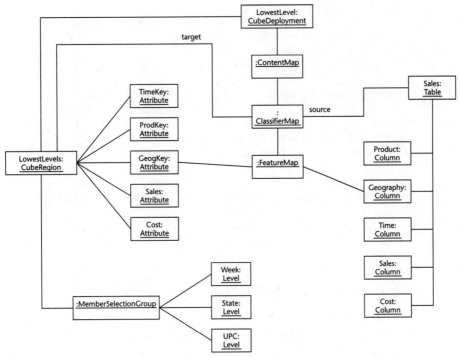

Figure 6.76 Map the Cube Region to the relational database: Geography key.

```
//map the cube region to the relational database
CubeDeployment lowestLevelCD =
    olapPackage.getCubeDeployment().createCubeDeployment();
lowestLevels.addCubeDeployment(lowestLevelCD);
ContentMap LLCM =
    olapPackage.getContentMap().createContentMap();
lowestLevelCD.addContentMap(LLCM);

ClassifierMap LLCFM =
    transformationPackage.getClassifierMap().createClassifierMap();
LLCM.addClassifierMap(LLCFM);
lowestLevels.addOwnedElement(LLCFM);
LLCFM.addTarget(lowestLevels);
LLCFM.addSource(salesFactTable);

FeatureMap prodKeyLLFM =
    transformationPackage.getFeatureMap().createFeatureMap();
LLCFM.addFeatureMap(prodKeyLLFM);
prodKeyLLFM.addSource(relSalesProdId);
prodKeyLLFM.addTarget(LLProdKey);
```

```
FeatureMap geogKeyLLFM =
   transformationPackage.getFeatureMap().createFeatureMap();
LLCFM.addFeatureMap(geogKeyLLFM);
geogKeyLLFM.addSource(relSalesGeogId);
geogKeyLLFM.addTarget(LLGeogKey);

FeatureMap timeKeyLLFM =
   transformationPackage.getFeatureMap().createFeatureMap();
LLCFM.addFeatureMap(timeKeyLLFM);
timeKeyLLFM.addSource(relsalesTimeId);
timeKeyLLFM.addTarget(LLTimeKey);

FeatureMap salesLLFM =
   transformationPackage.getFeatureMap().createFeatureMap();
LLCFM.addFeatureMap(salesLLFM);
prodKeyLLFM.addSource(relSales);
prodKeyLLFM.addTarget(LLSales);

FeatureMap costFM =
   transformationPackage.getFeatureMap().createFeatureMap();
LLCFM.addFeatureMap(costFM);
prodKeyLLFM.addSource(relCost);
prodKeyLLFM.addTarget(LLCost);
```

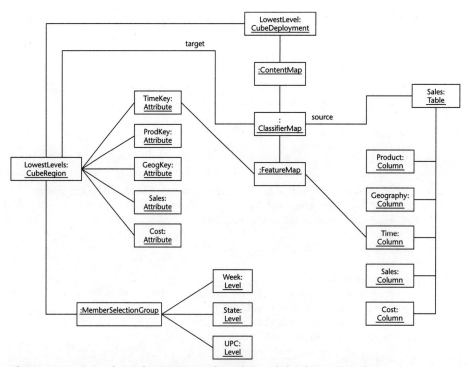

Figure 6.77   Map the Cube Region to the relational database: Time key.

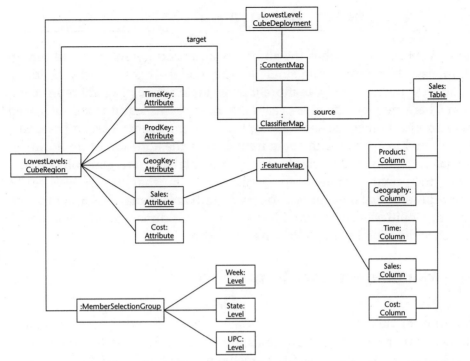

Figure 6.78   Map the Cube Region to the relational database: Sales (measure) attribute.

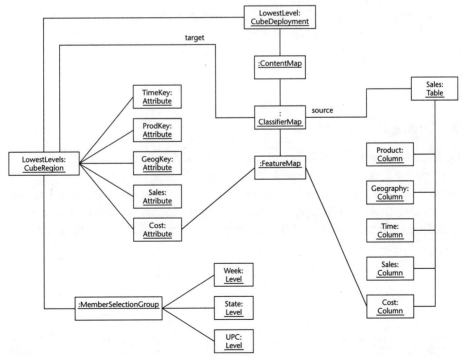

Figure 6.79   Map the Cube Region to the relational database: Cost (measure) attribute.

Creating a Second Deployment

The CWM metamodel has the ability to support different physical configurations, which represent a single logical model. This support was added to address the need to have more than a single active physical representation. There are many business cases that require this feature; one such need is to provide both a test and development environment. A second case that has started to appear with some frequency is the addition of multidimensional databases to the warehouse. These databases are generally configured to provide high-speed access to data that is analysis-ready. Multidimensional databases also provide advanced analytics and forecasting capabilities. CWM provides a core multidimensional metamodel, which is described in the following subsection.

The Multidimensional Metamodel

This CWM Multidimensional metamodel was purposely built as a generalization of different multidimensional databases and doesn't contain a sufficient representation for any existing database. Instead, the intent of the CWM designers was to provide a mechanism for individual database companies to specialize the CWM Multidimensional model with vendor-specific models. This was done to provide a convenient starting point for these vendors and to correctly link the multidimensional databases into the remainder of the model. In this example, a second deployment of the Product dimension will be provided by an extension to the Multidimensional Package of CWM. The core CWM Multidimensional metamodel is shown in Figure 6.80.

The Express Model

The Express metamodel is provided as a CWM extension example in volume 2 of the CWM specification. This metamodel is based on the core Multidimensional metamodel described above. In the case of the Express metamodel, there are two points in the model that are anchored by the core Multidimensional metamodel. An Express Dimension is a type of core

Dimension, and the dimensioned Express classes are specializations of DimensionedObject. This example shows how simple it is to add an entire metamodel to CWM. This feature of CWM can allow users of CWM to greatly extend the provided functionality. It is worth noting that these types of extensions are not generally interchangeable. They are, however, interchangeable among tools that understand the Express metamodel or can be used internally by the extending vendor. A portion of the extended Express metamodel is shown in Figure 6.81.

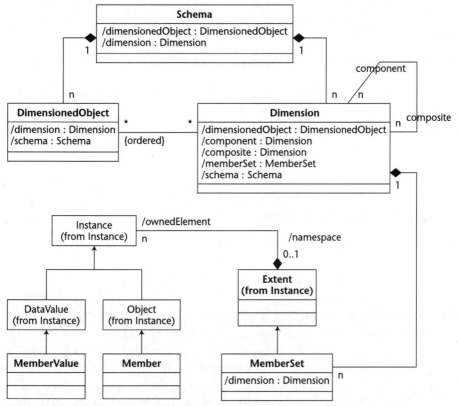

Figure 6.80　CWM Multidimensional metamodel.

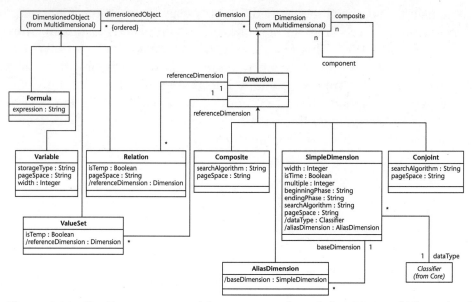

Figure 6.81 The Express metamodel as an extension of the CWM Multidimensional metamodel.

Creating the Express Objects

This example will use the Express metamodel to create a physical Express schema. This schema will parallel the functionality provided by the relational star-schema. In the case of Express, the Dimension object represents not only a Dimension but supplies a mechanism to store a Dimension member within the Dimension object itself. This can be thought of as the Dimension object having an internal attribute that represents its "ID" attribute and unique key. In Express, attributes are created as individual Express variables, which are "dimensioned" by their owning dimension. A hierarchy in Express is created as a separate dimension where the members of the hierarchy dimension become the hierarchies of an associated dimension. Creating a separate dimension where the members in this case denote levels creates levels in a similar fashion to hierarchies. The levels are added to the hierarchy by creating a variable that links the two dimensions together. Finally, a variable representing the ancestor relationships of the hierarchy is created to supply hierarchical navigation for the dimension. The Express instances are shown in Figure 6.82.

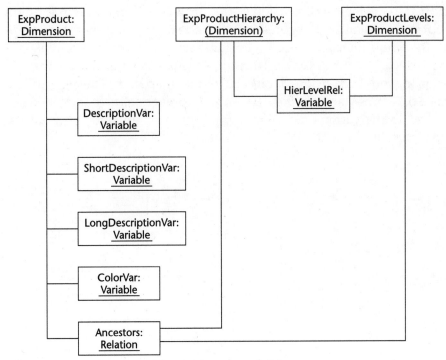

Figure 6.82   An instance of the Express metamodel.

Adding the Second Deployment

The Express physical structures can now be used to create a second deployment of the logical model. The process of mapping the logical model to the Express instances is very similar to the mapping already shown in this example. The main thing to note is that in the case of a multidimensional database, most of the mappings are one-to-one because the multidimensional database has a more natural representation of the logical model than a relational database. Figures 6.83 to 6.89 show the mapping of the logical model to the physical Express objects. For clarity, these instances, like the other mapping instance diagrams, have been separated from an overall set of diagrams. There are several points of interest in these mappings: The first is the use of a ClassifierFeatureMap. This feature is illustrated by mapping the Express Dimension to logical attribute. This mapping is done because of the nature of the Express Dimension object. As stated earlier, the Express Dimension can be thought to have an internal attribute, which represents its "ID" attribute. For this reason, the Dimension, which is a type of classifier, is mapped to the logical dimension's "ID" attribute. The second interesting concept in the instances in Figures 6.83 to 6.89 is that the Express objects represent the whole logical dimension in single structures. Because of this, it is often necessary to use an Express formula to isolate portions of the Express Dimension and Dimensioned objects in the mapping. Throughout the instance diagrams shown in the figures, an Express qualified data reference is applied to the various mappings with appropriate values to fulfill the desired mapping.

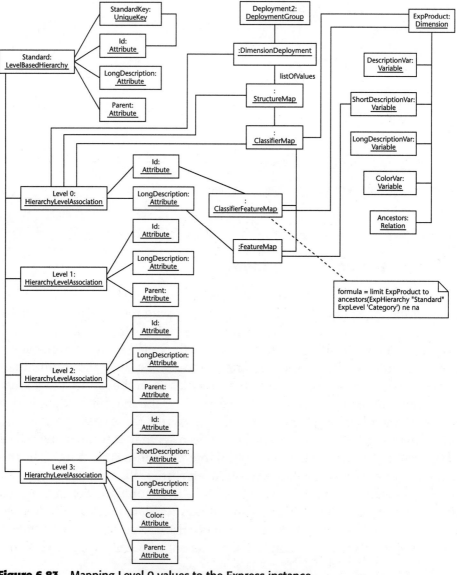

Figure 6.83 Mapping Level 0 values to the Express instance.

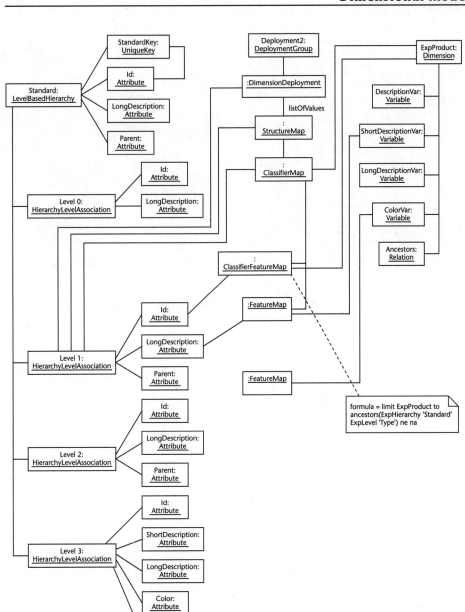

Figure 6.84   Mapping Level 1 values to the Express instance.

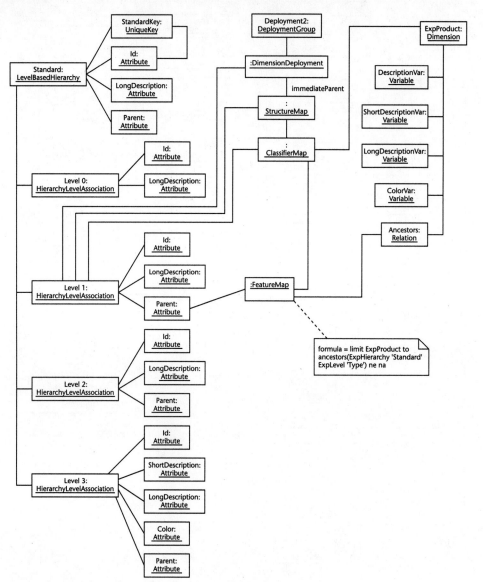

Figure 6.85 Mapping Level 1 parents to the Express instance.

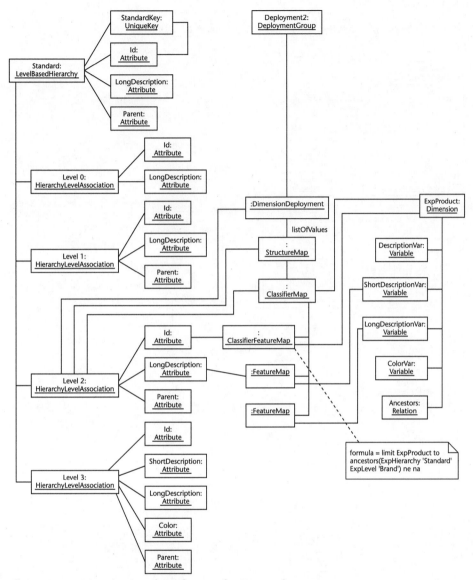

Figure 6.86   Mapping Level 2 values to the Express instance.

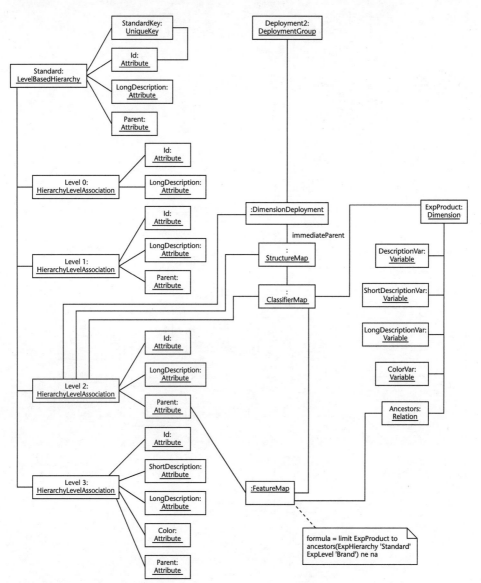

Figure 6.87 Mapping Level 2 parents to the Express instance.

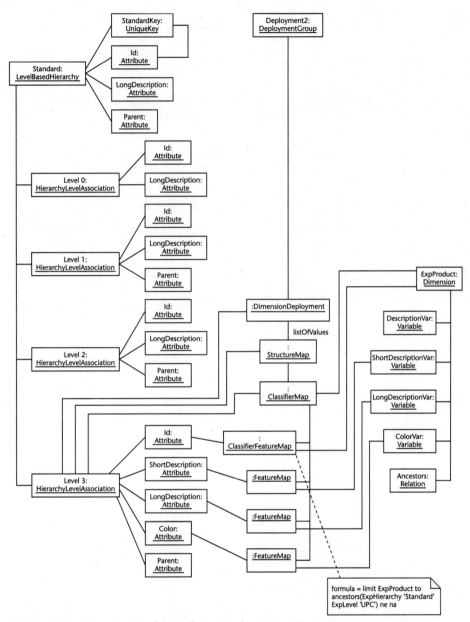

Figure 6.88 Mapping Level 3 attributes to the Express instance.

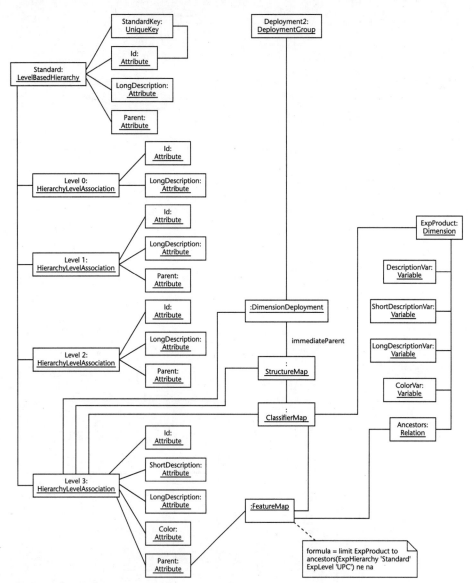

Figure 6.89 Mapping Level 3 parents to the Express instance.

A final note is that all of the previous mappings are ultimately associated with the second deployment, providing users of this system with a choice of physical representations for the single logical model.

Summary

This example has brought out many of the features available in the CWM metamodel. One of the key CWM features—package isolation—was illustrated in this example by the fact that only specific packages were used. Users of CWM are able to choose only those packages germane to a specific problem and remain CWM-compliant. A second important feature of CWM illustrated by this example is the reuse of common concepts. There were many examples of using attributes, measures, keys, classifierMaps, and featureMaps. As the example flowed from section to section, the same API calls were made over and over again, giving it context and correctness, but the overall number of API calls was kept to a minimum. The designers of CWM felt that this type of metamodel would decrease the overall learning curve of the CWM API and also serve as an example of metamodel reuse.

The OLAP portions of the example illustrate the enormous flexibility available in the OLAP metamodel. It clearly demonstrated the complete separation between the logical and physical model representations. This allows users of CWM to isolate the logical model requirements of the end user from the physical limitations of specific database systems.

The Resource packages in CWM contain several different types of physical metamodels. This example highlighted the Relational metamodel and the Multidimensional metamodel. The independent use of these two models in different portions of the example was another good illustration of package isolation. From the example, users of CWM can see that the physical representations available in CWM provide them with a complete definition for the various physical storage mechanisms. It was then shown that the logical and physical models are connected via deployments to form a complete OLAP system.

Finally, this example showed how an extension to CWM can be fit into the overall system. It is worth noting that this type of extension is not generally interchangeable because it represents a user-specific metamodel. That said, this extension is interchangeable by users with knowledge of the Express extension metamodel. The main point is that a user of CWM can extend the functionality provided by the base CWM metamodel with specific requirements. This example showed that the extended functionality could be modeled in such a way that it can use and reference the other portions of the CWM metamodel.

Please refer to this book's companion Web site for the formal specification of meta data interchange patterns that are relevant to this particular chapter.

Web-Enabled Data Warehouse Model

This chapter develops additional dimensional and operational concepts that allow the data warehouse to participate in a distributed, highly collaborative Web-based computing environment. The value of the Web-enabled data warehouse, or *data webhouse* (Kimball and Merz, 2000), is described. It is demonstrated how Common Warehouse Metamodel (CWM) can be used to model the situation in which a data warehouse is used to back-end a Web server, by providing new dimensional structures and other meta data constructs supporting clickstream analysis. We will show which core packages of the CWM architecture are most applicable in modeling a Web-enabled data warehousing environment. In a manner similar to the approach taken in Chapter 6, we will illustrate the construction of *logical models* of analysis concepts, *physical models* of data resources, and the various mappings and data transformations between the two. As with Chapters 5 and 6, examples of extending the core CWM metamodel to more adequately cover the additional domain semantics required by the Web environment are also demonstrated. Finally, several important formal patterns pertaining to the use of CWM in a Web-enabled data warehousing environment will be developed and entered into the pattern catalog on this book's companion Web site.

Given the rather complex nature of a complete, Web-enabled data warehouse, and the fact that the general relationship between data warehousing and Web Services computing models is still being established, this chapter emphasizes fundamental concepts rather than providing a complete Web model for data warehousing. Initial, logical dimensional structures are defined and constructed, and several important lower-level patterns are discovered and codified. The complete Web-enabled data warehouse and Web Services model (which is a topic of ongoing research) is located on the companion Web site. This model is versioned, with the current version representing the most evolved state of the Web-enabled data warehouse model. Readers should revisit the companion Web site regularly to obtain copies of this detailed model and emerging, related meta data patterns as they evolve.

Introducing the Web-Enabled Data Warehouse

The rapid evolution of the World Wide Web in recent years has resulted in the significant and rapid development of e-commerce as a major business paradigm. This has meant that data warehousing, which has traditionally been tasked with the problem of tying together many diverse legacy systems in order to support corporatewide business analysis, must now also account for the Web as both an informational resource and a delivery mechanism. As an information resource, the Web provides a wealth of strategic information that must somehow be brought into the data warehouse. As a delivery mechanism, the Web provides a highly ubiquitous and inexpensive medium for end-user analysis. Figure 7.1 illustrates this environment, in which the Web and data warehousing are deeply integrated. Achieving deep integration between the Web environment and data warehouse/Information Supply Chain (ISC) architectures requires, of course, extensive meta data modeling and the ability to integrate data warehousing and Web-based tools via common meta data. We will see subsequently how CWM can be used to provide this. We will also see how the pattern-based approach to meta data interchange benefits this application domain tremendously.

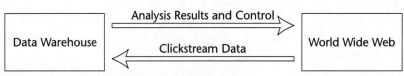

Figure 7.1 Web-enabled data warehouse.

The following subsections investigate further the dual nature of the Web-enabled data warehouse as both an information resource and analysis delivery mechanism, and underscore the challenges faced by supply chain implementers and integrators.

Merging the Web and the Data Warehouse

As an information resource (at the "front end" of the data warehouse), the Web provides a significant source of strategic information, largely in the form of *behavioral data*. In particular, this strategic information is inherent in the *clickstream*, the sequence of mouse clicks, key entries, and other events, triggered by a Web site end user as he or she navigates through a Web session. Clickstreams are accumulated by Web servers and stored in the Web server's log files. From the log file, the clickstream content may be imported into a data warehouse's dimensional store for subsequent analysis of the user's behavior. This analysis generally leads to the fine-tuning of the Web site's various promotions and presentations during future user sessions, optimized generally toward improving or customizing the user's Web experience, hopefully resulting in more successful sessions (higher volume of sales, upselling, and so forth).

However, such analysis is difficult to perform, as it involves extracting clickstream data from the various log files (often in a Web server vendor-specific format), and attempting to piece together multiple records that represent a single user session. And, of course, once the user sessions have been identified and assembled, one must determine how to move all this information into a dimensional data warehouse for analysis. Clearly, having a single common vision of meta data is necessary in order to do this in an efficient manner and to enhance the overall Return on Investment (ROI) of the data warehouse architecture when integrated with the Web. Some of the challenges facing modelers of this type of environment include:

- Modeling the Web site as a data resource
- Modeling the central dimensional store used by the data warehouse to analyze Web activity
- Modeling the mappings from the Web-based data resources to the dimensional store
- Modeling the extract-transform-load (ETL) used in the construction and loading of the Web-enabled data warehouse
- Modeling other operational and management processes of the Web-enabled data warehouse

As a delivery mechanism (at the back end of the data warehouse), the Web provides a ubiquitous and relatively inexpensive medium for communicating analysis results to business strategists and corporate decision-makers. This means that advanced analysis and reporting tools must be capable of interfacing with the data warehouse and any associated data marts via the Web. This includes:

- Advanced reporting applications
- Online Analytical Processing (OLAP) servers that provide custom- and purpose-built cubes used for what-if analyses
- Advanced visualization tools
- Browser-based clients for query formulation and submission

In general, such advanced analysis tools must be capable of running inside a Web browser so as to take advantage of thin-client and ultra-thin-client deployment strategies. Interactions with the central data warehouse must also heavily leverage languages such as eXtensible Markup Language (XML). That is, both the specifications of a query and any data result sets computed as part of query evaluation will be communicated between the client and the data warehouse via XML documents. These documents conform to established tag sets (that is, XML Document Type Definitions, or DTDs) that define the analysis components in terms of XML tags and attributes. Such tag sets might be developed, for example, as part of an overall model of analysis meta data and advanced analytic process models. We will see that CWM and the Object Management Group (OMG) meta-modeling architecture, in general, can perform a critical role in modeling these elements.

Finally, the Web-enabled data warehouse may also host intelligent, agent-based clients that automatically perform a number of analysis steps and make adjustments to the Web site to improve and optimize subsequent Web user sessions. Thus, the Web-enabled data warehouse or ISC takes on a cyclic, feedback-loop architecture, consisting of several very distinctive and recognizable information and control flows:

- An informational flow from various Web-oriented data resources into the data warehouse
- An informational flow from the data warehouse to analysis clients via the Web

- A control flow of queries and directives from certain client processes via the Web, back to the data warehouse

- A control flow of directives from the data warehouse back to the Web site front-ending the data warehouse

Figure 7.2 illustrates the data warehouse/ISC diagram from the introductory CWM book (Poole, 2002), as a Web-enabled information supply chain environment. The Web-enabled ISC exhibits two prominent usage characteristics relative to the Web: that is, the Web as a strategic information source (via clickstream analysis) and the Web as a delivery mechanism for advanced business analysis products.

The remaining subsections of this chapter will introduce the reader to the underlying concepts of a detailed CWM model of a Web-enabled data warehouse or ISC. This model will be loosely based on the more general model developed by Kimball and Merz (2000). This model will represent meta data that might be used to define, control, and drive such an environment. Figure 7.3 illustrates the various CWM metamodel packages that will be used in the construction of this model throughout the remainder of this chapter.

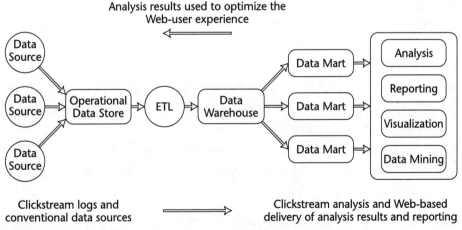

Figure 7.2 Web-enabled information supply chain.

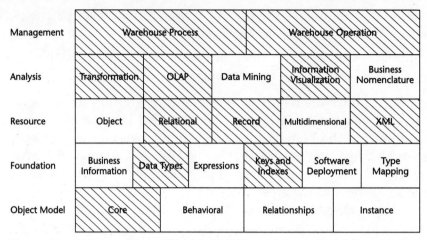

Management	Warehouse Process		Warehouse Operation	
Analysis	Transformation	OLAP	Data Mining	Information Visualization	Business Nomenclature
Resource	Object	Relational	Record	Multidimensional	XML
Foundation	Business Information	Data Types	Expressions	Keys and Indexes	Software Deployment	Type Mapping
Object Model	Core	Behavioral	Relationships	Instance

Figure 7.3 CWM packages utilized in building a Web-enabled information supply chain model.

Web-Enabled Dimensional Model

In this section, we will begin the construction of our complete Web-enabled data warehouse model by starting with the design of a central dimensional model for our Web-enabled data warehouse. The dimensional model is a crucial component of the Web-enabled data warehouse, forming the central, logical analysis store of the data warehouse. To this end, it must provide adequate dimensionality and measures that enable business analysis of the clickstream. It must also address a number of modeling issues, including the following:

- Establish a shared, logical model of the Web-enabled dimensional store
- Create the physical model of the underlying stores implementing the Web-enabled dimensional store
- Provide logical-to-physical mappings between the two models for the benefit of data warehouse tools and processes

The Logical Clickstream Dimensions

We will now actually use CWM to construct the logical dimensional model and, in the process, establish several useful patterns for model construction. Each logical dimension is developed in a separate and subsequent subsection. We first explain the motivation or purpose behind each dimension, then illustrate it in terms of a CWM instance diagram. Then we illustrate a code from our toolkit that demonstrates the actual construction of that portion of the model in terms of the Java interfaces of the CWM toolkit.

The logical dimensions that will define our Web-enabled data warehouse model—our "portfolio of conformed dimensions," according to Kimball and Merz (2000)—consists of the minimal set of dimensions required to perform effective clickstream analysis. Following the recommendations of Kimball and Merz (2000), we will construct the logical dimensions listed below. We will not necessarily build these dimensions in their entirety (that is, as they were originally defined in *The Data Webhouse Toolkit*) but will use a reasonable amount of detail to illustrate the use of CWM as a modeling language. The Web-enabled data warehouse dimensions, then, consist of the following:

- Time Dimension (actually, Date and Time of Day)
- Product Dimension
- Customer Dimension
- Page Dimension
- Event Dimension
- Session Dimension
- Referral Dimension
- Causal Dimension
- Entity Dimension

Note that the first three dimensions are fairly "conventional" (from a business viewpoint), while the remaining six dimensions can be classified as being of a "Web-oriented" nature. The key point here is that these dimensions collectively define the overall dimensionalities that we require for constructing useful analysis cubes in the Web-enabled information supply chain environment.

In the next section, we will identify those CWM packages that are required in order to build the logical clickstream dimensional model. This is always the first step in building a CWM model; that is, once you've determined what you need to model, you must then determine which CWM packages are required in order for you to build your model. Then we will briefly illustrate how to connect to a CWM meta data resource as the first step in building any CWM model. Since there are many possible implementations of CWM, this should be viewed as only one of many possible examples. It is an example based on current Java platform architecture. Following those two preliminaries, we will then proceed to build each of the logical Dimensions, adding them to a single, global Schema for the Web-enabled data warehouse.

CWM Packages and Interfaces

To understand the overall context for construction of the complete Web-enabled warehouse model, let's look at which packages of the CWM meta-model we intend to use. Briefly, we need to construct the following types of models:

- A logical dimensional model of the Web-enabled data warehouse
- A resource model of the underlying relational store supporting the logical dimensional model
- Mappings from the logical dimensional model to its physical realization
- A resource model of the Web server clickstream logs
- Definitions of transformation processes to load the clickstream data into the dimensional store
- Definitions of warehouse operations and processes that control the overall Web-enabled data warehouse

Therefore, we will be leveraging the following CWM packages in building this comprehensive Web-enabled data warehouse model:

- OLAP
- Relational
- Transformation
- Record
- Warehouse Operation
- Warehouse Process
- XML
- Information Visualization

We will use the OLAP metamodel to construct the logical model of the dimensional store. It is important to emphasize here that this is a purely logical model, and not a physical one. The logical model, as a piece of shared meta data, is crucial to the operation of the analysis tools. How this model resolves to its underlying physical resources must, of course, also be represented.

We assume that we are going to implement much of the physical dimensional model using relational database technology, so we will use the Relational package to model the physical realization in terms of a relation *star-schema* database.

The Transformation package is used to define the logical-to-physical mapping relating the logical dimensional model to the physical star-schema resource model. Transformation instances will also be used to define the data transformations between the physical resource model and the Web server log files used to collect clickstream data. Since the Web server log files are relatively simple, record-oriented files, we will use the Record package of CWM to model them.

The CWM Warehouse Operation and Process metamodels are used to model meta data representing those Web-enabled data warehouse management processes that invoke the transformations used to load the star-schema dimensional store from the clickstream logs.

Finally, we will use the CWM XML and Information Visualization metamodels to create meta data representing Web-enabled analysis inquiries, data responses, and visualization transformations (in terms of eXtensible Stylesheet Language Transformations [XSLT]).

Figure 7.3, introduced previously, shows the CWM architectural block diagram with the CWM packages used in this chapter (either directly or indirectly as a result of interpackage dependencies) shaded in. Note that a good part of the entire CWM metamodel is utilized. So the Web-enabled data warehouse model, as an example, provides considerable coverage in terms of usage of the CWM metamodel.

Subsequent sections will illustrate the complete construction of each of the major, logical dimensions of our Web-enabled data warehouse.

Building the Time Dimension

Kimball and Merz (2000) recommend factoring the Time Dimension into two separate dimensions: a Calendar Date dimension and a Time of Day dimension. This is done both for flexibility and for the ability to readily assign different properties to different granularities of time. However, in the interest of demonstrating the modeling power of CWM, as well as keeping this example relatively compact, let's instead introduce a hierarchical Time dimension where the hierarchies allow us to represent different properties at different levels of granularity within the same dimension. In particular, the levels of granularity represented are *time of day*, *date* (that is, day of calendar), and *quarter*.

This results in a single dimensional structure with the attributes described in Table 7.1. The unique key attribute, TimeID, is defined as a *surrogate key*, meaning a generated integer that guarantees the unique identification of its elements, but otherwise carries no semantic content. We shall formalize the specification of surrogate keys in the meta data patterns described toward the end of this chapter.

Table 7.1 Time Dimension

ATTRIBUTE	DATA TYPE
TimeID	Integer
DateType	String
CalendarType	String
DayOfWeek	Integer
DayNumberInWeek	Integer
DayNumberInMonth	Integer
DayNumberInYear	Integer
DayNumberInEpoch	Integer
Workday	Boolean
Holiday	Boolean
WeekDay	Boolean
LastDayInMonth	Boolean
WeekNumberInYear	Integer
WeekNumberInEpoch	Integer
Month	String
MonthAbbreviated	String
MonthNumberInYear	Integer
MonthNumberInEpoch	Integer
QuarterInYear	String
Year	String
FiscalPeriod	String
Season	String
Event	String
SecondsSinceMidnight	Integer
MinutesSinceMidnight	Integer
Hour	Integer
Minute	Integer
Second	Integer
TimeSpan	Integer

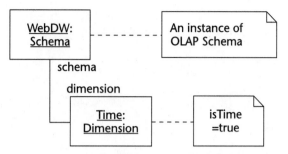

Figure 7.4   Instance diagram: Initial Time dimension and Schema.

The instance diagrams (see Figures 7.4, 7.6, and 7.8) show how this dimension is constructed as instances of classes from the CWM OLAP package. We shall follow the general approach outlined in Chapter 6, in which a logical dimensional model is first constructed using the CWM OLAP package.

Note that we model the Time Dimension instance as being owned by an instance of OLAP Schema named "WebDW." The Time Dimension is also explicitly tagged as a CWM Time Dimension. The code fragments shown in Figures 7.5, 7.7, and 7.9 are the actual Java code that initially constructs the Time Dimension and adds it to the Schema.

```
// Bootstrap the CWM Factory and create an OLAP Schema
CWMCompletePackage cwmFactory = new CWMCompletePackageImp();
OlapPackage olapPkg = cwmFactory.getOlap();
SchemaClass schemaClass = olapPkg.getSchema();
Schema schema = schemaClass.createSchema();
schema.setName( "WebDW" );

// Create the Time Dimension
DimensionClass dimensionClass = olapPkg.getDimension();
Dimension timeDimension = dimensionClass.createDimension();
timeDimension.setName( "Time" );
timeDimension.setTime( true );

// Add the Time Dimension to the OLAP Schema
Collection dimCol = schema.getDimension();
dimCol.add( timeDimension );
timeDimension.setSchema( schema );
```

Figure 7.5   Code fragment: Creating the initial Time dimension.

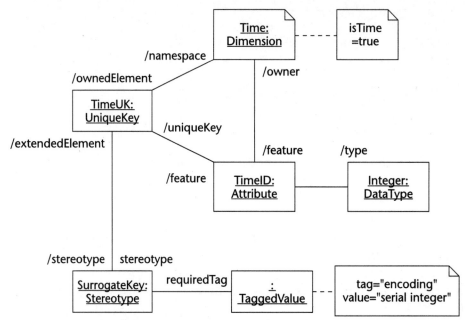

Figure 7.6 Instance diagram: Specifying the unique (surrogate) key.

If you look at the instance diagram in Figure 7.6 closely, and then refer to the formal definition of the Surrogate Key pattern at the end of this chapter, you will see that TimeID is indeed a realization of that pattern. The same will generally be true of the other dimensions constructed in this chapter.

```
// Get the necessary class factories

CorePackage corePkg = cwmFactory.getCore();
KeysIndexesPackage keysIndexesPkg = cwmFactory.getKeysIndexes();

AttributeClass attributeClass = corePkg.getAttribute();
DataTypeClass dataTypeClass = corePkg.getDataType();
UniqueKeyClass uniqueKeyClass = keysIndexesPkg.getUniqueKey();
StereotypeClass stereotypeClass = corePkg.getStereotype();
TaggedValueClass taggedValueClass = corePkg.getTaggedValue();
```

Figure 7.7 Code fragment: Creating the unique (surrogate) key.

```
// Create the primary key of the Time Dimension using the
// "surrogate key" pattern. Note that the data types we
// create here will be reused by other attributes.

DataType integerType = dataTypeClass.createDataType();
integerType.setName( "Integer" );

Attribute keyAttribute = attributeClass.createAttribute();
keyAttribute.setName( "TimeID" );
keyAttribute.setType( integerType );
keyAttribute.setNamespace( timeDimension );
List featureList = timeDimension.getFeature();
featureList.add( keyAttribute );

UniqueKey uniqueKey = uniqueKeyClass.createUniqueKey();
uniqueKey.setName( "TimeUK" );
List keyFeatureList = uniqueKey.getFeature();
keyFeatureList.add( keyAttribute );
uniqueKey.setNamespace( timeDimension );
Collection ownedElements = timeDimension.getOwnedElement();
ownedElements.add( uniqueKey );

// Create the "surrogate key" stereotype, as required by
// the "surrogate key" pattern.
// Note that this stereotype will be reused by other
// dimension keys.

Stereotype surrogateKeyStereotype = stereotypeClass.createStereotype();
surrogateKeyStereotype.setName( "SurrogateKey" );
Collection extendedElements =
surrogateKeyStereotype.getExtendedElement();
extendedElements.add( uniqueKey );

TaggedValue surrogateKeyTaggedValue =
taggedValueClass.createTaggedValue();
surrogateKeyTaggedValue.setTag( "encoding" );
surrogateKeyTaggedValue.setValue( "serial integer" );
surrogateKeyTaggedValue.setStereotype( surrogateKeyStereotype );

Collection requiredTags = surrogateKeyStereotype.getRequiredTag();
requiredTags.add( surrogateKeyTaggedValue );
```

Figure 7.7 Code fragment: Creating the unique (surrogate) key. *(continued)*

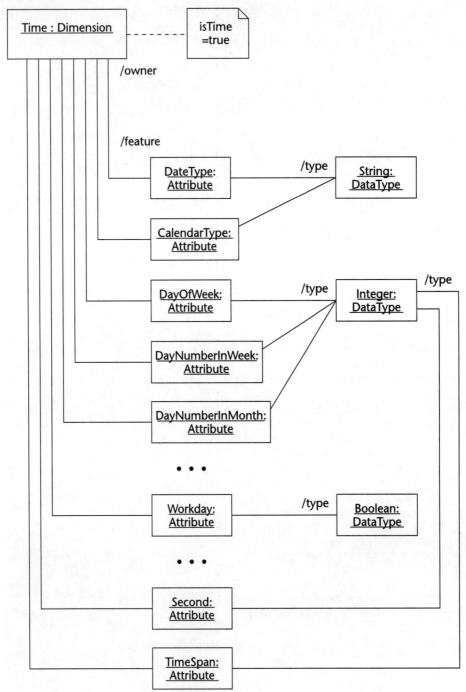

Figure 7.8 Instance diagram: Specifying the non-key dimension attributes.

```
// Create the non-key attributes and add them to the Time Dimension.
// Note that the data types created here will be re-used by other
// attributes.

DataType booleanType = dataTypeClass.createDataType();
booleanType.setName( "Boolean" );
DataType stringType = dataTypeClass.createDataType();
stringType.setName( "String" );

Attribute nonKeyAttribute = attributeClass.createAttribute();

nonKeyAttribute.setName( "DateType" );
nonKeyAttribute.setType( stringType );
nonKeyAttribute.setNamespace( timeDimension );
featureList.add( nonKeyAttribute );

nonKeyAttribute = attributeClass.createAttribute();
nonKeyAttribute.setName( "CalendarType" );
nonKeyAttribute.setType( stringType );
nonKeyAttribute.setNamespace( timeDimension );
featureList.add( nonKeyAttribute );

nonKeyAttribute = attributeClass.createAttribute();
nonKeyAttribute.setName( "DayOfWeek" );
nonKeyAttribute.setType( integerType );
nonKeyAttribute.setNamespace( timeDimension );
featureList.add( nonKeyAttribute );

nonKeyAttribute = attributeClass.createAttribute();
nonKeyAttribute.setName( "DayNumberInWeek" );
nonKeyAttribute.setType( integerType );
nonKeyAttribute.setNamespace( timeDimension );
featureList.add( nonKeyAttribute );

nonKeyAttribute = attributeClass.createAttribute();
nonKeyAttribute.setName( "DayNumberInMonth" );
nonKeyAttribute.setType( integerType );
nonKeyAttribute.setNamespace( timeDimension );
featureList.add( nonKeyAttribute );

// ...

nonKeyAttribute = attributeClass.createAttribute();
nonKeyAttribute.setName( "Workday" );
nonKeyAttribute.setType( booleanType );
nonKeyAttribute.setNamespace( timeDimension );
featureList.add( nonKeyAttribute );
```

Figure 7.9   Code fragment: Creating the non-key dimension attributes. *(continues)*

```
// ...

nonKeyAttribute = attributeClass.createAttribute();
nonKeyAttribute.setName( "Second" );
nonKeyAttribute.setType( integerType );
nonKeyAttribute.setNamespace( timeDimension );
featureList.add( nonKeyAttribute );

nonKeyAttribute = attributeClass.createAttribute();
nonKeyAttribute.setName( "TimeSpan" );
nonKeyAttribute.setType( integerType );
nonKeyAttribute.setNamespace( timeDimension );
featureList.add( nonKeyAttribute );
```

Figure 7.9   Code fragment: Creating the non-key dimension attributes. *(continued)*

Building the Customer Dimension

The Customer Dimension is a single dimensional structure with the attributes shown in Table 7.2.

Table 7.2   Customer Dimension

ATTRIBUTE	DATA TYPE
CustomerID	Integer
CustomerType	String
ISP	String
CookieID	Integer
LastChangeDatestamp	Integer

Table 7.2 *(Continued)*

ATTRIBUTE	DATA TYPE
LastChangeReason	String
Identifier	String
NameType	String
Salutation	String
FirstName	String
MiddleNames	String
LastName	String
Gender	String
IP_City	String
IP_State	String
IP_Country	String
CompanyName	String
DepartmentName	String
PrimaryPhone	String
FAX	String
EMAIL	String
WebSiteURL	String
AddressType	String
StreetNumber	String
StreetName	String
City	String
State	String
PostalCode	String
Region	String
Country	String

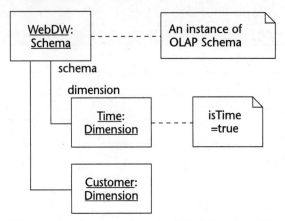

Figure 7.10 Instance diagram: Initial Customer Dimension.

The instance diagrams in Figures 7.10, 7.12, and 7.14 represent how this dimension appears when constructed as instances of classes from the CWM OLAP package. Note that the Customer Dimension instance is owned by an instance of OLAP Schema. The code fragments in Figures 7.11, 7.13, and 7.15 are the actual Java code that constructs the Customer Dimension.

```
// Create the Customer Dimension and add it to the Schema

Dimension customerDimension = dimensionClass.createDimension();
customerDimension.setName( "Customer" );

dimCol.add( customerDimension );
customerDimension.setSchema( schema );
```

Figure 7.11 Code fragment: Creating the initial Customer Dimension.

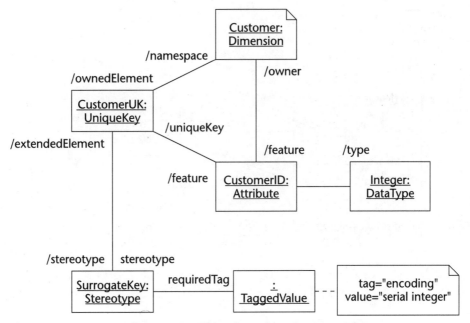

Figure 7.12   Instance diagram: Specifying the unique (surrogate) key.

```
// Create the primary key of the Customer Dimension using the
// "surrogate key" pattern

keyAttribute = attributeClass.createAttribute();
keyAttribute.setName( "CustomerID" );
keyAttribute.setType( integerType );
keyAttribute.setNamespace( customerDimension );
featureList = customerDimension.getFeature();
featureList.add( keyAttribute );

uniqueKey = uniqueKeyClass.createUniqueKey();
uniqueKey.setName( "CustomerUK" );
keyFeatureList = uniqueKey.getFeature();
keyFeatureList.add( keyAttribute );
uniqueKey.setNamespace( customerDimension );
ownedElements = customerDimension.getOwnedElement();
ownedElements.add( uniqueKey );

// Note that the stereotype is reused...
extendedElements.add( uniqueKey );
```

Figure 7.13   Code fragment: Creating the unique (surrogate) key.

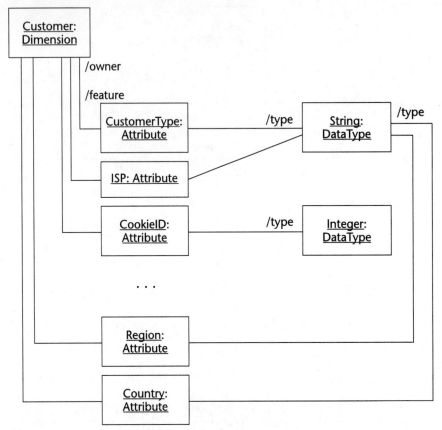

Figure 7.14 Instance diagram: Specifying the non-key dimension attributes.

```
// Create the non-key attributes and add them to the
// Customer Dimension.
// Note that the data types created previously are re-used.

nonKeyAttribute = attributeClass.createAttribute();

nonKeyAttribute.setName( "CustomerType" );
nonKeyAttribute.setType( stringType );
nonKeyAttribute.setNamespace( customerDimension );
featureList.add( nonKeyAttribute );

nonKeyAttribute = attributeClass.createAttribute();
nonKeyAttribute.setName( "ISP" );
nonKeyAttribute.setType( stringType );
nonKeyAttribute.setNamespace( customerDimension );
featureList.add( nonKeyAttribute );
```

Figure 7.15 Code fragment: Creating the non-key dimension attributes.

```
nonKeyAttribute = attributeClass.createAttribute();
nonKeyAttribute.setName( "CookieID" );
nonKeyAttribute.setType( integerType );
nonKeyAttribute.setNamespace( customerDimension );
featureList.add( nonKeyAttribute );

// ...

nonKeyAttribute = attributeClass.createAttribute();
nonKeyAttribute.setName( "Region" );
nonKeyAttribute.setType( stringType );
nonKeyAttribute.setNamespace( customerDimension );
featureList.add( nonKeyAttribute );

nonKeyAttribute = attributeClass.createAttribute();
nonKeyAttribute.setName( "Country" );
nonKeyAttribute.setType( stringType );
nonKeyAttribute.setNamespace( customerDimension );
featureList.add( nonKeyAttribute );
```

Figure 7.15 Code fragment: Creating the non-key dimension attributes. *(continued)*

Building the Product Dimension

The Product Dimension is a single dimensional structure with the attributes listed in Table 7.3.

Table 7.3 Product Dimension

ATTRIBUTE	DATA TYPE
ProductID	Integer
ProductType	String
SKU	String
Description	String
LastChangeDatestamp	String
LastChangeReason	String
Brand	String
Category	String
Manufacturer	String

(continues)

Table 7.3   Product Dimension *(Continued)*

ATTRIBUTE	DATA TYPE
Department	String
SystemType	String
Packaging	String
Width	Integer
Depth	Integer
Height	Integer
Stacking	String
Weight	Integer
StandardCost	String
StandardPrice	String
Buyer	String

The instance diagrams in Figures 7.16, 7.18, and 7.20 represent how this dimension appears when constructed as instances of classes from the CWM OLAP package. Note that the Product Dimension instance is owned by an instance of OLAP Schema. The code fragments shown in Figures 7.17, 7.19, and 7.21 are the actual Java code that constructs the Product Dimension.

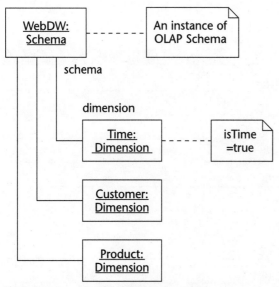

Figure 7.16   Instance diagram: Initial Product Dimension.

```
// Create the Product Dimension and add it to the Schema

Dimension productDimension = dimensionClass.createDimension();
productDimension.setName( "Product" );

dimCol.add( productDimension );
productDimension.setSchema( schema );
```

Figure 7.17   Code fragment: Creating the initial Product Dimension.

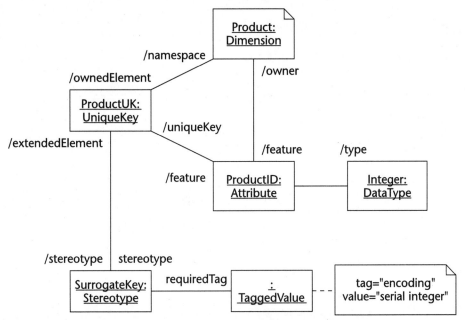

Figure 7.18   Instance diagram: Specifying the unique (surrogate) key.

```
// Create the primary key of the Product Dimension using the
// "surrogate key" pattern

keyAttribute = attributeClass.createAttribute();
keyAttribute.setName( "ProductID" );
keyAttribute.setType( integerType );
keyAttribute.setNamespace( productDimension );
featureList = productDimension.getFeature();
featureList.add( keyAttribute );
```

Figure 7.19   Code fragment: Creating the unique (surrogate) key. *(continues)*

```
uniqueKey = uniqueKeyClass.createUniqueKey();
uniqueKey.setName( "ProductUK" );
keyFeatureList = uniqueKey.getFeature();
keyFeatureList.add( keyAttribute );
uniqueKey.setNamespace( productDimension );
ownedElements = productDimension.getOwnedElement();
ownedElements.add( uniqueKey );

// Note that the stereotype is reused...
extendedElements.add( uniqueKey );
```

Figure 7.19   Code fragment: Creating the unique (surrogate) key. *(continued)*

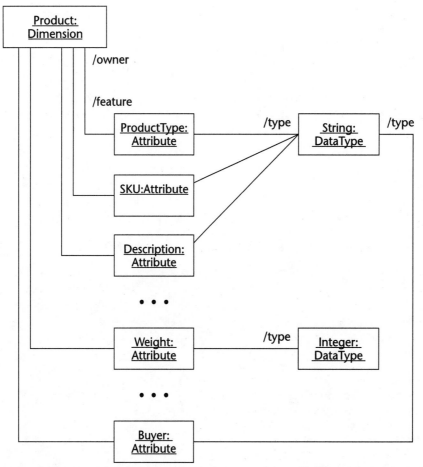

Figure 7.20   Instance diagram: Specifying the non-key dimension attributes.

```
// Create the non-key attributes and add them to the
// Product Dimension.
// Note that the data types created previously are re-used.

nonKeyAttribute = attributeClass.createAttribute();

nonKeyAttribute.setName( "ProductType" );
nonKeyAttribute.setType( stringType );
nonKeyAttribute.setNamespace( productDimension );
featureList.add( nonKeyAttribute );

nonKeyAttribute = attributeClass.createAttribute();
nonKeyAttribute.setName( "SKU" );
nonKeyAttribute.setType( stringType );
nonKeyAttribute.setNamespace( productDimension );
featureList.add( nonKeyAttribute );

nonKeyAttribute = attributeClass.createAttribute();
nonKeyAttribute.setName( "Description" );
nonKeyAttribute.setType( stringType );
nonKeyAttribute.setNamespace( productDimension );
featureList.add( nonKeyAttribute );

// ...

nonKeyAttribute = attributeClass.createAttribute();
nonKeyAttribute.setName( "Weight" );
nonKeyAttribute.setType( integerType );
nonKeyAttribute.setNamespace( productDimension );
featureList.add( nonKeyAttribute );

// ...

nonKeyAttribute = attributeClass.createAttribute();
nonKeyAttribute.setName( "Buyer" );
nonKeyAttribute.setType( stringType );
nonKeyAttribute.setNamespace( productDimension );
featureList.add( nonKeyAttribute );
```

Figure 7.21   Code fragment: Creating the non-key dimension attributes.

Building the Page Dimension

The Page Dimension describes the *page context* for a Web page *event*. The Page Dimension is a single dimensional structure with the attributes shown in Table 7.4.

Table 7.4 Page Dimension

ATTRIBUTE	DATA TYPE
PageID	Integer
Source	String
Function	String
Template	String
ItemType	String
GraphicsType	String
AnimationType	String
SoundType	String
FileName	String

The instance diagrams in Figures 7.22, 7.24, and 7.26 represent how this dimension appears when constructed as instances of classes from the CWM OLAP package. Note that the Page Dimension instance is owned by an instance of OLAP Schema. The code fragments in Figures 7.23, 7.25, and 7.27 are actual Java code that constructs the Page Dimension.

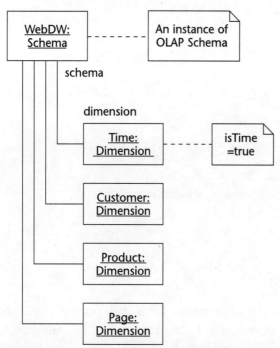

Figure 7.22 Instance diagram: Initial Page Dimension.

```
// Create the Page Dimension and add it to the Schema

Dimension pageDimension = dimensionClass.createDimension();
pageDimension.setName( "Page" );

dimCol.add( pageDimension );
pageDimension.setSchema( schema );
```

Figure 7.23   Code fragment: Creating the initial Page Dimension.

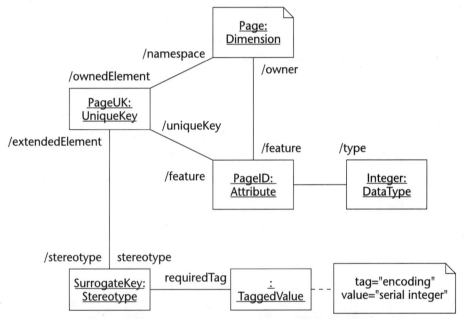

Figure 7.24   Instance diagram: Specifying the unique (surrogate) key.

```
// Create the primary key of the Page Dimension using the
// "surrogate key" pattern

keyAttribute = attributeClass.createAttribute();
keyAttribute.setName( "PageID" );
keyAttribute.setType( integerType );
keyAttribute.setNamespace( pageDimension );
featureList = pageDimension.getFeature();
featureList.add( keyAttribute );
```

Figure 7.25   Code fragment: Creating the unique (surrogate) key. *(continues)*

```
uniqueKey = uniqueKeyClass.createUniqueKey();
uniqueKey.setName( "PageUK" );
keyFeatureList = uniqueKey.getFeature();
keyFeatureList.add( keyAttribute );
uniqueKey.setNamespace( pageDimension );
ownedElements = pageDimension.getOwnedElement();
ownedElements.add( uniqueKey );

// Note that the stereotype is reused...
extendedElements.add( uniqueKey );
```

Figure 7.25   Code fragment: Creating the unique (surrogate) key. *(continued)*

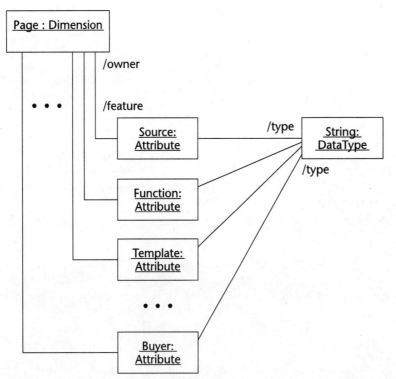

Figure 7.26   Instance diagram: Specifying the non-key dimension attributes.

```
// Create the non-key attributes and add them to the
// Page Dimension.
// Note that the data types created previously are re-used.

nonKeyAttribute = attributeClass.createAttribute();

nonKeyAttribute.setName( "Source" );
nonKeyAttribute.setType( stringType );
nonKeyAttribute.setNamespace( pageDimension );
featureList.add( nonKeyAttribute );

nonKeyAttribute = attributeClass.createAttribute();
nonKeyAttribute.setName( "Function" );
nonKeyAttribute.setType( stringType );
nonKeyAttribute.setNamespace( pageDimension );
featureList.add( nonKeyAttribute );

nonKeyAttribute = attributeClass.createAttribute();
nonKeyAttribute.setName( "Template" );
nonKeyAttribute.setType( stringType );
nonKeyAttribute.setNamespace( pageDimension );
featureList.add( nonKeyAttribute );

// ...

nonKeyAttribute = attributeClass.createAttribute();
nonKeyAttribute.setName( "Buyer" );
nonKeyAttribute.setType( stringType );
nonKeyAttribute.setNamespace( pageDimension );
featureList.add( nonKeyAttribute );
```

Figure 7.27   Code fragment: Creating the non-key dimension attributes.

Building the Event Dimension

The Event Dimension describes what happened on a particular page at a particular point in time. Note that in the case of dynamic pages based on XML, the semantics of the page are exposed to the Web server. Each field in an XML document can be labeled with a user-defined tag, and we need to capture that information in the Event Dimension (Kimball and Merz, 2000). The Event Dimension is a single dimensional structure with the attributes shown in Table 7.5.

Table 7.5   Event Dimension

ATTRIBUTE	DATA TYPE
EventID	Integer
EventType	String
EventContent	String

The instance diagrams in Figures 7.28, 7.30, and 7.32 represent how this dimension appears when constructed as instances of classes from the CWM OLAP package. Note that the Event Dimension instance is owned by an instance of OLAP Schema. The code fragments in Figures 7.29, 7.31, and 7.33 are the actual Java code that constructs the Event Dimension.

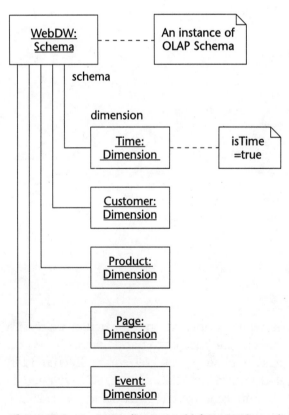

Figure 7.28   Instance diagram: Initial Event Dimension.

```
// Create the Event Dimension and add it to the Schema

Dimension eventDimension = dimensionClass.createDimension();
eventDimension.setName( "Event" );

dimCol.add( eventDimension );
eventDimension.setSchema( schema );
```

Figure 7.29   Code fragment: Creating the initial Event Dimension.

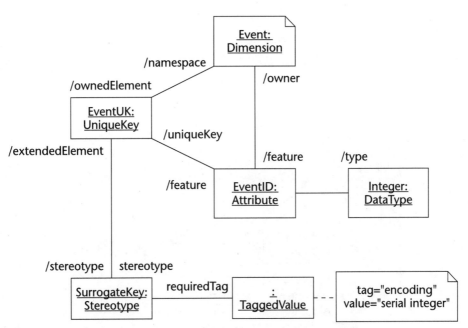

Figure 7.30   Instance diagram: Specifying the unique (surrogate) key.

```
// Create the primary key of the Event Dimension using the
// "surrogate key" pattern

keyAttribute = attributeClass.createAttribute();
keyAttribute.setName( "EventID" );
keyAttribute.setType( integerType );
keyAttribute.setNamespace( eventDimension );
featureList = eventDimension.getFeature();
featureList.add( keyAttribute );

uniqueKey = uniqueKeyClass.createUniqueKey();
uniqueKey.setName( "EventUK" );
keyFeatureList = uniqueKey.getFeature();
keyFeatureList.add( keyAttribute );
uniqueKey.setNamespace( eventDimension );
ownedElements = eventDimension.getOwnedElement();
ownedElements.add( uniqueKey );

// Note that the stereotype is reused...
extendedElements.add( uniqueKey );
```

Figure 7.31   Code fragment: Creating the unique (surrogate) key.

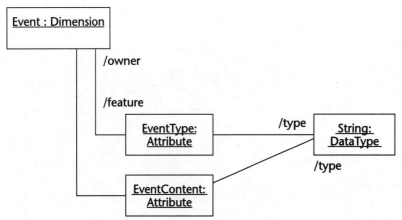

Figure 7.32   Instance diagram: Specifying the non-key dimension attributes.

```
// Create the non-key attributes and add them to the
// Event Dimension.
// Note that the data types created previously are re-used.

nonKeyAttribute = attributeClass.createAttribute();

nonKeyAttribute.setName( "EventType" );
nonKeyAttribute.setType( stringType );
nonKeyAttribute.setNamespace( eventDimension );
featureList.add( nonKeyAttribute );

nonKeyAttribute = attributeClass.createAttribute();
nonKeyAttribute.setName( "EventContent" );
nonKeyAttribute.setType( stringType );
nonKeyAttribute.setNamespace( eventDimension );
featureList.add( nonKeyAttribute );
```

Figure 7.33   Code fragment: Creating the non-key dimension attributes.

Building the Session Dimension

The Session Dimension describes one or more levels of diagnosis for the user's session as a whole. This dimension provides a way to group Web sessions for analysis (Kimball and Merz, 2000). The Session Dimension is a single dimensional structure with the attributes shown in Table 7.6.

Table 7.6   Session Dimension

ATTRIBUTE	DATA TYPE
SessionID	Integer
SessionType	String
LocalContext	String
SessionContext	String
ActionSequence	String
SuccessStatus	String
CustomerStatus	String

The instance diagrams in Figures 7.34, 7.36, and 7.38 represent how this dimension appears when constructed as instances of classes from the CWM OLAP package. Note that the Session Dimension instance is owned by an instance of OLAP Schema. The code fragments in Figures 7.35, 7.37, and 7.39 are the actual Java code that constructs the Session Dimension.

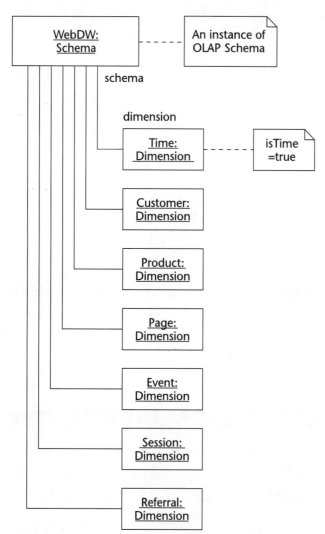

Figure 7.34   Instance diagram: Initial Session Dimension.

```
// Create the Session Dimension and add it to the Schema

Dimension sessionDimension = dimensionClass.createDimension();
sessionDimension.setName( "Session" );

dimCol.add( sessionDimension );
sessionDimension.setSchema( schema );
```

Figure 7.35   Code fragment: Creating the initial Session Dimension.

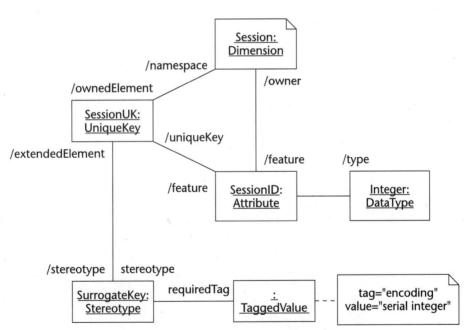

Figure 7.36   Instance diagram: Specifying the unique (surrogate) key.

```
// Create the primary key of the Session Dimension using the
// "surrogate key" pattern

keyAttribute = attributeClass.createAttribute();
keyAttribute.setName( "SessionID" );
keyAttribute.setType( integerType );
keyAttribute.setNamespace( sessionDimension );
featureList = sessionDimension.getFeature();
featureList.add( keyAttribute );

uniqueKey = uniqueKeyClass.createUniqueKey();
uniqueKey.setName( "SessionUK" );
keyFeatureList = uniqueKey.getFeature();
keyFeatureList.add( keyAttribute );
uniqueKey.setNamespace( sessionDimension );
ownedElements = sessionDimension.getOwnedElement();
ownedElements.add( uniqueKey );

// Note that the stereotype is reused...
extendedElements.add( uniqueKey );
```

Figure 7.37   Code fragment: Creating the unique (surrogate) key.

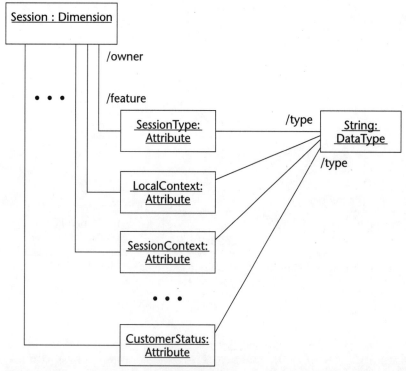

Figure 7.38   Instance diagram: Specifying the non-key dimension attributes.

```
// Create the non-key attributes and add them to the
// Session Dimension.
// Note that the data types created previously are re-used.

nonKeyAttribute = attributeClass.createAttribute();

nonKeyAttribute.setName( "SessionType" );
nonKeyAttribute.setType( stringType );
nonKeyAttribute.setNamespace( sessionDimension );
featureList.add( nonKeyAttribute );

nonKeyAttribute = attributeClass.createAttribute();
nonKeyAttribute.setName( "LocalContext" );
nonKeyAttribute.setType( stringType );
nonKeyAttribute.setNamespace( sessionDimension );
featureList.add( nonKeyAttribute );

nonKeyAttribute = attributeClass.createAttribute();
nonKeyAttribute.setName( "SessionContext" );
nonKeyAttribute.setType( stringType );
nonKeyAttribute.setNamespace( sessionDimension );
featureList.add( nonKeyAttribute );

// ...

nonKeyAttribute = attributeClass.createAttribute();
nonKeyAttribute.setName( "CustomerStatus" );
nonKeyAttribute.setType( stringType );
nonKeyAttribute.setNamespace( sessionDimension );
featureList.add( nonKeyAttribute );
```

Figure 7.39 Code fragment: Creating the non-key dimension attributes.

Building the Referral Dimension

The Referral Dimension describes how the customer may have arrived at the current page. The Web server log generally provides this information in the form of a Uniform Resource Locator (URL), referring to the previous page (Kimball and Merz, 2000). The Session Dimension is a single dimensional structure with the attributes shown in Table 7.7.

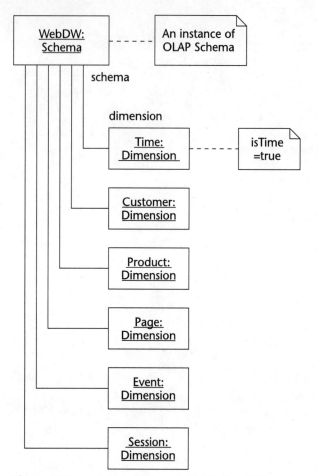

Figure 7.40 Instance diagram: Initial Referral Dimension.

Table 7.7   Referral Dimension

ATTRIBUTE	DATA TYPE
ReferralID	Integer
ReferralType	String
ReferralURL	URL
ReferralSite	URL
ReferralDomain	String
SearchType	String
Specification	String
Target	String

The instance diagrams in Figures 7.40, 7.42, and 7.44 represent how this dimension appears when constructed as instances of classes from the CWM OLAP package. Note that the Referral Dimension instance is owned by an instance of OLAP Schema. The code fragments shown in Figures 7.41, 7.43, and 7.45 are the actual Java code that constructs the Referral Dimension.

```java
// Create the Referral Dimension and add it to the Schema

Dimension referralDimension = dimensionClass.createDimension();
referralDimension.setName( "Referral" );

dimCol.add( referralDimension );
referralDimension.setSchema( schema );
```

Figure 7.41   Code fragment: Creating the initial Referral Dimension.

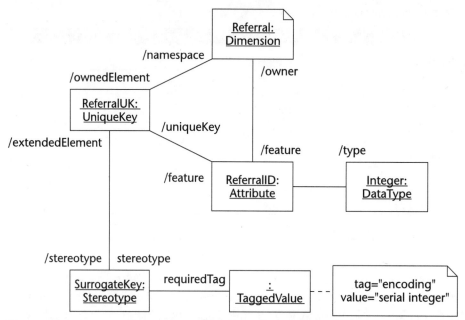

Figure 7.42   Instance diagram: Specifying the unique (surrogate) key.

```
// Create the primary key of the Referral Dimension using the
// "surrogate key" pattern

keyAttribute = attributeClass.createAttribute();
keyAttribute.setName( "ReferralID" );
keyAttribute.setType( integerType );
keyAttribute.setNamespace( referralDimension );
featureList = sessionDimension.getFeature();
featureList.add( keyAttribute );

uniqueKey = uniqueKeyClass.createUniqueKey();
uniqueKey.setName( "ReferralUK" );
keyFeatureList = uniqueKey.getFeature();
keyFeatureList.add( keyAttribute );
uniqueKey.setNamespace( referralDimension );
ownedElements = sessionDimension.getOwnedElement();
ownedElements.add( uniqueKey );

// Note that the stereotype is reused...
extendedElements.add( uniqueKey );
```

Figure 7.43   Code fragment: Creating the unique (surrogate) key.

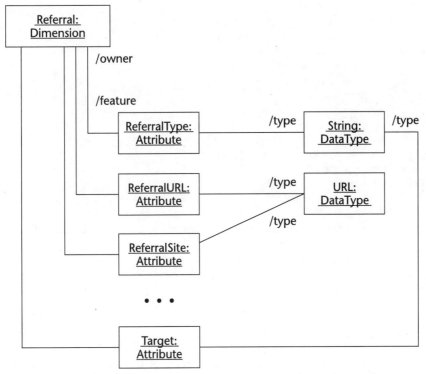

Figure 7.44   Instance diagram: Specifying the non-key dimension attributes.

```
// Create the non-key attributes and add them to the
// Referral Dimension.
// Note that the data types created previously are re-used,
// except for a "URL" data type, which needs to be created.

DataType urlType = dataTypeClass.createDataType();
urlType.setName( "URL" );

nonKeyAttribute = attributeClass.createAttribute();

nonKeyAttribute.setName( "ReferralType" );
nonKeyAttribute.setType( stringType );
nonKeyAttribute.setNamespace( referralDimension );
featureList.add( nonKeyAttribute );

nonKeyAttribute = attributeClass.createAttribute();
nonKeyAttribute.setName( "ReferralURL" );
nonKeyAttribute.setType( urlType );
nonKeyAttribute.setNamespace( referralDimension );
featureList.add( nonKeyAttribute );
```

Figure 7.45   Code fragment: Creating the non-key dimension attributes. *(continues)*

```
nonKeyAttribute = attributeClass.createAttribute();
nonKeyAttribute.setName( "ReferralSite" );
nonKeyAttribute.setType( urlType );
nonKeyAttribute.setNamespace( referralDimension );
featureList.add( nonKeyAttribute );

// ...

nonKeyAttribute = attributeClass.createAttribute();
nonKeyAttribute.setName( "CustomerStatus" );
nonKeyAttribute.setType( stringType );
nonKeyAttribute.setNamespace( referralDimension );
featureList.add( nonKeyAttribute );
```

Figure 7.45 Code fragment: Creating the non-key dimension attributes. *(continued)*

Building the Causal Dimension

The Referral Dimension describes the conditions of the marketplace at the moment of insertion of the measurement into the fact table (Kimball and Merz, 2000). The Causal Dimension is a single dimensional structure with the attributes shown in Table 7.8.

Table 7.8 Causal Dimension

ATTRIBUTE	DATA TYPE
CausalID	Integer
CausalType	String
PriceTreatment	String
AdType	String
WebType	String
RadioType	String
StoreDisplayType	String
MfgrPromoType	String
OtherCausalEvent	String

The instance diagrams in Figures 7.46, 7.48, and 7.50 represent how this dimension appears when constructed as instances of classes from the CWM OLAP package. Note that the Causal Dimension instance is owned by an instance of OLAP Schema. The code fragments shown in Figures 7.47, 7.49, and 7.51 are the actual Java code that constructs the Causal Dimension.

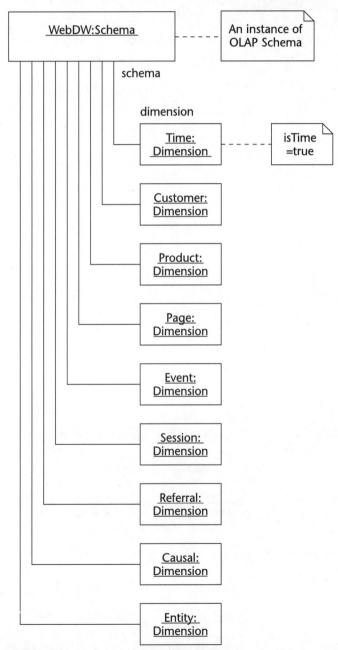

Figure 7.46   Instance diagram: Initial Causal Dimension.

```
// Create the Causal Dimension and add it to the Schema

Dimension causalDimension = dimensionClass.createDimension();
causalDimension.setName( "Causal" );

dimCol.add( causalDimension );
causalDimension.setSchema( schema );
```

Figure 7.47   Code fragment: Creating the initial Causal Dimension.

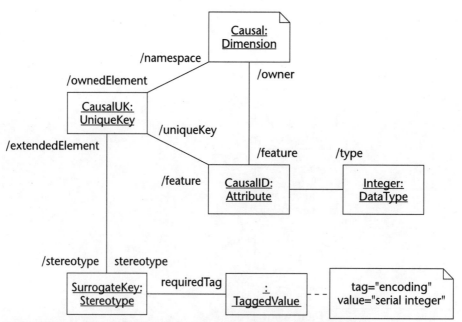

Figure 7.48   Instance diagram: Specifying the unique (surrogate) key.

```
// Create the primary key of the Causal Dimension using the
// "surrogate key" pattern

keyAttribute = attributeClass.createAttribute();
keyAttribute.setName( "CausalID" );
keyAttribute.setType( integerType );
keyAttribute.setNamespace( causalDimension );
featureList = causalDimension.getFeature();
featureList.add( keyAttribute );

uniqueKey = uniqueKeyClass.createUniqueKey();
uniqueKey.setName( "CausalUK" );
keyFeatureList = uniqueKey.getFeature();
keyFeatureList.add( keyAttribute );
uniqueKey.setNamespace( causalDimension );
ownedElements = causalDimension.getOwnedElement();
ownedElements.add( uniqueKey );

// Note that the stereotype is reused...
extendedElements.add( uniqueKey );
```

Figure 7.49 Code fragment: Creating the unique (surrogate) key.

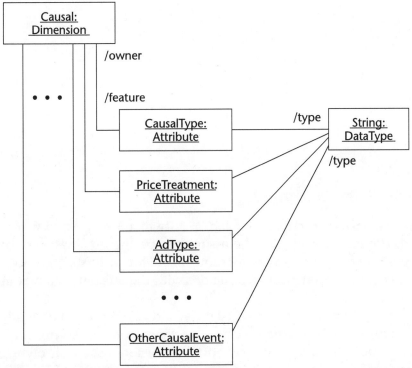

Figure 7.50 Instance diagram: Specifying the non-key dimension attributes.

```
// Create the non-key attributes and add them to the
// Causal Dimension.
// Note that the data types created previously are re-used.

nonKeyAttribute = attributeClass.createAttribute();

nonKeyAttribute.setName( "CausalType" );
nonKeyAttribute.setType( stringType );
nonKeyAttribute.setNamespace( causalDimension );
featureList.add( nonKeyAttribute );

nonKeyAttribute = attributeClass.createAttribute();
nonKeyAttribute.setName( "PriceTreatment" );
nonKeyAttribute.setType( stringType );
nonKeyAttribute.setNamespace( causalDimension );
featureList.add( nonKeyAttribute );

nonKeyAttribute = attributeClass.createAttribute();
nonKeyAttribute.setName( "AdType" );
nonKeyAttribute.setType( stringType );
nonKeyAttribute.setNamespace( causalDimension );
featureList.add( nonKeyAttribute );

// ...

nonKeyAttribute = attributeClass.createAttribute();
nonKeyAttribute.setName( "OtherCausalEvent" );
nonKeyAttribute.setType( stringType );
nonKeyAttribute.setNamespace( causalDimension );
featureList.add( nonKeyAttribute );
```

Figure 7.51   Code fragment: Creating the non-key dimension attributes.

Building the Entity Dimension

The Entity Dimension describes a business entity that is associated with a fact record. A business entity can be a supplier, partner, referrer, service provider, customer, or something else (Kimball and Merz, 2000). The Entity Dimension is a single dimensional structure with the attributes shown in Table 7.9.

The instance diagrams in Figures 7.52, 7.54, and 7.56 represent how this dimension appears when constructed as instances of classes from the CWM OLAP package. Note that the Entity Dimension instance is owned by an instance of OLAP Schema. The code fragments in Figures 7.53, 7.55, and 7.57 are the actual Java code that constructs the Entity Dimension.

Table 7.9 Entity Dimension

ATTRIBUTE	DATA TYPE
EntityID	Integer
EntityType	String
EntityName	String
IndustryCategory	String

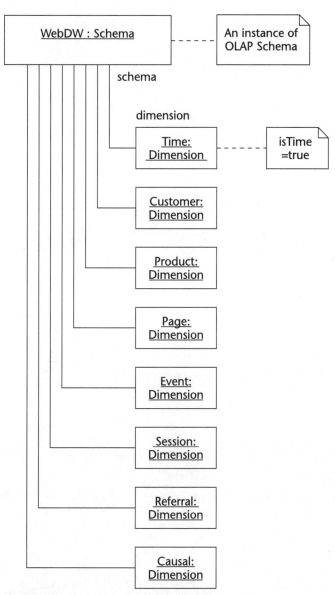

Figure 7.52 Instance diagram: Initial Entity Dimension.

```
// Create the Entity Dimension and add it to the Schema

Dimension entityDimension = dimensionClass.createDimension();
entityDimension.setName( "Entity" );

dimCol.add( entityDimension );
entityDimension.setSchema( schema );
```

Figure 7.53   Code fragment: Creating the initial Entity Dimension.

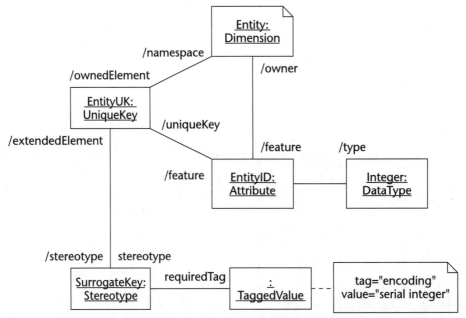

Figure 7.54   Instance diagram: Specifying the unique (surrogate) key.

```
// Create the primary key of the Entity Dimension using the
// "surrogate key" pattern

keyAttribute = attributeClass.createAttribute();
keyAttribute.setName( "EntityID" );
keyAttribute.setType( integerType );
keyAttribute.setNamespace( entityDimension );
featureList = entityDimension.getFeature();
featureList.add( keyAttribute );
```

Figure 7.55   Code fragment: Creating the unique (surrogate) key.

```
uniqueKey = uniqueKeyClass.createUniqueKey();
uniqueKey.setName( "EntityUK" );
keyFeatureList = uniqueKey.getFeature();
keyFeatureList.add( keyAttribute );
uniqueKey.setNamespace( entityDimension );
ownedElements = entityDimension.getOwnedElement();
ownedElements.add( uniqueKey );

// Note that the stereotype is reused...
extendedElements.add( uniqueKey );
```

Figure 7.55   Code fragment: Creating the unique (surrogate) key. *(continued)*

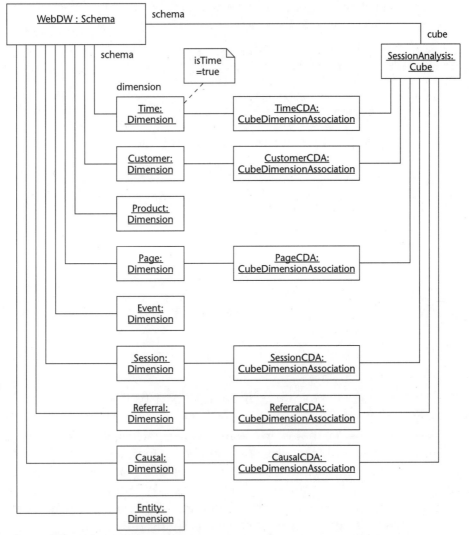

Figure 7.56   Instance diagram: Specifying the non-key dimension attributes.

```
// Create the non-key attributes and add them to the
// Entity Dimension.
// Note that the data types created previously are re-used.

nonKeyAttribute = attributeClass.createAttribute();

nonKeyAttribute.setName( "EntityType" );
nonKeyAttribute.setType( stringType );
nonKeyAttribute.setNamespace( entityDimension );
featureList.add( nonKeyAttribute );

nonKeyAttribute = attributeClass.createAttribute();
nonKeyAttribute.setName( "EntityName" );
nonKeyAttribute.setType( stringType );
nonKeyAttribute.setNamespace( entityDimension );
featureList.add( nonKeyAttribute );

nonKeyAttribute = attributeClass.createAttribute();
nonKeyAttribute.setName( "IndustryCategory" );
nonKeyAttribute.setType( stringType );
nonKeyAttribute.setNamespace( entityDimension );
featureList.add( nonKeyAttribute );
```

Figure 7.57   Code fragment: Creating the non-key dimension attributes.

Finally, we satisfy the requirements of the Local Type System and Local Stereotype patterns by placing the "Surrogate Key" Stereotype instance in the "WebDW" Schema, that is, in the innermost, enclosing Package of the Dimensions whose primary keys are qualified by that Stereotype. We also create a Type System to contain the Data Types defined thus far, and add this Type System to the Namespace of the "WebDW" Schema as well. The resulting object structure is illustrated in Figure 7.58, and the JMI source code used to build this structure is shown in Figure 7.59.

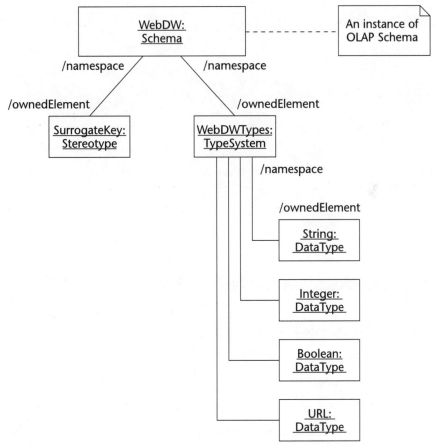

Figure 7.58   Instance diagram: Placement of Stereotype and Type System objects.

```
surrogateKeyStereotype.setNamespace( schema );
Collection schemaOwnedElements = schema.getOwnedElement();
schemaOwnedElements.add( surrogateKeyStereotype );


TypeMappingPackage typeMappingPkg = cwmFactory.getTypeMapping();
TypeSystemClass typeSystemClass = typeMappingPkg.getTypeSystem();
TypeSystem typeSystem = typeSystemClass.createTypeSystem();
typeSystem.setName( "WebDWTypes" );
Collection typeCol = typeSystem.getOwnedElement();
typeCol.add( stringType );
typeCol.add( integerType );
```

Figure 7.59   Code Fragment: Adding Stereotype and Type System objects to the OLAP Schema. *(continues)*

```
typeCol.add( booleanType );
typeCol.add( urlType );
stringType.setNamespace( typeSystem );
integerType.setNamespace( typeSystem );
booleanType.setNamespace( typeSystem );
urlType.setNamespace( typeSystem );

typeSystem.setNamespace( schema );
schemaOwnedElements.add( typeSystem );
```

Figure 7.59 Code Fragment: Adding Stereotype and Type System objects to the OLAP Schema. *(continued)*

The Logical Clickstream Analysis Cubes

Our Schema must also contain the following Cubes for analysis of the clickstream data represented by the Dimensions:

- Session Analysis Cube
- Page Analysis Cube
- Aggregation Cube

These Cubes are modeled using CWM and then constructed using the CWM Java Meta Data Interfaces (JMIs) in each of the subsequent subsections. We initially construct the three Cubes and add them to the "WebDW" Schema. Figure 7.60 shows the object diagram representing the expanded OLAP Schema.

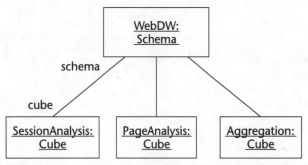

Figure 7.60 Instance diagram: Analysis Cubes added to Schema instance.

```
// Create the analysis cubes

CubeClass cubeClass = olapPkg.getCube();

Cube sessionAnalysisCube = CubeClass.createCube();
sessionAnalysisCube.setName( "SessionAnalysis" );

Cube pageAnalysisCube = CubeClass.createCube();
pageAnalysisCube.setName( "PageAnalysis" );

Cube aggregationCube = CubeClass.createCube();
aggregationCube.setName( "Aggregation" );

Collection cubeCol = schema.getCube();
cubeCol.add( sessionAnalysisCube );
sessionAnalysisCube.setSchema( schema );

cubeCol.add( pageAnalysisCube );
pageAnalysisCube.setSchema( schema );

cubeCol.add( aggregationCube );
aggregationCube.setSchema( schema );
```

Figure 7.61   Code Fragment: Creating the initial Analysis Cubes.

Next, in each of the following three subsections, we provide detailed definitions of each of the three Analysis Cubes.

Session Analysis Cube

The Session Analysis Cube tracks the measures listed in Table 7.10.

Table 7.10   Session Analysis Measures

ATTRIBUTE	DATA TYPE
SessionSeconds	Integer
PagesVisited	Integer
OrdersPlaced	Integer
UnitsOrdered	Integer
OrderDollars	Double

Figure 7.62 shows a CWM object model representing the Session Analysis Cube and its measures. Note that the Integer DataType may be reused from the Schema, but we will need to create a new Data Type of type "Double" for the OrderDollars Measure, and then add this Data Type to our local Type System instance.

Figure 7.63 shows the sequence of JMI calls used to construct the object structure of Figure 7.62.

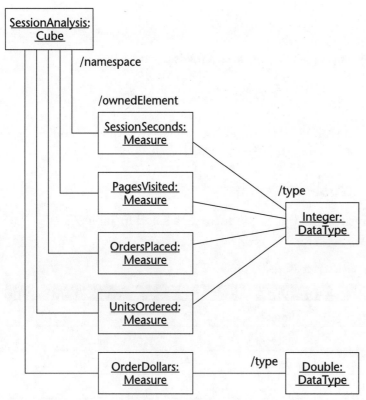

Figure 7.62   Instance Diagram: Session Analysis Cube.

```
MeasureClass measureClass = olapPkg.getMeasure();
Measure measure = measureClass.createMeasure();
measure.setName( "SessionSeconds" );
measure.setType( integerType );
List sessionFeatureList = sessionAnalysisCube.getFeature();
sessionFeatureList.add( measure );
measure.setOwner( sessionAnalysisCube );

measure = measureClass.createMeasure();
measure.setName( "PagesVisited" );
measure.setType( integerType );
sessionFeatureList.add( measure );
measure.setOwner( sessionAnalysisCube );

measure = measureClass.createMeasure();
measure.setName( "OrdersPlaced" );
measure.setType( integerType );
sessionFeatureList.add( measure );
measure.setOwner( sessionAnalysisCube );

measure = measureClass.createMeasure();
measure.setName( "UnitsOrdered" );
measure.setType( integerType );
sessionFeatureList.add( measure );
measure.setOwner( sessionAnalysisCube );

measure = measureClass.createMeasure();
measure.setName( "OrderDollars" );
measure.setType( doubleType );
sessionFeatureList.add( measure );
measure.setOwner( sessionAnalysisCube );
```

Figure 7.63   Code fragment: Construction of Session Analysis Cube.

The Session Analysis Cube is joined to the following dimensions:

- Time
- Customer
- Session
- Causal
- Page
- Referral

In CWM, this is modeled through the use of CubeDimensionAssociation objects, which make it possible for Cubes within a given Schema to share the Dimensions of that Schema. Figure 7.64 depicts how the Session Analysis Cube uses a specific subset of the total dimensionality defined by the "WebDW" OLAP Schema.

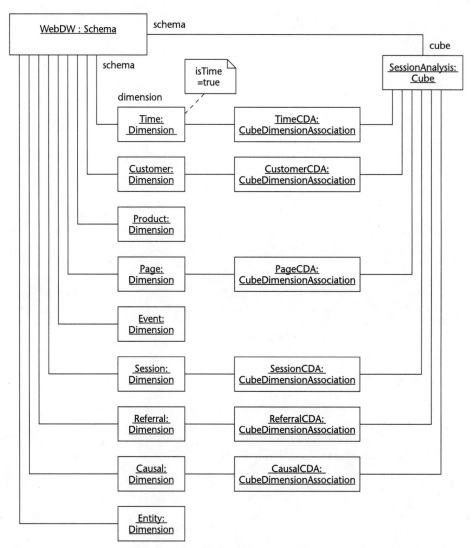

Figure 7.64 Instance diagram: Shared dimension usage by the Session Analysis Cube.

Table 7.11   Page Analysis Measures

ATTRIBUTE	DATA TYPE
PageSeconds	Integer
UnitsOrdered	Integer
OrderDollars	Double

Page Analysis Cube

The Page Analysis Cube is a clickstream fact table at the granularity of the individual page event. It must track the measures in Table 7.11.

Figure 7.65 shows a CWM object model representing the Page Analysis Cube and its measures. Note that both the Integer and Double DataTypes may be reused at this point.

Figure 7.66 shows the sequence of JMI calls used to construct the object structure of Figure 7.65.

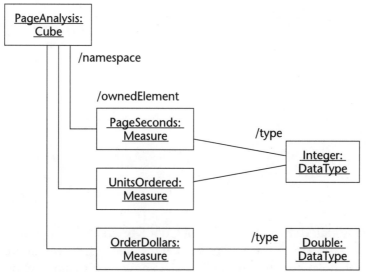

Figure 7.65   Instance Diagram: Page Analysis Cube.

```
measureClass = olapPkg.getMeasure();
measure = measureClass.createMeasure();
measure.setName( "PageSeconds" );
measure.setType( integerType );
List sessionFeatureList = sessionAnalysisCube.getFeature();
sessionFeatureList.add( measure );
measure.setOwner( pageAnalysisCube );

measure = measureClass.createMeasure();
measure.setName( "UnitsOrdered" );
measure.setType( integerType );
sessionFeatureList.add( measure );
measure.setOwner( pageAnalysisCube );

measure = measureClass.createMeasure();
measure.setName( "OrderDollars" );
measure.setType( doubleType );
sessionFeatureList.add( measure );
measure.setOwner( pageAnalysisCube );
```

Figure 7.66   Code fragment: Construction of Page Analysis Cube.

The Page Analysis Cube is joined to the following dimensions:

- Time
- Customer
- Event
- Session
- Causal
- Page
- Referral
- Product

In CWM, this is modeled through the use of CubeDimensionAssociation objects, which make it possible for Cubes within a given Schema to share the Dimensions of that Schema. Figure 6.67 depicts how the Session Analysis Cube uses a specific subset of the total dimensionality defined by the "WebDW" OLAP Schema.

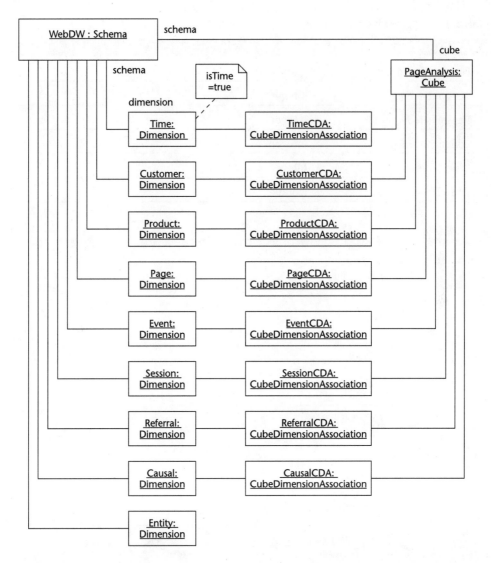

Figure 7.67 Instance diagram: Shared dimension usage by the Page Analysis Cube.

Aggregation Cube

The Aggregation Cube is a clickstream fact table at the granularity of demographic type by month by entry page by session outcome. It must track the measures in Table 7.12.

Table 7.12 Aggregation Measures

ATTRIBUTE	DATA TYPE
NumberSessions	Integer
SessionSeconds	Integer
PagesVisited	Integer
OrdersPlaced	Integer
UnitsOrdered	Integer
OrderDollars	Double

Figure 7.68 shows a CWM object model representing the Aggregation Cube and its measures.

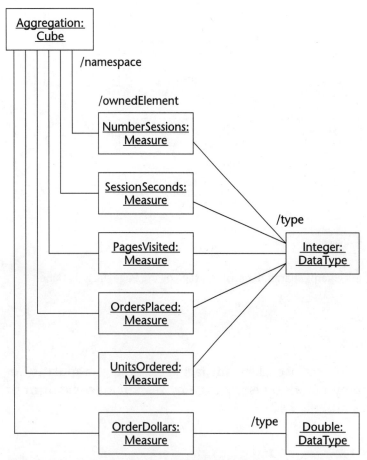

Figure 7.68 Instance Diagram: Aggregation Cube.

Figure 7.69 shows the sequence of JMI calls used to construct the object structure of Figure 7.68.

```
measureClass = olapPkg.getMeasure();
measure = measureClass.createMeasure();
measure.setName( "NumberSessions" );
measure.setType( integerType );
List sessionFeatureList = sessionAnalysisCube.getFeature();
sessionFeatureList.add( measure );
measure.setOwner( aggregationCube );

measure = measureClass.createMeasure();
measure.setName( "SessionSeconds" );
measure.setType( integerType );
sessionFeatureList.add( measure );
measure.setOwner( aggregationCube );

measure = measureClass.createMeasure();
measure.setName( "PagesVisited" );
measure.setType( integerType );
sessionFeatureList.add( measure );
measure.setOwner( aggregationCube );

measure = measureClass.createMeasure();
measure.setName( "OrdersPlaced" );
measure.setType( integerType );
sessionFeatureList.add( measure );
measure.setOwner( aggregationCube );

measure = measureClass.createMeasure();
measure.setName( "UnitsOrdered" );
measure.setType( integerType );
sessionFeatureList.add( measure );
measure.setOwner( aggregationCube );

measure = measureClass.createMeasure();
measure.setName( "OrderDollars" );
measure.setType( doubleType );
sessionFeatureList.add( measure );
measure.setOwner( pageAnalysisCube );
```

Figure 7.69   Code fragment: Construction of Aggregation Cube.

The Aggregation Cube joins the following dimensions:

- Time
- Page
- Demographics
- Session

Figure 6.70 depicts how the Aggregation Cube uses a specific subset of the total dimensionality defined by the "WebDW" OLAP Schema.

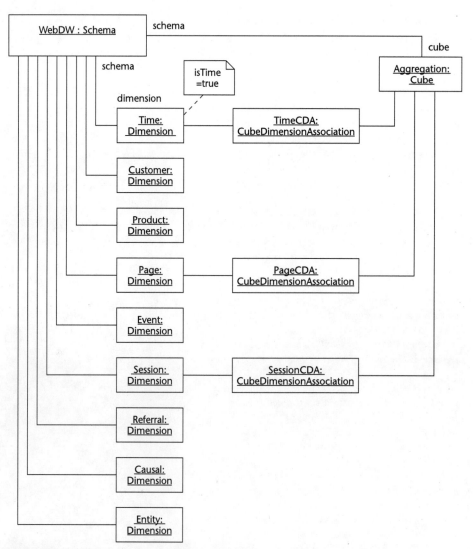

Figure 7.70   Instance diagram: Shared dimension usage by the Aggregation Cube.

New Meta Data Patterns Developed and Cataloged

This subsection now introduces four new CWM meta data interchange patterns. These patterns will be used extensively in the construction of the complete Web-enabled data warehouse and Web Services model. They consist of:

- Local Stereotype
- Local Type System
- Surrogate Key
- Star-Join

These patterns are formally specified in each of the following subsections, in the form of standard Pattern Catalog entries (see Chapter 4 and the Pattern Catalog on the companion Web site). These patterns were developed by applying the meta data interchange pattern development methodology presented in Chapter 4 to the modeling objectives of this chapter.

Local Stereotype, Version 1.0

URL

```
http://www.cwmforum.org/
```

Contributor

CWM Team

Structural Classification

Micro pattern

Usage Category

Structural, Typing

Intent

This pattern provides a simple, consistent way of organizing Stereotypes that have been defined locally within a given model.

Also Known As

N/A

Motivation

In situations where a Stereotype is defined within a model for the purpose of extending one or more model elements, the Stereotype is made an ownedElement of the most immediate Package containing all of the extended model elements. We refer to such Stereotypes as being *local* because they are defined locally within the model itself, and packaged together with the elements they extend. This is in contrast to Stereotypes that are defined externally to a given model (for example, in another repository extent), but are imported or referenced by that model for the purpose of extending model elements.

Applicability

This micro pattern is generally used in the construction of Domain patterns that specify the extension of certain model elements based on Stereotypes.

Projection

The Local Stereotype pattern is based on a sub-graph of the CWM meta-model consisting of the meta classes:

- org.omg.cwm.objectmodel.core.Package
- org.omg.cwm.objectmodel.core.ModelElement
- org.omg.cwm.objectmodel.core.Stereotypeand the associations
- org.omg.cwm.objectmodel.core.ElementOwnership
- org.omg.cwm.objectmodel.core.StereotypedElement

This sub-graph is illustrated in Figure 7.71.

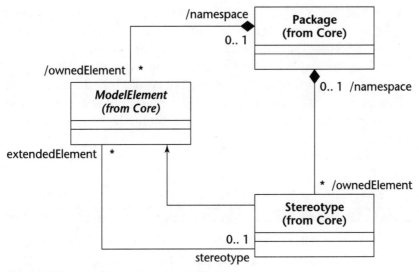

Figure 7.71   Local Stereotype projection.

Restriction

A *locally defined* Stereotype that extends one or more ModelElements is owned by the nearest or most immediate Package instance of the recursive Package containment hierarchy containing the ModelElements.

Note that this implies that local stereotypes are not imported, and not owned by some Package residing outside the recursive containment hierarchy. This also implies that the Stereotype could not possibly be defined externally to the ModelElement's containment hierarchy (that is, it could not be anything other than a locally defined Stereotype).

Usage

When processing an imported XML Metadata Interchange (XMI) model, the importing process checks each Package instance in the model for its collection of local Stereotypes. If such Stereotypes have been defined, each model element within the Package is tested for extension by one of the local Stereotypes. (Note that each must also be tested for extension by external Stereotypes, if the importing process is expecting this.) When exporting meta data via an XMI file, the exporting process simply stores all locally defined Stereotype instances in their most-immediate Package.

In essence, this pattern simply establishes a convenient and well-known place to park one's Stereotypes. It does not otherwise affect or modify their meaning, nor how Stereotyped elements are to be interpreted.

This pattern does not apply to Stereotypes defined in external Packages, that is, Packages that are not part of the recursive containment hierarchy of the ModelElements, or Packages whose owned Stereotypes are imported into some Package of the recursive containment hierarchy of the extended ModelElements.

Parameters

M2 PARAMETER	M1 VALUE	COMMENTS
Stereotype.ModelElement::name	User-defined	Value is arbitrary; up to the user.

Commentary

None

Consequences

N/A

Known Uses

N/A

Related Patterns

N/A

Sample Solution

Figure 7.72 illustrates an occurrence of the Local Stereotype pattern. In this case, two Stereotypes that encode class instances with the concept of color ("red" or "blue") are defined. Since "RedClasses" labels both "ABC" and "PQR," it is stored in the most-immediate Package instance containing both "ABC" and "PQR," while "BlueClasses" is stored in the Package instance containing the single object that this Stereotype applies to (that is, "XYZ").

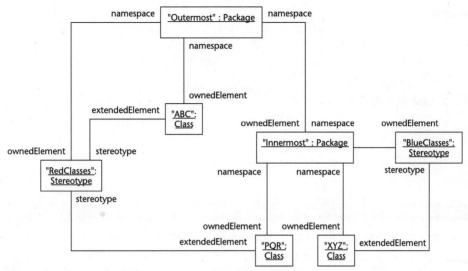

Figure 7.72   Instance diagram: Local Stereotype example.

Local Type System, Version 1.0

URL

    http://www.cwmforum.org/

Contributor

CWM Team

Structural Classification

Micro pattern

Usage Category

Structural, Typing

Intent

This pattern provides a simple, consistent way of organizing Data Types that have been defined locally within a given model.

Also Known As

N/A

Motivation

In situations where a number of Data Types are defined within a model for the purpose of typing the StructuralFeatures of Classifiers, the Data Type instances can be organized more effectively if they are pulled together into a single named TypeSystem instance. For convenience and uniformity of structure, this TypeSystem should then be placed within the most immediate Package whose Classifier instances utilize the TypeSystem's DataType instances.

Note that, in general, the explicit modeling of TypeSystems makes the use of modeled DataTypes less ambiguous. For instance, if a given Type-System instance models a well-known real-world type system, such as that of CORBA Interface Definition Language (IDL) or the Java programming language, there is a definition of those types that can readily be referred to. TypeSystem modeling also facilitates meta data reuse. For example, a single model of a particular language's data types can be developed, published, and reused by all models within a particular interchange environment. (In this case, though, the Local Type System pattern doesn't always apply, since TypeSystems are shared, but may not be defined locally. But to the extent that a TypeSystem might be defined within an interchanged model, an attempt should be made to follow this pattern.)

Applicability

This micro pattern is generally used in the construction of any Domain pattern that requires local modeling of data types.

Projection

The Local Type System pattern is based on a sub-graph of the CWM meta-model consisting of the meta classes:

- org.omg.cwm.objectmodel.core.Package
- org.omg.cwm.objectmodel.core.Classifier

- org.omg.cwm.objectmodel.core.StructuralFeature

- org.omg.cwm.objectmodel.core.DataType

- org.omg.cwm.foundation.typemapping.TypeSystemand the associations

- org.omg.cwm.objectmodel.core.ElementOwnership

- org.omg.cwm.objectmodel.core.ClassifierFeature

- org.omg.cwm.objectmodel.core.StructuralFeatureType

This sub-graph is illustrated in Figure 7.73.

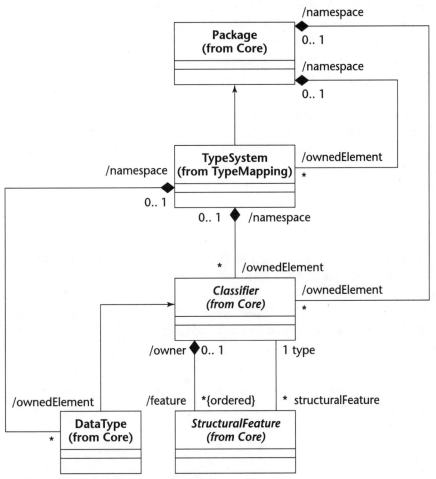

Figure 7.73   Local Type System projection.

Restriction

A *locally defined* TypeSystem instance that provides DataType instances to StructuralFeatures of Classifier instances defined within a given model is owned by the *nearest* or *most-immediate* Package instance in the recursive Package containment hierarchy of those Classifier instances.

Note that this implies that the TypeSystem instance is not imported, and not owned by some Package residing outside the recursive containment hierarchy of the Classifier instances that use it. It also implies that the Type-System could not possibly be defined externally to the Classifier instances' containment hierarchy (that is, it could not be anything other than a locally defined TypeSystem).

Usage

When processing an imported XMI model, the importing process checks each Package instance in the model for the presence of any locally defined TypeSystems. If such TypeSystem instances have been defined, each StructuralFeature of each Classifier instance within the Package is tested for classification/typing by one of the local TypeSystem's DataType instances. (Note that each StructuralFeature must also be tested for classification/typing by external DataTypes, if the import process expects this.) When writing an XMI export file, the exporting process simply stores all locally defined TypeSystem instances in the most-immediate Package of the recursive Package containment hierarchy.

In essence, this pattern simply establishes a convenient and well-known place to park one's DataTypes. It does not otherwise affect or modify their meaning, nor how DataTypes and typed StructuralFeatures are to be interpreted.

This pattern does not apply to DataTypes and TypeSystems defined in external Packages, that is, Packages that are not part of the recursive containment hierarchy of some set of Classifier instances. Nor does it apply to Packages whose owned DataTypes or TypeSystems are imported into some Package of the recursive containment hierarchy of the Classifier instances.

Parameters

M2 PARAMETER	M1 VALUE	COMMENTS
Package.ModelElement::name	User-defined.	Value is arbitrary; up to the user.

Commentary

None

Consequences

N/A

Known Uses

N/A

Related Patterns

N/A

Sample Solution

Figure 7.74 illustrates an occurrence of the Local Type System pattern. In this example, a partial model of the Java 2 type system is defined, consisting of the types java.lang.Object, int, and java.util.String. The Attributes of a number of CWM Classes use the Java types as their data types. These Classes are instantiated within two Package instances comprising the model. The "Java2" TypeSystem instance is contained by the nearest Package in the containment hierarchy of the model.

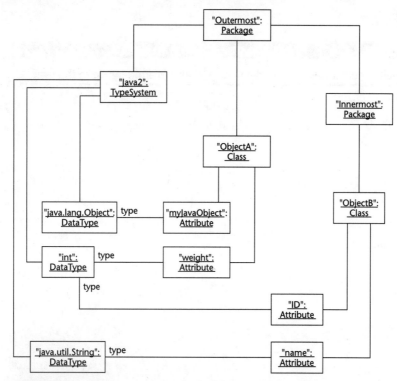

Figure 7.74   Instance Diagram: Local Type System example.

Surrogate Key, Version 1.0

URL

```
http://www.cwmforum.org/
```

Contributor

CWM Team

Structural Classification

Micro pattern

Usage Category

Structural

Intent

Provides a means for defining unique keys whose values are anonymous.

Also Known As

- Serial key
- Anonymous key

Motivation

Values of surrogate keys contain no semantic content; they are often referred to as being *opaque* to the applications using them, and are used specifically as a means of joining structures together. They have no meaning otherwise. How their values are generated is up to the underlying implementation or system, but has no meaning to end users of the joined structures. Often, surrogate values consist of unique, but otherwise anonymous, integer values.

Applicability

Surrogate keys are often used in data warehouses to construct the dimensional tables implementing the data analysis store. Whenever a dimensional lookup table needs to be modified, new surrogate key values are generated according to some established algorithm that guarantees unique values. New member records can easily be added to dimensional tables, and existing records may be updated or versioned in a straightforward manner because of the anonymous identities of the surrogate key values. Surrogate keys facilitate *graceful upgrades* to the dimensional structure of the data warehouse.

Projection

The Surrogate Key pattern is based on a sub-graph of the CWM metamodel consisting of the meta classes:

- org.omg.cwm.objectmodel.core.Class
- org.omg.cwm.objectmodel.core.Attribute
- org.omg.cwm.objectmodel.core.DataType
- org.omg.cwm.objectmodel.core.Stereotype
- org.omg.cwm.foundation.keysindexes.UniqueKey

and the associations

- org.omg.cwm.objectmodel.core.ElementOwnership
- org.omg.cwm.objectmodel.core.ClassifierFeature
- org.omg.cwm.objectmodel.core.StructuralFeatureType
- org.omg.cwm.objectmodel.core.StereotypedElement
- org.omg.cwm.objectmodel.core.StereotypeTaggedValues
- org.omg.cwm.foundation.keysindexes.UniqueFeature

This sub-graph is illustrated in Figure 7.75.

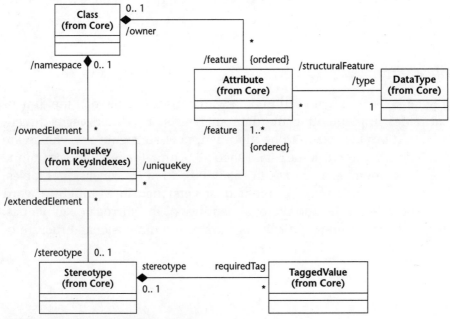

Figure 7.75 Surrogate Key Projection.

Restriction

There are two restrictions on instances of the projection:

- The Stereotype instance attached to the instance of UniqueKey must be named "surrogateKey."

- Optionally, a single TaggedValue instance may be attached to the Stereotype, identifying the encoding algorithm used to generate the key values. The tag attribute must be set to "encoding." The value attribute is supplied by the end user and not specified by the pattern.

These restrictions are formally expressed by the following Object Constraint Language (OCL) constraints:

```
context Stereotype inv: self.ModelElement::name = "surrogateKey"
context TaggedValue inv: self.tag = "encoding"
```

Usage

This pattern is typically used as a constructional or structural pattern in the realization of higher-level domain patterns that can benefit from the use of surrogate keys in structuring unique key relationships between objects.

Parameters

M2 PARAMETER	M1 VALUE	COMMENTS
Stereotype.ModelElement::name	"SurrogateKey"	Value is fixed.
TaggedValue.tag	"encoding"	Value is fixed.
TaggedValue.value	User-defined	Value is a user-supplied name of the surrogate key encoding or generation algorithm.

Commentary

None

Consequences

N/A

Known Uses

N/A

Related Patterns

Since Surrogate Key makes use of a Stereotype and (optional) Tagged-Value, this pattern is often combined with the Local Stereotype pattern, as a means of cleanly establishing where the Stereotype is stored in an interchange stream.

Sample Solution

Figure 7.76 illustrates an occurrence of the Surrogate Key pattern. In this example, a single surrogate key is defined as the Primary key of a simple Relational table. The corresponding XMI fragment shows how the table definition would appear in an XMI interchange stream.

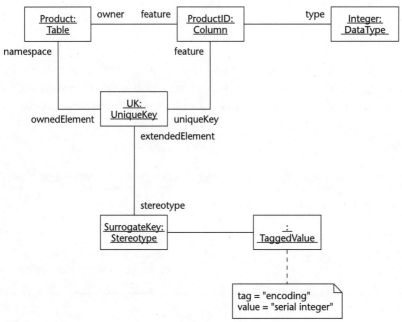

Figure 7.76 Instance diagram: Surrogate key example.

Star-Join, Version 1.0

URL

```
http://www.cwmforum.org/
```

Contributor

CWM Team

Structural Classification

Domain pattern

Usage Category

Interpretation

Intent

Provides a domain pattern for constructing and identifying instances of relational star-schemas.

Also Known As

- Star-schema
- Relational star-schema
- Dimensional star-schema

Motivation

The basic star-join design is used extensively in data warehousing as a means of organizing analysis data into a dimensional format. Star-joins are generally used to define relational schemas in such a manner that the dimensional nature of the stored data is readily apparent from the structure of the relational schema itself.

Applicability

This pattern is used whenever there is a need to interchange a relational model that is organized as a star-join or star-schema structure.

Projection

The Star-Join pattern is based on a sub-graph of the CWM metamodel consisting of the meta classes:

- org.omg.cwm.objectmodel.core.Stereotype
- org.omg.cwm.resource.relational.Table
- org.omg.cwm.resource.relational.Column
- org.omg.cwm.foundation.keysindexes.UniqueKey
- org.omg.cwm.foundation.keysindexes.KeyRelationship

and the associations

- org.omg.cwm.objectmodel.core.ElementOwnership
- org.omg.cwm.objectmodel.core.ClassifierFeature
- org.omg.cwm.objectmodel.core.StereotypedElement
- org.omg.cwm.foundation.keysindexes.UniqueFeature
- org.omg.cwm.foundation.keysindexes.KeyRelationshipFeatures
- org.omg.cwm.foundation.keysindexes.UniqueKeyRelationship

This sub-graph is illustrated in Figure 7.77.

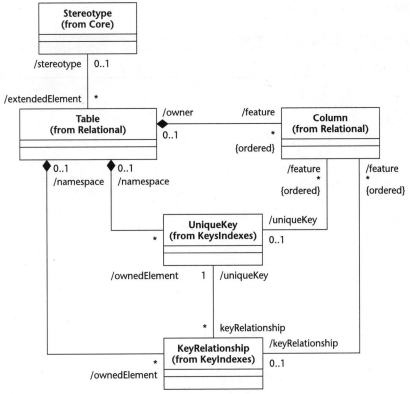

Figure 7.77   Star-Join projection.

Restriction

Restrictions on instances of the projection are as follows:

- There must be at least one relational Table (the *join table*) whose unique key values represent compositions of the unique key values of two or more other relational Tables. This relationship is made explicit through instances of the UniqueKey and KeyRelationship classes.

- Optionally, an instance of Stereotype may be attached to any Relational table serving as the join table of the star-schema, making its role explicit. This Stereotype's name must be set to the value "StarJoin."

Usage

N/A

Parameters

M2 PARAMETER	M1 VALUE	COMMENTS
Stereotype.ModelElement::name	"StarJoin"	Value is fixed.

Commentary

None

Consequences

N/A

Known Uses

N/A

Related Patterns

Surrogate Key is often used as a constructional and/or structural pattern in the realizations of the Star-Join domain pattern.

Sample Solution

Figure 7.78 illustrates an occurrence of the Star-Join pattern. In this example, a single Table instance called "Sales" serves as the Join table relating two other Tables called "Product" and "Time," respectively. This forms a very simple star schema that supports data warehouse analyses of tracking how sales figures relate to geographic regions, over time. The corresponding XMI fragment shows how the star-schema instance would appear in an XMI interchange stream.

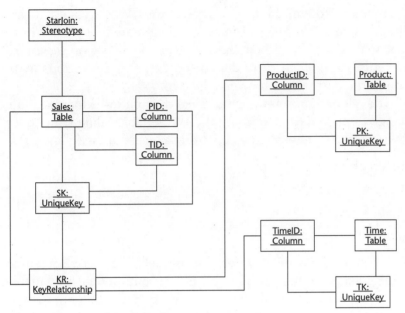

Figure 7.78   Instance diagram: Star-Join example.

Summary

We have described in this chapter the additional dimensional and operational concepts that allow the data warehouse to participate in a distributed, highly collaborative Web-based computing environment. We demonstrated how CWM can be used to model situations in which a data warehouse is used to back-end a Web server, providing new dimensional structures and other meta data constructs supporting clickstream analysis.

We also demonstrated which core packages of the CWM architecture are most applicable in modeling a Web-enabled data-warehousing environment. In particular, we illustrated the construction of *logical models* of analysis concepts, *physical models* of data resources, and the various mappings and data transformations between the two.

Finally, we developed four new, useful meta data patterns that facilitate the interchange of meta data describing the Web-enabled data warehouse and ISC environments. These standard patterns consist of the following:

- Local Stereotype
- Local Type System
- Surrogate Key
- Star-Join

The CWM Web-enabled data warehouse model is an active research topic. The current state of this model at any given point in time is available from the companion Web site. Also included are patterns that are discovered and codified as the model is developed. Readers should regularly visit the companion Web site to download the latest versions of the Web-enabled data warehouse model and Patterns Catalog.

CWM Metastore

The Common Warehouse Metamodel (CWM) is an interchange technology at heart. Its purpose is to promote the movement of meta data between diverse software tools from multiple vendors. Meta data interchange is the foundation for data movement between disparate tools and heterogeneous information systems, and data movement is the key to successful construction and management of modern data warehousing environments. The Information Supply Chain (ISC) metaphor discussed in earlier chapters captures and explores the central role of data and meta data movement in data warehousing environments.

CWM eases the effort involved in meta data interchange by providing a common format that data warehousing tools can use. To accomplish meta data interchange with CWM, tools must be able to both import and export meta data in the common CWM format. By using a common format for interchange, each tool can interchange meta data with all other CWM-aware tools. Once meta data has been exchanged, the receiving tool can use it to orchestrate movement of the data described by the received meta data.

In today's Web-aware world, CWM-mediated meta data interchange is accomplished by creating an eXtensible Markup Language (XML) document corresponding to the CWM Document Type Definition (DTD) and making that file available to receiving meta data tools. However, XML syntax is not an essential part of CWM interchanges. Using XML to encode meta data in CWM is really just a low-cost way to promote interchange among tools from different vendors. The attraction of XML syntax is its ability to encode meta data in simple, displayable characters that are not impeded by firewalls. But even without an XML representation, CWM meta data interchange can still occur. The exchange of instances of classes and association links that is the essence of a CWM meta data interchange can occur over any suitable communication medium and in any mutually accepted format.[1] Once a CWM meta data interchange has been created, it can be sent to any number of tools without knowledge of the creating tool.

Meta data interchange services the needs of a broad class of meta data-aware data warehousing applications, but not all. Some application systems need extensive control over individual meta data components. These environments often treat meta data itself as a strategic business asset. They want to control access to meta data, record a history of its evolution, track usage of meta data, and use it to generate other information system components such as programming interfaces. Central control and archiving of meta data are the provinces of *meta data repositories*. Repositories are software systems that store, control access to, record usage of, and generate new components from the meta data they own. Repositories can mediate the interchange of CWM meta data, but the key difference is that meta data repositories treat meta data as if they own it.

Do you need a meta data repository to exchange meta data with CWM? Certainly not, but they can be very useful in some application situations. Meta data interchange can be accomplished with nothing more complicated than a CWM DTD-compliant XMI interchange file; but interchange alone doesn't support a lot of interesting application needs like persistence, concurrency control, access control, versioning, life-cycle management, and so forth. From the point of view of meta data interchange, repositories can be thought of as "parking lots" on the ISC. Meta data can be placed in a repository parking lot, left there indefinitely, and applied to a diversity of purposes. While there, meta data can benefit from the more sophisticated capabilities of, but are also subject to the limitations imposed by, repositories. The chief limitations of repositories for most information processing environments are their substantial complexity and resource demands, aggravated by increased staff training costs. In other words, a repository can be an expensive place to park your meta data. What we'd really like for CWM is a meta data parking lot that doesn't cost so much.

---

[1] The notion that information exchange can occur regardless of the precise format in which the exchange is expressed is similar to the XML Information Set (W3C, 2001).

To meet the need for a less expensive meta data parking lot, this chapter describes a database that can be used to store CWM-encoded meta data. This database, though built on a commonly available relational database management system, preserves the object-oriented underpinnings of CWM that are essential to successful meta data interchange within the foundational framework of Unified Modeling Language (UML) and Meta Object Facility (MOF). This meta data store, which we call the CWM *Metastore*, offers sufficient data management functionality that it provides persistent storage and allows concurrent, transacted access to the complex meta data found in data warehousing environments, while still being substantially less costly to operate than a full-fledged repository. The Metastore, however, does not provide more advanced repository features such as versioning, life-cycle management, and source code generation. Figure 8.1 depicts the relative functionality and complexity of interchange files, the Metastore, and meta data repositories. If these more sophisticated services are part of your information processing needs, perhaps you should acquire one of the available meta data repository products. Otherwise, help yourself to the CWM Metastore.

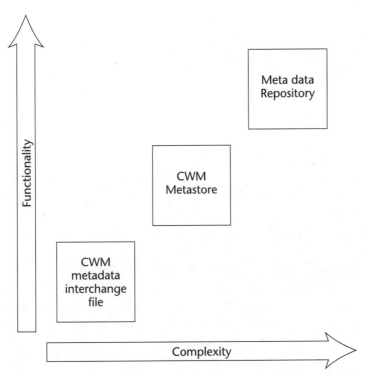

Figure 8.1   Feature and complexity relationships of CWM meta data stores.

Building a CWM Metastore

Because CWM is itself an object-oriented metamodel, you'd think that an object-oriented Database Management System (DBMS) would be the engine of choice for building a CWM metastore. While this is probably true from a strictly technical point of view, many object-oriented DBMSs have not met with much commercial success, so it's difficult to rely on their continued support and availability in the future. Furthermore, software development groups may not have sufficient staff that is aware of object-oriented DBMS techniques to design and effectively operate such systems. If you have the expertise to build a metastore on your favorite object-oriented DBMS, by all means do so. For the rest of us, this chapter shows how to map CWM's object-oriented metamodel onto a relational database. The broad commercial success of relational database management systems means most developers understand at least something about how relational databases are structured, and most organizations will have staff that knows how to operate them more or less effectively. These factors make a relational DBMS our engine of choice for the CWM Metastore.

Mapping CWM's object-oriented concepts onto relational tables requires dissecting CWM's classes and associations in ways that permit them to be mapped onto relational tables while preserving the logical structure of the meta data itself. The bulk of this chapter describes techniques, which we call *object-to-relational mapping patterns*, describing how different CWM object modeling constructs are mapped onto relational tables. Also, the mapping patterns for a few of the more interesting CWM modeling constructs are examined in some detail, a couple of implementation tradeoffs are explored, and suggestions for possible extensions are made. The chapter concludes with source listings for a complete program that populates the Metastore with a simple relational database schema, retrieves the schema from the Metastore, and displays it for view. A complete script file containing the CWM Metastore and the sources for the sample program are available on the companion Web site as described in the sidebar *Acquiring the CWM Metastore*.

Although you can download the CWM Metastore source, the object-to-relational mapping techniques used in the Metastore are intended primarily as illustrations of how the CWM metamodel can be deployed using commonly available software tooling. There are certainly other equally valid ways to accomplish the same end goals, and you are encouraged to explore them as well. There is no guarantee that the techniques described here are in any way either the best or fastest of available techniques. And although we have made reasonable efforts to ensure their correctness, we

**RETRIEVING INFORMATION FROM THE METASTORE
USING SQL STATEMENTS**

One obvious advantage of using a relational DBMS to implement the Metastore
is that it becomes possible to use Structured Query Language (SQL) data
manipulation statements to directly access the information in the Metastore
using an ad hoc query utility or other custom-written programs. While this is
certainly possible with the Metastore, please be aware that the mapping from
objects to tables fractionates the information in ways that require special
knowledge to correctly reassemble CWM instances from the Metastore.

This chapter provides the information you need to do such reassembly, but
you must understand these mapping techniques well before attempting to use
SQL SELECT, INSERT, UPDATE, and DELETE statements directly on the Metastore
database. To avoid these difficulties, the Metastore provides a large number
of stored procedures whose principal purpose is to encapsulate this special
knowledge into single operations that can be safely performed without risking
the structural integrity of data in the Metastore. Many of the examples in the
following text use these procedures to safely accomplish their tasks. Please do
likewise in your applications.

make no warrantee that they are, in fact, even correct! Rather, the Metastore should be treated as one possible way that you might deploy CWM in
your data warehousing solutions. Feel free to change and improve it as you
see fit and as your experience dictates, but you use it at your own risk.
Updates to the CWM Metastore source files may be posted on the companion Web site on an occasional basis; refer to the site for details.

The CWM Metastore is described in the Transact-Structured Query Language (often abbreviated T-SQL) defined by the Microsoft SQL Server 2000
relational database management system. Although these statements can, in
principle, be described using the appropriate language constructs of most
production-quality relational database management systems, SQL Server
2000's T-SQL language was selected for several reasons:

- Microsoft SQL Server is a widely used and well-understood relational database management system. Conversion of T-SQL scripts to
  the data description and manipulation languages of most other popular relational database management systems is a relatively straightforward process.

- Documentation of SQL Server's features and T-SQL language constructs is widely available. Many books, magazine articles, and other
  resources describing T-SQL are available from booksellers and online sources [Chappell & Trimble (2001), http://www.sqlmag.com].

- The batch-oriented, textual structure of T-SQL source language files allows the T-SQL source describing a complete implementation of the CWM Metastore database to be contained within a single file.

- The definition of the CWM Metastore must be in a script language that can be interpreted by a production-quality database management system. This DBMS serves as a means for developers to directly verify the correctness of the CWM Metastore object-to-relational mapping and as a foundation which developers can extend to meet the specific needs of their particular application.

Object-to-Relational Mapping Patterns

The mapping of concepts from the CWM model onto the components of a relational database occupies the bulk of this chapter. To avoid the tedium of describing in detail how every class, attribute, and association in CWM is mapped onto corresponding relational database components, we will take advantage of the fact that many CWM concepts can be mapped to relational database components using the same mapping technique. In this way, we can understand how major subsets of the several hundred CWM concepts can be mapped onto relational database components by simply examining one instance of the subset in detail. For example, by examining how the Table class from CWM's Relational package is mapped onto a relational database implementation in a CWM Metastore, we can learn a great deal about how *every* CWM class is mapped onto a relational database.

ACQUIRING THE CWM METASTORE

The relatively large number of classes, attributes, references, and associations in the combined packages of CWM means that the T-SQL script file describing a complete implementation of the CWM Metastore is quite large (in excess of 2 megabytes). Consequently, a complete listing of the T-SQL source is not included in the body of this book (at something like 1,800 pages, a full listing would increase the poundage of this volume nearly three times). However, you can download the complete listing from the book's accompanying Web site (http://www.wiley.com/compbooks/poole).

If you prefer to deploy the CWM Metastore using a different relational DBMS, you are free to do so, but you are responsible for doing this on your own. The authors cannot help you in this effort. Fortunately, though large, the CWM Metastore source is relatively straightforward and because SQL is a well-standardized language, migration to another commercial DBMS (such as Oracle's, for example) should be a relatively simple programming exercise.

In a sense, the object-to-relational mapping techniques described here can be directly compared to the notion of *templates* or *patterns* frequently used to describe commonalities in the structure of computer programs (Silverston, 2001). In CWM, an object-to-relational mapping pattern describes how a collection of structurally similar CWM concepts is mapped onto tables in the relational database that implements a CWM Metastore.

To anchor each mapping pattern firmly in CWM, we will examine an example of a specific instance of the pattern in detail. For each mapping pattern, a widely used CWM construct is selected for detailed examination from the collection of CWM constructs that use the pattern. For example, the Single-Valued Attribute pattern is described below by examining how the *precision* attribute of the Column class from CWM's Relational package is mapped onto a specific column (called *precision*) of a table (called *Relational_Column*) in the Metastore. Where a pattern is used by a limited subset of CWM constructs, a table listing the specific CWM constructs using the pattern is included so that other occurrences of the pattern can be unambiguously found.

Although the examples used to show how CWM constructs are mapped to relational database tables are taken from across the spectrum of CWM packages, there is a tendency to prefer examples from portions of CWM that are more widely understood in the industry and are expected to be frequently used in CWM implementations. As a result, many of the examples tend to focus on the CWM Relational package.

Each mapping pattern is described with a combination of graphical figures and code samples including, as appropriate, any or all of the following:

- UML diagrams of the CWM constructs whose mapping to relational tables is being described. In most cases, these diagrams are relevant fragments of diagrams that appear in the CWM specification document. These diagrams represent the source information used in the mapping process.

- Pictorial representations of the relational tables created by the mapping process. These tables depict the relational database constructs resulting from the mapping process.

- Statements from a relational database data definition language showing exactly how the tables can be created.

- Example SQL statements showing how data in the relational tables can be manipulated to accomplish specific purposes.

- Stored procedure definitions permitting information in the relational tables that make up the Metastore to be manipulated as if they are structured similarly to the CWM constructs to which they correspond. These stored procedures are particularly useful because they preserve the object structure of CWM even though a relational database is used to contain the Metastore. Also, they provide a way for external clients to manipulate information in the Metastore that minimizes the risk of unintentional data corruption.

A Field Guide to Object-to-Relational Mapping Patterns

This section is a tutorial guide to the diagramming techniques and source code fragments used to describe how CWM concepts (classes, attributes, associations, and so forth) are mapped onto SQL Server tables in the CWM Metastore. If you are already familiar with UML notation, general structure of relational tables, and syntactic conventions of the T-SQL language, you can safely skip over this section and move on to the discussion of specific mapping patterns that follows.

UML Notation Overview

Fragments of UML diagrams from the CWM specification serve as conceptual descriptions of the input to the mapping process. A brief overview of UML notation as it is used in the formal CWM specification document is provided in Figure 8.2. The figure shows a fragment of the CWM Relational package, and annotations in it identify the names and functions of specific parts of the diagram.

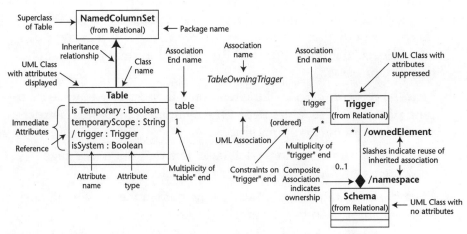

Figure 8.2   Summary of UML notation used to describe CWM concepts.

The figure shows that the Table class is a subclass of the NamedColumn-Set class and implies that Tables inherit (that is, have) all of the attributes of NamedColumnSets as well as *immediate attributes* listed within the Table class box itself. Classes may be drawn with their attributes shown, as for Table, or suppressed, as for NamedColumnSet and Trigger, if they are not relevant to the concept being described. The Schema class is shown with attributes visible even though the class has no immediate attributes. Sometimes, only the relevant subset of the immediate attributes of a class may be shown in the class box.

The UML association between Table and Trigger, represented by the horizontal line connecting their class boxes, identifies and orders the triggers that a particular table uses. Regardless of the name of this association, the model fragment shows that triggers are, in fact, owned by schemas. The solid diamond on the association line between the Trigger and Schema classes indicates this and implies that when a schema object is deleted, all of the triggers it owns are deleted as well. Slashes affixed to the end names of this association, /ownedElement and /namespace, indicate that it is a reuse of an association declared elsewhere in the CWM metamodel (in this case, it is the ElementOwnership association between ModelElement and Namespace in the Core package).

A slash is also used to visually distinguish attributes that are MOF references, as is the case for the /trigger reference of Table. References can be thought of as "pointers" to specific instances of another class (in this case, Trigger) connected via an association. There is a direct correspondence between the Trigger instances that the /trigger reference points to and the links of the TableOwningTrigger association in which the Table instance participates.

The definitive description of the CWM model is contained in an XML document that is compliant with the XMI (version 1.1) DTD definition. Both files are publicly available at www.omg.org. Fragments of the XML definition of CWM are introduced only when they contribute directly to an understanding of the mapping process. Because of their visual character, we prefer UML diagrams over XML fragments for describing CWM concepts.

Relational Table Notation

A diagrammatic representation of relational tables and T-SQL statements describing their creation serve as the output of the mapping process. The diagrams give quick visual summaries of the essential structure of tables resulting from the mapping process but are, of necessity, incomplete. T-SQL table creation statements complement the table diagrams and provide a complete description of the characteristics of the table in the Metastore. Figure 8.3 contains an example of a relational table diagram and labels its parts.

The Metastore table that stores instances of the Relational::Table class is used in the figure. The name of the table is constructed by concatenating the name of the CWM package containing the class and class name itself separated by an underscore character. If the CWM class is resident in an embedded package in CWM, all package names are used to construct the table name. Thus, the values of the Relational::Enumerations::Procedure-Type data type may be found in the Metastore table named Relational_ Enumerations_ProcedureType. This naming convention results in a unique name for each table and prevents confusion of similarly named classes in different packages (for example, several packages have a class named Schema).

A Metastore table is a collection of columns, and the order of columns in the table diagram has no significance. The shaded boxes at the top of each column contain the names of the Table attributes that reside in the columns. As discussed more fully below, only the values of immediate, single-valued attributes are mapped to columns defined directly in the Metastore table corresponding to a particular CWM class; the values of inherited and multi-valued attributes reside in other tables elsewhere in the Metastore. The ragged column on the right side of the table indicates that additional columns exist in the table but have not been shown in the figure because they are not relevant to the current situation. (Note, however, that the ragged column is purposefully misapplied in the figure—all columns of

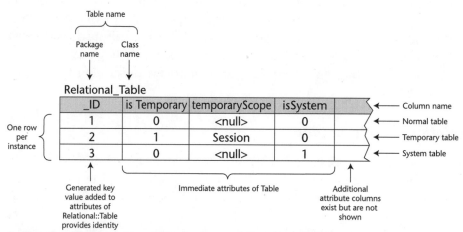

Figure 8.3   Diagrammatic representation of a Metastore table.

the Relational_Table table are already shown. It has been added here only to illustrate its significance when it appears on tables in other figures throughout the chapter.)

The object-to-relational mapping process may add columns to tables in the Metastore that are not part of the CWM definition itself. These columns are infrastructural in nature and do not contain values of CWM attributes. Rather, they contain values used to capture the mapping of objects onto relational tables in the Metastore. So that infrastructural columns introduced by the mapping process can be easily recognized, their names usually begin with an underscore ("_") character. The most important of infrastructural column is represented in Figure 8.3 by the _ID column. This column is added to every Metastore table representing some part of a CWM class and, as described later on, is involved in connecting the various parts of a single instance of a CWM class.

Each row in the table corresponds to a single instance of the CWM concept mapped to the Metastore table. The column values in a row show the current data values assigned to immediate, single-valued attributes of the instance. When it contributes to understanding of a point being discussed, specific data values may be given in some diagrams. For example, the figure shows three rows representing how attribute values are assigned to create normal, system, and temporary Table instances. An empty column value simply implies that the value for the column is not stated and does not imply that the data value is necessarily null. When data values are shown, any missing or otherwise null values are indicated by the <null> metatoken, as has been done for values of the temporaryScope attribute in the normal and system table rows in the figure.

To keep the diagrams of Metastore tables simple and understandable, some information about the structure of the tables, such as the data types of their columns, has been left out of the diagrams. Complete information about the structure of a Metastore table can be found in the T-SQL Create Table statement that created the table. Figure 8.4 shows an example table creation statement for Relational_Table and labels its parts.

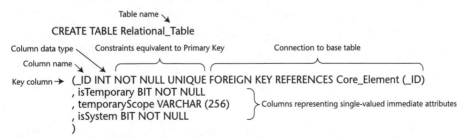

Figure 8.4 Table creation statements precisely define the structure of Metastore tables.

Table creation statements include columns representing the immediate, single-valued attributes of the class being mapped. Inherited attributes and multi-valued attributes reside in other tables within the Metastore and do not appear in the table creation statement itself. Reference attributes are handled differently (described below) and do not cause addition of columns to Metastore tables.

As described elsewhere in this chapter, the object-to-relational mapping process may add infrastructural columns to Metastore tables. A column named _ID is added to the creation statement of every table representing a CWM class and, if the table represents a sub-class, links this column to the base table using a foreign-key-based referential integrity constraint. Another infrastructural column is added to Metastore tables for each one-to-many association that uses the class as the type of its "many" end. No infrastructural columns of this latter type are added to the Relational_Table example shown in Figure 8.4, but they can be recognized in other tables because their names end with the characters "_ID."

Manipulating Data in Metastore Tables

In the following discussion of object-to-relational mapping patterns used by the Metastore, example T-SQL data manipulation statements are provided to show how data in Metastore tables is manipulated. These statements are the foundation of a set of T-SQL stored procedures created in the Metastore to preserve the object-oriented nature of CWM constructs even though the data has been mapped to relational tables. The structure of these stored procedures is described in more detail in the next section. These statements illustrate various techniques that manipulate data stored in Metastore tables.

T-SQL is a merger of traditional SQL language statements, much like those described by the SQL99 language standard, plus programming language like constructs providing for variable definitions, expressions, iteration constructs, and code modularization. Although you should refer to the Microsoft SQL Server documentation or any of a large number of fine books on the SQL language for precise details [for example, Melton and Simon (2002), Chappell and Trimble (2001)], we provide a very short primer on SQL language statements used to manipulate data in Metastore tables in Figure 8.5.

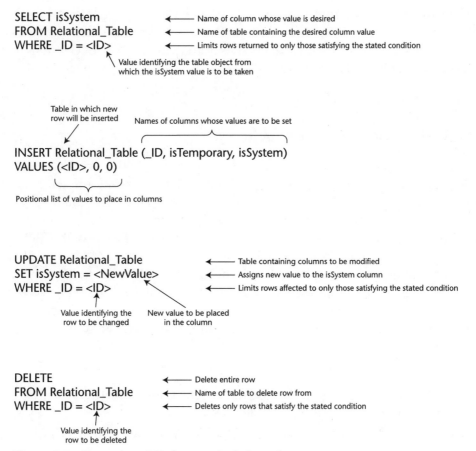

Figure 8.5   A very short SQL data manipulation primer.

Similar to most modern relational database management systems, there are four principal T-SQL statements that provide for data manipulation: SELECT, INSERT, UPDATE, and DELETE. SELECT statements retrieve data from the columns of tables and provide for the assembly of result sets that look and behave like tables. In contrast, INSERT, UPDATE, and DELETE statements alter the contents of database tables. The figure shows a simple example of each statement type as it is used to manipulate instances of CWM's Relational::Table class as mapped into the Metastore table called Relational_Table.

To ease the effort required to port the Metastore implementation from Microsoft SQL Server to some other relational database management system, product-specific constructs have been avoided wherever possible when creating SQL statements.

Preserving CWM's Object Structure

Because relational databases do not directly support the object-oriented UML and MOF concepts used to describe CWM, a Metastore implementation containing only the tables needed to store CWM concepts would suffer from a problem known to programmers as *impedance mismatch* (a term borrowed from electronics). Impedance mismatch means that users of the Metastore must understand both the object-oriented concepts of CWM and the relational database techniques used to implement the Metastore. Moreover, programmers and ad hoc users accessing a table-only Metastore would be required to mentally translate object-oriented operations onto an appropriate sequence of SQL statements every time they used the Metastore.

There are three important consequences that may result from significant impedance mismatch:

- Programs accessing the Metastore become more complex and, hence, more expensive, to create and maintain.

- The probability that programs and ad hoc updaters will inadvertently corrupt data in the Metastore increases dramatically.

- The risks that users will reach incorrect conclusions about information contained in the Metastore, and perhaps take inappropriate actions based thereon, go up substantially. This may happen if subtleties of the object-to-relational mapping used to create the Metastore are not fully understood when Metastore queries are constructed.

To mitigate these potential risks, the Metastore contains stored procedures whose purpose is to dramatically reduce impedance mismatch by preserving the object-oriented nature of CWM. These stored procedures encapsulate knowledge of the object-to-relational mapping techniques used in the creation of the Metastore so that they can be applied in a consistent manner for every Metastore user. Although the implementation of the Metastore described here does not directly do so, the security features of Microsoft SQL Server (and certainly most other production-quality relational database management systems) can be used to further prevent users from accessing data in Metastore tables directly, bypassing the safety features of the stored procedures.

An additional benefit of accessing the Metastore via its stored procedures is that they may tend to improve performance of Metastore accesses in distributed computing and client-server application architectures. This happens because stored procedures are executed on the same server where the database files are located. The result is minimized network traffic because data that does not satisfy the constraints of a requested operation need not be transmitted over the network.

The structure of a Transact-Structured Query Language (T-SQL) stored procedure is examined in Figure 8.6. The procedure in the figure reconstructs an instance of the Relational::Table class from the four Metastore tables across which it has been spread by the object-to-relational mapping process. The desired instance is identified via the @_ID parameter by providing the value in the _ID column of the desired instance. A sample T-SQL script in the figure shows how the stored procedure is called, how parameter values are passed, and how the stored procedure's result value is saved after execution. In the Metastore, all stored procedures return the value 0 if no error occurred during execution. A nonzero return value is the number of the first error that occurred. The meaning of returned error numbers can be found in the SQL Server documentation or, as shown in the figure, by calling the stored procedure provided in the Metastore that translates SQL Server error numbers into an understandable text message.

Stored procedure names are constructed in a consistent manner through the Metastore. They appear in the form

```
<function>_<package>_<construct>_<attribute>,
```

where <function> is a keyword indicating the nature of the operation that the stored procedure performs; <package> is the name of the CWM package containing the <construct>; <construct> is the name of the CWM data type, class, or association that is being operated upon; and <attribute> is a CWM attribute, reference, or association end name. The <attribute> portion of the name is included only if the stored procedure is specific to some attribute, reference, or association end. When the <attribute> portion is absent, the stored procedure function applies to the entire <construct>. Table 8.1 contains a list of the <function> names used in the Metastore. Examples of these functions will be examined throughout this chapter.

Table 8.1   Stored Procedure Function Keywords

<FUNCTION>	DESCRIPTION
Add	Add a role for a class
AllOfKind	Get all of the instances of a class without its subclasses
AllOfType	Get all of the instances of a class and all of its subclasses
Create	Create an instance of a class or a link in an association
Delete	Delete an instance of a class or a link from an association
Drop	Remove a role for a class
Exclude	Remove an instance of a class from a reference set
ExcludeAll	Remove all instances of a class from a reference set
Get	Get the value of some <attribute>, or all the single-valued <attribute> values of one instance of a class
GetAll	Get the single-valued <attribute> values of all instances of a class
GetCursor	Returns same result as the GetAll procedure in a T-SQL CURSOR variable. Used primarily to manipulate data within other T-SQL scripts.
Include	Add an instance of a class to a reference set
Set	Change the value of an <attribute>

The SELECT statement in the procedure in Figure 8.6 has three sections. The column list following the SELECT keyword indicates the column values to be returned and their order in the result set. Each column value is qualified by the name of the table containing the column to prevent ambiguous column names. The returned column value is known in the result set by the name following the AS keyword. The FROM clause lists tables that are referenced in either the column list or in the WHERE clause. The WHERE clause contains two types of expressions. The first expression, containing the input parameter @_ID, selects the desired row from the table where the stated column has the value currently in the @_ID parameter. The remainder of the expressions in the WHERE clause are relational join conditions that serve to reassemble the table instance from the various tables where its values have been placed by the object-to-relational mapping process.

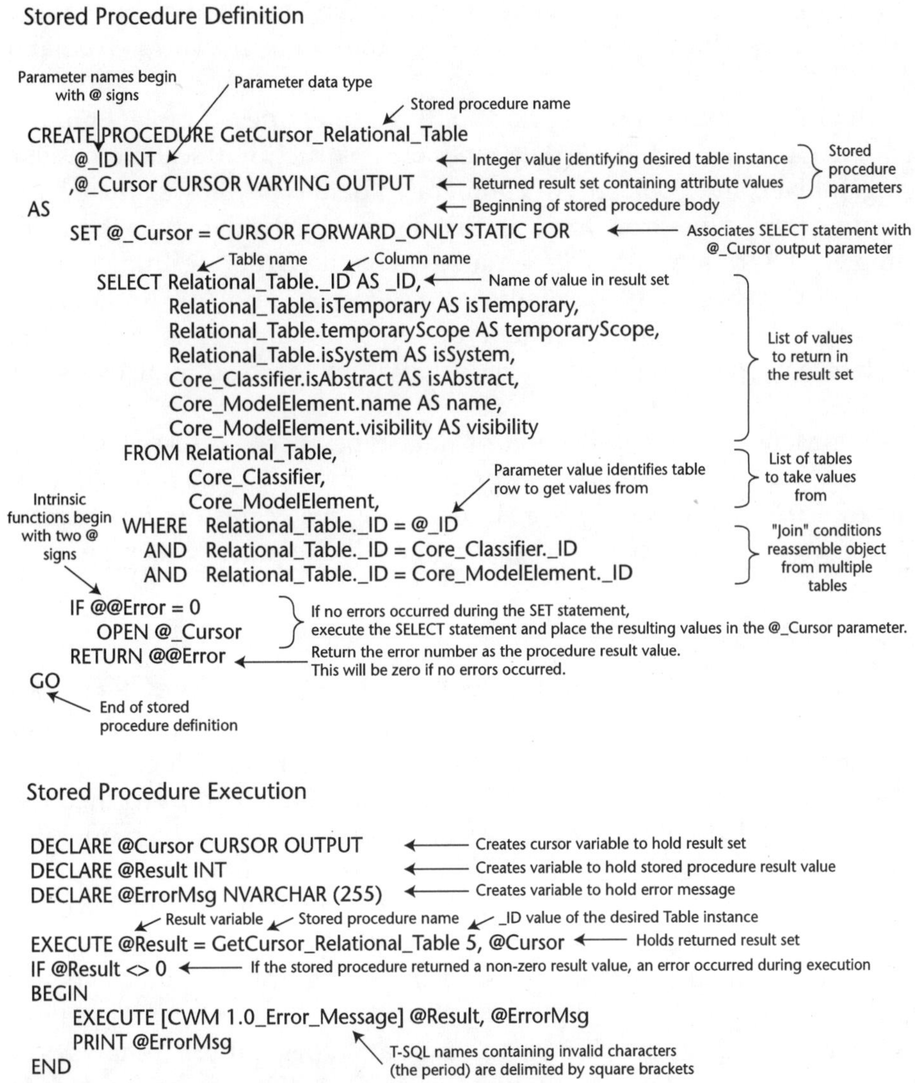

Stored Procedure Definition

Parameter names begin
with @ signs   Parameter data type
                                    Stored procedure name

CREATE PROCEDURE GetCursor_Relational_Table
    @_ID INT ←——————————— Integer value identifying desired table instance   Stored
    ,@_Cursor CURSOR VARYING OUTPUT ←——— Returned result set containing attribute values   procedure
AS   ←——— Beginning of stored procedure body   parameters
        SET @_Cursor = CURSOR FORWARD_ONLY STATIC FOR ←———— Associates SELECT statement with
                    Table name   Column name   @_Cursor output parameter
        SELECT Relational_Table._ID AS _ID, ←——— Name of value in result set
                Relational_Table.isTemporary AS isTemporary,
                Relational_Table.temporaryScope AS temporaryScope,   List of values
                Relational_Table.isSystem AS isSystem,   to return in
                Core_Classifier.isAbstract AS isAbstract,   the result set
                Core_ModelElement.name AS name,
                Core_ModelElement.visibility AS visibility
        FROM Relational_Table,   List of tables
                Core_Classifier,   Parameter value identifies table   to take values
                Core_ModelElement,   row to get values from   from
        Intrinsic
functions begin WHERE Relational_Table._ID = @_ID   "Join" conditions
with two @   AND   Relational_Table._ID = Core_Classifier._ID   reassemble object
signs   AND   Relational_Table._ID = Core_ModelElement._ID   from multiple
                                                                                    tables
        IF @@Error = 0   If no errors occurred during the SET statement,
            OPEN @_Cursor   execute the SELECT statement and place the resulting values in the @_Cursor parameter.
        RETURN @@Error ←————   Return the error number as the procedure result value.
GO   This will be zero if no errors occurred.
        End of stored
        procedure definition

Stored Procedure Execution

DECLARE @Cursor CURSOR OUTPUT   ←———— Creates cursor variable to hold result set
DECLARE @Result INT   ←———— Creates variable to hold stored procedure result value
DECLARE @ErrorMsg NVARCHAR (255)   ←—— Creates variable to hold error message
            Result variable   Stored procedure name   _ID value of the desired Table instance
EXECUTE @Result = GetCursor_Relational_Table 5, @Cursor ←——— Holds returned result set
IF @Result <> 0 ←———— If the stored procedure returned a non-zero result value, an error occurred during execution
BEGIN
        EXECUTE [CWM 1.0_Error_Message] @Result, @ErrorMsg
        PRINT @ErrorMsg
END   T-SQL names containing invalid characters
                                 (the period) are delimited by square brackets

Figure 8.6 Stored procedure anatomy and execution.

Data Type Mapping Patterns

Every CWM attribute has a data type. An attribute's data type limits the
values that the attribute may assume to those that are compatible with its
declared data type. For example, an attribute with the declared data type of

String can store textual values like "CWM is fun" and "blue" but cannot store numeric values, like 1.3 and 100, or the Boolean values, True and False.

Each CWM attribute falls into one of three categories: Simple, Enumerated, and Class-based. Simple data types are unstructured, scalar types like String, Integer, and Boolean. An enumerated data type allows an attribute to assume only values from a specific list defined by the data type itself. For example, a CWM attribute whose data type is the OrderingKind enumerated type can assume only the values "ok_ordered" and "ok_unordered." Attributes with a Class-based data type can be thought of as instances of the class named as the type embedded within the class that owns the attribute.

In the Metastore, the collection of data types used in CWM must be mapped to equivalent data types supported in the T-SQL language. If there is no directly corresponding T-SQL data type, the Metastore must create data structures necessary to allow it to mimic the required data type.

Simple Data Type Pattern

As an example of how simple data types are handled in CWM, Figure 8.7 shows ways the Integer data type is defined in various CWM documents. The definition of Integer starts in the formal specification document as a textual description of the data type. It is then sequentially transformed to a UML class labeled with the stereotype "<<datatype>>" in the model file, mapped to the typecode for the CORBA Interface Definition Language (IDL) "long" data type in the CWM XML file and, finally, converted to T-SQL's Integer primitive data type in the Metastore.

The Metastore takes advantage of the mapping of CWM data types to CORBA IDL typecodes in the CWM XML file to drive the mapping of CWM simple data types to T-SQL's native data types. Table 8.2 shows how CWM simple data types are mapped to CORBA IDL typecodes and, in turn, to T-SQL data types. In the table, CORBA IDL typecodes are represented by their XML Metadata Interchange (XMI) names, and the Count column indicates the number of attributes of that data type in CWM.

Enumerated Data Type Pattern

CWM enumerated data types are represented in UML as a class labeled with the "<<enumeration>>" stereotype. Values of the enumeration that an attribute of its type can assume, called *enumeration literals*, are listed in the lower section of the class box.

In the Metastore, a table is created to represent each CWM enumerated data type. Rows in enumerated data type tables have only one column, called _EnumLiteral, which contains the enumeration literal value. When the value of a column based on an enumerated data type is changed, the new value is verified against this table to maintain the integrity of the column's data.

In the formal CWM Specification:

Integer

Integer represents the predefined type of integers. An instance of Integer is an element in the (infinite) set of integers (…, –2, –1, 0, 1, 2, …).

The default for Integer is 0.

In the CWM model file:

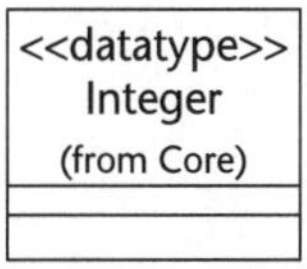

```
<<datatype>>
   Integer
  (from Core)
```

In the CWM XML file:

```
<Model:DataType xmi.id='a70' name='Integer' annotation='Integer represents the
    predefined type of integers. An instance of Integer is an element in the (infinite) set of
    integers (…, –2, –1, 0, 1, 2, …). &#10;&#10;&#10;&#10;The default for Integer is 0.'
    isRoot='true' isLeaf='true' isAbstract='false' visibility='public_vis'>
    <Model:DataType.typeCode>
      <XMI.CorbaTypeCode>
        <XMI.CorbaTcLong/>
      </XMI.CorbaTypeCode>
    </Model:DataType.typeCode>
</Model:DataType>
```

In the Metastore:

INTEGER

Figure 8.7   Representations of the CWM simple data type Integer.

Table 8.2 Mapping of CWM Simple Data Types

CWM DATA TYPE	CORBA IDL TYPECODE	T-SQL DATA TYPE	COUNT	REMARKS
Any	XMI.CorbaTcAny	VARCHAR(255)	2	Convert value to string
Boolean	XMI.CorbaTcBoolean	BIT	39	Values 0 and 1
Float	XMI.CorbaTcFloat	FLOAT	8	
Integer	XMI.CorbaTcLong	INTEGER	29	
Name Identifier	XMI.CorbaTcString	VARCHAR(128)	6	Max. length of T-SQL identifier
String	XMI.CorbaTcString	VARCHAR(255)	75	T-SQL max length is 8,000
Time	XMI.CorbaTcString	VARCHAR(255)	7	Convert to string representation
UnlimitedInteger	XMI.CorbaTcLong	INTEGER	1	Nonnegative integers; -1 = "unlimited"

The ProcedureType enumeration from the Relational package is used in Figure 8.8 and in the following text to illustrate the mapping of CWM enumerations to tables in the Metastore. The Metastore table has a three-part name because the ProcedureType enumeration is located in an embedded package, called Enumerations, within the Relational package definition in the CWM XML file.

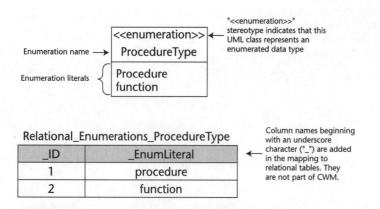

Figure 8.8 Enumerated data type mapping.

The T-SQL statements needed to create the Metastore table for the ProcedureType enumeration are shown below. The INSERT statements following the CREATE TABLE statement place enumeration literal values into the table once it has been created. The length of the _EnumLiteral column is limited to 128 characters because this is the maximum length of a T-SQL identifier.

```
CREATE TABLE Relational_Enumerations_ProcedureType
    (_EnumLiteral VARCHAR(128)
    )
GO


INSERT Relational_Enumerations_ProcedureType(_EnumLiteral)
    VALUES('procedure')
INSERT Relational_Enumerations_ProcedureType(_EnumLiteral)
    VALUES('function')
GO
```

The single stored procedure for the ProcedureType enumeration follows. In the GetAll_Relational_Enumerations_ProcedureType procedure, the "SELECT *" phrase is a SQL idiom that returns all columns of the table named in the FROM clause—in this case, simply the _EnumLiteral column.

```
CREATE PROCEDURE GetAll_Relational_Enumerations_ProcedureType
AS
    SELECT * FROM Relational_Enumerations_ProcedureType
    RETURN @@ERROR
GO
```

The following T-SQL code fragment shows how the GetAll_Relational_Enumerations_ProcedureType procedure can be used to list the enumeration literals for the ProcedureType enumeration.

```
EXECUTE GetAll_Relational_Enumerations_ProcedureType
```

The procedure returns the following results:

```
_EnumLiteral
------------
procedure
function
```

CWM has 25 enumerated data types declared in seven packages. A total of 29 attributes distributed across the same seven packages are based on enumerated data types.

Class-Based Data Type Pattern

The data type of an attribute may be the name of some other class in the model. This situation is illustrated in Figure 8.9 by the initialValue attribute of the Core::Attribute class, which has the data type Expression. This class-based data type refers to the Expression class, also in the Core package. The Expression class allows so-called black box expressions, that is, expressions for which CWM has no knowledge of internal structure, to be stored in CWM.

Expressions have two attributes: language and body. The language attribute contains the name of the language in which the body of the Expression is stated. For example, a T-SQL SELECT statement might be stored in an Expression instance by setting its attributes as follows:

```
body = "SELECT * FROM Relational_Table"          language = "T-SQL".
```

An appropriate way to think about the semantics of this declaration would be as an instance of the Expression class embedded within the Attribute class and given the name initialValue.

To store values for attributes with class-based data types, an instance of the class-based type is created. The key of this instance is then placed in an infrastructural column added to the table representing the class that owns the attribute. The name of the infrastructural column is constructed by appending the characters "_ID" to the name of the attribute. The infrastructural column is then associated with the instance of the class-based type by a foreign key constraint. The T-SQL statement that creates this situation for the example in Figure 8.9 is shown below.

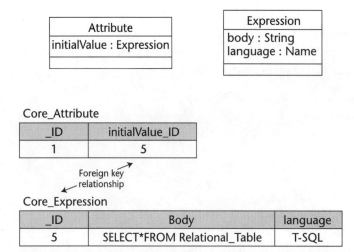

Figure 8.9 Class-based data type mapping.

```
CREATE TABLE Core_Attribute
  (_ID INT UNIQUE FOREIGN KEY REFERENCES Core_Element (_ID)
  ,initialValue_ID INT NOT NULL FOREIGN KEY REFERENCES
      Core_Expression(_ID)
  )
```

In the figure, an instance of Expression is created and assigned an _ID value = 5 (this value is selected by the Metastore automatically). The value of the Expression's _ID column (5) is then placed in the initialValue_ID column of the Core_Attribute table.

Table 8.3 summarizes the six CWM classes that are used as the class-based data type of 23 attributes.

Class Mapping Patterns

The UML class is a central metaphor used in the design of CWM. Every CWM concept is represented as a class in the formal specification document and in the accompanying model files. Basic capabilities of UML classes have been leveraged to complete the description of CWM classes. These basic capabilities include containment of multiple attributes, acting as the types of attributes, and anchoring the ends of associations. Consequently, representing the UML class correctly in the Metastore is of critical importance.

Previous sections have already given a number of hints about how CWM classes are mapped onto relational tables in the Metastore. Several important mapping principles were introduced, but only informally. Here, we briefly review these principles to emphasize the importance of their central role in mapping CWM classes to tables in the Metastore.

Table 8.3   CWM Class-Based Data Types

PACKAGE	CLASS	ATTRIBUTES
Core	BooleanExpression	3
Core	Expression	7
Core	Multiplicity	1
Core	ProcedureExpression	6
DataTypes	QueryExpression	2
Expressions	ExpressionNode	4

There is a one-to-many correspondence between a UML class and tables in the Metastore. Each class is represented by at least one table (see Figure 8.10). This table serves as the class's anchor table in the Metastore; accesses to instances of the class in the Metastore begin by referencing the row in the class's *anchor table*[2] that corresponds to the desired instance.

Depending on the kinds of attributes a class owns, additional tables may be added to the Metastore to enhance representation of the class. We have already seen how attributes with enumerated and class-based data types cause additional tables representing their data types to be linked to the base table. In a sense, rows in these other tables become part of the representation in the Metastore of the CWM class associated with the anchor table. We will see in this and in the following sections how other kinds of tables may be added as well to further enhance the representation of UML classes in the Metastore.

The data type relationships that we have examined so far are implemented in the Metastore using foreign key-based relationships between the anchor table and the appropriate data type tables. This notion will be extended so that, under appropriate circumstances, yet another kind of table—the intersection table—may be added to further enhance representation of a CWM class. Finally, the foreign key-based relationships will be adapted to prevent unintentional corruption of instances in the Metastore and to enforce the ownership semantics of composite relationships.

Table
isTemporary : Boolean
temporaryScope : String
/ trigger : Trigger
isSystem : Boolean

Relational_Table

_ID	isTemporary	temporaryScope	isSystem

Figure 8.10 The Table class and its anchor table in the Metastore.

[2] To minimize confusion, we will avoid referring to the anchor table of a class as its base table because that term has a specific, but different, meaning in some relational database management systems.

Perhaps that most basic mapping technique hinted at in previous sections is the notion of identity. *Identity* is the thread that ties together all the pieces of a CWM instance in the Metastore. When an instance is placed in the Metastore, its parts are distributed to multiple tables as required by the object-to-relational mapping patterns. With each piece is stored the identity of the instance to which it belongs. To reconstruct an instance, its identity is used so that its pieces can be found and reassembled correctly. Throughout the Metastore, infrastructural columns are added to tables to contain the relevant identity values. These identity columns can be recognized by their name, which either is _ID or is terminated with the characters _ID.

Usage of identity to connect the pieces of instances in the Metastore will continue to be elucidated throughout this section. Near the end, an example will be provided that summarizes the ways identity is used in the Metastore. In this chapter, identities will be gathered together to represent collections of instances to support the Metastore implementations of CWM associations and references.

Implementation of the Metastore takes advantage of a particular feature of Microsoft SQL Server to ease the creation of identity values. When the IDENTITY keyword is associated with a column definition, SQL Server generates a monotonically increasing integer value (starting at 1, by default) and automatically places the current value in the column every time a new row is created in the owning table. SQL Server guarantees that it will not generate the same number twice for a given table.

The Metastore defines IDENTITY columns on the primary key attributes (named _ID) in the tables corresponding to every CWM enumerated data type, to tables created to support multi-valued attributes, and to the table Core_Element. An important side effect of the way identity values are used to implement inheritance is that every CWM instance has a unique identity value regardless of which class it is an instance of, allowing every row in every Metastore table to be uniquely associated with one and only one instance.

Identity values in the Metastore have been created using the T-SQL INT data type (a common abbreviation of INTEGER). The numeric capacity of the INT data type and the way identity values are assigned in the Metastore interact to allow for a total of 2,147,483,647 separate CWM instances to be stored regardless of their class membership. If you feel your application is likely to overflow this limit, you can raise it by changing the data type of every column named _ID and every column with a name ending with the characters _ID from INT to BIGINT. This change must be made before the database is generated and will permit storage of 9,223,372,036,854,775,807 (nearly 10 quintillion!) individual instances.

Attribute Mapping Patterns

Attributes capture data values. Consequently, the most obvious mapping of CWM attributes in the Metastore would be to map each of them onto a column in the Metastore table corresponding to the CWM class. As we have seen in the previous examples, most CWM attributes are indeed mapped to columns in Metastore tables. However, a few CWM attributes require special handling because their characteristics do not map well to a single column in a relational table.

All CWM attributes have meta data characteristics, collectively called *multiplicity*. The multiplicity of an attribute specifies the minimum and maximum number of copies of an attribute value that an instance of a class can contain. These minimum and maximum numbers are usually referred to as an attribute's *lower* and *upper* bounds, respectively. An attribute cannot have fewer copies than its lower bound nor more copies than its upper bound. A lower bound of zero implies that the attribute is optional—it need not have a value at all—whereas an unspecified upper bound means that the attribute may exist in as many copies as needed—there is no limit. Of course, the lower bound must always be less than or equal to the upper bound. An attribute with an upper bound of one is called *single-valued* and an attribute with an upper bound greater than one is said to be *multi-valued*.

Multiplicity is a term derived from CWM's roots in the UML modeling language; those of you with database backgrounds may recognize these concepts by the name *cardinality*.

An attribute's multiplicity not only conveys its upper and lower bounds but also determines, if its upper bound is greater than one, whether the ordering of the values is significant for the attribute. If it is, the attribute is said to be *ordered*. The Metastore orders multiple values by insertion order. The first value stored will be the first value returned, the second will be returned next, and so forth. If you need to have values saved in some other order, you should arrange to store them in the order you want them back. If an attribute is unordered, no guarantees are made about the order in which multiple values will be returned. The section below called *Multi-Valued Attribute Patterns* covers the implementation of ordering more completely. The UML concept of attribute multiplicity is also capable of indicating if multiple values of an attribute must be unique, that is, whether any two of them can have the same value. CWM, however, has no unique attributes and does not use this feature.

Because they are owned by classes, CWM references are technically attributes of their owning class even if they do not capture an understandable data value. However, understanding the mapping of references into the Metastore first requires understanding details of the implementation of associations. Consequently, discussion of the references is deferred until after association implementation has been described.

There are 204 classes distributed across 21 packages in CWM.

Single-Valued Attribute Patterns

Single-valued attributes, those with a multiplicity upper bound of one, are mapped directly to columns of their owning class's anchor table. The attribute's name is used as the column name in the anchor table, and the attribute's data type is mapped to a T-SQL type as described in Table 8.2. Several examples of mapping single-valued attributes are shown in Figure 8.11 using the Relational::Column class to map its own attributes.

As with the Relational::Table examples above, the name of the attribute is not stored in a column's anchor table but in an inherited attribute, as will be described later. Similarly, the data type indication for each column is stored in another Metastore table.

The T-SQL CREATE TABLE statement for Relational_Column shows how attribute lower bounds are handled. Required attributes, those with a lower bound of one, can be recognized by the NOT NULL specification included in their definition. When this specification is present, SQL Server requires every row in the Relational_Column table to have a value for the columns isNullable, collationName, and characterSetName. Note that for string attributes (collationName and characterSetName in the example), an empty string is considered a non-null value. For optional attributes, with a lower bound of zero such as precision, scale, and length, the NOT NULL specification is missing and no value is required.

Relational_Column

_ID	precision	scale	isNullable	length	collationName	characterSetName	
91	<null>	<null>	columnNullable	<null>	"	"	← precision
92	<null>	<null>	columnNullable	<null>	"	"	← scale
93	<null>	<null>	columnNoNulls	<null>	"	"	← isNullable
94	<null>	<null>	columnNullable	<null>	"	"	← length
95	<null>	<null>	columnNoNulls	<null>	"	"	← collation-Name
96	<null>	<null>	columnNoNulls	<null>	"	"	← character-SetName

Figure 8.11   Single-valued attribute mapping.

```
CREATE TABLE Relational_Column
    (_ID INT NOT NULL UNIQUE FOREIGN KEY REFERENCES Core_Element (_ID)
    ,precision INT
    ,scale INT
    ,isNullable VARCHAR(128) NOT NULL
    ,length INT
    ,collationName VARCHAR(256) NOT NULL
    ,characterSetName VARCHAR(256) NOT NULL
    )
GO
```

For each single-valued, immediate attribute, the Metastore contains two stored procedures to permit manipulation of the attribute's data value in the Metastore. The procedures allow for the retrieval and setting of the attribute's current value. For example, the following procedures are defined for the precision column of the Relational_Column table.

```
CREATE PROCEDURE Get_Relational_Column_precision
    @_ID INT
    ,@_Value INT OUTPUT
AS
    SELECT @_Value = [precision] FROM Relational_Column WHERE _ID = @_ID
    RETURN @@Error
GO


CREATE PROCEDURE Set_Relational_Column_precision
    @_ID INT
    ,@_Value INT
AS
    UPDATE Relational_Column SET [precision] = @_Value WHERE _ID = @_ID
    RETURN @@Error
GO
```

You can see that for simple attributes, the Get and Set stored procedures are merely wrappers on the single SQL data manipulation statement required to effect the desired action. Similar pairs of stored procedures exist for the scale, length, isNullable, collationName, and characterSet-Name attributes. Because the literal values of enumerated data types are stored directly in anchor table columns, no special handling is required for attributes, like isNullable, which are based on them. Even though the Set procedures for enumerated types will accept any character string via their input parameters, only those strings that match the literal values defined for the enumerated type will be placed into the anchor table.

To illustrate usage of simple attribute procedures, the following T-SQL fragment sets the length column of the collationName attribute (i.e., the column with _ID = 95) to 10, but only if the length column value is currently null.

```
DECLARE @len INT
DECLARE @result INT
DECLARE @errMsg VARCHAR(255)
EXECUTE @result = Get_Relational_Column_length 95, @len OUTPUT
IF @result = 0 AND @len IS NULL
    EXECUTE @result = Set_Relational_Column_length 95, 10
IF @result <> 0
BEGIN
    EXECUTE [CWM 1.0_Error_Message] @result, @errMsg OUTPUT
    PRINT @errMsg
END
GO
```

The handling of class-typed attributes is different. For these attributes, the Get and Set procedures use the identity value of the instance of the class-based data type containing the information for the class-based attribute. This identity is then used to manipulate the attributes of the instance of the class-based data type directly via their own Get and Set procedures. The following discussion extends the example of class-based data types presented in Figure 8.9, illustrating how the initialValue attribute of the Core::Attribute class is mapped into the Metastore.

Two stored procedures are created for a class-based attribute. They get and set the value of the infrastructural column in the table representing the class owning the attribute. For the example, the text of these procedures follows.

```
CREATE PROCEDURE Get_Core_Attribute_initialValue
    @_ID INT
    ,@_Class_ID INT OUTPUT
AS
    SELECT @_Class_ID = initialValue_ID FROM Core_Attribute
        WHERE _ID = @_ID
    RETURN @@Error
GO


CREATE PROCEDURE Set_Core_Attribute_initialValue
    @_ID INT
    ,@_Class_ID INT
AS
    UPDATE Core_Attribute SET initialValue_ID = @_Class_ID
        WHERE _ID = @_ID
    RETURN @@Error
GO
```

The following T-SQL fragment illustrates how these stored procedures can be used to create the example shown in Figure 8.9. Details of the Create procedures used to make the Attribute instance and the Set procedures for the Expression attributes will be discussed in another section. For now, simply note that the Create_Core_Attribute procedure automatically creates the instance of Expression required to implement the initialValue attribute and places its _ID value into the initialValue_ID column of the attribute's row in the Core_Attribute table.

```
DECLARE @attrID INT
DECLARE @exprID INT
DECLARE @result INT
DECLARE @errMsg VARCHAR(255)
EXECUTE @result = Create_Core_Attribute @attrID OUTPUT
IF @result = 0
   EXECUTE @result = Get_Core_Attribute_initialValue @attrID,
      @exprID OUTPUT
IF @result = 0
   EXECUTE @result = Set_Core_Expression_body @exprID,
      'SELECT * FROM Relational_Table'
IF @result = 0
   EXECUTE @result = Set_Core_Expression_language @exprID, 'T-SQL'
If @result = 0
   SET @errMsg = 'OK'
ELSE
   EXECUTE [CWM 1.0_Error_Message] @result, @errMsg OUTPUT
   PRINT @errMsg
GO
```

CWM has 219 single-valued attributes. Forty-two of these are optional; the rest are required.

Multi-Valued Attribute Patterns

In contrast to single-valued attributes, which are mapped to columns, multi-valued attributes are each mapped to a separate table. These tables are linked to the class's anchor table using identity values in foreign keys and, together with the anchor table, make up the set of tables used to map CWM classes with multi-valued attributes into the Metastore.

CWM only has two examples of multi-valued attributes, and both of them reside in the same class—SoftwareDeployment::Machine. The host-Name and ipAddress attributes of this class are both optional multi-valued attributes. Also, both attributes are ordered and will help illustrate how the order of multiple data values is maintained. The UML diagram for this class and its corresponding Metastore tables are shown in Figure 8.12.

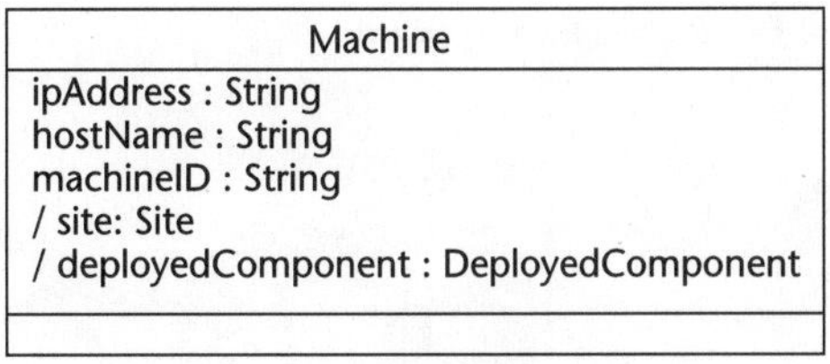

Machine
ipAddress : String hostName : String machineID : String / site: Site / deployedComponent : DeployedComponent

SoftwareDeployment_Machine

_ID	MachineID
1	Production
2	Test
3	Development

SoftwareDeployment_Machine_ipAddress

_ID	_Class_ID	_Value	_Ordinal
1	1	10.0.0.1	1
2	1	10.0.0.255	2
3	2	10.0.0.10	1
4	3	10.0.0.17	1

SoftwareDeployment_Machine_hostName

_ID	_Class_ID	_Value	_Ordinal
1	1	ProdServer	1
2	3	DevMaster	1
3	3	DevHost	2
4	2	TestHost	1

Figure 8.12 Multi-valued attribute mapping.

The example data in the rows of the Metastore tables in Figure 8.12 represent the network topology in Figure 8.13.

In tables created for multi-valued attributes, an infrastructural column (called _Class_ID in Figure 8.12) is added to link each row of the table to the appropriate owning row in the anchor table via a foreign key relationship. Even though both multi-valued attributes are optional, the _Class_ID foreign key must still be marked as NOT NULL. Optional multi-valued attributes that currently have no values can be recognized in the Metastore because their multi-valued tables will have no records in them.

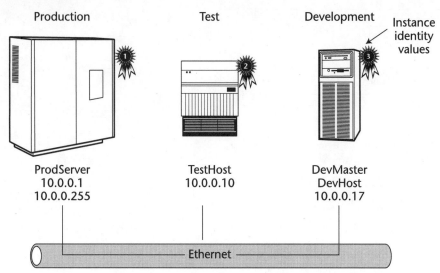

Figure 8.13 Network topology of example data in Figure 8.12.

The T-SQL definition of the set of tables used to implement Software-Deployment::Machine below shows how the tables and relationships in Figure 8.12 are created. An infrastructural column called _ID is added to the two multi-valued attribute tables as an identity-generating primary key. These column provide no immediate function other than permitting multiple instances with the same data value to be clearly distinguished. The data value for each row is stored in the _Value column. If the multi-valued attribute is ordered, the _Ordinal column will be present as well (in the example case, both attributes are ordered). Values in the _Ordinal column are used to preserve the order in which the multiple values of the attribute are added to the Metastore. The Get procedures for the attribute are returned in the order indicated by this column.

```
CREATE TABLE SoftwareDeployment_Machine
    (_ID INT NOT NULL UNIQUE FOREIGN KEY REFERENCES Core_Element (_ID)
    ,machineID VARCHAR(256)
    )
GO

CREATE TABLE SoftwareDeployment_Machine_ipAddress
    (_ID INT IDENTITY PRIMARY KEY
    ,_Class_ID INT NOT NULL FOREIGN KEY REFERENCES
        SoftwareDeployment_Machine(_ID)
    ,_Value VARCHAR(256)
```

```
    ,_Ordinal INT NOT NULL
    )
GO

CREATE TABLE SoftwareDeployment_Machine_hostName
    (_ID INT IDENTITY PRIMARY KEY
    ,_Class_ID INT NOT NULL FOREIGN KEY REFERENCES
       SoftwareDeployment_Machine(_ID)
    ,_Value VARCHAR(256)
    ,_Ordinal INT NOT NULL
    )
GO
```

The stored procedures for manipulating a multi-valued attribute are somewhat different than those for single-valued attributes. Like single-valued attributes, multi-valued attributes have a Get procedure. But unlike single-valued attributes, multi-valued attributes have a pair of procedures for manipulating attribute values instead of a single Set procedure. These procedures, called Include and Exclude, add and remove individual values to and from, respectively, the current set of values for the attribute in the Metastore. In the example that follows, the stored procedures for the ipAddress attribute are shown; similar procedures are provided for the hostName attribute.

Because the Get procedure must return a set of values, it returns a T-SQL result set rather than a simple data type. The result set rows contain an identity value and a data value taken from the _ID and _Value columns, respectively, of the multi-valued attribute table. The input parameter @_Class_ID contains the identity value of the row in the Machine class's anchor table for which multiple attribute values are requested. The ORDER BY clause is added only if the multi-valued attribute is ordered.

```
CREATE PROCEDURE Get_SoftwareDeployment_Machine_ipAddress
    @_Class_ID INT
AS
    SELECT _ID, _Value
       FROM SoftwareDeployment_Machine_ipAddress
       WHERE _Class_ID = @_Class_ID
       ORDER BY _Ordinal
    RETURN @@Error
GO
```

This T-SQL code exercises the ipAddress Get procedure by printing the IP addresses for the Production system (_ID = 1) in Figure 8.13. If an error occurs during execution, its number is returned in the @result variable and an appropriate message is displayed.

```
DECLARE @result INT
DECLARE @errMsg VARCHAR(256)
EXECUTE @result = Get_SoftwareDeployment_Machine_ipAddress 1
IF @result <> 0
BEGIN
    EXECUTE [CWM 1.0_Error_Message] @result, @errMsg OUTPUT
    PRINT 'Error: ' + @errMsg
END
GO
```

The _ID value returned in the following result set uniquely identifies the _Value within the multi-valued attribute table. It is provided so that the multiple attribute values can be individually distinguished even if the data in the _Value field duplicates that found in some other _Value field. Values of _ID are unique only within the multi-valued attribute table itself and should not be confused with the _Class_ID column that contains the identity value of the Machine instance to which the ipAddress belongs.

```
_ID     _Value
---     ------
 1      10.0.0.1
 2      10.0.0.255
```

Multi-valued attributes also have GetCursor procedures so that individual rows can be manipulated independently in T-SQL scripts. However, they do not have GetAll procedures since it makes little sense to retrieve all values of multi-valued attributes outside the context of their owning class instances.

GetCursor procedures return the same results as GetAll procedures except that their results are returned in T-SQL variables of type *cursor*. Cursors are pointer-like data structures that permit each row in the result to be manipulated independently. Because of the breadth of capabilities that cursors may provide, they can adversely affect application performance, especially in today's client-server, remote computing, and Web-based applications. To mitigate possible performance effects, the Metastore provides only the simplest and, hence, fastest kind of SQL Server cursors—forward-only, static cursors. Because they are the fastest form, T-SQL cursors of this kind are often called *firehose* cursors. Cursors execute on the database server itself and are, consequently, also called *server-side* cursors. GetCursor procedures are intended for use in other T-SQL scripts (that also execute on the database server); they are also used by the standalone T-SQL scripts in this chapter that demonstrate use of Metastore procedures. Application programs base their access on Get and GetAll procedures and do not directly use GetCursor procedures.

To continue our example, the definition of SoftwareDeployment_ Machine_ipAddress's GetCursor procedure is as follows:

```
CREATE PROCEDURE GetCursor_SoftwareDeployment_Machine_ipAddress
    @_Class_ID INT
    ,@_Cursor CURSOR VARYING OUTPUT
AS
    DECLARE @Error INT
    SET @_Cursor = CURSOR FORWARD_ONLY STATIC FOR
        SELECT _ID, _Value
            FROM SoftwareDeployment_Machine_ipAddress
            WHERE _Class_ID = @_Class_ID
            ORDER BY _Ordinal
    SELECT @Error = @@Error
    IF @Error = 0
    BEGIN
        OPEN @_Cursor
        SELECT @Error = @@Error
    END
    RETURN @Error
GO
```

The following T-SQL script shows how the values of a multi-valued attribute can be accessed, again using the Machine with the identity value 1.

```
DECLARE @result INT
DECLARE @name VARCHAR(256)
DECLARE @ID INT
DECLARE @Value VARCHAR(256)
DECLARE @cursor CURSOR
EXECUTE @result = Get_SoftwareDeployment_Machine_name 1, @name OUTPUT
IF @result = 0
    EXECUTE @result = GetCursor_SoftwareDeployment_Machine_ipAddress 1,
        @cursor OUTPUT
IF @result = 0
BEGIN
    PRINT 'The ' + @name ' machine is known by the IP addresses:'
    FETCH NEXT FROM @cursor INTO @ID, @Value
    WHILE @@Fetch_Status = 0
    BEGIN
        PRINT '    ' + @Value + ' (Metastore ID = ' +
                CONVERT(VARCHAR, @ID) + ')'
        FETCH NEXT FROM @cursor INTO @ID, @Value
    END
END
CLOSE @cursor
DEALLOCATE @cursor
GO
```

This T-SQL example script displays the following results:

```
The Production machine is known by the IP addresses:
    10.0.0.1 (Metastore ID = 1)
    10.0.0.255 (Metastore ID = 2)
```

The Include procedure that replaces the Set procedure of single-valued attributes accepts three parameters. @_Class_ID is the identity value of the Machine instance to which the ipAddress applies, and @_Value holds the new IP address value that is to be added. If the procedure completes successfully, the identity value of the newly created row in the multi-valued attribute table is returned in @_ID.

Because the ipAddress values are ordered, the first thing the Get procedure does is calculate the next value to assign to the _Ordinal column of the new row. By choosing the next _Ordinal value as one more than the highest _Ordinal value currently in the table for the class instance, the Get procedure ensures that the newly added value will be last in the list of values. This method of selecting the next _Ordinal value is also insensitive to missing _Ordinal values that may have been caused by intervening calls to the Exclude procedure. The _Ordinal value is never returned via any Metastore stored procedure. As previously noted, if you need a different ordering of values than insertion order, simply delete all the existing values and reinsert them in the order you desire to have them returned.

This Include procedure has the first example we have seen of explicit transaction handling. All of the previously shown Set procedures have been transacted as well, but, for reasons that will be discussed below, no specific transaction management statements were required. Details of transaction management are discussed in a later section. However, for now, simply note the unusual identifier Include_SoftwareDep_FD7F0B011608 in the transaction statements. This identifier is a "mangled" name produced by the Metastore because identifiers appearing in these locations have a maximum allowed length of 32 characters; the name you see is generated from the Include procedure name to ensure that this length maximum is enforced. The exact content of the identifier is not important as long as it is unique. A unique name mangling is created in every stored procedure that needs one.

```
CREATE PROCEDURE Include_SoftwareDeployment_Machine_ipAddress
    @_ID INT OUTPUT
    ,@_Class_ID INT
    ,@_Value VARCHAR(256)
AS
    DECLARE @Error INT
```

```
    DECLARE @MaxOrdinal INT
    SELECT @MaxOrdinal = MAX(_Ordinal)
        FROM SoftwareDeployment_Machine_ipAddress
        WHERE _Class_ID = @_Class_ID
    SELECT @Error = @@Error
    IF @Error = 0
    BEGIN
        BEGIN TRANSACTION Include_SoftwareDep_FD7F0B011608
        SELECT @Error = @@Error
        IF @Error = 0
        BEGIN
            INSERT SoftwareDeployment_Machine_ipAddress(_Class_ID, _Value,
                _Ordinal) VALUES (@_Class_ID, @_Value, @MaxOrdinal + 1)
            SELECT @Error = @@Error
            IF @Error = 0
                SET @_ID =
                    IDENT_CURRENT('SoftwareDeployment_Machine_ipAddress')
        END
    END
    IF @Error = 0
        COMMIT TRANSACTION Include_SoftwareDep_FD7F0B011608
    ELSE
        ROLLBACK TRANSACTION
    IF @@Error <> 0
        SELECT @Error = @@Error
    RETURN @Error
GO
```

The Exclude procedure for ipAddress is shown below. It simply deletes the row from the multi-valued table with the supplied @_ID value. This identity value is the value in the _ID column of the multi-valued table; it is not the identity of the class instance owning ipAddress value. The class instance's identity is not needed because the @_ID value is sufficient to safely delete the desired attribute value; this is a side effect of the IDENTITY property added to the _ID column of the multi-valued table in its CREATE TABLE statement. The Exclude procedure needs to do nothing special if the attribute columns are ordered.

```
CREATE PROCEDURE Exclude_SoftwareDeployment_Machine_ipAddress
    @_ID INT
AS
    DECLARE @Error INT
    BEGIN TRANSACTION Exclude_SoftwareDep_EC43DC0C1499
    SELECT @Error = @@Error
    IF @Error = 0
    BEGIN
        DELETE FROM SoftwareDeployment_Machine_ipAddress WHERE _ID = @_ID
        SELECT @Error = @@Error
```

```
      END
      IF @Error = 0
         COMMIT TRANSACTION Exclude_SoftwareDep_EC43DC0C1499
      ELSE
         ROLLBACK TRANSACTION
      IF @@Error <> 0
         SELECT @Error = @@Error
      RETURN @Error
   GO
```

Inheritance Pattern

Inheritance is a central feature of UML, and of object-oriented systems in general. It is the foundation upon which object reuse is built and the chief technique used to organize models of systems of many kinds. Inheritance organizes classes into inverted treelike structures called *generalization hierarchies* in which classes nearer the top of the hierarchy are more general in nature, and those nearer the bottom are more specific. The lower a class is in the generalization hierarchy, the more specifically and completely it defines those classes above it. Classes lower in the hierarchy are called subclasses of those classes that reside above them. Conversely, classes higher up the hierarchy are called superclasses of those classes below them. A subclass further specifies and defines its superclasses in two ways: by limiting instances of the superclass that can participate in the sub-classes, and by adding attributes that further characterize instances of the sub-class.

CWM makes extensive use of the inheritance features of UML to achieve its own ends as well. The shared features of CWM classes and the provision of CWM service models (such as generic capabilities like the ResponsibleParty class that are available in the Foundation layer), are delivered to all classes in CWM because they are attached to classes near the top of the CWM generalization hierarchy. A complete understanding of the implementation of inheritance is of critical importance to tool vendors and other developers creating general-purpose CWM solutions. Since visual examples often help in understanding the structure of a generalization hierarchy, the complete generalization hierarchy for the CWM Relational package appears in Figure 8.14.

Preservation of CWM's generalization hierarchy in the Metastore is essential, and the choice of how to implement the generalization hierarchy was perhaps the most crucial decision in the Metastore's development. The basic idea behind the representation of the generalization hierarchy is to map each class in the hierarchy to a separate table which, along with its immediate, single-valued attributes, is linked to its superclasses and subclasses by a shared identity value.

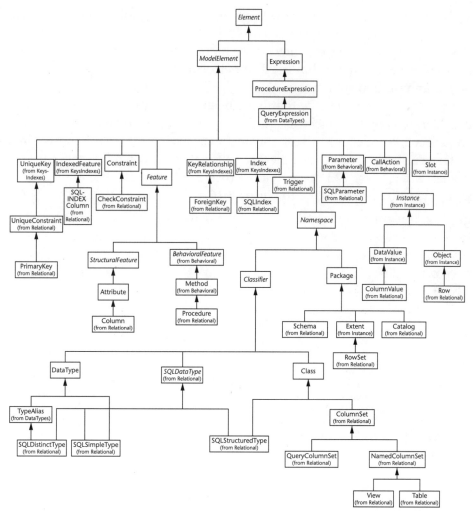

Figure 8.14   Relational generalization hierarchy.

Regardless of where a class resides in the generalization hierarchy, there is a separate table for each of its superclasses in the hierarchy. For example, from the Table class in Figure 8.14, we must traverse seven levels of super-classes to reach the top of the generalization hierarchy: NamedColumnSet, ColumnSet, Class, Classifier, Namespace, ModelElement, and Element. As we will see in a later example, there are separate anchor tables for each of these intermediate superclasses of Table named Relational_Named-ColumnSet, Relational_ColumnSet, Core_Class, Core_Classifier, Core_Namespace, Core_ModelElement, and Core_Element, respectively.

To explore how the generalization hierarchy is implemented, we will begin by examining a somewhat simpler section of Figure 8.14. This section, shown in Figure 8.15, is the inheritance hierarchy for the Relational::Trigger class. Triggers are tasks that may be performed at the completion of SQL data manipulation statements.

The pieces of an instance that have been spread around the generalization hierarchy by the object-to-relational mapping can be reassembled into an object by collecting all of the instance rows that share the desired instance's identity value. The pieces of a Relational::Trigger instance for the trigger with _ID = 273 are spread across the three tables making up its mapping into the Metastore in Figure 8.16.

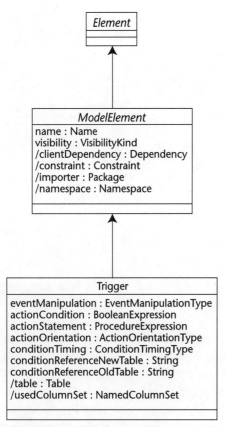

Figure 8.15 Relational::Trigger generalization hierarchy.

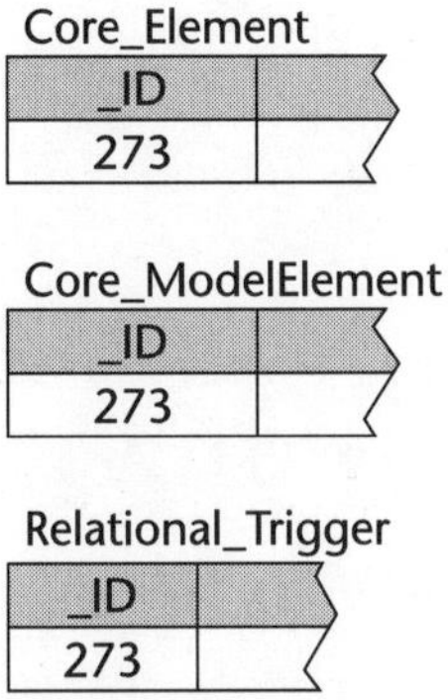

Core_Element

_ID	
273	

Core_ModelElement

_ID	
273	

Relational_Trigger

_ID	
273	

Figure 8.16   Metastore mapping of a Relational::Trigger.

The T-SQL creation statements for the Trigger's hierarchy that follow show how these tables are created and linked together via their identity values in the _ID column. The Core_Element table is the anchor table for the Core::Element class that serves the superclass of all other classes in CWM. Because it has no superclasses, Core_Element's _ID column is defined with the IDENTITY and PRIMARY KEY properties. Having a single table at the top of the generalization hierarchy means that every other CWM class is a sub-class, at some level, of Core::Element. Because creation of an instance of a class causes a row to be added to the class's anchor table and to the anchor tables of all of its superclasses, there is a row in Core_Element for *every* class instance in the Metastore. Consequently, the IDENTITY property on Core_Element's _ID column serves to guarantee that every instance will have a unique _ID value. This unique _ID value is then placed in the _ID column of the rows added to each of the intervening superclass anchor tables between Core_Element and the class being created. In our Relational::Trigger example in Figure 8.16, the _ID value of 273 was created when the Core_Element row was added and copied to the _ID columns of Core_ModelElement and Relational_Trigger in turn. Of course, for this technique to work, the Core_Element row must be created before the Core_ModelElement and Relational_Trigger rows.

```
CREATE TABLE Core_Element
  (_ID INT IDENTITY PRIMARY KEY
  ,_Kind_ID INT
  )
```

```
GO

CREATE TABLE Core_ModelElement
    (_ID INT NOT NULL UNIQUE FOREIGN KEY REFERENCES Core_Element (_ID)
    ,name VARCHAR(256) NOT NULL
    ,visibility VARCHAR(128) NOT NULL
    )
GO

CREATE TABLE Relational_Trigger
    (_ID INT NOT NULL UNIQUE FOREIGN KEY REFERENCES Core_Element (_ID)
    ,eventManipulation VARCHAR(128) NOT NULL
    ,actionCondition_ID INT NOT NULL FOREIGN KEY REFERENCES
        Core_BooleanExpression(_ID)
    ,actionStatement_ID INT NOT NULL FOREIGN KEY REFERENCES
        Core_ProcedureExpression(_ID)
    ,actionOrientation VARCHAR(128) NOT NULL
    ,conditionTiming VARCHAR(128) NOT NULL
    ,conditionReferenceNewTable VARCHAR(256) NOT NULL
    ,conditionReferenceOldTable VARCHAR(256) NOT NULL
    )
GO
```

The _ID columns in Core_ModelElement and Relational_Trigger are treated as foreign keys of Core_Element's _ID primary key column. This has been done so that SQL Server's referential integrity enforcement features can prevent an instance's Core_Element row from being deleted until after all of its sub-class rows have been deleted from all other tables in the Metastore. In this way, the presence of a row in the Core_Element table is sufficient to define the existence of an instance in the Metastore, and the Core_Element row must be the first row created, and the last row deleted, for that instance. This order of creation and deletion is visually combined with Relational::Trigger's generalization hierarchy and anchor tables in Figure 8.17.

For each class, a Get procedure is available to reconstruct an instance of the class by reassembling it from the various Metastore tables where its parts have been placed by the object-to-relational mapping. This procedure takes the identity value for the desired instance and returns a result set containing one row made up of all of the single-valued attribute values of the instance. For attributes with simple and enumerated data types, the value of the attribute is returned in the result set. For attributes with class-based data types, however, the result set contains the identity value of the type class instance containing the values. For these attributes, you must then use the identity value returned in the result set to retrieve the type class's instance values, using its own Get procedure.

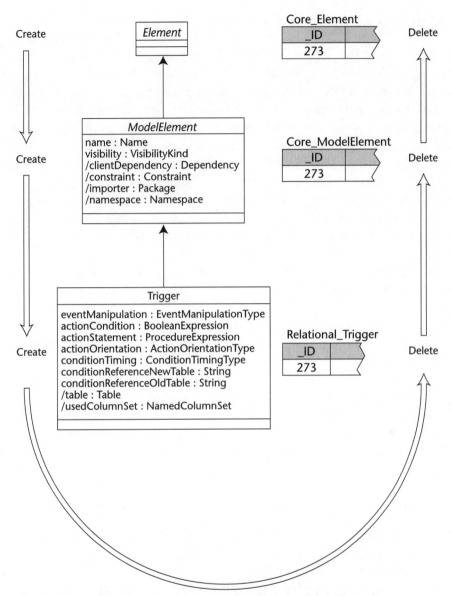

Figure 8.17   Inheritance mapping dictates creation and deletion order.

The Get procedure for the Trigger class, shown in Figure 8.18, illustrates how an instance is reassembled from the relevant Metastore tables. Annotations in the figure indicate the function of the various parts of the T-SQL SELECT statement that reassembles an instance of the Trigger class. The list of columns in the SELECT clause describes the structure of the single record result set that is returned. The name following the AS keyword for each column is used as the name of the attribute in the result set; these names are used in the code to manipulate attributes in the result set. The FROM clause contains the list of tables that holds pieces of the Trigger instance. You may notice that Core_Element, even though it clearly holds part of a Trigger instance (its identity value), is not part of the SELECT statement. This is because only tables that contain attributes of Trigger are needed to reconstruct an instance. Because Core_Element has only the identity value and no other attributes, the instance can be reassembled without Core_Element's participation. Even the instance's identity value is replicated in the Relational_Trigger table and can be obtained without reference to Core_Element. Similarly, any superclass's or sub-class's anchor table that exists to maintain the generalization hierarchy but contains no attributes is not needed to reconstruct the instance.

To ease the effort involved in scanning the Metastore for the presence of particular instances, the GetAll procedure returns the single-valued attributes for every instance in a class. For example, the GetAll_Relational_Trigger procedure returns a result set containing one row for each Trigger instance currently in the Metastore and is shown below. If you compare this procedure with the definition of the corresponding Get procedure, you will notice that the columns returned in the result set are the same in both cases. The procedure definitions differ in that GetAll is missing the @_ID parameter and the Relational_Trigger._ID = @_ID clause in the WHERE clause found in the Get procedure. Also, Get returns a single row whereas GetAll returns one row for each Trigger found in the Metastore.

```
CREATE PROCEDURE GetAll_Relational_Trigger
AS
    SELECT Relational_Trigger._ID AS _ID,
        Relational_Trigger.eventManipulation AS eventManipulation,
        Relational_Trigger.actionCondition_ID AS actionCondition_ID,
        Relational_Trigger.actionStatement_ID AS actionStatement_ID,
        Relational_Trigger.actionOrientation AS actionOrientation,
        Relational_Trigger.conditionTiming AS conditionTiming,
        Relational_Trigger.conditionReferenceNewTable AS
            conditionReferenceNewTable,
        Relational_Trigger.conditionReferenceOldTable AS
            conditionReferenceOldTable,
        Core_ModelElement.name AS name,
        Core_ModelElement.visibility AS visibility
    FROM Relational_Trigger,
        Core_ModelElement
    WHERE Relational_Trigger._ID = @_ID
      AND Relational_Trigger._ID = Core_ModelElement._ID
    RETURN @@Error
GO
```

```
CREATE PROCEDURE Get_Relational_Trigger
     @_ID INT
AS
                            Table name          Column name
     SELECT Relational_Trigger._ID AS _ID,          Name in result set
           Core_ModeElement.name AS name,
           Core_ModeElement.name.visibility AS visibility
           Relational_Trigger.eventManipulation AS eventManipulation,
           Relational_Trigger.actionCondition_ID AS actionCondition_ID,
           Relational_Trigger.actionStatement_ID AS actionStatement_ID,
           Relational_Trigger.actionOrientation AS actionOrientation,
           Relational_Trigger.conditionTiming AS conditionTiming,
           Relational_Trigger.conditionReferenceNewTable
              AS conditionReferenceNewTable,
           Relational_Trigger.conditionReferenceOldTable
              AS conditionReferenceOldTable,
        FROM Relational_Trigger,
             Core_ModelElement                             Selects the desired instance
           WHERE Relational_Trigger._ID = @_ID
             AND  Relational_Trigger._ID = Core_ModelElement._ID    Link Trigger and ModelElement rows
        Return   @@Error
GO
```

Figure 8.18   How the Get procedure reassembles an Instance of Relational::Trigger.

And finally, the GetCursor procedure is defined for classes so that every member of the class can be examined individually in T-SQL scripts. Notice that the SELECT statement is identical to the one in the corresponding GetAll procedure. The GetCursor procedure for Relational::Trigger is as follows:

```
CREATE PROCEDURE GetCursor_Relational_Trigger
    @_Cursor CURSOR VARYING OUTPUT
AS
    DECLARE @Error INT
    SET @_Cursor = CURSOR FORWARD_ONLY STATIC FOR
       SELECT Relational_Trigger._ID AS _ID,
          Relational_Trigger.eventManipulation AS eventManipulation,
          Relational_Trigger.actionCondition_ID AS actionCondition_ID,
          Relational_Trigger.actionStatement_ID AS actionStatement_ID,
          Relational_Trigger.actionOrientation AS actionOrientation,
          Relational_Trigger.conditionTiming AS conditionTiming,
          Relational_Trigger.conditionReferenceNewTable AS
              conditionReferenceNewTable,
          Relational_Trigger.conditionReferenceOldTable AS
              conditionReferenceOldTable,
          Core_ModelElement.name AS name,
          Core_ModelElement.visibility AS visibility
       FROM Relational_Trigger,
            Core_ModelElement
       WHERE Relational_Trigger._ID = Core_ModelElement._ID    IF @Error =
0
```

```
        BEGIN
            OPEN @_Cursor
            SELECT @Error = @@Error
        END
        RETURN @Error
    GO
```

Usage of the GetCursor_Relational_Trigger procedure is illustrated by the following T-SQL script for the instance in Figure 8.16 with _ID = 273. If the SELECT statement executes without error, GetCursor_Relational_ Trigger returns the cursor open and ready for use.

```
DECLARE @result INT
DECLARE @cursor CURSOR
DECLARE @ID INT
DECLARE @eventManip VARCHAR(128)
DECLARE @actStmtID INT
DECLARE @actCondID INT
DECLARE @actOrient VARCHAR(128)
DECLARE @condTiming VARCHAR(128)
DECLARE @refNewTable VARCHAR(255)
DECLARE @refOldTable VARCHAR(255)
DECLARE @name VARCHAR(255)
DECLARE @visKind VARCHAR(128)
DECLARE @lang VARCHAR(255)
DECLARE @body VARCHAR(255)
EXECUTE @result = Get_Relational_Trigger 273, @cursor OUTPUT
IF @result = 0
BEGIN
    FETCH NEXT FROM @cursor INTO @ID, @name, @visKind, @eventManip,
        @actCondID, @actStmtID, @actOrient, @condTiming, @refNewTable,
        @refOldTable
    WHILE @@Fetch_Status = 0
    BEGIN
        PRINT 'Trigger ' + @name + ' (ID=' + CONVERT(VARCHAR,@ID) + ')'
        PRINT 'visbility = ' + @visKind
        PRINT 'eventManipulation = ' + @eventManip
        EXECUTE @result = Get_Core_BooleanExpression_language @actCondID,
            @lang OUTPUT
        IF @result = 0
        BEGIN
            EXECUTE @result = Get_Core_BooleanExpression_body @actCondID,
                @body OUTPUT
            IF @result = 0
                PRINT 'actionCondition = (' + @lang + ') ' + @body
        END
        EXECUTE @result = Get_Core_ProcedureExpression_language
            @actStmtID, @lang OUTPUT      IF @result = 0
        BEGIN
            EXECUTE @result = Get_Core_ProcedureExpression_body @actStmtID,
```

```
            @body OUTPUT
        IF @result = 0
            PRINT 'actionStatement = (' + @lang + ') ' + @body
    END
    PRINT 'actionOrientation = ' + @actOrient
    PRINT 'conditionTiming = ' + @condTiming
    PRINT 'conditionReferenceNewTable = ' + @refNewTable
    PRINT 'conditionReferenceOldTable = ' + @refOldTable
    FETCH NEXT FROM @cursor INTO @ID, @name, @visKind, @eventManip,
        @actCondID, @actStmtID, @actOrient, @condTiming, @refNewTable,
        @refOldTable
    END
END
CLOSE @cursor
DEALLOCATE @cursor
GO
```

Much of the internal effort required to manage the content of the Metastore is related to the creation and deletion of instances in the generalization hierarchy. These tasks are managed by the Add and Drop procedures, respectively. These procedures are infrastructural in nature and under normal circumstances should not need to be directly accessed by Metastore users. However, knowing how they operate is essential to an understanding of how the Metastore works.

The Add procedure begins, if @_ID is not null, by counting the number of rows in the anchor table for the requested identity value received in the @_ID parameter. If a row already exists for the identity value, the procedure simply exits with an indication of no error. This is a simple check to prevent accidental creation of a second row for the instance, and is unnecessary if @_ID is null. After starting a transaction, the Add procedure for each immediate superclass is called, in the order indicated in Figure 8.17. The call to Add_Core_ModelElement recursively calls Add_Core_Element which assigns and returns the identity value for the new instance in its @_ID parameter. This value is then used by Add_Core_ModelElement so that the same identity value will be in the _ID columns of both superclass tables. Next, instances are created for each attribute that has a class-based data type. These instances are created by calling the appropriate Create procedures for the class-based types. The identity of each new instance is saved into a local variable for later placement into Trigger's anchor table record. Now that initial values are available for all of the columns in the new Relational_Trigger record, it is inserted into the table. Default values are placed into the columns for all non-null attributes with simple or enumerated data types, and the instance identity values previously saved are put in place for attributes with class-based data types. Lastly, the transaction is terminated with commit or rollback, as appropriate.

```
CREATE PROCEDURE Add_Relational_Trigger
   @_ID INT OUTPUT
AS
   DECLARE @actionCondition_ID INT
   DECLARE @actionStatement_ID INT
   DECLARE @Error INT
   DECLARE @Count INT
   IF @_ID IS NOT NULL
   BEGIN
      SELECT @Count = COUNT(*) FROM Relational_Trigger WHERE _ID = @_ID
      IF @Count > 0
         RETURN 0
   END
   BEGIN TRANSACTION Add_Relational_Trigger
   SELECT @Error = @@Error
   IF @Error = 0
      EXECUTE @Error = Add_Core_ModelElement @_ID OUTPUT
   IF @Error = 0
   BEGIN
      EXECUTE @Error = Create_Core_BooleanExpression
         @actionCondition_ID OUTPUT
      IF @Error = 0
         EXECUTE @Error = Create_Core_ProcedureExpression
            @actionStatement_ID OUTPUT
      IF @Error = 0
      BEGIN
         INSERT Relational_Trigger (_ID, eventManipulation,
                actionCondition_ID, actionStatement_ID,
               actionOrientation, conditionTiming,
                conditionReferenceNewTable, conditionReferenceOldTable)
            VALUES (@_ID, 'insert', @actionCondition_ID,
               @actionStatement_ID, 'row', 'before', '', '')
         SELECT @Error = @@Error
      END
   END
   IF @Error = 0
      COMMIT TRANSACTION Add_Relational_Trigger
   ELSE
      ROLLBACK TRANSACTION
   IF @@Error <> 0
      SELECT @Error = @@Error
   RETURN @Error
GO
```

The Drop procedure takes an @_ID parameter that contains the identity value of the Relation_Trigger instance to be removed. If the class has any attributes with class-based data types, the identity values for the attributes are retrieved by calling the appropriate Get procedures. If this process completes without error, a transaction is begun. The instances containing values for attributes with class-based data types are removed first by calling the Drop procedures for the classes and passing in the retrieved identity value. An internal utility procedure called DeleteLinks is then called for each locally attached association to remove any links in which the instance participates. This action also cleans up any references mapped to those associations. If the class has any multi-valued attributes (Relational::Trigger has none), the instances values are removed from them. Next, the row in the anchor table is directly removed with a DELETE statement, and the AllOfType row added by the Add procedure is removed. Finally, the transaction is completed as appropriate, and the Drop procedure returns.

```
CREATE PROCEDURE Drop_Relational_Trigger
    @_ID INT
    AS
    DECLARE @Error INT
    DECLARE @actionCondition_ID INT
    DECLARE @actionStatement_ID INT
    EXECUTE @Error = Get_Relational_Trigger_actionCondition
            @_ID, @actionCondition_ID OUTPUT
    IF @Error = 0
        EXECUTE @Error = Get_Relational_Trigger_actionStatement
                @_ID, @actionStatement_ID OUTPUT
    IF @Error = 0
    BEGIN
        BEGIN TRANSACTION Drop_Relational_Trigger
        SELECT @Error = @@Error
        IF @Error = 0 AND @actionCondition_ID IS NOT NULL
            EXECUTE @Error = Drop_Core_BooleanExpression
                @actionCondition_ID
        IF @Error = 0 AND @actionStatement_ID IS NOT NULL
            EXECUTE @Error = Drop_Core_ProcedureExpression
                @actionStatement_ID
        IF @Error = 0
        IF @Error = 0
            EXECUTE @Error = [CWM 1.0_DeleteLinks]
                'GetCursor_Relational_TriggerUsingColumnSet_usedColumnSet',
                'Delete_Relational_TriggerUsingColumnSet', @_ID
        IF @Error = 0
            EXECUTE @Error = [CWM 1.0_DeleteLinks]
                'GetCursor_Relational_TableOwningTrigger_table',
                'Delete_Relational_TableOwningTrigger', @_ID
        IF @Error = 0
        BEGIN
            DELETE FROM Relational_Trigger WHERE _ID = @_ID
            SELECT @Error = @@Error
        END
        IF @Error = 0
```

```
            EXECUTE @Error = Drop_Core_ModelElement @_ID
        IF @Error = 0
            COMMIT TRANSACTION Drop_Relational_Trigger
        ELSE
            ROLLBACK TRANSACTION
        IF @@Error <> 0
            SELECT @Error = @@Error
    END
    RETURN @Error
GO
```

In the XML file, UML classes have an attribute called isAbstract. Classes with isAbstract='true' are called *abstract* classes, and those with isAbstract='false', *concrete* classes. The following fragment from the CWM XML file demonstrates how this attribute appears in the Model:Class tag for the Core::Element class.

```
<Model:Class xmi.id='a3' name='Element'
    annotation='An element is an atomic constituent of a model. In the
        metamodel, an Element is the top metaclass in the metaclass
        hierarchy. Element is an abstract metaclass.&#10;&#10;'
    isRoot='false' isLeaf='false' isAbstract='true'
    visibility='public_vis' isSingleton='false'>
</Model:Class>
```

Instances can be created for concrete, but not for abstract, classes. Abstract classes are instantiated only when one of their concrete sub-classes is created. In the Metastore, concrete classes can be recognized because they have Create and Delete procedures. Abstract classes, such as Core::Element, do not have these procedures. The Create and Delete procedures call the Add and Drop procedures, respectively, of their concrete and abstract superclasses to create and delete complete instances. Relational::Trigger is a concrete class; its Create and Delete procedures are examined next.

The Create procedure calls the Add procedures for all of the class's supertypes in the top-down order required for instance creation described in Figure 8.17. Because the @_ID parameter is labeled for output, its value before the call to Add_Core_Element is null. This procedure returns the identity value in its @_ID parameter that will be assigned to each anchor table in the hierarchy by the subsequent Add procedure that calls for the intermediate superclasses. The final call to Add_Relational_Trigger actually creates the row in the Relational_Trigger table that represents the new Relational::Trigger instance.

```
CREATE PROCEDURE Create_Relational_Trigger
    @_ID INT OUTPUT
```

```
AS
    DECLARE @Error INT
    BEGIN TRANSACTION Create_Relational_Trigger
    SELECT @Error = @@Error
    IF @Error = 0
        EXECUTE @Error = Add_Relational_Trigger @_ID OUTPUT
    IF @Error = 0
    BEGIN
        UPDATE Core_Element
            SET _Kind_ID = 85
            WHERE _ID = @_ID
        SELECT @Error = @@Error
    END
    IF @Error = 0
        COMMIT TRANSACTION Create_Relational_Trigger
    ELSE
        ROLLBACK TRANSACTION
    IF @@Error <> 0
        SELECT @Error = @@Error
    RETURN @Error
GO
```

The Delete procedure is the inverse operation of the Create procedure. It simply calls the Drop procedure for the type. The Drop procedure recursively calls the Drop procedures for each superclass in the inverse order of the Add procedures, again as shown in Figure 8.17.

```
CREATE PROCEDURE Delete_Relational_Trigger
    @_ID INT
AS
    DECLARE @Error INT
    IF @Error = 0
        EXECUTE @Error = Drop_Relational_Trigger @_ID
    RETURN @Error
GO
```

There are other ways that inheritance could have been implemented. For example, inherited attributes could have been mapped directly into the rows of the anchor table. This technique would have resulted in a single table for each class and would have made for simpler reconstruction of instances. However, the trade-off is that these other architectures do not easily allow instances to change the roles (i.e., sub-classes) in which they participate. This ability, sometimes called "metamorphosis," makes it possible to, for example, change a relational table instance into a record definition instance without having to create a new instance; the relevant portion of CWM's generalization hierarchy is shown in Figure 8.19.

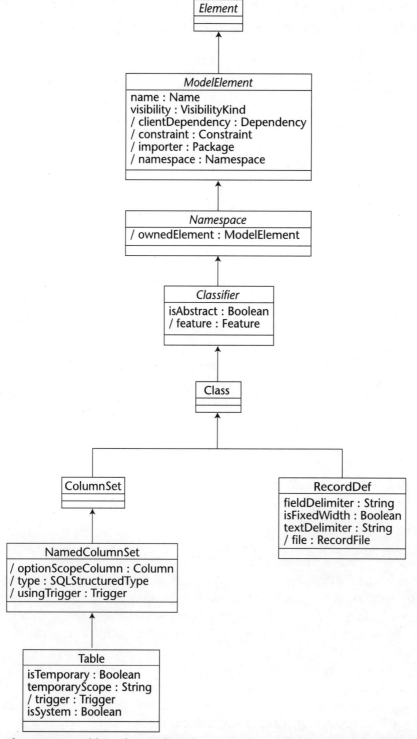

Figure 8.19 Table and RecordDef share a portion of the generalization hierarchy.

Metamorphosis is possible because each level in the generalization hierarchy has its own anchor table. If there were only a single row per instance, one would have to create the new instance, copy shared attribute values to the new instance (in our table to record example, three attribute values would be moved: name, visibility, and isAbstract), and delete the old instance. Although the shared attributes of the new instance would have the same values as they did in the old instance, the new instance has a different identity value. A side effect of this change in identity means that all of the association links in which the old instance participated would have to be found and changed to link to the new instance. The overhead and complexity of this search can be significant, so it was avoided in the Metastore by choosing to use separate tables for each level in the hierarchy. Although the multiple table design adds some overhead to the SELECT statements in the Get procedures, on the whole, the Metastore emphasizes flexibility over retrieval speed where both cannot be achieved simultaneously.

To wrap up this discussion of the implementation of inheritance, let's sum up everything we've said so far by taking a look at a fairly complete example. The example illustrates the complete contents of the Metastore for a simple relational table. The relevant portion of the CWM generalization hierarchy is shown in Figure 8.20 and contains sufficient classes and associations to accomplish the following tasks:

- Create a SQL data type.
- Create a column, assigning the SQL data type as the column's data type.
- Create an expression that defines the default value for the column.
- Create a table.
- Add the column to the table.

Our example places the definition of a simple table, named Person, into the Metastore. The Person table has one column called Name that is a VARCHAR column with a maximum length of 35 characters. The default value for the column is 'Doe, John'. The following T-SQL script might be used to create the example table in an application's SQL Server database (that is, not in the Metastore database).

```
CREATE TABLE Person
    (Name VARCHAR(35) DEFAULT 'Doe, John')
GO
```

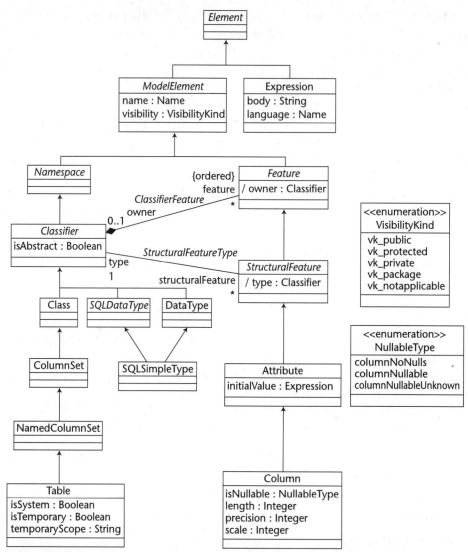

Figure 8.20 Relational table, column, and data type generalization hierarchy.

The following T-SQL script creates the necessary meta data entities in the Metastore and populates it with the definition of the Person table. Figure 8.21 shows what the contents of the relevant Metastore tables will look like after the script has completed successfully. Attribute values that are not explicitly set by the script but have values in their columns in the Metastore were set because they are the default values for those columns. The arrows in the figure mimic the inheritance hierarchy of Figure 8.20 that is implemented by the Metastore tables.

```
DECLARE @result INT
DECLARE @typeID INT
DECLARE @exprID INT
DECLARE @colID INT
DECLARE @tblID INT
BEGIN TRANSACTION Load_Person
SELECT @result = @@Error
/* Step 1: Create the VARCHAR data type and set its name attribute */
IF @result = 0
   EXECUTE @result = Create_Relational_SQLSimpleType @typeID OUTPUT
IF @result = 0
   EXECUTE @result = Set_Relational_SQLSimpleType_name @typeID,
'VARCHAR'
/* Step 2: Create the Name column and assign its attributes */
IF @result = 0
   EXECUTE @result = Create_Relational_Column @colID OUTPUT
IF @result = 0
   EXECUTE @result = Set_Relational_Column_name @colID, 'Name'
IF @result = 0
   EXECUTE @result = Set_Relational_Column_length @colID, 35
/* Step 3: Set the expression attributes for the column's initial value
*/
IF @result = 0
   EXECUTE @result = Get_Relational_Column_initialValue @colID,
      @exprID OUTPUT
IF @result = 0
   EXECUTE @result = Set_Core_Expression_body @exprID, 'Doe, John'
IF @result = 0
   EXECUTE @result = Set_Core_Expression_language @exprID, 'English'
/* Step 4: Associate the column with the data type */
IF @result = 0
   EXECUTE @result = Create_Core_StructuralFeatureType @colID, @typeID
/* Step 5: Create the Person table */
IF @result = 0
   EXECUTE @result = Create_Relational_Table @tblID OUTPUT
IF @result = 0
   EXECUTE @result = Set_Relational_Table_name @tblID, 'Person'
/* Step 6: Add the column to the table */
IF @result = 0
   EXECUTE @result = Create_Core_ClassifierFeature @tblID, @colID
IF @result = 0
   COMMIT TRANSACTION Load_Person
ELSE
   ROLLBACK TRANSACTION
GO
```

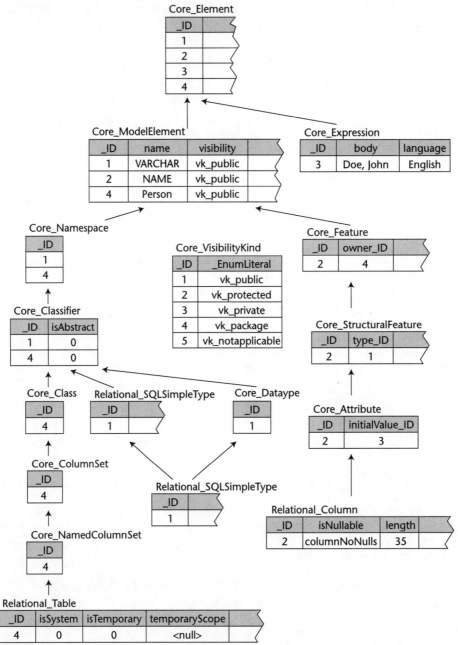

Figure 8.21 Contents of the Metastore after completion of the Load_Person T-SQL script.

The script, in Step 1, creates the SQLSimpleType instance for the column's data type and stores its identity value in @typeID. The call to Set_Relational_SQLSimpleType_name sets the name property of the @typeID instance to 'VARCHAR'. Because name is an attribute that a SQLSimpleType inherits from ModelElement, this call is really just a wrapper procedure that does nothing other than pass the call along to the Set_Core_ModelElement_name procedure to actually change the value stored in the name column of Core_ModelElement row with _ID = @typeID. For more details on wrapper procedures, see the sidebar *Accessing Inherited Attributes*.

In Step 2, the script creates the Column instance, assigns 'Name' to its inherited name attribute, and sets its length attribute to the value 35.

Step 3 sets the value of the Expression attributes for the initialValue attribute that the column inherits from Core::Attribute class definition. Recall that initialValue has a class-based data type and that the corresponding instance of Expression that holds the initialValue was automatically created by the Create_Relational_Column procedure. All we need to do here is retrieve the identity of the Expression instance from the initialValue_ID column of the Core_Attribute table into @exprID and use it to set Expression attributes as needed.

A link is created between the column instance (in @colID) and its data type instance (in @typeID) in Step 4 by the call to Create_Core_StructuralFeatureType. This call inserts a link into the StructuralFeatureType association between Core::StructuralFeature and Core::Classifier (how this stored procedure works is examined in a later section).

Step 5 creates the Relational::Table instance representing the Person table and sets its inherited name attribute to the string 'Person'.

Finally, Step 6 completes the process by creating a link in the Core::ClassifierFeature association by calling its Create procedure. This link represents the fact that the Person table has a column called Name.

Association Mapping Patterns

Associations are a UML device for representing relationships between instances of classes. We saw, in Figure 8.2, how associations are represented in UML class diagrams as lines connecting classes. One convenient way to think about associations is as classes that store information about relationships between other classes. Although some may contend that this way of thinking about associations is not semantically correct in every UML context, it works well enough for the purposes of the Metastore, and we will use it extensively here.

An important side effect of thinking about associations as a kind of class is that associations become, in a sense, independent entities within a CWM (we say that they are *first-class objects*). Although they cannot exist without the classes they connect, association links (that is, the instances of the association) can be manipulated independently of class instances, and the association itself can be queried independently of the connected classes. Also, like classes, associations are owned by CWM packages, but this does not limit them to connecting classes in the same package. Rather, associations may span package boundaries, connecting classes in separate packages. There are MOF rules (the details of which are beyond the scope of this chapter) that make this independent nature of associations necessary for accessing certain relationships that cross boundaries between packages residing in different MOF repositories. Fortunately for us, the Metastore does not have this problem directly because all of its instances reside within a single MOF repository (that is, the Metastore itself *is* a single MOF repository). However, it does have an impact on how CWM references were designed; these will be discussed in the *Reference Mapping Patterns* section of this chapter.

A simple-minded implementation of associations would leverage their classlike nature and map them into a table with two columns—one for each of the identity values of the related class instances. Each row in such a table represents one *link*—that is, a relationship between a specific instance of one of the connected classes and another specific instance of the other connected class. If one end of the association is ordered, a third column would need to be added for storing a value that preserves the ordering of links for that end. The ends of an association cannot both be ordered, so we won't ever need a second ordering column.

The simple-minded association table described so far would be able to hold the links for a single association. A further enhancement might be to add another column to contain the identity of the association to which a link refers; this column could contain, for example, the name of the association (although this might not be the most efficient thing to do). Finally, we might add a fifth column containing an identity value so that there would never be any confusion about which link was which.

Figure 8.22 contains a graphical representation of our simple-minded association table. The figure also shows how a set of instances would be stored in the association table for each of the three multiplicity patterns in which an association might exist. These multiplicity patterns are really just the well-known binary relationship types that have been discussed in nearly every database management textbook written in the last thirty or so years: one-to-one (1:1), one-to-many (1:N), and many-to-many (M:N). As noted earlier, you may also recognize these concepts by the name *cardinality*. In the first row of the table, the _Ordinal column is marked <null> because the notion of ordering links makes no sense for 1:1 associations.

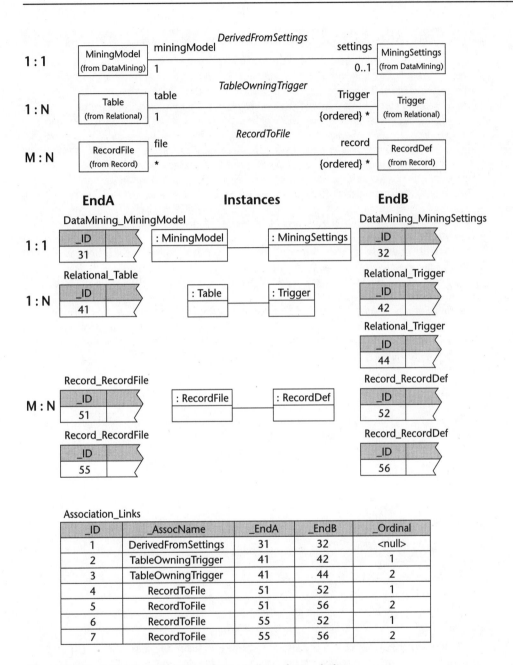

Figure 8.22 A simple-minded Implementation of associations.

ACCESSING INHERITED ATTRIBUTES

Perhaps the most frequently used attribute in CWM is the name attribute that nearly every CWM instance inherits from Core::ModelElement. Consequently, a convenient way to access inherited attributes is an important part of the Metastore. Although the Metastore could have insisted that users access the name attribute at the inheritance hierarchy level where it is declared, it seems much more direct and less confusing to simply call each class to access its inherited attributes AS IF they were immediate attributes. This is done in the Metastore by providing wrapper classes that simply pass along the call to the appropriate superclass in the hierarchy. For example, the intent of a user wanting to display the name of a Relational:: SQLSimpleType instance is much more clearly expressed by a call to Get_Relational_ SQLSimpleType_name than it would be by a call to Get_Relational_ModelElement_ name, even though ModelElement has the desired immediate attribute called name and SQLSimpleType does not.

Get and Set wrapper procedures are available for every inherited attribute at each level in the generalization hierarchy. These wrappers pass their requests directly on to the instance at the level where the attribute is defined; intermediate superclasses do not need to be involved and are bypassed. For example, the definitions of the Get and Set procedures for our SQLSimpleType example pass their request directly to Core::ModelElement and bypass the intermediate superclasses Core::Datatype, Core::Classifier, and Core::Namespace. The SQLSimpleType wrapper procedures are defined as follows:

```
CREATE PROCEDURE Get_Relational_SQLSimpleType_name
    @_ID INT
   ,@_Value VARCHAR(256) OUTPUT
AS
   DECLARE @Error INT
   EXECUTE @Error = Get_Core_ModelElement_name @_ID, @_Value OUTPUT
   RETURN @Error
GO


CREATE PROCEDURE Set_Relational_SQLSimpleType_name
    @_ID INT
   ,@_Value VARCHAR(256)
AS
   DECLARE @Error INT
   EXECUTE @Error = Set_Core_ModelElement_name @_ID, @_Value
   RETURN @Error
GO
```

Any of the following wrapper procedures would return the name of a SQLSimpleType instance. Each, except the last, passes its call to Get_Core_ ModelElement_name.

```
Get_Relational_SQLSimpleType_name
Get_Core_Datatype_name
Get_Core_Classifier_name
Get_Core_Namespace_name
Get_Core_ModelElement_name
```

Our simple-minded association table will work perfectly for all three multiplicity patterns. In fact, this is exactly the sort of structure we *must* use for M:N associations (at least when implementing them in a relational database). However, experience will quickly show that our table deserves the moniker "simple-minded" when it comes to 1:1 and 1:N associations. For these multiplicity patterns, our table introduces substantial overhead that can be avoided by selecting other implementation architectures. Fortunately, we can do much better from a performance perspective with these other techniques (Guck, 1988; Jagannathan, 1988). So, the implementation of associations described in this section is organized around the multiplicity patterns of associations. We will use techniques that are appropriate to each multiplicity type individually. This adds some complexity to the implementation, but the rewards in performance will be found worthwhile.

The following sections describe how each multiplicity pattern is mapped into tables in the Metastore and provides examples of the stored procedures available for each pattern. In the Metastore, association links are not lumped together into a single table as the simple-minded association implementation suggests. Rather, each association is mapped onto one (or more) tables. Sometimes these tables are already in the Metastore for other reasons, and sometimes the tables are added specially to support associations. Using multiple tables for associations actually tends to improve search performance for retrievals from them because fewer rows—only those relevant to the current association—need to be searched. CWM has 154 associations.

One-to-One Association Pattern

One-to-one associations can be handled directly without having to introduce another table into the Metastore. This is done by simply adding a column to each class's anchor table. These columns hold the identity values of related instances of the other connected class. Foreign key constraints are added to these columns to ensure that one end of the association link is not inadvertently deleted in an inconsistent manner. Placing columns in both connected tables allows the association link to be traversed in either direction with equal ease. The implementation of 1:1 associations is shown in Figure 8.23.

The figure shows the DerivedFromSettings 1:1 association from CWM's DataMining package. To understand how the association columns are added to the MiningModel and MiningSetting anchor tables, we need to start with the T-SQL for creating the tables themselves, which follows:

```
CREATE TABLE DataMining_MiningModel
    (_ID INT NOT NULL UNIQUE FOREIGN KEY REFERENCES Core_Element (_ID)
    ,function VARCHAR(256) NOT NULL
```

```
    ,algorithm VARCHAR(256) NOT NULL
    )
GO

CREATE TABLE DataMining_MiningSettings
    (_ID INT NOT NULL UNIQUE FOREIGN KEY REFERENCES Core_Element (_ID)
    ,function VARCHAR(256) NOT NULL
    ,algorithm VARCHAR(256) NOT NULL
    )
GO
```

As originally defined, anchor tables are created without the association columns in place. They are added at a later phase in the Metastore creation process. There is no CWM logical reason for doing things in this manner, but rather it makes for an easier implementation by avoiding a technical problem known as a *forward-reference*, that is, referring to something before it has been defined.

The following ALTER TABLE statements add the association columns:

```
ALTER TABLE DataMining_MiningSettings ADD miningModel_ID INT
ALTER TABLE DataMining_MiningSettings ADD
      FOREIGN KEY (miningModel_ID) REFERENCES
         DataMining_MiningModel(_ID)
ALTER TABLE DataMining_MiningModel ADD settings_ID INT
ALTER TABLE DataMining_MiningModel ALTER COLUMN settings_ID INT NOT NULL
ALTER TABLE DataMining_MiningModel ADD
      FOREIGN KEY (settings_ID) REFERENCES
         DataMining_MiningSettings(_ID)
GO
```

The settings_ID column has an additional ALTER TABLE statement to add the NOT NULL property because MiningSettings are required to have an association link to a MiningModel. No such constraint is defined for the MiningModel association end so a NOT NULL constraint is not needed because is NULL is the T-SQL default.

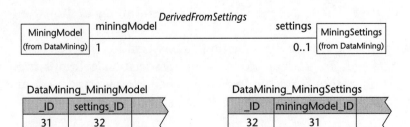

Figure 8.23   1:1 association mapping.

As hinted in the introduction to this section, ordering of 1:1 associations is not a meaningful concept so we need do nothing to provide for it in the Metastore.

A Get procedure is provided for each end of the association. Given the identity value of the instance on one end of an association, the identity value of the connected instance on the opposite end of the association is returned. One-to-one associations do not have GetAll or GetCursor procedures.

```
CREATE PROCEDURE Get_DataMining_DerivedFromSettings_miningModel
    @settings_ID INT
    ,@miningModel_ID INT OUTPUT
AS
    SELECT @miningModel_ID  = _ID
       FROM DataMining_MiningModel
       WHERE settings_ID = @settings_ID
    RETURN @@Error
GO


CREATE PROCEDURE Get_DataMining_DerivedFromSettings_settings
    @miningModel_ID INT
    ,@settings_ID INT OUTPUT
AS
    SELECT @settings_ID  = _ID
       FROM DataMining_MiningSettings
       WHERE miningModel_ID = @miningModel_ID
    RETURN @@Error
GO
```

To understand how to use these procedures, imagine you are standing on the MiningModel class box in Figure 8.23 and looking along the association line to the MiningSettings box at the other end of the association. The Get_DataMining_DerivedFromSettings_settings procedure, then, is a kind of telescope that lets you see along the association line to view the _ID value of the MiningSettings instance on the other side of the association. This imagery is shown in Figure 8.24. The telescopes on both ends of the association are the same—they both see a single identity value. Another useful way to think about this situation is to treat the settings end of the association as if it were an attribute of the MiningModel class, and the MiningModel end as if it were an attribute of the MiningSettings class.

Each association also has a Create and a Delete procedure. The procedures add a new link to, and delete an existing link from, the association, respectively. For both procedures, the identity values of the class instances on the ends must be provided via the appropriately named parameter.

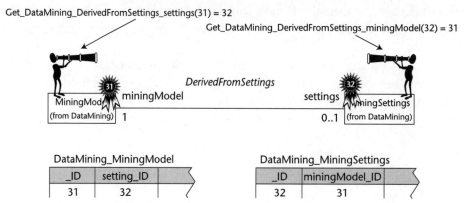

Figure 8.24   The telescope analogy for the Get procedure.

```
CREATE PROCEDURE Create_DataMining_DerivedFromSettings
    @miningModel_ID INT
   ,@settings_ID INT
AS
   DECLARE @Error INT
   IF @Error = 0
   BEGIN
      BEGIN TRANSACTION Create_DataMining_D_54F302E43EB3
      SELECT @Error = @@Error
      IF @Error = 0
      BEGIN
         UPDATE DataMining_MiningModel
            SET settings_ID = @settings_ID
         SELECT @Error = @@Error
      END
      IF @Error = 0
      BEGIN
         UPDATE DataMining_MiningSettings
            SET miningModel_ID = @miningModel_ID
         SELECT @Error = @@Error
      END
      IF @Error = 0
         COMMIT TRANSACTION Create_DataMining_D_54F302E43EB3
      ELSE
         ROLLBACK TRANSACTION
      IF @@Error <> 0
         SELECT @Error = @@Error
   END
   RETURN @Error
GO

CREATE PROCEDURE Delete_DataMining_DerivedFromSettings
```

```
    @miningModel_ID INT
    ,@settings_ID INT
AS
    DECLARE @Error INT
    IF @Error = 0
    BEGIN
        BEGIN TRANSACTION Delete_DataMining_D_8586CDCF1E9C
        SELECT @Error = @@Error
        IF @Error = 0
        BEGIN
            UPDATE DataMining_MiningModel SET settings_ID = Null
                WHERE _ID = @miningModel_ID
            SELECT @Error = @@Error
        END
        IF @Error = 0
        BEGIN
            UPDATE DataMining_MiningSettings SET miningModel_ID = Null
                WHERE _ID = @settings_ID
            SELECT @Error = @@Error
        END
        IF @Error = 0
            COMMIT TRANSACTION Delete_DataMining_D_8586CDCF1E9C
        ELSE
            ROLLBACK TRANSACTION
        IF @@Error <> 0
            SELECT @Error = @@Error
    END
    RETURN @Error
GO
```

CWM has five 1:1 associations. Although reflexive associations (those that link different instances of the same class) are valid for 1:1 associations, CWM has none.

One-to-Many Association Pattern

The one-to-many association pattern requires changes only to the anchor table on the *many-end* of the association; no changes are needed to the anchor table on the *one-end*. The many-end is the end that has a multiplicity upper bound greater than one. In the mapping of 1:N associations into the Metastore summarized in Figure 8.25, the trigger end is the many-end because it has an unlimited multiplicity upper bound. The asterisk on the trigger end is a multiplicity shorthand for 0..*, meaning the end may have zero or more instances. Likewise, the 1 on the table end is a shorthand for 1..1.

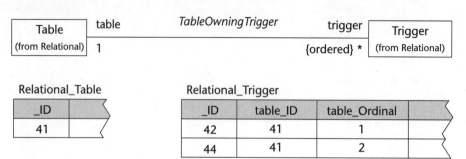

Figure 8.25   1:N association mapping.

A column is added to the anchor table on the many-end of the association to hold the identity value of an instance in the one-end. The column name is constructed by concatenating the name of the one-end (the table end, in the figure) with the _ID suffix. For each instance on the many-side of the association, its anchor table row holds the identity value of the related instance on the one-side.

If the many-end of the association is ordered, an additional column is added to the many-end anchor table to hold the ordinal value used to preserve the ordering of many-end instances. Its name is composed from the name of the many-end and the _Ordinal suffix. The _Ordinal column is optional and is only present if the corresponding many-end is ordered. It contains an integer value that is used to record the insertion order of the multiple many-end instances corresponding to the one-end instance. Specific values in the _Ordinal column are not visible to clients via the Metastore procedure interfaces. The creation statements for these tables show how these infrastructural columns are created.

```
CREATE TABLE Relational_Table
    (_ID INT NOT NULL UNIQUE FOREIGN KEY REFERENCES Core_Element (_ID)
    ,isTemporary BIT NOT NULL
    ,temporaryScope VARCHAR(256)
    ,isSystem BIT NOT NULL
    )
GO

CREATE TABLE Relational_Trigger
    (_ID INT NOT NULL UNIQUE FOREIGN KEY REFERENCES Core_Element (_ID)
    ,eventManipulation VARCHAR(128) NOT NULL
    ,actionCondition_ID INT NOT NULL FOREIGN KEY REFERENCES
        Core_BooleanExpression(_ID)
    ,actionStatement_ID INT NOT NULL FOREIGN KEY REFERENCES
        Core_ProcedureExpression(_ID)
```

```
    ,actionOrientation VARCHAR(128) NOT NULL
    ,conditionTiming VARCHAR(128) NOT NULL
    ,conditionReferenceNewTable VARCHAR(256) NOT NULL
    ,conditionReferenceOldTable VARCHAR(256) NOT NULL
    )
GO


ALTER TABLE Relational_Trigger ADD table_ID INT
ALTER TABLE Relational_Trigger ADD
      FOREIGN KEY (table_ID) REFERENCES Relational_Table(_ID)
ALTER TABLE Relational_Trigger ADD trigger_Ordinal INT
GO
```

As with 1:1 associations, a Get procedure is available for each end of a
1:N association. The definition of these association procedures follows:

```
CREATE PROCEDURE Get_Relational_TableOwningTrigger_table
    @trigger_ID INT
    ,@table_ID INT OUTPUT
AS
    SELECT @table_ID = table_ID
       FROM Relational_Trigger
       WHERE _ID = @trigger_ID
    RETURN @@Error
GO


CREATE PROCEDURE Get_Relational_TableOwningTrigger_trigger
    @table_ID INT
AS
    SELECT _ID
       FROM Relational_Trigger
       WHERE table_ID = @table_ID
       ORDER BY trigger_Ordinal
    RETURN @@Error
GO
```

There are a couple of noticeable differences from the 1:1 associations.
One thing to notice is that both Get procedures reference only the many-
side anchor table—the association is implemented completely without reference to the one-side anchor table. The second thing to notice is that the
many-end Get procedure, Get_Relational_TableOwningTrigger_trigger,
returns a set of identity values rather than a single value. If the association
end is ordered, the identity values returned in the set are ordered as specified by the table_Ordinal column; otherwise, the order of the identity values
is not defined. Elsewhere in this chapter, a list of identity values, like that
returned by the many-end Get procedure, is sometimes called a *reference set*
or a *result set*. When ordered, the word *list* is probably more accurate than
set because sets are unordered by definition.

Since it returns a set of identity values, the many-side of a 1:N association also has a GetCursor procedure. The GetCursor for the many-side of our example association is as follows:

```
CREATE PROCEDURE GetCursor_Relational_TableOwningTrigger_trigger
    @table_ID INT
    ,@_Cursor CURSOR VARYING OUTPUT
AS
    DECLARE @Error INT
    SET @_Cursor = CURSOR FORWARD_ONLY STATIC FOR
        SELECT _ID
            FROM Relational_Trigger
            WHERE table_ID = @table_ID
            ORDER BY trigger_Ordinal
    SELECT @Error = @@Error
    IF @Error = 0
    BEGIN
        OPEN @_Cursor
        SELECT @Error = @@Error
    END
    RETURN @Error
GO
```

Figure 8.26 adapts our telescope analogy to 1:N associations. However, this time the telescopes are not exactly alike. The one-side telescope, standing on the Table class, now sees a set (or possibly, a list) of identity values while the many-side telescopes, on the Trigger class, still see only a single identity value.

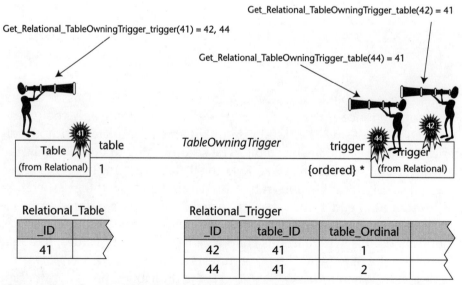

Figure 8.26 The telescope analogy for 1:M associations.

The Create procedure demonstrates how the _Ordinal column values are assigned. The _Ordinal value for a new link is determined by adding 1 to the maximum of the current _Ordinal column values for the one-side instance. This technique ensures that insertion order is preserved and has the useful property that both it and the ordering algorithm are insensitive to the deletion of rows with _Ordinal column values in the middle of the sequence. You can observe this in the Delete procedure by noticing the *absence* of any code to reassign values in the _Ordinal column.

```
CREATE PROCEDURE Create_Relational_TableOwningTrigger
    @table_ID INT
   ,@trigger_ID INT
AS
   DECLARE @Error INT
   DECLARE @MaxOrdinal INT
   SELECT @MaxOrdinal = MAX(trigger_Ordinal)
      FROM Relational_Trigger
      WHERE table_ID = @table_ID
   SELECT @Error = @@Error
   IF @Error = 0
   BEGIN
      UPDATE Relational_Trigger
         SET table_ID = @table_ID
            ,trigger_Ordinal = @MaxOrdinal + 1
         WHERE _ID = @trigger_ID
      SELECT @Error = @@Error
   END
   RETURN @Error
GO


CREATE PROCEDURE Delete_Relational_TableOwningTrigger
    @table_ID INT
   ,@trigger_ID INT
AS
   DECLARE @Error INT
   UPDATE Relational_Trigger
      SET table_ID = Null,
          trigger_Ordinal = Null
      WHERE table_ID = @table_ID
        AND _ID = @trigger_ID
   SELECT @Error = @@Error
   RETURN @Error
GO
```

There are 101 one-to-many associations in CWM. Fourteen of them are ordered, and two are reflexive. No associations are both ordered and reflexive.

Many-to-Many Association Pattern

Many-to-many associations are mapped onto intersection tables, much like the simple-minded association described in the introduction to this section. However, since each association is mapped to a separate table, there is no need to include the association name column, nor is a separate identity value column needed, in an M:N association table.

Our example for M:N association mapping uses the RecordToFile association from CWM's Record package as shown in Figure 8.27. One end of the association is ordered, so features to support ordering appear in the figure as well. Since ordering is optional, only M:N associations with an ordered end will have these features.

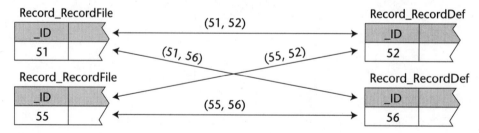

Record_RecordToFile		
file_ID	record_ID	record_Ordinal
51	52	1
51	56	2
55	52	1
55	56	2

Figure 8.27   M:N association mapping.

M:N associations are implemented without altering the anchor tables on either end. Association links are stored as rows in the association's table, which is created with the following T-SQL statement. The record_Ordinal column exists because the record end of the association is ordered. It contains integer ordinal values used to preserve the insertion order of Record-Def instances for a given RecordFile instance. _Ordinal columns in M:N tables are managed in a manner similar to the _Ordinal columns of 1:N associations as described above.

```
CREATE TABLE Record_RecordToFile
    (file_ID INT NOT NULL FOREIGN KEY REFERENCES Record_RecordFile(_ID)
    ,record_ID INT NOT NULL FOREIGN KEY REFERENCES Record_RecordDef(_ID)
    ,record_Ordinal INT
    )
GO
```

The Get procedures for both ends of an M:N association return sets of identity values as T-SQL cursor objects. These procedures also demonstrate the highly symmetrical nature of M:N associations. The only difference between them is the ORDER BY clause in Get_Record_RecordTo-File_record that sorts record instances by their record_Ordinal column values. Because both ends of the association return result sets, there are two GetCursor procedures as well.

```
CREATE PROCEDURE Get_Record_RecordToFile_file
    @record_ID INT
AS
    SELECT file_ID
        FROM Record_RecordToFile
        WHERE record_ID = @record_ID
    RETURN @@Error
GO


CREATE PROCEDURE GetCursor_Record_RecordToFile_file
    @record_ID INT
    ,@_Cursor CURSOR VARYING OUTPUT
AS
    DECLARE @Error INT
    SET @_Cursor = CURSOR FORWARD_ONLY STATIC FOR
        SELECT file_ID
            FROM Record_RecordToFile
            WHERE record_ID = @record_ID
    SELECT @Error = @@Error
    IF @Error = 0
```

```
       BEGIN
           OPEN @_Cursor
           SELECT @Error = @@Error
       END
       RETURN @Error
   GO


   CREATE PROCEDURE Get_Record_RecordToFile_record
       @file_ID INT
   AS
       SELECT record_ID
           FROM Record_RecordToFile
           WHERE file_ID = @file_ID
           ORDER BY record_Ordinal
       RETURN @@Error
   GO


   CREATE PROCEDURE GetCursor_Record_RecordToFile_record
       @file_ID INT
       ,@_Cursor CURSOR VARYING OUTPUT
   AS
       DECLARE @Error INT
       SET @_Cursor = CURSOR FORWARD_ONLY STATIC FOR
           SELECT record_ID
               FROM Record_RecordToFile
               WHERE file_ID = @file_ID
               ORDER BY record_Ordinal
       SELECT @Error = @@Error
       IF @Error = 0
       BEGIN
           OPEN @_Cursor
           SELECT @Error = @@Error
       END
       RETURN @Error
   GO
```

The symmetry of M:N associations also returns balance to their tele-scope diagram, but this time, each telescope sees a list of identity values (Figure 8.28).

Like their Get procedures, the Create and Delete procedures for M:N associations operate only on the association table; the class anchor tables on either end are unaffected by operations on the connecting association. The Create procedure generates a new _Ordinal value using the same technique described for 1:N associations. Also, multiplicity lower bounds greater than zero are interpreted for M:N associations as referring to the count of rows in the association table and have nothing to do with NOT NULL constraints as was the case for 1:1 associations.

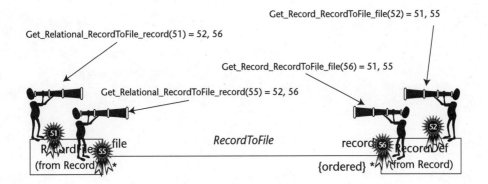

Record_RecordToFile Links

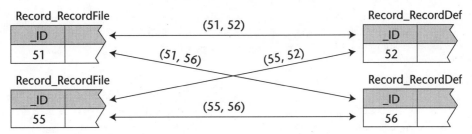

Figure 8.28 The M:N telescopes are symmetrical and see only lists.

Record_RecordToFile

file_ID	record_ID	record_Ordinal
51	52	1
51	56	2
55	52	1
55	56	2

```
CREATE PROCEDURE Create_Record_RecordToFile
    @file_ID INT
    ,@record_ID INT
AS
    DECLARE @Error INT
    DECLARE @MaxOrdinal INT
    SELECT @MaxOrdinal = MAX(record_Ordinal)
        FROM Record_RecordToFile
```

```
            WHERE record_ID = @record_ID
      SELECT @Error = @@Error
      IF @Error = 0
      BEGIN
         INSERT Record_RecordToFile (file_ID, record_ID, record_Ordinal)
            VALUES (@file_ID, @record_ID, @MaxOrdinal + 1)
         SELECT @Error = @@Error
      END
      RETURN @Error
   GO


   CREATE PROCEDURE Delete_Record_RecordToFile
       @file_ID INT
      ,@record_ID INT
   AS
      DECLARE @Error INT
      DELETE FROM Record_RecordToFile
         WHERE file_ID = @file_ID
           AND record_ID = @record_ID
      SELECT @Error = @@Error
      RETURN @Error
   GO
```

There are a couple of situations in CWM where naming conflicts occur when a class is owned by two different 1:N composite, ordered associations using the same end names[3]. In this situation, both associations cause a column to be added to the class's anchor table to hold the _Ordinal value. If both associations have the same end name, the added _Ordinal columns will have the same names as well, which is not allowed. The situation is resolved by promoting the mapping type of the second (and subsequent) association from 1:N to M:N. In CWM, the Behaviorial::EventParameter and OLAP::ValuedBasedHierarchyOwnsDimensionDeployments association are promoted to M:N to avoid such naming conflicts.

CWM has 48 M:N associations. Eleven of them have an ordered end, and ten are reflexive. No CWM association is both ordered and reflexive.

Using Association Patterns

Developing an understanding of several interesting association usage patterns in CWM will help improve your understanding of both the Metastore and its foundation technologies—UML and MOF. The association usage examples considered in this section will help you understand how associations are used by CWM, how they are mapped to relational tables in the

---

[3] Of course, a single instance of the class cannot be simultaneously owned via both associations because this would violate the semantics of composite associations.

Metastore, and how to interpret the meaning of some of the more interesting association usage patterns in CWM.

As with many things in life, CWM's greatest strength is also perhaps its greatest weakness. The choice to base CWM on UML and MOF provides great expressive power to the meta-modeler and is a foundation upon which robust software tools that use CWM for data warehousing meta data interchange can be built. However, power and expressiveness often come at a cost: increased complexity. Increased complexity is not in itself bad, especially considering the considerable benefits it brings to CWM. However, some users may find that these complexities occasionally get in the way of what seemingly ought to be straightforward tasks. This may be especially true of users who only need to do simple tasks, like exchanging a relational database schema. Although the CWM design team reduced complexity of the model wherever it could, some complexities simply had to stay so that CWM's other goals of power and expressiveness could be achieved. There are always compromises.

The purpose of this section, then, is to explore some of the remaining complexities in CWM in an attempt to demystify them a little. You may find that you will benefit from the explanations here whether you have a simple task or are a builder of a complex, model-driven software utility.

Association Ends as Sets of Identity Values

As we've already seen, an association connects two classes in CWM and represents a relationship between instances of the connected classes. Each association has a name, and each of its ends is named as well. Links are instances of associations, and when mapped into the Metastore, each link is represented as a pair of identity values, one from each of the connected classes. The Metastore takes advantage of association end names as vehicles for expressing queries about their association. The correct way to think about these queries is to consider an association end as a function that, given a parameter, returns a set of identity values. The parameter is an identity value representing the instance of interest from the class on one end of the association, and the returned identity value set contains related identity values from the class on the other end of the association. The order in which identity values are returned by an association end is meaningful only if the end has been declared as ordered in the CWM specification.

Figure 8.29 shows how the Relational::TableOwningTrigger association is mapped into Metastore tables. The data in the tables corresponds to the instance diagrams on the left side of the figure. As explained above, the multiplicity of the association ends determines how the association is implemented in the Metastore. TableOwningTrigger is a 1:N association, with its trigger end being the *many*-end. Links for this type of association are mapped directly into rows of the anchor table representing the class on the many-end of the association by adding a foreign key column to contain the identity value of the instance on the one end. In Figure 8.29, the table_ID column of the Relational_Trigger table was added to hold the identity value of the corresponding row in the Relation_Table table. Because the trigger end of the association is declared as ordered, the table_Ordinal column was also added to hold the ordinal value that maintains the insertion order of the Trigger instances. As the table shows, the physical ordering of rows is not important even when the end is ordered. This insensitivity to row order is a feature of the relational model itself and is not special to the Metastore.

In the lower right corner of the figure, the functionlike expressions show how association ends can be viewed as sets of values. For example, the first expression,

```
trigger(132) = {475, 586, 798}
```

treats the trigger end of the association as a function that accepts a parameter (132) that is the identity value of an instance of the Table class. The function result is a set of three identity values, each of which corresponds to a row in the Relational_Trigger table that is related to the Relational_Table row with the identity value of 132. Because the trigger end of the TableOwningTrigger association is ordered, the set of identity values returned is sorted according to the contents of the ordinal value in the table_Ordinal column.

The Metastore takes advantage of this view of association ends as functions that implement the association. Each association end has a Get stored procedure in the Metastore that returns a set of identity values for related instances on the other end of the association. For the TableOwningTrigger association, these procedures, Get_Relational_TableOwningTrigger_table and Get_Relational_TableOwningTrigger_trigger, have been shown above in the section on the mapping of 1:N associations. The following T-SQL script illustrates the use of the GetCursor_Relational_TableOwningTrigger_trigger procedure to return sets of identity values, using the example data from Figure 8.29.

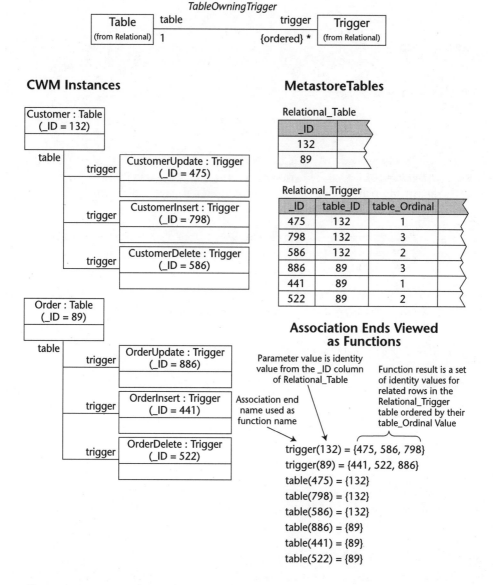

Figure 8.29 Association ends as sets of identity values.

```
DECLARE @result INT
DECLARE @tableID INT
DECLARE @triggerID INT
DECLARE @cursor CURSOR
DECLARE @name VARCHAR(255)
SET @tableID = 132
EXECUTE @result = GetCursor_Relational_TableOwningTrigger_trigger
    @tableID, @cursor OUTPUT
IF @result = 0
BEGIN
    EXECUTE @result = Get_Relational_Table_name @tableID, @name OUTPUT
    IF @result = 0
    BEGIN
        PRINT 'The class ' + @name + ' (_ID=' +
            CONVERT(VARCHAR, @tableID) + ') uses triggers:'
        FETCH NEXT FROM @cursor INTO @triggerID
        WHILE @@Fetch_Status = 0
        BEGIN
            EXECUTE @result = Get_Relational_Trigger_name @triggerID,
                @name OUTPUT
            IF @result = 0
                PRINT '      ' + @name + ' (_ID=' +
                    CONVERT(VARCHAR, @triggerID) + ')'
            FETCH NEXT FROM @cursor INTO @triggerID
        END
    END
END
CLOSE @cursor
DEALLOCATE @cursor
GO
```

The script produces the following output display:

```
The class Customer (_ID=132) uses triggers:
    CustomerUpdate (_ID=475)
    CustomerDelete (_ID=586)
    CustomerInsert (_ID=798)
```

Anchoring Services at ModelElement

For CWM, one of the chief attractions of UML is the multilevel inheritance hierarchy it provides. Multilevel abstraction in an inheritance hierarchy is attractive because, as one moves down the hierarchy, each level provides a more detailed and specific description of the reality being modeled. Designers and developers of model-based software tools leverage these multilevel abstractions to simplify their development processes and reduce the amount of work they must do. This is valuable for CWM and in the data warehousing domain because it makes it possible to build tools that can deal with highly heterogeneous data warehousing products and software environments with reasonable amounts of investment.

An important way that tool developers take advantage of the multilevel abstractions in an inheritance hierarchy is by anchoring associations, and thus the software services they represent, at relatively more abstract levels in the hierarchy (that is, anchoring associations to classes closer to the top of the hierarchy). By doing so, software services can be provided broadly within the resulting tool. An example of this is seen in the CWM's Core package (see Figure 8.30). Notice in the figure that associations from several other classes (Dependency, Constraint, Namespace, and Package) have one end anchored on the ModelElement class. Although not shown in the figure, two other CWM Core classes (Stereotype and TaggedValue) also have associations anchored on ModelElement. Each of these six classes provides some sort of general-purpose service within CWM: Dependency records dependencies between model elements, Constraints define rules on model elements, Namespaces define uniqueness of names, and Packages allow grouping of model elements. Because these classes are related to ModelElement by associations and because nearly every CWM class is a subclass of ModelElement,[4] nearly every instance in CWM has these services available to it.

Making general-purpose services available by anchoring associations on ModelElement is used even more widely within CWM. Six additional packages (BusinessInformation, Expressions, Transformation, InformationVisualization, BusinessNomenclature, and WarehouseOperations) also have associations directly attached to ModelElement, allowing their services to be generally available to every instance of any sub-class of ModelElement. In other words, these services are available to nearly every instance in a CWM respository.

Finding a Data Source

Anchoring associations on a common superclass is also used in situations that do not involve ModelElement. An important example of this is seen in the SoftwareDeployment package. The M:N DataManagerDataPackage association between SoftwareDeployment::DataManager and Core:: Package uses this modeling technique in a somewhat different way (see Figure 8.31).

---

[4] In fact, only eleven of CWM's 204 classes are not sub-classes of ModelElement: Element, Expression, ProcedureExpression, QueryExpression, Multiplicity, MultiplicityRange, ExpressionNode, FeatureNode, ConstantNode, ElementNode, and ModelElement itself. Except for ModelElement, all of these classes provide general-purpose services, and their instances do not have names.

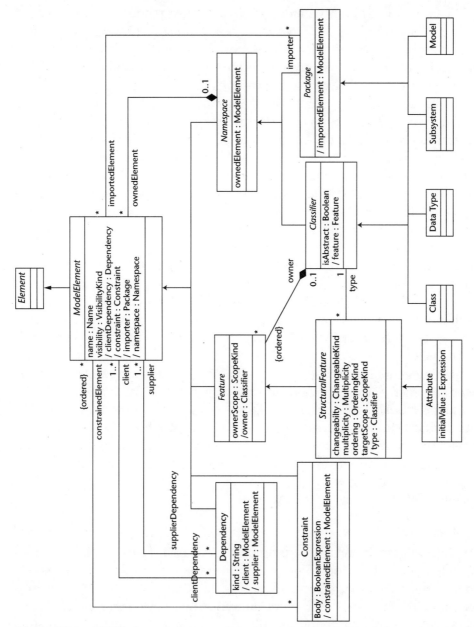

Figure 8.30 CWM's Core package anchors general-purpose associations close to the hierarchy's top.

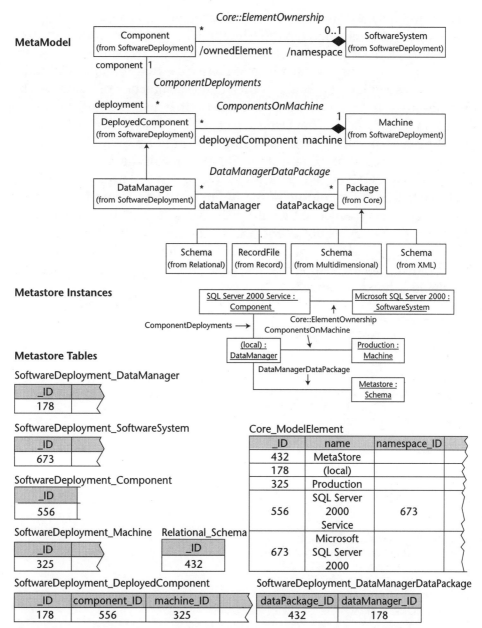

Figure 8.31 Locating a data source on a computer.

The DataManagerDataPackage association, which links the description of a data source (its *schema*) to the location on some computer where a physical instance of it resides, attaches to Package. By convention, every package in the Resource layer of CWM has a class that contains a logically complete description of a data resource that is a sub-class of Package. The four Resource layer sub-classes of Package that use this technique are shown in Figure 8.31. The DataManager class represents an installed instance of a data management software system like a relational database management system or a file system. For example, if the Metastore's relational schema itself is stored in the Metastore (this is certainly possible), the CWM instances in the middle of the figure would be found in the Metastore. These instances would result in the Metastore tables shown in the lower part of the figure (not every table or column value is depicted).

The following T-SQL script uses these classes and associations to display the location of the Metastore, assuming we already know that the identity value of its schema instance is 432:

```
DECLARE @result INT
DECLARE @schemaID INT
DECLARE @schemaName VARCHAR(255)
DECLARE @machineID INT
DECLARE @machineName VARCHAR(255)
DECLARE @dataManagerID INT
DECLARE @dataManagerName VARCHAR(255)
DECLARE @componentID INT
DECLARE @softwareSystemID INT
DECLARE @softwareSystemName VARCHAR(255)
DECLARE @cursor CURSOR
SET @schemaID = 432
EXECUTE @result = Get_Relational_Schema_name @schemaID, @schemaName
    OUTPUT
IF @result = 0
    EXECUTE @result =
        GetCursor_SoftwareDeployment_DataManagerDataPackage_dataManager
            @schemaID, @cursor OUTPUT
IF @result = 0
BEGIN
    FETCH NEXT FROM @cursor INTO @dataManagerID
    SELECT @result = @@Error
    IF @result = 0
        EXECUTE @result = Get_SoftwareDeployment_DataManager_name
            @dataManagerID, @dataManagerName OUTPUT
END
CLOSE @cursor
DEALLOCATE @cursor
IF @result = 0
    EXECUTE @result =
        Get_SoftwareDeployment_ComponentsOnMachine_machine
```

```
                    @dataManagerID, @machineID OUTPUT
   IF @result = 0
      EXECUTE @result = Get_SoftwareDeployment_Machine_name
         @machineID, @machineName OUTPUT
   IF @result = 0
      EXECUTE @result =
   Get_SoftwareDeployment_ComponentDeployments_component
         @dataManagerID, @componentID OUTPUT
   IF @result = 0
      EXECUTE @result = Get_Core_ElementOwnership_owner @componentID,
         @softwareSystemID OUTPUT
   IF @result = 0
      EXECUTE @result = Get_SoftwareDeployment_SoftwareSystem_name
         @softwareSystemID, @softwareSystemName OUTPUT
   IF @result = 0
      PRINT 'The ' + @schemaName + ' is located in the ' +
         @softwareSystemName + ' installation named ' + '''' +
         @dataManagerName + '''' + ' located on the ' + @machineName +
         ' server.'
   ELSE
   BEGIN
      EXECUTE [CWM 1.0_Error_Message] @result, @schemaName OUTPUT
      PRINT 'Error: ' + @schemaName
   END
   GO
```

Using the data in Figure 8.31, this example script produces the following displayed message:

```
The Metastore is located in the Microsoft SQL Server 2000 installation
named 'SQL Server 2000 Service' located on the Production server.
```

Reusing Inherited Associations

Another important advantage of anchoring associations near the top of the inheritance hierarchy is that these associations can be reused at lower levels in the metamodel. From the perspective of meta data tool developers, this is desirable because queries about the relationships represented by associations at higher levels in the hierarchy are simpler to formulate and produce a much greater coverage of instances in a single result set.

In CWM, there are three associations declared in the Core package that are reused heavily by other packages. These associations provide the general-purpose structuring capabilities of CWM that are reused by each of the Resource layer packages describing data sources and targets. The structure of this portion of CWM mimics equivalent structures in UML and MOF. An understanding of how these associations work in conjunction with the inheritance hierarchy is a key component of the knowledge that meta data tool vendors need to deploy successful CWM-based solutions.

Each of these associations will be examined in turn. Figure 8.32 depicts all three associations and the relevant parts of the CWM Core package's inheritance hierarchy. Because a central use of the associations is to enable CWM's aggregation and containment services, the chief clients of these services are shown in the figure as sub-classes of the Class and Attribute classes.

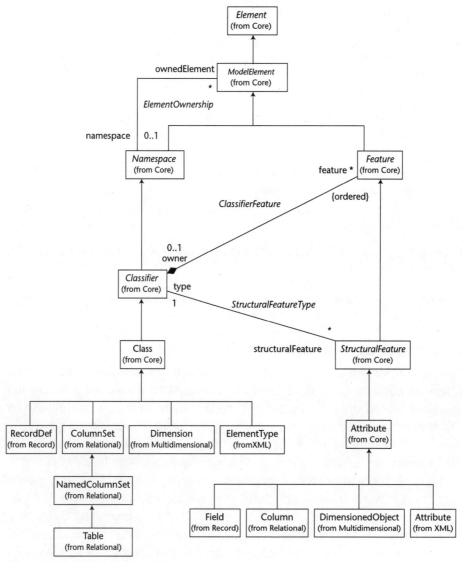

Figure 8.32   CWM's key associations.

The ClassifierFeature association connects a Classifier to the list of features that defines its structure. For a Table instance, this is the association that connects it to its Column instances. The same association is used to connect a Record::RecordDef instance to the Record::Field instances that define its structure, to connect an Olap::Dimension to its Olap::DimensionedObjects, and to connect an XML::ElementType to its attributes.

Notice that the association is a *composite* association, recognized by the filled-in diamond next to Classifier, meaning that Classifiers own the Features they are connected to via this association. The semantics of a composite relationship are such that when a Classifier instance (e.g., a Table) is deleted, all of the Features it owns (its Columns) are deleted as well. This sort of delete behavior will be familiar to relational database users under the name *cascade delete*. Cascade delete semantics are discussed later in this section.

At first glance, the *zero or one* multiplicity (0..1) of the ClassifierFeature association may seem to conflict with the notion of composite ownership which requires owned elements to have a single owner. How can a Table not own a Column? If the relational model does not allow unowned columns, why should CWM? Well, normally tables must, of course, own columns. Allowing a Feature like Column to have no owning Classifier was permitted to support a specific meta data discovery pattern in which Features might exist for a period of time without an owner. For example, meta data discovery tools, those that might load meta data into a CWM repository from external sources, might find it convenient to allow Features to exist unowned until some later point in the discovery process. This relaxed multiplicity was provided to support such usage.

The ordered constraint on the ownedElement end of this association is used to preserve the order of the Features owned by a Classifier instance. Although the order of columns in a relational table is, by definition, unimportant, maintaining the order of fields in a record is essential. As already described, the Metastore compromises these various ordering needs by maintaining the insertion order of instances for this association.

The second association, Core::StructuralFeatureType, identifies the data type of the StructuralFeature instances that are owned by Classifiers via the ClassifierFeature association. StructuralFeature is a sub-class of, and inherits the ClassifierFeature association from, the Feature class. As you can see in Figure 8.32, each of the data holder classes from the four Resource layer models are sub-classes of the Attribute class, which is itself a subclass of StructuralFeature. Instances of these classes (like Column) are owned by their corresponding aggregation classes (like Table) because they inherit the ClassifierFeature association from Feature and have a data type because they inherit the StructuralFeatureType association from StructuralFeature.

Data types are themselves instances of Classifier or one of its sub-classes, often Datatype. For example, the T-SQL integer data type, called INT in the code examples, would be placed into the Metastore by creating an instance of the class SQLSimpleType (itself a sub-class of Datatype and not shown in the figure) and setting its name attribute (that it inherits from ModelElement) to INT. Structured data types available in many programming languages (like COBOL 01 records, C structs, and PASCAL records) can be added by creating a Classifier instance for the type and associating it with the fields that make up its definition.

The ElementOwnership association indicates ownership relationships between any instance that belongs to the Namespace class or any of its many sub-classes and other instances of ModelElement. In principle, every ModelElement instance in a CWM repository, except the few that reside at the highest organizational levels (like Relational::Catalog instances), is owned by another instance that is a (sub-class of) Namespace. Although ElementOwnership has characteristics similar to ClassifierFeature, it differs in one important way—it does not maintain the order of its links. Consequently, ElementOwnership is used to capture general-purpose ownership relationships whereas ClassifierFeature captures the specific relationship between Classifiers and their features. Notice, also, that any Classifier instance can have features via the ClassifierFeature association and can own other instances via the ElementOwnership association.

Figure 8.33 shows what the contents of the Metastore might look like for a table in a relational database and for a fragment of an XML document. These tables exercise all three of the important associations. The ElementOwnership association is implemented by the namespace_ID column of the Core_ModelElement table; ClassifierFeature, by Core_Feature's owner_ID column; and StructuralFeatureType, by Core_StructuralFeature's type_ID column.

Deleting Ownership Associations

The notion of ownership is central to the organization of CWM. With the exception of a few instances, virtually every instance in a CWM is owned by some other instance. Instances that are not owned are normally restricted to a few classes. For example, in the Relational package, only instances of the Catalog class are typically not owned by some other instance. Catalogs own Schemas; Schemas own Tables and Views; Tables own Columns, Keys, and Triggers; and so forth. An instance may own other instances only if it belongs to the Namespace class or one of its subtypes. Catalogs, Schemas, and Tables, which are namespaces, can own other instances, but Columns and Triggers cannot because they are not namespaces. You can review the inheritance relationships for Relational classes in Figure 8.20.

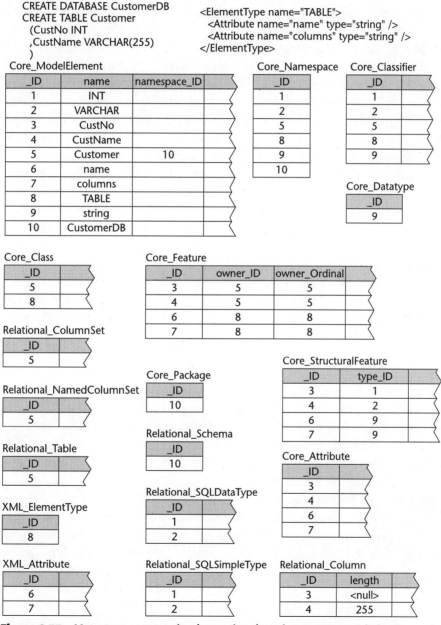

```
CREATE DATABASE CustomerDB
CREATE TABLE Customer
  (CustNo INT
  ,CustName VARCHAR(255)
  )
```

```
<ElementType name="TABLE">
  <Attribute name="name" type="string" />
  <Attribute name="columns" type="string" />
</ElementType>
```

Core_ModelElement

_ID	name	namespace_ID
1	INT	
2	VARCHAR	
3	CustNo	
4	CustName	
5	Customer	10
6	name	
7	columns	
8	TABLE	
9	string	
10	CustomerDB	

Core_Namespace

_ID
1
2
5
8
9
10

Core_Classifier

_ID
1
2
5
8
9

Core_Datatype

_ID
9

Core_Class

_ID
5
8

Core_Feature

_ID	owner_ID	owner_Ordinal
3	5	5
4	5	5
6	8	8
7	8	8

Relational_ColumnSet

_ID
5

Core_Package

_ID
10

Core_StructuralFeature

_ID	type_ID
3	1
4	2
6	9
7	9

Relational_NamedColumnSet

_ID
5

Relational_Schema

_ID
10

Relational_Table

_ID
5

Core_Attribute

_ID
3
4
6
7

XML_ElementType

_ID
8

Relational_SQLDataType

_ID
1
2

XML_Attribute

_ID
6
7

Relational_SQLSimpleType

_ID
1
2

Relational_Column

_ID	length
3	<null>
4	255

Figure 8.33 Metastore contents implementing three important associations.

Ownership relationships are depicted in CWM diagrams by associations with closed (filled-in) diamonds adjacent to the owning class. Instances of the class on the other end of the association are owned by instances of the class on the closed diamond end. Such associations are said to be *composite* because the owned instances can be thought of as parts of, or composing, their owning instance. Most ownership associations in CWM are actually re-usages of the two inherited associations discussed in the previous section: Core::ElementOwnership and Core::ClassifierFeature.

In UML terms, composite associations are of two types: strong (indicated by a closed diamond) and shared (open diamond). Strong associations imply exclusive ownership whereas shared implies multiple ownership. CWM uses only strong ownership association; it has no shared associations.

Strong ownership associations have, in relational database terms, *cascade delete* semantics. This means that when an owning instance is deleted, all of the instances it owns are deleted as well, recursively. The consequence is that deleting a single instance can, because of cascade delete semantics, delete entire trees of instances. Cascade delete semantics can be very dangerous if used carelessly. A single SQL DELETE statement can sometimes remove significant portions of a database. But used with care, they can greatly ease the effort required to build applications.

Figures 8.34 and 8.35 illustrate the effects of cascade delete semantics. Figure 8.34 shows the Relational package's composite association chain— Catalogs own Schemas that own Tables that own Columns—before a cascade delete operation is performed. In the accompanying instance diagram, the Partners catalog owns two database schemas, CustDB and EmpDB. Each schema owns two tables, and each table has two columns. Notice that columns are owned by the ClassifierFeature association whereas schemas and tables are owned via the ElementOwnership association. As discussed previously, this is because columns are features of their owning tables, but schemas and tables are not features of their owning instances. Classifier-Feature preserves the ordering of features, but ElementOwnership does not preserve the order of its ownedElements ends. The figure also shows the contents of the Metastore for the instance diagram.

Figure 8.35 shows the contents of the Metastore after the EmpDB Schema instance has been deleted. Because of the cascade delete behavior of composite ownership associations, not only was the EmpDB row in the Relational_Schema table deleted, but also the Employee and Department rows of Relational_Table and four rows in the Relational_Column table as well.

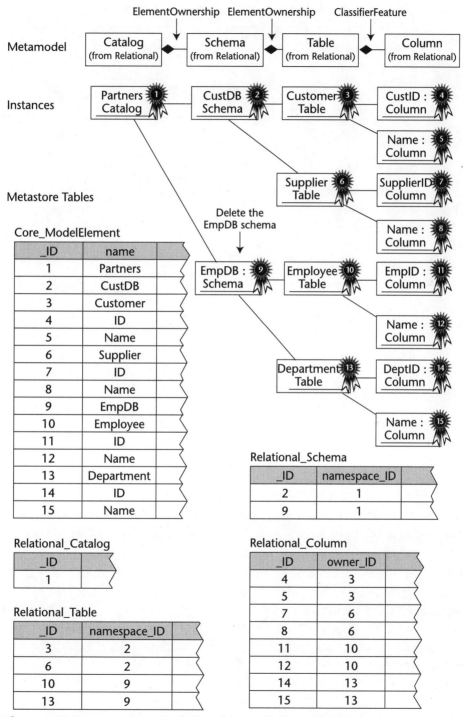

Figure 8.34   Metastore contents before deleting the EmpDB database.

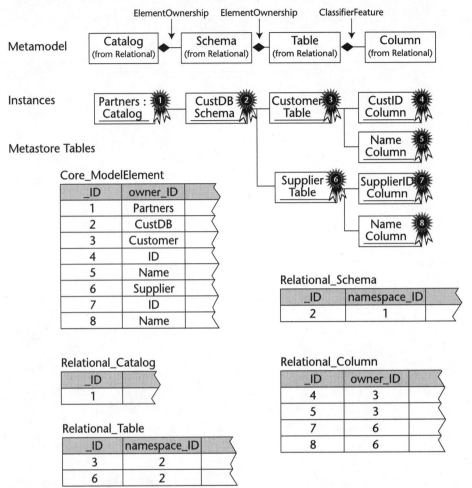

Figure 8.35 Metastore contents after deleting the EmpDB database.

SQL Server provides T-SQL syntax, an optional part of a FOREIGN KEY REFERENCES constraint, which would result in automatically cascaded delete operations. However, CWM cannot use T-SQL's syntax to accomplish cascade deletes. To guard against certain cascade delete definitions that cannot be implemented, SQL Server flags as errors any situations that would result in cyclic cascade delete chains. To do this, SQL Server analyzes the *definitional* structure of cascade delete chains. CWM contains several situations[5] that SQL Server interprets as cyclical cascade delete chains. CWM avoids the apparent logical inconsistencies via an Object Constraint

[5] See, for example, the apparent cyclical relationship involving three OLAP associations in Figure 11-2 of the formal CWM specification: OLAP::LevelBasedHierarchyOwnsHierarchyLevelAssociations, OLAP::HierarchyLevelAssociationOwnsDimensionDeployments, and OLAP::ValueBased HierarchyOwnsDimensionDeployments.

Language (OCL) constraint,[6] but such constraints are not directly expressed in the Metastore. In principle, these OCL constraints could be implemented, but in the Metastore, their implementation is left as an exercise for the more experienced developer.

Reflexive Associations

Reflexive associations link different instances of the same class. One classic example of a reflexive association is the marriage relationship between people. Both husband and wife are people and each of them is related to a spouse, also a person. Although the spouse relationship is (usually) 1:1, reflexive associations can occur in any of the three cardinality groups.

Figure 8.36 examines the InverseTransformationTask reflexive association from CWM's Transformation package. The association links a transformation task with its inverse transformation task—that is, the task that will undo its effects.

Visually, reflexive associations are drawn in the metamodel as association lines, both of whose ends are attached to the same class. Although this method of drawing reflexive associations may seem a bit bizarre at first, the instance diagram in the figure shows that it is really just a relationship between different instances of the same class.

Because it is an M:N association, InverseTransformationTask is represented in the Metastore by the Transformation_InverseTransformationTask table. Despite the somewhat unusual appearance of reflexive associations, there is nothing special about their representation in the Metastore—it is just another M:N association. The Metastore can even represent an instance linked to itself via a reflexive association. Although such situations can be represented in CWM (such as a symmetrical encryption algorithm that is its own inverse), you might wish to make sure that the semantics of the situation being modeled are well understood.

CWM has 12 reflexive associations. Two are 1:N, occurring in the BusinessNomenclature package; the rest are M:N and are found in various packages. There are no 1:1 reflexive associations in CWM.

Paired Associations

In several cases, CWM uses a pair of associations to link two classes. This usage pattern for associations implies that one of the linked classes is an *intersection class*. The term *intersection* is borrowed from the relational data model and implies that one of the classes represents a relationship between two instances of the other class. You may notice that this sounds a lot like the definition of reflexive association from the previous section, and, in fact, it is very similar. Indeed, these situations could have been modeled

---

[6] OCL constraint C-14 in chapter 11 of the formal CWM specification.

using a single reflexive association. Replacing a reflexive association with a class connected by a pair of associations provides CWM with capabilities similar in concept to those provided by UML's AssocationClass and by the Entity-Relationship model's Relationship entity—the ability to record attributes about a relationship between instances.

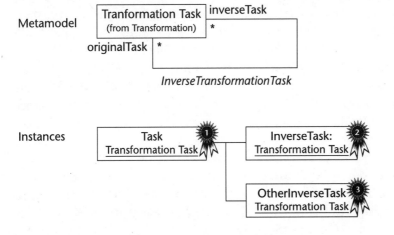

Metamodel

Tranformation Task (from Transformation) inverseTask *

originalTask *

InverseTransformationTask

Instances

Task / Transformation Task ❶

InverseTask: Transformation Task ❷

OtherInverseTask Transformation Task ❸

Metastore Tables

Core_ModelElement

_ID	name
1	Task
2	InverseTask
3	OtherInverseTask

Transformation_TransformationTask

_ID	
1	
2	
3	

Transformation_InverseTransformationTask

originalTask_ID	inverseTask_ID
1	2
1	3

Figure 8.36 The InverseTransformationTask reflexive association.

In CWM, intersection classes are convenient connection points that can be used to record information about relationships between instances. The information recorded can be either immediate attributes of the intersection class or relationships to other parts of the metamodel represented as associations connected to the intersection class. Often, the relationship being modeled is some sort of source and/or target dependency between instances of some class. Figure 8.37 examines one of these—the ClassifierMap from the Transformation package. (Other important intersection classes include Core::Dependency and TypeMapping::TypeMapping.)

The instance diagram in the middle of the figure illustrates the instances required if the Metastore were to store the relationship between the class Relational::Table (a Classifier) and the Metastore table Relational_Table (also a Classifier) that implements it. The unnamed ClassifierMap instance represents this relationship between these two instances.[7] The bottom portion of the figure shows the contents of some of the relevant Metastore tables for these instances.

The value of an intersection class does not reside completely within the class itself, but rather in the modeler's ability to use it as a connection point for other associations and as a superclass for classes that extend CWM into other usage domains. The ClassifierMap class, for example, has two immediate attributes and is attached to three other associations (not shown in the figure) that provide additional information about the relationship between a pair of Classifiers.

Figure 8.38 depicts how a ClassifierMap intersection class can be extended into a specific problem domain. In the figure, the MyClassifierMap class has been added as a sub-class of ClassifierMap. The new class has an additional attribute, whenCreated, recording the time at which the relationship was created. In an application, the MyClassifierMap class could be used anywhere the ClassifierMap class was allowed, providing additional information about the time of creation that wasn't recorded in the CWM metamodel itself.

---

[7] This example implies that the Metastore can contain the CWM metamodel and a description of the Metastore's own schema as well. Don't let the apparent circular quality of this idea distract you; it's perfectly legal for the Metastore to contain its own definition and that of CWM. In fact, the ability to store its own description is an important and sought-after characteristic of robust metamodels.

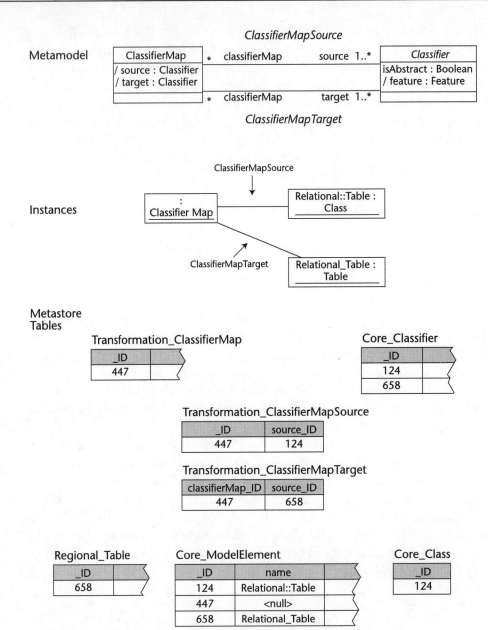

Figure 8.37   The intersection class Transformation::ClassifierMap.

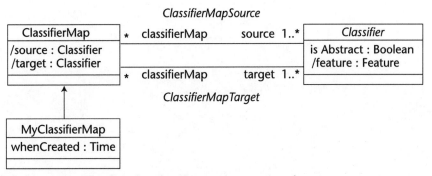

Figure 8.38   Extending the ClassifierMap intersection class.

Implementing OCL Constraints on Associations

Figure 8.39 summarizes the diagrammatic technique used in CWM's formal specification to indicate reuse of the Core::ClassifierFeature association to represent the fact that relational tables own columns. At the bottom of the figure, the ClassifierFeature association is redrawn between the Table and Column classes. A forward slash is prefixed to the association's end names to indicate that this is a reuse of an association inherited from higher up the inheritance hierarchy. Although the intent of this representation is that a table can own *only* columns in this way, there is nothing in the Metastore to prevent a Table instance from owning other sorts of instances as well. For example, there is nothing to prevent the Customer table instance from owning completely nonsensical instances—like XML attributes, for example.

UML provides a constraint definition language, called OCL, for describing additional rules about instances that are not expressed directly by the structure of the metamodel itself. Although the CWM specification does not specifically include it,[8] the appropriate OCL statement for our rule that tables can own only columns would be as follows:

```
context Table inv:
  self.ownedElement -> forAll(col | col.oclIsKindOf(Column)).
```

---

[8] And, arguably, should.

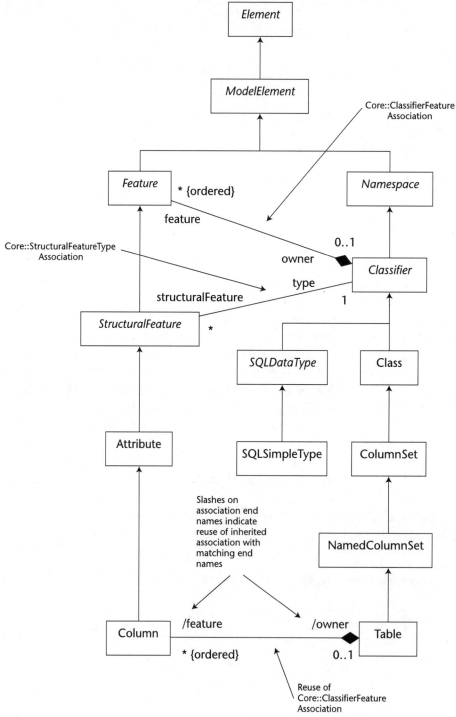

Figure 8.39 CWM association reuse.

Unfortunately, not many (in fact, very few) metamodel tools currently enforce OCL constraints. The Metastore, alas, is a member of this group. However, it can be instructive to see how enforcing an OCL constraint of this sort might be accomplished by a suitably ambiguous developer. An example of how the Create_Core_ClassifierFeature stored procedure might be modified to enforce this rule follows (lines added appear in boldface type):

```
CREATE PROCEDURE Create_Core_ClassifierFeature
    @owner_ID INT
   ,@feature_ID INT
AS
   DECLARE @Error INT
   DECLARE @MaxOrdinal INT
   -- Ensure that relational tables only own columns
   DECLARE @count INT
   SELECT @count = COUNT(*)
      FROM Core_Element
      WHERE _Kind_ID = 76   -- numeric value for Relational::Table
        AND   _ID = @owner_ID
   SELECT @Error = @@Error
   IF @Error = 0 AND @count > 0
   BEGIN    -- the owner is an instance of Relational::Table
      SELECT @count = COUNT(*)
         FROM Core_Element
         WHERE _Kind_ID = 83  -- numeric value for Relational::Column
            AND _ID = @feature_ID
      SELECT @Error = @@Error
      IF @Error <> 0  -- the SELECT statement failed
         RETURN @Error
      IF @count = 0   -- feature is not a Relational::Column instance
         RETURN 50001 -- return some other appropriate error number
      -- Otherwise, this is a legal pairing of a table and a column
      -- and the procedure may continue execution.
   END
   SELECT @MaxOrdinal = MAX(owner_Ordinal)
      FROM Core_Feature
      WHERE owner_ID = @owner_ID
   SELECT @Error = @@Error
   IF @Error = 0
   BEGIN
      UPDATE Core_Feature
         SET owner_ID = @owner_ID
            ,owner_Ordinal = @MaxOrdinal + 1
         WHERE _ID = @feature_ID
      SELECT @Error = @@Error
   END
   RETURN @Error
GO
```

The additional T-SQL code to enforce our rule about tables owning columns uses the Metastore's AllOfType service, described in more detail below, to discover if the owner and feature identity values are members of the Table and Column classes, respectively. Of course, the same result could have been achieved with a single, more complex SELECT statement, but this was not done here because the logical flow of the example would be less obvious.

CWM contains many reuses of the Core package's most important ownership associations: ElementOwnership and ClassifierFeature. The Relational package alone reuses ClassifierFeature in at least three different places, and ElementOwnership, at least 11 times. You can imagine the impact that full enforcement of all these sorts of rules would have on the complexity and performance of a product-quality implementation of the Metastore. There is little wonder that OCL has been fully implemented only occasionally. Perhaps a future revision of UML will provide improvements to these ideas that will promote wider acceptance of such integrity constraints without losing the substantial value derived from association reuse.

Using Associations to Capture Specific Rules

One final usage of associations in CWM that is worthy of some examination is shown in Figure 8.40. The example is from the OLAP package and illustrates how information about the deployment of a dimension is used to find related instances in the package's StructureMap class. Since the associations alone are not sufficient to completely capture the semantics required of the modeling situation, the three OCL rules taken from the CWM specification needed to complete the definition are shown as well. These OCL rules ensure that the collection of StructureMap instances owned by a DimensionDeployment contains two distinguished instances called its *immediate parent* and *list of values* instances. This example is instructive because it gives a hint as to the amount of work required to fully capture even moderately complicated rules in a metamodel.

The fact that DimensionDeployments may own StructureMap instances is captured by the composite association DimensionDeploymentsOwnStructureMaps. The collection of StructureMap instances owned by a DimensionDeployment may have two distinguished instances identified by the DimensionDeploymentHasListOfValues and DimensionDeploymentHasImmediateParent 1:1 associations. The OCL constraints ensure a DimensionDeployment instance having an identified immediate parent

StructureMap instance also has a list of values StructureMap instance that is not the immediate parent instance (C-10). The OCL constraints also ensure that the immediate parent and list of values StructureMap instances are members of the set of StructureMap instances owned by this DimensionDeployment (C-11 and C-12).

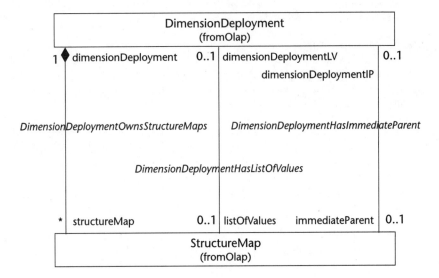

[C-10] Within a DimensionDeployment, an "immediate parent" StructureMap must always have an associated and distinct "list of values" StructureMap.

    context DimensionDeployment inv:
    self.immediateParent->notEmpty implies
      (self.listOfValues->notEmpty and self.listOfValues <> self.immediateParent)

[C-11] A StructureMap referenced as a "list of values" StructureMap must not reside outside of the DimensionDeployment's collection of StructureMaps.

    context DimensionDeployment inv:
    self. listOfValues->notEmpty implies self.structureMap->includes(self.listofValues)

[C-12] A StructureMap referenced as an "immediate parent" StructureMap must not reside outside of the DimensionDeployment's collection of StructureMaps.

    context DimensionDeployment inv:
    self.immediateParent->notEmpty implies self.structureMap->includes(self.immediateParent)

Figure 8.40 DimensionDeployments own StructureMaps with two distinguished instances.

Capturing all of this in the Metastore is challenging. For example, the stored procedure shown below might be added to the Metastore just to ensure that these constraints are enforced. A non-zero procedure result indicates that the DimensionDeployment instance with the identity value passed in the @dimensionDeployment_ID parameter does not satisfy the constraints.

```
CREATE PROCEDURE Validate_DimensionDeployment
    @dimensionDeployment_ID INT
AS
    DECLARE @failure INT
    DECLARE @result INT
    DECLARE @immediateParent_ID INT
    DECLARE @listOfValues_ID INT
    DECLARE @structureMap_ID INT
    DECLARE @cursor CURSOR
    SET @failure = 50001  -- or some other appropriate error number
    EXECUTE @result =
      Get_Olap_DimensionDeploymentHasImmediateParent_immediateParent
        @dimensionDeployment_ID, @immediateParent_ID OUTPUT
    IF @result = 0
      EXECUTE @result =
        Get_Olap_DimensionDeploymentHasListOfValues_listOfValues
          @dimensionDeployment_ID, @listOfValues_ID OUTPUT
    IF @result = 0 AND @immediateParent_ID IS NOT NULL
    BEGIN
      -- Enforce constraint C-10
      IF @listOfValues_ID IS NOT NULL
      BEGIN
        IF @listOfValues_ID = @immediateParent_ID
          SET @result = @failure
      END
      ELSE
        SET @result = @failure
      IF @result = 0
      BEGIN
        -- Enforce constraints C-11 and C-12
        EXECUTE @result =
      GetCursor_Olap_DimensionDeploymentOwnsStructureMaps_structureMap
          @dimensionDeployment, @cursor OUTPUT
        IF @result = 0
        BEGIN
          FETCH NEXT FROM @cursor INTO @structureMap_ID
          WHILE @@Fetch_Status = 0
          BEGIN
            -- Set IDs to null to indicate they were found
            IF @structureMap_ID = @listOfValues_ID
```

```
                        SET @listOfValues_ID = Null      -- C-11 met
                IF @structureMap_ID = @immediateParent_ID
                        SET @immediateParent_ID = Null   -- C-12 met
                FETCH NEXT FROM @cursor INTO @structureMap_ID
            END
            -- If either ID is not null, we failed
            IF @immediateParent_ID IS NOT NULL OR
                @listOfValues_ID IS NOT NULL
                SET @result = @failure
        END
        CLOSE @cursor
        DEALLOCATE @cursor
    END
  END
  RETURN @result
GO
```

Enforcing Association Multiplicities

In the general case, enforcing association multiplicities is a challenge of similar magnitude to enforcing OCL constraints. However, the task is eased somewhat for CWM because the upper multiplicity bound of CWM associations is either one or unlimited. Since unlimited upper bounds do not need to be enforced, multiplicities only need to be checked for 1:1 associations and for the one-end of 1:N associations—a relatively straightforward task. Similarly, multiplicity lower bounds only need to be checked for associations with a lower bound of one because a zero lower bound can never be violated. Also, upper bounds need to be checked only in association Create procedures, and lower bounds, only in association Delete procedures.

Unfortunately, there are other complexities that make enforcing association multiplicities difficult that cannot be so easily bypassed. When creating or deleting an association link, both of the class instances making up the link must be checked to ensure that the operation does not violate the multiplicity bounds of every association in which either instance participates. This includes not only the immediate associations of each instance but also every inherited association in which each instance might participate. This can become a problem because some CWM classes, especially those lower down in the inheritance hierarchy, may participate in a substantial number of classes (a Relational::Table instance might, for instance, participate in over 40 different associations).

> **NOTE** The Metastore source available on the Web site accompanying this book does not, at the time of this writing, enforce either OCL constraints or association multiplicities. Rather, the examples presented here are intended solely to illustrate the challenges that may be involved.
>
> If these problems can be addressed in some reasonable way at a future time, the Metastore source will be updated accordingly. However, we make no promises, and certainly do not guarantee, that this will ever happen. Please refer to the Web site for further information.

Reference Mapping Patterns

CWM inherits references from MOF; they are not part of UML. References are best thought of as attributes of classes that point to instances of another class that is the declared type of the reference. In practice, references are implemented by association ends. That is, a reference can be thought of as a surrogate for an association end, represented as an attribute of the opposite class. In a sense, a reference, then, is a kind of predefined select query on an association that returns only the association links relevant to the instance that owns the reference. (Remember: Because they are first-class objects, associations can be the targets of queries and updates just like any other Metastore class.) The Metastore takes advantage of this view of references in its implementation of them.

The implementation of references requires no additions to the data structures in the Metastore. Rather, they are implemented solely as stored procedures that pass along their requests to the appropriate association data structures or procedures, as discussed in the previous section. For example, the Get procedure for the file reference of the Record::RecordDef class, Get_Record_RecordDef_file, simply returns the identity values for the desired links by selecting them directly from the association's table. The exact SELECT statement used depends on the cardinality of the underlying association as discussed above.[9] It does this because it cannot return a cursor through the default result set used by Get procedures. The corresponding GetCursor procedure is shown as well, but notice that all it needs to do is pass along its call to the appropriate end of the underlying association end that implements the reference.

---

[9] For the example, you can convince yourself of this by comparing the SELECT statements in the Get procedures with the corresponding association Get procedures in the section above on the M:N association pattern.

```
CREATE PROCEDURE Get_Record_RecordDef_file
    @record_ID INT
AS
    SELECT file_ID
      FROM Record_RecordToFile
      WHERE record_ID = @record_ID
    RETURN @@Error
GO


CREATE PROCEDURE GetCursor_Record_RecordDef_file
    @record_ID INT
    ,@_Cursor CURSOR VARYING OUTPUT
AS
    DECLARE @Error INT
    EXECUTE @Error = GetCursor_Record_RecordToFile_file @record_ID,
      @_Cursor OUTPUT
    RETURN @Error
GO
```

The Get and GetCursor procedures for the opposing reference, Record::RecordFile::record, are similarly structured but work from the other end of the Record::RecordToFile association.

```
CREATE PROCEDURE Get_Record_RecordFile_record
    @file_ID INT
AS
    SELECT record_ID
      FROM Record_RecordToFile
      WHERE file_ID = @file_ID
      ORDER BY record_Ordinal
    RETURN @@Error
GO


CREATE PROCEDURE GetCursor_Record_RecordFile_record
    @file_ID INT
    ,@_Cursor CURSOR VARYING OUTPUT
AS
    DECLARE @Error INT
    EXECUTE @Error = GetCursor_Record_RecordToFile_record @file_ID,
      @_Cursor OUTPUT
    RETURN @Error
GO
```

GetCursor procedures only exist for a reference if it is multi-valued, that is, if its multiplicity upper bound is unlimited (recall that CWM has no association ends with specific upper bounds greater than one —that is, all of the upper bounds are either 1 or * for *many*).

Rather than have Set procedures like normal class attributes, references have Include, Exclude, and ExcludeAll procedures. These update procedures treat references more like sets of identity values (which they are) than traditional attributes. As with the Get procedures for references, Include and Exclude procedures simply pass along their calls to the appropriate association Create and Delete procedures, respectively, to get their jobs done.

```
CREATE PROCEDURE Include_Record_RecordDef_file
    @record_ID INT
    ,@file_ID INT
AS
    DECLARE @Error INT
    EXECUTE @Error = Create_Record_RecordToFile @record_ID = @record_ID,
        @file_ID = @file_ID
    RETURN @Error
GO


CREATE PROCEDURE Exclude_Record_RecordDef_file
    @record_ID INT
    ,@file_ID INT
AS
    DECLARE @Error INT
    EXECUTE @Error = Delete_Record_RecordToFile @record_ID = @record_ID,
        @file_ID = @file_ID
    RETURN @Error
GO
```

The above procedures use a different T-SQL calling sequence than other Metastore procedures. Each parameter is passed in the <parameter> = <value> form that T-SQL supports. When written this way, parameters are not positional—that is, they do not have to be listed in the same order in the procedure declaration. The parameter name is used to match up parameter values. Since there is no inherent way to infer the order of an association's end in the procedures that manipulate association links, using this technique means you don't have to look up the correct order when writing a call to the Create and Delete procedures. This is merely a convenience; there is no particular CWM reason for doing so.

The ExcludeAll procedure finds the current set of instances that a reference contains and then individually removes their association links from the underlying association. ExcludeAll procedures are really service procedures that are provided to simplify the writing of class Drop procedures, but they can also be used for other purposes in Metastore clients.

```
CREATE PROCEDURE ExcludeAll_Record_RecordDef_file
    @record_ID INT
AS
```

```
        DECLARE @Error INT
        DECLARE @file_ID INT
        DECLARE @_Cursor CURSOR
        BEGIN TRANSACTION ExcludeAll_Record_RecordDef
        SELECT @Error = @@Error
        IF @Error = 0
        BEGIN
            SET @_Cursor = CURSOR FORWARD_ONLY STATIC FOR
                SELECT file_ID
                    FROM Record_RecordToFile
                    WHERE record_ID = @record_ID
            SELECT @Error = @@Error
        END
        IF @Error = 0
        BEGIN
            OPEN @_Cursor
            SELECT @Error = @@Error
        END
        IF @Error = 0
        BEGIN
            FETCH NEXT FROM @_Cursor INTO @file_ID
            WHILE @@Fetch_Status = 0 and @Error = 0
            BEGIN
                EXECUTE @Error = Delete_Record_RecordToFile @record_ID,
                    @file_ID
                FETCH NEXT FROM @_Cursor INTO @file_ID
            END
        END
        CLOSE @_Cursor
        DEALLOCATE @_Cursor
        IF @Error = 0
            COMMIT TRANSACTION ExcludeAll_Record_RecordDef
        ELSE
            ROLLBACK TRANSACTION
        IF @@Error <> 0
            SELECT @Error = @@Error
        RETURN @Error
    GO
```

Figure 8.41 provides a graphical summary of the changes in the Record_RecordToFile association table that would occur after example calls to the above Include, Exclude, and ExcludeAll procedures.

The MOF specification contains a rule that affects how references are allocated in CWM. This *Reference Closure* rule is designed to prevent the creation of logically inconsistent states in MOF repositories. This MOF rule prevents the construction of circular reference chains—that is, a reference that ends up pointing to itself, possibly via other, intermediate references. The effect on CWM is that a reference may be missing when an association crosses package boundaries. Figure 8.42 provides an illustrative example.

RecordFile		RecordToFile		RecordDef
isSelfDescribing : Boolean recordDelimiter : Integer skipRecords : Integer / record : RecordDef	file *		record {ordered} *	fieldDelimiter : String isFixedWidth : Boolean textDelimiter : String / file : RecordFile

Record_RecordFile

_ID	
1	
2	
3	
4	

Record_RecordToFile

_ID	file_ID
10	1
11	1
12	2
13	2
13	3
11	3

Record_RecordDef

_ID	
10	
11	
12	
13	

After:
EXECUTE Include_Record_RecordDef_file
@file = 4, @record = 13

Record_RecordToFile

record_ID	file_ID
10	1
11	1
13	4
12	2
13	2
13	3
11	3

After:
EXECUTE Exclude_Record_RecordDef_file
@file = 3, @record = 11

Record_RecordToFile

record_ID	file_ID
10	1
11	1
13	4
12	2
13	2
13	3

After:
EXECUTE ExcludeAll_Record_RecordDef_file
@record = 13

Record_RecordToFile

record_ID	file_ID
10	1
11	1
12	2
11	3

Figure 8.41 Effects of Include, Exclude, and ExcludeAll procedures.

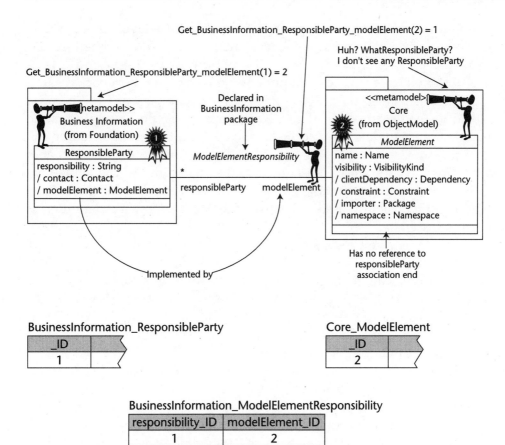

Get_BusinessInformation_ResponsibleParty_modelElement(2) = 1

Huh? WhatResponsibleParty?
I don't see any ResponsibleParty

Get_BusinessInformation_ResponsibleParty_modelElement(1) = 2

Declared in
BusinessInformation
package

<<metamodel>>
Core
(from ObjectModel)

hetamodel>>
Business Information
(from Foundation)

ModelElement

name : Name
visibility : VisibilityKind
/ clientDependency : Dependency
/ constraint : Constraint
/ importer : Package
/ namespace : Namespace

ResponsibleParty

responsibility : String
/ contact : Contact
/ modelElement : ModelElement

ModelElementResponsibility

responsibleParty   modelElement

Has no reference to
responsibleParty
association end

Implemented by

BusinessInformation_ResponsibleParty

_ID
1

Core_ModelElement

_ID
2

BusinessInformation_ModelElementResponsibility

responsibility_ID	modelElement_ID
1	2

Figure 8.42   References on associations that cross package boundaries.

In the figure, the ModelElementResponsibility association connects the ResponsibleParty class in the BusinessInformation package to the Model-Element class in Core. The association allows one to determine which ModelElement instances a ResponsibleParty instance has responsibility for. However, the absence of a reference in ModelElement that maps to the ReponsibleParty end of the association makes it impossible to directly see, from the perspective of a ModelElement instance, the ResponsibleParty instance. ModelElement has no reference to ResponsibleParty because, if it did, the requirements of the Reference Closure rule would not be met. That is, the references can be followed from ResponsibleParty to ModelElement, but not from ModelElement to ResponsibilityParty.

Another way of thinking about this situation that involves less meta-model mumbo-jumbo might go something like this: Core is the most fundamental package in CWM, and all other CWM packages and classes derive from it. As such, Core cannot refer to any other CWM package. If it did, the other packages would effectively become part of Core because they'd be required to define Core. Now, think of the BusinessInformation package as being defined *after* the Core package. BusinessInformation can inherit from Core classes and can create associations to them, but cannot alter Core in any way. Consequently, the definition of ModelElement cannot be directly extended to include another reference for the ModelElementResponsibility association because ModelElement's definition is already frozen.

MOF's Reference Closure rule is necessary because it allows logically consistent repositories to be constructed. However, it's pretty inconvenient in certain applications because it prevents some questions from being asked. For example, it's possible to ask a ResponsibleParty instance which ModelElements it has responsibility for, but it isn't possible to ask a ModelElement instance to identify its ResponsibleParty instances. Fortunately, there is a way out of this conundrum.

Because associations are first-class objects in CWM and have instances, called links, we can bypass the absence of a reference in ModelElement by rephrasing the question and redirecting it to the association. If we restate our question to ask the association to give us all of the instances of ResponsibleParty that are associated with the ModelElement that has identity value equal to 1, we get back the ResponsibleParty instance with identity value equal to 2 as our answer. This is precisely the answer we would have gotten if ModelElement had a reference that mapped to the ResponsibleParty end of the association, and we asked the ModelElement instance with identity value equal to 1 to identify its ResponsibleParty instances. We hinted at this earlier when we said that references are implemented by association ends. The unfortunate part of all this is that the query-former (that is, the end user or developer) must recognize the situation and know to ask a slightly different question of the association to get a useful answer.

MetaStore Services

The Metastore provides several general services intended to improve its ease of use. Transaction management services are built into the stored procedures wherever they are needed. The ClassMap service converts instance identity values into textual type names. The AllOfType services provide for retrieval of all instances of a class and are required for support of some programming interfaces, such as the Java Meta data Interface (JMI). Finally, a few error-handling services are provided.

Transaction Management Services

SQL Server provides an automatic transaction service that protects single INSERT, UPDATE, and DELETE statements. If no other actions are taken, each of these data-altering statements will be individually transacted. Consequently, Metastore procedures that use a single data update statement contain no transaction management logic. If a transaction has been started when the Metastore procedure is executed, its data update statement will be included in the previously existing transaction, and if no transaction has been started, the data update statement will be implicitly transacted by SQL Server.

An explicit transaction is started by a BEGIN TRANSACTION statement and ends when a COMMIT TRANSACTION or ROLLBACK TRANSACTION statement is encountered. All of the data update statements between these delimiting statements will happen or none of them will happen; no partial updates will be made. The COMMIT TRANSACTION statement is used to signal the correct end of a transaction, and ROLLBACK TRANSACTION is used to undo the effects of all the work done since the last BEGIN TRANSACTION statement.

Metastore procedures are constructed so that their transactions can be safely nested within other transactions, whether started by another Metastore procedure or by a Metastore client, and still produce the desired result. When nested within an outer transaction, BEGIN TRANSACTION and COMMIT TRANSACTION statements are largely ignored—the inner transaction, sequenced appropriately with other inner transactions, is applied to the database when the COMMIT TRANSACTION statement that matches the outer transaction is executed. The pairing between BEGIN TRANSACTION and COMMIT TRANSACTION statements in Metastore procedures can be recognized because they have the same identifier following the word TRANSACTION. The identifier is constructed from the procedure name and is mangled if needed so that it meets a 32-character limitation on transaction identifiers. ROLLBACK TRANSACTION statements have no transaction identifier and cause all transactions, including the outermost transaction, to fail. Any error conditions that result in an unbalanced count of BEGIN TRANSACTION and COMMIT TRANSACTION statements will ultimately cause the outer transaction to fail, thereby protecting the integrity of the Metastore.

ClassMap Service

The Metastore contains a table that maps the names of CWM classes onto integer values. These integer values are used in other Metastore procedures when a specific class needs to be referenced. The class map table is defined as follows:

```
CREATE TABLE [CWM_1.0_ClassMap]
    (_ID INT PRIMARY KEY
    ,Name VARCHAR(128)
    )
GO
```

Because the class map table does not exist in any particular package, its table name is constructed by prefixing the Metastore's name (here, "CWM_1.0") and an underscore to "ClassMap". Because the Metastore name contains a character not legal in T-SQL identifiers (the "."), the table name is delimited with square brackets so that the illegal character can be accommodated.

The class map table contains one row for every CWM class the Metastore supports. The _ID column contains a unique number assigned to the class, and the Name column contains the class name expressed in <package>. <class> form. Values in the _ID column are assigned in the order that classes are added to the class map table; the specific value assigned to a class is of no particular importance outside of the Metastore itself. These values are used internally by Metastore procedures to reference specific classes and are placed into the _Kind_ID column of the Core_Element table. They are used to speed work performed by the Drop and AllOfType procedures.

The GetKind_Core_Element procedure is provided to return the name of an instance's declared type—that is, the class in which it was originally created. The procedure is defined as follows:

```
CREATE PROCEDURE GetKind_Core_Element
    @_ID INT
    ,@_Kind VARCHAR(128) OUTPUT
AS
    SELECT @_Kind = [CWM_1.0_ClassMap]._Name
        FROM [CWM_1.0_ClassMap], Core_Element
        WHERE [CWM_1.0_ClassMap]._ID = Core_Element._Kind_ID
          AND Core_Element._ID = @_ID
    RETURN @@Error
GO
```

The GetKind_Core_Element can be called for any Metastore instance regardless of the subclass of Core::Element in which it was originally created. The following T-SQL script shows how this is done.

```
DECLARE @result INT
DECLARE @instanceID INT
DECLARE @className VARCHAR(256)
EXECUTE @result = Create_Relational_Table @instanceID OUTPUT
IF @result = 0
BEGIN
   EXECUTE @result = GetKind_Core_Element @instanceID, @className OUTPUT
   IF @result = 0
      PRINT 'Instance ' + CONVERT(VARCHAR, @instanceID) +
            ' is a ' + @className
END
```

If the table instance were created with an identity value of 349, this script would produce the following display:

```
Instance 349 is a Relational.Table
```

AllOfType Services

Some of the programming interfaces through which the Metastore can be accessed (such as JMI) provide specific functions for retrieval of all the instances in a particular class. Because support for these so-called AllOfType functions can be very expensive and error-prone if they are implemented without the assistance of the underlying data store, the Metastore contains stored procedures to ease their implementation.

AllOfType services are implemented using the _Kind_ID column of the Core_Element table. Each time a new instance is created, the class's Create procedure calls Add_Core_Element to create a new instance row in the Core_Element table and sets the _Kind_ID column of this to the numeric value from the class map table corresponding to Core.Element. After the Add procedures have been called for each of the intervening superclasses, the Create procedure sets the _Kind_ID column of the instance's Core_Element row to the class map numeric value for the new instance. For the Relational::Table example of Figure 8.21, the Core_Element table would contain, after the Load_Person script completes, the rows shown in Figure 8.43 (only class map rows relevant to the example are included in the figure).

CWM_1.0_ClassMap

_ID	Name
15	Core.Expression
76	Relational.Table
81	Relational.SQLSimpleType
83	Relational.Column

Core_Element

_ID	Kind_ID
1	81
2	83
3	15
4	76

Figure 8.43 Contents of the Core_Element table after the Load_Person script completes.

The JMI interface defines two operations for each class that can make use of the Metastore's AllOfType services: allOfType<class> and allOfKind <class>. To understand the Metastore's AllOfType and AllOfKind procedures that support these JMI operations, consider the CWM Record package classes, and their anchor tables, shown in Figure 8.44.

The Metastore provides AllOfType and AllOfKind procedures for each class. The AllOfType procedure below returns the set of all Record::Field class instances. In terms of Figure 8.44, the set of returned instances contains the identity values 123 and 124. In contrast, the AllOfKind procedure returns the set of instances that are instances *only* of Field; that is, the returned set contains instance 123, but not instance 124, because it is also an instance of Record::FixedOffsetField. For the FixedOffsetField class, both procedures return instance 124 only.

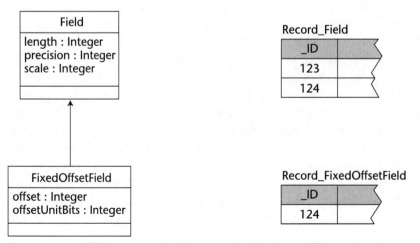

Figure 8.44 AllOfType example classes and tables from the Record package.

The text of the AllOfType and AllOfKind procedures for Field are shown below. Field is class number 96, and FixedOffsetField is class number 98. The SELECT statement in AllOfType_Record_Field selects instances that are of either the Field or FixedOffsetField types.

```
CREATE PROCEDURE AllOfType_Record_Field
AS
    SELECT _ID FROM Core_Element
        WHERE _Kind_ID IN
            (96, 98)
    RETURN @@Error
GO


CREATE PROCEDURE AllOfKind_Record_Field
AS
    SELECT _ID
        FROM Core_Element
        WHERE _Kind_ID = 96
    RETURN @@Error
GO
```

Error-Handling Services

Each Metastore procedure returns a number as its result. If this number is zero, no errors were detected during the procedure or in any procedures that the outermost procedure may have called. If the returned number is non-zero, an error occurred during execution. The Metastore provides two utility procedures that translate this number into a textual description of the error and into another number that indicates the severity of the error that occurred. These procedures are convenience procedures that simply use existing T-SQL techniques for translating error numbers to messages and severities.

```
CREATE PROCEDURE [CWM 1.0_Error_Message]
    @_ID INT
    ,@_Description NVARCHAR(255) OUTPUT
AS
    SELECT @_Description = description FROM master..sysmessages
        WHERE error = @_ID
    RETURN @@Error
GO

CREATE PROCEDURE [CWM 1.0_Error_Severity]
    @_ID INT
```

```
    ,@_Severity INT OUTPUT
AS
    SELECT @_Severity = severity FROM master..sysmessages
        WHERE error = @_ID
    RETURN @@Error
GO
```

The vast majority of non-zero error numbers returned by Metastore procedures will be SQL Server error numbers generated by SQL Server itself. Error numbers originating in the Metastore will have error numbers greater than 50,000. Error numbers less than this value are from SQL Server. The meaning of SQL Server error numbers and severity level numbers can be found by consulting the Microsoft SQL Server product documentation.

Using the Metastore in Applications

We conclude this chapter with a complete example of an application program. The application creates objects in the Metastore for a small relational database schema called MyCompany. The schema contains two tables, each of which has two columns. The necessary association links are also created to correctly represent the ownership and type relationship between various components of the schema. All three of the central CWM associations discussed previously are used: Core::ElementOwnership, Core::Classifier-Feature, and Core::StructuralFeatureType. The example is written in Microsoft Visual Basic 6 and uses Active Data Objects (ADO) version 2.7 (although most earlier versions should work as well). You can obtain the machine-readable source file for this example from this book's companion Web site.

As you peruse the example, note that there are procedures for each of the kinds of stored procedures (CWMCreate, for example) described in the text. Organizing an application around these stored procedures seems to provide a very readable program listing.

Following the program listing, Figure 8.45 shows the contents of the Metastore after the example application has completed execution.

```
VERSION 5.00
Begin VB.Form Form1
    Caption         =   "CWM VB Demo"
    ClientHeight    =   3150
    ClientLeft      =   60
    ClientTop       =   450
    ClientWidth     =   4710
```

```
      LinkTopic        =    "Form1"
      ScaleHeight      =    3150
      ScaleWidth       =    4710
      StartUpPosition =    3   'Windows Default
      Begin VB.TextBox Text1
         BeginProperty Font
            Name              =    "MS Sans Serif"
            Size              =    8.25
            Charset           =    0
            Weight            =    400
            Underline         =    0     'False
            Italic            =    0     'False
            Strikethrough     =    0     'False
         EndProperty
         Height            =    3135
         Left              =    0
         MultiLine         =    -1    'True
         TabIndex          =    0
         Text              =    "Form1.frx":0000
         Top               =    0
         Width             =    4695
      End
   End
End
Attribute VB_Name = "Form1"
Attribute VB_GlobalNameSpace = False
Attribute VB_Creatable = False
Attribute VB_PredeclaredId = True
Attribute VB_Exposed = False
'CWM Metastore Demonstration, Microsoft Visual Basic 6 with ADO 2.7
'This demonstration program adds the following relational database to the
'Metastore. The schema created is displayed in the multiline text box
'control Text1.

'CREATE DATABASE MyCompany
'
'CREATE TABLE Person
'    (personID INT
'    ,name VARCHAR(255)
'    )
'
'CREATE TABLE Department
'    (deptID INT
'    ,name VARCHAR(255)
'    )

Option Explicit

Private oConn As New ADODB.Connection
```

```
Private Function CWMCreate(ByVal sClass As String) As Long
    'Create an instance of the <sClass> class
    Dim oCmd As New ADODB.Command
    Dim retParam As ADODB.Parameter
    Dim idParam As ADODB.Parameter

    With oCmd
        .ActiveConnection = oConn
        .CommandText = "Create_" & sClass
        .CommandType = adCmdStoredProc
        Set retParam = _
            .CreateParameter("_Return", adInteger, adParamReturnValue)
        .Parameters.Append retParam
        Set idParam = .CreateParameter("@_ID", adInteger, adParamOutput)
        .Parameters.Append idParam
        .Execute
        If retParam.Value = 0 Then
            CWMCreate = idParam.Value
        Else
            CWMCreate = -retParam.Value
        End If
    End With
End Function

Private Function CWMGetSVAttr(ByVal sAttr As String, _
            ByVal idValue As Long, _
            ByVal adType As ADODB.DataTypeEnum) As Variant
    'Get the <sAttr> attribute of the <idValue> instance of
    'type <adType>
    Dim oCmd As New ADODB.Command
    Dim retParam As ADODB.Parameter
    Dim idParam As ADODB.Parameter
    Dim valParam As ADODB.Parameter

    With oCmd
        .ActiveConnection = oConn
        .CommandText = "Get_" & sAttr
        .CommandType = adCmdStoredProc
        Set retParam = _
            .CreateParameter("_Return", adInteger, adParamReturnValue)
        .Parameters.Append retParam
        Set idParam = .CreateParameter("@_ID", adInteger, adParamInput)
        idParam.Value = idValue
        .Parameters.Append idParam
        Set valParam = .CreateParameter("@_Value", adType, _
            adParamOutput)
        If adType = adVarChar Then valParam.Size = 255
        .Parameters.Append valParam
        .Execute
        If retParam.Value = 0 Then
```

```
                CWMGetSVAttr = valParam.Value
            Else
                CWMGetSVAttr = -retParam.Value
            End If
        End With
End Function


Private Function CWMSetSVAttr(ByVal sAttr As String, _
            ByVal idValue As Long, _
            ByVal attrValue As Variant) As Long
    'Set the <sAttr> attribute of the <idValue> instance to <attrValue>
    Dim oCmd As New ADODB.Command
    Dim retParam As ADODB.Parameter
    Dim idParam As ADODB.Parameter
    Dim valParam As ADODB.Parameter
    Dim adType As ADODB.DataTypeEnum

    With oCmd
        .ActiveConnection = oConn
        .CommandText = "Set_" & sAttr
        .CommandType = adCmdStoredProc
        Set retParam = _
            .CreateParameter("_Return", adInteger, adParamReturnValue)
        .Parameters.Append retParam
        Set idParam = .CreateParameter("@_ID", adInteger, adParamInput)
        idParam.Value = idValue
        .Parameters.Append idParam
        adType = If(VarType(attrValue) = vbInteger, adInteger, _
            adVarChar)
        Set valParam = .CreateParameter("@_Value", adType, adParamInput)
        If adType = adVarChar Then valParam.Size = Len(attrValue)
        valParam.Value = attrValue
        .Parameters.Append valParam
        .Execute
        CWMSetSVAttr = retParam.Value
        If CWMSetSVAttr > 0 Then CWMSetSVAttr = -CWMSetSVAttr
    End With
End Function


Private Function CWMDataType(ByVal sName As String) As Long
    'Create a SQL data type called <sName>
    Dim oCmd As New ADODB.Command
    Dim retParam As ADODB.Parameter
    Dim idParam As ADODB.Parameter

    With oCmd
        .ActiveConnection = oConn
        .CommandText = "Create_Relational_SQLSimpleType"
        .CommandType = adCmdStoredProc
        Set retParam = _
```

```
                    .CreateParameter("_Return", adInteger, adParamReturnValue)
            .Parameters.Append retParam
            Set idParam = .CreateParameter("@_ID", adInteger, adParamOutput)
            .Parameters.Append idParam
            .Execute
            If retParam.Value = 0 Then
                'Set the type's name
                CWMSetSVAttr "Relational_SQLSimpleType_name", _
                    idParam.Value, sName
                CWMDataType = idParam.Value
            Else
                CWMDataType = -retParam.Value
            End If
        End With
    End Function


    Private Function CWMLink(ByVal sAssoc As String, _
                ByVal End1 As String, ByVal ID1 As Long, _
                ByVal End2 As String, ByVal ID2 As Long) As Long
        'Create a link in the <sAssoc> association between end <End1>
        'with value <ID1> and end <End2> with value <ID2>.
        Dim oCmd As New ADODB.Command
        Dim retParam As ADODB.Parameter
        Dim param1 As ADODB.Parameter
        Dim param2 As ADODB.Parameter

        With oCmd
            .ActiveConnection = oConn
            .CommandText = "Create_" & sAssoc
            .CommandType = adCmdStoredProc
            Set retParam = _
                .CreateParameter("_Return", adInteger, adParamReturnValue)
            .Parameters.Append retParam
            Set param1 = _
                .CreateParameter("@" & End1 & "_ID", adInteger, _
                    adParamInput)
            param1.Value = ID1
            .Parameters.Append param1
            Set param2 = _
                .CreateParameter("@" & End2 & "_ID", adInteger, _
                    adParamInput)
            param2.Value = ID2
            .Parameters.Append param2
            .Execute
            CWMLink = retParam.Value
            If CWMLink > 0 Then CWMLink = -CWMLink
        End With
    End Function


    Private Function CWMGetMVLinks(ByVal sAssoc As String, _
                ByVal endName As String, _
                ByVal endID As Long) As ADODB.Recordset
```

```
            'Return a recordset of identity values for instanced linked
            'to the <endID> instance via the <sAssoc> association.
            Dim oCmd As New ADODB.Command
            Dim retParam As ADODB.Parameter
            Dim idParam As ADODB.Parameter

            With oCmd
                .ActiveConnection = oConn
                .CommandText = "Get_" & sAssoc
                .CommandType = adCmdStoredProc
                Set retParam = _
                    .CreateParameter("_Return", adInteger, adParamReturnValue)
                .Parameters.Append retParam
                Set idParam = _
                    .CreateParameter("@" & endName & "_ID", adInteger, _
                        adParamInput)
                idParam.Value = endID
                .Parameters.Append idParam
                Set CWMGetMVLinks = .Execute
            End With
        End Function


        Private Function CWMGetSVLink(ByVal sAssoc As String, _
                    ByVal end1Name As String, _
                    ByVal end2Name As String, ByVal end2ID As Long) As Long
            'Return the identity value of the single link in the <sAssoc>
            'association that references the <idEnd2> instance on its
            '<endName2> end.
            Dim oCmd As New ADODB.Command
            Dim retParam As ADODB.Parameter
            Dim end1Param As ADODB.Parameter
            Dim end2Param As ADODB.Parameter

            With oCmd
                .ActiveConnection = oConn
                .CommandText = "Get_" & sAssoc & "_" & end1Name
                .CommandType = adCmdStoredProc
                Set retParam = _
                    .CreateParameter("_Return", adInteger, adParamReturnValue)
                .Parameters.Append retParam
                Set end2Param = _
                    .CreateParameter("@" & end2Name & "_ID", adInteger, _
                        adParamInput)
                end2Param.Value = end2ID
                .Parameters.Append end2Param
                Set end1Param = _
                    .CreateParameter("@" & end1Name & "_ID", adInteger, _
                        adParamOutput)
                .Parameters.Append end1Param
                .Execute
                If retParam.Value = 0 Then
                    CWMGetSVLink = end1Param.Value
```

```
            Else
                CWMGetSVLink = -retParam.Value
            End If
        End With
    End Function


Private Sub Form_Load()
    Const indent = "    "
    Dim rsTableLink As ADODB.Recordset
    Dim rsColumnLink As ADODB.Recordset
    Dim dbID As Long
    Dim personID As Long
    Dim deptID As Long
    Dim colID As Long
    Dim intID As Long
    Dim varcharID As Long
    Dim tableID As Long
    Dim typeID As Long
    Dim delim As String

    'Connect to the Metastore
    With oConn
        .Provider = "sqloledb"
        .Properties("Data Source").Value = "(local)"
        .Properties("Initial Catalog").Value = "CWM 1.0"
        .Properties("User ID").Value = "sa" 'provide your login name
        .Properties("Password").Value = ""   'and password here
        .CursorLocation = adUseClient
        .Open
    End With

    'Create SQL Server data types
    intID = CWMDataType("INT")
    varcharID = CWMDataType("VARCHAR")

    'Create the database
    dbID = CWMCreate("Relational_Schema")
    CWMSetSVAttr "Relational_Schema_name", dbID, "MyCompany"

    'Create the Person table
    personID = CWMCreate("Relational_Table")
    If personID > 0 Then
        'Assign the table's name
        CWMSetSVAttr "Relational_Table_name", personID, "Person"
        'Make the database the owner of the table
        CWMLink "Core_ElementOwnership", "ownedElement", personID, _
            "namespace", dbID
        'Add the personID column
        colID = CWMCreate("Relational_Column")
        If colID > 0 Then
            CWMSetSVAttr "Relational_Column_name", colID, "personID"
            CWMLink "Core_StructuralFeatureType", "structuralFeature", _
```

```
            colID, "type", intID
        CWMLink "Core_ClassifierFeature", "owner", personID, _
            "feature", colID
    End If
    'Add the name column
    colID = CWMCreate("Relational_Column")
    If colID > 0 Then
        CWMSetSVAttr "Relational_Column_name", colID, "name"
        CWMSetSVAttr "Relational_Column_length", colID, 255
        CWMLink "Core_StructuralFeatureType", "structuralFeature", _
            colID, "type", varcharID
        CWMLink "Core_ClassifierFeature", "owner", personID, _
            "feature", colID
    End If
End If

'Create the Deparment table
deptID = CWMCreate("Relational_Table")
If deptID > 0 Then
    'Assign its name and ownership
    CWMSetSVAttr "Relational_Table_name", deptID, "Department"
    CWMLink "Core_ElementOwnership", "ownedElement", deptID, _
        "namespace", dbID
    'Add the deptID column
    colID = CWMCreate("Relational_Column")
    If colID > 0 Then
        CWMSetSVAttr "Relational_Column_name", colID, "deptID"
        CWMLink "Core_StructuralFeatureType", "structuralFeature", _
            colID, "type", intID
        CWMLink "Core_ClassifierFeature", "owner", deptID, _
            "feature", colID
    End If
    'Add the name column
    colID = CWMCreate("Relational_Column")
    If colID > 0 Then
        CWMSetSVAttr "Relational_Column_name", colID, "name"
        CWMSetSVAttr "Relational_Column_length", colID, 255
        CWMLink "Core_StructuralFeatureType", "structuralFeature", _
            colID, "type", varcharID
        CWMLink "Core_ClassifierFeature", "owner", deptID, _
            "feature", colID
    End If
End If

'Display contents of the Metastore
Text1.Text = "CREATE DATABASE " & _
    CWMGetSVAttr("Relational_Schema_name", dbID, adVarChar) & vbCrLf
'Get the tables owned by the database via the ElementOwnership
'association
Set rsTableLink = _
    CWMGetMVLinks("Core_ElementOwnership_ownedElement", _
        "namespace", dbID)
```

```
    If Not rsTableLink.EOF Then
        'Process each table
        Do While Not rsTableLink.EOF
            tableID = rsTableLink("_ID")
            Text1.Text = Text1.Text & vbCrLf & "CREATE TABLE " & _
                CWMGetSVAttr("Relational_Table_name", tableID, _
                    adVarChar)
            delim = "("
            'Find the table's columns via the ClassifierFeature
            'association
            Set rsColumnLink = _
                CWMGetMVLinks("Core_ClassifierFeature_feature", _
                    "owner", tableID)
            Do While Not rsColumnLink.EOF
                'Add each column to the display text
                colID = rsColumnLink("feature_ID")
                Text1.Text = Text1.Text & vbCrLf & indent & delim & _
                    CWMGetSVAttr("Relational_Column_name", _
                        colID, adVarChar)
                'Get the column's data type via the
                'StructuralFeatureType association
                typeID = CWMGetSVLink("Core_StructuralFeatureType", _
                    "type", "feature", colID)
                Text1.Text = Text1.Text & " " & _
                    CWMGetSVAttr("Relational_SQLSimpleType_name", _
                        typeID, adVarChar)
                If typeID = varcharID Then
                    'Add the length for VARCHAR columns
                    Text1.Text = Text1.Text & "(" & _
                        CWMGetSVAttr("Relational_Column_length", _
                            colID, adInteger) & ")"
                End If
                delim = ","
                rsColumnLink.MoveNext
            Loop
            Text1.Text = Text1.Text & vbCrLf & indent & ")" & vbCrLf
            rsTableLink.MoveNext
        Loop
    End If

    'We're done
    oConn.Close
End Sub
```

Core_Namespace

_ID	
1	
2	
3	
4	
9	

Core_ModelElement

_ID	name	namespace_ID	
1	INT	<null>	
2	VARCHAR	<null>	
3	MyCompany	<null>	
4	Person	3	
5	personID	4	
7	name	4	
9	Department	3	
10	deptID	9	
12	name	9	

Core_Element

_ID	
1	
2	
3	
4	
5	
6	
7	
8	
9	
10	
11	
12	
13	

Core_Feature

_ID	owner_ID	feature_Ordinal	
5	5	1	
7	7	2	
10	10	1	
12	12	2	

Core_Expression

_ID	
6	
8	
11	
13	

Core_Classifier

_ID	
1	
2	
4	
9	

Core_Datatype

_ID	
1	
2	

Core_StructuralFeature

_ID	type_ID	
5	1	
7	2	
10	1	
12	2	

Core_Class

_ID	
4	
9	

Relational_SQLDatatype

_ID	
1	
2	

Relational_Column

_ID	length	
5	<null>	
7	255	
10	<null>	
12	255	

Relational_ColumnSet

_ID	
4	
9	

Relational_SQLSimpleType

_ID	
1	
2	

Relational_NamedColumnSet

_ID	
4	
9	

Relational_Table

_ID	
4	
9	

Core_Attribute

_ID	initialValue_ID	
5	6	
7	8	
10	11	
12	13	

Figure 8.45   Contents of the Metastore after the example program ends.

Summary

This chapter defined a relatively "low-cost" meta data store or repository that can be used to store CWM-encoded meta data, and presented the SQL script required to generate its structures. We have seen that this database, built on top of a commonly available relational database management system, still preserves the object-oriented underpinnings of CWM that are essential to successful meta data interchange within the foundational framework of UML and MOF.

The CWM Metastore offers a sufficient level of data management functionality, and provides persistent storage for (as well as allowing for concurrent, transacted access to) the complex meta data found in data warehousing environments. Its relative simplicity, however, means that it is substantially less costly to build, operate, and maintain than a full-fledged repository. It does not, however, provide more advanced repository features such as versioning, life-cycle management, and source code generation. Developers wishing this level of meta data management and control will need to construct additional service layers above the core persistence architecture of the CWM Metastore.

PART

Three

Implementation and Deployment

Integration Architecture

The preceding chapters have described domain-specific applications of Common Warehouse Metamodel (CWM) in considerable detail. In particular, we have seen that CWM is a standard specification for defining data warehousing and business analysis meta data in terms of descriptive models. We've used CWM in that capacity to develop models of four representative domain areas: Data Warehousing, Dimensional Modeling, Web-Enabled Data Warehousing, and the CWM Metastore model. We've demonstrated that CWM is independent of any particular technology, and it is obvious that the models developed in the previous four chapters are capable of existing outside of the various software products that use them as the basis for integration.

Chapter 6 of *Common Warehouse Metamodel: An Introduction to the Standard for Data Warehouse Integration* (Wiley, 2002) provided a much broader description of how CWM relates to the overall problem of building a comprehensive meta data integration solution. In particular, that chapter delved into the implications that CWM has for both meta data management strategies and meta data integration architectures. It also described the necessary architectural components required to deploy CWM integration solutions in the data warehousing and business analysis environments.

In this chapter, we will briefly summarize those results, in order to convey the understanding that, given a choice of vertical domain models, one may then co-opt a specific subset of the architectural methodology for the purposes of specifying a concrete meta data management strategy and integration architecture centered on CWM. Note that the various logical, domain modeling solutions are largely orthogonal to issues of integration architecture. For example, the CWM Metastore model developed in Chapter 8 is realizable as the central hub repository described more abstractly in the following summarization.

Developing a Meta Data Integration Architecture

In the Introductory CWM book (Poole, 2002), we described at length the importance of establishing a coherent and sound meta data management strategy prior to defining the meta data integration architecture. We described how the meta data management strategy must identify all of the meta data sources, their life-cycle roles, the owners of meta data, the agreed-upon semantics of the meta data, and the measurable goals for reuse and sharing. We also showed where CWM, as an anticipated component of the meta data integration architecture, provides direct support for many of the essential characteristics of such a strategy.

This subsection delves further into the concept of the meta data integration architecture. As suggested previously, any meta data integration architecture is largely a realization or implementation of a meta data management strategy. We show the advantages that CWM provides as the standard infrastructure for a model-driven approach to meta data integration. CWM supports the overall integration architecture; it simplifies the integration and ensures its effectiveness (that is, results in the best-possible implementation of a coherent meta data management strategy).

Survey of Architectural Patterns

Like a meta data management strategy, any particular meta data integration architecture is specific to its target environment. Integration architectures must possess complete specificity to be effective but must also be founded on sound principles if they are to work. Whereas a sound meta data management strategy must adhere to certain essential characteristics, as elaborated in (Poole, 2002), sound meta data integration architecture must also be based on certain essential design patterns that have been proven to solve the problem. We define our architecture by selecting one of these proven patterns and then tailoring it to our specific implementation or environment. We also demonstrate how the model-based integration approach taken by CWM helps us to define superior concrete architectures from the more general architectural patterns.

The term *architecture* can be regarded as the use of abstract models or high-level specifications that describe something to be constructed. In Chapter 2, we described at great length how meta data is essentially an abstract model of data and how a metamodel like CWM is very much an abstract model of meta data in a particular domain. We likened models to architectural blueprints for the building of a house. We also noted that one particular model or blueprint does not necessarily provide all the viewpoints required by the various contractors involved in constructing a house. For example, we need an electrical blueprint for the electrical contractor, a plumbing blueprint for the plumber, a framing blueprint for the builder, and so on. Each of these blueprints is a separate model of the house, and, collectively, they define the overall architecture of the house. Each blueprint defines a separate and necessary viewpoint on the overall architecture. No single description of the house's architecture is sufficient for all contractors.

Also, no single expression of a meta data integration architecture is sufficient for all purposes. We need to deal with several specific architectural viewpoints to provide a comprehensive description of our meta data integration solution. Two of the key viewpoints are as follows:

- Meta data interconnection architecture
- Meta data life-cycle architecture

Meta Data Interconnection Architecture

A *meta data interconnection architecture* (*topology*) describes, from a high level, the physical meta data interchange connections established between software products and tools within the deployment of an actual data warehouse or ISC.

Figure 9.1 illustrates a simple meta data interchange scenario between several data warehouse tools. A modeling tool is used to define a data warehouse model consisting of a relational database schema, transformation mappings from a source operational system to a relational database, and an Online Analytical Processing (OLAP) analysis application and its mapping to the relational schema. Portions of this model are exported to an Extraction, Transfer, and Loading (ETL) tool, a relational database engine, and an OLAP server. In each case, this meta data needs to be translated to three different formats that each of the three target tools can understand (each flow line in the diagram is implemented by a productwise meta data bridge). Finally, a reporting tool imports the meta data that it needs to facilitate its analysis reporting and data drill-down capabilities. The sources of this meta data are the ETL tool, relational database, and OLAP server. Productwise meta data bridges are used to translate the ETL, relational, and OLAP meta data into some format that is intelligible to the reporting tool.

Figure 9.2 shows the same scenario, except with a meta data repository included as the central clearinghouse for managing and publishing all meta data relevant to the software tools comprising the data warehouse. Note that this has the effect of simplifying the scenario somewhat. The modeling tool is still the primary source of meta data for the data warehouse, and the ETL is still both a consumer and a secondary source of meta data. Neither the relational database, the OLAP server, nor the ETL tool need serve as a direct meta data source to the analytic reporting tool. Instead, each tool obtains its meta data from the repository. Note that fewer productwise meta data bridges are required. Furthermore, these bridges translate between tool-specific formats and a single format defined by the repository product. So, their overall complexity is somewhat reduced.

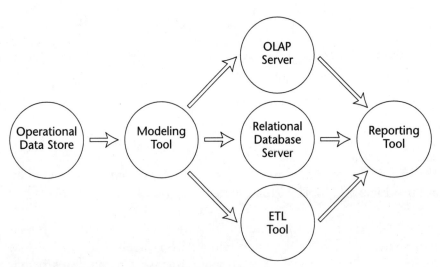

Figure 9.1 Simple meta data interchange scenario.

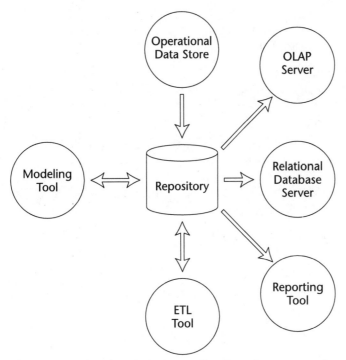

Figure 9.2   Repository-based meta data interchange scenario.

Figure 9.1 is an example of a *point-to-point*, or *network*, meta data inter-connection architecture, and Figure 9.2 illustrates a *hub-and-spoke*, or *centralized*, meta data interconnection architecture. We can abstract these two meta data interconnection architectures into two general patterns. Figure 9.3 shows a generalization of the point-to-point interconnection architecture involving four software tools (denoted as T1, T2, T3, and T4). Because this diagram represents the most general case, we assume that any of the tools can equally be producers or consumers of meta data. Each link in the diagram represents a meta data bridge joining a pair of tools, and it is assumed that each bridge is bidirectional. (We also can assume that each link is composed of two unidirectional bridges.)

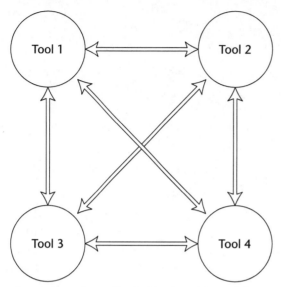

Figure 9.3 Generalized point-to-point model.

Similarly, Figure 9.4 illustrates a generalization of the hub-and-spoke meta data interconnection architecture consisting of four tools interconnected via a central meta data repository. Notice that the number of required meta data bridges has been reduced from six to four. In general, the point-to-point model requires a total of n (n [ms] 1) / 2 bidirectional meta data bridges to interconnect n tools; whereas the generalized hub-and-spoke model requires n bidirectional bridges to interconnect n tools. This should give some indication of why point-to-point bridge building can be such an expensive and complex undertaking when the number of tools that need to be interconnected is large. For 100 tools, the generalized point-to-point solution requires 4,950 bidirectional bridges; whereas the generalized hub-and-spoke solution requires only 100 bidirectional bridges to fully interconnect all tools.

This illustration is something of a *worst-case* scenario, in which we naively assume that each tool requires to be interconnected to every other tool. In any real-world situation, this is usually not going to be the case. This example, however, does serve to illustrate the fact that, *on average*, point-to-point interconnections using productwise meta data bridges (for example, a bridge that performs a custom mapping between one proprietary metamodel and another) can be expected to be far more expensive than an equivalent hub-and-spoke solution. This is because a hub-and-spoke solution introduces a single, common metamodel (that is, implemented by the repository) with which tools need to interface. Each tool requires a single meta data bridge that translates between its own proprietary metamodel and a single metamodel defined by the central meta data repository product.

Note that, although we've reduced overall cost by standardizing on a particular, repository-based metamodel, we have still not provided the ideal, *minimal-cost* solution. This is because the common metamodel is still proprietary to the meta data repository. Each meta data bridge is required to translate between productwise metamodels. We need fewer bridges, and the bridges are somewhat less complex, because the interface to the repository is the same for each bridge. If we wanted to substitute another vendor's repository product, however, we would need to acquire a whole new collection of bridges, unless the other vendor's repository implemented the same metamodel and interfaces as the previous vendor's. This is precisely what CWM enables us to have—a common and product-independent meta data and interface definition that we can use to construct meta data interchange architectures in a plug-and-play and minimal-cost fashion. Before considering how CWM enhances meta data integration architectures, let's consider several more variations on the basic meta data interconnection topologies.

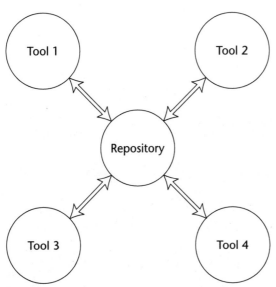

Figure 9.4 Generalized hub-and-spoke model.

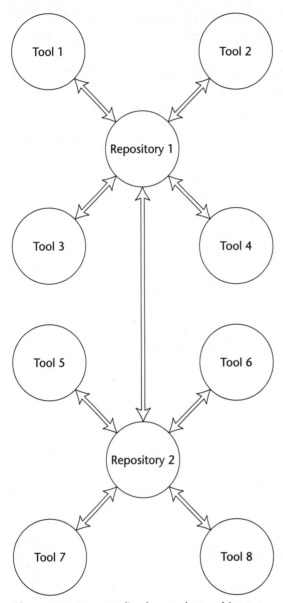

Figure 9.5   Decentralized meta data architecture.

Figure 9.5 illustrates an interconnection architecture in which two hub-and-spoke topologies are connected together via their repositories. We generally refer to this type of meta data integration architecture as being *distributed, decentralized,* or *federated*. (Note that a point-to-point topology is inherently decentralized, but here we use the term *decentralized* to refer to repository-oriented topologies.) The two repositories in Figure 9.5 are interconnected via a meta data bridge. If the repositories implement different metamodels and interfaces, the bridge is another productwise bridge that must be capable of translating meta data between the two metamodels. If each repository implements the same metamodel and interfaces, or some subset of the same metamodel, the bridge represents a simple, physical connection between repositories.

A number of reasons exist for building this form of meta data integration architecture. In the case of dissimilar metamodels, the architecture still provides a single, managed environment for meta data. A meta data client of repository R1 (in Figure 9.5) can have access to meta data defined in repository R2, assuming that the bridge properly maps this meta data between the two metamodels. This architecture might be used to combine two different business domains, with different descriptive metamodels, such as a sales domain and a manufacturing domain. In this case, either repository is primarily responsible for servicing meta data clients of its supported domain. Each repository maintains meta data specific to its particular metamodel and domain. Whenever necessary, meta data clients are still able to access and share meta data from the foreign domain (as long as adequate metamodel mapping and translation is provided). This approach facilitates cross-domain sharing and reuse of meta data.

In other situations, it may be advantageous to physically partition a single, common metamodel and distribute it across several repositories. For example, tools requiring only certain subsets of the overall data warehouse or ISC meta data might be designed as going to one particular repository hosting only that meta data. This might be done to ensure the efficient use of processing cycles and network bandwidth in a multitier environment. An analysis tier might host a repository containing meta data specific to analysis and visualization only, and the dimensional data warehouse itself might reside on a different tier with its own meta data repository defining the data warehouse and ETL processes. In any case, the entire meta data integration architecture is based on a single metamodel that gives it both semantic unity and simplified interconnections. We sometimes refer to this scenario as *model distribution*.

Yet another scenario supported by decentralized meta data integration architectures is that of *controlled meta data replication*. We stated in our requirements for a meta data integration strategy that redundant meta data definitions should be avoided or minimized. In certain situations, however, replication of meta data is necessary. For example, when the meta data repositories are geographically dispersed, it might be necessary to replicate some meta data between repositories to ensure adequate response times for the meta data clients at a remote location. This replication is acceptable, as long as a specific policy is in place that defines how and when meta data is to be replicated and how modifications are to be handled. Usually, modification to the meta data is restricted to one particular repository and that repository is designated as the master repository, with respect to any replicated meta data at other points in the topology.

Figure 9.6 illustrates a variation on the decentralized model that supports the model distribution paradigm in a specific way. This variation is referred to as a *hierarchical* or *star* topology. Note that this is essentially a hub-and-spoke architecture in which the central repository hub has other repositories as its client tools. In this case, the *root* repository implements common portions of the metamodel (and corresponding meta data instances) that are common to the overall meta data environment. Each of the *leaf* repositories implements one or more specific subsets of the common metamodel and stores meta data instances corresponding to those subsets only. A given meta data client primarily accesses the leaf repository hosting the meta data in which it is primarily interested, but also has access to the global meta data stored in the root, as well as any subset meta data stored by other leaf-level repositories.

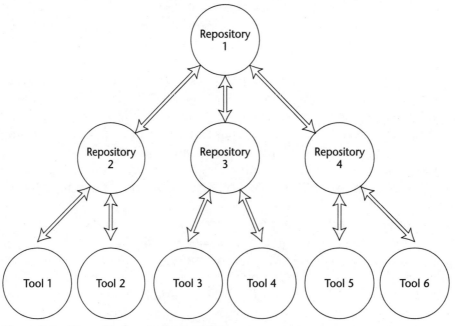

Figure 9.6   Hierarchical meta data architecture.

Note that this architecture gives us the ability to optimize the use of system resources (that is, processing cycles and network bandwidth) based on the principle of *locality of reference*. A given client usually accesses a single, specific leaf-level repository most of the time for its meta data needs. On occasion, the client may need to go to the global root or one or more of the other leaf-level repositories. Most of the time, the client's meta data requirements can be satisfied by one particular repository, and that repository can be colocated on the same physical computing tier as the client (or on a tier close by). So the majority of the client's meta data requests do not impact the rest of the interconnection architecture. However, a single, common, and consistent metamodel (and corresponding collection of meta data) can be maintained and centrally administered. Although the metamodel and its meta data instances are physically distributed across the interconnection topology, a single, logical definition of the metamodel and a single, logical collection of instances exist. The computing environment is optimized (from a performance perspective), and meta data redundancy is eliminated.

Note that CWM's highly decoupled architecture, based on packaged metamodels with clean package separation and minimal interpackage dependencies (see Chapter 4, "Meta Date Interchange Patterns"), greatly facilitates model distribution. For example, if the interconnection architecture shown in Figure 9.5 represents a distributed metamodel, two CWM-enabled repositories would be deployed in this environment. One repository would support some subset of the CWM metamodel packages (and corresponding meta data instances). The other repository would support some other subset of CWM metamodel packages and their meta data instances. Collectively, the distributed metamodel represents a single metamodel that is logically coherent, yet physically partitioned. The implementation of hierarchical architectures based on CWM, such as the one shown in Figure 9.6, is also facilitated by CWM's modular architecture.

We will demonstrate in a subsequent section how CWM relates to the integration topologies presented here. In particular, we will show that CWM enables these various architectural patterns to be physically deployed with minimal implementation complexity and cost, far less than what is currently possible with productwise, or repository-productwise meta data bridges. First, we need to consider the other key perspective on meta data integration architecture—*meta data life-cycle architecture*.

Meta Data Life-Cycle Architecture

In the preceding subsection on meta data management strategy, we alluded to the fact that a distinct meta data life cycle consists of the following activities:

- Authoring
- Publishing
- Owning
- Consuming
- Managing

Authoring generally implies the creation of new meta data. *Publishing* consists of somehow making the existence and location of meta data known to the environment at large or to specific interested parties. *Owning* refers to some specific tool or process asserting certain privileges regarding how a piece of meta data is used. *Consuming* refers to a tool reading meta data and using it for some purpose, usually to effect its own internal operations or to build its internal information structures. Finally, *managing* refers to the overall management and control of meta data, including modifying, extending, and controlling its access by other tools or processes.

Corresponding to the meta data life-cycle activities are a corresponding set of meta data life-cycle *roles:*

- Author
- Publisher
- Owner
- Consumer
- Manager

Each role describes how a particular software tool (or type of software tool) usually functions in some specified meta data integration architecture. For example, a modeling tool usually plays the role of meta data author. A repository often plays the role of publisher and usually the role of manager, as well. An analysis tool (for example, an OLAP server or reporting or visualization tool) is more often than not a consumer of meta data.

Note that these roles are not hard and fast. Specific software products and tools may assume different roles at different points in time. In many cases, roles may overlap. For example, the author of a particular model may also continue as the model's owner and manager. Or, the author may relinquish management of the model to a repository but still continue as the model's owner and have certain access privileges regarding the model.

These roles are clearly important to any meta data management strategy as well as its related meta data integration architecture. In fact, the roles define another viewpoint on the meta data integration architecture, one more behavioral in nature, and not necessarily readily apparent from the interconnection topology alone. We refer to this as the meta data life-cycle architecture. This architecture defines the overall meta data flow and behavioral characteristics of our meta data integration architecture; whereas the interconnection topology tends to define the static structure of the meta data integration architecture.

Consider again the meta data interchange scenario illustrated in Figure 9.1. A point-to-point interconnection topology capable of supporting this interchange is shown in Figure 9.7. Each of the links connecting the various tools is assumed to be a single, productwise, bidirectional meta data bridge (for now, anyway). Figure 9.8 depicts the meta data life-cycle architecture supporting the interchange scenario. Now, a number of important points are revealed by the life-cycle architecture. The flow of meta data defining the life cycle is from left to right in the diagram. So it appears that the meta data bridges implementing the point-to-point network need only be unidirectional, although still productwise. (Note, however, that some other life-cycle flow could easily impose other requirements on the same interconnection architecture, including the use of bidirectional bridges or mixtures of both bidirectional and unidirectional bridges.)

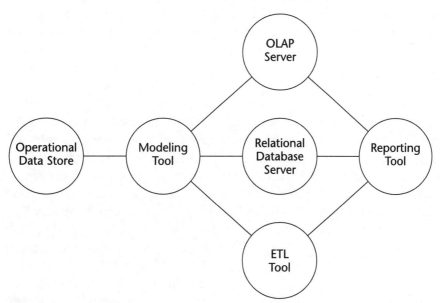

Figure 9.7   Point-to-point interconnection architecture.

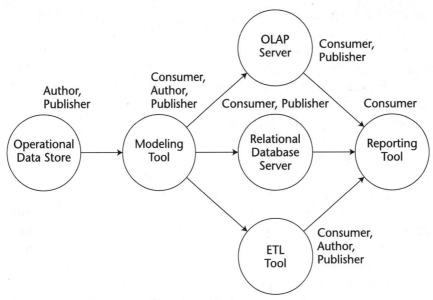

Figure 9.8 Point-to-point life-cycle architecture.

The various life-cycle roles of the participating tools are also shown in Figure 9.8. The operational data store is both an author and publisher, in the sense that its major role is to define and introduce *new* meta data to the environment. The modeling tool is the primary consumer of the Open Data Services (ODS) meta data. The modeling tool, via its meta data bridge to the ODS, captures enough essential meta data describing the ODS information structures to build a model mapping the ODS to the relational store. The modeling tool also creates new meta data in the form of a comprehensive warehouse model defining the relational database and OLAP schemas. So, the modeling tool plays the roles of consumer of published meta data, author of new meta data, and publisher of the combined model. The relational database and OLAP server are primarily consumers of meta data and republishers of existing meta data; that is, they use the meta data they import from the modeling tool to build their internal information structures, and then forward that same meta data on to the reporting tool. The ETL tool is a consumer, author, and publisher and republisher, because it generates some new meta data as a by-product of its data transformation, cleansing, and normalization process. Finally, the reporting tool only consumes meta data made available by the relational database, OLAP server, and ETL tool.

One of the roles obviously missing from Figure 9.8 is that of meta data manager. Quite a bit of authoring, publishing, and consumption of meta data goes on in this life cycle, but there does not appear to be any clear ownership or management functionality roles assumed by any of these tools. Given the interconnection architecture and the necessary life-cycle flow, no one particular tool in this environment really seems suitable to assume this role. We will see how this situation changes when we introduce a centralized interconnection architecture.

Recall that Figure 9.2 showed the same meta data interchange scenario originally illustrated in Figure 9.1, but introduced a central repository, converting the point-to-point interconnection architecture to a centralized one. Figure 9.9 shows the meta data interconnection architecture supporting this interchange scenario, and Figure 9.10 illustrates the equivalent, centralized life-cycle architecture (based on the same life-cycle flow implied by the interchange scenario of Figure 9.1).

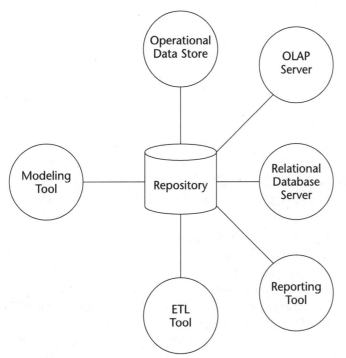

Figure 9.9 Centralized interconnection architecture.

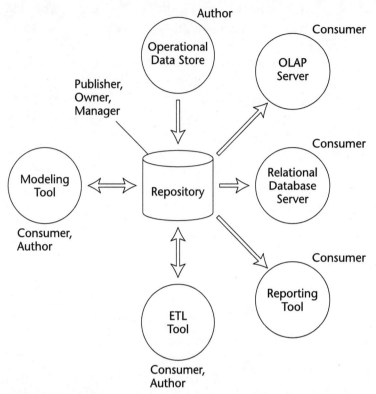

Figure 9.10 Centralized life-cycle architecture.

Note that in this case, the roles are far more crisply defined than in the previous depiction of the life cycle. The ODS and modeling tools are clearly the primary authors of meta data in this environment. Although it is true that the modeling tool also consumes ODS meta data to perform its authoring function, its more dominant role is that of meta data author, although we have labeled it as both a consumer and an author. The repository clearly plays the roles of publisher and manager and will consider it to be the owner of the meta data, as well. (One could also stipulate that the modeling tool and ODS share ownership of the meta data and that the repository manages the meta data on behalf of these two tools. For this example, declaring the repository the owner of all meta data is simpler.) The ETL tool is both a consumer and an author, and this is emphasized by the presence of a bidirectional bridge between the ETL tool and repository. The relational database, OLAP server, and reporting tools are now strictly consumers of meta data. The relational database and OLAP server are no longer both consumers and republishers of meta data (a rather bothersome and clearly extraneous term that the point-to-point topology forced us to use).

Before taking up the discussion of how CWM enhances these various interconnection and life-cycle architectures, let's briefly consider several of the important nuances often associated with these various approaches.

We described the use of meta data bridges as a means of implementing the links shown in the preceding diagrams. We also said that a given meta data bridge is either unidirectional or bidirectional. A unidirectional bridge is capable of transporting meta data in one direction only, from source tool to target tool. A bidirectional bridge is capable of transporting meta data in both directions and is generally equivalent to two unidirectional bridges between the same tools. A bidirectional bridge (or two unidirectional bridges) is typically deployed between two tools that need to switch between the roles of source and target. For example, in one particular interchange scenario, Tool A might be a publisher of meta data, and Tool B is a consumer; although in another interchange scenario occurring within the same environment, Tool A is the consumer of meta data published by Tool B.

To facilitate meta data transfers, a bridge must be capable of translating between the proprietary metamodels of its source and target tools, assuming that they have different metamodels. Obviously, if they share a common metamodel and common interfaces for meta data, the transfer of meta data from the source tool to the target tool is straightforward and requires the use of a much simpler form of bridge, which we will term an *adapter*.

Certain behavioral nuances of meta data bridges or adapters need to be decided upon when specifying the meta data integration architecture. These behavioral features concern the initiation of the actual meta data transfer or flow and are generally categorized as the following:

- Import-export
- Push-pull
- Request-response
- Subscribe-notify

Import and *export* often refer to the general nature of the behavior of the bridge or adapter with respect to a particular tool with which the bridge interfaces. A tool currently acting as a meta data producer in some capacity is said to export its meta data via the bridge or adapter. A meta data consumer is said to import its meta data via the bridge or adapter. This generally means that the processing logic of the bridge generally reads meta data from the tool's proprietary meta data interfaces, in the case of a meta data export operation, or writes to the tool's proprietary meta data interfaces, in the case of a meta data import operation.

Push and *pull* are concepts almost synonymous with import and export, except that they more closely describe a meta data transfer from the viewpoint of the initiator of the transfer, rather than from the viewpoint of how the bridge interfaces with the source or target tool. If the source tool initiates the overall transfer process to a target tool, the transfer is usually referred to as a *meta data push*. If the target tool initiates the transfer process, it is usually called a *meta data pull*. If neither source nor target initiates the transfer, the terms *push* and *pull* still apply but are relative to the process initiating the transfer. That is, the initiating process pulls the meta data from the source and pushes it to the target (relatively speaking). This is illustrated in Figure 9.11.

Request-response is essentially the opposite of the push-pull. In this case, a meta data target issues a request to a meta data source for some specific meta data instance. The source then transmits the requested meta data instance to the target, and the target imports the instance. Note that the request-response paradigm tends to be more message-oriented and synchronous than the push-pull or import-export paradigms, which are batch-oriented and asynchronous in nature. The request-response paradigm also offers more opportunity for finer-grained interchanges, because the meta data target has an opportunity to request precisely what meta data elements it needs from the source. Figure 9.12 depicts the request-response paradigm.

Finally, *subscribe-notify* refers to the capability of a meta data target to request (subscribe) that a meta data source notify it when some specific meta data instance is modified or otherwise made available in some published form. The source notifies the target that the requested instance is available, and the target issues a request for the instance using the fine-grained request-response paradigm (unless the notification message also includes a copy of the requested instance). This is shown in Figure 9.13.

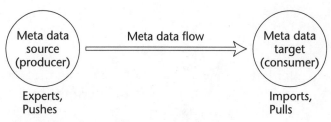

Figure 9.11 Push-pull interchange protocol.

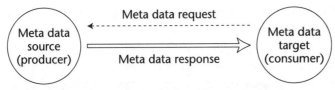

Figure 9.12   Request-response interchange protocol.

Note that these various behavioral classifications apply primarily to the initiation of meta data movement between source and target tools and do not describe how metamodel mapping or meta data translation is to be performed. These behavioral classifications represent, however, an extremely important aspect of the meta data integration architecture, because they define the dynamic capabilities and overall robustness of the architecture. For example, consider a situation in which the various data warehousing or Information Supply Chain (ISC) tools are all served by a single central repository. The repository has subscribe-notify capabilities built into it, and tools subscribe for notifications whenever any meta data instances in which they have a vested interest are modified. An administrator uses a modeling tool or repository front-end management tool to alter a particular instance of meta data. All affected tools are then notified of the change, and each requests a fresh copy of the modified instance. Each tool incorporates this new version of the meta data into its internal information structures and gracefully reintegrates itself into the overall ISC environment.

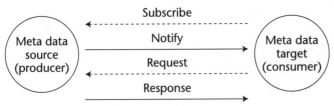

Figure 9.13   Subscribe-notify interchange protocol.

This sort of dynamic meta data architecture is sometimes referred to as an *active repository* environment (although it requires the various tools participating in the environment to be just as active as the repository itself). Numerous advantages exist to such an architecture, including the central administration of changes to meta data, the automatic propagation of those changes to any affected tools, and the opportunity that each tool has to adjust its internal models accordingly and to reintegrate back into the environment. David Marco classifies this sort of meta data integration architecture as *bidirectional meta data*. He also discusses another variation of this behavior, referred to as *closed-loop meta data*, in which modified operational meta data is automatically applied to the affected operational system. Marco suggests that these types of meta data architecture will become quite prevalent in the near future (see Marco, 2000, pp. 311–314). Figure 9.14 illustrates a dynamic, centralized architecture, based on the active repository concept.

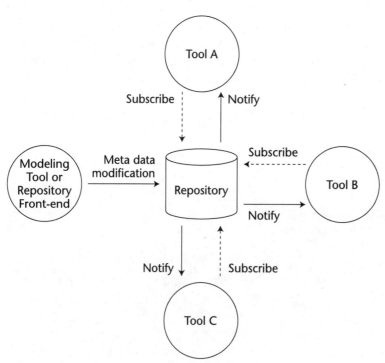

Figure 9.14 Dynamic centralized architecture.

CWM-Based Meta Data Integration Architecture

In the preceding subsections, we investigated meta data integration architectural patterns in considerable detail. We noted that two key viewpoints exist for any meta data integration architecture:

- Meta data interconnection architecture
- Meta data life-cycle architecture

The meta data interconnection architecture defines the static connections between the various tools of a meta data-driven environment. The life-cycle architecture defines the general behavior and flow requirements of the meta data interchange process, embellishing the static interconnection topology with additional information on the dynamics of the overall meta data integration architecture.

Each static connection or link in the interconnection topology represents a meta data bridge, a software process that enables the flow of meta data between meta data source and target components. In addition to transferring meta data, the bridge is responsible for translating meta data between source and target components in situations when the components have dissimilar, internal metamodels and proprietary meta data interfaces. We saw that the construction of a meta data bridge is a complex and expensive process, mainly because a large number of bridges must be implemented to integrate a wide variety of tools. We also saw that providing a meta data repository helps to mitigate this cost somewhat, because the repository, as a central hub for all meta data management and interactions, offers a single metamodel with which all tools integrate. Bridges are used to link tools with the common repository, rather than to link individual tools in a pairwise fashion. Although this solution helps to lower development costs and to provide a higher degree of meta data sharing and reuse, it is still not the ideal solution. The meta data repository is another software tool with a proprietary metamodel and interface, and repositories from different vendors are not guaranteed to be compatible in this regard.

Now that we have a thorough understanding of the problem, let's investigate why and how CWM resolves this last remaining roadblock to achieving cost-effective meta data integration in the data warehousing and business intelligence environments.

As described throughout previous chapters, CWM is a comprehensive metamodel defining data warehousing and business analysis concepts and relationships. Meta data is represented as formal models (that is, instances of the CWM metamodel), and these models are both technology- and platform-neutral (as is the CWM metamodel itself). CWM is compliant with Object Management Group's (OMG's) Meta Object Facility. This means that standard rules exist for mapping CWM instances to both eXtensible Markup Language (XML) [via the XML Metadata Interchange (XMI) standard] and language-independent programmatic interfaces [via Meta Object Facility (MOF) and Interface Definition Language (IDL)]. The XML format is used for bulk interchange (based on the push-pull and request-response paradigms discussed earlier), and programmatic Application Programming Interfaces (APIs) based on the CWM IDL provide a standard programming model for meta data access.

CWM provides both a standard metamodel and a related collection of standard meta data interfaces (both stream-based and programmatic). Any repository product provides this as well. So what advantages does CWM offer us? The key point about CWM is that the metamodel is completely independent of any conceivable implementation. The CWM metamodel exists independently of, and outside of, all technology platforms and products. And so do any instances of CWM. Therefore, using CWM, we can formulate highly expressive and semantically complete models of information structures (meta data) that can exist outside of any particular software product or tool. Meta data, therefore, is no longer confined to the proprietary metamodels and interfaces of specific products. Data warehousing meta data is liberated from products and tools and can exist on its own, as a valuable information resource in its own right.

CWM models can be constructed to any required degree of complexity. They can be sufficiently descriptive to be used as the basis for building the internal implementation models of a wide variety of data warehousing products and tools. Conversely, a given product or tool can easily export its internal meta data in the form of a standard CWM model, with little or no information loss, because the CWM metamodel is semantically rich. The meta data interfaces defined by CWM (both the XML and programmatic APIs) are also completely independent of any particular implementation or product, because they are based on standard mappings of the CWM metamodel.

All CWM-enabled software products, tools, applications, repositories, and so on, share a single, common metamodel that is totally independent of any particular implementation model. And all CWM-enabled products also implement the same common interfaces for meta data interchange. This means that any CWM-aware software component can readily understand the meta data instances exposed by another CWM-enabled component and can access that meta data through the standard set of CWM meta data interfaces.

This has profound implications for meta data bridges. In an environment consisting of CWM-enabled tools, the heavyweight, productwise bridges we discussed earlier can be replaced with lightweight bridges termed *CWM adapters*. An adapter is a piece of software that understands the CWM metamodel, as well as the internal metamodel and proprietary meta data interfaces of the software product for which the adapter is written. One side of the adapter, the *public side*, implements the CWM standard interfaces. The other end of the adapter connects to the product-specific interfaces. Processing logic within the adapter translates between CWM-compliant meta data instances and product-specific meta data. A CWM adapter for a given software product or tool need be written only once. This represents considerable savings over the development of productwise bridges, even when the bridge is targeted toward a repository product. A CWM-enabled product can readily integrate into any environment consisting of other CWM-enabled products and tools.

So let's investigate how CWM enhances the various meta data integration architectures described earlier. Consider the point-to-point meta data interchange scenario first defined in Figure 9.1. Figure 9.8 shows a life-cycle architecture describing the interchange. Each directed link in this diagram represents a unique, product-to-product bridge facilitating meta data interchange between pairs of products, along with the various life-cycle roles ascribed to each product instance. Figure 9.10 illustrates the equivalent centralized version of the life cycle, in which a meta data repository is introduced as the central meta data hub. The architecture is simplified to the extent that the bridges now interconnect product-specific metamodels and interface with the common metamodel and interface supplied by the repository. The life-cycle roles ascribed to the products are also simpler in this case.

Figure 9.15 illustrates the point-to-point life-cycle architecture resulting from enabling each of the tools pictured in Figure 9.8 with CWM adapters (for example, the large arrows that had represented productwise meta data bridges in Figure 9.8 now represent lightweight CWM adapter modules in Figure 9.15). Note that the actual meta data interchange *flow* between the products in Figure 9.15 is still exactly the same as the flow defined by the connecting bridges in Figure 9.8. However, from an *interface and metamodel mapping* perspective, all tools are integrated via a single, logical CWM infrastructure layer. For example, the ODS is supplying meta data to the modeling tool using standard CWM meta data interfaces, and the modeling tool is supplying its meta data to its various consumers via the same standard interfaces. All of this meta data (actually, various portions of a single CWM model) is consistent with the single CWM common metamodel. In principle, each tool participating in this architecture has only one metamodel that is publicly exposed to the CWM metamodel.

Standardization on the CWM metamodel and interfaces provides a point-to-point topology with a *logical central hub*. This hub is more conceptual than it is physical but provides essentially the same benefits as if we had introduced a physical central hub (that is, a meta data repository). For a collection of CWM-enabled tools, deploying a point-to-point architecture is no more expensive than building a centralized architecture. (The control and management advantages of the repository are missing, but for a relatively small number of interconnected tools, a strong requirement may not exist for central meta data management to justify the cost of a repository, anyway.)

What happens if we use a CWM-enabled repository to convert the point-to-point architecture into a centralized one? By saying that the repository is CWM-enabled, we mean that the repository's metamodel *is* the CWM metamodel and that the meta data stored in the repository consists of instances of the CWM metamodel. Note that how the metamodel and meta data storage schema is physically implemented under the covers (for example, as a relational database schema) doesn't really matter. Access to repository meta data must also be available via the standard CWM meta data interfaces (both via XML and programmatically). The repository must also provide a set of *system level* interfaces not defined by CWM, such as an interface for establishing a connection to the repository.

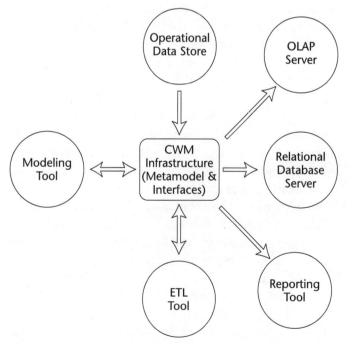

Figure 9.15   CWM-enabled point-to-point architecture.

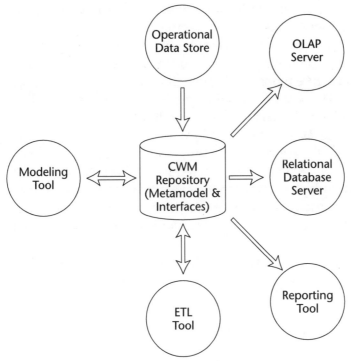

Figure 9.16   CWM-enabled centralized architecture.

Figure 9.16 shows the centralized life-cycle architecture of Figure 9.10 with a CWM-enabled repository. Note that very little difference exists between this physically centralized architecture and the logically centralized architecture. In fact, from the perspective of standard meta data interfaces based on a common metamodel, essentially no difference exists between the two. Only the sources and targets of the meta data flows are different. There are going to be differences in terms of system-level interfaces. For example, the interface used to connect to the repository probably will be different from the interface that would be used to connect to the OLAP server.

A need also exists to provide process-oriented interfaces for initiating the various types of interchange paradigms (for example, push-pull, request-response, subscribe-notify). These interfaces and their semantics are also outside the scope of the CWM specification. However, it is possible to hide the differences between the various system-level interfaces of various tools by providing a relatively simple *control framework* for the tools participating in a given environment. The basic control framework defines a number of fairly simple interfaces for implementing the basic meta data interchange sessions and interactions typically required in an integrated environment. A more complex control framework might implement the functionality required by completely automatic, dynamic, meta data environments (such as an active repository). Note that in a purely Web-centric environment using XML-based interchanges, supporting system-level interfaces are less problematic, as they are generally standardized in terms of the various Web services, interfaces, and protocols.

Figure 9.17 illustrates the concept of a CWM-enabled meta data environment. Two software tools, A and B, are enabled for CWM-based meta data interchange via CWM adapters. Adapter logic reads or writes tool-specific meta data (that is, meta data conforming to the internal metamodel of the tool) via each tool's proprietary meta data interfaces. Tool-specific meta data is translated to and from equivalent CWM meta data, according to a precisely defined mapping between CWM and tool-specific metamodels.

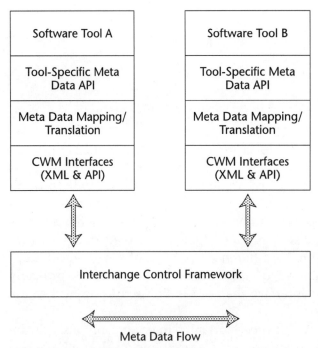

Figure 9.17 CWM-enabled meta data environment.

(This mapping is defined as a part of the adapter module specification itself, and there are many possible ways, from a software engineering perspective, to design and implement this mapping logic.) CWM-compliant meta data is then somehow exposed to the interchange control framework. Note that the interchange control framework is not specified in any way by the CWM standard. Rather, it consists of the collection of system-level processes provided by the overall data warehouse or ISC implementation that manages and initiates meta data interchange and transfer. Such an overall control framework is necessary in any meta data-driven environment.

Crafting Your Own CWM Architectural Solutions

Note that CWM is a specification, not an implementation. However, this book provides a considerable amount of information that should enable you to begin designing and building your own CWM integration solutions. In particular, the CWM Metastore is an ideal starting point to begin prototyping any of the more abstract integration architectures described in the preceding subsections. One can readily envision an implementation of the Metastore serving the role of a central repository hub. Much of the logic required to implement the various interchange and publish-subscribe protocols that make access to the Metastore more dynamic is not provided by our sample implementation and must be developed. But the CWM Metastore is perhaps one of the best possible (and simplest!) starting points for at least building prototypes of such architectural solutions.

Furthermore, generalized control framework and adapter-based solutions can be developed based on the concepts presented in this Chapter and also explicated in Chapter 11.

Summary

In this chapter, we discussed the need for a comprehensive meta data management strategy, acknowledging that no technology-based solution (including CWM) is assured success without an overall strategy guiding its application. We surveyed the various patterns for meta data integration architectures and described both interconnection topologies and meta data interchange life cycles. We also examined why current approaches to deploying meta data integration architectures (for example, via the building of meta data bridges) are complex and costly. We also demonstrated that CWM, as a model-based approach to meta data integration, simplifies the complexity and costs associated with building meta data integration architectures (regardless of interconnection topologies and life-cycle behaviors).

Finally, we described how the abstract architectural patterns and concepts presented here can be readily combined with more concrete implementation artifacts, such as custom-built adapters, control frameworks, and even the CWM Metastore as a basic centralized repository for storing, maintaining, and publishing, a collection of CWM models (for example, instances of any of the vertical models defined in this book).

Please visit the companion Web site regularly for the latest, concrete, integration architecture models being developed and published by the CWM Team.

Interface Rendering

The preceding chapters have described domain-specific applications of Common Warehouse Metamodel (CWM) in considerable detail. We've used CWM in that capacity to develop models of four representative domain areas: Data Warehousing, Dimensional Modeling, Web-Enabled Data Warehousing, and a Meta Data Repository model. Then, in Chapter 9, we adopted a specific subset of the abstract methodology presented in *Common Warehouse Metamodel: An Introduction to the Standard for Data Warehouse Integration* (Wiley, 2002) for the purposes of specifying a concrete meta data management strategy and integration architecture centered on CWM. We showed how the various models, especially the CWM Meta Store Model, might be used in the realization of the concrete architectural design presented here.

In this chapter, we delve into the the Java programmatic Application Programming Interfaces (API) that will represent our programmatic contract for the access to the CWM meta data described throughout the book. We illustrate the process of translating CWM metaclasses to Java interfaces using the Java Metadata Interface (JMI) standard, which is an industry standard mapping of the Object Management Group's (OMG's) Meta Object Facility (MOF) to the Java programming language. The reader is informally guided through steps that might be performed by an automated MOF utility in generating Java interfaces representing the CWM metaclasses.

Note, however, that it is not necessary to study the entire collection of JMI interfaces generated from CWM. Investigating a few fundamental ones, such as those generated from classes of the CWM Core and Relational models, will suffice to give the reader a general idea of the "look and feel" of JMI. For a complete JMI rendering of the entire CWM that you can readily compile, please visit the companion Web site.

CWM Core Classes and JMI Mappings

In the following sections, we will discuss the classes of the CWM Core metamodel and their JMI mappings. This is necessary in order to understand the CWM Relational classes and their JMI mappings.

ModelElement, Namespace, and Package

The class diagram of the CWM Core metamodel is shown in Figure 10.1. For now, we will focus our attention on the following three classes: ModelElement, Namespace, and Package, which appear in the upper right-hand corner. Even though Namespace is not directly inherited by any of the CWM Relational classes, it is included here since it is inherited by Package and Classifier (which we will discuss later). Please note that Namespace owns ModelElements and has a reference "ownedElement" to its owned ModelElements. ModelElement also has a reference "namespace" to its owner Namespace.

The JMI mappings for ModelElement, Namespace, and Package are shown in Figure 10.2. Please note:

- The ModelElement interface provides methods to get/set its name, to manipulate associated Dependencies and Constraints, and to get/set its owner Namespace. Since all CWM Relational interfaces inherit from the ModelElement interface, they all support these methods.

- The Namespace interface provides methods to manipulate its owned ModelElements.

- The Package interface inherits from the Namespace interface. The PackageClass interface provides methods to create new Packages. (The PackageClass interface therefore serves as the "factory" interface for Package.)

- Since both ModelElement and Namespace are abstract, their JMI mappings do not provide "factory" methods.

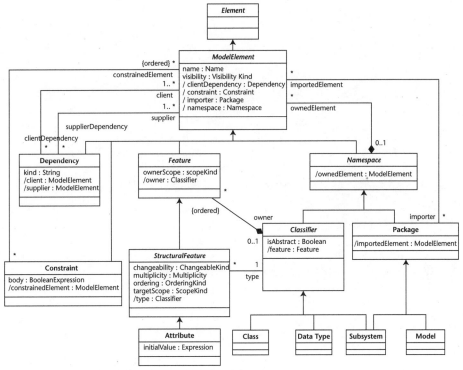

Figure 10.1   Class diagram: Core Metamodel.

```
public interface ModelElement extends RefObject, Element
{
    public String getName() throws MOFERROR;
    public void setName(String value) throws MOFERROR;

    public String getVisibility() throws MOFERROR;
    public void setVisibility(String value) throws MOFERROR;

    public Collection getClientDependency() throws MOFERROR;
    public void setClientDependency(Collection value) throws MOFERROR;
    public void addClientDependency(Dependency value) throws MOFERROR;
    public void modifyClientDependency(Dependency newValue,
        Dependency oldValue) throws MOFERROR, NotFoundException;
    public void removeClientDependency(Dependency value)
        throws MOFERROR, NotFoundException;

    public Collection getConstraint() throws MOFERROR;
```

Figure 10.2   JMI mappings: ModelElement, Namespace, and Package. *(continues)*

```
        public void setConstraint(Collection value) throws MOFERROR;
        public void addConstraint(Constraint value) throws MOFERROR;
        public void modifyConstraint(Constraint newValue, Constraint
oldValue)
            throws MOFERROR, NotFoundException;
        public void removeConstraint(Constraint value)
            throws MOFERROR, NotFoundException;

        public Collection getImporter() throws MOFERROR;
        public void setImporter(Collection value) throws MOFERROR;
        public void addImporter(Package value) throws MOFERROR;
        public void modifyImporter(Package newValue, Package oldValue)
            throws MOFERROR, NotFoundException;
        public void removeImporter(Package value)
            throws MOFERROR, NotFoundException;

        public Namespace getNamespace() throws MOFERROR;
        public void setNamespace(Namespace value) throws MOFERROR;
}
public interface ModelElementClass extends RefClass
{
        public List allOfTypeModelElement();
}

public interface Namespace extends RefObject, ModelElement
{
        public Collection getOwnedElement() throws MOFERROR;
        public void setOwnedElement(Collection value) throws MOFERROR;
        public void addOwnedElement(ModelElement value) throws MOFERROR;
        public void modifyOwnedElement(ModelElement newValue,
            ModelElement oldValue) throws MOFERROR, NotFoundException;
        public void removeOwnedElement(ModelElement value)
            throws MOFERROR, NotFoundException;
}
public interface NamespaceClass extends RefClass
{
        public List allOfTypeNamespace();
}

public interface Package extends RefObject, Namespace
{
        public Collection getImportedElement() throws MOFERROR;
        public void setImportedElement(Collection value) throws MOFERROR;
        public void addImportedElement(ModelElement value) throws MOFERROR;
        public void modifyImportedElement(ModelElement newValue,
            ModelElement oldValue) throws MOFERROR, NotFoundException;
        public void removeImportedElement(ModelElement value)
            throws MOFERROR, NotFoundException;
```

Figure 10.2   JMI mappings: ModelElement, Namespace, and Package.

```
}
public interface PackageClass extends RefClass
{
    public List allOfTypePackage();
    public List allOfKindPackage();

    public Package createPackage() throws MOFERROR;
    public Package createPackage(String name, String visibility)
        throws MOFERROR;
}
```

Figure 10.2 JMI mappings: ModelElement, Namespace, and Package. *(continued)*

Classifier, Class, Datatype, and Attribute

We will now turn our attention to the following classes: Classifier, Class, Datatype, Feature, StructuralFeature, and Attribute, which appear on the lower middle part of Figure 10.1. Among these, Feature and StructuralFeature are intermediary classes whose uses are normally hidden. Please note that Classifier owns Features and has a reference "feature" to its owned Features. Feature also has a reference "owner" to its owner Classifier. StructuralFeature has a reference "type" to the Classifier that is its data type.

The JMI mappings for Classifier, Class, Datatype, and Attribute are shown in Figure 10.2. Also included are those for Feature and StructuralFeature. Please note:

- The Classifier interface inherits from the Namespace interface and provides additional methods to manipulate its owned Features.

- The Class interface inherits from the Classifier interface. The ClassClass interface provides methods to create new Classes.

- The Datatype interface inherits from the Classifier interface. The DatatypeClass interface provides methods to create new Datatypes.

- The Feature interface provides methods to get/set its owner Classifier.

- The StructuralFeature interface inherits from the Feature interface and provides additional methods to get/set its attributes (e.g., multiplicity) and its type Classifier.

- The Attribute interface inherits from the StructuralFeature interface. The AttributeClass interface provides methods to create new Attributes.

```
public interface Classifier extends RefObject, Namespace
{
    public Boolean isAbstract() throws MOFERROR;
    public void setIsAbstract(Boolean value) throws MOFERROR;
    public boolean isAbstractValue() throws MOFERROR;
    public void setIsAbstract(boolean value) throws MOFERROR;

    public List getFeature() throws MOFERROR;
    public void setFeature(List value) throws MOFERROR;
    public void addFeature(Feature value) throws MOFERROR;
    public void addBeforeFeature(Feature value, Feature before)
        throws MOFERROR, NotFoundException;
    public void modifyFeature(Feature newValue, Feature oldValue)
        throws MOFERROR, NotFoundException;
    public void removeFeature(Feature value)
        throws MOFERROR, NotFoundException;
}
public interface ClassifierClass extends RefClass
{
    public List allOfTypeClassifier();
}

public interface Class extends RefObject, Classifier
{
}
public interface ClassClass extends RefClass
{
    public List allOfTypeClass();
    public List allOfKindClass();

    public Class createClass() throws MOFERROR;
    public Class createClass(String name, String visibility,
        Boolean isAbstract) throws MOFERROR;
}

public interface DataType extends RefObject, Classifier
{
}
public interface DataTypeClass extends RefClass
{
    public List allOfTypeDataType();
    public List allOfKindDataType();

    public DataType createDataType() throws MOFERROR;
    public DataType createDataType(String name, String visibility,
        Boolean isAbstract) throws MOFERROR;
}

public interface Feature extends RefObject, ModelElement
```

Figure 10.3 JMI Mappings: Classifier, Class, Datatype, and Attribute.

```
{
    public String getOwnerScope() throws MOFERROR;
    public void setOwnerScope(String value) throws MOFERROR;

    public Classifier getOwner() throws MOFERROR;
    public void setOwner(Classifier value) throws MOFERROR;
}
public interface FeatureClass extends RefClass
{
    public List allOfTypeFeature();
}

public interface StructuralFeature extends RefObject, Feature
{
    public String getChangeability() throws MOFERROR;
    public void setChangeability(String value) throws MOFERROR;
    public org.omg.java.cwm.objectmodel.core.Multiplicity
        getMultiplicity() throws MOFERROR;
    public void setMultiplicity(
        org.omg.java.cwm.objectmodel.core.Multiplicity value)
        throws MOFERROR;
    public String getOrdering() throws MOFERROR;
    public void setOrdering(String value) throws MOFERROR;
    public String getTargetScope() throws MOFERROR;
    public void setTargetScope(String value) throws MOFERROR;

    public Classifier getType() throws MOFERROR;
    public void setType(Classifier value) throws MOFERROR;
}
public interface StructuralFeatureClass extends RefClass
{
    public List allOfTypeStructuralFeature();
}

public interface Attribute extends RefObject, StructuralFeature
{
    public org.omg.java.cwm.objectmodel.core.Expression
getInitialValue()
        throws MOFERROR;
    public void setInitialValue(
        org.omg.java.cwm.objectmodel.core.Expression value)
        throws MOFERROR;
}
public interface AttributeClass extends RefClass
{
    public List allOfTypeAttribute();
    public List allOfKindAttribute();

    public Attribute createAttribute() throws MOFERROR;
```

Figure 10.3   JMI Mappings: Classifier, Class, Datatype, and Attribute. *(continues)*

```
      public Attribute createAttribute(String name, String visibility,
          String ownerScope, String changeability,
          org.omg.java.cwm.objectmodel.core.Multiplicity multiplicity,
          String ordering, String targetScope,
          org.omg.java.cwm.objectmodel.core.Expression initialValue)
          throws MOFERROR;
  }
```

Figure 10.3 JMI Mappings: Classifier, Class, Datatype, and Attribute. *(continued)*

Method and Parameter

The class diagram of the CWM Behavior metamodel is shown in Figure 10.4. We will focus our attention only on the following three classes: BehavioralFeature, Method, and Parameter, which appear on the left and in the middle of the figure. Please note that BehavioralFeature owns Parameters and has a reference "parameter" to its owned Parameters. Parameter also has a reference "behavioralFeature" to its owner BehavioralFeature. Parameter has a reference "type" to the Classifier that is its data type.

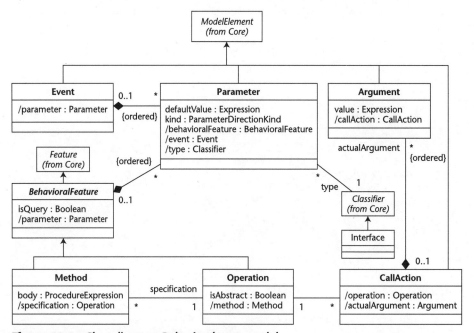

Figure 10.4 Class diagram: Behavioral metamodel.

The JMI mappings for Method and Parameter are shown in Figure 10.5. Also included are those for BehavioralFeature. Please note:

- The BehavioralFeature interface inherits from the Feature interface and provides additional methods to manipulate its owned Parameters.

- The Method interface inherits from the BehavioralFeature interface and provides additional methods to get/set its body. The Method-Class interface provides methods to create new Methods.

- The Parameter interface provides methods to get/set its attributes (e.g., kind), its owner BehavioralFeature and its type Classifier. The ParameterClass interface provides methods to create new Parameters.

```
public interface BehavioralFeature extends RefObject, Feature
{
    public Boolean isQuery() throws MOFERROR;
    public void setIsQuery(Boolean value) throws MOFERROR;
    public boolean isQueryValue() throws MOFERROR;
    public void setIsQuery(boolean value) throws MOFERROR;

    public List getParameter() throws MOFERROR;
    public void setParameter(List value) throws MOFERROR;
    public void addParameter(Parameter value) throws MOFERROR;
    public void addBeforeParameter(Parameter value, Parameter before)
        throws MOFERROR, NotFoundException;
    public void modifyParameter(Parameter newValue, Parameter oldValue)
        throws MOFERROR, NotFoundException;
    public void removeParameter(Parameter value)
        throws MOFERROR, NotFoundException;
}
public interface BehavioralFeatureClass extends RefClass
{
    public List allOfTypeBehavioralFeature();
}

public interface Method extends RefObject, BehavioralFeature
{
    public org.omg.java.cwm.objectmodel.core.ProcedureExpression
getBody()
        throws MOFERROR;
    public void setBody(
        org.omg.java.cwm.objectmodel.core.ProcedureExpression value)
        throws MOFERROR;
    public Operation getSpecification() throws MOFERROR;
    public void setSpecification(Operation value) throws MOFERROR;
```

Figure 10.5 JMI Mappings: Method and Parameter. *(continues)*

```
}
public interface MethodClass extends RefClass
{
    public List allOfTypeMethod();
    public List allOfKindMethod();

    public Method createMethod() throws MOFERROR;
    public Method createMethod(String name, String visibility,
        String ownerScope, Boolean isQuery,
        org.omg.java.cwm.objectmodel.core.ProcedureExpression body)
        throws MOFERROR;
}

public interface Parameter extends RefObject, ModelElement
{
    public org.omg.java.cwm.objectmodel.core.Expression
getDefaultValue()
        throws MOFERROR;
    public void setDefaultValue(
        org.omg.java.cwm.objectmodel.core.Expression value)
        throws MOFERROR;
    public String getKind() throws MOFERROR;
    public void setKind(String value) throws MOFERROR;

    public BehavioralFeature getBehavioralFeature() throws MOFERROR;
    public void setBehavioralFeature(BehavioralFeature value)
        throws MOFERROR;

    public Event getEvent() throws MOFERROR;
    public void setEvent(Event value) throws MOFERROR;

    public Classifier getType() throws MOFERROR;
    public void setType(Classifier value) throws MOFERROR;
}
public interface ParameterClass extends RefClass
{
    public List allOfTypeParameter();
    public List allOfKindParameter();

    public Parameter createParameter() throws MOFERROR;
    public Parameter createParameter(String name, String visibility,
        org.omg.java.cwm.objectmodel.core.Expression defaultValue,
        String kind) throws MOFERROR;
}
```

Figure 10.5   JMI Mappings: Method and Parameter. *(continued)*

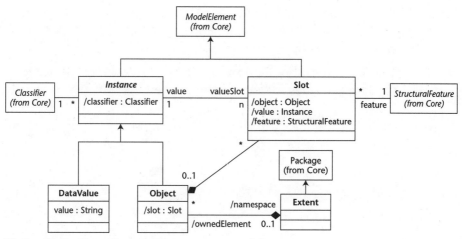

Figure 10.6   Class diagram: Instance metamodel.

Instances

The class diagram of the CWM Instance metamodel is shown in Figure 10.6. Please note that Instance can be either DataValue or Object. Instance has a reference "classifier" to the Classifier of which it is an instance. Object owns Slot and has a reference "slot" to its owned Slots. Slot also has a reference "object" to its owner Object. In addition, Slot has a reference "feature" to the StructuralFeature that specifies it and a reference "value" to the Instance that is its value. Extent owns Object and has an inherited reference "ownedElement" to its owned Objects. Object also has an inherited reference "namespace" to its owner Extent.

The JMI mappings for Instance, DataValue, Object, Slot, and Extent are shown in Figure 10.7. Please note:

- The Instance interface provides methods to get/set the Classifier of which it is an instance.

- The DataValue interface inherits from the Instance interface and provides additional methods to get/set its value. The DataValueClass interface provides methods to create new DataValues.

- The Object interface inherits from the Instance interface and provides additional methods to manipulate its owned Slots. The ObjectClass interface provides methods to create new Objects.

- The Slot interface provides methods to get/set its owner Object, its specifying StructuralFeature, and the Instance that is its value. The SlotClass interface provides methods to create new Slots.

- The Extent interface inherits from the Package interface. The Extent-Class interface provides methods to create new Extents.

```
public interface Instance extends RefObject, ModelElement
{
    public Classifier getClassifier() throws MOFERROR;
    public void setClassifier(Classifier value) throws MOFERROR;
}
public interface InstanceClass extends RefClass
{
  public List allOfTypeInstance();
}


public interface DataValue extends RefObject, Instance
{
    public String getValue() throws MOFERROR;
    public void setValue(String value) throws MOFERROR;
}
public interface DataValueClass extends RefClass
{
    public List allOfTypeDataValue();
    public List allOfKindDataValue();

    public DataValue createDataValue() throws MOFERROR;
    public DataValue createDataValue(String name, String visibility,
        String value) throws MOFERROR;
}


public interface Object extends RefObject, Instance
{
    public Collection getSlot() throws MOFERROR;
    public void setSlot(Collection value) throws MOFERROR;
    public void addSlot(Slot value) throws MOFERROR;
    public void modifySlot(Slot newValue, Slot oldValue)
        throws MOFERROR, NotFoundException;
    public void removeSlot(Slot value) throws MOFERROR,
NotFoundException;
}
```

Figure 10.7   JMI Mappings: Instance metamodel.

```
public interface ObjectClass extends RefClass
{
    public List allOfTypeObject();
    public List allOfKindObject();

    public Object createObject() throws MOFERROR;
    public Object createObject(String name, String visibility)
        throws MOFERROR;
}

public interface Slot extends RefObject, ModelElement
{
    public Object getObject() throws MOFERROR;
    public void setObject(Object value) throws MOFERROR;

    public Instance getValue() throws MOFERROR;
    public void setValue(Instance value) throws MOFERROR;

    public StructuralFeature getFeature() throws MOFERROR;
    public void setFeature(StructuralFeature value) throws MOFERROR;
}
public interface SlotClass extends RefClass
{
    public List allOfTypeSlot();
    public List allOfKindSlot();

    public Slot createSlot() throws MOFERROR;
    public Slot createSlot(String name, String visibility)
        throws MOFERROR;
}

public interface Extent extends RefObject, Package
{
}
public interface ExtentClass extends RefClass
{
    public List allOfTypeExtent();
    public List allOfKindExtent();

    public Extent createExtent() throws MOFERROR;
    public Extent createExtent(String name, String visibility)
        throws MOFERROR;
}
```

Figure 10.7   JMI Mappings: Instance metamodel. *(continued)*

Keys and Indexes

The class diagram of the CWM Keys and Indexes metamodel is shown in Figure 10.8. Please note that UniqueKey and KeyRelationship both are owned by Class through the inherited Namespace-ModelElement association discussed previously. They may be related to each other and, when they are, each has a reference to the other, namely "keyRelationship" and "uniqueKey," respectively. UniqueKey has a reference "feature" to the StructuralFeatures that form the unique key. Similarly, KeyRelationship also has a reference "feature" to the StructuralFeatures that form the key relationship. Index owns IndexedFeature and has a reference "indexedFeature" to its owned IndexedFeatures. IndexedFeature also has a reference "index" to its owner Index. In addition, Index has a reference "spannedClass" to the Class that is spanned by it, and IndexedFeature has a reference "feature" to the StructuralFeature that is being indexed.

The JMI mappings for UniqueKey, KeyRelationship, Index, and IndexedFeature are shown in Figure 10.7. Please note:

- The UniqueKey interface provides methods to manipulate the StructuralFeatures that form the unique key and the KeyRelationships that are paired with it. The UniqueKeyClass provides methods to create new UniqueKeys.

- The KeyRelationship interface provides methods to manipulate the StructuralFeatures that form the key relationship and to get/set the UniqueKey with which it is paired. The KeyRelationshipClass provides methods to create new KeyRelationships.

- The Index interface provides methods to get/set its attributes (e.g., isUnique), to manipulate its owned IndexedFeatures and to get/set its spanned Class. The IndexClass interface provides methods to create new Indexes.

- The IndexedFeature interface provides methods to get/set the StructuralFeature that is being indexed and its owner Index. The IndexedFeatureClass interface provides methods to create new IndexedFeatures.

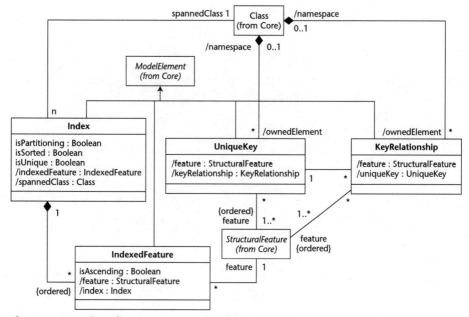

Figure 10.8   Class diagram: Keys and Indexes metamodel.

```
public interface UniqueKey extends RefObject, ModelElement
{
    public List getFeature() throws MOFERROR;
    public void setFeature(List value) throws MOFERROR;
    public void addFeature(StructuralFeature value) throws MOFERROR;
    public void addBeforeFeature(StructuralFeature value,
        StructuralFeature before) throws MOFERROR, NotFoundException;
    public void modifyFeature(StructuralFeature newValue,
        StructuralFeature oldValue) throws MOFERROR, NotFoundException;
    public void removeFeature(StructuralFeature value)
        throws MOFERROR, NotFoundException;

    public Collection getKeyRelationship() throws MOFERROR;
```

Figure 10.9   JMI Mappings: Keys and Indexes. *(continues)*

```
        public void setKeyRelationship(Collection value) throws MOFERROR;
        public void addKeyRelationship(KeyRelationship value) throws
MOFERROR;
        public void modifyKeyRelationship(KeyRelationship newValue,
            KeyRelationship oldValue) throws MOFERROR, NotFoundException;
        public void removeKeyRelationship(KeyRelationship value)
            throws MOFERROR, NotFoundException;
}
public interface UniqueKeyClass extends RefClass
{
        public List allOfTypeUniqueKey();
        public List allOfKindUniqueKey();

        public UniqueKey createUniqueKey() throws MOFERROR;
        public UniqueKey createUniqueKey(String name, String visibility)
            throws MOFERROR;
}


public interface KeyRelationship extends RefObject, ModelElement
{
        public List getFeature() throws MOFERROR;
        public void setFeature(List value) throws MOFERROR;
        public void addFeature(StructuralFeature value) throws MOFERROR;
        public void addBeforeFeature(StructuralFeature value,
            StructuralFeature before) throws MOFERROR, NotFoundException;
        public void modifyFeature(StructuralFeature newValue,
            StructuralFeature oldValue) throws MOFERROR, NotFoundException;
        public void removeFeature(StructuralFeature value)
            throws MOFERROR, NotFoundException;

        public UniqueKey getUniqueKey() throws MOFERROR;
        public void setUniqueKey(UniqueKey value) throws MOFERROR;
}
public interface KeyRelationshipClass extends RefClass
{
        public List allOfTypeKeyRelationship();
        public List allOfKindKeyRelationship();

        public KeyRelationship createKeyRelationship() throws MOFERROR;
        public KeyRelationship createKeyRelationship(String name,
            String visibility) throws MOFERROR;
}


public interface Index extends RefObject, ModelElement
{
        public Boolean isPartitioning() throws MOFERROR;
        public void setIsPartitioning(Boolean value) throws MOFERROR;
```

Figure 10.9 JMI Mappings: Keys and Indexes.

```
        public boolean isPartitioningValue() throws MOFERROR;
        public void setIsPartitioning(boolean value) throws MOFERROR;
        public Boolean isSorted() throws MOFERROR;
        public void setIsSorted(Boolean value) throws MOFERROR;
        public boolean isSortedValue() throws MOFERROR;
        public void setIsSorted(boolean value) throws MOFERROR;
        public Boolean isUnique() throws MOFERROR;
        public void setIsUnique(Boolean value) throws MOFERROR;
        public boolean isUniqueValue() throws MOFERROR;
        public void setIsUnique(boolean value) throws MOFERROR;

        public List getIndexedFeature() throws MOFERROR;
        public void setIndexedFeature(List value) throws MOFERROR;
        public void addIndexedFeature(IndexedFeature value) throws MOFERROR;
        public void addBeforeIndexedFeature(IndexedFeature value,
            IndexedFeature before) throws MOFERROR, NotFoundException;
        public void modifyIndexedFeature(IndexedFeature newValue,
            IndexedFeature oldValue) throws MOFERROR, NotFoundException;
        public void removeIndexedFeature(IndexedFeature value)
            throws MOFERROR, NotFoundException;

        public Class getSpannedClass() throws MOFERROR;
        public void setSpannedClass(Class value) throws MOFERROR;
}
public interface IndexClass extends RefClass
{
        public List allOfTypeIndex();
        public List allOfKindIndex();

        public Index createIndex() throws MOFERROR;
        public Index createIndex(String name, String visibility,
            Boolean isPartitioning, Boolean isSorted, Boolean isUnique)
            throws MOFERROR;
}

public interface IndexedFeature extends RefObject, ModelElement
{
        public Boolean isAscending() throws MOFERROR;
        public void setIsAscending(Boolean value) throws MOFERROR;

        public StructuralFeature getFeature() throws MOFERROR;
        public void setFeature(StructuralFeature value) throws MOFERROR;
        public Index getIndex() throws MOFERROR;
        public void setIndex(Index value) throws MOFERROR;
}
public interface IndexedFeatureClass extends RefClass
{
```

Figure 10.9   JMI Mappings: Keys and Indexes. *(continues)*

```
    public List allOfTypeIndexedFeature();
    public List allOfKindIndexedFeature();

    public IndexedFeature createIndexedFeature() throws MOFERROR;
    public IndexedFeature createIndexedFeature(String name,
        String visibility, Boolean isAscending) throws MOFERROR;
}
```

Figure 10.9 JMI Mappings: Keys and Indexes. *(continued)*

CWM Relational Classes and JMI Mappings

We are now ready to discuss the CWM Relational classes and their JMI mappings.

Catalog and Schema

The class diagram of Catalog, Schema, and their owned classes is shown in Figure 10.10. For now we will focus our attention only on Catalog and Schema. We will discuss their owned classes in the subsequent sections. Please note that Catalog owns Schema through the inherited Namespace-ModelElement association discussed previously. Similarly, Schema owns NamedColumnSet, SQLIndex, Procedure, and Trigger through the inherited Namespace-ModelElement association as well.

The JMI mappings for Catalog and Schema are shown in Figure 10.11. Please note:

- The Catalog interface inherits from the Package interface. The CatalogClass interface provides methods to create new Catalogs.

- The Schema interface inherits from the Package interface. The SchemaClass interface provides methods to create new Schemas.

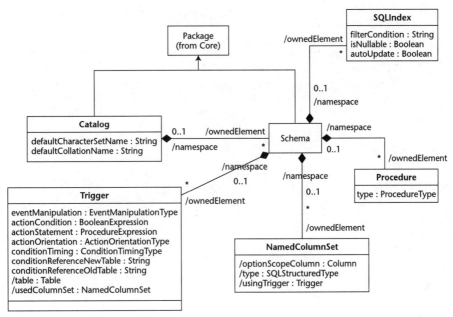

Figure 10.10 Class diagram: Catalog, Schema, and owned classes.

```
public interface Catalog extends RefObject, Package
{
    public String getDefaultCharacterSetName() throws MOFERROR;
    public void setDefaultCharacterSetName(String value) throws
MOFERROR;
    public String getDefaultCollationName() throws MOFERROR;
    public void setDefaultCollationName(String value) throws MOFERROR;
}
public interface CatalogClass extends RefClass
{
    public List allOfTypeCatalog();
```

Figure 10.11 JMI mappings: Catalog and Schema. *(continues)*

```
    public List allOfKindCatalog();

    public Catalog createCatalog() throws MOFERROR;
    public Catalog createCatalog(String name, String visibility,
        String defaultCharacterSetName, String defaultCollationName)
        throws MOFERROR;
}

public interface Schema extends RefObject, Package
{
}
public interface SchemaClass extends RefClass
{
    public List allOfTypeSchema();
    public List allOfKindSchema();

    public Schema createSchema() throws MOFERROR;
    public Schema createSchema(String name, String visibility)
        throws MOFERROR;
}
```

Figure 10.11 JMI mappings: Catalog and Schema. *(continued)*

Table, View, QueryColumnSet, and Column

The class diagram of Table, Column, and SQL data types is shown in Figure 10.12. For now we will ignore the three classes on the right-hand side that deal with SQL data types and the CheckConstraint class that appears in the upper left-hand corner. Please note that the top-most class in the inheritance hierarchy for Table and View is ColumnSet, which owns Columns through the inherited Classifier-Feature association discussed previously. Therefore, ColumnSet has a reference "feature" to its owned Columns and Column has a reference "owner" to its owner ColumnSet. Table and View both inherit from NamedColumnSet, which in turn inherits from ColumnSet. QueryColumnSet, which represents the meta data of the result set returned from a SQL query, also inherits from ColumnSet. Going back to Figure 10.10, please note that Schema owns Named-ColumnSet and, therefore, Table and View.

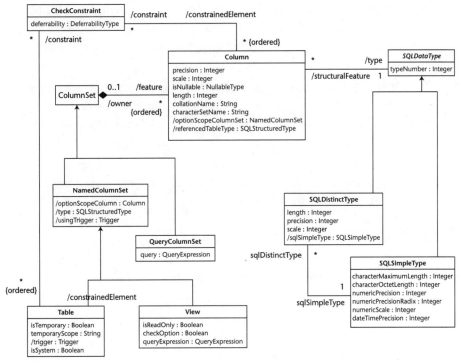

Figure 10.12   Class diagram: Table, Column, and SQL data types.

The JMI mappings for Table, View, QueryColumnSet, and Column are shown in Figure 10.13. JMI mappings are also included for ColumnSet and NamedColumnSet. Please note:

- The ColumnSet interface inherits from the Class interface. The ColumnSetClass interface provides methods to create new ColumnSets. (These methods, however, are not used directly since ColumnSet is abstract in general.)

- The NamedColumnSet interface inherits from the ColumnSet interface and provides additional methods to manipulate its attributes (e.g., usingTrigger). The NamedColumnSetClass interface provides methods to create new NamedColumnSets. (These methods, however, are not used directly since NamedColumnSet is abstract in general.)

- The QueryColumnSet interface inherits from the ColumnSet interface and provides additional methods to get/set its associated SQL query expression. The QueryColumnSetClass interface provides methods to create new QueryColumnSets.

- The Table interface inherits from the NamedColumnSet interface and provides additional methods to manipulate its attributes (e.g., Trigger). The TableClass interface provides methods to create new Tables.

- The View interface inherits from the NamedColumnSet interface and provides additional methods to get/set its associated SQL query expression and attributes (e.g., isReadOnly). The ViewClass interface provides methods to create new Views.

- The Column interface inherits from the Attribute interface and provides additional methods to get/set its attributes (e.g., Precision). The ColumnClass interface provides methods to create new Columns.

```
public interface ColumnSet extends RefObject, Class
{
}
public interface ColumnSetClass extends RefClass
{
    public List allOfTypeColumnSet();
    public List allOfKindColumnSet();

    public ColumnSet createColumnSet() throws MOFERROR;
    public ColumnSet createColumnSet(String name, String visibility,
        Boolean isAbstract) throws MOFERROR;
}


public interface NamedColumnSet extends RefObject, ColumnSet
{
    public Collection getOptionScopeColumn() throws MOFERROR;
    public void setOptionScopeColumn(Collection value) throws MOFERROR;
    public void addOptionScopeColumn(Column value) throws MOFERROR;
    public void modifyOptionScopeColumn(Column newValue, Column
oldValue)
        throws MOFERROR, NotFoundException;
    public void removeOptionScopeColumn(Column value)
        throws MOFERROR, NotFoundException;

    public SQLStructuredType getType() throws MOFERROR;
```

Figure 10.13 JMI mappings: Table, View, QueryColumnSet, and Column.

```
      public void setType(SQLStructuredType value) throws MOFERROR;

      public Collection getUsingTrigger() throws MOFERROR;
      public void setUsingTrigger(Collection value) throws MOFERROR;
      public void addUsingTrigger(Trigger value) throws MOFERROR;
      public void modifyUsingTrigger(Trigger newValue, Trigger oldValue)
          throws MOFERROR, NotFoundException;
      public void removeUsingTrigger(Trigger value)
          throws MOFERROR, NotFoundException;
}
public interface NamedColumnSetClass extends RefClass
{
      public List allOfTypeNamedColumnSet();
      public List allOfKindNamedColumnSet();

      public NamedColumnSet createNamedColumnSet() throws MOFERROR;
      public NamedColumnSet createNamedColumnSet(String name,
          String visibility, Boolean isAbstract) throws MOFERROR;
}

public interface QueryColumnSet extends RefObject, ColumnSet
{
      public org.omg.java.cwm.foundation.datatypes.QueryExpression
          getQuery() throws MOFERROR;
      public void setQuery(
          org.omg.java.cwm.foundation.datatypes.QueryExpression value)
          throws MOFERROR;
}
public interface QueryColumnSetClass extends RefClass
{
      public List allOfTypeQueryColumnSet();
      public List allOfKindQueryColumnSet();

      public QueryColumnSet createQueryColumnSet() throws MOFERROR;
      public QueryColumnSet createQueryColumnSet(String name,
          String visibility, Boolean isAbstract,
          org.omg.java.cwm.foundation.datatypes.QueryExpression query)
          throws MOFERROR;
}

public interface Table extends RefObject, NamedColumnSet
{
      public Boolean isTemporary() throws MOFERROR;
      public void setIsTemporary(Boolean value) throws MOFERROR;
      public boolean isTemporaryValue() throws MOFERROR;
      public void setIsTemporary(boolean value) throws MOFERROR;
      public String getTemporaryScope() throws MOFERROR;
      public void setTemporaryScope(String value) throws MOFERROR;
      public Boolean isSystem() throws MOFERROR;
```

Figure 10.13   JMI mappings: Table, View, QueryColumnSet, and Column. *(continues)*

```
        public void setIsSystem(Boolean value) throws MOFERROR;
        public boolean isSystemValue() throws MOFERROR;
        public void setIsSystem(boolean value) throws MOFERROR;

        public List getTrigger() throws MOFERROR;
        public void setTrigger(List value) throws MOFERROR;
        public void addTrigger(Trigger value) throws MOFERROR;
        public void addBeforeTrigger(Trigger value, Trigger before)
            throws MOFERROR, NotFoundException;
        public void modifyTrigger(Trigger newValue, Trigger oldValue)
            throws MOFERROR, NotFoundException;
        public void removeTrigger(Trigger value)
            throws MOFERROR, NotFoundException;
}
public interface TableClass extends RefClass
{
        public List allOfTypeTable();
        public List allOfKindTable();

        public Table createTable() throws MOFERROR;
        public Table createTable(String name, String visibility,
            Boolean isAbstract, Boolean isTemporary, String temporaryScope,
            Boolean isSystem) throws MOFERROR;
}

public interface View extends RefObject, NamedColumnSet
{
        public Boolean isReadOnly() throws MOFERROR;
        public void setIsReadOnly(Boolean value) throws MOFERROR;
        public boolean isReadOnlyValue() throws MOFERROR;
        public void setIsReadOnly(boolean value) throws MOFERROR;
        public Boolean isCheckOption() throws MOFERROR;
        public void setCheckOption(Boolean value) throws MOFERROR;
        public boolean isCheckOptionValue() throws MOFERROR;
        public void setCheckOption(boolean value) throws MOFERROR;

        public org.omg.java.cwm.foundation.datatypes.QueryExpression
            getQueryExpression() throws MOFERROR;
        public void setQueryExpression(
            org.omg.java.cwm.foundation.datatypes.QueryExpression value)
            throws MOFERROR;
}
public interface ViewClass extends RefClass
{
        public List allOfTypeView();
```

Figure 10.13   JMI mappings: Table, View, QueryColumnSet, and Column.

```
    public List allOfKindView();

    public View createView() throws MOFERROR;
    public View createView(String name, String visibility,
        Boolean isAbstract, Boolean isReadOnly, Boolean checkOption,
        org.omg.java.cwm.foundation.datatypes.QueryExpression
        queryExpression) throws MOFERROR;
}

public interface Column extends RefObject, Attribute
{
    public Long getPrecision() throws MOFERROR;
    public void setPrecision(Long value) throws MOFERROR;
    public Long getScale() throws MOFERROR;
    public void setScale(Long value) throws MOFERROR;
    public String getIsNullable() throws MOFERROR;
    public void setIsNullable(String value) throws MOFERROR;
    public Long getLength() throws MOFERROR;
    public void setLength(Long value) throws MOFERROR;
    public String getCollationName() throws MOFERROR;
    public void setCollationName(String value) throws MOFERROR;
    public String getCharacterSetName() throws MOFERROR;
    public void setCharacterSetName(String value) throws MOFERROR;
    public NamedColumnSet getOptionScopeColumnSet() throws MOFERROR;
    public void setOptionScopeColumnSet(NamedColumnSet value)
        throws MOFERROR;
    public SQLStructuredType getReferencedTableType() throws MOFERROR;
    public void setReferencedTableType(SQLStructuredType value)
        throws MOFERROR;
}
public interface ColumnClass extends RefClass
{
    public List allOfTypeColumn();
    public List allOfKindColumn();

    public Column createColumn() throws MOFERROR;
    public Column createColumn(String name, String visibility,
        String ownerScope, String changeability,
        org.omg.java.cwm.objectmodel.core.Multiplicity multiplicity,
        String ordering, String targetScope,
        org.omg.java.cwm.objectmodel.core.Expression initialValue,
        Long precision, Long scale, String isNullable, Long length,
        String collationName, String characterSetName)
        throws MOFERROR;
}
```

Figure 10.13   JMI mappings: Table, View, QueryColumnSet, and Column. *(continued)*

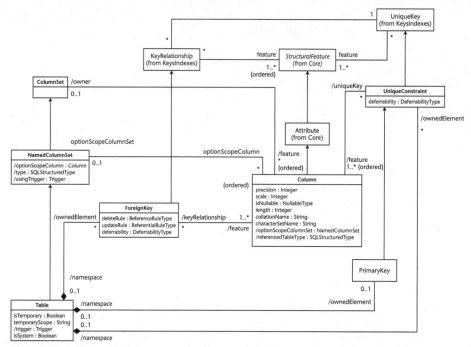

Figure 10.14   Class diagram: UniqueConstraint, PrimaryKey, and ForeignKey.

UniqueConstraint, PrimaryKey, and ForeignKey

The class diagram of UniqueConstraint, PrimaryKey, and ForeignKey is shown in Figure 10.14. We will focus our attention only on these three classes here. All other classes shown in the figure have been discussed previously. Please note that UniqueConstraint, PrimaryKey, and ForeignKey are all owned by Table through the inherited Namespace-ModelElement association discussed previously. PrimaryKey inherits from UniqueConstraint, which in turn inherits from UniqueKey; ForeignKey inherits from KeyRelationship. Both UniqueKey and KeyRelationship have been discussed previously.

The JMI mappings for UniqueConstraint, PrimaryKey, and ForeignKey are shown in Figure 10.15. Please note:

- The UniqueConstraint interface inherits from the UniqueKey interface. The UniqueConstraintClass interface provides methods to create new UniqueConstraints.

- The PrimaryKey interface inherits from the UniqueConstraint interface. The PrimaryKeyClass interface provides methods to create new PrimaryKeys.

- The ForeignKey interface inherits from the KeyRelationship interface and provides additional methods to get/set its attributes (for example, deleteRule). The ForeignKeyClass interface provides methods to create new Foreignkeys.

```
public interface UniqueConstraint extends RefObject, UniqueKey
{
    public String getDeferrability() throws MOFERROR;
    public void setDeferrability(String value) throws MOFERROR;
}
public interface UniqueConstraintClass extends RefClass
{
    public List allOfTypeUniqueConstraint();
    public List allOfKindUniqueConstraint();

    public UniqueConstraint createUniqueConstraint() throws MOFERROR;
    public UniqueConstraint createUniqueConstraint(String name,
        String visibility, String deferrability) throws MOFERROR;
}

public interface PrimaryKey extends RefObject, UniqueConstraint
{
}
public interface PrimaryKeyClass extends RefClass
{
    public List allOfTypePrimaryKey();
    public List allOfKindPrimaryKey();

    public PrimaryKey createPrimaryKey() throws MOFERROR;
    public PrimaryKey createPrimaryKey(String name, String visibility,
        String deferrability) throws MOFERROR;
```

Figure 10.15 JMI mappings: UniqueConstraint, PrimaryKey, and ForeignKey. *(continues)*

```
    }

    public interface ForeignKey extends RefObject, KeyRelationship
    {
      public String getDeleteRule() throws MOFERROR;
      public void setDeleteRule(String value) throws MOFERROR;
      public String getUpdateRule() throws MOFERROR;
      public void setUpdateRule(String value) throws MOFERROR;
      public String getDeferrability() throws MOFERROR;
      public void setDeferrability(String value) throws MOFERROR;
    }
    public interface ForeignKeyClass extends RefClass
    {
        public List allOfTypeForeignKey();
        public List allOfKindForeignKey();

        public ForeignKey createForeignKey() throws MOFERROR;
        public ForeignKey createForeignKey(String name, String visibility,
            String deleteRule, String updateRule, String deferrability)
            throws MOFERROR;
    }
```

Figure 10.15 JMI mappings: UniqueConstraint, PrimaryKey, and ForeignKey. *(continued)*

SQLIndex and SQLIndexColumn

The class diagram of SQLIndex and SQLIndexColumn is shown in Figure 10.16. We will focus our attention only on these two classes here. All other classes shown in the figure have been discussed previously. Please note that SQLIndex inherits from Index and SQLIndexColumn inherits from IndexedFeature. Both Index and IndexedFeature have been discussed previously. Note in Figure 10.10 that Schema owns SQLIndex. Also, as can be inferred from Figure 10.8, SQLIndex owns SQLIndexColumn and has a reference "indexedFeature" to its owned SQLIndexColumns. SQLIndexColumn also has a reference "index" to its owner SQLIndex. In addition, SQLIndex has a reference "spannedClass" to the Table that is spanned by it, and SQLIndexColumn has a reference "feature" to the Column that is being indexed.

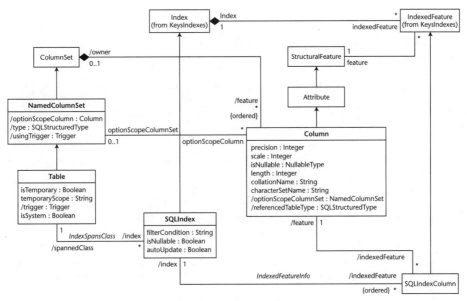

Figure 10.16   Class diagram: SQLIndex and SQLIndexColumn.

The JMI mappings for SQLIndex and SQLIndexColumn are shown in Figure 10.17. Please note:

- The SQLIndex interface inherits from the Index interface and provides additional methods to get/set its attributes (e.g., isNullable). The SQLIndexClass interface provides methods to create new SQLIndexes.

- The SQLIndexColumn interface inherits from the IndexedFeature interface. The SQLIndexColumnClass interface provides methods to create new SQLIndexColumns.

```
public interface SQLIndex extends RefObject, Index
{
    public String getFilterCondition() throws MOFERROR;
    public void setFilterCondition(String value) throws MOFERROR;
    public Boolean isNullable() throws MOFERROR;
```

Figure 10.17   JMI Mappings: SQLIndex and SQLIndexColumn. *(continues)*

```
        public void setIsNullable(Boolean value) throws MOFERROR;
        public boolean isNullableValue() throws MOFERROR;
        public void setIsNullable(boolean value) throws MOFERROR;
        public Boolean isAutoUpdate() throws MOFERROR;
        public void setAutoUpdate(Boolean value) throws MOFERROR;
        public boolean isAutoUpdateValue() throws MOFERROR;
        public void setAutoUpdate(boolean value) throws MOFERROR;
    }
    public interface SQLIndexClass extends RefClass
    {
        public List allOfTypeSQLIndex();
        public List allOfKindSQLIndex();

        public SQLIndex createSQLIndex() throws MOFERROR;
        public SQLIndex createSQLIndex(String name, String visibility,
            Boolean isPartitioning, Boolean isSorted, Boolean isUnique,
            String filterCondition, Boolean isNullable, Boolean autoUpdate)
            throws MOFERROR;
    }


    public interface SQLIndexColumn extends RefObject, IndexedFeature
    {
    }
    public interface SQLIndexColumnClass extends RefClass
    {
        public List allOfTypeSQLIndexColumn();
        public List allOfKindSQLIndexColumn();
        public SQLIndexColumn createSQLIndexColumn() throws MOFERROR;
        public SQLIndexColumn createSQLIndexColumn(String name,
            String visibility, Boolean isAscending) throws MOFERROR;
    }
```

Figure 10.17   JMI Mappings: SQLIndex and SQLIndexColumn. *(continued)*

SQL Data Types

The class diagram of SQLDataType, SQLSimpleType, and SQLDistinctType
was shown in Figure 10.12. The class diagram of SQLStructuredType is
shown in Figure 10.18. In addition, as was shown in in Chapter 5 in Figure 5.7,
SQLSimpleType inherits from SQLDataType and DataType; SQLDistinct-
Type inherits from SQLDataType and TypeAlias; and SQLStructuredType
inherits from SQLDataType and Class. In Figure 10.12, please note that
SQLDistinctType has a reference "sqlSimpleType" to its base SQLSimple-
Type. In Figure 10.18, it is seen that SQLStructuredType owns Columns

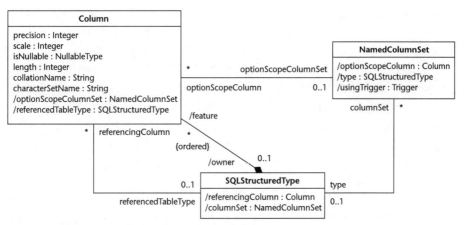

Figure 10.18 Class diagram: SQL Structured Type.

through the inherited Classifier-Feature association discussed previously. NamedColumn Set (e.g., typed table) can be defined in terms of SQLStructuredType, in which case, NamedColumnSet has a reference "type" to SQLStructuredType and SQLStructuredType has a reference "ColumnSet" to NamedColumnSet. Also, Column can be of SQL REF type, in which case, Column has a reference "referencedTableType" to SQLStructuredType and SQLStructuredType has a reference "referencingColumn" to Column. Additionally, Column can be scoped to a certain typed table, in which case, Column has a reference "optionScopeColumnSet" to NamedColumnSet, and NamedColumnSet has a reference "optionScopeColumn" to Column.

The JMI mappings for SQLDataType, SQLSimpleType, SQLDistinctType, and SQLStructuredType are shown in Figure 10.19. Also included is the JMI mapping for TypeAlias (from the DataTypes package). Please note:

- The SQLDataType interface inherits from the Classifier interface and provides additional methods to get/set the SQL type number.

- The TypeAlias interface inherits from the DataType interface and provides additional methods to get/set its base type Classifier. The TypeAliasClass interface provides methods to create new TypeAliases.

- The SQLSimpleType interface inherits from the SQLDataType and DataType interface, and provides additional methods to get/set its attributes (e.g., characterMaximumLength). The SQLSimpleTypeClass interface provides methods to create new SQLSimpleTypes.

- The SQLDistinctType interface inherits from the SQLDataType and TypeAlias interfaces, and provides additional methods to get/set its base SQLSimpleType and optional attributes (e.g., length). The SQLDistinctTypeClass interface provides methods to create new SQLDistinctTypes.

- The SQLStructuredType interface inherits from the SQLDataType and Class interfaces, and provides additional methods to manipulate its optional references (e.g., referencingColumn). The SQLStructuredTypeClass interface provides methods to create new SQLStructuredTypes.

```
public interface SQLDataType extends RefObject, Classifier
{
    public Long getTypeNumber() throws MOFERROR;
    public void setTypeNumber(Long value) throws MOFERROR;
}
public interface SQLDataTypeClass extends RefClass
{
    public List allOfTypeSQLDataType();
}


public interface TypeAlias extends RefObject, DataType
{
    public Classifier getType() throws MOFERROR;
    public void setType(Classifier value) throws MOFERROR;
}
public interface TypeAliasClass extends RefClass
{
    public List allOfTypeTypeAlias();
    public List allOfKindTypeAlias();

    public TypeAlias createTypeAlias() throws MOFERROR;
    public TypeAlias createTypeAlias(String name, String visibility,
        Boolean isAbstract) throws MOFERROR;
}


public interface SQLSimpleType extends RefObject, SQLDataType, DataType
{
    public Long getCharacterMaximumLength() throws MOFERROR;
    public void setCharacterMaximumLength(Long value) throws MOFERROR;
    public Long getCharacterOctetLength() throws MOFERROR;
    public void setCharacterOctetLength(Long value) throws MOFERROR;
    public Long getNumericPrecision() throws MOFERROR;
    public void setNumericPrecision(Long value) throws MOFERROR;
    public Long getNumericPrecisionRadix() throws MOFERROR;
```

Figure 10.19 JMI Mappings: SQL Data Types.

```
    public void setNumericPrecisionRadix(Long value) throws MOFERROR;
    public Long getNumericScale() throws MOFERROR;
    public void setNumericScale(Long value) throws MOFERROR;
    public Long getDateTimePrecision() throws MOFERROR;
    public void setDateTimePrecision(Long value) throws MOFERROR;
}
public interface SQLSimpleTypeClass extends RefClass
{
    public List allOfTypeSQLSimpleType();
    public List allOfKindSQLSimpleType();

    public SQLSimpleType createSQLSimpleType() throws MOFERROR;
    public SQLSimpleType createSQLSimpleType(String name,
        String visibility, Boolean isAbstract, Long typeNumber,
        Long characterMaximumLength, Long characterOctetLength,
        Long numericPrecision, Long numericPrecisionRadix,
        Long numericScale, Long dateTimePrecision) throws MOFERROR;
}

public interface SQLDistinctType extends RefObject, SQLDataType,
TypeAlias
{
    public Long getLength() throws MOFERROR;
    public void setLength(Long value) throws MOFERROR;
    public Long getPrecision() throws MOFERROR;
    public void setPrecision(Long value) throws MOFERROR;
    public Long getScale() throws MOFERROR;
    public void setScale(Long value) throws MOFERROR;

    public SQLSimpleType getSqlSimpleType() throws MOFERROR;
    public void setSqlSimpleType(SQLSimpleType value) throws MOFERROR;
}
public interface SQLDistinctTypeClass extends RefClass
{
    public List allOfTypeSQLDistinctType();
    public List allOfKindSQLDistinctType();

    public SQLDistinctType createSQLDistinctType() throws MOFERROR;
    public SQLDistinctType createSQLDistinctType(String name,
        String visibility, Boolean isAbstract, Long typeNumber,
        Long length, Long precision, Long scale) throws MOFERROR;
}

public interface SQLStructuredType extends RefObject, SQLDataType, Class
{
    public Collection getReferencingColumn() throws MOFERROR;
    public void setReferencingColumn(Collection value) throws MOFERROR;
    public void addReferencingColumn(Column value) throws MOFERROR;
```

Figure 10.19 JMI Mappings: SQL Data Types. *(continues)*

```
        public void modifyReferencingColumn(Column newValue, Column oldValue)
            throws MOFERROR, NotFoundException;
        public void removeReferencingColumn(Column value)
            throws MOFERROR, NotFoundException;

        public Collection getColumnSet() throws MOFERROR;
        public void setColumnSet(Collection value) throws MOFERROR;
        public void addColumnSet(NamedColumnSet value) throws MOFERROR;
        public void modifyColumnSet(NamedColumnSet newValue,
            NamedColumnSet oldValue) throws MOFERROR, NotFoundException;
        public void removeColumnSet(NamedColumnSet value)
            throws MOFERROR, NotFoundException;
}
public interface SQLStructuredTypeClass extends RefClass
{
        public List allOfTypeSQLStructuredType();
        public List allOfKindSQLStructuredType();

        public SQLStructuredType createSQLStructuredType() throws MOFERROR;
        public SQLStructuredType createSQLStructuredType(String name,
            String visibility, Boolean isAbstract, Long typeNumber)
            throws MOFERROR;
}
```

Figure 10.19 JMI Mappings: SQL Data Types. *(continued)*

Stored Procedure

The class diagram of Procedure and SQLParameter is shown in Figure 10.20. Please note that Procedure owns SQLParameter through the inherited BehavioralFeature-Parameter association discussed previously. Going back to Figure 10.10, please note that Schema owns Procedure.

The JMI mappings for Procedure and SQLParameter are shown in Figure 10.21. Please note:

- The Procedure interface inherits from Method and provides additional methods to get/set its type (i.e., "function" or "procedure"). The interface ProcedureClass provides methods to create new Procedures.

- The SQLParameter interface inherits from Parameter. The SQLParameterClass interface provides methods to create new SQLParameters.

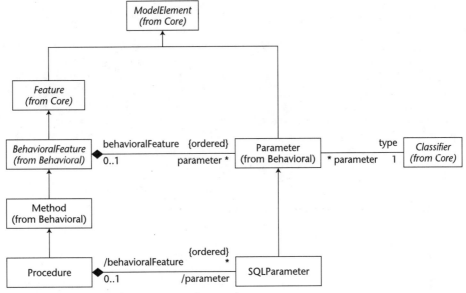

Figure 10.20   Class diagram: Stored Procedure.

```
public interface Procedure extends RefObject, Method
{
    public String getType() throws MOFERROR;
    public void setType(String value) throws MOFERROR;
}
public interface ProcedureClass extends RefClass
{
    public List allOfTypeProcedure();
    public List allOfKindProcedure();

    public Procedure createProcedure() throws MOFERROR;
    public Procedure createProcedure(String name, String visibility,
        String ownerScope, Boolean isQuery,
        org.omg.java.cwm.objectmodel.core.ProcedureExpression body,
        String type) throws MOFERROR;
}


public interface SQLParameter extends RefObject, Parameter
{
```

Figure 10.21   JMI Mappings: Stored Procedure. *(continues)*

```
}
public interface SQLParameterClass extends RefClass
{
    public List allOfTypeSQLParameter();
    public List allOfKindSQLParameter();

    public SQLParameter createSQLParameter() throws MOFERROR;
    public SQLParameter createSQLParameter(String name, String
visibility,
        org.omg.java.cwm.objectmodel.core.Expression defaultValue,
        String kind) throws MOFERROR;
}
```

Figure 10.21 JMI Mappings: Stored Procedure. *(continued)*

Trigger

The class diagram of Trigger is shown in Figure 10.22. Please note Schema owns Trigger, as shown previously in Figure 10.10. Trigger has a reference "table" to the Table it is associated with and a reference "usedColumnSet" to the ColumnSet used in its expression.

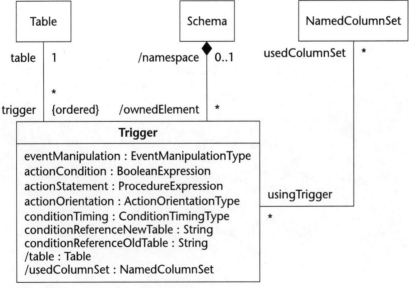

Figure 10.22 Class diagram: Trigger.

The JMI mapping for Trigger is shown in Figure 10.23. Please note:

■ The Trigger interface provides methods to get/set its attributes (e.g., actionCondition) and associated Table, and to manipulate the ColumnSet used in its expression. The TriggerClass interface provides methods to create new Triggers.

```
public interface Trigger extends RefObject, ModelElement
{
    public String getEventManipulation() throws MOFERROR;
    public void setEventManipulation(String value) throws MOFERROR;
    public org.omg.java.cwm.objectmodel.core.BooleanExpression
        getActionCondition() throws MOFERROR;
    public void setActionCondition(
        org.omg.java.cwm.objectmodel.core.BooleanExpression value)
        throws MOFERROR;
    public org.omg.java.cwm.objectmodel.core.ProcedureExpression
        getActionStatement() throws MOFERROR;
    public void setActionStatement(
        org.omg.java.cwm.objectmodel.core.ProcedureExpression value)
        throws MOFERROR;
    public String getActionOrientation() throws MOFERROR;
    public void setActionOrientation(String value) throws MOFERROR;
    public String getConditionTiming() throws MOFERROR;
    public void setConditionTiming(String value) throws MOFERROR;
     public String getConditionReferenceNewTable() throws MOFERROR;
    public void setConditionReferenceNewTable(String value)
        throws MOFERROR;
    public String getConditionReferenceOldTable() throws MOFERROR;
    public void setConditionReferenceOldTable(String value)
        throws MOFERROR;

    public Table getTable() throws MOFERROR;
    public void setTable(Table value) throws MOFERROR;
    public Collection getUsedColumnSet() throws MOFERROR;
    public void setUsedColumnSet(Collection value) throws MOFERROR;
    public void addUsedColumnSet(NamedColumnSet value) throws MOFERROR;
    public void modifyUsedColumnSet(NamedColumnSet newValue,
        NamedColumnSet oldValue) throws MOFERROR, NotFoundException;
    public void removeUsedColumnSet(NamedColumnSet value)
        throws MOFERROR, NotFoundException;
}
public interface TriggerClass extends RefClass
{
    public List allOfTypeTrigger();
```

Figure 10.23   JMI Mappings: Trigger. *(continues)*

```
    public List allOfKindTrigger();

    public Trigger createTrigger() throws MOFERROR;
    public Trigger createTrigger(String name, String visibility,
        String eventManipulation,
        org.omg.java.cwm.objectmodel.core.BooleanExpression
        actionCondition,
        org.omg.java.cwm.objectmodel.core.ProcedureExpression
        actionStatement, String actionOrientation, String
conditionTiming,
        String conditionReferenceNewTable,
        String conditionReferenceOldTable) throws MOFERROR;
}
```

Figure 10.23   JMI Mappings: Trigger. *(continued)*

Relational Instances

The class diagram of RowSet, Row, and ColumnValue was shown previously in Figure 5.8. Please note that RowSet inherits from Extent; Row inherits from Object; and ColumnValue inherits from DataValue.

The JMI mappings for RowSet, Row, and ColumnValue are shown in Figure 10.24. Please note:

- The RowSet interface inherits from the Extent interface. The RowSet-Class interface provides methods to create new RowSets.

- The Row interface inherits from the Object interface. The RowClass interface provides methods to create new Rows.

- The ColumnValue interface inherits from the DataValue interface. The ColumnValueClass interface provides methods to create new ColumnValues.

```
public interface RowSet extends RefObject, Extent
{
}
public interface RowSetClass extends RefClass
{
    public List allOfTypeRowSet();
    public List allOfKindRowSet();

    public RowSet createRowSet() throws MOFERROR;
    public RowSet createRowSet(String name, String visibility)
```

Figure 10.24   JMI Mappings: Relational Instances.

```
            throws MOFERROR;
    }

    public interface Row extends RefObject, Object
    {
    }
    public interface RowClass extends RefClass
    {
        public List allOfTypeRow();
        public List allOfKindRow();

        public Row createRow() throws MOFERROR;
        public Row createRow(String name, String visibility) throws
    MOFERROR;
    }

    public interface ColumnValue extends RefObject, DataValue
    {
    }
    public interface ColumnValueClass extends RefClass
    {
        public List allOfTypeColumnValue();
        public List allOfKindColumnValue();

        public ColumnValue createColumnValue() throws MOFERROR;
        public ColumnValue createColumnValue(String name, String visibility,
            String value) throws MOFERROR;
    }
```

Figure 10.24   JMI Mappings: Relational Instances. *(continued)*

Relational Package Proxy

The package proxy interface generated for the CWM Relational package is shown in Figure 10.25. Please note that this interface provides methods for accessing all contained classes.

```
    public interface RelationalPackage extends RefPackage
    {
      // Nested packages
        public EnumerationsPackage getEnumerations() throws MOFERROR;

      // Clustered packages

      // Classes
```

Figure 10.25   JMI Mappings: Relational Package Proxy. *(continues)*

```
    public CatalogClass getCatalog() throws MOFERROR;
    public SchemaClass getSchema() throws MOFERROR;
    public ColumnSetClass getColumnSet() throws MOFERROR;
    public NamedColumnSetClass getNamedColumnSet() throws MOFERROR;
    public TableClass getTable() throws MOFERROR;
    public ViewClass getView() throws MOFERROR;
    public QueryColumnSetClass getQueryColumnSet() throws MOFERROR;
    public SQLDataTypeClass getSQLDataType() throws MOFERROR;
    public SQLDistinctTypeClass getSQLDistinctType() throws MOFERROR;
    public SQLSimpleTypeClass getSQLSimpleType() throws MOFERROR;
    public SQLStructuredTypeClass getSQLStructuredType() throws MOFERROR;
    public ColumnClass getColumn() throws MOFERROR;
    public ProcedureClass getProcedure() throws MOFERROR;
    public TriggerClass getTrigger() throws MOFERROR;
    public SQLIndexClass getSQLIndex() throws MOFERROR;
    public UniqueConstraintClass getUniqueConstraint() throws MOFERROR;
    public ForeignKeyClass getForeignKey() throws MOFERROR;
    public SQLIndexColumnClass getSQLIndexColumn() throws MOFERROR;
    public PrimaryKeyClass getPrimaryKey() throws MOFERROR;
    public RowClass getRow() throws MOFERROR;
    public ColumnValueClass getColumnValue() throws MOFERROR;
    public CheckConstraintClass getCheckConstraint() throws MOFERROR;
    public RowSetClass getRowSet() throws MOFERROR;
    public SQLParameterClass getSQLParameter() throws MOFERROR;

  // Associations
    public TriggerUsingColumnSet getTriggerUsingColumnSet()
        throws MOFERROR;
    public TableOwningTrigger getTableOwningTrigger() throws MOFERROR;
    public ColumnSetOfStructuredType getColumnSetOfStructuredType()
        throws MOFERROR;
    public ColumnRefStructuredType getColumnRefStructuredType()
        throws MOFERROR;
    public ColumnOptionsColumnSet getColumnOptionsColumnSet()
        throws MOFERROR;
    public DistinctTypeHasSimpleType getDistinctTypeHasSimpleType()
        throws MOFERROR;
}
```

Figure 10.25 JMI Mappings: Relational Package Proxy. *(continued)*

CWM Transformation Classes and JMI Mappings

For convenience, we will break the discussion of CWM Transformation classes into three groups: (1) Transformation; (2) TransformationTask, TransformationStep, and TransformationActivity; and (3) TransformationMap and its components (ClassifierMap, ClassifierFeatureMap, and FeatureMap).

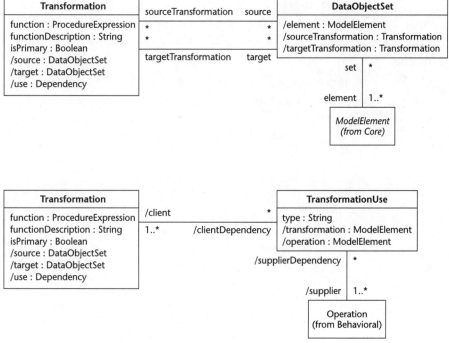

Figure 10.26   Class diagram: Transformation.

Transformation

The class diagram of Transformation and its associated classes is shown in Figure 10.26. Please note that Transformation is optionally associated with source and target DataObjectSets. This is due to the fact that certain types of Transformation (e.g., TransformationMap, to be discussed later) are associated with their own specific source and target ModelElements. Please also note that Transformation may be defined using existing Operations (e.g., an existing program) through TransformationUse, which is an "association" class.

The JMI mappings for Transformation and its associated classes are shown in Figure 10.27. Please note:

■ The Transformation interface inherits from the Namespace interface and provides additional methods to manipulate its attributes (e.g., Function), its source and target DataObjectSets, and the Operations that it uses (through TransformationUse). The TransformationClass interface provides methods to create new Transformations.

- The DataObjectSet interface provides methods to manipulate its associated ModelElements (i.e., the "data objects") and source and target Transformations. The DataObjectSetClass interface provides methods to create new DataObjectSets.

- The TransformationUse interface inherits from the Dependency interface and provides additional methods to manipulate its associated Transformations and Operations. The TransformationUseClass interface provides methods to create new TransformationUses.

```
public interface Transformation extends RefObject, Namespace
{
    public org.omg.java.cwm.objectmodel.core.ProcedureExpression
        getFunction() throws MOFERROR;
    public void setFunction(
        org.omg.java.cwm.objectmodel.core.ProcedureExpression value)
        throws MOFERROR;
    public String getFunctionDescription() throws MOFERROR;
    public void setFunctionDescription(String value) throws MOFERROR;
    public Boolean isPrimary() throws MOFERROR;
    public void setIsPrimary(Boolean value) throws MOFERROR;
    public boolean isPrimaryValue() throws MOFERROR;
    public void setIsPrimary(boolean value) throws MOFERROR;
    public Collection getSource() throws MOFERROR;

    public void setSource(Collection value) throws MOFERROR;
    public void addSource(DataObjectSet value) throws MOFERROR;
    public void modifySource(DataObjectSet newValue, DataObjectSet
        oldValue) throws MOFERROR, NotFoundException;
    public void removeSource(DataObjectSet value) throws MOFERROR,
        NotFoundException;
    public Collection getTarget() throws MOFERROR;
    public void setTarget(Collection value) throws MOFERROR;
    public void addTarget(DataObjectSet value) throws MOFERROR;
    public void modifyTarget(DataObjectSet newValue, DataObjectSet
        oldValue) throws MOFERROR, NotFoundException;
    public void removeTarget(DataObjectSet value) throws MOFERROR,
        NotFoundException;

    public Collection getUse() throws MOFERROR;
    public void setUse(Collection value) throws MOFERROR;
    public void addUse(Dependency value) throws MOFERROR;
    public void modifyUse(Dependency newValue, Dependency oldValue)
throws
        MOFERROR, NotFoundException;
    public void removeUse(Dependency value) throws MOFERROR,
    NotFoundException;
```

Figure 10.27   JMI Mappings: Transformation.

```
}
public interface TransformationClass extends RefClass
{
    public List allOfTypeTransformation();
    public List allOfKindTransformation();

    public Transformation createTransformation() throws MOFERROR;
    public Transformation createTransformation(String name, String
        visibility,
org.omg.java.cwm.objectmodel.core.ProcedureExpression
        function, String functionDescription, Boolean isPrimary)
        throws MOFERROR;
}

public interface DataObjectSet extends RefObject, ModelElement
{
    public Collection getElement() throws MOFERROR;
    public void setElement(Collection value) throws MOFERROR;
    public void addElement(ModelElement value) throws MOFERROR;
    public void modifyElement(ModelElement newValue, ModelElement
        oldValue) throws MOFERROR, NotFoundException;
    public void removeElement(ModelElement value)
        throws MOFERROR, NotFoundException;

    public Collection getSourceTransformation() throws MOFERROR;
    public void setSourceTransformation(Collection value) throws
MOFERROR;
    public void addSourceTransformation(Transformation value)
        throws MOFERROR;
    public void modifySourceTransformation(Transformation newValue,
        Transformation oldValue) throws MOFERROR, NotFoundException;
    public void removeSourceTransformation(Transformation value)
        throws MOFERROR, NotFoundException;
    public Collection getTargetTransformation() throws MOFERROR;
    public void setTargetTransformation(Collection value) throws
MOFERROR;
    public void addTargetTransformation(Transformation value)
        throws MOFERROR;
    public void modifyTargetTransformation(Transformation newValue,
        Transformation oldValue) throws MOFERROR, NotFoundException;
    public void removeTargetTransformation(Transformation value)
        throws MOFERROR, NotFoundException;
}
public interface DataObjectSetClass extends RefClass
{
    public List allOfTypeDataObjectSet();
    public List allOfKindDataObjectSet();

    public DataObjectSet createDataObjectSet() throws MOFERROR;
```

Figure 10.27 JMI Mappings: Transformation. *(continues)*

```
      public DataObjectSet createDataObjectSet(String name,
          String visibility) throws MOFERROR;
}

public interface TransformationUse extends RefObject, Dependency
{
    public String getType() throws MOFERROR;
    public void setType(String value) throws MOFERROR;

    public Collection getTransformation() throws MOFERROR;
    public void setTransformation(Collection value) throws MOFERROR;
    public void addTransformation(ModelElement value) throws MOFERROR;
    public void modifyTransformation(ModelElement newValue, ModelElement
        oldValue) throws MOFERROR, NotFoundException;
    public void removeTransformation(ModelElement value) throws
MOFERROR,
        NotFoundException;
    public Collection getOperation() throws MOFERROR;
    public void setOperation(Collection value) throws MOFERROR;
    public void addOperation(ModelElement value) throws MOFERROR;
    public void modifyOperation(ModelElement newValue, ModelElement
        oldValue) throws MOFERROR, NotFoundException;
    public void removeOperation(ModelElement value) throws MOFERROR,
        NotFoundException;
}
public interface TransformationUseClass extends RefClass
{
    public List allOfTypeTransformationUse();
    public List allOfKindTransformationUse();

    public TransformationUse createTransformationUse() throws MOFERROR;
    public TransformationUse createTransformationUse(String name, String
        visibility, String kind, String type) throws MOFERROR;
}
```

Figure 10.27   JMI Mappings: Transformation. *(continued)*

TransformationTask, TransformationStep, and TransformationActivity

The class diagram of TransformationTask, TransformationStep, TransformationActivity, and their associated classes is shown in Figure 10.28. Please note that a TransformationTask is associated with one or more Transformations, although this is not shown in the diagram. Also, Transformation Steps can be connected to each other either explicitly through StepPrecedence or implicitly through PrecedenceConstraint.

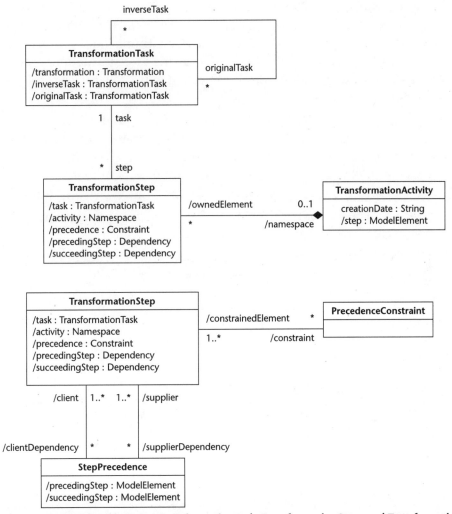

Figure 10.28   Class diagram: TransformationTask, TransformationStep, and Transformation-Activity.

The JMI mappings for TransformationTask, TransformationStep, TransformationActivity, and their associated classes are shown in Figure 10.29. Please note:

- The TransformationTask interface inherits from the Component interface and provides additional methods to manipulate its associated Transformations as well as any original and inverse TransformationTasks, if they exist. The TransformationTaskClass interface provides methods to create new TransformationTasks.

- The TransformationStep interface provides methods to get/set its associated TransformationTask and owning TransformationActivity, and methods to manipulate PrecedenceConstraints and preceding/succeeding StepPrecedences. The TransformationStep-Class interface provides methods to create new Transformation-Steps.

- The TransformationActivity interface inherits from the Subsystem interface and provides additional methods to manipulate its owned TransformationSteps. The TransformationActivityClass interface provides methods to create new TransformationActivities.

- The PrecedenceConstraint interface inherits from the Constraint interface. The PrecedenceConstraintClass interface provides methods to create new PrecedenceConstraints.

- The StepPrecedence interface inherits from the Dependency interface and provides additional methods to manipulate its preceding/succeeding TransformationSteps. The StepPrecedence-Class interface provides methods to create new StepPrecedences.

```java
public interface TransformationTask extends RefObject, Component
{
    public Collection getTransformation() throws MOFERROR;
    public void setTransformation(Collection value) throws MOFERROR;
    public void addTransformation(Transformation value) throws MOFERROR;
    public void modifyTransformation(Transformation newValue,
        Transformation oldValue) throws MOFERROR, NotFoundException;
    public void removeTransformation(Transformation value)
        throws MOFERROR, NotFoundException;

    public Collection getInverseTask() throws MOFERROR;
    public void setInverseTask(Collection value) throws MOFERROR;
    public void addInverseTask(TransformationTask value) throws
MOFERROR;
    public void modifyInverseTask(TransformationTask newValue,
        TransformationTask oldValue) throws MOFERROR, NotFoundException;
    public void removeInverseTask(TransformationTask value)
        throws MOFERROR, NotFoundException;
    public Collection getOriginalTask() throws MOFERROR;
    public void setOriginalTask(Collection value) throws MOFERROR;
    public void addOriginalTask(TransformationTask value) throws
MOFERROR;
    public void modifyOriginalTask(TransformationTask newValue,
        TransformationTask oldValue) throws MOFERROR, NotFoundException;
    public void removeOriginalTask(TransformationTask value)
```

Figure 10.29 JMI Mappings: TransformationTask, TransformationStep, and Transformation-Activity.

```
            throws MOFERROR, NotFoundException;
}
public interface TransformationTaskClass extends RefClass
{
    public List allOfTypeTransformationTask();
    public List allOfKindTransformationTask();

    public TransformationTask createTransformationTask() throws
MOFERROR;
    public TransformationTask createTransformationTask(String name,
String
        visibility, Boolean isAbstract) throws MOFERROR;
}

public interface TransformationStep extends RefObject, ModelElement
{
    public TransformationTask getTask() throws MOFERROR;
    public void setTask(TransformationTask value) throws MOFERROR;
    public Namespace getActivity() throws MOFERROR;
    public void setActivity(Namespace value) throws MOFERROR;

    public Collection getPrecedence() throws MOFERROR;
    public void setPrecedence(Collection value) throws MOFERROR;
    public void addPrecedence(Constraint value) throws MOFERROR;
    public void modifyPrecedence(Constraint newValue, Constraint
oldValue)
        throws MOFERROR, NotFoundException;
    public void removePrecedence(Constraint value) throws MOFERROR,
        NotFoundException;

    public Collection getPrecedingStep() throws MOFERROR;
    public void setPrecedingStep(Collection value) throws MOFERROR;
    public void addPrecedingStep(Dependency value) throws MOFERROR;
    public void modifyPrecedingStep(Dependency newValue, Dependency
        oldValue) throws MOFERROR, NotFoundException;
    public void removePrecedingStep(Dependency value) throws MOFERROR,
        NotFoundException;
    public Collection getSucceedingStep() throws MOFERROR;
    public void setSucceedingStep(Collection value) throws MOFERROR;
    public void addSucceedingStep(Dependency value) throws MOFERROR;
    public void modifySucceedingStep(Dependency newValue, Dependency
        oldValue) throws MOFERROR, NotFoundException;
    public void removeSucceedingStep(Dependency value) throws MOFERROR,
        NotFoundException;
}
public interface TransformationStepClass extends RefClass
{
    public List allOfTypeTransformationStep();
```

Figure 10.29   JMI Mappings: TransformationTask, TransformationStep, and Transformation-Activity. *(continues)*

```
    public List allOfKindTransformationStep();

    public TransformationStep createTransformationStep() throws
MOFERROR;
    public TransformationStep createTransformationStep(String name,
String
        visibility) throws MOFERROR;
}

public interface TransformationActivity extends RefObject, Subsystem
{
    public String getCreationDate() throws MOFERROR;
    public void setCreationDate(String value) throws MOFERROR;

    public Collection getStep() throws MOFERROR;
    public void setStep(Collection value) throws MOFERROR;
    public void addStep(ModelElement value) throws MOFERROR;
    public void modifyStep(ModelElement newValue, ModelElement oldValue)
        throws MOFERROR, NotFoundException;
    public void removeStep(ModelElement value) throws MOFERROR,
        NotFoundException;
}
public interface TransformationActivityClass extends RefClass
{
    public List allOfTypeTransformationActivity();
    public List allOfKindTransformationActivity();

    public TransformationActivity createTransformationActivity() throws
        MOFERROR;
    public TransformationActivity createTransformationActivity(String
        name, String visibility, Boolean isAbstract, String
creationDate)
        throws MOFERROR;
}

public interface PrecedenceConstraint extends RefObject, Constraint
{
}
public interface PrecedenceConstraintClass extends RefClass
{
    public List allOfTypePrecedenceConstraint();
    public List allOfKindPrecedenceConstraint();

    public PrecedenceConstraint createPrecedenceConstraint() throws
```

Figure 10.29   JMI Mappings: TransformationTask, TransformationStep, and Transformation-Activity.

```
        MOFERROR;
    public PrecedenceConstraint createPrecedenceConstraint(String name,
        String visibility,
        org.omg.java.cwm.objectmodel.core.BooleanExpression body)
        throws MOFERROR;
}

public interface StepPrecedence extends RefObject, Dependency
{
    public Collection getPrecedingStep() throws MOFERROR;
    public void setPrecedingStep(Collection value) throws MOFERROR;
    public void addPrecedingStep(ModelElement value) throws MOFERROR;
    public void modifyPrecedingStep(ModelElement newValue, ModelElement
        oldValue) throws MOFERROR, NotFoundException;
    public void removePrecedingStep(ModelElement value) throws MOFERROR,
        NotFoundException;
    public Collection getSucceedingStep() throws MOFERROR;
    public void setSucceedingStep(Collection value) throws MOFERROR;
    public void addSucceedingStep(ModelElement value) throws MOFERROR;
    public void modifySucceedingStep(ModelElement newValue, ModelElement
        oldValue) throws MOFERROR, NotFoundException;
    public void removeSucceedingStep(ModelElement value) throws
MOFERROR,
        NotFoundException;
}
public interface StepPrecedenceClass extends RefClass
{
    public List allOfTypeStepPrecedence();
    public List allOfKindStepPrecedence();

    public StepPrecedence createStepPrecedence() throws MOFERROR;
    public StepPrecedence createStepPrecedence(String name, String
        visibility, String kind) throws MOFERROR;
}
```

Figure 10.29 JMI Mappings: TransformationTask, TransformationStep, and Transformation-Activity. *(continued)*

TransformationMap and Its Components

The class diagram of TransformationMap and its component classes is shown in Figure 10.30. It can be seen that TransformationMap owns ClassifierMap, which in turn owns FeatureMap and ClassifierFeatureMap.

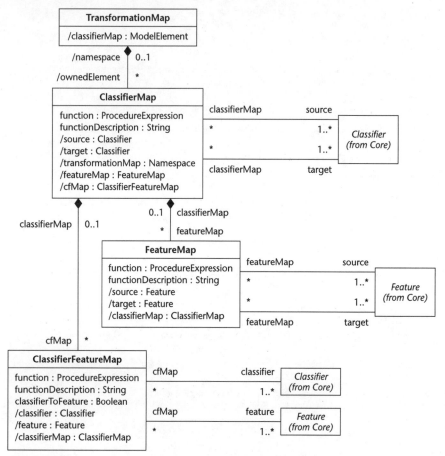

Figure 10.30 Class diagram: TransformationMap and its components.

The JMI mappings for TransformationMap and its component classes are shown in Figure 10.31. Please note:

- The TransformationMap interface inherits from the Transformation interface and provides additional methods to manipulate its owned ClassifierMaps. The TransformationMapClass interface provides methods to create new TransformationMaps.

- The ClassifierMap interface inherits from the Namespace interface and provides additional methods to get/set its function and function description, to manipulate its source and target Classifiers, to get/set its owning TransformationMap, and to manipulate its owned FeatureMaps and ClassifierFeatureMaps. The ClassifierMap-Class interface provides methods to create new ClassifierMaps.

- The FeatureMap interface provides methods to get/set its function and function description, to manipulate its source and target Features, and to get/set its owning ClassifierMap. The FeatureMap-Class interface provides methods to create new FeatureMaps.

- The ClassifierFeatureMap interface provides methods to get/set its function and function description, to manipulate its source/target Classifiers and Features, and to get/set its owning ClassifierMap. The ClassifierFeatureMapClass interface provides methods to create new ClassifierFeatureMaps.

```
public interface TransformationMap extends RefObject, Transformation
{
    public Collection getClassifierMap() throws MOFERROR;
    public void setClassifierMap(Collection value) throws MOFERROR;
    public void addClassifierMap(ModelElement value) throws MOFERROR;
    public void modifyClassifierMap(ModelElement newValue, ModelElement
        oldValue) throws MOFERROR, NotFoundException;
    public void removeClassifierMap(ModelElement value) throws MOFERROR,
        NotFoundException;
}
public interface TransformationMapClass extends RefClass
{
    public List allOfTypeTransformationMap();
    public List allOfKindTransformationMap();

    public TransformationMap createTransformationMap() throws MOFERROR;
    public TransformationMap createTransformationMap(String name, String
        visibility,
org.omg.java.cwm.objectmodel.core.ProcedureExpression
        function, String functionDescription, Boolean isPrimary)
        throws MOFERROR;
}

public interface ClassifierMap extends RefObject, Namespace
{
    public org.omg.java.cwm.objectmodel.core.ProcedureExpression
        getFunction() throws MOFERROR;
    public void setFunction(
        org.omg.java.cwm.objectmodel.core.ProcedureExpression
        value) throws MOFERROR;
    public String getFunctionDescription() throws MOFERROR;
    public void setFunctionDescription(String value) throws MOFERROR;

    public Collection getSource() throws MOFERROR;
    public void setSource(Collection value) throws MOFERROR;
```

Figure 10.31   JMI Mappings: TransformationMap and its components. *(continues)*

```
        public void addSource(Classifier value) throws MOFERROR;
        public void modifySource(Classifier newValue, Classifier oldValue)
            throws MOFERROR, NotFoundException;
        public void removeSource(Classifier value) throws MOFERROR,
            NotFoundException;
        public Collection getTarget() throws MOFERROR;
        public void setTarget(Collection value) throws MOFERROR;
        public void addTarget(Classifier value) throws MOFERROR;
        public void modifyTarget(Classifier newValue, Classifier oldValue)
            throws MOFERROR, NotFoundException;
        public void removeTarget(Classifier value) throws MOFERROR,
            NotFoundException;

        public Namespace getTransformationMap() throws MOFERROR;
        public void setTransformationMap(Namespace value) throws MOFERROR;
        public Collection getFeatureMap() throws MOFERROR;
        public void setFeatureMap(Collection value) throws MOFERROR;
        public void addFeatureMap(FeatureMap value) throws MOFERROR;
        public void modifyFeatureMap(FeatureMap newValue, FeatureMap
oldValue)
            throws MOFERROR, NotFoundException;
        public void removeFeatureMap(FeatureMap value) throws MOFERROR,
            NotFoundException;
        public Collection getCfMap() throws MOFERROR;
        public void setCfMap(Collection value) throws MOFERROR;
        public void addCfMap(ClassifierFeatureMap value) throws MOFERROR;
        public void modifyCfMap(ClassifierFeatureMap newValue,
            ClassifierFeatureMap oldValue) throws MOFERROR,
NotFoundException;
        public void removeCfMap(ClassifierFeatureMap value) throws MOFERROR,
            NotFoundException;
}
public interface ClassifierMapClass extends RefClass
{
        public List allOfTypeClassifierMap();
        public List allOfKindClassifierMap();

        public ClassifierMap createClassifierMap() throws MOFERROR;
        public ClassifierMap createClassifierMap(String name, String
            visibility,
org.omg.java.cwm.objectmodel.core.ProcedureExpression
            function, String functionDescription) throws MOFERROR;
}

public interface FeatureMap extends RefObject, ModelElement
{
        public org.omg.java.cwm.objectmodel.core.ProcedureExpression
            getFunction() throws MOFERROR;
        public void setFunction(
```

Figure 10.31   JMI Mappings: TransformationMap and its components.

```
            org.omg.java.cwm.objectmodel.core.ProcedureExpression value)
        throws MOFERROR;
    public String getFunctionDescription() throws MOFERROR;
    public void setFunctionDescription(String value) throws MOFERROR;

    public Collection getSource() throws MOFERROR;
    public void setSource(Collection value) throws MOFERROR;
    public void addSource(Feature value) throws MOFERROR;
    public void modifySource(Feature newValue, Feature oldValue) throws
        MOFERROR, NotFoundException;
    public void removeSource(Feature value) throws MOFERROR,
        NotFoundException;
    public Collection getTarget() throws MOFERROR;
    public void setTarget(Collection value) throws MOFERROR;
    public void addTarget(Feature value) throws MOFERROR;
    public void modifyTarget(Feature newValue, Feature oldValue) throws
        MOFERROR, NotFoundException;
    public void removeTarget(Feature value) throws MOFERROR,
        NotFoundException;

    public ClassifierMap getClassifierMap() throws MOFERROR;
    public void setClassifierMap(ClassifierMap value) throws MOFERROR;
}
public interface FeatureMapClass extends RefClass
{
    public List allOfTypeFeatureMap();
    public List allOfKindFeatureMap();

    public FeatureMap createFeatureMap() throws MOFERROR;
    public FeatureMap createFeatureMap(String name, String visibility,
        org.omg.java.cwm.objectmodel.core.ProcedureExpression function,
        String functionDescription) throws MOFERROR;
}

public interface ClassifierFeatureMap extends RefObject, ModelElement
{
    public org.omg.java.cwm.objectmodel.core.ProcedureExpression
        getFunction() throws MOFERROR;
    public void setFunction(
        org.omg.java.cwm.objectmodel.core.ProcedureExpression value)
        throws MOFERROR;
    public String getFunctionDescription() throws MOFERROR;
    public void setFunctionDescription(String value) throws MOFERROR;
    public Boolean isClassifierToFeature() throws MOFERROR;
    public void setClassifierToFeature(Boolean value) throws MOFERROR;
    public boolean isClassifierToFeatureValue() throws MOFERROR;
    public void setClassifierToFeature(boolean value) throws MOFERROR;

    public Collection getClassifier() throws MOFERROR;
```

Figure 10.31 JMI Mappings: TransformationMap and its components. *(continues)*

```
      public void setClassifier(Collection value) throws MOFERROR;
      public void addClassifier(Classifier value) throws MOFERROR;
      public void modifyClassifier(Classifier newValue, Classifier
oldValue)
          throws MOFERROR, NotFoundException;
      public void removeClassifier(Classifier value) throws MOFERROR,
          NotFoundException;
      public Collection getFeature() throws MOFERROR;
      public void setFeature(Collection value) throws MOFERROR;
      public void addFeature(Feature value) throws MOFERROR;
      public void modifyFeature(Feature newValue, Feature oldValue) throws
          MOFERROR, NotFoundException;
      public void removeFeature(Feature value) throws MOFERROR,
          NotFoundException;

      public ClassifierMap getClassifierMap() throws MOFERROR;
      public void setClassifierMap(ClassifierMap value) throws MOFERROR;
}
public interface ClassifierFeatureMapClass extends RefClass
{
      public List allOfTypeClassifierFeatureMap();
      public List allOfKindClassifierFeatureMap();

      public ClassifierFeatureMap createClassifierFeatureMap() throws
          MOFERROR;
      public ClassifierFeatureMap createClassifierFeatureMap(String name,
          String visibility,
          org.omg.java.cwm.objectmodel.core.ProcedureExpression function,
          String functionDescription, Boolean classifierToFeature)
          throws MOFERROR;
}
```

Figure 10.31   JMI Mappings: TransformationMap and its components. *(continued)*

CWM WarehouseProcess Classes and JMI Mappings

The class diagram of WarehouseProcess, WarehouseActivity, and WarehouseStep is shown in Figure 10.32. Also shown is ProcessPackage. Please note that both WarehouseActivity and WarehouseStep inherit from WarehouseProcess. ProcessPackage is the "top" class and it owns WarehouseActivity, which in turn owns WarehouseStep. Please also note that WarehouseActivity is always associated with TransformationActivity and, likewise, WarehouseStep is associated with TransformationStep.

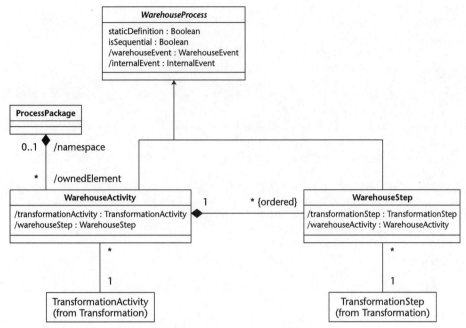

Figure 10.32 Class diagram: Warehouse Process, Activity, and Step.

The JMI mappings for WarehouseProcess, WarehouseActivity, WarehouseStep, and ProcessPackage are shown in Figure 10.33. Please note:

- The WarehouseProcess interface provides methods to get/set its attributes (e.g., isSequential) and to manipulate warehouse events.

- The WarehouseActivity interface inherits from the WarehouseProcess interface and provides additional methods to get/set its associated TransformationActivity and to manipulate its owned WarehouseSteps. The WarehouseActivityClass interface provides methods to create new WarehouseActivities.

- The WarehouseStep interface inherits from the WarehouseProcess interface and provides additional methods to get/set its associated TransformationStep and its owning WarehouseActivity. The WarehouseStepClass interface provides methods to create new WarehouseSteps.

- The ProcessPackage interface inherits from the Package interface and the ProcessPackageClass interface provides methods to create new ProcessPackages.

```
public interface WarehouseProcess extends RefObject, ModelElement
{
    public Boolean isStaticDefinition() throws MOFERROR;
    public void setStaticDefinition(Boolean value) throws MOFERROR;
    public boolean isStaticDefinitionValue() throws MOFERROR;
    public void setStaticDefinition(boolean value) throws MOFERROR;
    public Boolean isSequential() throws MOFERROR;
    public void setIsSequential(Boolean value) throws MOFERROR;
    public boolean isSequentialValue() throws MOFERROR;
    public void setIsSequential(boolean value) throws MOFERROR;

    public Collection getWarehouseEvent() throws MOFERROR;
    public void setWarehouseEvent(Collection value) throws MOFERROR;
    public void addWarehouseEvent(WarehouseEvent value) throws MOFERROR;
    public void modifyWarehouseEvent(WarehouseEvent newValue,
        WarehouseEvent oldValue) throws MOFERROR, NotFoundException;
    public void removeWarehouseEvent(WarehouseEvent value) throws
        MOFERROR, NotFoundException;
    public Collection getInternalEvent() throws MOFERROR;
    public void setInternalEvent(Collection value) throws MOFERROR;
    public void addInternalEvent(InternalEvent value) throws MOFERROR;
    public void modifyInternalEvent(InternalEvent newValue, InternalEvent
        oldValue) throws MOFERROR, NotFoundException;
    public void removeInternalEvent(InternalEvent value) throws MOFERROR,
        NotFoundException;
}
public interface WarehouseProcessClass extends RefClass
{
    public List allOfTypeWarehouseProcess();
}

public interface WarehouseActivity extends RefObject, WarehouseProcess
{
    public TransformationActivity getTransformationActivity()
        throws MOFERROR;
    public void setTransformationActivity(TransformationActivity value)
        throws MOFERROR;

    public List getWarehouseStep() throws MOFERROR;
    public void setWarehouseStep(List value) throws MOFERROR;
    public void addWarehouseStep(WarehouseStep value) throws MOFERROR;
    public void addBeforeWarehouseStep(WarehouseStep value, WarehouseStep
        before) throws MOFERROR, NotFoundException;
    public void modifyWarehouseStep(WarehouseStep newValue, WarehouseStep
        oldValue) throws MOFERROR, NotFoundException;
    public void removeWarehouseStep(WarehouseStep value) throws MOFERROR,
```

Figure 10.33 JMI Mappings: Warehouse Process, Activity, and Step.

```
            NotFoundException;
}
public interface WarehouseActivityClass extends RefClass
{
    public List allOfTypeWarehouseActivity();
    public List allOfKindWarehouseActivity();
    public WarehouseActivity createWarehouseActivity() throws MOFERROR;
    public WarehouseActivity createWarehouseActivity(String name, String
        visibility, Boolean staticDefinition, Boolean isSequential) throws
        MOFERROR;
}


public interface WarehouseStep extends RefObject, WarehouseProcess
{
    public TransformationStep getTransformationStep() throws MOFERROR;
    public void setTransformationStep(TransformationStep value)
        throws MOFERROR;

    public WarehouseActivity getWarehouseActivity() throws MOFERROR;
    public void setWarehouseActivity(WarehouseActivity value)
        throws MOFERROR;
}
public interface WarehouseStepClass extends RefClass
{
    public List allOfTypeWarehouseStep();
    public List allOfKindWarehouseStep();

    public WarehouseStep createWarehouseStep() throws MOFERROR;
    public WarehouseStep createWarehouseStep(String name,
        String visibility, Boolean staticDefinition, Boolean
isSequential)
        throws MOFERROR;
}


public interface ProcessPackage extends RefObject, Package
{
}
public interface ProcessPackageClass extends RefClass
{
    public List allOfTypeProcessPackage();
    public List allOfKindProcessPackage();

    public ProcessPackage createProcessPackage() throws MOFERROR;
    public ProcessPackage createProcessPackage(String name,
        String visibility) throws MOFERROR;
}
```

Figure 10.33   JMI Mappings: Warehouse Process, Activity, and Step. *(continued)*

Summary

In this chapter, we examined the actual implementation of the Java programmatic API that was used in previous chapters as the basis for our programmatic contract for the access to CWM meta data. We described the process of translating CWM metaclasses to Java interfaces using the Java Metadata Interface (JMI) standard, which is an industry standard mapping of the OMG's Meta Object Facility (MOF) to the Java programming language. For each relevant CWM class, we provided a simple overview of the algorithm that would normally be performed by an automated MOF utility to generate Java interfaces representing the CWM metaclasses.

CHAPTER 11

Implementation Development

The previous chapters described in detail the technical aspects of creating a full-service, Common Warehouse Metamodel (CWM)-based meta data integration environment such as one might construct around a central CWM Metastore. This chapter defines the overall realization approach used in supporting CWM interfaces, their extensions, and import and export adapters.

CWM Implementation

CWM provides a common foundation for data warehouse vendors and tools for the interoperability and interchange of meta data and possibly data. This common foundation was developed with no specific vendor tool in mind but rather represents a set of features and functions commonly found in many data warehousing tools. Tool vendors and application developers are provided with a standard set of items by the Object Management Group (OMG) as part of the CWM specification.

Figure 11.1 depicts the materials supplied by the OMG as part of the CWM specification. The specification itself has a complete set of objects and object definitions. In addition to the specification, the OMG supplies four other components with CWM. The complete CWM metamodel in Unified

Modeling Language (UML) notation is a set of UML diagrams that graphically demonstrates the CWM metamodel. An eXtensible Markup Language (XML) file that describes the CWM model is a Meta Object Facility (MOF) 1.3 compliant version of the CWM metamodel serialized into an XML document. The CWM Document Type Definitions (DTD) is a file that users of CWM can use to validate CWM interchange documents. Finally, the OMG also supplies a set of files that contain an IDL representation of the CWM metamodel.

CWM is not intended to solve all the problems faced by all the data warehousing tools and tool vendors in a single model. Rather, CWM is intended to provide a common representation of many of the commonly used features and functionalities provided by many vendors and vendor tools. In many cases, CWM represents a lowest common denominator from the various tools analyzed to produce the CWM model. The model contains no vendor-specific representations or vendor-specific models. Given this approach, how then would a vendor (even a CWM working group member vendor) use CWM in the creation of a tool or to integrate into an existing tool? The first task for the vendor is to understand how the concepts in CWM were modeled and how those concepts relate to a tool-specific concept or, in some cases, concepts. The second task is understanding the vocabulary and nomenclature used by CWM, the model, and model definitions defined in the CWM specification. Note that these terms and object definitions may or may not match the way a specific vendor uses the same term or object. Therefore, vendors implementing CWM must take great care when using objects and object definitions to ensure semantic usage equivalence.

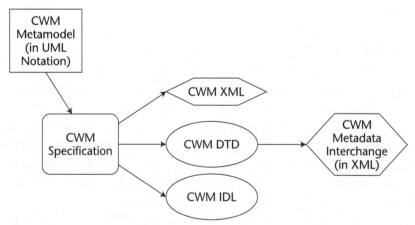

Figure 11.1 Materials supplied by the OMG for implementing CWM.

Extending CWM

As we just saw, CWM is a model that represents the common features and functionality available from various data warehouse tools. This approach to the model provides *Vendors* and *Tools* with common definitions, but probably lacks the complete set of information that an existing tool or new tool would need to fully operate. The users of CWM will have to extend the given definitions to provide their tool with tool-specific definitions required to operate. The extension of CWM can be categorized into two types:

- Simple Extensions
- Modeled Extensions

Simple Extensions to CWM

The built-in extension mechanism consists of using "Stereotypes" and "Tagged Values." This mechanism allows a user to assign any number of either "Stereotypes" and/or "Tagged Values" to any object. CWM's built-in extension mechanism is generally used to augment the object definitions with "simple" additions or to assign semantic roles to objects in the system. Users can extend the object definitions by using the Tagged Value object. The CWM user can add any number of objects like attributes with associated values to any specific object instance. Stereotypes are used to connote some special object instance usage or meaning specific to a tool. The stereotypes can be shared across Tools and Vendors, but this level of interoperability is beyond the scope of CWM and is only an agreement between two parties, which is not enforceable by the CWM model. The implementation of the stereotype mechanism can be provided as a single "Tagged Value" or by a set of "Tagged Values," which as a group carries the semantic meaning intended for a specific stereotype.

For a more complete understanding of these extension mechanisms, let's examine different scenarios of using Tagged Values and Stereotypes by looking at concrete examples. In the following examples, we will introduce the concept of an object instance. An *object instance* is a specific use of an object definition. It also contains the operational data described by the object definition.

Tagged Values

Let's assume that we need to extend the definition of some Relational Table to include several database-specific attributes of that Table. Let's also assume that the model contains no vendor-specific properties. Thus, we will augment the model to add these properties. In this example, a Tool needs to capture auxiliary information about the Table not directly supplied by CWM. In this particular case, the information fits nicely as a set of "Tagged Values" associated with the Relational Table object instance.

To create the extension, we start with the definition of a Relational Table from CWM. The Table object has a single attribute "name," which is of type string, and the Table can contain any number of Column objects. At runtime, a specific instance of the Table object can be created as, say, the Product table with two columns: ProductId and Description. Adding additional properties that are not otherwise supplied by the CWM model augments the runtime instance.

CWM object definitions can be augmented with tool-specific information not native to the CWM model. Tools and vendors can use this mechanism to store a wide variety of auxiliary information in CWM that is necessary for specific Tools to operate.

Another motivation for extending CWM might consist of enabling a tool to use either Tagged Values or Stereotypes to connote a specific *semantic meaning*. Staying with Tagged Values, consider the case in which a tool would like to identify that a particular Column in the table described above should be used as the default display Column of the Table. A tool requires that one of the Columns be identified as the display Column at Table creation time, because noncreation portions of the tool expect that a column is set up to play this role. The tool considers this meta data extension crucial to its operation, and a Table definition is not complete without the assignment of the default display Column. In this case, a Tagged Value can be used to associate a particular Column to be used by a tool under the circumstances defined by the tool. By adding the Tagged Value, the Column instance now carries the additional semantics required by the tool.

Stereotypes

Stereotypes can have much the same effect as Tagged Values on CWM objects; however, they have a broader definition in CWM in that a Stereotype can contain any number of Tagged Values and can contain constraints. The latter mechanism gives a Stereotype the appearance of creating a new virtual metamodel construct. Stereotypes are most useful in defining semantic roles to instances of CWM objects. These roles will generally have a Tagged Value or a set of Tagged Values that further specify and/or qualify the desired role. To fully understand how to use a Stereotype, let's examine the following example: A Tool supports the definition of a periodic *dimension*. In order for a *dimension* to be periodic, it must supply the type of periodicity, the periodic unit, and further identify two *dimension attributes* (by name) to be associated with a Dimension's periodicity. One of the *dimension attributes* will represent the period of a dimension member, and another *dimension attribute* will represent the number of periodic units in the period.

The Stereotype definition, called the "Periodic Stereotype," is now added. This Stereotype is attached to the Dimension instance and will contain four Tagged Values. There will be a Tagged Value for type of periodicity, the unit of periodicity, the name of the dimension attribute that contains the period, and the name of the dimension attribute that contains the number of periodic units in the period.

The CWM built-in extension mechanism is provided to overcome some of the Tool-specific meta data requirements that were removed from the generic object model. The extension mechanism works well for a variety of uses (some are mentioned directly above); however, there are shortcomings of using both Stereotypes and Tagged Values. Some of those issues are listed here:

- The Tool itself must define and police the usage of both the Stereotype and Tagged Value mechanism.

- Stereotypes and Tagged Values are not directly interchangeable. The semantic usage of these constructs is not conveyed in their definition. Therefore, Tools may interpret the information differently.

- The Stereotype definitions can change from release to release, making it necessary for a Tool to either handle both definitions of the Stereotype or to upgrade existing definitions.

- Tagged Values can have different semantic meaning for different Tools. In this case, a Tagged Value may be used by more than one Tool. If different Tools are using the Tagged Values differently, one Tool may inadvertently change a value expected by the other Tool.

- The Stereotype and Tagged Values definitions will not be directly available through model-defined Application Programming Interface (API) definitions. This means that when looking at the definition of an object, an implementer must know that certain constructs that they are looking for are "wrapped" in a Tagged Value and are not directly available as an API call.

Modeled Extensions

To alleviate the shortcomings of Stereotypes and Tagged Values, or if the required model changes go beyond "simple" extensions, a Tool will need to employ a more robust mechanism to extend the CWM model. To achieve this endeavor, the Vendor can extend the CWM model using standard Object Oriented (OO) techniques. There are a number of OO techniques from which Vendors could choose to implement an extended CWM; however, we will only present one such mechanism here called *Inheritance*. It is important to understand that this is not the only OO technique available, but that it is straightforward and serves to help understand how to extend the model. The CWM specification is delivered as a set of components that can help the Vendor to define the extensions. These components include the following:

- A specification describing the CWM object definitions
- A MOF 1.3 compliant XML file describing the CWM model

To fully examine this technique, we will use the above Relational Table example and implement the extended functionality using OO inheritance. The example above has been augmented to show an extension not directly possible using just Tagged Values or Stereotypes. We have added an association between the Table definition and one or more WidgetAs. The first step to extending the model using inheritance is to start with either an implementation of the CWM specification or by loading the supplied model file into some OO-capable modeling tool. The second step is to actually extend the definition. This activity can be done by writing code directly against the initial implementation or by using a modeling tool to graphically capture the extensions to the model. If we had started with some initial implementation of CWM, the implementer may have decided not to use a modeling tool, but instead extend the code directly using some software development tool.

Modeling extensions to CWM is the preferred mechanism for additions that go beyond just simple extensions. In addition to providing extension capability beyond simple Tagged Values, it provides a cleaner programming model. Notice in the above example that the data types of several of the added class attributes are not String, but reflect the implementer's desired data type. Notice also that additional methods are generated for the class extensions. This type of extension mechanism makes the programming interface to the extended class more in line with a standard class interface definition.

Interoperability using CWM

The CWM team consisted of a number of leading Vendors in the data warehouse space. One of the main purposes of CWM is to provide interoperability between these Vendors. Interoperability among Vendors will allow the End-Users to purchase Tools and Applications from Vendors that will cooperate with each other. End-Users can then buy best-of-breed Tools from a variety of Vendors without the cost of duplicated and/or separate administration.

Tools can interoperate by exchanging their meta data in a commonly understood format. In order to provide interoperability, there has to be some common understanding of the interchanged data and a common transport mechanism. CWM can be used to satisfy both interoperability requirements. First, the CWM model provides for the common under-standing of the meta data semantics. Secondly, the CWM specification pro-vides a DTD, which governs the serialization of instances of CWM objects into an XML file. To illustrate how CWM facilitates and promotes interoperability among different tools, consider the following initial scenario.

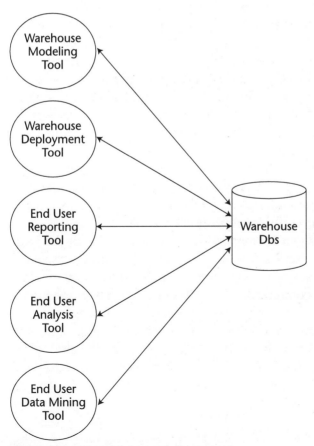

Figure 11.2   A set of data warehouse tools.

Figure 11.2 depicts a sample data warehouse; a client has chosen a variety of different tools to perform various tasks within the data warehouse. There is a modeling tool to plan the logical and physical implementation of the data warehouse. There is a data warehouse deployment tool to manage and control the creation, production, and maintenance of the data warehouse. This tool may include the ability to schedule and implement the various transactions and transformations needed by an operational data warehouse. There is also a suite of end-user reporting and analysis tools. These tools range from simple reporting to complex data analysis and data mining.

As we move from tool to tool in Figure 11.2, we discover a great deal of meta data overlap among the various tools. The meta data about the warehouse is replicated and used by the different tools in different ways with different purposes. In Figure 11.2, the various tools shown must produce and maintain their own meta data information. As an example of common meta data information that could be shared, consider the meta data of the modeling tool. This tool might allow a user to graphically design both the logical and physical schema of the data warehouse. These definitions could include very detailed information about the construction of the physical data warehouse deployment. The deployment tool could certainly use this deployment information. In the above scenario, however, the tools are not connected. Thus, there is no process or methodology to share the deployment information. The above scenario contains many other possible opportunities for the tools to share meta data information and administration. Another opportunity for sharing meta data in Figure 11.2 comes from the end-user reporting and analysis tools. These tools could benefit from the knowledge about how the data warehouse was designed and constructed. If these definitions could have been made available, the reporting and analysis tools wouldn't need to provide administration components to capture the physical deployment of the warehouse and could concentrate on providing administration only for reporting and analysis.

CWM can be used as the vehicle to provide interoperability for the various data warehouse tools described above. If we alter the above scenario to include CWM, we can provide the common bond needed to allow the data warehouse applications to cooperate and work together to share meta data information.

By including CWM in the data warehouse scenario, the tools can now interoperate with each other by importing and exporting their meta data information to and from the CWM common representation. Any tool that either imports or exports meta data can participate in this sharing methodology.

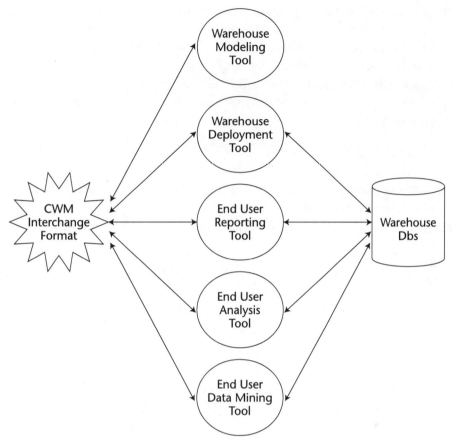

Figure 11.3   Using CWM to provide interoperability among data warehousing tools.

The main benefactors of interoperability are the clients. From an operational perspective, the end user benefits from this because the administration of the data warehouse has become simpler and more manageable. End users may not have to repeat the same administration tasks over and over as they deploy tool after tool. Instead, the end user will export the meta data definitions from one tool and import those definitions into a second tool. This process will give the second tool a jump-start on its configuration process. To illustrate this point, the end user could select the modeling tool to construct the logical and physical implementation of the data warehouse. In addition, the end user may enter specific deployment information via this modeling tool based on ease of use and presentation of information through this tool. When it comes time to deploy the data warehouse, the end user needs to use the data warehouse deployment tool. Now the information from the design tool can be loaded directly into the deployment tool via CWM. This negates the need for the end user to reenter all the deployment information just added via the modeling tool.

To cement the importance of interoperability, consider a more complete example of data warehouse administration and operations that can be improved using CWM:

- A DBA uses a modeling tool to graphically design a data warehouse.

- The DBA uses the same tool to document and design a set of transformations to cleanse the raw data and produce a data mart for reporting and analysis.

- The DBA uses CWM to export the above designs and transformations to the common format.

- The DBA uses a deployment and scheduling tool to create and deploy the above designs. By importing the exported meta data definitions, a job is created based on the definitions from the design tool and scheduled for execution.

- The job is run, and the data warehouse is created.

- The DBA can now use the same exported meta data to jump-start the reporting and analysis tools. The DBA imports the definitions into the tool, and the tool is automatically ready to run.

- In this scenario, we can see that CWM can provide interoperability across a wide range of tasks in the data warehouse. CWM can be used to provide interoperability across the spectrum of tasks from concept to design to deployment to reporting and analysis.

Adapter Construction

The model-based approach to meta data integration eliminates or significantly reduces the cost and complexities associated with the traditional point-to-point meta data integration architectures based on meta data bridges. It provides the same benefit to central repository-based, hub-and-spoke-style meta data architectures, as well. Both types of meta data integration architecture were elaborated on in Chapter 9, "Integration Architecture." In point-to-point architectures, the model-based approach eliminates the need to build multiple meta data bridges that interconnect each pair of product types that need to be integrated. Instead, each software product implements an *adapter* (a layer of software logic) that understands the common metamodel, on the one hand, and the internal implementation metamodel of the product, on the other hand.

The adapter is, of course, another form of a meta data bridge, but one that only needs to be written once for a given product, because all products agree on the common metamodel. This is in sharp contrast to the traditional meta data bridging approach, in which pairwise bridges are built for every pair of product types that are to be integrated. So the model-based solution clearly reduces the costs and complexities of building point-to-point meta data architectures, enhancing the overall Return on Investment (ROI) of the Information Supply Chain (ISC) or data warehouse effort.

Figure 11.4 illustrates a conceptual architecture for a CWM-based integration environment based on the use of tool-specific adapters. In that diagram, the architectural layers labeled "Meta Data Mapping/Translation" and "CWM Interfaces (XML & API)" generally form what we think of as software-based adapters.

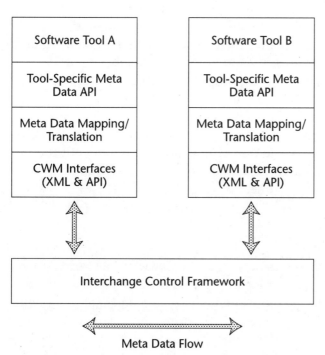

Figure 11.4 CWM adapter-based meta data interchange architecture.

This subsection covers a number of commonly used techniques for implementing interoperability frameworks and adapters to provide CWM-enabled tool suites.

Interoperability Frameworks for CWM

Interoperability using CWM is done primarily via an XML document that contains instances of CWM objects. A number of techniques are available to tool vendors and tool implementers to provide interoperability using CWM. Those techniques can be categorized into two predominant implementation mechanisms:

- Transform direct
- Transform indirect

Transform Direct

In the direct transform method, a tool will transform the XML interchange instances directly into tool-specific objects. At no time will there be an implementation of a CWM object in memory. Using this method, a definition is read from the file, a tool-specific object is created, and the data is transferred to the tool object directly from the XML stream.

Figure 11.5 depicts a typical interchange of meta data using the direct transform method. The key to this method is the use of some type of mapping methodology. This type of interchange works best when a one-to-one mapping is available from a CWM object to a tool-specific object. It is possible to use this method when the mapping is not one to one, but the following section provides a better mechanism when the CWM to tool object definitions are other than one to one.

Transform Indirect

Some sort of bridge, which moves data from the CWM model format to the tool's specific format, defines the indirect mechanism. This mechanism is good for existing tools that want to interchange data and meta data with other tools that support CWM without rewriting the existing tool meta data model. In this approach, the tool generally reads the interchange document into some intermediate form, which is then transformed into the tool-specific representation by mapping the CWM model to the tool-specific model.

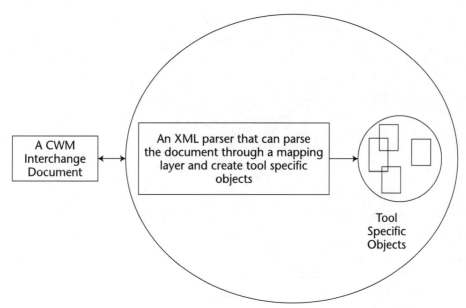

Figure 11.5   Transform-direct interoperability.

To illustrate how tools can use CWM in an indirect implementation, consider hub-and-spoke architecture first with CWM as the hub and some set of tools as the spokes. Indirect transformation would be an ideal choice for a vendor who needs to integrate a number of tools via CWM. A straightforward way to implement this would be to create an implementation of the CWM object model. This set of classes then would be populated by some CWM interchange document. The document instances would be read directly into the CWM class implementations. After the document was reconstructed in memory, the in-memory copy could be traversed moving the meta data from the CWM model definition to a tool-specific representation.

As shown in Figure 11.6, a vendor could use this approach to integrate a single tool or any number of tools. This approach reuses the code to move the document into memory. The vendor creates a new mapping to integrate a different tool.

In some instances, vendors will already have an integration strategy which uses a hub-and-spoke architecture. In this case, the preceding architecture would change: The hub model would become a vendor-specific model created to provide interchange among existing tools, and CWM would become a new spoke. This is shown in Figure 11.7. When this was done, the preexisting interchange mechanism would enable all tools supported by the hub with CWM.

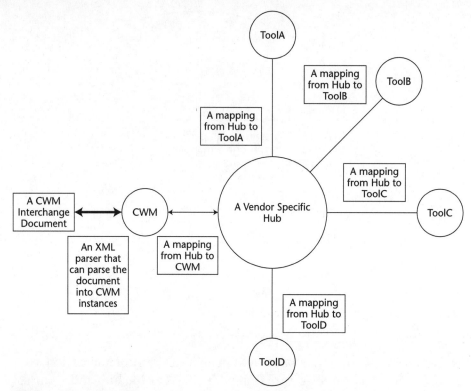

Figure 11.6 Hub-and-spoke architecture based on CWM.

In a bridging architecture, the flow of data usually is done as a single iso-lated task. Figures 11.6 and 11.7 give no indication as to the direction that the data will flow, with one notable exception. The portion of the bridge that reads and writes the CWM Interchange Document must be bidirec-tional if a vendor wants compatibility both to and from any specific tool. In a number of instances, bidirectionality of the CWM spoke is not necessary:

Timing.   A tool may implement only one side of the bridge to gain speed to market.

End-user-based reporting tools.   This class of tool may not need to write back to the CWM format because the definitions used by these tools use the predefined warehouse and build on top. It is not intended that the added definitions be shared.

Warehouse authoring tools.   This class of tool may be concerned only with creating the warehouse. It may not be able, or consider it appro-priate, to enable users to change the warehouse definitions outside the context of this type of tool.

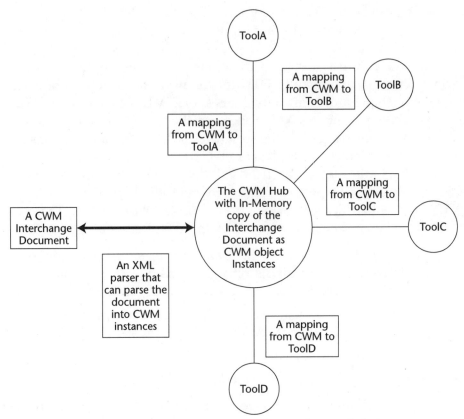

Figure 11.7   Hub-and-spoke architecture based on vendor-specific hub.

Extending to Web Services

This subsection summarizes the basic mechanisms required for transforming a CWM implementation into a provider of Web-based meta data services.

CWM and W3C Standards

In *Common Warehouse Metamodel: An Introduction to the Standard for Data Warehouse Integration* (Wiley, 2002), we described how XML, which is a W3C standard (see W3C.org), is a foundation technology for CWM. XML provides the universal format for interchanging CWM meta data. The XML specification defines the well-formedness rules for XML documents, the grammar rules for DTDs, and the validity rules for validating XML documents against its DTDs. In addition, the XML Namespace specification defines the mechanism for providing namespace support in XML documents and DTDs.

Recently the W3C has adopted XML Schema as a standard. XML Schema provides an alternative way to DTD for defining the structures of XML documents. There are many advantages of XML schema over DTD. Because of these advantages, XML Schema, rather than DTD, is expected to be used in the future to define the structures of XML documents, particularly those used to interchange data or meta data. As discussed previously, XML Metadata Interchange (XMI) 2.0 will define rules that can be used to automatically generate the CWM XML Schema Definition (XSD).

XML Protocol, which originated from Simple Object Access Protocol (SOAP), is a standard being developed by the W3C that intends to define:

- An envelope to encapsulate XML data for transfer in an interoperable manner that allows for distributed extensibility, evolvability, as well as intermediaries like proxies, caches, and gateways

- An operating system-neutral convention for the content of the envelope when used for Remote Procedure Call (RPC) applications

- A mechanism to serialize data based on XML Schema datatypes

- A nonexclusive mechanism layered on an HTTP transport

Web Services Definition Language (WSDL) is a proposal made to the W3C for standardization. WSDL is an XML format for describing network services as a set of endpoints operating on messages containing either document-oriented or procedure-oriented information. The operations and messages are described abstractly and then bound to a concrete network protocol and message format to define an endpoint. Related concrete endpoints are combined into abstract endpoints (services). WSDL is extensible to allow descriptions of endpoints and their messages regardless of what message formats or network protocols are used to communicate. Both XML Protocol and WSDL (or whatever is eventually standardized by the W3C in its place) are expected to become the foundation technologies for the CWM Web Services to be discussed in the next section.

Support for meta data search and query has been lacking for some time. The one exception is that for relational meta data, in which case one can use SQL for search and query, assuming that one has access to the schema tables. However, no such support exists for meta data represented in UML, not even standardized UML-based search or query languages. XPath and XQuery provide hope for such support, at least via the XML views of such meta data, with XPath used for simple search and XQuery used for search and query.

XPath is a W3C standard. The primary purpose of XPath is to address parts of an XML document. In support of this primary purpose, it also provides basic facilities for manipulation of strings, numbers, and booleans. XPath uses a compact, non-XML syntax to facilitate use of XPath within URLs and XML attribute values. XPath operates on the abstract, logical structure of an XML document, rather than its surface syntax. XPath gets its name from its use of a path notation as in URLs for navigating through the hierarchical structure of an XML document.

XQuery is an XML query language standard being developed by the W3C. It is designed to be a small, easily implemented language in which queries are concise and easily understood. It is also flexible enough to query a broad spectrum of XML information sources, including both databases and documents. XQuery provides for a human-readable query syntax, and XQueryX (the XML representation of XQuery) provides an XML-based query syntax. XQuery relies on path expressions defined in XPath for navigating hierarchical documents.

The relationships between CWM and XML, XML Schema, XML Protocol, WSDL, XPath, as well as XQuery are summarized in Table 11.1.

Table 11.1   CWM and W3C Standards

CATEGORY	STANDARD	BASE TECHNOLOGY FOR CWM
W3C	XML	XML document definition
		XML DTD definition
	XML schema	XML schema structures and datatypes definitions (future)
	XML Protocol	XML messaging protocol (future)
	WSDL	Web Services interface definition language (future)
	Xpath	XML Pattern language (future)
	XQuery	XML query language (future)

CWM Meta Data Interchange Patterns RFP

The construction and semantics of the CWM metamodel are such that the metamodel covers a broad spectrum of uses in the data warehouse. This design enables a user to interchange meta data for many diverse portions of the CWM metamodel. This flexibility, although expressively powerful, is at the same time problematic for tool implementers. The metamodel has no way to describe what a valid unit of interchange should be. As a result, it is possible to receive a portion of the CWM metamodel without sufficient context to reliably interchange the meta data. This was brought to light when the CWM team produced the CWM Enablement Showcase. To solve this issue, the participants agreed on what a valid unit of transfer was for the context of the Showcase. This methodology needs to be formalized for CWM.

Meta data interchange patterns are structural patterns for interchanged meta data content between typical Data Warehouse (DW) and Batch Interactive (BI) tools, which serve to constrain the total universe of possible meta data content that can be interchanged. They simplify tool construction and logic because an importing tool, for example, knows in advance what to look for. (Its search space is constrained to specific structural patterns, and it knows what the top-level anchor points are for patterned content.) Similarly, exporting tools also have a guideline to follow in structuring their meta data for export. The CWM Meta Data Interchange Patterns Request for Proposal (RFP), therefore, solicits proposals for a complete specification of the syntax and semantics of typical CWM meta data interchange patterns.

CWM Web Services RFP

CWM describes the interchange of meta data. This is necessary but not necessarily sufficient for interchanging DW/BI meta data over the Web. The major characteristic of the Web is that it consists of massive, asynchronous, and loosely and infrequently connected clients and servers. In such an environment, it is much more desirable and efficient to interchange information (including meta data) using a request-response model and in coarse-grained manners. CWM defines fine-grained metamodels for access and interchange of DW/BI meta data, using XML to interchange meta data and IDL to access meta data. CWM does not, however, define typical meta data interchange patterns nor define standard meta data interchange (request-response) protocols. Specifically, CWM does not define an enablement architecture that allows loosely coupled interchange of DW/BI meta data over the Web.

The CWM Web Services RFP, therefore, solicits proposals for the following:

- A complete specification of the syntax and semantics of standard CWM meta data interchange (request-response) protocols that is based on typical CWM meta data interchange patterns (as requested in the CWM Meta Data Interchange Patterns RFP)

- A complete specification of the syntax and semantics of a CWM Web Services API that allows the loosely coupled interchange of CWM meta data over the Web and that is based on the standard CWM meta data interchange protocols

This RFP is expected to solicit proposals that specify the protocols one can use to request specific patterns for interchange and to express the desired results of interchange, and the APIs one can use to do so over the Web. The Web Services API is expected to be dependent on the CWM interchange format (the CWM DTD) and be consistent with it.

Developing Automated Meta Data Driven Environments

This subsection provides an illustration of how relatively small-scale CWM meta data integration architectures, such as the one developed throughout this book, might evolve into large-scale, enterprise-wide, and highly automated meta data solutions.

The Vision

The proposed near-term vision is that of an environment in which efficient and nearly seamless interoperability between diverse applications, tools, and databases is achieved through the interchange of shared models. Components participating in this environment leverage standard services provided by implementations of Management Domain Architecture (MDA) standards that enable them to expose and interchange their meta data as instances of well-defined models. These platform services have standard definitions that are expressed via standard programming models (such as APIs), which are automatically generated from platform-independent models.

The Importance of Shared Meta Data

Meta data is critical to all aspects of interoperability within any heterogeneous environment. In fact, meta data *is* the primary means by which interoperability is achieved (interoperability is largely facilitated by standard APIs, but ultimately requires shared meta data as the definitions of system semantics and capabilities). Any MDA-based system must have the ability to store, manage, and publish both application- and system-level meta data (including descriptions of the environment itself). Applications, tools, databases, and other components plug into the environment and discover meta data descriptions pertaining to the environment. Similarly, a component or product introduced into the environment can also publish its own meta data to the rest of the environment. Having an abundance of shared, descriptive meta data (*ubiquitous meta data*) facilitates software interoperability among platform components in very specific ways, including:

- Data interchange, transformation, and type mapping between dissimilar data resources can be driven by formal, product-independent meta data descriptions of the transformations, data types, and type-system mappings.

- Schema generation can be based on shared meta data descriptions of common schema elements. For example, both a relational database and an OLAP server can build their own internal representations of a dimensional model, according to a standard, meta data-based definition of "dimension" published to the environment. Having common meta data definitions facilitates data interchange between subsystems, because there is a common understanding of what the data means.

- Business intelligence and visualization functions can utilize meta data in the processing and formatting of data for analysis and display. Meta data descriptions confer the "higher level of meaning" on data items that analysts and reporting users need in order to make sense of data points and results (e.g., definitions of business terms, glossaries, taxonomies, nomenclatures, and so on, are a part of the shared meta data).

- Software components with no prior knowledge of each other's capabilities, interfaces, and data representations can interoperate once they've established a meta data "handshake," in which each exposes its features and assesses those of the other. Note that this exchange of knowledge does not always need to be complete, but to the extent that components can make sense of each other's capabilities, they can interact with one another. In the absence of specific knowledge, components might rely on standard defaults, or may be able to refer to some other source of information to fill the knowledge gaps.

A CWM-based system does not require that *internal representations* of meta data within applications, tools, and databases be modified to correspond to the shared definitions. Product-specific internals and programming models remain as they are. Shared meta data consists of *externalized* definitions that are interchanged between participating components. These external definitions are readily understood by components that agree on the metamodel describing the meta data (e.g., CWM). External definitions are highly generic, but also possess sufficient *semantic completeness* (with respect to the problem domains that components need to address) and are, therefore, understood by a wide range of participants. Highly product-specific meta data that does not fit the generic model is handled through the use of extension mechanisms that are predefined as part of the generic models (e.g., the use of UML extension mechanisms, such as tagged values, stereotypes, and constraints).

To ensure that shared meta data is readily understood by all participating components, an MDA-based system requires its components to standardize on each of the following:

- A formal language (syntax and semantics) for representing meta data.
- An interchange format for exchanging and publishing meta data.
- A programming model for meta data access and discovery. This must include generic programming capabilities for dealing with meta data of an unknown nature.
- Mechanisms for extending each of the above.
- An optional meta data *service* of some form, where published meta data resides. Note that there is no strict requirement that such a service be provided; i.e., components are always free to interchange meta data in a point-to-point fashion, without the use of an intervening service.

Common Services and Programming Models

In addition to shared meta data, another key building block of interoperable systems is the standardization of common system- and application-level services, along with the application programming interfaces (APIs) used to access these services. A standard API defines a *standard programming model* of the services it represents. This form of standardization simplifies clients and facilitates the integration of new components into the MDA-based environment. Clients using common services have a smaller footprint and are less complex, because they only need to be coded to one interface, regardless of how services are actually implemented in a particular deployment. Conversely, service providers implementing standard APIs are readily available for use by a large number of clients.

Platform Specification

The final building block of the near-term system vision is the *platform specification*. This is basically the complete definition of the meta data interoperability and interchange strategies, common services, and standard APIs that any instance of an MDA-based system is capable of supporting. Each MDA-based system instance includes a *descriptor* that specifies those features actually supported by that particular deployment. Software tools for specifying and integrating system components generate the descriptor, and tools for configuring, installing, and bootstrapping an instance of the system are driven by the descriptor.

Overview of the Long-Term Vision

The long-term vision for MDA-oriented system architectures includes software capable of automatic discovery of properties of its environment and adaptation to that environment by various means, including dynamic modification of its own behavior. This is an ambitious vision that builds significantly on experiences and insights gained from implementing the near-term vision. It represents a migration of the near-term vision (i.e., meta data-based interoperability) to that of systems whose behavior is largely determined at run time by the Adaptive Object Models (AOMs). The following points summarize the main characteristics of the long-term vision.

Knowledge-Based Orientation

System functionality will gradually become more knowledge-based and capable of automatically discovering common properties of dissimilar domains, making intelligent decisions based on those discoveries, and drawing and storing resulting inferences. In general, "knowledge" is supported by an advanced and highly evolved concept of ubiquitous meta data, in which the ability to act upon, as well as revise, knowledge at run time is provided through AOMs.

Our ability to engineer such systems will come about largely as the result of our extensive experiences with the use of metamodels and ontologies in influencing system behavior and decision-making. We will eventually learn how to build systems in which a considerable amount of domain knowledge is pushed up into higher abstraction levels. Systems will understand how to efficiently extract and act on that information.

Another factor contributing to the development of knowledge-based systems will be the future availability of far more effective reflective capabilities, as provided by programming language implementations, as well as repository and middleware services, and, most importantly, generalized meta data management, authoring, and publishing services. The current state -of -the art of reflection generally allows for static program introspection. Future reflective capabilities will efficiently support not only introspection, but also dynamic modification of both structure and behavior.

Dynamic Architecture

Experiences gained in the development and deployment of meta data-driven systems based on extensible object models will ultimately result in the development of systems that can directly interpret models and modify their own behavior accordingly, rather than explicitly mapping external views of shared meta data to implementation models.

In the future, this mapping process will be discarded, and models will be interpreted directly by software. This is the promise of the areas of dynamic objects and AOMs. In this paradigm, changing the model directly changes software behavior, resulting in complete runtime extensibility. For example, publishing a new version of a model in a repository causes all software systems in the environment to automatically adjust their own behaviors to reflect the changes. Note that a highly evolved concept of meta data is critical to this sort of architecture. Meta data (i.e., the Adaptive Object Model) is updated while the system is executing, and the resulting changes to system behavior and structure take effect as soon as the running system is ready to expose those changes.

Adaptive Systems

The architectures and capabilities described above will produce a general class of highly dynamic and self-organizing systems that can act directly on domain knowledge and behave intelligently without having to be told how. Such systems can readily accommodate unforeseen changes in the environment and react appropriately without the need for programmer intervention (e.g., when dynamic and largely unstructured data resources are brought into the environment). When systems do need to be modified, this is accomplished by altering the system model. This may be performed by domain experts who are not necessarily software specialists, or, in many cases perhaps, by the system itself.

Summary

In this chapter, we saw that the CWM metamodel was constructed as a common set of features and functionality from a variety of existing data warehouse tools. Due to the fact that the model only represents a common set of features, there is a built-in extension mechanism. This internal mechanism is good for "simple" changes to the CWM metamodel. For larger, more complex changes, CWM users should model their changes using standard OO techniques.

The CWM metamodel provides interoperability among data warehousing tools by providing a standard XML definition for meta data interchange. Tools can interoperate by exchanging meta data definitions via files compliant with the CWM DTD. Tool extensions of the CWM metamodel can be either private or intended for interchange. If the extensions are intended for interchange, they must be interchanged using the built-in mechanism of tagged values and stereotypes.

We also introduced some of the approaches used in constructing CWM interoperability frameworks and adapters, and how they are used in the construction of CWM-enabled meta data integration architectures.

The following are some of the implementation issues encountered when using either direct or indirect transform implementations of CWM. These experiences were taken from some of the teams that produced the interoperability demonstration.

- Transform Indirect, using CWM, as the hub in a hub-and-spoke architecture is a good and flexible overall design.

- Transform Direct works best when there is a preexisting tool that has a one-to-one mapping between its object definitions and CWM.

- Transform Direct is a good choice when only a single point of interoperability is required and the mapping of tools to CWM is one-to-one or very close.

- If writing a new tool, use the CWM model directly, if possible. The interoperability decision, Transform Direct or Transform Indirect, is then based more on whether single or multiple points of interoperability exist.

Both Transform Direct and Transform Indirect interoperability is provided by an isolated XML file. In general, no information as to what came before the intended interchange exists, or there will be subsequent interchanges. Implementers should be aware that to provide complete round-trip interoperability, they must take into consideration how to merge into a preexisting set of CWM objects.

Finally, we briefly surveyed the core OMG MDA standards (i.e., UML, MOF, XMI and CWM) and discussed the current attempts at mapping these standards to J2EE, as examples of standard translations of *Platform Independent Models* to *Platform Specific Models* (PIM-to-PSM translations), translations that are currently under development. These forthcoming APIs will provide the initial building blocks for a new generation of systems based on the model-driven architecture concept. The progression of these initial MDA realizations to AOMs is the next logical step in this evolution.

CHAPTER 12

Conclusions

When IBM, Oracle, and Unisys proposed the Common Warehouse Model (CWM) standardization effort to the Object Management Group (OMG) in May 1998, meta data interchange had been identified for some time as one of the most critical problems facing the data warehousing industry.

The CWM standardization effort has been a resounding success, after three and a half years of intense collaboration and hard work among eight cosubmitting companies: IBM, Unisys, NCR, Hyperion, Oracle, UBS, Genesis, and Dimension EDI. The OMG adopted CWM as an available technology, which means that it has gone through the finalization process and at least one submitting company was able to demonstrate an implementation, in April 2001. Not only that, but CWM has become a showcase technology for the OMG as well as a core component of its new strategic direction on Model Driven Architecture (MDA), as shown in Figure 12.1.

In this last chapter, we will discuss three important topics on CWM that illustrate its success, the reason for its success, and its relationship and significance to other industry standards on meta data. First, we will discuss CWM Enablement Showcase, which clearly demonstrates CWM's success for enabling meta data interchange among data warehousing and business intelligence tools and repositories. Second, we will discuss the model-driven approach used in CWM, which is a major reason for its success and which serves as proof of its existence for the OMG's new strategic direction on MDA. Third, we will discuss the relationship and significance of CWM to other relevant standards, both existing and emerging from OMG, W3C, and the Java community. Finally, we will conclude the book by peeking into the future evolution of CWM.

CWM and MDA

Many reasons exist for the success of CWM. Foremost is the willingness of major vendors to work together and develop a commonly agreed upon meta data interchange standard for data warehousing and business intelligence. Technically, the keys to the success of CWM are Unified Modeling Language (UML) and eXtensible Markup Language (XML). UML provides a single and powerful modeling language for modeling all types of warehouse meta data; XML provides a simple and universal data format for interchanging all these types of warehouse meta data. By nature, data warehousing deals with a very complex environment that involves many different types of data resources (relational, record-based, object-oriented, multidimensional, and XML), various types of transformation and analysis tools [Extraction, Transfer and Loading (ETL), Online Analytical Processing (OLAP), data mining, information visualization, and business nomenclature], as well as warehouse process and warehouse operation management. UML is capable of modeling the meta data for all of these entities, thus serving as the single modeling language. Also by nature, data warehousing involves many different tools from many different vendors, big and small. Therefore, for meta data interchange to be successful and prevalent, the interchange format used must be universal and must be cheap to implement and support. XML is ideal for this purpose, because it *is* simple, universal, and cheap to implement and support.

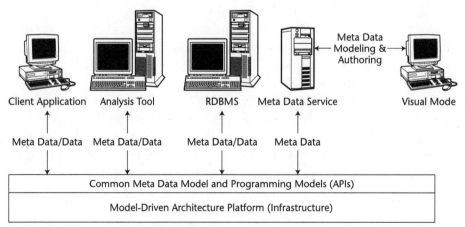

Figure 12.1 Model-driven architecture.

UML and XML by themselves, however, are not sufficient for the success of CWM. UML is a modeling language for meta data; XML is an interchange format for meta data. They are disjointed entities. To bring them together so that one can start with modeling meta data using UML and end up with interchanging meta data so modeled in XML, CWM uses a model-driven approach as shown in Figure 12.2. The development of the CWM specification starts with the CWM metamodel, which is represented in UML notation using a tool such as Rational Rose. When the CWM metamodel is developed, it is used to develop the CWM specification in text form by adding English text and Object Constraint Language (OCL) constraints where appropriate. The CWM metamodel is further used to automatically generate a CWM XML, a CWM Document Type Definition (DTD), and a CWM IDL, according to XML Metadata Interchange (XMI) and Meta Object Facility (MOF), respectively. The CWM XML document is generated per the MOF DTD and represents a formal, tool-independent definition of the CWM metamodel. The CWM DTD can be used to validate XML documents used to interchange CWM meta data. The CWM IDL defines a language-independent API for accessing CWM meta data. In the future, as discussed in the next section, a CWM Java interface also will be generated per Java Meta Data Interface (JMI), which will define a Java API for accessing CWM meta data.

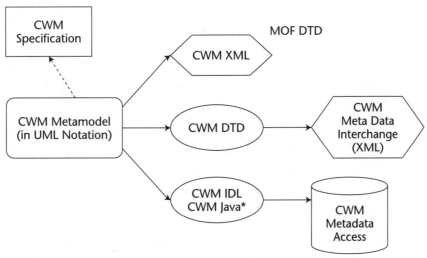

Figure 12.2   CWM model-driven approach.

The essence of the CWM model-driven approach is that everything starts with the CWM metamodel and, with the exception of the text-based CWM specification, everything is automatically generated. Anytime that something needs to be changed, the change is first made in the CWM metamodel and then propagated manually to the CWM specification and automatically to CWM XML, CWM DTD, and CWM IDL. This not only ensures consistency among all the CWM artifacts but it also enhances understanding because one only needs to focus on the CWM metamodel (and the CWM specification for OCL constraints).

Partly as a result of the success of the CWM model-driven approach, the OMG has recently embarked on a new strategic direction on MDA as shown in Figure 12.1. MDA addresses integration and interoperability spanning the life cycle of a software system from modeling and design, to component construction, assembly, integration, deployment, management, and evolution. The following are definitions of models and their subtypes in MDA:

Model. A formal specification of the function, structure, and behavior of a software system

Platform-independent model. A model that abstracts away technological and engineering details

Platform-specific model. A model that contains technological and engineering details

Although platform-specific models are needed to implement such models, platform-independent models are useful for two basic reasons. First, by abstracting the fundamental structure and meaning, they make it easier to validate the correctness of the model. Second, by holding the essential structure and meaning of the system invariant, they make it easier to produce implementations on different platforms.

Three basic ways exist to construct a platform-specific model from a platform-independent model:

- A person could study the platform-independent model and manually construct a platform-specific model.

- An algorithm could be applied to the platform-independent model resulting in a skeletal platform-specific model that is manually enhanced by a person.

- An algorithm could be applied to the platform-independent model resulting in a complete platform-specific model.

Fully automated transformations from platform-independent models to platform-specific models are feasible only in certain constrained environments.

The CWM metamodel, specification, and generated artifacts fit in with MDA very well and can be looked at from two different perspectives. From the technology platform perspective (that is, if we think of XML, CORBA, and Java as different technology platforms), the relationships between the platform-independent model (the CWM metamodel and specification) and platform-specific models (CWM XML, CWM DTD, CWM IDL, and, in the future, CWM Java) are shown in Figure 12.3. All platform-specific models in this case are fully automatically generated from the platform-independent model. From the product platform perspective (that is, if we think of DMSII, IMS, Essbase, Express, and so on as different product platforms), the relationships between the platform-independent model (the CWM metamodel and specification) and platform-specific models (DMSII, IMS, Essbase, Express, and so on) are shown in Figure 12.4. All platform-specific models in this case are constructed by people from the platform-independent model.

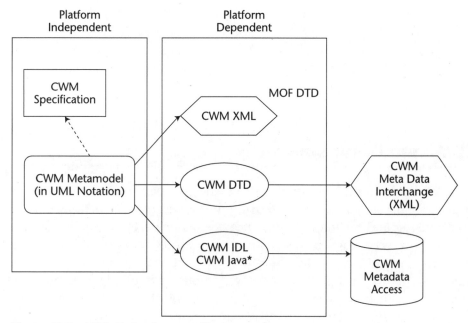

Figure 12.3 MDA: Technology-specific perspective.

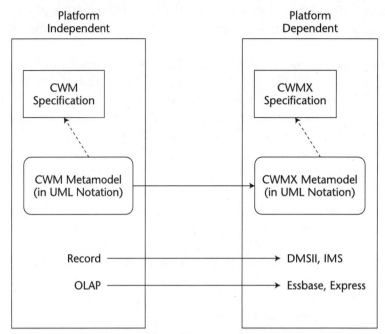

Figure 12.4 MDA: Product-specific perspective.

The model-driven architecture approach, exemplified by the UML, MOF, and CWM standards, provides a modeling infrastructure that can serve as the backbone for deeply-integrated and highly autonomous systems. See (Poole, 2001) for some advanced perspectives on this application of MDA.

CWM and Other Standards

For CWM to continue its initial success and prosper, it must evolve with other relevant standards, both existing and emerging. Even though data warehousing and business intelligence are major parts of an enterprise's information technology infrastructure, they are only parts of that infrastructure and not the whole. Therefore, CWM, being the meta data interchange standard for data warehousing and business intelligence, must be consistent with and complement other relevant standards in the enterprise's information technology infrastructure.

OMG Standards

As discussed in Chapter 3, "Modeling Meta Data Using CWM," the following OMG standards are foundation technologies for CWM: UML, IDL, MOF, and XMI. These together form the core meta data standards adopted by the OMG. UML and MOF, together with CWM, also form the core components of the OMG MDA.

UML provides the UML notation and OCL as part of the metamodeling language for CWM. In addition, the UML metamodel, or a subset of it, was used as the design basis for the CWM Object Model package, which serves as both the base metamodel as well as the object metamodel for CWM. Specifically, the Object Model package was derived from the UML Foundation, Common_Behavior, and Model_Management packages.

IDL provides an interface definition language for use in the CORBA environment. It is programming-language independent. Any programming language that has a defined IDL mapping and CORBA support can be used to implement IDL interfaces.

MOF provides the metamodeling architecture for CWM. Specifically, the MOF model provides the semantics of the metamodeling language for CWM; the MOF reflective interfaces provide generic APIs for accessing CWM meta data; and the MOF-to-IDL mapping provides the mechanism to generate CWM IDL interfaces for accessing CWM meta data.

XMI provides the meta data interchange mechanism for CWM. Specifically, XMI defines rules that can be used to automatically generate the CWM DTD, which can be used to validate any XML documents that contain CWM meta data. XMI also defines rules that can be used to generate XML documents that contain CWM meta data and that is valid per the CWM DTD. In the future, with the adoption by the OMG of XMI 2.0, XMI will, in addition, define rules that can be used to automatically generate the CWM XML Schema Definition (XSD), which can be used to validate any XML documents that contain CWM meta data.

At the time of this writing, the OMG Analysis and Domain Task Force (OMG ADTF) is strongly considering the next generation of MOF and UML standards (that is, MOF 2.0 and UML 2.0). The objectives of these efforts is ultimately to unify both MOF and UML with a common modeling infrastructure. Once this has been established, it is most likely that CWM will be revised to leverage these improvements in its underpinning technologies. To track the current status of these efforts, readers should regularly visit the OMG Web site at http://www.omg.org/.

Java Standards

In Chapter 3 we mentioned that Java has been the most widely used implementation platform for CWM and, therefore, is a foundation technology for CWM. A major reason for this is because Java can be written once and run anywhere. In particular, J2EE has been the implementation platform of choice because of its support for enterprise computing, including Web technologies such as servlets and JSP that can work seamlessly with XML.

An important standard being developed through the Java Community Process (JCP) (see JCP.org) is Java Meta Data Interface (JMI), which will have direct relevance to CWM in the near future. JMI intends to specify a pure Java API that supports the creation, storage, retrieval, and interchange of meta data. The API is expected to implement the functionality of MOF in a way that will be compatible with the J2EE platform. Although today one can use the MOF-to-IDL mapping and then the IDL-to-Java mapping to generate a Java API for CWM, that API is appropriate for use only in a CORBA environment. The API is nonintuitive to Java programmers, and it does not take advantage of the Java language or J2EE environment. After JMI is standardized, we should expect that, in the future, CWM Java will be automatically generated per JMI and published as part of the CWM specification, in a similar manner to CWM IDL.

All the standards we have discussed so far are existing or emerging foundation technologies for CWM. Two emerging standards, however, are technologies that derive, at least in part, from CWM. These are Java OLAP Interface (JOLAP) and Java Data Mining API (JDM).

JOLAP intends to specify a pure Java API for the J2EE environment that supports the creation, storage, access, and maintenance of data and meta data in OLAP systems (for example, OLAP servers and multidimensional databases). The goal is to provide for OLAP systems what Java Database Connectivity (JDBC) did for relational databases. JOLAP intends to have a close alignment with JMI and the CWM OLAP and multidimensional metamodels so that it can directly support the construction and deployment of data warehousing and business intelligence applications, tools, and platforms based on OMG open standards for meta data and system specification.

JDM intends to specify a pure Java API for the J2EE environment that supports the building of data-mining models, the scoring of data-using models, as well as the creation, storage, access, and maintenance of data and meta data-supporting data mining results and select data transformation. The goal is to provide for data mining systems what JDBC did for relational databases. JDM intends to have a close alignment with JMI and the CWM data-mining metamodel, so that it can directly support the construction and deployment of data warehousing and business intelligence applications, tools, and platforms based on OMG open standards for meta data and system specification.

The Future of CWM

CWM was adopted by the OMG as an Available Specification in April 2001. As a result, a CWM Revision Task Force (RTF) has been formed to solicit public comments on the specification and to revise it based on resolutions of the comments and on feedback from CWM implementations. The following metamodels are expected to go through major revisions:

Data mining. To incorporate feedback from the result of the JDM standardization effort

XML. To extend the metamodel to cover the new XML Schema specification adopted by the W3C

Separately, two RFPs were issued by the OMG in April 2001 to enhance CWM: CWM Meta Data Interchange Patterns RFP and CWM Web Services RFP. These two RFPs intend to enhance the ease of using CWM for meta data interchange and to enable such interchange using the new Web Services computing paradigm.

More recently, efforts within the OMG to reconcile differences between the MOF and UML core models may result in a new core meta-metamodel that will effectively serve the purposes of both. In this case, the CWM core ObjectModel will most likely be replaced with the new MOF common core.

Summary

Acceptance and support for CWM in the industry are rapidly growing for two reasons: the decision by the Meta Data Coalition (MDC) in September 2000 to fold its meta data standardization effort into the OMG, and the fact that Java Community Process (JCP) is extending OMG meta data standards into the Java platform (for example, JMI, JOLAP, and JDM). One should not be surprised to find CWM providing the common solution to warehouse meta data integration problems in the very near future. Looking a little further into the future, as W3C adopts newer standards on XML (for example, XQuery, XML Protocol, and WSDL) and as CWM evolves (that is, the

CWM RTF, the CWM Meta Data Interchange Patterns RFP, and the CWM Web Services RFP) to incorporate these technologies, warehouse meta data integration using CWM should become even easier and more powerful.

Finally, the patterns-based approach to CWM integration (as a general modeling practice), and the overall development and publishing of representative, vertical domain models, as we've presented in this book, together offer what is perhaps one of the richest approaches to using CWM in the construction of comprehensive integration solutions.

Bibliography

Booch, Grady. (1991). *Object-Oriented Design with Applications*. Redwood City, CA: Benjamin/Cummings, Inc.

Booch, Grady. (1994). *Object-Oriented Analysis and Design with Applications, 2nd Edition*. Reading, MA: Addison Wesley Longman, Inc.

Booch, Grady, James Rumbaugh, and Ivar Jacobson. (1999). *The Unified Modeling Language User Guide*. Reading, MA: Addison Wesley Longman, Inc.

Borges, Jorge Luis. (1962). "The Library of Babel." In *Labyrinths: Selected Stories and Other Writings*. New York: New Directions.

Chang, Dan, and Dan Harkey. (1998). *Client/Server Data Access with Java and XML*. New York: John Wiley & Sons, Inc.

Chappell, D., and J. H. Trimble, Jr. (2001). *A Visual Introduction to SQL, 2nd Edition*. New York: John Wiley & Sons, Inc.

Common Warehouse Metamodel Specification. (2001). Needham, MA: Object Management Group. Internet: www.omg.org/technology/cwm/index.htm or www.cwmforum.org/spec.htm.

Gamma, Erich, Richard Helm, Ralph Johnson, and John Vlissedes. (1995). *Design Patterns: Elements of Reusable Object-Oriented Software*. Reading, MA: Addison Wesley Longman, Inc.

Grand, Mark. (1998). *Patterns in Java: A Catalog of Reusable Design Patterns Illustrated with UML, Volume 1*. New York: John Wiley & Sons, Inc.

Grand, Mark. (1999). *Patterns in Java, Volume 2*. New York: John Wiley & Sons, Inc.

Guck, R. L., B. L. Fritchman, J. P. Thompson, and D. M. Tolbert. (1988). "SIM: Implementation of a Database Management System Based on a Semantic Data Model." In *Data Engineering, Vol. 11, No. 2.* pp. 23-32.

Hubert, Richard, and David A. Taylor. (2001). *Convergent Architecture: Building Model Driven J2EE Systems with UML.* New York: John Wiley & Sons, Inc.

Inmon, William H. (1996). *Building the Data Warehouse, 2nd Edition.* New York: John Wiley & Sons, Inc.

Jagannathan, D., R. L. Guck, B. L. Fritchman, J. P. Thompson, and D. M. Tolbert. (1988). "SIM: A Database System Based on a Semantic Data Model." In *Proceedings of the ACM SIGMOD International Conference on Management of Data,* Chicago, IL, 1-3 June. pp. 46-55.

Kimball, Ralph. (1996). *The Data Warehouse Toolkit.* New York: John Wiley & Sons, Inc.

Kimball, Ralph, Laura Reeves, Marge Ross, and Warren Thornthwaite. (1998). *The Data Warehouse Lifecycle Toolkit: Expert Methods for Designing, Developing, and Deploying Data Warehouses.* New York: John Wiley & Sons, Inc.

Kimball, Ralph, and Richard Merz. (2000). *The Data Webhouse Toolkit: Building the Web-Enabled Data Warehouse.* New York: John Wiley & Sons, Inc.

Marco, David. (2000). *Building and Managing the Meta Data Repository: A Full Lifecycle Guide.* New York: John Wiley & Sons, Inc.

Marinescu, Floyd. (2002). *EJB Design Patterns: Advanced Patterns, Processes, and Idioms.* New York: John Wiley & Sons, Inc.

Melton, J., and A. R. Simon. (2002). *SQL:1999.* San Francisco: Morgan Kaufmann, Inc.

Poole, John. (2000). "The Common Warehouse Metamodel as a Foundation for Active Object Models in the Data Warehousing Environment." ECOOP 2000 Workshop on Metadata and Active Object Models. Internet: www.adaptiveobjectmodel.com/ECOOP2000/ or www.cwmforum.org/paperpresent.htm.

Poole, John. (2001). "Model-Driven Architecture: Vision, Standards, and Emerging Technologies." ECOOP 2001 Workshop on Metamodeling and Adaptive Object Models. Internet: www.adaptiveobjectmodel.com/ECOOP2001/ or www.omg.org/mda/presentations.htm.

Poole, John, Dan Chang, Douglas Tolbert, and David Mellor. (2002). *Common Warehouse Metamodel: An Introduction to the Standard for Data Warehouse Integration.* New York: John Wiley & Sons, Inc.

Rumbaugh, James, Ivar Jacobson, and Grady Booch. (1999). *The Unified Modeling Language Reference Manual.* Reading, MA: Addison Wesley Longman, Inc.

Silverston, Len. (2001). *The Data Model Resource Book: A Library of Universal Data Models for All Enterprises, Volumes 1 & 2*. New York: John Wiley & Sons, Inc.

Sunyé, Gerson, Alain Le Guennec, and Jean-Marc Jézéquel. (2000). "Design Patterns Application in UML." Proceedings of the 14th European Conference on Object-Oriented Programming. *Lecture Notes in Computer Science #1850*. Berlin: Springer-Verlag.

Thomsen, Erik. (1997). *OLAP Solutions: Building Multidimensional Information Systems*. New York: John Wiley & Sons, Inc.

Tolbert, Doug. (2000). "CWM: A Model-Based Architecture for Data Warehouse Interchange." Workshop on Evaluating Software Architectural Solutions 2000. University of California at Irvine. Internet: www.cwmforum.org/paperpresent.htm.

W3C. (2001). XML Information Set. Internet: www.w3.org/TR/xml-infoset.

Warmer, Jos, and Anneke Kleppe. (1999). *The Object Constraint Language: Precise Modeling with UML*. Reading, MA: Addison Wesley Longman, Inc.

Index

extending CWM *(continued)*
  meta data reuse, 67–71
  Stereotypes, 71–73
  Tagged Values, 71–73
Inheritance, 648
issues, 647–648
modeled extensions, 648
object-oriented techniques, 648
periodic dimensions, 647
simple extensions, 645–648
Stereotypes, 645–648
Tagged Values, 645–646
to Web services, 657–661
Extensible Markup Language.
  See XML
extension pattern category, 154
extensions, 22
Extent class, 33, 595–597

F
Feature class, 589–592
FeatureMap class, 635–638
FeatureNode class, 40–41
features
  architecture, 29
  classifier equality, 99–101, 105
  connecting Classifiers to, 515–516
  meta data (*see* StructuralFeature
    class)
finding data sources, 509–513
first-class objects, 487–488
FixedOffsetField class, 50
ForeignKey class, 610–612
foreign keys
  adding, 288
  architecture, 42
  columns, 183–184
  exporting relational meta data,
    196–199
  meta data, exporting, 196–199
  PopulationFact table, 293
  retrieving description of foreign key
    columns, 183–184
  SalesFact table, 292

forward references, 492
Foundation layer
  Business Information package, 34–36
  DataProvider class, 44
  DataTypes package, 36–39
  DeployedComponent class, 44
  DeployedSoftwareSystem class, 44
  Description class, 34–36
  Document class, 34–36
  ExpressionNode class, 40–41
  Expressions package, 39–41
  FeatureNode class, 40–41
  Index class, 42–43
  KeyRelationship class, 42–43
  Keys and Indexes package, 41–43
  metamodel, 88
  overview, 18
  ResponsibleParty class, 34–36
  Software Deployment package,
    43–44
  SoftwareSystem instances, 44
  TypeMapping package, 44–46
  TypeSystem class, 45–46
  UniqueKey class, 42–43
frameworks
  CWM-based integration architecture,
    581–583
  interoperability, 654–657
functional expressions, 40–41
future of CWM, 661–666, 677

G
Gamma, Erich, 144
Generalization class, 32
generalization hierarchies, 468–474
generalizations, 81, 86
generation pattern category, 155
geography dimension, defining, 242,
  258–261
geography keys, 272
geography levels, defining, 247–248
geography lookup table, 283–284
Geography Lookup table keys, 290
GetAll procedure, 474–476

standard geography hierarchy keys, 276
Standard hierarchy, defining, 251
standardization
  CWM and model-driven architecture, 670–674
  meta data formats, 7–9
  models, 672
  platform-independent models, 672–674
  platform-specific models, 672–674
standard product hierarchy, defining, 253–255
standard programming model, 663–664
standards
  CWM, 657–659
  future requirements, 663
  IDL, 675
  Java, 676–677
  JDM, 676–677
  JOLAP, 676
  meta data search and query, 658–659
  MOF, 675
  OMG, 675
  UML, 675
  W3C, 657–659
  WSDL, 658–659
  XMI, 658–659, 675
  XML Namespace, 658–659
  XML Protocol, 658–659
  XML Schema, 658–659
  XPath, 659
  XQuery, 659
  XSD, 658–659
standard time hierarchy keys, 277
Star-Join pattern, 425–429
star topology, 566–567
static structure model *vs.* MOF Model, 87
static structures
  aggregation, 81
  associations, 81

attributes, 81
classes, 81
Compositions, 81
core elements, 81–82
dependencies, 81
generalizations, 81
modeling, 80–82
objects, 81
operations, 81
realizations, 81
shared aggregation, 81
StepExecution class, 65–66
StepPrecedence, 54–57
StepPrecedence class, 630–633
Stereotypes, 71–73, 645–648
Stored Procedure class, 618–620
stored procedure parameter and result columns, 187–188
string data types, 38
struct (C language) data types, 38
structural classification, patterns, 153–154, 163
structural classification, pattern template, 159
StructuralFeature class, 29, 589–592
structural modeling, 80–82
structural pattern category, 155
structural resolution, 153–154
structured vocabulary. *See* Business Nomenclature package
sub-components of Cube, 305–306
subscribe-notify adapters, 574–575
subsets, patterns, 146
subset space, 146
subtype-oriented parameters, 156
summarizing data. *See* Information Visualization package
supported standard SQL types, 185
Surrogate Key pattern, 420–424
surrogate keys, 357
synonyms, 63
syntactic validation, 140–141